INTERROGATING HUMAN ORIGINS

Interrogating Human Origins encourages new critical engagements with the study of human origins, broadening the range of approaches to bring in postcolonial theories, and begin to explore the decolonisation of this complex topic.

The collection of chapters presented in this volume creates spaces for expansion of critical and unexpected conversations about human origins research. Authors from a variety of disciplines and research backgrounds, many of whom have strayed beyond their usual disciplinary boundaries to offer their unique perspectives, all circle around the big questions of what it means to be and become human. Embracing and encouraging diversity is a recognition of the deep complexities of human existence in the past and the present, and it is vital to critical scholarship on this topic.

This book constitutes a starting point for increased interrogation of the important and wide-ranging field of research into human origins. It will be of interest to scholars across multiple disciplines, and particularly to those seeking to understand our ancient past through a more diverse lens.

Martin Porr is Associate Professor of Archaeology and a member of the Centre for Rock Art Research + Management at the University of Western Australia (UWA). His research has so far concentrated on aspects related to Palaeolithic European art, Australian rock art, human origins and postcolonial approaches to archaeological research. He has conducted fieldwork in Germany, Thailand, Australia, India and the Philippines.

Jacqueline M. Matthews is a professional archaeologist with Cultural Heritage Management Australia and has wide-ranging experience working with Indigenous communities across Australia. She completed her master's thesis at the University of Western Australia, focused on the application of ontological and postcolonial theories to Australian archaeology, which led to a research interest in the role of Australia in global debates about human origins.

ARCHAEOLOGICAL ORIENTATIONS

Series Editors:
Gavin Lucas, *University of Iceland, Iceland*
Christopher Witmore, *Texas Tech University, USA*

An interdisciplinary series that engages our on-going, yet ever-changing, fascination with the archaeological, *Archaeological Orientations* investigates the myriad ways material pasts are entangled with communities, animals, ecologies and technologies, past, present or future. From urgent contemporary concerns, including politics, violence, sustainability, ecology, and technology, to long-standing topics of interest, including time, space, materiality, memory and agency, *Archaeological Orientations* promotes bold thinking and the taking of risks in pressing trans-disciplinary matters of concern.

Ruin Memories
Materialities, Aesthetics and the Archaeology of the Recent Past
Edited by Bjørnar Olsen and Þóra Pétursdóttir

Elements of Architecture
Assembling Archaeology, Atmosphere and the Performance of Building Spaces
Edited by Mikkel Bille and Tim Flohr Sorensen

Reclaiming Archaeology
Beyond the Tropes of Modernity
Edited by Alfredo González-Ruibal

Interrogating Human Origins
Decolonisation and the Deep Human Past
Edited by Martin Porr and Jacqueline M. Matthews

For more information on this series please visit: https://www.routledge.com/Archaeological-Orientations/book-series/ARCHOR.

INTERROGATING HUMAN ORIGINS

Decolonisation and the Deep Human Past

Edited by Martin Porr and Jacqueline M. Matthews

Routledge
Taylor & Francis Group

LONDON AND NEW YORK

First published 2020
by Routledge
2 Park Square, Milton Park, Abingdon, Oxon OX14 4RN

and by Routledge
52 Vanderbilt Avenue, New York, NY 10017

Routledge is an imprint of the Taylor & Francis Group, an informa business

British Library Cataloguing in Publication Data
A catalogue record for this book is available from the British Library

Library of Congress Cataloging-in-Publication Data
Names: Porr, Martin, editor. | Matthews, Jacqueline M.
Title: Interrogating human origins : decolonisation and the deep human past / edited by Martin Porr and Jacqueline M. Matthews.
Description: Abingdon, Oxon ; New York, NY : Routledge, 2020. | Series: Archaeological orientations ; 4 | Includes bibliographical references and index.
Identifiers: LCCN 2019039113 (print) | LCCN 2019039114 (ebook) | ISBN 9781138300415 (hardback) | ISBN 9781138300439 (paperback) | ISBN 9780203731659 (ebook) | ISBN 9781000761610 (adobe pdf) | ISBN 9781000761771 (mobi) | ISBN 9781000761931 (epub)
Subjects: LCSH: Human beings–Origin. | Decolonization. | Postcolonialism.
Classification: LCC GN281 .I684 2020 (print) | LCC GN281 (ebook) | DDC 569.9–dc23
LC record available at https://lccn.loc.gov/2019039113
LC ebook record available at https://lccn.loc.gov/2019039114

ISBN: 9781138300415 (hbk)
ISBN: 9781138300439 (pbk)
ISBN: 9780203731659 (ebk)

Typeset in Bembo
by Taylor & Francis Books

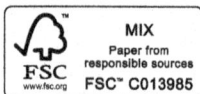

MIX
Paper from
responsible sources
FSC
www.fsc.org   FSC™ C013985

Printed in the United Kingdom
by Henry Ling Limited

CONTENTS

ILLUSTRATIONS

Figures

Tables

CONTRIBUTORS

Rebecca Rogers Ackermann is a biological anthropologist, Professor in the Department of Archaeology, Director of the Human Evolution Research Institute, and Deputy Dean of Transformation in the Science Faculty, University of Cape Town. Her research focusses on evolutionary process, and specifically how gene flow, drift and selection interact to produce skeletal diversity through time, with a particular focus on human evolution.

Kay Anderson is Emeritus Professor of Cultural Geography at the Institute for Culture & Society, Western Sydney University, and an elected Fellow of the Social Sciences Academies of Australia and the UK. She has published widely in the field of race historiography, including the award-winning *Vancouver's Chinatown* (McGill-Queens University Press, 1991) and *Race and the Crisis of Humanism* (Routledge, 2007).

Sheela Athreya is an Associate Professor of Anthropology at Texas A&M University. Her research focuses on quantitative analyses of the craniofacial morphology of Middle and Late Pleistocene humans, particularly in southern and eastern Eurasia. She conducts fieldwork in India, Sri Lanka and China, examining the evolutionary history of *Homo sapiens*.

Parth R. Chauhan is a faculty member in the Department of Humanities and Social Sciences at the Indian Institute of Science Education and Research, Mohali, India. He obtained his Ph.D., M.A. and B.A. degrees from Sheffield University (UK), Deccan College and Post-graduate Research Institute (India) and Rutgers University (USA), respectively. His research area is the palaeoanthropology of India including Palaeolithic and Mesolithic time periods.

Iain Davidson is Emeritus Professor at the University of New England (New South Wales). Born and educated in the UK, Ph.D. on Spanish Paleolithic. Australian by choice. Principal employment at the University of New England, research on stone tools, rock art, and language origins. Chair of Australian Studies at Harvard, 2008–9. Undertook consultancies for all of Australia's major industries – once – with and on behalf of Kalkadoon, Darug, Wonnarua, Yulluna and Mitakoodi peoples.

Robin Dennell is currently Emeritus Research Professor at the Department of Archaeology, University of Exeter, and his main academic interest is human evolution in Asia, and particularly in China. He has conducted extensive fieldwork in Bulgaria, Iran, Pakistan and China. He is author of *The Palaeolithic Settlement of Asia* (Cambridge University Press, 2009) and co-editor of *Southern Asia, Australia and the Search for Human Origins* (together with Martin Porr; Cambridge University Press, 2014). He is also a Fellow of the British Academy.

Joe Dortch is an archaeologist with diverse experience in academic research and heritage management. He completed his Ph.D. at the University of Western Australia on Aboriginal responses to glacial-period environmental changes in southwestern Australia. Since then he has investigated archaeological evidence for Late Pleistocene faunal extinctions, researched past Aboriginal burning and landscape management in southwestern Australia, and collaborated with geneticists and Aboriginal stakeholders on ancient and modern DNA analysis. He holds an adjunct research position at the University of Western Australia and currently advises Rio Tinto on managing the company's Aboriginal heritage responsibilities in parts of the Pilbara, Western Australia.

Amanda Esterhuysen is an Associate Professor of Archaeology and Head of the Origins Centre in the School of Geography, Archaeology and Environmental studies, University of the Witwatersrand. Her principal research focus is the recent historical past, and contemporary issues affecting the practice of archaeology. She was a member of the late Kadar Asmal's Ministerial History project (2000), and more recently served on the Minister of Education's History Task Team (2018–2020). She has a particular interest in the teaching of evolution in South Africa and has a long association with the Cradle of Humankind World Heritage Site (CoHWHS).

Ursula K. Frederick is a researcher and practitioner of visual arts and archaeology based at the Australian National University. She is currently a recipient of an Australian Research Council Discovery Early Career Research Award (DE DE170101351), investigating the role that creative practice and other visualising strategies may play in the production of archaeological knowledge and heritage discourse. In addition to publishing her research in books and journals, Ursula regularly shows her artwork in group and solo exhibitions.

Jonathan Marks is Professor of Anthropology at the University of North Carolina at Charlotte. Although initially trained in genetics, his interests are eclectic, and he has published widely in science and humanities journals. Among other books, he is the author of *What It Means to be 98% Chimpanzee* (2002) and *Is Science Racist?* (2017).

Jacqueline M. Matthews is a professional archaeologist with Cultural Heritage Management Australia and has wide-ranging experience working with Indigenous communities across Australia. She completed her master's thesis at the University of Western Australia, focused on the application of ontological and postcolonial theories to Australian archaeology, which led to a research interest in the role of Australia in global debates about human origins.

John McNabb is a Palaeolithic archaeologist with interests in stone tools, the Acheulean, cognitive evolution and in the history of human origins research and how its findings were translated for public consumption. He is also interested in the history of science fiction. He is unusual for an academic as he does not like talking about himself. He is Welsh, and damned proud of it.

Ian J. McNiven is Professor of Indigenous Archaeology at Monash Indigenous Studies Centre (Monash University, Melbourne) and the Australian Research Council Centre of Excellence for Australian Biodiversity and Heritage. He specialises in the archaeology of Australian Indigenous societies, with a major research interest in coastal societies and ritual and spiritual relationships with the sea.

Allison Mickel is Assistant Professor of Anthropology in the Department of Sociology and Anthropology at Lehigh University. Her research focuses on how local communities have impacted and been affected by the long history of archaeological work in the Middle East. Mickel received her Ph.D. in anthropology from Stanford University in 2016.

Craig Muller received his Ph.D. in history and postgraduate diploma in archaeology from the University of Western Australia, and has authored numerous publications on Aboriginal history and archaeology. The research for the contribution to this volume was conducted while Craig was a postdoctoral researcher with the Centre for GeoGenetics at the University of Copenhagen. Craig is currently an Honorary Research Fellow with the University of Western Australia.

Martin Porr is Associate Professor of Archaeology and a member of the Centre for Rock Art Research + Management at the University of Western Australia. His research has so far concentrated on aspects related to Palaeolithic European art, Australian rock art, human origins and postcolonial approaches to archaeological research. He has conducted fieldwork in Germany, Thailand, Australia, India and the Philippines.

Paulette F. Steeves Ph.D. (Cree-Metis) is an Assistant Professor in History and a nominee for a Canada Research Chair in Healing and Reconciliation at Algoma University in Ontario. Steeves argues that Indigenous peoples were present in the Western Hemisphere as early as 130,000 years ago, and possibly much earlier. Her research links global human migrations during the Pleistocene to the Americas.

ACKNOWLEDGEMENTS

Like many books, the present volume also developed over a considerable period and involved many collaborators, who provided important input along the way. We, the editors of this volume, first convened a session on 'Decolonising Human Origins' at the Theoretical Archaeology Group Conference at the University of Manchester in 2014. We were able to extend and deepen the engagement with this theme at a Wenner-Gren Foundation workshop that we hosted at the University of Western Australia (UWA) in October 2015. We want to acknowledge the support that was received by the Wenner-Gren Foundation to make that meeting possible, which provided many crucial elements that are developed in this volume. We are also grateful for the extra support provided through a Special Grant from the Deputy Vice Chancellor of Research at UWA (Professor Robyn Owens) and the UWA Institute of Advanced Studies on this occasion.

We want to thank the editors of the Archaeological Orientations series at Routledge, Chris Witmore and Gavin Lucas, for their enthusiasm, patience, advice and support. They really made this volume possible in its current form.

Important aspects of this volume were developed and written while one of us (MP) was based at Tübingen University (Germany) as a Senior Research Fellow of the Alexander von Humboldt Foundation from 2015 to 2017. MP wants to acknowledge the academic inspiration and support provided by Miriam Haidle, Nicholas Conard, Andrew Kandel and Niels Weidtmann during this time.

Finally, we are grateful to our friends and family for supporting us during the work on this volume. We also want to thank our many Indigenous collaborators and friends, who have provided inspiration for this overall project.

As current and former researchers at the University of Western Australia, we acknowledge the Whadjuk Noongar people as the Traditional Owners of the land on which the University's main campus is situated, and all other Traditional Owners of land on which any of its campuses are located. The Traditional Owners, past, present and emerging, remain the spiritual and cultural custodians of their land, and continue to practise their values, languages, beliefs and knowledge. Always was, always will be.

SECTION 1

Introduction

1

INTERROGATING AND DECOLONISING THE DEEP HUMAN PAST

Martin Porr and Jacqueline M. Matthews

Introduction

Even though archaeology is often regarded as a relatively recent discipline, it already has a long and complicated global history. It is widely recognised and accepted that archaeology is closely connected to the development of Western modernity, nationalism and imperialism. These latter aspects particularly influenced archaeology in its formative period during the nineteenth century, and they have left a strong legacy. The nineteenth century was also the time during which the understanding of human history and ethnographic variability was fundamentally reconfigured through a complex interaction between the emerging fields of archaeology and anthropology. Parallel developments include the establishment of the deep antiquity of humanity, which became widely accepted together with the recognition of biological evolution, extinct archaic hominins and, more generally, deep links between humanity and the rest of the natural world. These developments took place in a setting that was politically and socio-economically dominated by European nations and their empires. Possibly the most significant expression of this dominance was the system of global European colonialism, which reached its greatest extent in the late nineteenth century and deeply affected the European political and intellectual landscape, and the perception of the world, its people and their histories. In this text, we use the terms European and Western colonialism to refer to the colonial system of global economic exploitation that was established by European nations from the sixteenth century onwards and subsequently also included the United States as an active force (Nayar 2015b).

Today, it is widely accepted that archaeology's history is closely related to Western colonial expansions and the subsequent denigration of colonised peoples (Gosden 2004; 2012; Liebmann & Rizvi 2008; Lydon & Rizvi 2012). Together with the large number of other disciplines that comprise the 'academy', archaeology is recognised to be a product of colonial Western ideology and discourse, and indeed important and positive developments have been undertaken by uncovering the ongoing influences of these historical and intellectual configurations (Bruchac, Hart & Wobst 2010; McNiven & Russell 2005). Important discussions about historical and contemporary influences of colonialism and the applicability of postcolonial thought to different aspects of global archaeology are ongoing and continue to make important contributions to this field (Hamilakis 2009; 2012; Hamilakis & Duke 2007; Moro-Abadía 2006). More generally and despite much diversity in approaches, a recognition of the importance of reflexivity towards archaeological methods and theories has been a central element within the discipline for some time now. It is generally accepted that our subjectivities are inescapable and that an understanding of the relationships between the different forces impacting on any practitioner is necessary to conduct good research (see for example contributions in Hodder 2012).

However, it seems noteworthy that there is only limited engagement with these aspects of archaeological theory and practice in the fields that traditionally are concerned with human origins or human evolution, Palaeolithic archaeology, and palaeoanthropology. Even if we understand 'human origins' research very broadly, it is noticeable that contributions dealing with these themes are virtually absent in the postcolonial or decolonising literature within archaeology (see for example Bruchac, Hart & Wobst 2010; Gosden 2012; Liebmann & Rizvi 2008; Lydon & Rizvi 2012; McNiven & Russell 2005; Rizvi 2015). We appear to be faced with a situation in which important and significant sections of archaeology remain largely unaffected by some of the most significant theoretical developments to influence our field in recent decades. This situation is unsatisfactory because it is these sections of archaeology that tend to make a range of universalist claims about humanity's past, how 'we' became human, what it means to be human and so on.

As we will outline in this chapter, similar universal claims by mostly Western scientists, politicians, administrators and writers have been at the core of postcolonial critique for a long time. This volume aims to fill a gap in critical archaeological analysis and research history. It is aimed at exploring connections and entanglements between the study of human origins and human evolution, and Western colonialism and its critique. However, we also recognise the numerous links that exist between postcolonialism and other critical developments that have gained traction throughout the second half of the twentieth century, e.g. poststructuralism, critical theory and Marxist approaches (McLeod 2007; Young 2001). More recently, the influence of Indigenous philosophies and non-Western intellectual contributions has increased the engagement with ontological dimensions of scientific inquiry, so-called new animism and new materialism, as well as post-humanist approaches (Alberti 2016; Alberti et al. 2011; Alberti & Marshall 2009). These latter developments are broadly related to postcolonial thought through the challenge of established Western science, its epistemologies, ontology and practices, as well as the related intellectual and political dominance of the West (Blaser 2013b; 2014; Coole & Frost 2010; Grusin 2015; Tsing 2015). The contributions in this volume, consequently, approach the theme in different ways and from different perspectives. Some make explicit reference to postcolonial literature; some do not. They all, however, closely interrogate human origins and human becoming in a theoretically-informed fashion that centres an awareness of the socio-economic and historical conditions of archaeological practice.

Research, knowledge and the postcolonial critique

The idea of decolonisation as an intellectual endeavour grew out of the political and socio-economic upheavals after World War II during which many of the formal and institutionalised structures of Western colonialism were dismantled (see for example contributions in

Ashcroft, Griffiths & Tiffin 1995; Bhambra 2014; Young 2001). These developments reconfigured the power relationships between colonisers and colonised and opened new spaces in which it became possible to critically engage with and analyse the mechanisms that had created, justified and perpetuated the system of Western colonialism. The intellectual roots of such an explicitly critical postcolonial movement or postcolonialism can be identified in a wave of anticolonial literature between the 1930s through to the 1960s. These were to a large extent embedded in or even initiated the complex movements of decolonisation, political independence and national liberation (Bhabha 1994; Said 1978; Spivak 1999). Just as Western or European colonialism was not a monolithic ideology and found different expressions in different parts of the world, reactions, responses and critical engagements were also variable (Bhambra 2014; Young 2001). Despite some significant differences, 'postcolonial' or approaches with a decolonising agenda often share a challenge against 'traditional colonialist epistemologies, questioning the knowledge about and the representation of colonised "Others" that has been produced in colonial and imperial contexts' (Liebmann 2008, p. 5). Postcolonial studies are known for their critique of Eurocentrism, nationalism, colonial ideologies and economic determinism. They tend to concentrate on subaltern agency and culture as a central mechanism in the creation of social formations (Chibber 2013, p. 4).

Postcolonial approaches raise profound issues related to the knowability of social forms and causalities. These approaches can be regarded as a reflection of critical reflexive dimensions that have been a central force, directly and indirectly, affecting all fields of comparative studies of human societies in a wider sense of the term. They stem not only from postcolonial critique but more broadly through the so-called crisis of representation (Clifford & Marcus 1986; Marcus & Fischer 1986) and the cultural turn (Chibber 2013, p. 1). Largely replacing Marxist materialism as the dominant theoretical framework, these aspects have particularly impacted cultural or social anthropology from the late 1970s onwards, and the criticism of colonial discourses necessitated a critique of the objectifying epistemology of anthropology itself. Recursively, the critique of the construction of 'the Other' through such discourses leads toward the emergence of cultural critique, which takes seriously where the dominant ideas that direct thought and practice emerge from and on what basis their validity is accepted. A critical reflexive dimension has since been a central force that has directly and indirectly affected the social sciences and literary studies in a wider sense of the term. One of the key characteristics of postcolonialism was its rapid movement from literature and literary studies to many other academic and non-academic fields. From around the end of the twentieth century, postcolonialism 'was no longer a purely disciplinary phenomenon' (Chibber 2013, p. 2).

Postcolonialism developed out of the resistance against colonial power structures and it 'marks the moment where the political and cultural experience of the marginalized periphery developed into a more general theoretical position that could be set against western political, intellectual and academic hegemony and its protocols of objective knowledge' (Young 2001, p. 65). Hence, the project of Subaltern Studies has been a key catalyst for the postcolonial movement since the early 1980s (Chaturvedi 2000; Ludden 2002). Postcolonial approaches consequently often stress the subjective, personal and individual experience as an important element and causal factor in social processes and formations. In this way, the insights from the periphery have been employed to critique the narratives that have originated from the centre. Postcolonial theory operates on the assumption that intellectual and cultural traditions from former colonies or other suppressed social contexts can be deployed against the heritage of colonialism and its ideologies in the West itself (Young 2001, p. 65). Postcolonialism has developed not only into a collection of analytical approaches, but also a transdisciplinary and global cultural critique of social practices. Therefore, it has been argued that postcolonialism does not present a coherent theory and methodology. It rather presents a critical and political agenda that employs a range of shifting theories and methods (Chibber 2013, p. 3). It is broadly committed to political ideals of transnational social justice and against hegemonic economic imperialism.

Over the last few decades, postcolonialism has shifted its focus together with changes in the global political and economic systems. The end of the European political colonial system and the end of the Cold War produced new forms of domination, which have been described as capitalist economic imperialism. Postcolonialism today operates within these structures, as a critical response to its conditions, and has to 'contend with a complex adversary whose power is dispersed through a wide range of globalized institutions and practices' (Young 2001, p. 59). Consequently, the focus has more recently shifted to uncovering and exposing the imperialist system of economic, political and cultural domination with a particular emphasis on the subtle mechanisms of the latter. This tendency is linked to the cultural orientation of postcolonial critique mentioned above that found an early reflection in the idea of the 'decolonisation of the mind' (Ngugi 1986), which has now become an important element in a wide range of disciplines. For example, social anthropology has recently been suggested as 'being the theory/practice of the permanent decolonization of thought' (Viveiros de Castro 2014, p. 40). Through a serious engagement with Indigenous worldviews and directions from Indigenous scholars, this orientation understands the Western framework of ontology, epistemology and knowledge as a product of its own specific conditions and consequently denies its ability and authority to explain and describe humanity as a whole. This critique has been applied to several analytical fields, for example, the conceptualisation of social space and time, the division between nature and culture, humanity and animality and notions of causal relationships and material effects (Bhambra 2014; Kohn 2013; Mignolo 2011). Postcolonialism is, therefore, concerned with dislocating, questioning and displacing Western knowledge and its dominance, which includes Western historicist history as the dominant narrative that includes and ultimately replaces all other narratives (Chakrabarty 2000).

As mentioned above, the intellectual side of decolonisation has always been entangled with political and economic aspects related to independence movements and calls for social justice and sovereignty. Accordingly, postcolonialism has also deeply impacted the practical and ethical aspects of research (Tuck & Yang 2012). These aspects, of course, take different forms across different disciplines in the natural and social sciences. They range from the establishment of consultation and permission protocols to the collaborative control of research materials and results as well as collaboratively authored publications. However, despite many positive developments and legislative changes, Indigenous authors continue to stress that these aspects still need a lot of work. As Tuhiwai Smith (2012, p. 232) has argued, 'scientific research remains inextricably linked to European imperialism and colonialism [...] The word itself, "research", is probably one of the dirtiest words in the indigenous world's vocabulary.' This devastating assessment is based on the long experience of objectification of Indigenous people by Western scientists. Whereby, science became another facet of the extractive and exploitative practices of European domination:

It appals us that the West can desire, extract and claim ownership of our ways of knowing, our imagery, the things we create and produce, and then simultaneously reject the people who created and developed those ideas and seek to deny them further opportunities to be creators of their own culture and own nations.

(Tuhiwai Smith 2012, p. 240)

While these aspects cannot be discussed in greater detail here, it is important to stress that the postcolonial movement necessitates a critical engagement with knowledge production, knowledge hierarchies and knowledge institutions, which is important for the theory and practice of all fields of archaeology as well. As Rizvi (2008, p. 108) has argued, to 'decolonise does not only index a choice to change the discipline but also in a very real way, is a desire to safeguard ourselves from recreating forms of imperial knowledge production'.

Archaeology and the postcolonial critique

Together with social and biological/physical anthropology, archaeology has deep intellectual and historical links with the rise of Western modernity, imperialism and colonialism (Gosden 1999; 2004). Going back to key developments during the Enlightenment, these disciplines are connected by their aim to describe and explain human biological and cultural variability in the past and the present without reference to religious or mystical principles. As Gosden (2012, p. 251) has outlined, these disciplines are consequently characterised by a tension between human unity and universality on the one hand and local cultural variability and difference on the other. Consequently, adopting a postcolonial perspective 'resonates strongly with the possible dissonance between difference and equality or unity', which is a motive directly relevant to the theme of this volume. It is not necessary to repeat here a detailed overview of the history of postcolonial influences on archaeology (see for example Liebmann & Rizvi 2008; Lydon & Rizvi 2012). Mirroring the complexity of developments in other fields, postcolonialism as a movement in archaeology has been equally diverse and situational and can be understood as 'an active intervention that emerges from particular histories, interrogates the status quo, and moves consciously towards decolonization politically, intellectually and economically' (Nicholas & Hollowell 2007, p. 62).

The influence of postcolonial elements in archaeology has grown considerably in the last two decades. The field can be broadly divided into three interconnected areas: the history of colonialism itself, development of Indigenous archaeologies and collaborative projects with Indigenous communities, and the critical analysis of colonialism's influence on archaeological narratives. These areas are elaborated on throughout the rest of this section.

Archaeological methods have been employed to better understand the history of colonialism itself and its different mechanisms across the continents. In this case, postcolonial archaeology is a sub-field of historical archaeology that itself is broadly understood as the archaeology of the modern world system that originated with European colonialism during the last 500 years (Paterson 2011). This field also has a critical dimension and obvious links exist with the postcolonial aim of accessing and reconstructing subaltern narratives and perspectives (cf. Spivak 1999). Archaeology can play a key role in understanding the different dimensions and mechanisms of colonialism that fundamentally involved the control and exploitation of spaces, time, bodies, resources and boundaries. These aspects apply particularly to the forms of colonialism in the last 200 years, which caused historically unusual devastation and histories that are not recorded in official written records (Gosden 2012, p. 256). Therefore, these analyses are often done together with or initiated by Indigenous communities.

The development of Indigenous archaeologies or collaborative archaeological projects with Indigenous communities is thus the second significant area of postcolonial influences on archaeology. This aspect is related to postcolonialism's critique of existing contemporary power structures and the ambition to develop interventionalist methodologies for the analysis of the subjective and material conditions of the postcolonial era and an activist engagement that creates positive political positions and new forms of political identity (Young 2001, p. 58). Cooperative relationships between archaeologists and Indigenous people and communities have taken many forms and have followed a range of aims. There is also a considerable variability related to disciplinary histories, colonial traditions, and national as well as bureaucratic trajectories (Colwell-Chanthaphonh 2012).

Within Australia, close interactions with Indigenous communities highlight the inescapable political dimension of routine archaeological practice. Professional archaeological work undertaken on Indigenous archaeology or cultural heritage often stems from the recognition of a particular Indigenous community's status within Native Title or other land rights legislation. Professional archaeologists, working to 'manage' Indigenous cultural heritage in these contexts, often collaborate on decisions about the preservation of Indigenous cultural heritage in the face of potential threats from development. Their work is not a neutral and disinterested practice, and it is done with the knowledge that it can have dramatic and irreversible consequences; not just physically for tangible heritage places, it can also have wide-ranging political implications for the Indigenous community in question. For example, archaeological evidence and reasoning have demonstrated potential to be used as evidence in Indigenous Native Title claims (Godwin 2005; Gosden 2012, p. 252; Veth 2010). These negotiations always take place within specific administrative and legal frameworks that are often far removed from the 'traditional' sovereignty and laws of the Indigenous communities affected.

Today, virtually all nations have legislation in place that provides at least some protection to Indigenous, historical and archaeological heritage. One of the most well-known examples of such legislation is the Native American Graves and Repatriation Act (NAGPRA) in the United States in 1990. This legislation formalised some developments of collaborative engagements between Native American groups and Cultural Resource Management companies. It also intensified Indigenous participation in archaeological and heritage management projects and initiated extensive discussions around repatriation issues in the United States (Colwell 2017). These debates have not been without problems, but collaborative projects are now the norm rather than the exception. Comparable legislation to protect Indigenous heritage has also been introduced in many other countries, which initiated complex engagements about the access to archaeological sites and evidence, and the treatment of artefacts and human remains (Colwell-Chanthaphonh 2012, pp. 271–272). Again, these discussions have ultimately been about forms and control of knowledge, cultural and social values and the understanding of history.

These processes can, for example, be seen in the debates and controversies around the oldest human remains that have so far been discovered in Australia. In 1969, Jim Bowler and a team of geologists and archaeologists discovered the human remains eroding from the shores of ancient Lake Mungo, Willandra Lakes, New South Wales (Stern 2015). Analysis showed that these remains belonged to a woman who had lived in the region about 40,000 years ago (Bowler, Thorne & Polach 1972). The discovery and dating of the human remains – that became affectionally known as Mungo Lady – fundamentally changed the perception of the deep human past of Australia and influenced the global academic community. This situation was enhanced by the discovery of another individual in 1974, who became known as Mungo Man (Bowler & Thorne 1976). Although Australia was never seriously considered to be an origin region for humanity, early occupation dates from the continent have consequences for the interpretation of global human evolution. At the time of their discovery, the Lake Mungo human remains were the oldest known anatomically modern humans outside of Africa. However, statements like these immediately establish the significance of the remains in relation to a global narrative of human origins and a universal understanding of humanity. But the remains also have a local significance. In 1973, Alice Kelly, one of the Aboriginal Elders of the local Mutthi Mutthi people, wrote a letter of concern and asked why she was not consulted about the archaeological work and the removal of human remains. She wrote that Lady Mungo belonged to her tribal people and any excavations had to be stopped (Griffiths 2018, p. 133). However, only in 1988, and after many further interventions by the local Paakantji, Mutthi Mutthi and Ngyiampaa people, was an embargo put in place on fieldwork activities. In 1992, the remains of Mungo Lady were handed back to local Elders. In November 2017, Mungo Man was also returned to his ancestral country – together with the remains of more than a hundred further individuals from the Willandra Lakes that had been stored for many decades in universities and museums in Canberra and Sydney (Lambert 2018, p. 245). At the time of writing (April 2019), both Mungo Lady and Mungo Man are set to be reburied near to their original discovery locations in a unanimous decision by the Willandra Lakes Aboriginal Advisory Group (Perkins 2018).

Today, the Willandra Lakes World Heritage Site is widely regarded as a positive and powerful example of collaborative work between archaeologists, physical anthropologists and Indigenous communities, and the opportunities that come from respectfully navigating different cultural perspectives, values and understandings of temporality (Allbrock & McGrath 2015; Lawrence 2006). The collaborations and engagements that have been going on for a considerable amount of time – sometimes over many decades – also seem to produce significant convergences between so-called scientific and Indigenous perspectives. In 2004, Mutthi Mutthi Elder Mary Pappin wrote that: 'I believe that Mungo Lady came to walk with our people to help us with our struggle and to tell the rest of the world about our cultural identity with that land.' Similarly, Jim Bowler reflected on the personal dimensions of having lived together with Mungo Man for 42 years: 'I owe a great debt to Mungo Man. He has changed me, and he is capable of changing everyone else' (quoted in Griffiths 2018, p. 140). Here, it seems that the boundary between these two knowledge systems becomes porous and the encounter allows space for reflection on their similarities and differences, which can only be beneficial for future encounters and negotiations. Rizvi (2016) has explored these aspects in relation to the phenomenological creation of identity through the process of archaeological research, which draws on the relationships she constructs as a researcher with monuments, artefacts, non-humans and other people. Key to her argument is the idea of 'decolonisation as care', which refers to a reflexive mindfulness towards herself and her engagement with archaeological material: 'This can maintain one's livelihood and sense of self. And through alliances and creating kin with others (human/non-human), we maintain and protect ourselves. And ultimately, that care for and with others is also self-care' (Rizvi 2016, p. 94).

The healing powers of collaborative archaeological and heritage work have been documented and explored more recently in several contexts across the globe (Bruchac, Hart &

Wobst 2010; Schaepe et al. 2017; Smith & Wobst 2005). In the spirit of postcolonial studies' key aim of making visible hidden and suppressed narratives, archaeology can access evidence that had previously escaped the attention of official histories and historiographies. These studies can consequently be turned against the dominant discourse, and many Indigenous communities have acknowledged this potentially empowering dimension of archaeological practice.

The engagement with Indigenous communities has also contributed to the development of theoretical reflection within archaeology about archaeology's ontological position and epistemologies (Colwell 2016). This aspect relates to the final and third area where postcolonialism influences archaeology: the critical investigation and reflection of hitherto unrecognised tropes of colonialism in archaeological narratives. Engagement with Indigenous communities has necessitated new discussions about the meaning and significance of oral traditions and histories. Under the influence of the New Archaeology, this aspect was largely excluded from archaeological reasoning, and it only started to gain attention in the course of the above-mentioned legal changes. Over time, however, oral evidence is increasingly recognised as a source of novel hypotheses and propositions that contribute to the understanding of the phenomena of history (Colwell-Chanthaphonh 2012, pp. 274–275). This recognition includes, for example, the possibility that oral traditions accurately record deep-time historical and environmental events – as has been argued for North America (Echo-Hawk 2000) and Australia (Nunn 2018; Nunn & Reid 2016). The integration of archaeological or scientific and Indigenous accounts of the past is not unproblematic. Certainly, cultural differences must be navigated and considered as well. In the postcolonial tradition, these differences are taken seriously and related to deep cultural differences and ontologies, which, for example, explain the importance of myth and narratives for Indigenous worldviews (Porr & Matthews 2016).

The recognition of these deep differences also constitutes a problem and a challenge for collaborations between researchers and Indigenous communities. How should these differences be approached? These questions have supported engagement with the notion of multivocality in archaeological research and interpretation. Often, scientific and Indigenous interpretations are now presented alongside each other to acknowledge multiple viewpoints and perspectives appropriately. Such an approach has been employed for a long time in heritage and museum contexts. However, also in publications, multivocality has been integrated with co-authorship arrangements (Bruchac, Hart & Wobst 2010; Colwell 2016; Oobagooma et al. 2016; Porr & Bell 2012). The benefits of these initiatives seem to be very straightforward, but issues of representation and power imbalances persist. The translation of oral and embodied Indigenous knowledge into writing is always a complicated process that needs to be carefully navigated (Porr 2018). Still, the active engagement with different knowledge systems allows for reflection on archaeology's own ontological basis and methodological practices (Wylie 2008). While a deeper concern with the implications of a deeply integrated Indigenous archaeology has only just started (McNiven 2016), current developments have initiated a rethink of the discipline to allow a greater plurality in the approaches towards history and its connections with other critical strands within the social sciences.

These aspects connect the postcolonial influences in archaeology with the postprocessual critique from the 1980s onwards (see overview and references in Hodder 2012). The various theoretical and methodological links within this wider field cannot be discussed in greater detail here. However, numerous intellectual relationships exist between key areas of postcolonial critique and postprocessual archaeology in relation to critical (Marxist) theory (Leone, Potter Jr & Shackel 1987; Miller & Tilley 1984), feminism (Conkey & Gero 1997; Gero & Conkey 1991) and poststructuralism (Bapty & Yates 1990). However, explicit references to postcolonial literature and themes remain rare (but see Moro-Abadía 2006). Possibly the most explicit engagement with postcolonial themes was presented by Trigger in his extensive assessments of different aspects of the global history of archaeology (Trigger 1984; 1989; 2008); Trigger's Marxist orientation aligns him closely with postcolonial intellectual aims and strands of thought. The influences of imperialism, nationalism, racism and colonialism on the development of the discipline of archaeology form cornerstones of Trigger's groundbreaking critical study *A History of Archaeological Thought*, which has become a classic of archaeological literature (Trigger 1989). Its influence remains strong and it continues to influence new generations of archaeologists (Habu, Fawcett & Matsunaga 2008). The treatment of Palaeolithic archaeology and palaeoanthropological research, however, remains underdeveloped. In his main work, Trigger discusses the development of Palaeolithic archaeology in Europe in relation to the establishment of the antiquity of humanity and the acceptance of Darwinism (Trigger 1989, pp. 94–101). He further drew attention to the problematic imposition of European chronological schemes onto the African evidence in the context of colonial archaeology in the early twentieth century (Trigger 1989, pp. 135–136). He subsequently argued that early research into human origins in East and South Africa was mostly conducted to uncover the origins of modern European society rather than establish a link with the African continent and its people. This argument seems to point to an unusually critical reading of this research tradition and seems to suggest links to the idea of 'origins research' as proposed by Gamble and Gittins (Gamble & Gittins 2004; see below). However, the argument remains strangely unelaborated and suggestive (Trigger 1989, p. 136).

Postcolonial approaches and human origins

At this stage, it can be concluded that despite numerous positive developments in the wider field of archaeology, there has been very little explicit engagement with postcolonial literature and themes within the field of human origins studies, palaeoanthropology and Palaeolithic archaeology. We argue that this is a problematic situation because postcolonial writers have critically engaged with a wide range of terms and concepts that also form key aspects of research into the deep human past and human origins. In this section, we outline several relevant aspects of postcolonial contributions and approaches to human origins research, and we explicitly acknowledge that this is only a very preliminary collection of examples and suggestions. So far, these aspects have hardly been brought into explicit correspondence with each other. However, at the same time, there are critical strands available within archaeology that can be brought into this discussion, even though they do not explicitly reference postcolonial literature. These will be discussed in the following section.

Foundational texts of postcolonial studies contain elements that are not only relevant to archaeological interpretation and practice in general, but in particular to Palaeolithic archaeology and palaeoanthropology. Said's (1999 [orig. 1978]) ground-breaking thesis *Orientalism* not only elucidated the origins and perpetuations of the Western idea of the 'Orient', which has been variously applied to the societies and nations of the Near East, Russia, India, East and Southeast Asia. The significance of Said's work is in uncovering the intellectual and discursive processes that have contributed and continue to contribute to the construction of the Other in the Western popular and academic imagination. Said also showed how these processes are far from free-floating semantic relationships but are deeply entangled with material and economic conditions and structures. As such, they are intimately and deeply connected to the asymmetric power relationships that have characterised the colonial system. In this respect, Said has deep intellectual links with the critical theories of Foucault and other poststructuralist thinkers. The Orient, like any cultural category, does not have an independent objective existence. It is constantly created – consciously and unconsciously – and dialectically bound to the construction of the Occident, the West, itself. These insights have obvious applications for any historical and comparative social science. As Dennell demonstrates in this volume and elsewhere, orientalist ideas have had a fundamental structuring impact on Palaeolithic archaeology and the interpretation of the global archaeological record for most of the twentieth century.

In his later work, *Culture and Imperialism* (Said 1994), Said explored the fundamental links between cultural forms and practices, and the creation and perpetuation of imperial structures in France, the United Kingdom and the United States. He particularly concentrated on the role of the novel in the nineteenth and early twentieth centuries. Said's underlying aim was to uncover and analyse the significance of narratives in these processes. It is clear that such aspects are deeply entangled with power relationships. The ability to construct and disseminate certain narratives and block others from emerging is an important element in the relationship between culture and empire. Subsequently, in the processes of decolonisation, narratives and their reconfiguration into counternarratives played a similarly crucial role (Said 1994, p. xiii). These insights show some significant links with Anderson's (2006 [orig. 1983]) seminal analysis of the origins and spread of Western nationalism. In the latter case, Anderson wove together the elements of cultural expressions, narratives, nationalism and the construction of imagined communities. Anderson also emphasised the importance of time and history in these contexts, and these aspects are also explored by several authors in this volume.

For archaeology, Trigger (Trigger 1984; 1989) famously engaged with these issues and revealed the role of archaeology in the creation of national identities during the nineteenth and twentieth centuries. However, any reference to Palaeolithic archaeological evidence and interpretations as well as human origins is minimal in this context and not in relation to critical processes of identity construction or nationalism. Nevertheless, the importance of narrative structures in the construction of the deep human past has been seminally analysed by Landau (1991). She demonstrated the value of a systematic literary approach towards writing about human evolution. Landau was able to uncover similar narrative sequences that have deep links to Western cultural traditions of story-telling. They also appear to be largely unaffected by constantly growing empirical archaeological evidence. A related argument has subsequently been made by Stoczkowski (2002), who also observed that interpretations of human evolution were very resilient in the light of changing and expanding empirical data during the formative phase of archaeology and beyond. He further made the case that explanations of human evolution and origins were guided by a few complementary assumptions that are generally not made explicit and are rather regarded as self-evident: environmental determinism, materialism, utilitarianism and individualism (Stoczkowski 2002, pp. 16–17). These elements can certainly be regarded as fundamental building blocks of the modern Western ontology (Descola 2013) and we have argued elsewhere that they have structured recent views of so-called modern human origins in a problematic and universalising fashion (Porr & Matthews 2017). However, these elements can also be used as points of departure to explore a postcolonial critique of human evolution further because they also form crucial aspects within the postcolonial literature in relation to the understanding of human societies, identities and histories, cultural and biological difference.

In his discussion of Frantz Fanon's work, Bhabha (1994) drew attention to Fanon's critique of modernity's universal understanding of humanity itself. Fanon was very clear about the importance of this aspect within the ideology and mechanisms of colonialism. The 'white world' is governed by an ontology with hierarchical forms of rationality and universality that function to authorise 'the human' within a temporality of emergence. However, this emergence is unequally distributed and not accessible to everyone: 'Despite the pedagogies of human history, the performative discourse of the liberal West, its quotidian conversation and comments, reveal the cultural supremacy and racial typology upon which the universalism of Man is founded' (Bhabha 1994, p. 340). Fanon stressed, therefore, the historicity of modernity's most precious and universal symbol, humanity itself. This ideology also creates a progressive myth of humanity that constantly interprets cultural difference in temporal terms and creates an unbridgeable 'belatedness of the black man': 'You come too late, much too late, there will always be a world – a white world between you and us' (Fanon, quoted in Bhabha 1994, p. 339).

In his foundational text for postcolonial studies, *The Location of Culture*, Bhabha (1994) himself extensively engaged with the entanglements of temporality, modernity, race and colonialism. He made the case that modernity, as a fundamentally temporal concept, is constantly struggling with the establishment of its own historicity. Modernity emerges as a form of interrogation and a 'tension between the pedagogy of the symbols of progress, historicism, modernisation, homogeneous empty time, the narcissism of organic culture, the onanistic search for the origins of race' (Bhabha 1994, p. 350). The time-lag mentioned above remains a key element for the discourse of modernity between the 'epochal event of modernity as the symbol of the continuity of progress, and the interruptive temporality of the sign of the present' (Bhabha 1994, p. 350). For the future, he consequently argued for a diversity of temporalities and cultural understandings of time with rhythms that are sometimes swift and sometimes slow. Most significant for the topic of this volume, he concluded that a postcolonial perspective on history must do nothing less than change the understanding of humanity and history itself:

> What is crucial to such a vision of the future is the belief that we must not merely change the narratives of our histories, but transform our sense of what it means to live, to be, in other times and different spaces, both human and historical.
>
> *(Bhabha 1994, p. 367)*

A key element of Chakrabarty's (2000) *Provincializing Europe* is also the critical engagement with the universalising tendencies of Western thought and the effects on historical narratives. He noted that Western philosophers and thinkers have produced theories that embrace the entirety of humanity for a very long time. However, at the same time, these theories 'have been produced in relative, and sometimes absolute, ignorance of the majority of humankind – that is, those living in non-Western cultures' (Chakrabarty 2000, p. 29). For example, Marx's writings provide not only a universal theory to explain historical processes and developments. Chakrabarty also drew attention to the fact that Marx explicitly argued that these universal insights could only have been achieved within bourgeois or European societies. With specific reference to India, Chakrabarty consequently argued that Western historical writing is full of value judgements about achievements and successes. Equally, it often centrally contains references to 'absences' or 'the failure of a history to keep an appointment with its destiny' (Chakrabarty 2000, p. 31).

In a more recent paper, Chakrabarty (2011) reflected on the impact of his influential book and the possibility of history in the face of radically different forms of temporalities, knowledge production and 'necessary political anomalies of postcolonial societies'. Is history possible for societies that have no tradition of writing? Can material and archaeological evidence fully substitute historical and written documents? These considerations draw attention to the in-built inequalities of history as an academic discipline and as a form of knowledge production. If the possibility of history depends on the presence of written records, the world necessarily becomes divided into history-rich and history-poor societies. This distinction is embedded into asymmetrical power relationships and struggles for legitimacy and political representation (Chakrabarty 2011, p. 246). Anderson (2006, p. 46) has stressed that written history and its dissemination through different media is closely connected with nationhood and modern bureaucratic societies. As such, it became an important field of contestation during processes of decolonisation during the twentieth century. These considerations draw attention to the necessity to deeply engage with other forms of historical knowledge and, by extension, other forms of constructing the human past and human origins. Chakrabarty (2011, p. 48) did not reduce these questions to a discussion of whether history and myths should be considered as equally valid forms of knowledge (see for example Porr & Matthews 2016). He rather used this historical moment as an opportunity for reflection on the nature and limits of historical knowledge and its conditions of possibility. Such a movement must consequently include engagement with non-materialist and non-utilitarian causalities, and deep ontological difference and alterity.

In this context, numerous Indigenous scholars or those working with Indigenous people are increasingly challenging the Western epistemology of historical writing and reconstruction (Rifkin 2017). For example, Watts (2013) elaborated from her position as an Anishnaabe and Haudenosaunee woman the critical importance of origin narratives for her worldview and being, which are constantly tested against the colonial frame. She described a Haudenosaunee Creation Story that details how Sky Woman became curious and fell from a hole in the sky:

> On her descent, Sky Woman fell through the clouds and air towards water below. During her descent, birds could see this falling creature and saw she could not fly. They came to her and helped to lower her slowly to waters beneath her. The birds told Turtle that she must need a place to land, as she possessed no water legs. Turtle rose up, breaking through the surface so that Sky Woman could land on Turtle's back. Once landed, Sky Woman and Turtle began to form the earth, the land becoming an extension of their bodies.
>
> *(Watts 2013, p. 21)*

It is important to emphasise that according to Watts (2013 p. 21), these are not narratives that only serve as illustrations of moral and ethical standards of society. She was affirmative that the event that is described is 'not imagined or fantasized'. It is 'not lore, myth or legend': 'This is what happened.' For a long time, social anthropology, archaeology and other social sciences have grappled with such understandings of the past that seemingly contradict Western epistemologies and an understanding of history as a linear sequence of events. While the Western understanding of linear time is often presented as scientific or physical, it needs to be stressed that in modern physics, time is not an independent category or container in which events take place and can easily be ordered sequentially. Einstein established that time is always relative to an observer of an event and in quantum physics, processes do not have a determined direction or sequence (Rovelli 2018). Apart from these fundamental insights, time is in modern physics simply what a clock reads. It does not exist independently from forms of measurement, perception and experience. These insights possibly enable a more serious engagement with Indigenous notions of time and history, which also has an impact on notions of human origins (see Porr this volume).

Elsewhere, one of us discussed the challenges of navigating the relationships between Indigenous knowledge and current archaeological views of modern human origins within an Australian context. Bringing these aspects together in a balanced fashion requires the recalibration of several fundamental notions related to the conception of humanity, origins and identity (Porr 2015). In Australia, the discussion around these issues has been dominated by the notion of the Dreamtime or Dreaming (Stanner 1958), which has been used as a summary term to describe Aboriginal relational place-based philosophies with multiple and intersecting temporalities (James 2015; Oobagooma et al. 2016). Origin narratives play vital roles within these worldviews. But they do not refer to a distant past; rather, as Stanner (1968) famously outlined, they are located in the *every-when*, collapsing the Western understanding of linear time and spatiality. Rose (2004) has described the experience with her Aboriginal teachers in Northern Australia (Victoria River) as dizzying, because it is guided by a sense of historical inversion. Life is oriented towards origins rather than towards a future state: 'It seems that we face Dreaming, and live our lives moving closer to Dreaming; those behind us walk in our footsteps, as we walk in the steps of those who precede us' (Rose 2004, p. 54). Following Chakrabarty (2011; see above), we suggest that these are further insights that allow reflection upon the conditions and potentials of historical knowledge, which also includes archaeology and other approaches to humanity's deep past (Porr 2018). The resilience of Aboriginal communities is crucial to acknowledge in this space; however, that does not absolve the non-Indigenous scholarly community from their responsibility in addressing the enduring power imbalances that they benefit from and (albeit unwittingly) perpetuate. Among others, Muecke (2004) has drawn attention to the devastating and ongoing effects of Western views of history that are linked to the working of modern bureaucracy and administration as well as general social and economic pressures. Mirroring a gruesome and genocidal practice in the context of colonial economic exploitation and political domination, he has argued that Western linear temporality is 'history's poison blanket' (Muecke 2004, p. 24): 'From the beginning, history has been wielded against Aboriginal peoples as something they, along with other non-Western peoples, lacked.'

Muecke's analysis can be linked to a wider critique of the philosophical foundations of Western modernity that has been a core element of postcolonial studies and literature for several decades. As was mentioned above, archaeology has been widely recognised as a product of modernity and its ontological and epistemological dimensions (Thomas 2004). However, fewer authors have discussed the link between modernity and colonialism in the context of deep time archaeology (González-Ruibal 2013). We argue that such a discussion needs to be expanded and extended to all periods of archaeological research. There is little doubt that key aspects of archaeological reasoning have received extensive scrutiny already in this respect. Such scrutiny includes, for example, the progressive character of modernity's understanding of history according to which 'the modern future is one that is pure and full of light and its past, by contrast, is replete with superstition, outdatedness or error' (Muecke 2004, p. 25). These elements continue to influence the interpretation of humanity's deep past (Porr & Matthews 2017) and there are obvious and well-known links to the postcolonial critique of the interpretation of cultural and historical difference (Chakrabarty 2011; Fabian 1983; Trüper, Chakrabarty & Subrahmanyam 2015).

In the context of this volume, we draw attention to the fact that these critiques are part of a much wider reassessment of the foundations of modernity and scientific practice. Such a reassessment affects the core of the project of human evolution and human origins because it questions the notion of nature, the definition of humanity and, hence, the conceptualisation of human/animal/environment interactions. Within the social sciences, many authors have examined the close connections between the intellectual basis of Western modernity that originated with the Enlightenment in the eighteenth century, European colonialism and capitalism. The work of Latour, in particular, has provided important inspirations in this respect. Such discussions have opened a critical space for an assessment of scientific practices and the underlying assumptions about objects and subjects, agency, materiality and the constitution of knowledge as well as an extensive debate about the Western idea of nature and its relationship with modernity (Latour 1993; 2004; 2013). Descola has also extensively criticised the enhanced position that is usually afforded to Western naturalism and has made the case to view it as only one worldview among others (Descola 2013; 2014; see also Sahlins 1996; 2014). This theme has obvious connections to Chakrabarty's (2000) historically focussed *Provincializing Europe*. In Latin American anthropology and sociology, similar ideas have been developed recently in a much more fundamental fashion and with explicit reference to the processes and intellectual dimensions of European colonialism. Quijano proposed in 1989/1990 the notion of 'coloniality' (see Mignolo 2011, p. xx; Quijano 2007) to differentiate it from 'colonialism'. For Quijano colonialism describes the 'formal system of political domination by Western European societies' (Quijano 2007, p. 168) and coloniality refers to cultural forms of domination and the 'colonisation of the imagination' (Quijano 2007, p. 169). Quijano argued that global structures of domination persisted after the end of formal political domination as intersubjective constructions that were presented as objective or scientific, as natural phenomena, rather than as products of power relationships.

Mignolo has recently explored the concept of coloniality more extensively and regarded it as 'the darker side of Western modernity' (Mignolo 2011), which also functions as an 'anchor of decolonial thinking and doing in the praxis of living' (Mignolo & Walsh 2018, p. 2703). For Mignolo, Western modernity is inseparable from the logic of coloniality, which is consequently also expressed as modernity/coloniality. Coloniality is the symbolic and cultural matrix that was established during the Renaissance and refined and elaborated during the Enlightenment. Coloniality has persisted until the present day and has undergone its most recent transformation when modernity was absorbed by neoliberal globalisation (see also Moore 2015; Moore 2016). The important aspect here is the close association between fundamental intellectual and universalising features of modernity and colonialism. These include the notions of rationality, time, history, space, humanity, materiality, life and so on. According to Mignolo, these elements form not only the basis of modern colonial exploitation and political power structures but also the basis of the dominant Western paradigms of knowledge. Consequently, decoloniality (as opposed to decolonisation) requires a much more radical movement away from the macro-narratives of modernity and its ontological assumptions (Mignolo & Walsh 2018, p. 2764).

The nexus between the Western understanding of nature and knowledge regimes has recently gained more traction (Green 2013). We argue that these debates have a range of important consequences, both for the relationship between scientific practice and other knowledge regimes, and the reading of the deep past. Blaser (e.g. 2013a) stressed in this context the ontological dimension of observable differences that are not inter-cultural, i.e. they do not involve different cultures that relate to the world in different ways. Rather, these conflicts are based on different ontologies. This recognition means that they involve variable ways of generating a multiplicity of realities (Viveiros de Castro 2014). These processes are again deeply political and entangled in power structures and struggles. Western dominance is established by the assumption of the elevated ability of Western ontology to represent nature and the viewpoints of other cultures and peoples, in other words, by a superior ability to correctly distinguish between nature and culture. In addition to the critiques outlined above, the elevated position of Western ontology and science has been critically analysed by many authors from a philosophical and sociological perspective (Bourdieu 2000; Descola 2013; Latour 1993; Stengers 2000). In this context, it is important to recognise the relationship between ontologies and political power structures, which impact on the construction of historical narratives (Blaser 2013b) and the notions of knowledge and indigeneity (Blaser 2014). Consequently, conflicts about the uses of the environment, history, heritage and resources are often not just political conflicts about different interests. These conflicts can be viewed within a framework of political ontology and cosmopolitics (Blaser 2013a; Stengers 2010; 2011).

At this stage, we want to highlight that some Indigenous scholars have criticised recent contributions of the so-called ontological turn that have put forward a post-humanist or new materialist perspective. Despite their intention to challenge established forms of Western academic knowledge production, it is clear that many contributions to the ontological turn directly benefit from, perpetuate and leave intact such power structures. Todd (2016) has drawn attention to the fact that the debates and contributions mentioned above rarely engage with the work of Indigenous philosophers and thinkers 'in their own right, not just disembodied representatives of an amorphous Indigeneity that serves European intellectual or political purposes' (Todd 2016, p. 7). This important critique draws attention to the difficulties of challenging, transforming and decolonising academic processes and their political economy. It also emphasises the necessity to break with established forms of academic communication and representation in content as well as in form and practice to take seriously different ways of knowledge creation and preservation (Porr & Bell 2012).

Critiques of human origins

In this section, we discuss some critiques that have been put forward in the context of human origins studies itself, i.e. Palaeolithic archaeology and palaeoanthropology, that show some links with elements of the postcolonial critique. Generally, authors have not made these connections explicit; however, we suggest that this could be established in future work. The areas we address here do not constitute a complete list in this respect. Rather, we aim to show that there is a range of existing possibilities for further valuable and critical inquiries and explorations within the space outlined in this volume.

Possibly, the most significant theme in the study of human origins that connects to post-colonial critique is racism. Racism continues to be a major focus of postcolonial literature and studies with myriad contributions and analyses (Nayar 2015a; 2015b; Young 2001) and it features prominently within foundational texts of postcolonialism (Appiah 1998; Bhabha 1994; Fanon 1967). Within biological anthropology, race and racism have of course been critically discussed for a long time, and the rejection of racist epistemologies can be regarded as one of the most important developments in the field during the twentieth century (Marks 2008). Approaches within the field are today are far more reflective of the complex appreciation of human cultural and biological differences (Lahr 2016; Marks 2018). However, racist ideologies continue to plague the public imagination of human variability and questions remain about deeper essentialist orientations of biological anthropology (Corbey 2005; Corbey & Lanjouw 2013; Marks 2009; 2017).

During the nineteenth century and large parts of the twentieth century, racist ideologies also dominated the understanding of human evolution and origins (Marks 2012). Some of the founding figures of palaeoanthropology, such as Raymond Dart and Philip Tobias, also engaged in racist practices and perpetuated racist theories, an aspect that has only recently received greater attention and scrutiny (Kuljian 2016). The end of World War II is generally regarded as a watershed moment in the rejection of scientific racism and it also had an impact on the understanding of human evolution (Proctor 2003; Schwartz 2006). However, racist views continued to have a significant influence, within both public and academic spheres. For example, in his book *The Origin of Races*, Coon (1962) not only argued that the human races he perceived had evolved separately into *Homo sapiens* at different times. His argument was also used by American segregationists, actively supported by Coon himself as president of the American Association of Physical Anthropologists, to argue that African Americans were unfit for full participation in American society (Jackson 2001).

These legacies continued to plague one of the key debates in palaeoanthropology during the twentieth century. After World War II, it became more and more generally accepted that the deep roots of humanity must be in Africa. Discoveries in East and South Africa cemented this view and eventually led to the rejection of Asia as an alternative origin region, an interpretation which was favoured by most authors before World War II (Dennell 2001). However, the question of the origins of modern humans or *Homo sapiens* remained (and remains) a conundrum with much greater longevity.

In the last few decades, discussions of this topic have been dominated by antagonism between Out of Africa and multiregional models of so-called modern human origins. It is not possible to provide here a comprehensive or even a basic overview of this complex debate (Mellars & Stringer 1989; Smith & Ahern 2013; Stringer 2011; Wolpoff & Caspari 1997). The accusation of racism was raised against the multiregional understanding of modern human origins very quickly after its first major elaboration in the 1980s (overview in Wolpoff & Caspari 1997; Wolpoff, Xinzhi & Thorne 1984). The understanding of multiregional evolution is based on a range of conceptual elements and class of models:

> Multiregional Evolution describes the pattern of Pleistocene human evolution as the long-term evolution of central (African) and peripheral populations in a global polytypic species lineage that, in recent times, is no longer polytypic [...] The key aspects of multiregional pattern combine global evolutionary changes under selection as adaptive

genes disperse with regional continuity. [...] Multiregional models are structured as networks and not as trees.

(Caspari & Wolpoff 2013, p. 356)

Historically, this model took significant inspiration from the pre-World War II ideas of Weidenreich, who based his understanding of human evolution heavily on the analysis of fossils from Indonesia and China (e.g. Weidenreich 1946). Weidenreich understood his propositions as explicitly anti-racist, which is also related to his personal experience as a German Jew, who was removed from his position at the University of Frankfurt in 1935 (Hartkopf 2012, p. 57; Hertler 2002). Recent proponents of multiregional evolutionary models share this conviction (Caspari & Wolpoff 1994). However, at the same time, the model was placed by its critics close to the older tradition of polygenism that proposed a parallel, independent and potentially uneven development of human 'races'. The discussion became particularly charged with the publication of the Mitochondrial Eve model in 1987 (Cann, Stoneking & Wilson 1987) and the tensions between palaeoanthropological, archaeological and genetic readings of human evolution have persisted within the study of human evolution since then. Again, it is not possible here to provide a full overview of these issues. However, it seems significant that accusations of racism have been raised against all proponents in this context at some stage, which might point to deeper issues related to biological essentialism and the politics of anthropological knowledge production (Marks 2015; 2017; McManus 2017).

While proponents of the Out of Africa model of human origins originally suggested that the availability of genetic data would finally mean the end of multiregional models (Stringer 2011), this situation has significantly changed in recent years. In the light of more and more archaeological, anthropological and genetic data, Stringer (2014) had to counter the impression that the pendulum of models of modern human origins was going back to multiregionalism a few years later. Most recently, however, the idea of multiregionalism has now been more openly embraced, at least for the African continent (Galway-Witham & Stringer 2018). Following the redating of the Jebel Irhoud (Morocco) evidence (Richter et al. 2017), most researchers have started to reject a single origin point for modern humans and rather envisage these processes to have taken place 'in subdivided populations across Africa' (Scerri et al. 2018). Related questions have been raised about Asian evidence for some time (Dennell 2015; Dennell & Porr 2014). While these discussions mostly focus on anatomical and morphological features and processes, similar questions about origins and timings have been raised about the so-called behavioural origins, which now also appear to have no clear location in either space or time in Africa (Brooks et al. 2018; Potts et al. 2018). In this volume, we do not want to attempt to keep up with these rapidly changing developments. We rather want to emphasise the need to move beyond the search for more evidence and supplement the work in the field with deep critical considerations of key concepts and assumptions.

In the context of modern human origins, there has been a small number of valuable contributions, which can be linked to elements in postcolonial critique and can be explored further. Related to the theme of racism, is the element of essentialism that has been viewed from two different angles. Biological essentialism has been discussed in the biological sciences for a long time and is related to the understanding of the species concept, which also has a continuing impact on the study of human evolution and origins (Corbey & Lanjouw 2013; McManus 2017). Clearly, in relation to the latter, this aspect takes on a particular significance in relation to the nature of human exceptionalism. Several authors have drawn attention to the fact that current discussions continue to be plagued by historical legacies in this respect that can be traced back to European Enlightenment philosophies (Porr 2014). This tradition defined humanity in a humanistic and essentialist fashion along modern and Western categories. Post-World War II and post-racist conceptions of (modern) human origins seem to reproduce eighteenth-century ideas in an attempt to preserve an ideal human exceptionality in the face of biological variability (Ingold 2004). Both Darwin and Wallace struggled with these issues, and the resulting tensions have been preserved in recent discussions about modern human origins (McManus 2017; Porr 2014; Proctor 2003; Schwartz 2017).

As Ingold (Ingold 2000; 2004; 2006; 2007) has repeatedly discussed, current models generally continue to rest on the Western division between nature and culture implicitly. Projected back into the deep past, this differentiation is transformed into a distinction between biological evolution and human history. Both phases are separated by a mythical origin juncture, which created the unique human essence that distinguishes humans from the rest of nature. This understanding almost necessarily creates a progressive understanding of human history that is characterised by a movement out of or emancipation from nature. This process becomes overwhelmingly technologically driven and defined through an increase in material and economic complexity over time (Porr & Matthews 2017). Again, it is not possible to discuss here the numerous issues involved and the underlying assumptions that usually escape consideration. The latter include the dialectical and dichotomous definition of nature and humanity (see for example Descola 2013). As mentioned above, they also include a range of orientations that have implicitly guided approaches to human origins for the last 200 years and which continue to steer research and imagination towards the same range of questions, theories and methodologies (Stoczkowski 2002; Wagner 2016, p. 133). Consequently, they are producing similarly teleological visions of the deep human past. The critical analysis of these aspects in relation to the definition of human beings, their morality and the 'proper' course of history have played key roles in the postcolonial critique for many decades.

In the spirit of critical postcolonial literary studies, links can be drawn in this context to Landau's (1991) now classic analysis of recurring structures of human origin narratives (see also Landau, 1984). Landau followed a comparative literary science approach to detect similarities between scientific expositions of human evolution and European myths and folktales from the nineteenth to the twentieth centuries. A key element identified by Landau was the hero narrative, which presents human evolution as a mastery of successive challenges leading towards an ultimate goal. Invariably, the latter is Western civilisation, and the narrative structure consequently is guided by an intrinsic teleological determinism in which elements are not presented as they occurred but how they contributed to the outcome of the narrative (Landau 1991, p. 42). These ideas have more recently been developed further by Gamble and Gittins (Gamble 2007; Gamble & Gittins 2004), who also emphasised that the Palaeolithic is most often studied within a framework of 'origins research' that aims to establish the origins of features or elements of later periods of human history. Furthermore, Moser (1992; 1998; 2003) has demonstrated comparable processes (with explicit references to colonial influences) in the realm of the visual representation of human evolution and extinct hominins in publications and exhibitions. These considerations draw attention to questions about the reality of archaeological reconstructions of human origins and their authority to elucidate the story of all humans. Consequently, Landau (1991, p. 185) reflected on palaeoanthropology's recursive experimental and creative potential, and the possibility for it to become a form of cultural criticism (cf. Marcus & Fischer 1986).

Landau (1991 p. 184) admitted that one of the major limitations of her work was the neglect of the influence of gender on theories of human origins. Indeed, we want to stress here that feminist approaches have played an important role in reflecting on human origins and adding an important critical dimension to this field of research. Seminal books and edited collections in this context were published in the 1980s and 1990s (Conkey & Gero 1997; Dahlberg 1983; Gero & Conkey 1991), partly as a reaction to the perceived bias of the economic emphasis encapsulated in the image of 'Man the Hunter' (Lee & DeVore 1968). The critique was foremost directed at the use of stereotypical views of men and women in the deep past, and their respective contributions to human evolution. However, from the beginning, it was recognised that these biases needed to be seen in relation to discourses affecting the politics and practices of anthropology and the underrepresentation of women and their voices (Zihlmann 1987). These aims clearly show some alliance with the post-colonial emphasis on the politics of oppression and repression. As outlined above, the postcolonial movement has from the beginning attempted to create space for marginalised subjects and voices. Accordingly, women have also significantly contributed to the development of postcolonial literature and, more recently, drawn attention to the longevity of patriarchal structures that affect so-called critical literature itself (Lewis & Mills 2003; McLaren 2017).

There is little doubt that these issues remain relevant in the study of human origins as well. This relevance includes primatology and related debates about the most appropriate models of human evolution (Hrdy 2009a; 2009b). From outside of the disciplinary boundaries of Palaeolithic archaeology or palaeoanthropology, Haraway's work is also very relevant. Haraway initially analysed the hidden assumptions guiding the understanding of gender and race in modern science and human evolution from a feminist perspective (see for example Haraway 1989). More recently, Haraway has expanded her approach in a post-humanist, anti-essentialist and anti-universalist direction that explicitly echoes some key aspects of the postcolonial movement in their aim to find local solutions that fully take difference into account:

> How can general knowledge be nurtured in postcolonial worlds committed to taking difference seriously? Answers to these questions can only be put together in emergent practices, i.e., in vulnerable, on-the-ground work that cobbles together non-harmonious agencies and ways of living that are accountable both to their disparate inherited histories and to their barely possible but absolutely joint futures.
>
> *(Haraway 1989, p. 7)*

Archaeology, human origins, and the end of humanity

Public and academic debates have recently focused on the ends of the world. These conversations appear to be different from the apocalyptic scenarios of the Cold War and its threat of sudden and devastating nuclear annihilation. Still, the collapse of civilisation and the end of human life as we know it on a global scale is a major current theme. In contrast to earlier discourses, which appear to be a part of virtually all known human societies at some time, current exchanges concentrate on the threat of environmental deterioration and eventual catastrophe, and on the dangers of global pollution, breakdown of ecosystems and climate change (Danowski & Viveiros de Castro 2017; Morton 2013). The term that crystallises these ideas is the Anthropocene. The literature about this term and its problems and implications are already inconceivably large (Lewis & Maslin 2018; Moore 2016). In short, the Anthropocene has been proposed to describe the current geological epoch, which is characterised by the global and irreversible impact of human activity. The term has been proposed to reflect the fact that humanity has become a geological force. The definition of the beginning of the Anthropocene is still a hotly debated topic. In a recent discussion, Lewis and Maslin (2015, p. 173) have distinguished between three principal approaches to this issue, which each refer to a different global geological boundary marker, a Global Stratotype Section and Point (GSSP) or 'golden spike'. The first is defined by the impact of early extensive farming and the presence of unusually high levels of atmospheric methane. The second is the so-called Orbis GSSP, which records a sudden drop of atmospheric carbon dioxide around 1610 as a result of the devastation created by the European colonisation of the New World. The respective golden spike is explained by the reforestation of previously cultivated lands in South and Central America as a result of the mostly disease-related deaths of up to 50 million people (Lewis & Maslin 2015, p. 175). The third GSSP is presented by a marked spike of atmospheric ^{14}C as a result of nuclear bomb detonations in the mid-1960s. This marker is also generally related to the 'Great Acceleration' of human impacts on the environment after World War II, mostly as a result of an unprecedented expansion in human population and industrial technologies (Lewis & Maslin 2015, p. 176).

The Anthropocene and the related global challenges and changes have created extensive discussions within the social sciences. They have further focussed debates about a reconfiguration of the understanding of nature, the character, responsibility and role of science, and current and past interrelationships between humanity and the environment (Green 2013; Latour 2013; 2017a; 2017b; Povinelli 2016; Stengers 2015; Tsing 2015). At the same time, the concept of the Anthropocene has also received criticism. Some authors have noted that the idea of a new human-dominated geological epoch creates the illusion of a global, unified and progressive temporality. It cuts through innumerable processes and patterns of social–environmental relationships to homogenise past complexities (Bauer & Ellis 2018; Simon 2017; Todd 2015). Another critique has been raised at the deep understanding of the origin of the Anthropocene, which underestimates the significance of modern capitalism for the current condition of the planet. Moore (2016) has consequently coined the term Capitalocene to reflect this focus (see also Moore 2015).

Discussions about the consequences of the Anthropocene for archaeological theory and practice have also been going on for some time (Ion 2018; Lane 2015; Pétursdóttir 2017; Solli et al. 2011). In a recent critical review of the concept from an archaeological perspective, González-Ruibal (2018) asserted that the concept needs to be approached with a focus on the analysis of power, inequality and conflict. A geological perspective will only homogenise and naturalise these social complexities. Entangled in these considerations is the critique of the idea of the Anthropocene as human-made, which 'blames all humans equally for a specific effect of modernity and capitalism' (González-Ruibal 2018, p. 1). In this form, the Anthropocene appears again as the consequence of a universalist and progressive understanding of history. It also appears as the consequence of an essentialist understanding of humanity that relates the Anthropocene to the existence of the *Anthropos*. It is therefore slightly surprising that the Pleistocene is generally absent from discussions about the origins of the Anthropocene. This absence, however, is rather the consequence of an implicit omnipresence. In the face of global environmental deterioration and unrestricted resource exploitation, the Pleistocene hunter-gatherer has acquired a Rousseauian status again as humanity's innocent condition before the invention of agriculture that supposedly triggered the inevitable temporality of the Anthropocene. Living hunter-gatherers are now again celebrated as the last remnants of a lost world, a lost Garden of Eden: 'The last communities whose mode of production would never have led to the Anthropocene are disappearing, and with them important lessons about alternative temporalities and potential futures' (González-Ruibal 2018, p. 7). The environmental dystopia of modernity has produced the Pleistocene utopia of sustainable economic and social simplicity.

Although this understanding is morally appealing and comforting, it is as generalising and homogenising as the mainstream view of the Anthropocene. Current archaeological and palaeoanthropological approaches to human origins are seemingly not well equipped to participate in these discussions and reflect on these complex interrelationships. The narratives that are presented to explain particularly modern human origins continue to perpetuate an understanding that is still overwhelmingly guided by the four vectors that were identified by Stoczkowski (2002) almost 20 years ago: environmental determinism, materialism, utilitarianism and individualism (see also Ingold 2000). The vision of human origins is generally technocentric, expansionist and, in short, generally formulated in modernist terms. Taking today's mainstream narratives of modern human origins seriously, we are forced to conclude that the origins of the Anthropocene are also the origins of humanity, contained within humanity's Species Being (Gosden 1994) and the foundation of an inevitable temporality that is linked to human nature or the innate capacities of humanity (Porr 2014; Sahlins 2008). Largely undetected by recent re-evaluations, it is consequently a continuation of a historical and social intellectual project that has been at the core of the critique of the postcolonial movement for a long time (Porr & Matthews 2017). The concern with human origins must engage with its own intellectual basis and history. It must become more reflective and critical regarding the deep influences that structure its concepts, explanations and terminologies. Together with the authors in this volume, we argue that the study of human origins should take the challenge of the postcolonial critique and related critical movements seriously. There is no single framework, no single approach, that will provide better imaginations of the past, present and future of human beings and their environments. Not even these categories should be left untouched; they must also be open to critique. The understanding of human origin needs to embrace diversity; ontological, philosophical, epistemological, methodological diversity to reflect human diversity, or, rather, the diversity of life itself (Viveiros de Castro 2013). Interrogating and decolonising human origins is not a project about the deep past. It is also a project for the future.

Structure of the volume

This volume is not intended to be a comprehensive treatment of all of the possible intersections between the study of human origins and postcolonial thought. In contrast, we hope that this collection of papers will create spaces for an expansion of critical and unexpected conversations about the conceptualisation of human origins. This conceptualisation itself is a slippery area that depends on the perspective and focus of the research in question. The notion of 'human origins' has variously referred to different periods, to fossil and archaeological evidence. Recently, the discussions within palaeoanthropology and Palaeolithic archaeology have been dominated by the behavioural and anatomical origins of so-called modern humans (Hoffecker 2017; Kaifu et al. 2015; Marean 2015; Mellars et al. 2007;

Reyes-Centeno 2016). Many authors have approached this aspect in different ways over time, and it is clear that the taxonomy and definition of humans has always been treated differently from other animals. It is a social and cultural issue that directly affects human identity and values (Marks 2015). The first section of this volume consequently deals with the definition of the human being and its historical legacies with a specific focus on the latter's entanglements with ideologies that have been underlying Western colonialism.

The postcolonial movement has to a large extent been a critical literary movement. It continues to heavily depend on literary analyses and the production of critical literature, including novels and reflective political essays. In this spirit, the second section of the volume contains reflections on the narrative and aesthetic dimensions of the engagement with human origins. This section also includes an exploration of the origins of civilisation as an origin of humanity, an aspect that remains implicit in most recent approaches to human evolution and their progressive and technologically focused structures (Porr & Matthews 2017). Implicated in the progressive understanding of human history is also a uniform understanding of time in which all societies exist or have existed. Time and temporality consequently are further key aspects of this section, which are related to a crucial area of critique in the postcolonial movement.

The perception of progressive human history, driven by technological and material developments, is itself a product of the competition between imperial nations during the nineteenth and early twentieth centuries. It is consequently not surprising that human origins have also been part of nationalistic movements as well as racial interpretations of human history or evolution. The third section of this volume engages with these issues and also relates the theme of human origins to current political developments.

Within human origins research and throughout archaeology, the analysis of DNA has increased rapidly in recent years, and it has seemingly transformed our understanding of the human past forever (Ermini et al. 2015; Nielsen et al. 2017). The final section of the volume, therefore, reflects on the social dimensions of genetic data and their complicated connections to a variety of present and historical influences (Marks 2013; Nelson 2016). The increased use of DNA necessitates new ethical engagements and considerations, which also need to take the complex realities of Indigenous identities seriously (TallBear 2013).

Throughout this volume, we have tried to include a wide range of perspectives from different parts of the world. However, we are very much aware of the fact that the diversity of approaches presented here needs to be further increased in the future, and this is especially the case with the involvement of Indigenous scholars and alternative forms of scholarly expression. Embracing and encouraging diversity is a recognition of the deep complexities of human existence in the past and the present, and it is vital to critical scholarship on this topic.

References

Alberti, B 2016, 'Archaeologies of ontology', *Annual Review of Anthropology*, vol. 45, pp. 163–179.

Alberti, B, Fowles, S, Holbraad, M, Marshall, Y & Witmore, CL 2011, '"Worlds otherwise". Archaeology, anthropology, and ontological difference', *Current Anthropology*, vol. 52, no. 6, pp. 896–911.

Alberti, B & Marshall, Y 2009, 'Animating archaeology: local theories and conceptually open-ended methodologies', *Cambridge Archaeological Journal*, vol. 19, no. 3, pp. 344–356.

Allbrock, M & McGrath, A 2015, 'Collaborative histories of the Willandra Lakes', in A McGrath & MA Jebb (eds), *Long history, deep time. Deepening histories of place*, ANU Press, Canberra, pp. 241–252.

Anderson, B 2006, *Imagined communities. Reflections on the origin and spread of nationalism*, Verso, London.

Appiah, KA 1998, 'The illusions of race', in EC Eze (ed.), *African philosophy: an anthology*, Blackwell, Oxford, pp. 275–290.

Ashcroft, B, Griffiths, G & Tiffin, H (eds) 1995, *The postcolonial studies reader*, Routledge, New York.

Bapty, I & Yates, T (eds) 1990, *Archaeology after structuralism: post-structuralism and the practice of archaeology*, Routledge, London.

Bauer, AM & Ellis, EC 2018, 'The Anthropocene divide: obscuring understanding of social-environmental change', *Current Anthropology*, vol. 59, no. 2, pp. 209–227.

Bhabha, HK 1994, *The location of culture*, Routledge, London.

Bhambra, GK 2014, 'Postcolonial and decolonial dialogues', *Postcolonial Studies*, vol. 17, no. 2, pp. 115–121.

Blaser, M 2013a, 'Notes towards a political ecology of "environmental" conflicts', in L Green (ed.), *Contested ecologies: dialogues in the south on nature and knowledge*, HSRC Press, Cape Town, pp. 13–27.

Blaser, M 2013b, 'Ontological conflicts and the stories of peoples in spite of Europe', *Current Anthropology*, vol. 54, no. 4, pp. 547–568.

Blaser, M 2014, 'Ontology and indigeneity: on the political ontology of heterogeneous assemblages', *Cultural Geographies*, vol. 21, no. 1, pp. 49–58.

Bourdieu, P 2000, *Pascalian meditations*, Stanford University Press, Stanford, CA.

Bowler, J & Thorne, A 1976, 'Human remains from Lake Mungo: discovery and excavation of Lake Mungo III', in RL Kirk & A Thorne (eds), *The origin of the Australians*, Australian Institute for Aboriginal Studies, Canberra, pp. 127–138.

Bowler, J, Thorne, A & Polach, HA 1972, 'Pleistocene man in Australia: age and significance of the Mungo skeleton', *Nature*, vol. 240, no. 5375, pp. 48–50.

Brooks, AS, Yellen, JE, Potts, R, Behrensmeyer, AK, Deino, AL, Leslie, DE, Ambrose, SH, Ferguson, JR, d'Errico, F, Zipkin, AM, Wittaker, S, Post, J, Veatch, EG, Foecke, K & Clark, JB 2018, 'Long-distance stone transport and pigment use in the earliest Middle Stone Age', *Science*, vol. 360, no. 6384, pp. 90–94.

Bruchac, MM, Hart, SM & Wobst, HM (eds) 2010, *Indigenous archaeologies: a reader in decolonization*, Left Coast Press, Walnut Creek, CA.

Cann, RL, Stoneking, M & Wilson, AC 1987, 'Mitochondrial DNA and human evolution', *Nature*, vol. 325, pp. 31–36.

Caspari, R & Wolpoff, MH 1994, 'Weidenreich, Coon, and multiregional evolution', *Human Evolution*, vol. 11, no. 3–4, pp. 261–268.

Caspari, R & Wolpoff, MH 2013, 'The process of modern human origins: the evolutionary and demographic changes giving rise to modern humans', in FH Smith & JCM Ahern (eds), *The origins of modern humans: biology reconsidered*, John Wiley & Sons, New York, pp. 355–391.

Chakrabarty, D 2000, *Provincializing Europe: postcolonial thought and historical difference*, Princeton University Press, Princeton, NJ.

Chakrabarty, D 2011, 'The politics and possibility of historical knowledge: continuing the conversation', *Postcolonial Studies*, vol. 14, no. 2, pp. 243–250.

Chaturvedi, V (ed.) 2000, *Mapping subaltern studies and the postcolonial*, Verso, London.

Chibber, V 2013, *Postcolonial theory and the specter of capital*, Verso, London.

Clifford, J & Marcus, GE (eds) 1986, *Writing culture: the poetics and politics of ethnography*, University of California Press, Berkeley.

Colwell-Chanthaphonh, C 2012, 'Archaeology and Indigenous collaboration', in I Hodder (ed.), *Archaeological theory today*, 2nd edn, Polity Press, Cambridge, pp. 267–291.

Colwell, C 2016, 'Collaborative archaeologies and descendant communities', *Annual Review of Anthropology*, vol. 45, pp. 113–127.

Colwell, C 2017, *Plundered skulls and stolen spirits: inside the fight to reclaim Native America's culture*, University of Chicago Press, Chicago, IL.

Conkey, MW & Gero, JM 1997, 'Programme to practice: gender and feminism in archaeology', *Annual Review of Anthropology*, vol. 26, pp. 411–437.

Coole, D & Frost, S (eds) 2010, *New materialisms: ontology, agency, and politics*, Duke University Press, Durham, NC.

Coon, CS 1962, *The origin of races*, Random House, New York.

Corbey, R 2005, *The metaphysics of apes: negotiating the animal–human boundary*, Cambridge University Press, Cambridge.

Corbey, R & Lanjouw, A (eds) 2013, *The politics of species: reshaping our relationships with other animals*, Cambridge University Press, Cambridge.

Dahlberg, F (ed.) 1983, *Woman the gatherer*, Yale University Press, New Haven, CT.

Danowski, D & Viveiros de Castro, E 2017, *The ends of the world*, Polity Press, London.

Dennell, RW 2001, 'From Sangiran to Olduvai, 1937–1960: the quest for "centres" of hominid origins in Asia and Africa', in R Corbey & W Roebroeks (eds), *Studying human origins: disciplinary history and epistemology*, Amsterdam University Press, Amsterdam, pp. 44–66.

Dennell, RW 2015, 'Palaeoanthropology: *Homo sapiens* in China 80,000 years ago', *Nature*, vol. 526, no. 7575, pp. 647–648.

Dennell, RW & Porr, M (eds) 2014, *Southern Asia, Australia and the search for human origins*, Cambridge University Press, Cambridge.

Descola, P 2013, *Beyond nature and culture*, University of Chicago Press, Chicago, IL.

Descola, P 2014, 'Modes of being and forms of predication', *HAU: Journal of Ethnographic Theory*, vol. 4, no. 1, pp. 271–280.

Echo-Hawk, R 2000, 'Ancient history in the New World: integrating oral traditions and the archaeological record in deep time', *American Antiquity*, vol. 65, pp. 267–290.

Ermini, L, Der Sarkissian, C, Willerslev, E & Orlando, L 2015, 'Major transitions in human evolution revisited: a tribute to ancient DNA', *Journal of Human Evolution*, vol. 79, pp. 4–20.

Fabian, J 1983, *Time and the Other: how anthropology makes its object*, Columbia University Press, New York.

Fanon, F 1967, *Black skin, white masks*, Paladin, London.

Galway-Witham, J & Stringer, C 2018, 'How did *Homo sapiens* evolve?', *Science*, vol. 360, no. 6395, pp. 1296–1298.

Gamble, CS 2007, *Origins and revolutions: human identity in earliest prehistory*, Cambridge University Press, Cambridge.

Gamble, CS & Gittins, E 2004, 'Social archaeology and origins research: a Paleolithic perspective', in L Meskell & RW Preucel (eds), *A companion to social archaeology*, Blackwell, Malden, MA, pp. 96–118.

Gero, JM & Conkey, MW (eds) 1991, *Engendering archaeology: women and prehistory*, Blackwell, Oxford.

Godwin, L 2005, '"Everyday archaeology": archaeological heritage management and its relationship to native title in development-related processes', *Australian Aboriginal Studies*, vol. 1, pp. 74–83.

González-Ruibal, A 2018, 'Beyond the Anthropocene: defining the age of destruction', *Norwegian Archaeological Review*, vol. 51, no. 1–2, pp. 10–21.

González-Ruibal, A (ed.) 2013, *Reclaiming archaeology: beyond the tropes of modernity*, Routledge, New York.

Gosden, C 1994, *Social being and time*, Blackwell, Oxford.

Gosden, C 1999, *Anthropology and archaeology: a changing relationship*, Routledge, London.

Gosden, C 2004, *Archaeology and colonialism: cultural contact from 5000 BC to the present*, Cambridge University Press, Cambridge.

Gosden, C 2012, 'Post-colonial archaeology', in I Hodder (ed.), *Archaeological theory today*, 2nd edn, Polity, Cambridge, pp. 251–266.

Green, L (ed.) 2013, *Contested ecologies: dialogues in the south on nature and knowledge*, HSRC Press, Cape Town.

Griffiths, B 2018, *Deep time dreaming: uncovering ancient Australia*, Black Inc, Carlton, Australia.

Grusin, R (ed.) 2015, *The non-human turn*, University of Minnesota Press, Minneapolis.

Habu, J, Fawcett, C & Matsunaga, JM (eds) 2008, *Evaluating multiple narratives: beyond nationalist, colonialist, imperialist archaeologies*, Springer, New York.

Hamilakis, Y 2009, 'The "war on terror" and the military–archaeology complex: Iraq, ethics, and neo-colonialism', *Archaeologies*, vol. 5, no. 1, pp. 39–65.

Hamilakis, Y 2012, 'Are we postcolonial yet? Tales from the battlefield', *Archaeologies*, vol. 8, no. 1, pp. 67–76.

Hamilakis, Y & Duke, P (eds) 2007, *Archaeology and capitalism: from ethics to politics*, Left Coast Press, Walnut Creek, CA.

Haraway, D 1989, *Primate visions: gender, race, and nature in the world of modern science*, Routledge, New York.

Hartkopf, H 2012, *Franz Weidenreich: arzt, politiker, menschenforscher*, Verlag regionalkultur, Ubstadt-Weiher, Germany.

Hertler, C 2002, 'Menschenrassen und das problem der variabilität – ein Lösungsvorschlag von Franz Weidenreich', *Anthropologischer Anzeiger*, vol. 60, no. 1, pp. 81–94.

Hodder, I (ed.) 2012, *Archaeological theory today*, Polity Press, Cambridge.

Hoffecker, J 2017, *Modern humans: their African origin and global dispersal*, Columbia University Press, New York.

Hrdy, SB 2009a, *Mothers and others: the evolutionary origins of mutual understanding*, Harvard University Press, Cambridge, MA.

Hrdy, SB 2009b, *The woman that never evolved*, Harvard University Press, Cambridge, MA.

Ingold, T 2000, *The perception of the environment: essays in livelihood, dwelling and skill*, Routledge, London.

Ingold, T 2004, 'Beyond biology and culture: the meaning of evolution in a relational world', *Social Anthropology*, vol. 12, no. 2, pp. 209–221.

Ingold, T 2006, 'Against human nature', in N Gontier, JP van Bendegem & D Aerts (eds), *Evolutionary epistemology, language and culture*, Springer, Dordrecht, pp. 259–281.

Ingold, T 2007, 'The trouble with "evolutionary biology"', *Anthropology Today*, vol. 23, no. 2, pp. 13–17.

Ion, A 2018, 'A taphonomy of a dark Anthropocene: a response to Þóra Pétursdóttir's OOO inspired "archaeology and Anthropocene"', *Archaeological Dialogues*, vol. 25, no. 2, pp. 191–203.

Jackson, JPJ 2001, '"In ways unacademical": the reception of Carleton S. Coon's *The Origin of Races*', *Journal of the History of Biology*, vol. 34, pp. 247–285.

James, D 2015, '*Tjukurpa* time', in A McGrath & MA Jebb (eds), *Long history, deep time: deepening histories of place*, ANU Press, Canberra, pp. 33–46.

Kaifu, Y, Izuho, M, Goebel, T, Sato, H & Ono, A (eds) 2015, *Emergence and diversity of modern human behavior in Paleolithic Asia*, Texas A&M University Press, College Station.

Kohn, E 2013, *How forests think: toward an anthropology beyond the human*, University of California Press, Berkeley.

Kuljian, C 2016, *Darwin's hunch: science, race and the search for human origins*, Jacana Media, Auckland Park, South Africa.

Lahr, MM 2016, 'The shaping of human diversity: filters, boundaries and transitions', *Philosophical Transactions of the Royal Society B*, vol. 371, no. 20150241, pp. 1–12.

Lambert, DM 2018, 'Owning the science: the power of partnerships', *Griffiths Review*, vol. 60, pp. 244–255.

Landau, M 1984, 'Human evolution as narrative', *American Scientist*, vol. 72, pp. 262–268.

Landau, M 1991, *Narratives of human evolution*, Yale University Press, New Haven, CT.

Lane, PJ 2015, 'Archaeology in the age of the Anthropocene: a critical assessment of its scope and societal contributions', *Journal of Field Archaeology*, vol. 40, no. 5, pp. 485–498.

Latour, B 1993, *We have never been modern*, Harvard University Press, Cambridge, MA.

Latour, B 2004, *Politics of nature: how to bring the sciences into democracy*, Harvard University Press, Cambridge, MA.

Latour, B 2013, *An inquiry into modes of existence: an anthropology of the moderns*, Harvard University Press, Cambridge, MA.

Latour, B 2017a, *Facing Gaia: eight lectures on the new climatic regime*, Polity Press, Cambridge.

Latour, B 2017b, *Où atterrir? Comment s'orienter en politique*, La Découverte, Paris.

Lawrence, H (ed.) 2006, *Mungo over millennia: the Willandra landscape and its people*, Maygog Publishing, Rosny Park.

Lee, RB & DeVore, I (eds) 1968, *Man the hunter*, Aldine, Chicago, IL.

Leone, MP, Potter Jr, PB & Shackel, PA 1987, 'Toward a critical archaeology', *Current Anthropology*, vol. 28, no. 3, pp. 283–302.

Lewis, R & Mills, S (eds) 2003, *Feminist postcolonial theory: a reader*, Routledge, New York.

Lewis, SL & Maslin, MA 2015, 'Defining the Anthropocene', *Nature*, vol. 519, pp. 171–180.

Lewis, SL & Maslin, MA 2018, *The human planet: how we created the Anthropocene*, Pelican, London.

Liebmann, M 2008, 'Introduction: the intersections of archaeology and postcolonial studies', in M Liebmann & UZ Rizvi (eds), *Archaeology and the postcolonial critique*, Altamira Press, Lanham, MD, pp. 1–20.

Liebmann, M & Rizvi, UZ (eds) 2008, *Archaeology and the postcolonial critique*, Altamira Press, Lanham, MD.

Ludden, D (ed.) 2002, *Reading subaltern studies*, Anthem Press, London.

Lydon, J & Rizvi, UZ (eds) 2012, *Handbook of postcolonial archaeology*, Left Coast Press, Walnut Creek, CA.

Marcus, GE & Fischer, MMJ 1986, *Anthropology as cultural critique: an experimental moment in the human sciences*, University of Chicago Press, Chicago, IL.

Marean, CW 2015, 'An evolutionary anthropological perspective on modern human origins', *Annual Review of Anthropology*, vol. 44, no. 1, pp. 533–556.

Marks, J 2008, 'Race: past, present, and future', in BA Koenig, SS-J Lee & SS Richardson (eds), *Revisiting race in a genomic age*, Rutgers University Press, New Brunswick, NJ, pp. 21–38.

Marks, J 2009, 'The nature of humanness', in B Cunliffe, C Gosden & RA Joyce (eds), *The Oxford handbook of archaeology*, Oxford University Press, Oxford, pp. 237–253.

Marks, J 2012, 'Why be against Darwin? Creationism, racism, and the roots of anthropology', *Yearbook of Physical Anthropology*, vol. 55, pp. 95–104.

Marks, J 2013, 'The nature/culture of genetic facts', *Annual Review of Anthropology*, vol. 42, pp. 247–267.

Marks, J 2015, *Tales of the ex-apes: how we think about human evolution*, University of California Press, Oakland.

Marks, J 2017, *Is science racist?* Polity, Cambridge.

Marks, J 2018, 'An evolving, evolutionary science of human differences', in M Meloni, J Cromby, D Fitzgerald & S Lloyd (eds), *The Palgrave handbook of biology and society*, Palgrave Mcmillan, London, pp. 123–141.

McLaren, MA (ed.) 2017, *Decolonizing feminism: transnational feminism and globalization*, Rowman & Littlefield, New York.

McLeod, J (ed.) 2007, *The Routledge companion to postcolonial studies*, Routledge, London.

McManus, S 2017, 'Biological explanations and their limits: paleoanthropology among the sciences', in JH Schwartz (ed.), *Rethinking human evolution*, MIT Press, Cambridge, MA, pp. 31–52.

McNiven, I 2016, 'Theoretical challenges of Indigenous archaeology: setting an agenda', *American Antiquity*, vol. 81, no. 1, pp. 27–41.

McNiven, I & Russell, L 2005, *Appropriated pasts: Indigenous peoples and the colonial culture of archaeology*, Altamira Press, Oxford.

Mellars, P, Boyle, K, Bar-Yosef, O & Stringer, C (eds) 2007, *Rethinking the human revolution: new behavioural and biological perspectives on the origin and dispersal of modern humans*, McDonald Institute for Archaeological Research, Cambridge.

Mellars, P & Stringer, C (eds) 1989, *The human revolution: behavioural and biological perspectives in the origins of modern humans*, Edinburgh University Press, Edinburgh.

Mignolo, WD 2011, *The darker side of western modernity: global futures, decolonial options*, Duke University Press, Durham, NC.

Mignolo, WD & Walsh, CE 2018, *On coloniality: concepts, analytics, praxis*, Duke University Press, Durham, NC.

Miller, D & Tilley, C (eds) 1984, *Ideology, power and prehistory*, Cambridge University Press, Cambridge.

Moore, JW 2015, *Capitalism in the web of life: ecology and the accumulation of capital*, Verso, London.

Moore, JW (ed.) 2016, *Anthropocene or Capitalocene? Nature, history, and the crisis of capitalism*, PM Press, Oakland, CA.

Moro-Abadía, O 2006, 'The history of archaeology as a "colonial discourse"', *Bulletin of the History of Archaeology*, vol. 16, no. 2, pp. 4–17.

Morton, T 2013, *Hyperobjects: philosophy and ecology after the end of the world*, University of Minnesota Press, Minneapolis.

Moser, S 1992, 'The visual language of archaeology: a case study of the Neanderthals', *Antiquity*, vol. 66, no. 253, pp. 831–844.

Moser, S 1998, *Ancestral images: the iconography of human origins*, Cornell University Press, Ithaca, NY.

Moser, S 2003, 'Representing archaeological knowledge in museums: exhibiting human origins and strategies for change', *Public Archaeology*, vol. 3, no. 1, pp. 3–20.

Muecke, S 2004, *Ancient & modern: time, culture and Indigenous philosophy*, UNSW Press, Sydney.

Nayar, PK 2015a, *The postcolonial studies dictionary*, Wiley-Blackwell, Chichester.

Nayar, PK (ed.) 2015b, *Postcolonial studies: an anthology*, Wiley-Blackwell, Chichester.

Nelson, A 2016, *The social life of DNA: race, reparations, and reconciliation after the genome*, Beacon Press, Boston.

Ngugi, WTO 1986, *Decolonising the mind: the politics of language in African literature*, J Currey, London.

Nicholas, GP & Hollowell, J 2007, 'Ethical challenges to a postcolonial archaeology', in Y Hamilakis & P Duke (eds), *Archaeology and capitalism: from ethics to politics*, Left Coast Press, Walnut Creek, CA, pp. 59–82.

Nielsen, R, Akey, JM, Jakobsson, M, Pritchard, JK, Tishkoff, S & Willerslev, E 2017, 'Tracing the peopling of the world through genomics', *Nature*, vol. 541, pp. 302–310.

Nunn, PD 2018, *The edge of memory: ancient stories, oral tradition and the post-glacial world*, Bloomsbury Sigma, London.

Nunn, PD & Reid, NJ 2016, 'Aboriginal memories of inundation of the Australian coast dating from more than 7,000 years ago', *Australian Geographer*, vol. 47, no. 1, pp. 11–47.

Oobagooma, J, Umbagai, L, Doohan, K & Porr, M 2016, 'Yooddooddoom: a narrative exploration of the camp and the sacred place, daily life, images, arranged stones and Lalai beings', *Hunter Gatherer Research*, vol. 2, no. 3, pp. 345–374.

Paterson, A 2011, *A millennium of culture contact*, Routledge, New York.

Perkins, M 2018, 'Mungo Man remains to be reburied on country', *Sydney Morning Herald*, 18 December. Available from: https://www.smh.com.au/national/mungo-man-remains-to-be-rebur ied-on-country-20181218-p50n1i.html [3 April 2019].

Pétursdóttir, Þ 2017, 'Climate change? Archaeology and Anthropocene', *Archaeological Dialogues*, vol. 24, no. 2, pp. 175–205.

Porr, M 2014, 'Essential questions: "modern humans" and the capacity for modernity', in RW Dennell & M Porr (eds), *Southern Asia, Australia and the search for human origins*, Cambridge University Press, Cambridge, pp. 257–264.

Porr, M 2015, 'Lives and lines: integrating molecular genetics, the "origins of modern humans" and Indigenous knowledge', in A McGrath & MA Jebb (eds), *Long history, deep time: deepening histories of place*, ANU Press, Canberra, pp. 203–219.

Porr, M 2018, 'Country and relational ontology in the Kimberley, Northwest Australia: implications for understanding and representing archaeological evidence', *Cambridge Archaeological Journal*, vol. 28, no. 3, pp. 395–409.

Porr, M & Bell, HR 2012, '"Rock-art", "animism" and two-way thinking: towards a complementary epistemology in the understanding of material culture and "rock-art" of hunting and gathering people', *Journal of Archaeological Method and Theory*, vol. 19, pp. 161–205.

Porr, M & Matthews, JM 2016, 'Thinking through story', *Hunter Gatherer Research*, vol. 2, no. 3, pp. 249–274.

Porr, M & Matthews, JM 2017, 'Post-colonialism, human origins and the paradox of modernity', *Antiquity*, vol. 91, no. 358, pp. 1058–1068.

Potts, R, Behrensmeyer, AK, Faith, JT, Tryon, CA, Brooks, AS, Yellen, JE, Deino, AL, Kinyanjui, R, Clark, JB, Haradon, CM, Levin, NE, Meijer, HJ, Veatch, EG, Owen, RB & Renaut, RW 2018, 'Environmental dynamics during the onset of the Middle Stone Age in eastern Africa', *Science*, vol. 360, no. 6384, pp. 86–90.

Povinelli, EA 2016, *Geontologies: a requiem to late liberalism*, Duke University Press, Durham, NC.

Proctor, RN 2003, 'Three roots of human recency: molecular anthropology, the refigured Acheulean, and the UNESCO response to Auschwitz', *Current Anthropology*, vol. 44, no. 2, pp. 213–239.

Quijano, A 2007, 'Coloniality and modernity/rationality', *Cultural Studies*, vol. 21, no. 2–3, pp. 168–178.

Reyes-Centeno, H 2016, 'Out of Africa and into Asia: fossil and genetic evidence on modern human origins and dispersals', *Quaternary International*, vol. 416, pp. 249–262.

Richter, D, Grün, R, Joannes-Boyau, R, Steele, TE, Amani, F, Rué, M, Fernandes, P, Paynal, J-P, Geraads, D, Ben-Ncer, A, Hublin, J-J & McPherron, SP 2017, 'The age of the hominin fossils from Jebel Irhoud, Morocco, and the origins of the Middle Stone Age', *Nature*, vol. 546, pp. 293–296.

Rifkin, M 2017, *Beyond settler time: temporal sovereignty and Indigenous self-determination*, Duke University Press, Durham, NC.

Rizvi, UZ 2008, 'Conclusion: archaeological futures and the postcolonial critique', in L Liebmann & UZ Rizvi (eds), *Archaeology and the postcolonial critique*, AltaMira Press, Lanham, MD.

Rizvi, UZ 2015, 'Decolonizing archaeology: on the global heritage of epistemic laziness', in O Kholeif (ed.), *Two days after forever: a reader on the choreography of time*, Sternberg Press, Berlin, pp. 154–164.

Rizvi, UZ 2016, 'Decolonization as care', in AP Pais & CF Strauss (eds), *Slow reader: a resource for design thinking and practice*, Valiz, Amsterdam, pp. 85–95.

Rose, DB 2004, *Reports from a wild country: ethics for decolonisation*, University of New South Wales Press, Sydney.

Rovelli, C 2018, *The order of time*, Allen Lane, London.

Sahlins, M 1996, 'The sadness of sweetness: the native anthropology of western cosmology', *Current Anthropology*, vol. 37, no. 3, pp. 395–428.

Sahlins, M 2008, *The western ilusion of human nature*, Prickly Paradigm Press, Chicago, IL.

Sahlins, M 2014, 'On the ontological scheme of "Beyond nature and culture"', *HAU: Journal of Ethnographic Theory*, vol. 4, no. 1, pp. 281–290.

Said, EW 1978, *Orientalism*, Pantheon Books, London.

Said, EW 1994, *Culture and imperialism*, Vintage Books, London.

Scerri, EML, Thomas, MG, Manica, A, Gunz, P, Stock, JT, Stringer, C, Grove, M, Groucutt, HS, Timmermann, A, Rightmire, GP, d'Errico, F, Tryon, CA, Drake, NA, Brooks, AS, Dennell, RW, Durbin, R, Henn, BM, Lee-Thorp, J, deMenocal, P, Petraglia, MD, Thompson, JC, Scally, A & Chikhi, L 2018, 'Did our species evolve in subdivided populations across Africa, and why does it matter?', *Trends in Ecology & Evolution*, vol. 33, no. 8, pp. 582–594.

Schaepe, DM, Angelbeck, B, Snook, D & Welch, JR 2017, 'Archaeology as therapy: connecting belongings, knowledge, time, place, and well-being', *Current Anthropology*, vol. 58, no. 4, pp. 502–533.

Schwartz, JH 2006, 'Race and the odd history of human paleontology', *The Anatomical Record Part B: The New Anatomist*, vol. 289B, pp. 225–240.

Schwartz, JH (ed.) 2017, *Rethinking human evolution*, MIT Press, Cambridge, MA.

Simon, ZB 2017, 'Why the Anthropocene has no history: facing the unprecedented', *The Anthropocene Review*, vol. 4, no. 3, pp. 239–245.

Smith, C & Wobst, HM (eds) 2005, *Indigenous archaeologies: decolonizing theory and practice*, Routledge, London.

Smith, FH & Ahern, JCM (eds) 2013, *The origins of modern humans: biology reconsidered*, Wiley, Hoboken, NJ.

Solli, B, Burström, M, Domanska, E, Edgeworth, M, González-Ruibal, A, Holtorf, C, Lucas, G, Oestigaard, T, Smith, L & Witmore, C 2011, 'Some reflections on heritage and archaeology in the Anthropocene', *Norwegian Archaeological Review*, vol. 44, no. 1, pp. 40–88.

Spivak, GC 1999, *A critique of postcolonial reason: toward a history of the vanishing present*, Harvard University Press, Cambridge, MA.

Stanner, WEH 1958, 'The Dreaming', in W Lessa & E Vogt (eds), *Reader in comparative religion: an anthroplogical approach*, Harper and Row, New York, pp. 158–167.

Stanner, WEH 1968, *After the Dreaming*, Australian Broadcasting Commission, Sydney.

Stengers, I 2000, *The invention of modern science*, University of Minnesota Press, Minneapolis.

Stengers, I 2010, *Cosmopolitics I*, University of Minnesota Press, Minneapolis.

Stengers, I 2011, *Cosmopolitics II*, University of Minnesota Press, Minneapolis.

Stengers, I 2015, *In catastrophic times: resisting the coming barbarism*, Open Humanities Press, London.

Stern, N 2015, 'The archaeology of the Willandra', in A McGrath & MA Jebb (eds), *Long history, deep time: deepening histories of place*, ANU Press, Canberra, pp. 221–240.

Stoczkowski, W 2002, *Explaining human origins: myth, imagination and conjecture*, Cambridge University Press, Cambridge.

Stringer, C 2011, *The origin of our species*, Allen Lane, London.

Stringer, C 2014, 'Why we are not all multiregionalists now', *Trends in Ecology & Evolution*, vol. 29, no. 5, pp. 248–251.

TallBear, K 2013, *Native American DNA: tribal belonging and the false promise of genetic science*, University of Minnesota Press, Minneapolis.

Thomas, J 2004, *Archaeology and modernity*, Routledge, New York.

Todd, Z 2015, 'Indigenizing the Anthropocene', in H Davis & E Turpin (eds), *Art in the Anthropocene: encounters among aesthetics, politics, environments and epistemologies*, Open Humanities Press, London, pp. 241–254.

Todd, Z 2016, 'An Indigenous feminist's take on the ontological turn: "ontology" is just another word for colonialism', *Journal of Historical Sociology*, vol. 29, no. 1, pp. 4–22.

Trigger, B 1984, 'Alternative archaeologies: nationalist, colonialist, imperialist', *Man*, vol. 19, pp. 355–370.

Trigger, B 1989, *A history of archaeological thought*, Cambridge University Press, Cambridge.

Trigger, B 2008, '"Alternative archaeologists" in historical perspective', in J Habu, C Fawcett & JM Matsunaga (eds), *Evaluating multiple narratives: beyond nationalist, colonialist, and imperialist archaeologies*, Springer, New York, pp. 187–195.

Trüper, H, Chakrabarty, D & Subrahmanyam, J (eds) 2015, *Historical teleologies in the modern world*, Bloomsbury Academic, London.

Tsing, AL 2015, *The mushroom at the end of the world: on the possibility of life in capitalist ruins*, Princeton University Press, Princeton, NJ.

Tuck, E & Yang, KW 2012, 'Decolonization is not a metaphor', *Decolonization: Indigeneity, Education & Society*, vol. 1, no. 1, pp. 1–40.

Tuhiwai Smith, L 2012, *Decolonizing methodologies: research and Indigenous peoples*, 2nd edn, Zed Books, London.

Veth, P 2010, 'Australian and international perspectives on Native Title, archaeology and the law', in J Lydon & UZ Rizvi (eds), *Handbook of postcolonial archaeology*, Left Coast Press, Walnut Creek, CA, pp. 267–284.

Viveiros de Castro, E 2013, 'Economic development and cosmopolitical re-involvement', in L Green (ed.), *Contested ecologies: dialogues in the south about nature and knowledge*, HSRC Press, Cape Town, pp. 28–41.

Viveiros de Castro, E 2014, *Cannibal metaphysics: for a post-structural anthropology*, Univocal, Minneapolis, MN.

Wagner, R 2016, *The invention of culture*, 2nd edn, University of Chicago Press, Chicago, IL.

Watts, V 2013, 'Indigenous place-thought and agency amongst humans and non-humans (First Woman and Sky Woman go on a European world tour!)', *Decolonization: Indigeneity, Education & Society*, vol. 2, no. 1, pp. 20–34.

Weidenreich, F 1946, *Apes, giants and man*, University of Chicago Press, Chicago, IL.

Wolpoff, MH & Caspari, R 1997, *Race and evolution*, Simon & Schuster, New York.

Wolpoff, MH, Xinzhi, W & Thorne, A 1984, 'Modern *Homo sapiens* origins: a general theory of hominid evolution involving fossil evidence from East Asia', in FH Smith & F Spencer (eds), *The origins of modern humans: a world survey of the fossil evidence*, Liss, New York, pp. 411–483.

Wylie, A 2008, 'The integrity of narratives: deliberative practice, pluralism, and multivocality', in J Habu, C Fawcett & JM Matsunaga (eds), *Evaluating multiple narratives: beyond nationalist, colonialist, and imperialist archaeologies*, Springer, New York, pp. 201–212.

Young, RJC 2001, *Postcolonialism: an historical introduction*, Blackwell, Oxford.

Zihlmann, AL 1987, 'Sex, sexes, and sexism in human origins', *Yearbook of Physical Anthropology*, vol. 30, pp. 11–19.

SECTION 2

Definition of the human and its colonial legacy

2

IMHO

Inventing modern human origins

Iain Davidson

IDK: introducing defined knowledge

IDK is LOL-speak for I Don't Know. Knowledge of the past, like all knowledge, depends on the meanings of the words used in acquiring and maintaining it. Part of coming to know things is learning to name them. Too often we take for granted the definitions of the basic concepts, yet it turns out that often they derive from a prior history with quite political origins that impact what we think we know. As an example of this, my use of the first person is intended to show that I am aware of the subjectivity I bring to this piece. But it is also open to the criticism that I am writing as an old white male of certain education, privilege and background. My view is that it is better to be open about both of those things than to conceal them behind impersonal passive (aggressive) language.

There are two related but different issues in the study of human origins. On the one hand is biological evolution of humans and our ancestors, traditionally studied through the analysis of fossilised skeletal remains; on the other is the evolution of hominin and human behaviour, traditionally studied from archaeological evidence including stones and bones. It turns out that there are questions about classification in both domains, and these questions turn on the fact that both researchers studying skeletons and those studying behaviour use language composed of words, and hence classifications and concepts, defined by conventions. All of those classifications and concepts have history about how the conventions were originally defined: they derive from the history of the disciplines in the societies in which they arose, and from common usages among the general public of those societies. In most cases, those societies were actively engaged in colonialism during the period when the disciplines were developed, and the evidence was viewed through a corresponding cultural filter. The words and concepts of the discipline of archaeology carry the marks of colonialism. A modern approach to archaeohistory needs to look carefully at the colonial legacy in the interpretations that imbue our disciplines. At the same time, the concepts of postcolonialism and decolonisation can also be examined for their subjectivities and theoretical contexts.

Darwin once wrote that 'all observation must be for or against some view if it is to be of any service' (Shermer 2001, p. 38). At some stage all scholars have to formulate some views to argue 'for or against' if our data are to serve in telling any sort of story about the basic elements of long-term history. Many of the theoretical assumptions that have made it possible to tell a story have been less carefully examined than some of the data. Even postcolonial arguments have not escaped criticisms similar to those we mete out to writings unreflective about the underlying colonial thinking. Liebmann (2008, pp. 11–13) summarised arguments that postcolonialism is neo-colonialist, concluding that there is some possibility that archaeology might contribute to postcolonial theory which avoids that obvious paradox. This chapter will suggest that there are special reasons why that may be impossible. Edward Said (1995, p. 10), the great Palestinian pioneer of postcolonial thinking, wrote:

> No one has ever devised a method for detaching the scholar from the circumstances of life, from the fact of [their] involvement (conscious or unconscious) with a class, a set of beliefs, a social position, or from the mere activity of being a member of a society.

The import of that statement is that no one can escape their own cultural biases. We can be aware that we have them, though, and work to minimise the extent to which our work (in this case archaeohistory) is no more than a reflection of those biases.

FWIW: finding which issue is which

For some scholars 'human origins' is about the origins of people who are like us in every respect – the only creatures that can be called human – and exhibit what Noble and I called 'modern human behaviour' (Noble & Davidson 1996). This behavioural definition is only one of three general understandings of the phrase 'human origins' (for a recent discussion giving priority to skeletal classification rather than behavioural, see Smith & Wood 2017). A second branch of study is about how humans became distinct from what some people call 'other' apes with which we share a Last Common Ancestor – all creatures that physical anthropologists classify as belonging to the genus *Homo* would be called human (Marks 2015) – the *Homo* definition. These distinctions, while not self-evident, are easy enough to define. In addition to recognising these two categories of investigation of the biology of human origins, Smith & Wood (2017) defined a third that is somewhat more esoteric and primarily of interest to professionals in the business of fossils: a technical discrimination of the emergence of members of the genus *Homo* from the group of fossils that are not ancestors of apes, yet not so close to humans, such as Australopithecines and the like – the non-*Homo* definition. In all cases the dividing lines are not essential facts of nature. They are instead artefacts of the analysis – as shown by controversies about the appropriate classification of some fossils (e.g. Gibbons 2011) – a product of scholars' theoretical preoccupations or intuitions. Moreover, understanding of the relationships among proposed classifications depends heavily on the methods used to derive them (e.g. Collard & Wood 2000; Gibbs, Collard & Wood 2000), and the sometimes subjective reasons for choosing them.

The reality is that, if Darwin was right, and on this he could not have been otherwise, there can be no hard and fast boundaries between species through time, much less between genera. A mother (of any species past or present) could not have given birth to a male offspring to whom she was so distantly related that they would not have been able, give or take an incest taboo, to have produced offspring. So, the boundaries are things that are created in the process of study depending on what is being studied and why, and on the assumptions that are brought to bear on the study. The classifications are those of all-too-human scholars (scientists if you will) and are not given by biology or a god (or Linnaeus) as immutable for all time (for one appropriate reassessment of current taxonomic approaches see Antón, Potts & Aiello 2014). Even the dividing lines between the three categories of inquiry about human origins are deeply subjective. That lack of essence in the categories means that the chosen classifications are always subjective.

Although we might agree that the three categories of origin recognised by Smith and Wood – Behavioural, *Homo* and non-*Homo* – are relevant to the study of human biology, without accepting that they necessarily identify essences of human evolution, we also need to understand that there were behavioural changes during that process, even when only considering skeletons. The nature of evolution is such that we understand that such changes occurred in both the human line and the ape line, and presumably in the line that links fossil creatures[1] that are not on either line back to a Last Common Ancestor (Duda & Zrzavý 2013). Looking at human origins in relation to behavioural variables might legitimately take into account a whole different set of issues or achievements. These include the emergence of stone tools used for cutting (Davidson 2019), the mastery and making of fire (Wrangham 2009), hunting of prime age animals (Davidson 1989; Stiner 1994), symbolic communication (Davidson & Noble 1989; Henshilwood et al. 2002), marking of places with ochre or by engraving (Brumm et al. 2017), the creation of pictures and art (Davidson 2013), navigation beyond the sight of land (Davidson & Noble 1992) and grinding grains (Revedin et al. 2010) (which really means the modification of plant material to make it edible). All humans have, or have the capacity to achieve, these things; not all human ancestors had the characteristic and may not have had the capacity for it. Concentrating on the biological aspects of human evolution alone is a subjective choice that seems to ignore the most distinctive aspects of humanity – those behaviours that made us all cultural (Davidson 2016).

In addition to the emergence of those elements of cultural behaviour (or something like them) that are found among all human societies, it is probably the case that all humans have the capacity for permanent settlement (Hardy-Smith & Edwards 2004) (though the political imposition of settlement on nomads has not always been successful) and agriculture (in some form or other) (e.g. Pascoe 2014; Zeder 2015) (though the political imposition of agriculture on people whose subsistence is otherwise has not always been successful) but not all have them. These two behaviours were restricted to relatively small numbers of people and places until very recently (in the timescale of human evolution), however much they may be the norm in dominant societies nowadays. To add sedentism and agriculture to the initial list would allow the reader to think that somehow the process of behavioural evolution led inexorably to these anomalous behaviours and then to all of the subsequent differentiation among human populations. In reality, such achievements were not inevitable, but the colonialist narrative, being constructed in societies that had those achievements, has said they were.

There is a consequence of this historical context of writing the narrative of human achievement: the narrative has been distorted by two errors. First, in many colonies, the earliest systematic observations followed the destruction of the society and economy of the colonised 'Other' either accidentally through disease or deliberately as a result of an ideology of disdain and superior fire power – what Walter Roth (1984, p. 41) referred to in saying 'what with privation, disease, alcohol, and lead, the whole community has been annihilated'.

The second is the confirmation bias that resulted from the ingrained attitudes to Other people that did not allow the colonists to interpret the equivalences between what they saw and what was done in their own society. Recent scholarship has shown that early European explorers of Australia reported environmental management behaviour that can be described as agricultural, but denied that this was what it was (Gammage 2011; Pascoe 2014).

This is not the place, nor I the scholar, to point to the subsequent appearance of other key features that flowed from sedentism and agriculture: the demographic effects of agriculture; the hunger for, and conflict over, land that this generated; individual transferrable ownership of land, plants, animals and other property; the relationship between stored foods and records of stores using notations systems; and the capacity to write down origin stories around all of that. Arguably the expansion of population and agriculture, and the writing (not just the telling) of stories is the beginning of the expansionary practices that were mimicked millennia later in post-mediaeval colonisation. And along with, on one hand, written histories of how the colonists arrived at their own achievements and, on the other, those expansionary practices came an assumption of the inevitability of colonisation as the destiny of those colonists.

That narrative has led members of the general public (and far too many anthropologists for our own good) to ask questions such as: 'In 1492, were most of the tribes inhabiting the Americas *already* [my emphasis] farmers or *still* [my emphasis] hunter-gatherers?' The adverbs in that question appear to have little weight, but betray that the dominant narrative derived from the archaeohistory of Europe has led the inheritors of that narrative to regard those others as failures with all the apparent comforts of racist judgment. One could ask a counter-factual question on behalf of the invaded: 'Why could the colonists not survive as hunter-gatherers and why had they chosen to adopt agriculture that is so destructive of the environment?' In reality, the dominant behavioural achievement of humans has been flexibility (Veth et al. 2011) – the fact that humans can choose or create many different, cultural, ways of being human.

FYI: finding usable information

The subjective nature of the classification of hominins and of the key issues in the biological evolution in the hominin line(s) raise similar questions to the subjectivity in the behavioural issues: each question requires a disentanglement of preconceptions and subjectivities in order to work out what, exactly, is the relevant (i.e. usable) theoretical and hence empirical domain.

This means that there can be no objective agreement on how to identify such a thing as human origins: the concept is something we invent among the community of scholars. As such it is subject to two particular influences; first, how are the problems we study understood among the general public, who do not study them but consume the narratives we construct in addressing them; and second, how does the history of investigations linger in the understandings of those who do study those questions? It would be absurd to say that there is no such thing as human origins: the general public – our audience – expect us (anthropologists studying the past) to be able to answer such questions as 'where do we come from?' To claim there is no such thing as human origins would be absolutist in precisely the same way as the rejection of all of classic anthropology on the grounds that it was written by people from colonial powers (e.g. Hage 2017).

Modern humans are clearly different in form and behaviour from our other ancestors known only from archaeology – though recent studies are obscuring that clarity.

Anthropological theorising claims that we shared a succession of common ancestors (see, for example, Grabowski & Jungers 2017), first with monkeys, then with apes and finally with other hominins all of which went on to their own different histories. In the process, only some of them ended with identifiable modern species. That being so, it is 'self-evident' that we are different from all of them, and not only because we have evolved since those ancestors but because they have too (e.g. Duda & Zrzavý 2013; Grabowski & Jungers 2017).

Studying the deep past is a description of parts of the process of evolution. Consumers of the science that we produce expect us to be able to draw boundaries that define the important stages of that process (such as the Upper Palaeolithic). One part of the issue is where we draw the boundaries; another part is the reason we draw them where we do. We use the bounded entities (say, the different species of *Homo*) to tell a story about them as actors or characters who did things in the past according to a plot that we discern. The stages we define become the boundaries of that particular narrative. Who or what the actors are depends on the subjectivities of identifications of species or other groupings. With even greater subjectivity, the plot is determined by the reasons we define those entities and not others. Our classifications have an element of arbitrariness, and the entities we define in that way become agents and events in the plot of the archaeohistory that we construct. Each of those narratives is an invention of ours, and, so far as we know, none of the other entities, ancient or modern, be they monkey, ape or Australopithecine, is or has been capable of such inventions. The emergence of that difference is part of the narrative – the plot of the story that I am telling. The differences become obvious when contrasting the beginning of the process and its end, but the boundaries may be subjective at any point on the continuum.

This chapter is about Inventing Modern Human Origins, and for that I define what I mean by 'modern human' – those humans characterised by communication using symbols (Noble & Davidson 1991) – in contrast to Porr and Matthews (2017) who discussed modern human origins in the context of postcolonial theory, without, I think, attending to the definition of 'modern human'. This definition of Modern Human Behaviour (MHB) is different from the meaning used by Smith and Wood (2017, pp. 671–672) who define the question in skeletal terms – the appearance of Modern Human Anatomy (MHA). Of course, in what is now a familiar trope, what constitutes modernity depends on the field of study. Noble and I concentrated on the initial emergence of modern human behaviour – that is, the behaviour of the first people to be called 'modern humans' – and, in doing so, argued that modernity was closely tied to our perceptions at that time of the earliest emergence of art in the Upper Palaeolithic of Western Europe (Davidson & Noble 1989). In this, we were undoubtedly influenced by the sense that this art somehow marked the most significant step in the evolution of MHB. But we were also unreflective of the fact that vast regions of the world had barely been examined archaeologically, and none had been researched as intensively as Western Europe. The dated finds from Blombos, South Africa (Henshilwood & Sealy 1997), Nawarla Gabarnmang, Australia (David et al. 2013), Sulawesi (Aubert et al. 2014), Trinil, Java (Joordens et al. 2015) and Shuidonggou, China (Pitarch Marti et al. 2017) had not been published.

There are other, barely related, definitions of modernity. Art also features in the definition of that modernity identified with the European Renaissance (Eisenstein 1983), as well as that celebrated (more widely) in the early twentieth century (Habermas 1981). In all three of these cases, there were precursors in the record from before what is called modernity. But we should expect that. Indeed, since those innocent days of the late 1980s, when Noble and I began researching the issue, the data from the archaeology of periods earlier than the Upper Palaeolithic of Europe have expanded enormously, particularly but not only outside Europe, and in ways that demand scrutiny of the definition of 'art' (discussion of the relevant literature can be found in Davidson 2017). The dividing lines between the categories of inquiry are deeply subjective: they depend on the available data, but also on the ideas that are brought to bear on those data. In all three of these cases in which the word modernity is at issue, what is defined as modern is the choice of those on the modern side of the dividing line. At the boundaries of Middle Ages and of the twentieth century, there is a political element to that definition – 'modern-ness' was seen as an element of the progress towards what was morally and socially advanced – they are properly seen as colonialist or orientalist claims. That is a more difficult argument to run for the archaeological emergence of modern human behaviour, since there are no surviving protagonists of the alternative. That does not prevent controversy, since there are advocates for the modern-ness of human behaviour at various different dates in various different places. All people are modern, but all modern people are modern in their own way.

CU: colonialism unpacked

Many of the theoretical assumptions that have made it possible to tell a story have been less carefully examined than some of the data. Postcolonial critiques will not escape criticisms similar to those with which we castigate writings unreflective of the colonial origins of their thinking. This volume is devoted to 'decolonisation of the deep past' precisely because of such thinking. The concepts of postcolonialism and decolonisation can also be examined for their subjectivities and theoretical contexts. If it is true that 'The process of decolonization deconstructs systems of power' (Henry, Angelbeck & Rizvi 2017, p. 29) then it is important to assess what happens when decolonisation is successfully achieved. It is not that there are no subsequent relations of power, but that the location of the power will have changed. In a sense, the decolonisers will have become the new colonisers and a new struggle will ensue. Anomalous situations arise. It has been suggested that all early observation of Others might have been tainted by colonialist points of view, especially given the close relations between anthropology and colonial administration from the very beginning (McDougall & Davidson 2008). While acknowledging the difficulty, Hage (2017) argued that it is not impossible to discern the valuable observations from the overlay of assumptions derived from the colonial status of the anthropologists. The point of a postcolonial critique is to recognise such assumptions and remove their destructive influences.

The essential starting point for decolonisation and a postcolonial critique must be a definition of colonialism – on the assumption that 'decolonisation' refers to a process of undoing colonialism, and postcolonialism is what comes next. It is a field that is already the subject of a substantial theoretical literature, even in archaeology (Liebmann & Rizvi 2008; Lydon & Rizvi 2016; Porr & Matthews 2017), but given that such discussions often generate their own internal logic, in the spirit of the return to first principles of definitions for other branches of archaeological study, it is worth going back to first principles here too. Many others have defined the context of their engagement with postcolonial thought, including the authors in the cited volumes, but here the first principles are all that is needed.

Dictionaries, of course, have always had the function of providing authority for the conventional meanings of words, so it is sightly ironic to appeal to one here – the more so when it is a dictionary produced by non-Indigenous power-holders in a colonial society. The *Macquarie Dictionary* (Macquarie 2006) defines colonialism as: 'the policy of a nation seeking to extend or retain its authority over other peoples or territories'. It is experienced both at the level of state institutions and at the level of individual freedoms. My previous discussion (Davidson 2011) related only to the second of these – how I, as a citizen of a colonising country, interacted with archaeologists first in Spain (while I was a citizen of the UK) and then with Aboriginal people in Australia (after I became Australian). At the individual level, a colonial attitude is one in which a person (or people) from outside 'the colony' seeks to exert power or influence over those indigenous to it. But the issue is how to transfer that idea from the politics and reality of interactions between peoples and territories to the context of ideas about the science of human origins and the history we write about it. How literally we take the resulting metaphors is a very subjective matter.

In this discussion, the concept of 'colonising' extends to considering the way in which the authority of previous ideas about the past retains its influence over interpretations of the past despite changes in available knowledge (data and ideas). Those ideas were generally conceived by people from nations that engaged in colonising foreign places and killing or subjugating their inhabitants and exerting power over the survivors, yet, in colonised places, the past is that of the Indigenous inhabitants. This is much more akin to Said's concept of Orientalism as 'a style of thought based upon an ontological and epistemological distinction made between "the Orient" and (most of the time) "the Occident"' (Said 1995, p. 2). In the case of human origins, the distinction is between an 'us' (people of the present day) and an Other 'them' (people of the past defined in one of the ways discussed above). In a previous paper, I invoked L. P. Hartley's (1953, p. 1) saying that 'The past is a foreign country. They do things differently there,' pointing out that, in consequence we are all from somewhere else – we are all culturally different from the people of the past (Davidson 2011). We are all 'Other' to someone, past or present. Said's third status of Orientalism is 'as a Western style for dominating, restructuring, and having authority over the Orient' (Davidson 2011, p. 3). The analogy with the practice of twenty-first century archaeology is the persistence of tropes and expectations derived from nineteenth-century archaeology – how practice defined by people in the colonising West defined what progress was and permitted (but did not justify) judgments about the status of Others based on the fact that they had not made the same sort of change. The judgment was really about difference, but the colonialist style and language made it one of relative moral worth. The history of postcolonial theory is full of language about the desirability of overturning power structures that subjugated one group of people or peoples (Patterson 2008). Postcolonial theory and decolonisation are themselves knowledge claims that they are morally or socially more progressive than earlier claims mired in colonial thinking. For example, for Rizvi (2008, p. 197), 'Postcolonial research is a confession of enduring political inequality; it is a condition that continues until the disparities created by colonialism, often recast into neocolonial frameworks, are deconstructed.' But a sense of moral superiority was a primary motivation of colonial thinking, and thus postcolonial theory runs the risk of being recursively guilty of the thing it attacks, unless the practitioners are aware of, and mediate, that danger. To be fair, most of them are aware and do mediate the danger.

One approach to such deconstruction emphasises the way in which standard typologies 'exert control over forms of knowledge' (Henry, Angelbeck & Rizvi 2017, p. 28) as has been the case from the very beginning of archaeology. The initial archaeological research that established standard frameworks of the past, such as that of Savagery, Barbarism and Civili-sation – and here the moral worth is defined by the vernacular meanings of the chosen words – is best known from mid-nineteenth century scholars like Tylor (1871) and Morgan (1877), but was certainly identifiable in the eighteenth century (Barnard 2014). Darwin's friend John Lubbock, who was not only British but a baronet,[2] mined the evidence of 'travellers and naturalists' about other people to define the characteristics of the 'lowest in the scale of civilization' among the accounts of living peoples (Lubbock 1913, pp. 445–446 of the first edition of 1865) in his quest to illustrate the narrative of prehistoric times by the sleight of hand of using such evidence to 'throw some light on the remains of savage life in ages long gone by' (1865, p. viii). The purpose of prehistory was to paint pictures of progress.

A classification of the archaeological evidence (e.g. Stone Age, Bronze Age, Iron Age) was created as an empirical generalisation about excavated materials presented in European museum displays that was then said to indicate a chronology, and after some resistance, generally adopted by Western Europeans (Rowley-Conwy 2007). The hierarchical sequence was consequently taken as a fundamental fact about the past by those nations and their peoples most heavily involved in colonial exploitation of the rest of the world. It is arguable that the general acceptance within the colonising powers of a hierarchy of ages enabled them to define these as stages of progress in the emergence of their modern societies. The term 'Stone Age' became a pejorative label that Australian archaeologists stopped using a long time ago (Gorman 2018), at least in part because its use meant that colonialists could look down on Indigenous societies such as those in Sahul[3] or the Americas that had neither bronze nor iron. But that value judgment depended on assumptions about the inevitability of change of a particular sort that the colonists alone would call progress.

The people who promoted such judgments arrogantly looted the antiquities of the coun-tries of the East Mediterranean to fill the collections they kept in their country estates and the museums in their capital cities (for a discussion of the 'biography' of the Parthenon Marbles, see Hamilakis 1999). And when the opportunity arose they extended their rapacious appe-tites to the art and artefacts of Africa (e.g. Curtis 2010), Australia (e.g. Griffiths 1996), and other colonised countries (for a discussion of many of the legacies of colonial construction of museum collections and recent responses to that history, see Lynch & Alberti 2010). Out-rageously, the looting continues (Al-Hussainy & Matthews 2008). Such arrogance is matched by the unwillingness of those museums, until recently, to contemplate restoring the cultural heritage of others to its rightful place and the subjectivity with which, in true Orientalist fashion, they assert their ownership and their sole capacity to care for what they call the 'heritage of all mankind' (Porr 2017). As Hartwig Fischer, director of the British Museum in London, told the *Guardian*, his museum is 'a museum of the world for the world' (excluding, presumably, those countries that want their heritage returned) (Higgins 2018).

The power of the colonising countries, and the fact that their archaeological work was initiated early, established the frameworks that have been a dominant influence on almost all that has been written about the process of human evolution since the nineteenth century. The study of human evolution in the present day must be seen as colonised literally from the colonising countries (Britain, France, Germany, particularly) and from European 'science' of the nineteenth century – a foreign country in Hartley's terms. Underlying those frameworks were other preconceptions derived from the limitations of knowledge in those European countries that stemmed from their attitudes to Christianity and to Classical Greece and Rome – and influenced by the holdings of art and archaeological artefacts from those sources in the museums of colonising countries. Attitudes to Classical Greece and Rome entailed belief in the fundamental importance of knowledge and art from those places and their intellectual life, partly because the more recent Europeans were largely ignorant of the importance of Sumerian, Chinese, Islamic or, indeed, any other sources of knowledge.

Two of the most influential philosophical approaches to the historical emergence of civil society have some common features in this regard. Englishman Hobbes (1660, ch. XIII) and Frenchman Rousseau (1999), whose philosophies were rather different, both writing after colonies from their countries had followed those established by the Spanish in the Americas, seemed to ignore the emerging knowledge of non-European societies that had reached Europe ever since the earliest stages of European colonisation. Rather they based their arguments on general knowledge of the Bible and the classics, but more especially on thought experiments, what we might more reasonably call guesses or speculations. This was despite the fact that, more than half a century before Hobbes published, Frenchman Montaigne (1580, e.g. ch. XXV) had drawn conclusions (albeit very limited and largely inaccurate) from the evidence of the native inhabitants of the Americas. Early speculations about the behaviour of 'other people' very often depended on the subjectivities of people of the colonial powers, what Said, quoted at the beginning of this chapter, called their 'circumstances of life,' rather than on the accumulating knowledge about how other people constructed their worlds. And the influence of such ideas themselves persisted rather more than it ought.

LOL: language or language-as-we-know-it

Such considerations of the persistence of classification schemes as they applied to people of the past and Others in the present derive from the characteristics of languages as systems of conventional communication. And it was the emergence of such conventions that defined modern human behaviour (Noble & Davidson 1991).

Our paper of 1991 (Noble & Davidson 1991) was (one of) the first to use the phrase 'modern human behaviour' to mean the behaviour of humans who were the earliest modern humans in the archaeological record (some previous scholars had used it to refer to the behaviour of people in the present day) and certainly the first to define what might be meant by the phrase. We defined modern human behaviour as distinguished by the use of language, and, in a move that was unusual for people writing about language origins, we also defined language. The definition we chose was: 'the symbolic use of communicative signs' (p. 224). We concluded (p. 246) that:

> the colonisation of Australia and the Americas, ... world-wide changes in the technol-
> ogy of stone and especially bone tools, the first documented evidence for ritual and the
> disposal of the dead ... regional variation in style ... social differentiation ... and the
> emergence of both fisher-gatherer-hunters ... and agriculturalists ... can be attributed to
> the greater information flow, planning depth and conceptualisation consequent upon the
> emergence of language.

Even this degree of dependence on a definition that derives from modern humans could be seen as some sort of colonial project – imposing a view of what humans are. In reality, it is just the discourse that is necessary for unambiguous communication – to disambiguate the meaning of a signal for its emitter and its receiver. The decolonisation of the origins of modern humans cannot ignore that convention and its potentially colonial nature.

It would have been possible to address the question of what constituted modern human behaviour in a different way (for a more recent, and more disinterested discussion see Nowell 2010). We could have taken the archaeological evidence associated with the earliest finds of skeletal remains said to be of modern humans and stated that this was what constituted modern human behaviour. We might have ended up demonstrating that modern human skeletal form did not guarantee that the associated behaviour would be like that of present day people. Alternatively, we could have looked at present day (i.e. modern) humans and tried to define what behavioural characteristics are common to all people alive today (and we might then have said exactly what we did say: that the only common features are a product of being language-using species). In reality, the behavioural characteristics do not go in lockstep with the skeletal features for a simple reason: they relate to different domains – one is a biological classification (or 'biopolitical' as Jon Marks [2016] would have it), the other a cultural or behavioural one. Smith and Wood (2017, p. 672) emphasised the 'science' involved in investigating major questions in biological anthropology such as:

> When, where, how and why did we acquire the morphology that enables the distinctive behaviors of modern humans, such as our upright posture, bipedal locomotion, manual dexterity, theory of mind and the ability to communicate and plan using complex spoken language?

The important point here is that for biological anthropologists morphology comes first (it is the position from which they seek to colonise the subject), aspects of mind and its products, including 'complex spoken language',[4] are 'enabled' by that. Putting it gently, it may be that there are more complex relationships among these features. The systemic interaction between features of mind and body may be an important part of the natural selection involved in the evolution of both anatomy and behaviour. Understanding whether there are such complex relationships and how they work requires more sophisticated theoretical frameworks – it requires a decolonisation of the subject from the power of the anatomists. The point is that the objects of study in human origins research are not only matters of empirical investigation, but need to be put into a theoretical context (see, especially, Barnard 2010), not least because there is often a link between the story we want to tell about material found in the archaeological record and what is found. How they are linked influences what needs to be looked for.

These points are well illustrated by a discussion of the concept of 'anatomically modern *Homo sapiens*'. Brown (1990) showed how Australian Aboriginal skeletal material did not fit within the range of variation used by others (Day and Stringer, Stringer and Andrews, and Groves – originals not seen for this chapter[5]), oriented to Europe and Africa, to define 'anatomically modern *Homo sapiens*'. Brown acknowledged that the other authors did not intend for their criteria to be applied in such a way that modern human skeletal remains might be excluded (Stringer 2012), but in the present context that is not the point. The colonising power used a definition that excluded the people from the colony. There are three other points: first, that made by Brown (1990, p. 69): 'At best these anatomical definitions of "anatomically modern *Homo sapiens*" are inappropriately titled – at worst they may make a significant section of the modern human population think less of this subject area, and its practitioners, than they do already', referring, of course, to Aboriginal Australians;

second, we need to recognise that the claims that biological descriptions of skeletal remains from deep time are scientific and hence uninfluenced by any other considerations are, at best, hollow, such that many of us might also think less of this subject area; and third, the unconscious, and hence unwitting, biases that lead to such errors (or worse those that are made consciously) stem from a privileging of particular materials, ideas, and approaches that hardly ever work against the interests of those who have power over the practices of science and the presentation of its results. Another colonialism.

Scholars using behavioural definitions do not escape criticism, however. In tracing the impact of the emergence of language on perception, Davidson and Noble (1989) began from the idea that there was an important marker of language in the cave art of Western Europe. With hindsight this was part of the 'colonialist' mindset. Since the end of the nineteenth century, the art of the Upper Palaeolithic of Western Europe has been said to be early in the history of art, to the extent that the absence of similar art (in any medium) in some regions, betokened their impoverishment rather than the exceptional nature of Western Europe (Davidson 2012). By the end of our initial exploration of the subject that marker was no longer important.

One of the reasons for beginning with European cave art was that the psychologist Gibson (1966; 1979) had speculated that the emergence of language and the emergence of art were likely related, and Noble and I produced another speculation about a scenario by which that might have happened (Noble & Davidson 1996, ch. 8). What was 'colonialist' about our attitude was a lazy assumption, both authors having been educated in Western Europe and not thinking of 'detaching [ourselves] from the circumstances of life', that somehow or other the Western European archaeological sequence represented important stages in the evolution of all human behaviour, so that all narratives of human evolution would include a stage somewhat equivalent to European cave art. The evidence was already there that the sequence was different in different parts of the world (Davidson 1997; 2012) but the notion that Europe set the pattern has continued, and was still much in evidence when paintings were found in Sulawesi that pre-dated the earliest in Europe (Brumm et al. 2017). The recent publication of earlier paintings from Borneo likewise makes reference to the European evidence (Aubert et al. 2018).

Following the analysis of the issues by Noble and myself (Noble & Davidson 1996), there was some move towards identifying modern human behaviour through identification of a series of traits. This approach reached its zenith and subsequent demise through the comprehensive analysis by McBrearty and Brooks (2000) which sought to show, in good decolonial fashion, that many of the traits that defined modernity in Europe were present in Africa much earlier and never occurred as a single package. This was not a reconsideration of the appropriateness of defining modernity on European evidence. d'Errico (2003) showed that the traits occurred in a piecemeal fashion in Europe and the Near East, as well as Africa, so that in replacing a frankly colonialist attitude with a different chauvinism McBrearty and Brooks did not do much to resolve the historical question of what modern human behaviour is or how it emerged.

Unpacking these three attempts to get a purchase on the most momentous events in the evolution of human behaviour (Nowell 2010), what stands out is that none of us did very well. The outstanding thing about the trait lists is that some of the traits emerged before the supposed appearance of anatomically modern humans, most appeared long after the appearance of modern humans (defined either by skeletal remains or by the statistics of genetic sequences), and none of the traits appeared during the period of emergence of modern humans. This situation is not much changed by refining claims about the date of appearance of anatomically modern humans (e.g. Richter et al. 2017; Schlebusch et al. 2017).

The idea that modern human anatomy indicates modern human behaviour is pernicious, but by now the reader should realise that the boundaries of either category of 'modern human' should be viewed critically. Archaeological signatures have been transformed by the discoveries in southern Africa, far away from Europe and much older than any evidence there of bone tools (Henshilwood et al. 2001), beads (d'Errico, Henshilwood, Vanhaeren & Niekerk 2005), ochre with patterned engravings (Henshilwood, d'Errico & Watts 2009; Mackay & Welz 2008), paint mixing kits (Henshilwood et al. 2011; Villa et al. 2015), heat treatment of stone artefacts (Brown et al. 2009; Wadley & Prinsloo 2014), evidence of complex hafting technology (Charrié-Duhaut et al. 2013; Wadley, Williamson & Lombard 2004), and ostrich egg-shells with engraved patterns around a carefully prepared opening (Texier et al. 2010). A comprehensive review of evidence for early beads and ornaments shows that they were widespread across the world with the earliest presence of modern humans (Wei et al. 2016). Some have argued that they might not be beads and suggest, instead that they were materials used for counting (Coolidge & Overmann 2012; Overmann 2016). The distinction is a nicety, because, as with all of this other new evidence, the importance is not just symbolism or language, but the nature of cognition that can displace the process of production by several steps from the use and any possible function.

What has been difficult for a simple model (e.g. Davidson & Noble 1989) has been the discovery that European Neandertals appear to have engaged in substantial behaviour that looks like symbol use, including ochre use (e.g. Roebroeks et al. 2012), feather use (e.g. Blasco & Peresani 2016; Peresani et al. 2011), use of shells (e.g. Zilhão et al. 2010), use of ornaments (Caron et al. 2011), rock marking (e.g. Rodríguez-Vidal et al. 2014), the creation of rock structures deep inside a cave (Jaubert et al. 2016) and mark making with ochre inside caves (Hoffmann et al. 2018). There is no doubt that this presents a challenge. One view would be that despite several hundred thousand years (0.35 million years) of separate evolution, Neandertals and humans converged on similar solutions to the problems of living. Explaining how that was possible, without invoking a teleological progress, is more difficult.

Another view would be that the abilities of modern humans were present but latent before the species diverged. Some support for such a view could be provided by accepting as indicators of such ability the modified pebble from Berekhat Ram (d'Errico & Nowell 2000; Marshack 1997) and the scratched shell from Trinil, in Java (Joordens et al. 2015). At the moment the support is not strong because these are isolated cases, and any argument for the symbolic status of marking requires that there be conventions – and conventions cannot be identified unless there is some repetition of the acts of marking.

It is likely that the Trinil example is instructive here. The marked shell was collected in the 1890s as evidence of food-gathering. At that time no one thought of looking for 'art' among the products of *Homo erectus*. Art was known from marked bones of the Upper Palaeolithic of Europe associated with modern humans, though this find was made some years before everyone accepted that there was already cave art. As with some of the reassessments of Neandertal materials (e.g. Soressi & d'Errico 2007), it seems likely that Eurocentric and 'sapiens-centric' blinkers made a difference to what was looked for and found outside the existing expectations. It is not difficult to believe that more has already been found, but was not seen before being concealed in museums.

Much more careful attention has been paid to symbols (and other signs) in the archae-ological record (Culley 2016; Kissel & Fuentes 2017), but comparatively little attention has been paid to the cognitive models that would account for these uncertainties. In a model of cognitive systems it has been suggested that ambiguities are to be expected at the evolu-tionary boundary between cognitive system states and that the structure of the interacting subsystems and the mechanism by which they evolved might almost predict that there should be some convergence despite long separation (Barnard, Davidson & Byrne 2016). This way of approaching the issues allows discussion of the evolution of cognitive systems (Davidson 2019).

WTF: writing true fiction

One of the most amusing comments by Darwin on the nature of science reflected on the relations between data and theory in the service of reaching conclusions about a subject. In a letter to Henry Fawcett (Shermer 2001) he said:

> About thirty years ago there was much talk that geologists ought only to observe and not theorize; and I well remember someone saying that at this rate a man might as well go into a gravel-pit and count the pebbles and describe the colours. How odd it is that anyone should not see that all observation must be for or against some view if it is to be of any service!
>
> *(Shermer 2001)*

If we pay too much attention to the sorts of difficulty I have been outlining, we will find that we can do little more than an equivalent of counting pebbles (though we might want to ponder the dividing lines between gravel and pebbles and cobbles) and describing the colours (where there is probably more substantial disagreement on boundaries). At some stage it is necessary to formulate some views to argue for or against if the data are to serve in telling any sort of story about those 'pebbles'. The point of the catalogue of uncertainties about the basic elements that contribute to the views archaeologists have about the past is that many of the theoretical assumptions that have made it possible to tell a story have been less carefully examined than some of the data.

There are important constraints on the telling of stories (famously elaborated, for archae-ologists, by Landau 1984). There must be actors or agents, so we need names of species or the cultural equivalent. And there must be events, so we need classification of stages in the process. Landau (1993, pp. 5–10), for example identified the different arrangement of the events of arboreality, terrestriality, bipedalism, encephalisation and civilisation. The writers of archaeohistory must also be critical about both the actors and the events.

There is nothing fixed about the species – they are products of our expectation that there should be species – but it would be impossible to talk about the variation among fossils without some names. Moreover, the names of biological entities cannot and need not be completely arbitrary, but there is a possibility of defining entities based on some principles of biological relatedness. As the discussion of sufficient definitions of modern human skeletons showed, there are often historical legacies involved. Cultural stages and the names we give them mimic the expectation that there was an older history similar to that brief episode of the period of written record which writes of times such as the Dark Ages and the Middle

Ages, despite the implicit judgment about the periods implied in the names. These are names that scholars make up and give. But that is not a reason to avoid telling stories. At the beginning of her analysis Landau (1993, pp. 2–3) said of the constraints imposed by the fact of telling stories: 'scientists may free themselves from these bonds, first, by realizing that they tell stories and, second, by recognizing that they may put them to good purpose. … they can be serviceable creatures'.

The result is that there will always be a need for classifications to define both actors and events that form the basis for constructing a narrative. Many of the names used to write archaeohistory were invented in the nineteenth century and there was room for disagreement about what sorts of entities they were. The subjectivity of the definitions of the actors and events of narratives about the past has depended both on the nature of the data available and on the theoretical assumptions that have been brought to bear. The moral of the story I have been telling is that we have to be aware of the way in which our histories, and our unexamined biases, may determine the nature of the narratives we construct.

Many of those biases will reflect the history of concepts that originated in political contexts that gave rise in the colonies to relationships of colonialist and Indigenous people who might be called subaltern. The word 'subaltern', of course, is given to the colonised in recognition that the colonial attitude remains one that regards them as somehow inferior – but more importantly leaves them as having less access to power despite attempts to minimise the colonial attitude. That means that narratives reflect subconscious attitudes of power. Just as importantly, all peoples have concepts of their past, and often there are cultural differences between colonialist and colonised about the nature of the past and their relationships with it. Thirdly, the idea that that past is a foreign country means that both colonist and colonised 'seek … to extend or retain its authority over [the] peoples or territories' of that foreign country.

This analysis and that conclusion make it very unlikely that there might be objectively identifiable key stages in the study of such a process of emergence. It is more likely that that objectivity will change through time as we gain more understanding of the histories of the studies and the biases that affected them. The process of arriving at any particular narrative of archaeohistory will be iterative or involve selection. Such approaches are all correct at some level (assuming goodwill and fair-dealing in the scholarship) and are all wrong at other levels. As a result, an approach that can be called scientific may be impossible, or else it needs to constantly question its classifications, the actors or agents it creates and their roles in narratives that can be written about their relationships and archaeohistories.

NSFW: new synthesis for 'where-to-next?'

This may sound like a critique that leaves no room for optimism, by suggesting that most approaches to the archaeohistory of human origins have been impossibly trapped in the legacy of past interpretive frameworks that were themselves dominated by attitudes fostered by perceptions of self-worth in colonial societies. Such a dismal view is not my intention.

Rather I suggest we need to move beyond the problems posed by the European record and attitudes so that we can consider how to explain the related phenomena when they occur outside Europe without appearing to judge them in European and colonial terms.

I have sought to show that almost all of the problems of archaeohistory are contingent on the assumptions built in to interpretations, whether they concentrate on 'purely' biological aspects through the study of fossil skeletons, or on behavioural ones that dominated the record culturally, and probably had important selective effects biologically.

The important point about these assumptions is that made by Said in the extract already presented above: it is very difficult to 'detach … the scholar from the circumstances of life', but good scholarship requires us to review constantly the unconscious bias and assumptions that we bring to the data. So in looking at the influences on stories about modern human origins, there are issues about how to define modern, human and modern human. There are also issues about how to define an origin as a discontinuity in a continuous process. Finally, there are issues about the structural constraints on telling stories, including many studies that suggest that, as Landau (1993) found, examining early archaeohistorical narratives, there is a limited number of plots taken by fictional narratives (Booker 2004; Reagan et al. 2016), and what we are up against is the tendency of the nineteenth-century legacy to skew the narrative towards only one of those identified – a 'rags to riches' tale (Booker 2004; Reagan et al. 2016, p. 5) of the rise of modern humans.

In a recent re-examination of the work of several scholars puzzling with the evolution of cognition (culminating with the emergence of modern humans) it was possible to show the evolution of cognitive archaeology by gradual processes that involved an initial approximation, a re-assessment that showed new variations on the previous story, the selection of particular variants and construction of a new story, followed by a new re-assessment and so on (Davidson 2019). The point is that we stagger crab-wise towards more acceptable narratives of the past. Each time, we consider the previous ideas and look at them critically, then apply them to data that may be absolutely new or simply the old data seen in light of the new ideas. Generally speaking we do not go back to old ideas, and once we have identified the influence of the authority that derived from colonial ideas, we are unlikely to go back. We will not go back to the ideas from Western European colonising nations; nor will we go back to the authority derived from the 'foreign country' of past archaeological practice.

Acknowledgments

Thank you to all the people who showed an interest, commented, sustained or otherwise helped me while writing this paper: Helen Arthurson, Elisabeth Culley, Ramona Koval, David Mayes, Martin Porr, Lauren Santini, and Pat Shipman. In addition, the comments of two readers identified only from their initials were very helpful.

Notes

1 There is a vocabulary problem here because some were ancestral to modern humans, some were not; some were ancestral to modern apes, some were not. They probably fit into the category 'hominins' – a category invented by scholars who classify fossils – but to classify them as such is to pre-empt that interpretation. They were certainly creatures.

2 Later a baron – a nicety that was doubtless important to him, but is lost on me. It presumably implies that someone attributed superiority to him, but we might now be extremely dubious about the objective worth of such an attribution.

3 The continent that is the normal condition of Australia and New Guinea except during brief intervals of high sea-level when the islands are separated. The separation of these islands is a fact of recent geography that is enhanced by acceptance of the separateness of the nation states that occupy all or parts of them.

4 To which we must ask whether there is any spoken language that is *not* complex. In reality this cluster of words is just a way of avoiding having to address the questions of what the authors mean by language.
5 But I am grateful to Chris Stringer for sharing his memory of this dispute with me on Facebook (pers. comm. 2 November 2017).

References

Al-Hussainy, A & Matthews, R 2008, 'The archaeological heritage of Iraq in historical perspective', *Public Archaeology*, vol. 7, no. 2, pp. 91–100.

Antón, SC, Potts, R & Aiello, LC 2014, 'Evolution of early *Homo*: an integrated biological perspective', *Science*, vol. 345, no. 6192, pp. 1–15.

Aubert, M, Brumm, A, Ramli, M, Sutikna, T, Saptomo, EW, Hakim, B, Morwood, MJ, van den Bergh, GD, Kingsley, L & Dosseto, A 2014, 'Pleistocene cave art from Sulawesi, Indonesia', *Nature*, vol. 514, no. 7521, pp. 223–227.

Aubert, M, Setiawan, P, Oktaviana, AA, Brumm, A, Sulistyarto, PH, Saptomo, EW, Istiawan, B, Ma'rifat, TA, Wahyuono, VN, Atmoko, FT, Zhao, J-X, Huntley, J, Taçon, PSC, Howard, DL & Brand, HEA 2018, 'Palaeolithic cave art in Borneo', *Nature*, vol. 564, pp. 254–257.

Barnard, A 2014, 'Defining hunter-gatherers: enlightenment, romantic and social evolutionary perspectives', in V Cummings, P Jordan & M Zvelebil (eds), *Oxford handbook of the archaeology and anthropology of hunter gatherers*, Oxford University Press, Oxford, pp. 43–54.

Barnard, PJ 2010, 'Current developments in inferring cognitive capabilities from the archaeological traces left by stone tools: caught between a rock and a hard inference', in A Nowell & I Davidson (eds), *Stone tools and the evolution of human cognition*, University Press of Colorado, Boulder, pp. 207–226.

Barnard, PJ, Davidson, I & Byrne, RW 2016, 'Toward a richer theoretical scaffolding for interpreting archaeological evidence concerning cognitive evolution', in T Wynn & F Coolidge (eds), *Cognitive models in palaeolithic archaeology*, Oxford University Press, Oxford, pp. 45–67.

Blasco, R & Peresani, M 2016, 'Humankind and the avian world: zooarchaeological evidence for inferring behavioural evolutionary signatures', *Quaternary International*, vol. 421, pp. 1–5.

Booker, C 2004, *The seven basic plots: why we tell stories*, A&C Black, London.

Brown, KS, Marean, CW, Herries, AIR, Jacobs, Z, Tribolo, C, Braun, D, Roberts, DL, Meyer, MC & Bernatchez, J 2009, 'Fire as an engineering tool of early modern humans', *Science*, vol. 325, no. 5942, pp. 859–862.

Brown, P 1990, 'Osteological definitions of "anatomically modern" *Homo sapiens*: a test using modern and terminal Pleistocene, *Homo sapiens*', *Proceedings of the Australasian Society for Human Biology*, vol. 3, pp. 51–74.

Brumm, A, Langley, MC, Moore, MW, Hakim, B, Ramli, M, Sumantri, I, Burhan, B, Saiful, AM, Siagian, L, Suryatman, Sardi R, Jusdi A, Abdullah, Mubarak, AP, Hasrianti, H, Oktaviana, AA, Adhityatama, S, van den Bergh, GD, Aubert, M, Zhao, J-x, Huntley, J, Li, B, Roberts, RG, Saptomo, EW, Perston, Y & Grün, R 2017, 'Early human symbolic behavior in the Late Pleistocene of Wallacea', *Proceedings of the National Academy of Sciences*, vol. 114, pp. 4105–4110.

Caron, F, d'Errico, F, Del Moral, P, Santos, F & Zilhão, J 2011, 'The reality of Neandertal symbolic behavior at the Grotte du Renne, Arcy-sur-Cure, France', *PLoS ONE*, vol. 6, no. 6, pp. 215–245.

Charrié-Duhaut, A, Porraz, G, Cartwright, CR, Igreja, M, Connan, J, Poggenpoel, C & Texier, P-J 2013, 'First molecular identification of a hafting adhesive in the Late Howiesons Poort at Diepkloof Rock Shelter (Western Cape, South Africa)', *Journal of Archaeological Science*, vol 40, no. 9, pp. 3506–3518.

Collard, M & Wood, B 2000, 'How reliable are human phylogenetic hypotheses?', *Proceedings of the National Academy of the Sciences*, vol. 97, pp. 5003–5006.

Coolidge, FL & Overmann, KA 2012, 'Numerosity, abstraction, and the emergence of symbolic thinking', *Current Anthropology*, vol. 53, no. 2, pp. 204–225.

Culley, EV 2016, *A semiotic approach to the evolution of symboling capacities during the Late Pleistocene with implications for claims of modernity in early human groups*, PhD Thesis, Arizona State University.

Curtis, NG 2010, 'Repatriation from Scottish museums: learning from NAGPRA', *Museum Anthropology*, vol. 33, no. 2, pp. 234–248.

d'Errico, F 2003, 'The invisible frontier: a multiple species model for the origin of behavioral modernity', *Evolutionary Anthropology*, vol. 12, pp. 188–202.

d'Errico, F & Nowell, A 2000, 'A new look at the Berekhat Ram figurine: implications for the origins of symbolism', *Cambridge Archaeological Journal*, vol. 10, no. 1, pp. 123–167.

d'Errico, F, Henshilwood, C, Vanhaeren, M & Niekerk, KV 2005, 'Nassarius kraussianus shell beads from Blombos Cave: evidence for symbolic behaviour in the Middle Stone Age', *Journal of Human Evolution*, vol. 48, no. 1, pp. 3–24.

David, B, Barker, B, Petchey, F, Delannoy, J-J, Geneste, J-M, Rowe, C, Eccleston, M, Lamb, L & Whear, R 2013, 'A 28,000 year old excavated painted rock from Nawarla Gabarnmang, northern Australia', *Journal of Archaeological Science*, vol. 40, no. 5, pp. 2493–2501.

Davidson, I 1989, *La economía del final del Paleolítico en la España oriental*, Diputación Provincial, Valencia.

Davidson, I 1997, 'The power of pictures', in M Conkey, O Soffer, D Stratmann & NG Jablonski (eds), *Beyond art: Pleistocene image and symbol*, California Academy of Sciences, San Francisco, pp. 128–158.

Davidson, I 2011, '"Somos todos de fuera" – we are all from somewhere else. Thoughts on the responsibilities of archaeologists', in N Bicho (ed.), *História, Teoria e Método da Arqueologia. Actas do IV Congresso de Arqueologia Peninsular, Universidade do Algarve, Faro, Portugal*, pp. 245–250.

Davidson, I 2012, 'Symbolism and becoming a hunter-gatherer', in 'L'art pléistocène dans le monde / Pleistocene art of the world / Arte pleistoceno en el mundo, Actes du Congrès IFRAO, Tarascon-sur-Ariège, septembre 2010, Symposium "Signes, symboles, mythes et idéologie …"'. Special issue of *Préhistoire, Art et Sociétés, Bulletin de la Société Préhistorique Ariège-Pyrénées*, Book: pp. 292–293 CD: pp. 1689–1705.

Davidson, I 2013, 'Origins of pictures: an argument for transformation of signs', in K Sachs-Hombach & JRJ Schirra (eds), *Origins of pictures. Anthropological discourses in image science*, Halem, Cologne, pp. 15–45.

Davidson, I 2016, 'Stone tools: evidence of something in between culture and cumulative culture?', in MN Haidle, NJ Conard & M Bolus (eds), *The nature of culture, vertebrate paleobiology and paleoanthropology*, Springer, Netherlands, pp. 99–120.

Davidson, I 2017, 'Paleolithic art', in J Jackson (ed.), *Oxford bibliographies in anthropology*, Oxford University Press, New York.

Davidson, I 2019, 'Evolution of cognitive archaeology through evolving cognitive systems', in KA Overmann & F Coolidge (eds), *Squeezing minds from stones*, Oxford University Press, Oxford, pp. 79–101.

Davidson, I & Noble, W 1989, 'The archaeology of perception: traces of depiction and language', *Current Anthropology*, vol. 30, no. 2, pp. 125–155.

Davidson, I & Noble, W 1992, 'Why the first colonisation of the Australian region is the earliest evidence of modern human behaviour', *Archaeology in Oceania*, vol. 27, pp. 135–142.

Duda, P & Zrzavý, J 2013, 'Evolution of life history and behavior in hominidae: towards phylogenetic reconstruction of the chimpanzee–human last common ancestor', *Journal of Human Evolution* vol. 65, no. 4, pp. 424–446.

Eisenstein, EL 1983, *The printing revolution in early modern Europe*, Cambridge University Press, Cambridge.

Gammage, B 2011, *The biggest estate on Earth*, Allen & Unwin, Sydney.

Gardner, BT & Gardner, RA 1985, 'Signs of intelligence in cross-fostered chimpanzees', *Philosophical Transactions of the Royal Society of London, B*, vol. 308, pp. 159–176.

Gibbons, A 2011, 'Who was *Homo habilis* – and was it really *Homo*?', *Science*, vol. 332, no. 6036, pp. 1370–1371.

Gibbs, S, Collard, M & Wood, B 2000, 'Soft-tissue characters in higher primate phylogenetics', *Proceedings of the National Academy of the Sciences*, vol. 97, no. 20, pp. 11130–11132.

Gibson, JJ 1966, *The senses considered as perceptual systems*, Houghton Mifflin, Boston.

Gibson, JJ 1979, *The ecological approach to visual perception*, Houghton Mifflin, Boston.

Goddard, C, Wierzbicka, A & Fabréga, H 2014, 'Evolutionary semantics: using NSM to model stages in human cognitive evolution', *Language Sciences*, vol. 42, pp. 60–79.

Gorman, A 2018, 'Australian archaeologists dropped the term "Stone Age" decades ago, so should you', *The Conversation*. Available from: https://theconversation.com/australian-archaeologists-dropped-the-term-stone-age-decades-ago-and-so-should-you-47275 [2 April 2019].

Grabowski, M & Jungers, WL 2017, 'Evidence of a chimpanzee-sized ancestor of humans but a gibbon-sized ancestor of apes', *Nature Communications*, vol. 8, no. 1, p. 880.

Griffiths, T 1996, *Hunters and collectors. The antiquarian imagination in Australia*, Cambridge University Press, Cambridge.

Habermas, J 1981, 'Modernity versus postmodernity', *New German Critique*, vol. 22, pp. 3–14.

Hage, G 2017, '"Anthropology is a white colonialist project" can't be the end of the conversation', *Media Adiversitied*, Available from: https://mediadiversified.org/2017/09/04/anthropology-is-a-white-colonialist-project-cant-be-the-end-of-the-conversation/amp/ [16 September 2017].

Hamilakis, Y 1999, 'Stories from exile: fragments from the cultural biography of the Parthenon (or "Elgin") Marbles', *World Archaeology*, vol. 31, no. 2, pp. 303–320.

Hardy-Smith, T & Edwards, PC 2004, 'The garbage crisis in prehistory: artefact discard patterns at the Early Natufian site of Wadi Hammeh 27 and the origins of household refuse disposal strategies', *Journal of Anthropological Archaeology*, vol. 23, no. 3, pp. 253–289.

Hartley, LP 1953, *The go-between*, Penguin, Harmondsworth.

Henry, ER, Angelbeck, B & Rizvi, UZ 2017, 'Against typology: a critical approach to archaeological order', *The SAA Archaeological Record*, vol. 17, no. 1, pp. 28–32.

Henshilwood, C, d'Errico, F, Vanhaeren, M, van Niekerk, K & Jacobs, Z 2004, 'Middle Stone Age shell beads from South Africa', *Science*, vol. 304, no. 5669, p. 404.

Henshilwood, CS, d'Errico, F & Watts, I 2009, 'Engraved ochres from the Middle Stone Age levels at Blombos Cave, South Africa', *Journal of Human Evolution*, vol. 57, no. 1, pp. 27–47.

Henshilwood, CS, d'Errico, F, Marean, CW, Milo, RG & Yates, R 2001, 'An early bone tool industry from the Middle Stone Age at Blombos Cave, South Africa: implications for the origins of modern human behaviour, symbolism and language', *Journal of Human Evolution*, vol. 41, pp. 631–678.

Henshilwood, CS, d'Errico, F, Niekerk, KLv, Coquinot, Y, Jacobs, Z, Lauritzen, S-E, Menu, M & García-Moreno, R 2011, 'A 100,000-year-old ochre-processing workshop at Blombos Cave, South Africa', *Science*, vol. 334, pp. 219–222.

Henshilwood, CS, d'Errico, F, Yates, R, Jacobs, Z, Tribolo, C & Duller, GA 2002, 'Emergence of modern human behavior: Middle Stone Age engravings from South Africa', *Science*, vol. 295, pp. 1278–1280.

Henshilwood, CS & Dubreuil, B 2011, 'The Still Bay and Howiesons Poort, 77–59ka: symbolic material culture and the evolution of mind during the African Middle Stone Age', *Current Anthropology*, vol. 52, no. 3, pp. 361–400.

Henshilwood, CS & Sealy, J 1997, 'Bone artefacts from the Middle Stone Age at Blombos Cave, Southern Cape, South Africa', *Current Anthropology*, vol. 38, no. 5, pp. 890–895.

Higgins, C 2018, 'British Museum director Hartwig Fischer: "There are no foreigners here-the museum is a world country"', *The Guardian*. Available from: https://www.theguardian.com/culture/2018/apr/13/british-museum-director-hartwig-fischer-there-are-no-foreigners-here-the-museum-is-a-world-country [14 April 2018].

Hobbes, T 1660, *The Leviathan*. Available from: http://www.jrbooksonline.com/pdf_books_added2009-2/levithian.pdf [6 September 2017].

Hoffmann, DL, Standish, CD, García-Diez, M, Pettitt, PB, Milton, JA, Zilhão, J, Alcolea-González, JJ, Cantalejo-Duarte, P, Collado, H, de Balbín, R, Lorblanchet, M, Ramos-Muñoz, J, Weniger, G-Ch & Pike, AWG 2018, 'U-Th dating of carbonate crusts reveals Neandertal origin of Iberian cave art', *Science*, vol. 359, no. 6378, pp. 912–915.

Jaubert, J, Verheyden, S, Genty, D, Soulier, M, Cheng, H, Blamart, D, Burlet, C, Camus, H, Delaby, S, Deldicque, D, Edwards, RL, Ferrier, C, Lacrampe-Cuyaubère, F, Lévêque, F, Maksud, F, Mora, P, Muth, X, Régnier, É, Rouzaud, J-N & Santos, F 2016, 'Early Neanderthal constructions deep in Bruniquel Cave in southwestern France', *Nature*, vol. 534, pp. 111–114.

Joordens, JCA, d'Errico, F, Wesselingh, FP, Munro, S, de Vos, J, Wallinga, J, Ankjaergaard, C, Reimann, T, Wijbrans, JR, Kuiper, KF, Mucher, HJ, Coqueugniot, H, Prie, V, Joosten, I, van Os,

B, Schulp, AS, Panuel, M, van der Haas, V, Lustenhouwer, W, Reijmer, JJG & Roebroeks, W 2015, 'Homo erectus at Trinil on Java used shells for tool production and engraving', *Nature*, vol. 518, no. 7538, pp. 228–231.

Kissel, M & Fuentes, A 2017, 'Semiosis in the Pleistocene', *Cambridge Archaeological Journal*, vol. 27, no. 3, pp. 397–412.

Landau, M 1984, 'Human evolution as narrative', *American Scientist*, vol. 72, pp. 262–268.

Landau, M 1993, *Narratives of human evolution*, Yale University Press, New Haven, CT.

Liebmann, MJ 2008, 'Introduction: the intersections of archaeology and postcolonial studies', in L Liebmann & UZ Rizvi (eds), *Archaeology and the postcolonial critique*, AltaMira Press, Lanham, MD, pp. 1–20.

Liebmann, L & Rizvi, UZ (eds) 2008, *Archaeology and the postcolonial critique*, AltaMira Press, Lanham, MD.

Lubbock, J 1913, *Prehistoric times as illustrated by ancient remains and the manners and customs of modern savages*, 7th edn, Williams and Norgate, London.

Lydon, J & Rizvi, UZ (eds) 2016, *Handbook of postcolonial archaeology*, Routledge, London.

Lynch, BT & Alberti, SJMM 2010, 'Legacies of prejudice: racism, co-production and radical trust in the museum', *Museum Management and Curatorship*, vol. 25, no. 1, pp. 13–35.

Mackay, A & Welz, A 2008, 'Engraved ochre from a Middle Stone Age context at Klein Kliphuis in the Western Cape of South Africa', *Journal of Archaeological Science*, vol. 35, pp. 1521–1532.

Macquarie 2006, *Macquarie concise dictionary*, Macquarie University, Sydney.

Marks, J 2015, *Tales of the ex-apes: how we think about human evolution*, University of California Press, Berkeley.

Marks, J 2016, 'The units of scientific anthropological origin narratives', *Anthropological Theory*, vol. 16, no. 2–3, pp. 285–294.

Marshack, A 1997, 'The Berekhat Ram figurine – a late Acheulian carving from the Middle East', *Antiquity*, vol. 71, no. 272, pp. 327–337.

McBrearty, S & Brooks, AS 2000, 'The revolution that wasn't: a new interpretation of the origin of modern human behavior', *Journal of Human Evolution*, vol. 39, no. 5, pp. 453–563.

McDougall, R & Davidson, I 2008, 'Introduction', in R McDougall & I Davidson (eds), *The Roth family, anthropology and colonial administration*, Left Coast Press, Walnut Creek, CA, pp. 11–28.

Montaigne, MEde 1580, *Essays*, trans. J Florio (1603). Available from: www.mises.ch/library/Montaigne_Essays_Florio_Translation.pdf [6 September 2017].

Morgan, LH 1877, *Ancient society; or, researches in the lines of human progress from savagery, through barbarism to civilization*, Henry Holt & Company, New York.

Noble, W & Davidson, I 1991, 'The evolutionary emergence of modern human behaviour: language and its archaeology', *Man: Journal of the Royal Anthropological Institute*, vol. 26, no. 2, pp. 223–253.

Noble, W & Davidson, I 1996, *Human evolution, language and mind*, Cambridge University Press, Cambridge.

Nowell, A 2010, 'Defining behavioral modernity in the context of Neandertal and anatomically modern human populations', *Annual Review of Anthropology*, vol. 39, no. 1, pp. 437–452.

Overmann, KA 2016, 'The role of materiality in numerical cognition', *Quaternary International*, vol. 405, pp. 42–51.

Pascoe, B 2014, *Dark emu. Black seeds: agriculture or accident?* Magabala Books, Broome, Australia.

Patterson, TC 2008, 'A brief history of postcolonial theory and implications for archaeology', in L Liebmann & UZ Rizvi (eds), *Archaeology and the postcolonial critique*, AltaMira Press, Lanham, MD, pp. 21–34.

Peresani, M, Fiore, I, Gala, M, Romandini, M & Tagliacozzo, A 2011, 'Late Neandertals and the intentional removal of feathers as evidenced from bird bone taphonomy at Fumane Cave 44 ky B.P., Italy', *Proceedings of the National Academy of Sciences*, vol. 108, no. 10, pp. 3888–3893.

Pitarch Martí, A, Wei, Y, Gao, X, Chen, F & d'Errico, F 2017, 'The earliest evidence of coloured ornaments in China: the ochred ostrich eggshell beads from Shuidonggou Locality 2', *Journal of Anthropological Archaeology*, vol. 48, Supplement C, pp. 102–113.

Porr, M 2017, 'Colonialism, coloniality and opportunities for necessary engagement, critique and reflection. A comment on the current debate around the Humboldt Forum in Berlin'. Available from: www.decolonisinghumanorigins.com/2017/09/commentonhumboldtforumdebate.html [2 April 2019].

Porr, M & Matthews, JM 2017, 'Post-colonialism, human origins and the paradox of modernity', *Antiquity*, vol. 91, no. 358, pp. 1058–1068.

Reagan, AJ, Mitchell, L, Kiley, D, Danforth, CM & Dodds, PS 2016, 'The emotional arcs of stories are dominated by six basic shapes', *European Physical Journal Data Science*, vol. 5, no. 1, p. 31.

Revedin, A, Aranguren, B, Becattini, R, Longo, L, Marconi, E, Lippi, MM, Skakun, N, Sinitsyn, A, Spiridonova, E & Svoboda, J 2010, 'Thirty thousand-year-old evidence of plant food processing', *Proceedings of the National Academy of Sciences*, vol. 107, no. 44, pp. 18815–18819.

Richter, D, Grün, R, Joannes-Boyau, R, Steele, TE, Amani, F, Rué, M, Fernandes, P, Raynal, J-P, Geraads, D & Ben-Ncer, A 2017, 'The age of the hominin fossils from Jebel Irhoud, Morocco, and the origins of the Middle Stone Age', *Nature*, vol. 546, no. 7657, pp. 293–296.

Rizvi, UZ 2008, 'Conclusion: archaeological futures and the postcolonial critique', in L Liebmann & UZ Rizvi (eds), *Archaeology and the postcolonial critique*, AltaMira Press, Lanham, MD, pp. 197–203.

Rodríguez-Vidal, J, d'Errico, F, Giles Pacheco, F, Blasco, R, Rosell, J, Jennings, RP, Queffelec, A, Finlayson, G, Fa, DA, Gutiérrez López, JM, Carrión, JS, Negro, JJ, Finlayson, S, Cáceres, LM, Bernal, MA, Fernández Jiménez, S & Finlayson, C 2014, 'A rock engraving made by Neanderthals in Gibraltar', *Proceedings of the National Academy of Sciences*, vol. 111, no. 37, pp. 13303–13306.

Roebroeks, W, Sier, MJ, Nielsen, TK, De Loecker, D, Parés, JM, Arps, CES & Mücher, HJ 2012, 'Use of red ochre by early Neandertals', *Proceedings of the National Academy of Sciences*, vol. 109, no. 6, pp. 1889–1894.

Roth, WE 1984, *Ethnological studies among the North-West-Central Queensland Aborigines*, Facsimile edn, Hesperian Press, Carlisle, Australia.

Rousseau, J-J 1999, *Discourse on the origin of inequality*, Oxford University Press, Oxford.

Rowley-Conwy, P 2007, *From genesis to prehistory: the archaeological three age system and its contested reception in Denmark, Britain, and Ireland*, Oxford University Press, Oxford.

Said, EW 1995, *Orientalism*, Penguin Books, London.

Schlebusch, CM, Malmström, H, Günther, T, Sjödin, P, Coutinho, A, Edlund, H, Munters, AR, Vicente, M, Steyn, M, Soodyall, H, Lombard, M & Jakobsson, M 2017, 'Southern African ancient genomes estimate modern human divergence to 350,000 to 260,000 years ago', *Science*, vol. 358, no. 6363, pp. 652–655.

Shermer, M 2001, 'Colorful pebbles and Darwin's dictum: science is an exquisite blend of data and theory', *Scientific American*, vol. 284, no. 4, p. 38.

Smith, RJ & Wood, B 2017, 'The principles and practice of human evolution research: are we asking questions that can be answered?', *Comptes Rendus Palevol*, vol. 16, no. 5–6, pp. 670–679.

Soressi, M & d'Errico, F 2007, 'Pigment, gravures, parures: les comportements symboliques controversés des Néandertaliens', in B Vandermeersch & B Maureille (eds), *Les néandertaliens. Biologie et cultures*, Editions CTS, Paris, pp. 297–309.

Stiner, MC 1994, *Honor among thieves. A zooarchaeological study of Neandertal ecology*, Princeton University Press, Princeton, NJ.

Stringer, C 2012, 'Evolution: what makes a modern human', *Nature*, vol. 485, no. 7396, pp. 33–35.

Texier, PJ, Porraz, G, Parkington, J, Rigaud, JP, Poggenpoel, C, Miller, C, Tribolo, C, Cartwright, C, Coudenneau, A, Klein, R, Steele, T & Verna, C 2010, 'A Howiesons Poort tradition of engraving ostrich eggshell containers dated to 60,000 years ago at Diepkloof Rock Shelter, South Africa', *Proceedings of the National Academy of Sciences*, vol. 107, no. 14, pp. 6180–6185.

Tylor, EB 1871, *Primitive culture: researches into the development of mythology, philosophy, religion, language, art, and custom*, John Murray, London.

Veth, P, Stern, N, McDonald, JJ, Balme, J & Davidson, I 2011, 'The role of information exchange in the colonisation of Sahul', in R Whallon, WA Lovis & RK Hitchcock (eds), *Information and its role in hunter-gatherer bands*, Cotsen Institute of Archaeology Press, Los Angeles, CA, pp. 203–220.

Villa, P, Pollarolo, L, Degano, I, Birolo, L, Pasero, M, Biagioni, C, Douka, K, Vinciguerra, R, Lucejko, JJ & Wadley, L 2015, 'A milk and ochre paint mixture used 49,000 years ago at Sibudu, South Africa', *PLoS ONE*, vol. 10, p. 6.

Wadley, L & Prinsloo, LC 2014, 'Experimental heat treatment of silcrete implies analogical reasoning in the Middle Stone Age', *Journal of Human Evolution*, vol. 70, pp. 49–60.

Wadley, L, Williamson, B & Lombard, M 2004, 'Ochre in hafting in Middle Stone Age southern Africa: a practical role', *Antiquity*, vol. 78, pp. 661–675.

Wei, Y, d'Errico, F, Vanhaeren, M, Li, F & Gao, X 2016, 'An early instance of Upper Palaeolithic personal ornamentation from China: the freshwater shell bead from Shuidonggou 2', *PLoS ONE*, vol. 11, p. 5.

Wrangham, RW 2009, *Catching fire: how cooking made us human*, Basic Books, New York.

Zeder, MA 2015, 'Core questions in domestication research', *Proceedings of the National Academy of Sciences*, vol. 112, no. 11, pp. 3191–3198.

Zilhão, J, Angelucci, DE, Badal-García, E, d'Errico, F, Daniel, F, Dayet, L, Douka, K, Higham, TFG, Martínez-Sánchez, MJ, Montes-Bernárdez, R, Murcia-Mascarós, S, Pérez-Sirvent, C, Roldán-Garía, C, Vanhaeren, M, Villaverde, V, Wood, R & Zapata, J 2010, 'Symbolic use of marine shells and mineral pigments by Iberian Neandertals', *Proceedings of the National Academy of Sciences*, vol. 107, no. 3, pp. 1023–1028.

3

MODERN ONTOLOGIES OF THE 'MORE-THAN-ANIMAL' HUMAN

Provincialising humanism for the present day

Kay Anderson

Introduction: figuring the human

The belief that people are categorically or essentially different from all other animals has long shaped human self-image and regard in the philosophical traditions of western-derived cultures. In today's context, of deepening ecological concern, it is a belief that is also generating efforts of critique across numerous disciplinary platforms in the academy, from those invoking the post-human, non-human and trans-human, to those summoning the hybridity and materiality of all beings and things. The productive intervention of the environmental humanities, in particular, has been to restore voice and agency to all manner of nonhuman entities and beings, and so to think culture (language, intelligence and more) beyond a narrow humanist conception and across species lines.[1]

Yet despite diverse efforts to undo the anthropocentrism of worldviews that 'centre' human agency, subjectivity, need and desire,[2] little rigorous critical attention has been given across the social sciences, philosophy, cultural studies, and the humanities to the very idea of human distinction itself. Beyond critical appeals to the genetic facts of human biological kinship with nonhuman animals[3] and, differently, to assertions of the 'fantasy' of human exceptionality (Bennett 2010, p. ix), the premise of human distinction is characteristically dismissed out of hand as either scientifically flawed or as vain mythology. In John Gray's (2003, p. 31) words, the notion of human exception is a 'decaying scrap of Christian myth'. And its conceit is usually considered to be all the more deluded for having just persisted 'despite Darwin', in the words of Lynn White's (1967) influential paper *The Historical Roots of Our Ecological Crisis*. As Bruno Latour (1999, p. 8), too, glosses, 'we haven't moved an inch since Descartes'. Accordingly, he laments, 'the [human] mind is still in its vat, excised from the rest, disconnected, and contemplating … the world'.

Displaced to the realm of mythology as immaterial, then, as well as abstracted from both history and geography as an archaic, eternal, and essentially unchanging, belief, the very idea of human exceptionality has not been sufficiently turned into a problem. Not in itself has it been adequately considered a matter for political critique in the field of epistemology. Yet the implications of dismissing the *historicity* of the thesis of human exceptionality have been significant. For not only has it delayed critical re-evaluation of a key inherited assumption of colonial modernity traced in this chapter: that, of a uniquely human claim to *intelligence* conceived with animality as its constitutive other. The dismissal has also blocked imagining of alternative modes of human relation with the diversity of the earth's life-forms: with non-human life-forms to be sure, and as the environmental humanities remind us, but also of modes of relation of the earth's Indigenous cultures whose epistemic worlds have been muted beneath referential frameworks that anthropologists, in particular, have long since sought to decolonise (e.g. Fabian 1983; Viveiros de Castro 1998; Wolf 1982). Such worlds have also been silenced by sciences, of, for example, Palaeolithic archaeology and human evolutionary studies (Porr 2015; Porr & Matthews 2017) in ways that give false certainty to enduring models of human 'origins' and human nature that are themselves in need of precisely the comprehensive problematisation attempted by this volume and elsewhere (Porr 2014).

The idea of human distinction requires some specification, however, beyond its (dubious and by now much disputed) presumption of a unique and superior species being. These premises have been the target of a genre of critical enquiry that names itself 'post-humanist' in acknowledging that human subjects are defined not by some autonomous essence but by the networks in which they participate. In the words of Jennifer Carlson (2014) 'what we take to be human nature is actually an interspecies relationship, born of countless interactions across different forms of life.' The human and nonhuman are thus conceived on the same material and horizontal plane in various registers of post-humanism.[4] The problem is not only, however, the arrogance of the 'quantum leap between humans and all other organisms' (Bennett 2010, p. 68) that has been presumed to exist in the Christian and Cartesian logics informing western philosophical humanism. For typically, human beings – or, more precisely, those from European-derived cultures – tend to believe not only that there are characteristics 'proper to the human' (Lestel 2015, p. 61) that afford them a special claim to a 'unique sort of uniqueness' (Fernandez-Armesto 2004, p. 36). Going further, and more precisely here, such humans typically believe they are, or *become, human as they transcend some animal-like condition* (Glendinning 2000). That is, they tend to conceive of themselves as separated and elevated not only over an external nature of life-forms 'out there'. In addition, they imagine themselves as having transcended an interiorised animality that is considered a defining essence of human nature. Compared to other life-forms, then, humans in the western cultural tradition have more or less held tight to the proposition that they are in some sense *irreducible* to animal nature.

This more specific humanist idea – that *the human realises itself in taking distance from animal nature* – is the critical focus of this chapter, as it aims to unsettle the manifestly variable figure of the *more-than-animal* human. This is a figure that will be found inseparable from the power-differentiated dynamics of modern European colonialism, and, much more specifically here, the nineteenth-century practices of craniometry and other studies of the size and shape of human and animal skulls in the centuries beyond. The interjection of this particular *entanglement with empire* into critiques of humanism in the social sciences and humanities is far from incidental. The 'nonhuman turn' (Grusin 2015) has worked hard to elicit the sense in which 'the human' has always co-evolved with the nonhuman and, thus, that in our very indistinction from the nonhuman 'we have never been only human' (Pyyhtinen & Tamminen 2011, p. 137). This 'nonhuman turn' has, however, been curiously and arguably notoriously silent on the implication of certain power dynamics – namely, of colonialism – in reproducing the dualist knowledges that were made in the image of Eurocentric humanism (as above, since at least the 1980s in anthropology and postcolonial studies). More specifically, while modernist ontologies that pit human (culture) and nonhuman (nature) against each other have indeed been productively troubled by recent recuperations of the nonhuman in the likes of 'non' and 'more-than' human studies, strangely still occluded from critical view is the ontological infra-structure of Eurocentric animality tropes that historically informed the modern making of the figure of 'the human' that has been under contestation.

Some years ago, the book *Race and the Crisis of Humanism* (Anderson 2007), sought to think narratives of 'the human' in connection with the rise of the idea of racial difference and hierarchy in western thought. The project entailed an attempt to conceive the often-opposed categories of nature, race, and the human as historically entwined ontologies. Substantively – to summarise briefly here – the focus was British colonial encounters with Australia, a place and people that seemed to disturb Christian Enlightenment optimism in the capacity of all people everywhere to separate themselves from nature. It was not only that the Australian Aborigine was negatively regarded as primitive, as many representational critiques of the 'indigene-as-savage' had already amply demonstrated in postcolonial studies and elsewhere (see Anderson 2007, pp. 14–22, 27–32). Rather, *Race and the Crisis of Humanism* sought to elicit the sense in which 'The Australian' put into question the prevailing Enlightenment notion of savagery as a *surpassable* stage of human development. And therein lay its thesis: that increasingly deterministic elaborations of the race idea across the nineteenth century arose out of this specifically southern crisis for Enlightenment humanism. For, if, so the speculation went, Australia's Indigenous people could not improve their lands and distance themselves from a state of nature, perhaps there were *innate* reasons why – as a *people* – they never could or would.

This chapter charts further iterations of the Eurocentric representation of the human as a nature-transcendent being – where nature is conceived as both the external environment of life-forms 'out there' as well as an internal animal-like state. Through a series of historical vignettes, including of present day human exceptionalists, it continues the task of pro-blematising what it means (and might yet mean) to be human-among-other-beings. Con-sistent, however, with the claim above regarding the *historicity* of humanist thought, the target is no pre-set template of critique. Following Latour's (2005) rejection of overly linguistic conceptions of social constructivism, Eurocentric humanism is not conceived here as some abstract regime or 'amorphous imperial soup' (Harris 2004, p. 179) to be 'revealed' behind every habit of mind and practice in the many various theatres of European empire. Instead, its shifting and situated formulation will be tracked and amplified within three quite distinct historical moments of 'crisis' in which was put into question the very notion and status of the human as a being beyond animal nature. Elicited in this way will be the *contingent* rather than *irresistible* character of the thesis of human distinction. For although this idea exhibits an apparently stubborn resilience across a succession of centuries, the purpose here is not to rehearse a familiar story of human exceptionality's endurance – as if it were a cherished fan-tasy or blind vanity that will eternally and everywhere defy change. Instead the narrative plot in the antipodean perspective of what follows is *precisely the opposite*: to evoke the anxiety, and with it, the manifest variability and instability of humanism's improvisations. This is done in order to stimulate a sense of the radical potential for humanism's *reconsideration* amidst the urgent ecological challenges of the twenty-first century.

Intellectual histories of western humanist thought in relation to nature (from Glacken's 1967 seminal *Traces on the Rhodian Shore* through to the likes of the more recent, Smith 2015) have tended to gloss the significance of the moment in the late eighteenth to early nineteenth centuries when a specifically *anatomical* strand of humanism came to challenge earlier Cartesian and theological versions. This oversight might not be so important, it will be suggested, except that it was precisely in the rise of what has elsewhere been coined 'anatomical humanism' (Anderson & Perrin 2013), that comprehensively colonial accounts of certain people became constitutively enrolled in an idea of the human that is sustained to the present day.

First is a focus on Georges Cuvier's attribution in the early 1800s of 'intelligence' to beings who walked upright. At a time when prevailing assumptions about the uniqueness of the human were troubled by the discovery of the great apes, the discussion of this episode will take a disproportionate amount of the chapter's space since it was a formative moment in the emergence of a physical – rather than, as for previous centuries, metaphysical – conception of human uniqueness. The discussion then turns to Alfred Wallace's later nineteenth-century response to the profound threat posed to humanism by the assertion of an evolutionary continuity from apes to humans: in his claims for a distinct form of human *mental* evolution. Third, and finally, the chapter presents a summary account of today's human exceptionalists, for whom human 'intelligence' – now understood as a kind of brain power – is taken to hold the key to averting ecological catastrophe, in another anxious, and arguably reckless, re-assertion of the capacity of human beings to transcend the nonhuman world.

It bears restating that the aim in charting moments of humanist crisis and reaffirmation is not to reiterate critiques of colonial representations of Indigenous people as closer-to-nature. Given the persistent tendency to discern in colonial erasures of Indigenous peoples the same bestialising languages as operate in regimes of human mastery over animals, it seems important to emphasise not just a distance, but a departure, from that familiar line of representationalist critique.[5] Of course a commonality of oppressions, at once racialised and speciesist, may well be apprehended in the various dehumanising regimes that cast Indigenous people beyond the fold of apparently more civilised humans, in Australia, as elsewhere. But despite attention in this chapter to colonial characterisations of racialised subjects, their classification and status as 'not-quite-human' is definitively not the line of argument to be pursued. The point here is not the, by now, widely stated one: that Indigenous people *should* have been admitted to the category of the human. Rather, and more precisely, it is that the culture-specific figuration of the human does itself demand critique and revision.[6] This is a line of problematisation that chimes with valuable calls growing out of political ontology in the field of anthropology and geography to take seriously 'other' ontologies beyond the singular (modern humanist) one to which this chapter's critical focus is devoted (e.g. Blaser 2014; Sundberg 2014; and others in Cameron, de Leeuw & Desbiens 2014). Such works take issue with the common relativist presumption that there are competing perspectives and epistemologies on *one*, universal, real world, instead calling attention to the *multiplicity* of real worlds and their potentialities.

The challenge, then, is to continue to unsettle the terms through which ideas, technologies and governmentalities of human distinction came to be formulated and assembled. In so doing the all-too familiar account of human exceptionality's invariance and straightforward continuity can be disrupted with vignettes of the acute tension that signals humanism's capacity for radical reconsideration. It is a task we shall see requires close attention to modern epistemologies of a particularly formative discourse – of 'intelligence' – in each of this chapter's framing instances of humanism's fundamental instability.

'The peculiar distinction of the erect attitude': George Cuvier and the discovery of the great apes

The nineteenth-century field of comparative anatomy, as the study of physical differences and similarities between life-forms, transformed the anatomical observations of the classificatory science of natural history. Right at the start of that century, the French anatomist and palaeontologist, Georges Cuvier (1802), developed a comparative approach to biology. And it is in his work – together with the intellectual struggles with which he was grappling – that can be found the beginnings of a shift away from a metaphysical understanding of the human as an exalted being whose defining characteristic was a soul or mind.[7] The idea of a 'great chain of being' was coming under scrutiny, and with it 'disappears', Michel Foucault (1985, p. 292) argues, 'the possibility of deploying a great natural order which would extend continuously from the simplest and most inert of things to the most living and the most complex'.

Cuvier was to be a key proponent of a different, *distinctively modern*, formulation of human exception from animal nature. For although he saw the human as a 'purely physical being' to be studied within the domain of comparative anatomy alone, he nonetheless wished to uphold as 'absolute' the distinction between brute and animal mind (Carson 2007, p. 79). Indeed, it was the apparent incongruity between these observations that prompted him to conjecture: 'With so much resemblance in the structure of the nervous system … why is there so vast a difference as to the total result, between man and the most perfect animal?' (1802, p. 125). The following presentation of the political framework in which Cuvier's science was emerging, greatly condenses (of necessity) his attempt to address this question.

It was exactly in order to answer it that Cuvier turned to *racialised* skull readings and did, himself, contribute to the emerging 'science' of craniometry. This he did in the attempt to formulate an idea of intelligence that was qualitatively different in beings that walk upright. Of course nineteenth-century craniometry extended to a wide array of enquiries, into idiocy, genius, and criminality among other characteristics.[8] To be noted in passing here, too, is the important observation via Elizabeth Fee (1979) that craniometry involved almost exclusively the study of male skulls – an intriguing bias in itself, though one that cannot be taken up further here.[9] But it was racial craniometry most diagnostically, and more specifically for Cuvier, Dutch anatomist Petrus Camper's infamous measure of the facial profile (Meijer 1999), that appeared to offer the most promising method for formulating an account of the *mental* significance of human uprightness.

In the context of the discovery of the great apes, the massive gulf that Descartes had once asserted between human and animals was progressively becoming a problem, not least for Linneaus (1735) who wrote in the margins of *Systema naturae* that 'surely Descartes never saw an ape' (cited in Agamben 2004, p. 23). Linnaeus' infamous assertion that he could find no physical way to categorically distinguish between humans and the great apes, had been premised upon his assumption that 'orang-utangs' (a generic term at the time to refer to chimpanzees and other great apes) walked upright. That assumption was later overturned, however, following the French anatomist Louis Jean Marie Daubenton's (1764) comparison of the heads and faces of humans and 'orang-utangs'. With the arrival at the end of the eighteenth century into Europe of many more apes, Daubenton proposed that it was bipedalism or two-handedness that could be regarded as a distinctively human trait. But by the time of Cuvier's earliest writings, with Cartesian and Christian accounts of human distinction increasingly being called into question, it was still unclear as to precisely how this characteristic of human verticality could explain 'so vast a difference' between humans and other animals (1802, p. 125).

In Cuvier's (1840, p. 45) words, 'man is the only animal truly bimanous and biped. The whole body of Man is modified for the vertical position ... designed to be supported by the feet only'. However, the mere fact of uprightness could not alone explain human exceptionality. Here Cuvier proposed a thesis (in a context when phrenologists like Franz Joseph Gall were beginning to situate the mind in the brain) to the effect that the verticality of the facial profile – as linked to uprightness – was indicative of the relative anatomical dominance of the brain. Continuing, he observed that the *more* upright a being and the *more* vertical its facial profile, the *larger* its brain must be in proportion to its senses. For if the brain, which Cuvier defined as 'the instrument by which the mind reflects and thinks' is itself larger in a head more vertically positioned, the more it can be said to 'prevail', in his words, 'over those two senses of smell and taste [and so of nose and mouth] ... which act with the greatest force on animals' (1802, pp. 2–4).

Cuvier's hypothesis, then, was that the facial angle constituted – to quote Claude Blanckaert (1987, p. 434) – 'a physiological measure of intelligence', with intelligence defined as the extent to which a more basic, sensorial, animal-like, existence had been *superseded*. It was this endowment that afforded the essential, more-than-animal, nature, of the human. For, in the distinctly humanist terms of the formulation of intelligence at stake, one notes the categorical distinction being posed between the characteristics attributed to animality and those of humanity in a cultural and philosophical lineage that refused to admit continuity between such registers.[10] And crucially, here, the conception of intelligence being developed by Cuvier was acquiring its substance from notions of racialised difference and hierarchy that would later be comprehensively discredited by generations of critique of colonial 'ideologies of Western dominance' (e.g. Adas 1989). For a new hierarchical principle was needed if human superiority/exceptionality was to be freshly established beyond the metaphysical paradigm of the great chain of being. Enter here then: 'race' as *method*.

Take this statement of Cuvier in a paper with Geoffroy Saint Hilaire in 1795: 'In the various races of man, one observes the same series of relationships as in the various species of animals, between the projection of the skull and [that degree of] ... intelligence', adding immediately, 'none of the peoples with a depressed forehead and prominent jaws have ever furnished subjects generally equal to Europeans' (cited in Jahoda 1998, p. 77). Here, however, Cuvier was not just claiming that those people with 'a depressed forehead and prominent jaws' were inferior. The scopic regimes of colonial stereotyping had already targeted and dramatised variability in the physiognomic features of the world's people (Schiebinger 1993/ 2004).[11] More precisely, here, the supposed fact of this inferiority was being invoked as proof of the anatomical relationship Cuvier was trying to establish, overall, between head shape and intelligence. For without it, Cuvier's argument that the facial angle was a measure of some nature-surpassing capacity would remain unsubstantiated. It is, rather, then, that Cuvier was mobilising this supposed inferiority in order to demonstrate a general anatomical relationship – *stretching across human and ape* – between head shape and intelligence. Cuvier's invocation of an apparently self-evident racial hierarchy thus provided the basis upon which his comparative research could contend that certain anatomies – distinctly upright ones – were more 'intelligent' than other anatomies. In this sense, it was the very knowledge embedded in racial stereotypes and colonial accounts of non-Europeans that came to found the far-reaching modern contention that a uniquely human mentality was the product of a uniquely human anatomy.

Cuvier's English follower, William Lawrence, too, drew on race in his own assertion that the moral and intellectual phenomena of man are the offspring, not of some 'immaterialist' principle, but of 'physical organization'. For Lawrence, as for Cuvier, the 'predominance' in the human 'of the organ of thought and reflection [the brain], over the instruments employed in external sensation [mouth and nose]', is linked, again via Camper's facial angle, to the 'peculiar distinction of the erect attitude' (Lawrence 1819, p. 475). Lawrence declares this from observations of 'the Negro structure' and 'the Caucasian model', noting that insofar as 'the intellectual characters are reduced, the animal features are enlarged and exaggerated'. He then continues: 'This inferiority of organisation is attended with corresponding inferiority of faculties; which may be proved ... by every fact in the past history and present condition of Africa' (Lawrence 1819, p. 364).

For both Lawrence and Cuvier – among others (Thomas Soemmering, for example, in Germany) – the exceptionality of the human was attributed not to some meta-physical idea of mind, but to the distinctive, if variable, nature of the human body itself. Indeed if, as Cuvier maintained, 'intelligence ... is in constant proportion to the relative size of the brain', this was quite literally because: '[t]he more *elevated* the nature of the animal, the more volu-minous is the brain' (1840, pp. 95–96, emphasis added). Via the intensely invested project of racial craniometry, then, the exceptionality of the human had come to be attributed to the variable but nonetheless, distinctive, size and shape of the human brain.

'A distinct order of being': evolutionism and Alfred Wallace in colonial context

The idea that the human was essentially *more than* a mere human animal was constituted anew in the late nineteenth century while remaining indebted to Cuvier's anatomical studies. For although Cuvier's interpretation of the facial angle was eventually refuted (see for example, Blanckaert 1987, p. 447), the identification of human distinction with an idea of intelligence – conceived as a physical attribute of the brain and related to uprightness – informed subsequent elaborations of human uniqueness. Such elaborations were by no means seamlessly stitched together, however. Indeed, a profound sense of struggle and contradiction is to be discerned in the deeply fraught efforts to adapt the explicitly secular thinking of evolutionism in a way that preserved the thesis of human exceptionality (Ingold 2004). So, rather than conceive of such efforts as just another abstract iteration of fantasies of human supremacy, the following discussion seeks to capture the persisting *precarity* of the humanist thesis of intelligence, as forged within evolutionary conceptions of human origins and development that were themselves informed by turbulent experiences of culture-contact.

Evolutionary continuity with the apes notwithstanding, numerous arguments were pro-posed, later in the nineteenth century, in order to try and explain the intellectual 'gap' that many perceived between humans and (other) animals. Evolutionists themselves, despite their significant differences, did not in general relinquish the belief that mental and moral faculties were unique to human beings as a species (Bowler 1989). For, regardless of whether it was an increase in brain capacity that was considered to have led to bipedalism or, as Darwin himself argued, the adoption of an upright posture that – in freeing the hands for tool use – in turn stimulated cerebral development, the distinct path of human evolution was regularly conceived as a movement 'up' from the ape (Landau 1984). But it is important here to emphasise the fraught dependence of such new arguments upon Cuvier's own – *already racially inflected* – account of human exceptionality, with its anatomical invocation of uprightness, two-handedness and brain power.

Co-discoverer of evolution, Alfred Russell Wallace, before his turn to spiritualism, provided one of the most influential arguments for the human's distinct evolutionary path. In his well-known piece titled '*The Origin of the Human Races and the Antiquity of Man Deduced from Natural Selection*', Wallace (1864) drew on Herbert Spencer's claim that it was through their use or disuse that certain faculties evolved or diminished. Wallace pursued this claim in order to extend the argument – traced in this chapter to early nineteenth-century comparative anatomy – that the human brain, and with it intelligence, developed in the surpassing of a sensory and animal-like existence. Like Cuvier – for whom human uprightness released the hands for 'the arts' – Wallace too (but writing in the 1860s) considered that it was the human being's 'erect posture, with the consequent freeing of the hands' that provided 'the crucial difference between mankind and the apes' (1864, p. clxviii).

For Wallace, though, it was 'the development of the brain that was the [most] significant step in human evolution'. Accepting what he called the 'striking resemblances' between the bodily structures of humans and apes, Wallace argued that at a certain point in humanity's evolution 'the power [of natural selection] that had modified the human body would have transferred to the brain and skull – the organ of the mind'. And so, continued Wallace, 'man's body will have remained ... the same', whilst 'his brain ... would have increased in size and complexity and his cranium will have undergone corresponding changes in form' (1864, p. cixix).

It was an argument for a distinct form of human *mental* evolution that for Wallace offered an entirely new basis for placing, as he said, 'man apart ... as in some degree a new and distinct order of being' (1864, p. clxvii). Wallace's logic, then, extended the thesis of natural selection across species – human and nonhuman – to a particular discourse of human history and development that came to exempt the human from the full implications of an acknowledged ape ancestry. For 'ability to transcend nature' was now referred to a distinctively human path of cognitive development in which those humans with apparently less ability for surpassing nature were scripted as stuck in a state of 'mere physicality' – an arrested state that robbed them of the agency and competency not only to adapt but ultimately to survive. So, for Thomas Huxley (1897, p. 109), in his well-known diagrammatic 'sections of the skulls of Man and various apes', 'the Australian' was the very referential limit of the human, seeming to vindicate the apparently self-evident fact that the faculty of mind, as located in the skull, was the agent of a distinctively human trajectory of evolutionary development.[12]

Wallace's case for the relative autonomy of human culture was widely adopted in late nineteenth-century and early twentieth-century anthropological and sociological accounts. Take as examples the American anthropologist, W. J. McGee, who 'saw advancements through culture gradients from savagery to civilization as indicative of a corresponding cranial development'; as well as his compatriot Lewis Henry Morgan who maintained that with cultural development, 'the human mind necessarily grew and expanded', such that there was a 'gradual enlargement of the brain itself, particularly of the cerebral portion' (cited in Haller 1971, pp. 714–718). It is, then, something of Wallace's argument for the autonomy of human culture that is evident in the more general claims of many nineteenth-century evolutionary anthropologists that 'the process of biological evolution gradually began to give way to a new level of development stimulated by the feedback loop between culture and intelligence' (Bowler 1989, p. 152).

Few scientific projects were to prove as devastating for Australia's Aboriginal people as evolutionary craniometry. This was a project that was not only perniciously racist, as many critics have already amply demonstrated, in its invidious theorisation of, and justificatory practices towards, 'stone age man' (e.g. Bowdler 2014; Markus 1994; Turnbull 2012). It was also, as has been suggested here, fundamentally humanist, in drawing on stereotypes of Indigenous people in order to try to demonstrate anew the physical existence of a uniquely human capacity to surpass nature. To that extent, the ongoing reciprocity of racism and humanism that has been tracked in this chapter brings into fresh focus a critical conceptualisation of the idea of race that supplements its currently useful theorisation in the humanities and social sciences. For, beyond those critical characterisations of 'race' as a sociological, inter-subjective dynamic among power-differentiated human groupings, the idea of race can also be critically thought in more ecological terms: as intimately bound to a succession of anxious efforts to maintain the privilege of the human over all other life-forms.

'Only humans can reach for the stars': geo-engineering and human exceptionality today

Such efforts to clarify the physical basis of the nature-transcending human were by no means stable. Craniometry never managed to fix a concept of intelligence to the different skulls of the world's people and the practice of skull-measuring fell into scientific disrepute from around the end of the nineteenth century (only to experience a revival in the pre-World War II era, and again, later, with the likes of physical anthropologist Carleton Coon's controversial *The Origin of Races* in 1962). Nevertheless, it is upon anatomical arguments about the distinctiveness of the human brain that ideas about the exceptionality of human intelligence continued to rely. In a contemporary context of deepening concern about the ecological devastation of the planet, formulations of the more-than-animal nature of the human have again been reasserted.

Today's threat of ecological catastrophe is provoking much reconsideration of the place of the human in relation to nature. Among it, somewhat paradoxically, we see a concern about accelerating anthropogenic change alongside a renewed commitment to the idea that humans possess a unique capacity to 'control their environment' (Gray 2003, p. 4). Clive Hamilton (2013), for example, has called attention to what he calls the 'techno fix of geo-engineering': of attempts to modify the Earth's environment and control global warming via grand technological intervention, such as obstructing solar radiation with space-based mirrors; or, in Australia, covering endangered coral reefs with shade cloth and using electrical currents to stimulate their growth.

Such more or less grandiose projects of geo-engineering risk inflecting evolutionary narrations of this, the so-called 'age of humans' (Kress & Stine 2017), with all-too-familiar intimations of human mastery. Moreover, as this chapter has attempted to demonstrate for earlier time periods, this new thesis of the 'reign of man' (Stengers 2013, p. 171) risks being construed in terms of 'the human' writ large across the globe – as if a singular Eurocentric discourse of 'the human' actually commands the status of a universal species-being. As Chakrabarty (2009) argues of this illusion, all humanity becomes implicated equally in the production of a geophysical era that was, in historical terms, asymmetrically produced under conditions of modern colonialism. In the Australian context, such understandings of the human species as a 'unified force' whose technological ingenuity can be entrusted to rescue depleted nature (for example, waterways like the Murray-Darling Basin), continues to alienate diverse Indigenous modes of relation to such resources (Weir 2009; more generally see, Gibson, Fincher & Rose 2015; Taylor et al. 2015; and on modes of being, knowing, and crucially, 'not-knowing' Arctic lands and people, see Cameron 2015).

But what is the basis of this reinvigorated commitment to the idea that, in John Gray's (2003, p. 4) words, 'humans can free themselves from the limits that frame the lives of other animals'? Upon what basis is contemporary human exceptionalist Kenan Malik (2001) now claiming that it is 'in our very nature as human' to be able to transcend it?

It would be easy to answer this question with reference to a characterisation of humanism as an enduring 'fantasy', to use a word from Jane Bennett (2010, p. ix). So deluded, she states, is the conceit 'of human uniqueness in the eyes of God', it will ceaselessly find modes of dignifying itself. In this logic, the best retort, then, is to pour scorn and dismiss it out of hand. But how useful are counters to humanism that gloss its very contingency and complexity by seeing it as coincident with Christian vanity or naivete? Or that miss its very anxiety by reducing it to the confident expression of a steadfast human pride. How far do they help comprehend and challenge the dubious baggage that haunts 'our' very particular conception of that cherished capacity for 'intelligence'? And, importantly here, do they not also overlook the sense in which, as Rose and Abi-Rached (2013, p. 2) state in their book on the new brain sciences, that 'for at least the past century' humanism has been premised – not on lingering Christian ideas of the soul or Cartesian notions of immaterial mind. Instead it has found a footing, they state, in the claim 'that human beings are freed from their biology by virtue of that biology'.

As will now be briefly indicated, contemporary claims about the unique mental abilities of humans can be traced to precisely the kind of nineteenth-century anatomical arguments initiated by Cuvier, with the rise of European colonial modernity, and the problematisation of human distinctiveness presented by the discovery of the great apes. That is: it is in a physical – not metaphysical – understanding of human exceptionality that geo-engineering and other recent invocations of humanity's genius to save the earth put their faith and confidence. A more exhaustive and transformative critique of humanism, then, must attend to its complex (as well as violent) inheritances, the elucidation of which can render it susceptible to precisely the scrutiny it now urgently warrants.

Raymond Tallis, a British philosopher and neuro-scientist, accounts for what he sees as our 'fundamental difference from other creatures' with reference to the argument that: 'Although other animals assume the upright position from time to time, only man is overwhelmingly bipedal' (2011, p. 6). In his book *Aping Mankind* he distinguishes his argument for human exceptionalism from an old 'belief that we are immaterial ghosts in the material machine of the mind or the body' (2011, p. 11). Instead he argues that, as for 'most explanations of our differences', real clarification hinges 'on the fact that we have bigger brains' (2011, p. 215). Wesley J. Smith, bio-ethicist at the Human Exceptionalism Centre at the Discovery Institute in Seattle, similarly talks up (in prolific blogs) the uniqueness of the human brain. This he traces not to 'the mind of God, or some other mechanism', but to 'a rational examination of the difference of the only species that has transcended the tooth-and-claw world of naked natural selection' (cited in Murchison 2010). This line of argument bears witness to the increasingly pervasive legacy of what was noted earlier in the chapter, in the nineteenth-century shift from mind to brain. In the twenty-first-century throes of what has been referred to as today's condition of 'neuro-mania' (Tallis 2011), echoes of the early nineteenth-century obsession with the head and with the size and shape of the skull are hard to miss.

Sandy Starr of the Progress Educational Trust in London links human exceptionality to 'the size and complexity of the brain' that has evolved, he states, 'more rapidly in humans than … in any other species, including apes' (2004). So although brain science today is often associated with the claim that humans are purely material, some notion of the specialness of the human brain and its evolution is often articulated by neuroscientists themselves. The neuroscientist described by Richard Dawkins as the Marco Polo of Neuroscience, V.S. Ramachandran, writes in *The Tell-Tale Brain: A Neuroscientist's Quest for What Makes Us Human* (2011, p. 4) that although '[h]umans are apes, we are still … something unique … unprecedented … transcendent …. Any ape can reach for a banana, but only humans can reach for the stars'. Again, though, for Ramachandran, as for Tallis, the argument that 'the human … is indeed unique and distinct from that of the ape by a huge mental gap … is entirely compatible with [the] claim that we are biological' (2011, p. 12).

Conclusion

Tracing the emergence of a specific idea of human distinction to the early nineteenth century, the argument of this chapter has been that it was in the attempt to correlate supposed knowledge about the inferiority of certain peoples with their physical – and, above all, cranial – features, that an anatomical notion of intelligence came to be formulated. Centrally, then, it is the modern colonial assumption that certain modes of life are superior to others which remains embedded in a culturally specific concept of 'intelligence' – as that attribute considered to be qualitatively different in beings that walk upright, and that have more developed brains. To that extent, the entangled histories and ontologies of humanism and colonialism haunt contemporary ideas of intelligence as just one of their many damaging legacies and inheritances.

We have to admit, environmental feminist Val Plumwood (2009, p. 123) wrote, of 'other kinds of minds', not simply, she argues, in order to restore to nonhumans the dignity they lost when they were 'expunged', as she calls it, of mind and intelligence. But also, because 'we' (or at least those of 'us' of a western cultural tradition) urgently need to overcome the still lingering idea that being human means rising above our worldly, and indeed our animal, existence. Human intelligence can be thought anew: beyond illusions of transcendence in its humanist and colonialist baggage, as a means to help us acknowledge our limits and 're-join the rest of the world' (Taylor & Instone 2015, p. 139). For the human that is above or beyond nature is not the *only* possibility of human being to be admitted or acknowledged. 'Real-world humanity', in Ingold's (2010, p. 514) words, has never come 'ready made' by 'received species- or culture-specific attributes', but is something 'continually' – and variously – 'worked at'. In this perspective, Indigenous modalities of being and becoming human can also be thought anew, not 'merely' as forms of worlding or modes of existence to be catalogued as 'different'. Instead – in all their incommensurability with settler cultures, as well as diversity among each other – they multiply the very referential points of the human's own humanity and narration. Likewise, a story of 'intelligence' that rethinks the figure of the human as a historical and ongoing contestation, refuses to essentialise its colonial imposition.

It requires humanism to be closely historicised and attentively decolonised in the presence of others, nonhuman and human, as tuned to twenty-first-century matters of ecological concern in, this, our shared colonial present.

Acknowledgments

Research for this chapter was undertaken with the support of the Australia Research Council Discovery Program, DP110104298 'Decolonising the Human: Towards a Postcolonial Ecology'. Thanks to Dr Colin Perrin for his input throughout the research and writing, and to Martin Porr and Jacqueline Matthews for their intellectual engagement across disciplinary boundaries.

Notes

1 An ever-burgeoning field of 'animal studies' has restored a sense of agency and singularity to the life and minds of animals and their various forms of interrelation with humans across time periods and cultures (see the 'Minding Animals' and *Humananimalia* initiatives as just two interventions). More object-centred philosophies mobilise, analytically, the materiality of nonhuman entities, understood in a variety of ways in terms of bodies, technologies, organic and geophysical systems, also affectivity (see for example the recently launched Minnesota University Press book series on the 'nonhuman turn'). Recently, too, 'multispecies ethnography' focuses on the relations of multiple organisms including plants, viruses, human, and nonhuman animals, highlighting the human as an emergent becoming or 'corporeality that comes into being relative to multispecies assemblages, rather than a biocultural given' (Ogden, Hall & Tanita 2013, p. 6). For a recent example, see Hartigan (2014).

2 On posthumanism as a philosophy that resists centring the human as the sovereign agent of the earth, and which critiques the various boundary-making practices by which the human is distinguished from its 'others' (animals, plants or things), see by way of example, including of the field's diversity, of what can be here only a greatly abbreviated list: Plumwood (1993); Castree & Nash (2006); Braun (2004); Haraway (2008); Wolfe (2009); Hawkins & Potter (2009); Bennett (2010); Nimmo (2010); Latimer & Miele (2013); Braidotti (2014; 2016); Sundberg (2014). Symptomatic of the proliferating field since publication of a first volume in 2017, see *Journal of Posthuman Studies*.

3 The evidence of ethologists and geneticists regarding the capacities of nonhuman animals for tool-use, language, reason, digital dexterity and other traits once considered exceptional to the human, is often a starting point in countering the perpetual differentiation of culture from the realm of animal-kind (see for example Lestel 2014).

4 See note 2.

5 For a development of this point, see Anderson and Perrin (2008).

6 See also the writings of black feminist Sylvia Winter about the imperial, gendered and racial bases on which a more general notion of the human, as a supposedly universal category (Man), has been framed (McKittrick 2014; also, Jackson 2013). In contrast, this chapter offers a more specific critique – of the modern colonial invocation of the human who 'stands' above nature – condensing the significantly more detailed account in Anderson and Perrin (2018).

7 See H. Price's (2012) reassessment of 'chain of being' thought to indicate the demise of this belief system for comparative anatomists like Cuvier and the rise of new, specifically modern, understandings of human distinctiveness.

8 Although race occupied an unenviably privileged place in the elaboration of an anatomical notion of intelligence, craniometrists also studied the heads of 'geniuses', of scientists, philosophers and artists. See, for example, Hecht (2006) and Rafter (2009).

9 Non-white female bodies, on the other hand, were more commonly studied and documented in the nineteenth century. The most classic discussion and critique of such colonial accounts is Gilman's (1985) analysis of the circulation of Cuvier's anatomical descriptions of the 'Hottentot Venus'. Regarding the gendered character of craniometry – a subject as complex as its racialised foundation and which therefore requires its own study – see Fee (1979) as well as Schiebinger (1993/2004).

10 For an attempt to counter the long lineage of negative understandings of animality as it has been opposed to humanity, see Lestel (2014).
11 Note that Schiebinger's primary interest in such hierarchical representations is framed in terms of the race, gender and class differentiations of colonial 'identity politics'. This chapter's framing of race within an ecological domain of 'the human' supplements narrower critiques of craniometry that emphasise that science's role in turning 'race' into a supposedly innate condition (on racial craniometry as a legitimatory discourse of colonialism and slavery, see for example, Stepan 1982, Gould 1996, and on the well-known skull collecting practices and propositions of Samuel Morton, George Gliddon and Josiah Nott in the US, and later grave-robbing practices against Native Americans, see Fabian [2010]). More generally, on the past and ongoing role of various sciences in reproducing the fiction of race, see, more recently, Marks (2017).
12 By way of nuance here, Huxley did defend the thesis of human–animal continuity from Richard Owen's neuro-anatomy which argued the interior structure of the human brain was different in a sufficient number of ways to claim a dichotomous contrast between human and ape (Browne 2003, p. 154). Regarding the sense in which numerous post-Darwinian nineteenth-century accounts of Australia, as a 'museum of living antiquities', drew on earlier Enlightenment depictions of Australia's peculiarity in the 1700s and 1800s, which in turn informed depictions of the land's Indigenous people as 'hidebound, from a civilisation point of view' – in particular the Tasmanian as, in the words of Edward Tylor (1894), stuck in such an arrested state as to supply 'the rudest picture known' of 'a savage people' – see Anderson (2007, pp. 157–189).

References

Adas, M 1989, *Machines as the measure of man: science, technology and ideologies of western dominance*, Cornell University Press, Ithaca, NY and London.

Agamben, G 2004, *The open: man and animal*, Stanford University Press, Stanford, CA.

Anderson, K 2007, *Race and the crisis of humanism*, Routledge, London and New York.

Anderson, K & Perrin, C 2008, 'Beyond savagery: the limits of Australian Aboriginalism', *Cultural Studies Review*, vol. 14, pp. 147–169.

Anderson, K & Perrin, C 2013, 'Up from the ape: colonialism, craniometry and the emergence of anatomical humanism', in T Bennett (ed.), *Challenging the humanities*, Australian Academy of the Humanities in association with Australian Scholarly Publishing, Melbourne.

Anderson, K & Perrin, C 2018, 'Removed from nature: the rise of a modern ontology of human exceptionality', *Environmental Humanities*, vol. 10, pp. 447–472.

Bennett, J 2010, *Vibrant matter: a political ecology of things*, Duke University Press, Durham, NC.

Blanckaert, C 1987, 'Les vicissitudes de l'angle facial et les debuts de la craniometrie (1765–1875)', trans. C Perrin, *Revue de synthese*, vol. 108, pp. 417–453.

Blaser, M 2014, 'Ontology and indigeneity: on the political ontology of heterogeneous assemblages', *Cultural geographies*, vol. 2, pp. 49–58.

Bowdler, S 2014, '"Rattling the bones": the changing contribution of the Australian archaeological record to ideas about human evolution', in RW Dennell & M Porr, *Southern Asia, Australia, and the search for human origins* (eds), Cambridge University Press, Cambridge, pp. 21–32.

Bowler, P 1989, *Theories of human evolution: a century of debate*, Johns Hopkins University Press, Baltimore, MD.

Braidotti, R 2014, *The posthuman*, Polity Press, Cambridge.

Braidotti, R 2016, 'The contested posthumanities', in R Braidotti & P Gilroy (eds), *Conflicting humanities*, Bloomsbury, London and New York, pp. 9–46.

Braun, B 2004, 'Modalities of posthumanism', *Environment and Planning A*, vol. 3, no. 6, pp. 1341–1363.

Browne, J 2003, 'Classification in science', in J Heilbron (ed.), *The Oxford companion to the history of modern science*, Oxford University Press, Oxford, pp. 153–154.

Cameron, E, De Leeuw, S & Desbiens, C 2014, 'Editorial and special issue on "Indigeneity and Ontology"', *Cultural Geographies*, vol. 21, pp. 19–26.

Cameron, E 2015, *Far off Metal River: Inuit lands, settler stories, and the making of the contemporary Arctic*, UBC Press, Vancouver.

Carlson, R 2014, 'John Hartigan on multispecies ethnography'. Available from: http://blog.castac.org/2014/08/john-hartigan-on-multispecies-ethnography/ [2 April 2019].

Carson, J 2007, *The measure of merit: talents, intelligence, and inequality*, Princeton University Press, Princeton, NJ.

Castree, N & Nash, C 2006, 'Editorial and special issue on "posthuman geographies"', *Social & Cultural Geography*, vol. 7, pp. 501–504.

Chakrabarty, D 2009, 'The climate of history: four theses', *Critical Inquiry*, vol. 35, pp. 197–222.

Coon, C 1962, *The origin of races*, Alfred A. Knopf, New York.

Cuvier, G 1802, *Lectures on comparative anatomy*, Longman & Rees, London.

Cuvier, G 1840, *The animal kingdom*, S. Orr & Co, London.

Daubenton, L 1764, 'Memoire sur les differences de la situation du grand trou occipital dans l'homme et dans les animaux', in *Histoire de l'Académie Royale des Sciences avec les Mémoires de Mathématique et de Physique* [History of the Royal Academy of Sciences with the memories of mathematics and physics], Paris, pp. 568–579. Trans. MC Meijer (n.d.) as 'Memoir on the different positions of the occipital foramen in man and animals'. Available from: http://petruscamper.com/daubenton.htm [2 April 2019].

Fabian, A 2010, *The skull collectors: race, science and America's unburied dead*, University of Chicago Press, London.

Fabian, J 1983, *Time and the other: how anthropology makes its object*, Columbia University Press, New York.

Fee, E 1979, 'Nineteenth-century craniology: the study of the female skull', *Bulletin of the History of Medicine*, vol. 53, pp. 415–433.

Fernandez-Amesto, F 2004, *So you think you're human: a brief history of humankind*, Oxford University Press, Oxford.

Foucault, M 1985, *The order of things*, Routledge, London and New York.

Gibson, K, Fincher, R & Rose, D (eds) 2015, *Manifesto for living in the Anthropocene*, Punctum Books, New York.

Gilman, S 1985, 'Black bodies, white bodies: towards an iconography of female sexuality in late Victorian art, medicine, and literature', *Critical Inquiry*, vol. 12, pp. 204–242.

Glacken, C 1967, *Traces on the Rhodian Shore: nature and culture in western thought from ancient times to the end of the eighteenth century*, University of California Press, Berkeley.

Glendinning, S 2000, 'From animal life to city life', *Angelaki: Journal of the Theoretical Humanities*, vol. 5, pp. 19–30.

Gould, SJ 1996, *The mismeasure of man*, WW Norton, New York.

Gray, J 2003, *Straw dogs*, Granta Books, London.

Grusin, R 2015, *The nonhuman turn*, University of Minnesota Press, Minneapolis.

Haller, J 1971, 'Race and the concept of progress in nineteenth century American ethnology', *American Anthropologist*, vol. 73, pp. 710–724.

Hamilton, C 2013, *Earthmasters: the dawn of the age of climate engineering*, Yale University Press, New Haven, CT.

Haraway, D 2008, *When species meet*, Minnesota University Press, Minneapolis.

Harris, C 2004, 'How did colonialism dispossess? Comments from an edge of empire', *Annals of the Association of American Geographers*, vol. 94, pp. 165–182.

Hartigan, R 2014, *Aesop's anthropology: a multispecies approach*, University of Minnesota Press, Minneapolis.

Hawkins, G & Potter, E 2009, 'Naturecultures: introduction', *Australian Humanities Review*, vol. 46, pp. 39–41.

Hecht, J 2006, *The end of the soul: scientific modernity, atheism and anthropology in France*, Columbia University Press, New York.

Huxley, T 1897, *Man's place in nature and other anthropological essays*, Macmillan, London and New York.

Ingold, T 2004, 'Beyond biology and culture: the meaning of evolution in a relational world', *Social Anthropology*, vol. 12, pp. 209–221.

Ingold, T 2010, 'What is human being?', *American Anthropologist*, vol. 112, pp. 513–514.

Jackson, ZI 2013, 'Review: Animal: new directions in the theorisation of race and posthumanism', *Feminist Studies*, vol. 39, pp. 669–685.

Jahoda, G 1998, *Images of savages: ancient roots of modern prejudice in western culture*, Routledge, London.

Kress, WJ & Stine, J 2017, *Living in the Anthropocene: Earth in the Age of Humans*, Smithsonian Books, in association with Smithsonian Institution Scholarly Press, Washington, DC.

Landau, M 1984, *Narratives of human evolution*, Yale University Press, New Haven, CT.

Latimer, J & Miele, M 2013, 'Naturecultures? Science, affect and the non-human', *Theory, Culture & Society*, vol. 30, pp. 5–31.

Latour, B 1999, *Pandora's hope*, Harvard University Press, Cambridge, MA.

Latour, B 2005, *Re-assembling the social*, Oxford University Press, Oxford.

Lawrence, W 1819, *Lectures on physiology*, J. Callow, London.

Lestel, D 2014, 'The infinite debt of the human towards the animal', *Angelaki: Journal of the Theoretical Humanities*, vol. 19, pp. 171–181.

Lestel, D 2015, 'Like the fingers of the hand: thinking the human in the texture of animality', in L MacKenzie & S Posthumus (eds), *French thinking about animals*, Michigan State University Press, East Lansing, pp. 61–73.

Malik, K 2001, 'Materialism, mechanism and the human mind', *New Humanist*, vol. 116, pp. 2–3.

Marks, J 2017, *Is science racist?* Polity, Cambridge.

Markus, A 1994, *Australian race relations 1788–1993*, Allen & Unwin, Melbourne.

Mckittrick, K 2014, *Sylvia Winter: on being human as praxis*, Duke University Press, Durham, NC.

Meijer, MC 1999, *Race and aesthetics in Petrus Camper's anthropology*, Editions Rodopi, Amsterdam.

Murchison, W 2010, 'Wesley J. Smith v. Matthew Scully: animal rights and wrongs', *The Human Life Review*, vol. 36, no. 2.

Nimmo, R 2010, *Milk, modernity and the making of the human*, Routledge, London and New York.

Ogden, L, Hall, B & Tanita, K 2013, 'Animals, plants, people, and things: a review of multispecies ethnography', *Environment and Society: Advances in Research*, vol. 4, pp. 5–24.

Plumwood, V 2009, 'Nature in the active voice', *Australian Humanities Review*, pp. 112–129.

Plumwood, V 1993, *Feminism and the mastery of nature*, Routledge, London.

Porr, M 2014, 'Essential questions: "modern humans" and the capacity for modernity', in RW Dennell & M Porr (eds), *Southern Asia, Australia and the Search for Human Origins*, Cambridge University Press, Cambridge, pp. 257–264.

Porr, M 2015, 'Lives and lines: integrating molecular genetics, the "origins of modern humans" and Indigenous knowledge', in A McGrath & MA Jebb (eds), *Long history, deep time: deepening histories of place*, Australian National University Press and Aboriginal History, Inc, Canberra, pp. 203–219.

Porr, M & Matthews, JM 2017, 'Post-colonialism, human origins and the paradox of modernity', *Antiquity*, vol. 91, pp. 1058–1068.

Price, H 2012, 'Do brains think? Comparative anatomy and the end of the great chain of being in 19th century Britain', *History of the Human Sciences*, vol. 25, pp. 32–50.

Pyyhtinen, O & Tamminen, S 2011, 'We have never been only human: Foucault and Latour on the question of the anthropos', *Anthropological Theory*, vol. 11, pp. 135–152.

Rafter, N 2009, *The origins of criminology: a reader*, Routledge, London.

Ramachandran, VS 2011, *The tell-tale brain: a neuroscientist's quest for what makes us human*, Norton, New York.

Rose, N & Abi-Rached, J 2013, *Neuro: the new brain sciences and the management of the mind*, Princeton University Press, Princeton, NJ.

Schiebinger, L 1993/2004, *Nature's body: sexual politics and the making of modern science*, Pandora, London.

Smith, JH 2015, *Nature, human nature, and human difference: race in early modern philosophy*, Princeton University Press, Princeton, NJ.

Starr, S 2004, 'What makes us exceptional?', *Spiked Science*, December.

Stengers, I 2013, 'Matters of cosmopolitics: on the provocations of Gaïa, in conversation with Heather Davis and Etienne Turpin', in E Turpin (ed.), *Architecture in the anthropocene: encounters among design, deep time, science and philosophy*, Open Humanities Press, Ann Arbor, MI, pp. 171–183.

Stepan, N 1982, *The idea of race in science: Great Britain 1800–1960*, Macmillan, London.

Sundberg, J 2014, 'Decolonising posthumanist geographies', *Cultural Geographies*, vol. 21, pp. 33–47.

Tallis, R 2011, *Aping mankind: neuromania, Darwinitis and the misrepresentation of humanity*, Acumen, Manchester.

Taylor, A, Pacini-Ketchabaw, V, De Finney, S & Blaise, M 2015, 'Inheriting the ecological legacies of settler colonialism', *Environmental Humanities*, vol. 7, pp. 129–132.

Taylor, A & Instone, L 2015, 'Thinking about inheritance through the figure of the anthropocene, from the antipodes and in the presence of others', *Environmental Humanities*, vol. 7, pp. 133–150.

Turnbull, P 2012, 'The "Aboriginal" Australian brain in the scientific imagination, c. 1820–1880', *Somatechnics*, vol. 2, pp. 171–197.

Tylor, EB 1894, 'On the Tasmanians as representatives of Palaeolithic Man', *Journal of the Anthropological Institute of Great Britain and Ireland*, vol. 23, pp. 141–152.

Viveiros De Castro, E 1998, 'Cosmological deixis and Amerindian perspectivism', *Journal of the Royal Anthropological Institute*, vol. 4, pp. 469–488.

Wallace, A 1864, 'The origin of human races and the antiquity of man deduced from the theory of "natural selection"', *Journal of the Royal Anthropological Institute*, vol. 2, pp. clviii–clxxxvii.

Weir, J 2009, *Murray River country: an ecological dialogue with traditional owners*, Aboriginal Studies Press, Canberra, ACT.

White, L 1967, 'The historical roots of our ecological crisis', *Science*, vol. 155, pp. 1203–1207.

Wolf, ER 1982, *Europe and the people without history*, University of California Press, Berkeley.

Wolfe, C 2009, *What is posthumanism?*, University of Minnesota Press, Minneapolis and London.

4

COLONIALISM AND NARRATIVES OF HUMAN ORIGINS IN ASIA AND AFRICA

Sheela Athreya and Rebecca Rogers Ackermann

Introduction: the 'othering' of Asia and Africa

The concept of 'otherness,' or alterity, has been a part of academic discourse since George Herbert Mead's 1934 *Mind, Self and Society*. Within this discourse, Edward Saïd's *Orientalism* (1978) and V. Y. Mudimbe's *The Idea of Africa* (1994) were watershed works that implicated Europeans in constructing Asian and African identities and histories as 'other,' i.e., culturally marginalised and devalued in contrast to the European West. Both Saïd and Mudimbe tracked the historical developments over the course of many centuries that produced an Asia and an Africa that shared primitive, infant-like identities. In some respects, Asia's and Africa's constructed identities differed. For Asia, what Saïd calls the Oriental was described as fallen, irrational, stubborn, and alien, and Asia more broadly was remote, stagnant and unchangeable. European culture gained strength by setting itself up in contradistinction to the constructed identity of the Orient; framing the latter as inferior was necessary as a foil to create Western superiority. European knowledge about the Orient gave them the power and the privilege to speak for Asians (Saïd 1978). For Africa, its people were considered ape-like, savage, barbaric, and sexualised, and its resources a commodity to be acquired; it was a continent in need of civilising. Mudimbe refers to the 'blank slate' perception of Africa as *terra nullis*. He shows how this characterisation allowed European colonists to rationalise paternalistic colonial policies that replaced African cultures and identities with their own. Whereas in Asia the civilisation was no longer (i.e. fallen), in Africa the civilisation never was (Mudimbe 1994).

In addition to this, Saïd and Mudimbe showed that Western scholars were engaged in the deliberate homogenisation of both continents, reducing their vast diversity and complex histories into singular, geographically and temporally bounded entities to be described, owned, and to varying degrees controlled.

> The point is that in each of these cases the Oriental is 'contained' and 'represented' by dominating frameworks ... But at the outset one can say that so far as the West was concerned during the 18th and 20th centuries, an assumption had been made that the

Orient and everything in it was, if not patently inferior to, then in need of corrective study by the West.

(Saïd 1978, pp. 40–41)

Only from the 18th century on is there, thanks to the Enlightenment, a 'science' of difference: anthropology. It 'invents' an idea of Africa. Colonialism will elaborate upon the idea.

(Mudimbe 1994, p. 30)

This clear and longstanding practice of otherisation has been at the heart not just of Western sociopolitical policies and agendas, but also the ostensibly objective practice of Western science (Palladino & Worboys 1993).

Our thesis in this chapter is that human origins research is not immune to these influences, and therefore cannot be divorced from the stereotypes upon which this sociopolitical landscape of othering, as described by Saïd, Mudimbe, and others, was built. Because the unfolding of human origins research not only happened over the time period when these Asian and African identities were being created but was also focused directly on the material resources – both fossil and human – of these two continents, these colonialist ideologies are baked into human origins research and narratives. Indeed, we argue that these colonial ideologies, and the language and practices that perpetuate them, persist over time despite often radical shifts in the details of the location, timing, and ordering of evolutionary events. Our intent is not only to unpack this relationship between colonialism and human origins research, but to offer a means for future reflection and self-correction.

The emergence and construction of human origins narratives in colonial Asia and Africa

The debate over an African versus Asian origin of humans has deep roots in the history of evolutionary theory and provides insight into how prevailing social norms influenced scientific opinion about the 'humanness' of people from those regions. Long before Darwin, early natural historians were organising their understanding of human variation through the lens of 'otherness'. Polygenism and degeneracy theory took as their starting points the belief that non-Europeans were biologically inferior to whites, and sought merely to explain why. This view initially emerged from a Christian theological agenda but was reworked as a biological argument after the Darwinian revolution to explain the sub-human origins of Africans, Asians, and Native Americans (Popkin 1974; Sussman 2014).

Following the publication of *On the Origin of Species*, Darwin himself explored human evolution in more depth in *The Descent of Man* (1871), where he noted the similarities between African apes and humans. He posited, based on this shared anatomy, that our ancestors most likely came from Africa – a view that had been expressed earlier by Huxley (1863). Darwin's assertion within the context of his newly developed evolutionary theory was significant because it implied that humanity's deepest roots were African, and were shared by all living populations. While his contemporaries agreed with his theory of evolution, not all of them agreed with the idea of Africa's fundamental humanity and thus weighed in based what they thought of the 'civility' of the various ape species, filtered through what they thought of the humanity of Asians versus Africans. Victorian perceptions of Asians as more civilised than Africans no doubt played into their preferences as well.

A main player in the early debate about the locality of human origins was Ernst Haeckel, whose own estimations of comparative anatomy situated the roots of humankind in Asia, not Africa – specifically in a now-sunken land in the Indian Ocean which he referred to as 'so-called Paradise, cradle of the human race'. In his widely translated *History of Creation* (Haeckel 1876) he embraced Darwin's theory of evolution and the idea of an 'ape-man', and was the first to refer to it as *Pithecanthropus*, a name that would later be assigned to the earliest finds of what is now referred to as *Homo erectus*. His focus on Asia was shared by Wallace (1889), who in his essay *Darwinism Applied to Man*, noted the widespread distribution of phenotypically similar populations deriving from North Asia, notably Native Americans and Pacific Islanders. This belief led him to argue that Asia gave rise to our ancestors who then dispersed into Africa, Western Europe, and the Americas. The idea of an Asian root for the human tree was fleshed out in the most detail by biologist St George Jackson Mivart, who emphasised the similarities between humans and gibbons and downplayed those seen between humans and African apes (Mivart 1873). He, therefore, gave great weight to traits such as the human-like liver of gibbons (vs. the 'brutal' liver of gorillas), the apparent chin and 'aquiline nose' of the siamang and Hoolock gibbon, their propensity to walk bipedally when on the ground and, most notably, their monogamy. The seemingly civilised gibbons were thus a more appealing ancestor to (Western European male) humans, and this played a significant factor in shifting the focus from Africa to Asia in the search for the 'missing link'.

Ultimately, this focus on Asia's superiority to Africa in general, and the 'civilised' nature of the gibbon in particular, influenced one of the most instrumental figures in early palaeoanthropology, Dutch naturalist Eugène Dubois. As Shipman and others have shown, based on his belief in our gibbon ancestry (and the fact that Indonesia was Dutch colony), Dubois homed in on Southeast Asia in his search for human ancestors (Shipman 2001; Shipman & Storm 2002; Trinkaus & Shipman 1992). Dubois' discovery of the Trinil skullcap on Java, Indonesia in 1891 and his billing of it as the 'missing link' received a great deal of attention and led to further explorations in the region. Throughout the early 1900s, palaeontological research in East Asia by Westerners was extremely common and formed the basis for Osborn's Central Asia Theory of human origins (Osborn 1926), an idea that had first been proposed by W. D. Matthew (1914). Prominent Western palaeontologists such as Anderssen, Zdansky, Osborn, Tielhard de Chardin, and Black situated their research within this framework, which posited that the Central Asian plateau was the most likely place to find the most 'advanced' forms of early humans (see Dennell 2018). They thus devoted their fieldwork labor to studying ancient geological deposits throughout South, Southeast, and East Asia to search for evidence of early human evolution.

This early debate on the African vs. Asian roots of human ancestry reflects two phenomena that shaped palaeoanthropology from its inception. First, following the transition from theological to naturalistic explanations of human biology and origins, natural historians nonetheless continued promoting an agenda of European superiority using the veil of science to justify their views on the inferiority of non-Europeans. And second, as Saïd and Mudimbe point out, they actively constructed an interpretive framework for the study of the peoples in these regions, founded on a colonialist hierarchy that placed Europe above Asia, and situated Africa at the bottom.

Interpretations of early fossil finds in the 1910s and 1920s illustrate this hierarchy well. The Piltdown fossil (later revealed as a hoax) from Sussex, England was reported in 1912, and promoted as evidence of the European epicenter of human origins (Keith 1925; Trinkaus & Shipman 1992). When *actual* hominin fossils were discovered at the Broken Hill mine in Zambia in 1921 that again raised the possibility that Africa could have played a role in human evolution, researchers positioned them as younger than Neanderthals, thereby retaining the centrality of Europe and the marginalisation of Africa in how they storied the origin of humans (Keith 1925; Woodward 1922; see also Henke 2007). None of the British scholars reporting on the Broken Hill cranium following its discovery conceived of the true antiquity that humans had in Africa (Gregory 1927; MacCurdy 1922; Osborn 1927; Woodward 1922) and asserted their support of Piltdown as the earliest evidence of human antiquity.

The earliest truly ancient hominin in the fossil record came in 1925 with announcement of the Taung child (*Australopithecus africanus*) from South Africa. The Australian-born Raymond Dart had gone to South Africa in 1922 to take up the post of chair of anatomy at the University of the Witwatersrand. He, along with Robert Broom, a Scottish doctor who had settled in South Africa, was the first to recognise that this fossil provided the first solid evidence of the connection between African apes and humans, i.e., the 'missing link' or 'ape-man' in Africa. But despite being a prominent news story, Dart's *A. africanus* specimen was seen by many as representing nothing more than 'the extreme southward thrust of the chimpanzee stock after it had separated from man' (Gregory 1927, p. 399), and moreover was initially downplayed in part because it was an anomalous find from an otherwise barren continent (Reader 1988), sidelined by the Piltdown specimen that was more consistent with the narrative about European vs. African roots of humanity. In addition, soon after Dart announced his find from Taung, the first 'Peking Man' skulls were excavated from Zhou-koudian in northeastern China. The wealth of discoveries there, along with additional fossil crania emerging from Java beginning in 1931, effectively rendered both Dart's southern ape of Africa and the Broken Hill skull from Zambia mere side-notes in global models of human evolution for decades. Although some anthropologists were willing to contemplate the possibility that Dart and Broom were right in situating ancient human origins in Africa (Gregory & Hellman 1938; Le Gros Clark 1947; Leakey 1936), it took until the 1950s, with the revelation that Piltdown was a hoax along with an active East African program in palaeoanthropology by the Leakeys, for most scholars to shift their focus more fully to Africa.

Assumptions about the centrality of Europe were also brought to bear on questions about the recent direct ancestry of *H. sapiens* (i.e. modern human origins). Henry Fairfield Osborn, Marcellin Boule and Aleš Hrdlička were the main players in a debate about whether Europe vs. Asia was the 'cradle of *Homo sapiens*'. This debate was largely centred on the connection between recent humans and Asian *H. erectus* versus European Neanderthals (Hrdlička 1921; Woodward 1922). Osborn was certain that Europe had been peopled from the east (Osborn 1926), a view supported by Boule (Spencer & Smith 1981), while Hrdlička firmly main-tained that Asia lacked any evidence of early humans, that present-day Asian populations had always been the inhabitants of the region, and that they showed no evidence of admixture with any outside groups (Hrdlička 1921). From this, he determined that the region had been peopled from southwestern Europe – his cradle of 'mankind' – in part because the southern and eastern populations (his so-called Negritos and Malays) were too weak physically and mentally to have done so (Hrdlička 1921, p. 537). In addition, Hrdlička pointed to the (then-believed) deep antiquity of the Heidelberg mandible and Neanderthal remains to further support the fact that Europe had the deepest roots of our species (Hrdlička 1921; 1926). In doing so, he summarily rejected Osborn's Central Asia theory, along with Boule's belief that Neanderthals were an extinct side branch, and the general belief that our species had deep roots anywhere other than in Southwestern Europe.

Hrdlička's commitment to the European origins of *H. sapiens*, and his scepticism that later, gracile Upper Palaeolithic humans could have come from Africa or Asia, were profound enough that he rejected Black's interpretations of the Zhoukoudian fossils, considering them mere 'Neandertalers' (Hrdlička 1930). He ultimately proposed the 'Neanderthal Phase of Man' to argue for a unilineal evolution of *H. sapiens* within Europe from Neanderthals, excluding the possibility of any outside contributions (Hrdlička 1927). Although he had very little support for his unilineal model (Spencer & Smith 1981), his focus on Europe as the unique birthplace of *H. sapiens* was shared by other prominent anthropologists of the day (Howell 1957; Elliot Smith in Henke 2007; Keith 1929). The emerging evidence relevant to recent human evolution from East and South Africa, as well as Southwest and Southeast Asia, was dismissed as unreliable (Spencer & Smith 1981) and the narrative of modern *H. sapiens* evolution did not shift its focus from Europe in a substantial way until the 1980s.

These examples from Africa and Asia illustrate the racist context in which our understanding of human origins arose. If our ancestry was found to be European – as was argued by Hrdlička, Keith and others – then Europe could be lauded as the source of modernness, with Africa and Asia considered more primitive (and incapable of producing modern people), and therefore marginalised, and deemed irrelevant in the narrative of human origins. But if our ancestry was found to be either African or Asian, then ironically those continents could still be portrayed as primitive, an act that served to maintain the relatively more evolved, modern status of Europeans. In addition, as we discuss in detail in the next section the simultaneous study of Indigenous people in colonial contexts, the sourcing of their bodies for collections, and painting of them as primitive or wild (i.e. part of the local fauna), even as endangered species in need of protection (Sysling 2015), served to further establish and reinforce a hierarchy. In essence, European scientists were actively placing Africans and Asians outside the definition of 'real human', situating them as missing links between primitive fossil hominins and the more evolved living Europeans. In both scenarios, the othered, primitive identities of these continents and their people served to dehumanise them and maintain this status relative to the West.

Nineteenth- and twentieth-century studies of the bodies of living peoples: models for 'primitive' ancestors

Throughout the nineteenth and early twentieth century, as the fossil discoveries relevant to human evolution emerged and multiplied, concurrent studies of living human diversity rooted in a racist ideology were also being conducted. These aimed to support both the anatomical and psychological/intellectual superiority of white people over others (Gould 1996; Sussman 2014; Wolpoff & Caspari 1997). Physical anthropologists and researchers from cognate disciplines, including those who were themselves interested in human origins and hunting for fossil remains, were not just observers to this phenomenon, but were at the vanguard of these studies. These scientists were often directly engaged in body collecting and in research on living Indigenous peoples – both physical and ethnographic – which they argued was for the purpose of understanding our more primitive ancestors and modelling what human ancestral hunter-gatherer societies might have been like (Fuchs 2012; Gordon 1992; Henderson 2014; Kuljian 2016). In other words, living people of colour were studied because they were believed to be less evolved, even less human, and thus to provide insight into our early ancestors (Fabian 2010; Gordon 1992; Perignuey 1915). This philosophy is most strikingly evidenced in how anthropological collections around the world were formed by the field's then-luminaries. Aleš Hrdlička, Samuel Morton, and Paul Broca, for example, viewed the bodies of non-whites as theirs for the taking, engaging in collection practices that included stealing bodies from burial places, battlefields, and hospital wards (Broca 1865; Dias 2012; Fabian 2010; Hrdlička 1904). European and North American museums and zoos began to collaborate with prominent scientists to include displays of living people from non-western societies, often called 'human zoos'.

The assistance that scientists provided in this treatment of living people as animals played out dramatically in Southern Africa, where the Indigenous people referred to as 'Bushmen' and 'Hottentots' had been objects of scientific curiosity for decades. German anthropologist Eugen Fischer traveled to colonial Namibia to study the Herero and Nama peoples who had survived a German genocide and were imprisoned in concentration camps by Germany's Second Reich (these served as prototypes for the camps later used in the Holocaust) (Madley 2005). Fischer worked in conjunction with the National Socialist Party to conduct eugenic studies on mixed European-African children. These people were of particular interest for what they could reveal about the importance of keeping Europe 'pure'; Southern Africans were widely seen as being of unique relevance for their primitive, perhaps even animal-like character (Hambly 1937; Madley 2005). Many palaeoanthropologists even believed these populations might be the 'missing link' between humans and apes (see Kuljian 2016 and references therein; Gordon 1992).

For that reason, Broom became a collector of 'Bushmen' remains, often under dubious circumstances (Reader 1988). Dart's research interests also eventually expanded from fossils and bones to living people. The year after the Piltdown discovery was announced, a skull that came to be known as 'Boskop Man' – literally bush-head man – was described by Broom as a possible ancestor to the 'more or less degenerate Bushman' (quoted in Strkalj 2000). Dart later took up this argument about the fossil and declared that living Indigenous South Africans represented the ancestral stock from which humans were derived (Dart 1925). Following that, he participated on expeditions such as the University of the Witwatersrand's Kalahari Bushmen Expedition of 1936, where he and colleagues generated morphological data, photographs and face masks from local people to whom they gave nicknames or numbers (Kuljian 2016). These masks continued to be made into the 1980s by Tobias, and form the Raymond A. Dart Collection of African Life and Death Masks, which numbers over 1,000.

The morphological data taken on these expeditions included physical measurements such as head shape, but also gave special attention to the bodies of South African women, especially their genitalia. In fact, the earliest physical anthropology undertaken in South Africa, and the first academic interest in its inhabitants, centred on Khoe and San female genitalia (Cuvier 1817; Galton 1889). Dart's views, along with his contemporaries, and their work in the Kalahari, were in keeping with the hyper-sexualised stereotypes about Africans that pervaded colonial science. This obsession with genitalia was not only an extension of ideologies from earlier Victorian times but also added a sexist element into the already racist exploitation of the native peoples (Gordon-Chipembere 2011).

Perhaps the most profound example of the lasting effect that this sexist treatment of African bodies has had on palaeoanthropology is the fate of Sarah Baartman, the Khoe woman who had been brought to Europe in the early 1800s and put on display in London and Paris as an example of a 'living savage'. After her death in 1816, Georges Cuvier created a plaster cast of her body, which went on display, along with her skeleton, in French museums until as late as the 1970s. Baartman had been given the nickname of 'The Hottentot Venus', a name that invoked the Roman goddess of love (Scully & Crais 2008) but reduced her to a mere object, focusing entirely on her sexual organs and sexuality (Gordon-Chipembere 2011). At the same time, Upper Palaeolithic female figurines were being uncovered in Hungary, Germany, and elsewhere in Central Europe, and described as fertility objects, having 'exaggerated' breasts and buttocks. They were called 'Venus' figurines in reference to Baartman's sexualised nickname (Fuchs 2012), connecting the primitiveness of Sarah Baartman to these prehistoric figures. The term 'Venus figurines' continues to be used in academic publications on Palaeolithic art despite critiques of its racist, sexist origin (Gindhart 2008; White 2006). All of this is illustrative of how in Africa the study of human origins has from the outset been inseparable from the study of 'primitive people', and continues to be an extension of what has been playing out on the global stage for some time.

The commodification of bodies by the various Asian colonial powers was similar. In India, for example, the British administration viewed the *adivasis*, i.e. the so-called tribal populations who do not exist within the organised religious structure of Indian society, as the aboriginal inhabitants of India (Briggs 1852; Crawfurd 1868; Hodgson 1848). They were thus taken as objects to be surveyed and studied scientifically as part of the wild landscape along with the flora, fauna, and geological formations (Pels 1999) – much like the Africans had been studied as natural objects (Hambly 1937; Smith 1935). The British government set up formal offices such as the Geological Survey of India and Anthropological Survey of India to oversee the natural resources that were now possessed as part of the jewel in the empire's crown. In short, the bodies of Indians were objectified and studied by the British as part of taking inventory of their colonial possessions, and controlling their history[1] (Pels 1998; 1999).

In the Spanish, Portuguese, German, French, Italian and Dutch colonies, the commodification of colonised bodies was directly related to the growing science of anthropology in Europe and North America. There was a high demand for skeletal remains, especially skulls, from around the world (as also seen in Africa, see above), and major figures in the history of physical anthropology such as Paul Broca and Aleš Hrdlička let their needs be known to potential suppliers (Broca 1865; Hrdlička 1904). These included colonial administrators, explorers, doctors and especially members of the military who were instructed to collect bodies from hospitals, battlefields (after massacres from quelling uprisings or rebellions in the colonial states) and graveyards – all in the name of racial science (Dias 2012; Roque 2011). Roque (2011) compellingly argues that the demand for bodies from India, Indonesia, Macau, Timor, Taiwan, and other colonies throughout Asia and Oceania by British, French, Portuguese, Italian, German and Dutch scientists, was not simply to increase scientific knowledge about human variation. First, the bones were used by Broca, Topinard, Morton and others to 'scientifically' demonstrate the racial ideologies of the day. And second, the agenda was also to recreate the Oriental's or African's history and identity through the lens of the white man. Museum curators were not just overseeing collections of bones, they were also actively constructing a new history for these populations as 'savages', thus erasing or obscuring their humanity and history, and redefining them as 'other' – as primitive representatives in 'man's march towards civilization' (Roque 2011, p. 5).

Transition to the current narrative of human origins: lingering effects of the colonial past

The supporting role that scientists, including physical anthropologists, played in the colonial policies that contributed to the Holocaust led to a reckoning in the decades following the end of World War II. The eugenics movement that linked scientists with the genocidal actions of the Third Reich lost massive amounts of support in both the US and Europe. Racist ideologies weren't entirely abandoned in physical anthropology but were transformed, as evidenced by the publication of Carleton Coon's *Origin of Races* in 1962. There, he argued that the five purported races had deep roots in their respective geographical regions, and that Africans had crossed the threshold to modern humanity last, Europeans and Asians first. The implications were clear and led to a complete programmatic revision for physical anthropologists, what Washburn (1951) called 'the New Physical Anthropology'. This saw a shift away from race-based typological studies and a focus on evolutionary processes. However, as Caspari (2003) has shown, essentialist and typological ideas remained embedded in palaeoanthropology, reconfigured as the study of populations as clades.

In 1987, a seminal paper published in *Science* by geneticists Rebecca Cann, Mark Stoneking and Allan Wilson situated the root of the human species in Africa (Cann, Stoneking & Wilson 1987). In spite of its typological framing of human evolution, it nonetheless appealed to a community of scholars eager to embrace a post-racial narrative by supporting an African root of humanness (e.g. Caspari 2007; Gould 1987; 1988 cited in Wolpoff & Caspari 1997). This paper also put the final nail in the coffin for the 'pre-sapiens' and unilineal European models of *Homo sapiens* evolution of the previous six decades, and firmly shifted the narrative of recent human evolution to Africa. What emerged was a model that emphasised Africa as the source of humanity, with the original (modern) human female (because the research was based on mitochondrial data) cast by the popular press as 'African Eve'. Africa was no longer considered relevant primarily as a mere receptacle of primitive living people (and primitive extinct hominins), it was now the source of all humans. This fundamental shift from viewing Africa as the 'other' to being central to all human identities was a major turning point in palaeoanthropological narratives and had a wide-reaching effect. At the turn of the twenty-first century former South African president Thabo Mbeki declared, 'We are all Africans.'

This new narrative was problematic, however, because it implicitly marginalised archaic Asians and Europeans (i.e. Neanderthals). A debate raged around which Pleistocene people, from which region, were our direct ancestors, and which were not. In the Out of Africa model, only the African lineage led to modern people, with early humans dispersing around the Old World and replacing other hominins who lived there. In other models such as the 'Afro-European *sapiens*' hypothesis (Bräuer 1984), both Africa and Europe contributed to the origin of modern people. The Multiregional Evolution model was the most diametrically opposed to Out of Africa,[2] and postulated that all regions contributed in some degree to the evolution of *Homo sapiens* (Wolpoff, Wu & Thorne 1984). This model had emerged earlier out of observations made by Australasian scholars regarding evolutionary phenomena in their parts of the world (e.g. Thorne 1981; Wu 1988), and was a reconfiguration of the trellis model that Weidenreich had developed decades earlier (Weidenreich 1947). Throughout the 1990s, the so-called 'modern human origins debate' dominated Late Pleistocene studies in palaeoanthropology, frequently making news headlines and becoming canon in anthropology textbooks. The intensity and staying power of the debate reflects a certain intellectual stagnation in palaeoanthropology – nearly 30 years later, discussions of *H. sapiens* evolution are still framed as being part of this debate.

The Out of Africa model was ultimately more widely accepted and has dominated the literature over recent decades; its success has as much to do with the sociopolitical dimensions of palaeoanthropology as the actual data (Caspari 2007; Wolpoff & Caspari 1997). It has come to be defined by a set of 'facts', which although taken as universally agreed upon, are open to debate and carry echoes of colonialism and western superiority. First, humans are said to have a single origin in a single location, often referred to (even in scientific publications) in Biblical terms. This single population was supremely successful, and alone had the flexibility and adaptability to disperse throughout the globe replacing existing 'archaic' groups. Second, so-called 'archaic' groups were not modern, by definition; they were implicitly less able, backwards, stagnant, or on the verge of extinction. Although the population history of our origins has been argued on the basis of fossil morphology to be more complex than this (e.g. Caspari & Wolpoff 2013; Trinkaus 2005; Wu 2004), and genetic studies have supported these assertions (e.g. Fu et al. 2015; Fu et al. 2013; Templeton 2002), nonetheless these narratives persist.

Within the Out of Africa narrative of *H. sapiens* evolution, the Asian data continue to be cast within an Orientalist framework. The cradle of *H. sapiens*, once to be found in the Swanscombe or Piltdown fossils from northwestern Europe, is now believed to be in Africa, while the Zhoukoudian and Ngandong fossils are seen as dead ends (or at best, being on the evolutionary trajectory of living East Asians and Australians respectively). With few exceptions, East Asia is seen as an irrelevant player in the evolution of extant *H. sapiens* – possibly (in certain formulations) a recipient of unidirectional west-to-east migrations but not a producer of genetic innovation or modernity for the Western world. This continues to reflect a view of East Asia that has persisted since colonial times of a region that is remote, isolated, closed off and inaccessible (Darwin 2008). It has been cast for the past 80 or so years as (in Movius's words) a marginal region of 'cultural retardation' (Movius 1948, p. 411) that had made very little contribution to humankind.

Today, scientists continue to echo the colonialist mindset, not only viewing Asian *Homo erectus* itself as stagnant, but also Asian research as ethnocentric and therefore irrelevant to current models of human evolution (see Qiu 2016). Models developed from within the region, such as Wu's 'continuity with hybridization' (Wu 1988; 2004) have been overlooked entirely. The recent embrace of a narrative of human evolution that entails both a measure of continuity and hybridisation (e.g. Ackermann, Mackay & Arnold 2016; Galway-Witham & Stringer 2018) has largely occurred because of scientific observations and interpretive models developed by Western researchers; the current discourse contains little or no mention of the non-Western scholars who have been making similar observations based on their own data for decades. So while the *data* from Asia and other marginalised regions are now given authority within the human origins story – a seemingly progressive development – no authority is actually given to the scientific observations or interpretive models developed by scholars from those regions. That authority remains exclusively in the hands of Western scientists.

In addition, as with original models of human origins, current studies continue to fall back on the notion that living Africans – hunter-gatherers in particular – are appropriate primitive models for early humans. While a few critiques of this assumption exist (Kelly 2013; Schrire 1980; Testart et al. 1988) for the most part, prehistorians have not critically examined the colonialist elements of the 'Man the Hunter' model. The implicit assumptions of evolutionary primitiveness that accompany these studies are perpetuated by recent high-profile research on African societies within the framework of human evolution. These studies compare Africans including Ju/'hoansi and Hadza – and indeed several foraging societies from colonised countries – to apes in order to determine the 'deep social structure of humankind' (Chapais 2011; 2013; Hill et al. 2011). Similarly, a recent feature article in *Science* portrayed the Hadza as subjects of study precisely for the insight they give into human evolution.

> Times are hard for the Hadza, who include some of the last people on the planet to live as nomadic hunter-gatherers. Their way of life has been a magnet for researchers for 60 years, and the subject of hundreds of scholarly papers, because it may offer the closest analog to the way our African ancestors lived.
>
> *(Gibbons 2018, p. 700)*

The article also included references to their drunkenness, a dead baby, diarrhoea, and other indicators that they are not capable of modernity. Living hunter-gatherers are often treated as having social structures that have remained unchanged since the early days of human evolution, and thus serve as effective telescopes to our past, despite the fact that these societies have been reconstituting themselves and their organisational rules for thousands, if not tens of thousands of years (Appadurai 1988; Kopytoff 1987). These assumptions of primitiveness and stagnation have been present since the earliest contact between Europeans and Africans and served as the basis for imperial policy (Mudimbe 1994).

The Out of Africa/Replacement narrative also carries imperialist overtones, as portrayed in both the popular press and in scientific publications. For example, recently in both *Scientific American* and the *Journal of Human Evolution*, palaeoanthropologist Curtis Marean (Marean 2014; 2015a) modelled *Homo sapiens* evolution and dispersals as being the product of one African population's unique intellectual superiority coupled with their advanced weaponry and hyperprosocial behaviour (i.e. hyper-ingroup cooperation/outgroup hostility). Upon dispersing with this advanced bio-behavioural repertoire, they encountered archaic populations with whom they engaged in territorial conflicts and ultimately whom they replaced. Marean describes this process:

> [M]odern humans were equipped to respond to any environmental crisis with flexible social connections and technology. They became alpha predators on land, and, eventually, sea. This ability to master any environment was the key that finally opened the door out of Africa and into the rest of the world ... Archaic human groups that could not join together and hurl weapons did not stand a chance against this new breed ...
>
> *(Marean 2015a, p. 9)*

In his response to reader comments on the male-centric nature of his model, Marean stated in his online post:

> Such events are penetrating, brutal, bloody affairs, and the killing and butchery that ensue is the product of weapons and men.
>
> *(Marean 2015b)*

In sum, and based on previous work arguing the same (e.g. Bowles 2009; Bowles & Gintis 2011), the story of human history is that we are inherently conflict-oriented and programmed to 'otherise' members outside our group and that this violent nature, along with our intellectual and technological superiority, is largely the domain of men, and is what ultimately led to our success as a species.

This retelling of European colonial expansionism in biological terms presumes that populations that had been living in Eurasia for over a million years were less well-adapted to their own environments. Indeed, the Out of Africa narrative, in general, perpetuates the view that one group is adaptively superior to another. Even within Africa, much of the debate has focused on which region can claim to be the root of living people, once again, the implication being that a single population of Africans had superior capabilities, cognitive or otherwise, that alone made it superior to other Africans (but see Hublin et al. 2017; Scerri et al. 2018). As above, modern human origins research often neatly packages this narrative of success with male domination and violence at its core – echoing imperialist models of bloody expansionism over inferior groups. The imagery associated with human origins research often powerfully captures this male-dominated, violent and racially charged space, both through the ubiquitous portrayal of humans evolving into a white man, often with weapons (Figure 4.1), and representations of Africans as violent, virile, and primitively clad (Figure 4.2). Additionally, these depictions invariably collapse numerous complex temporalities into a small number of actors, locations, and characteristics in service of a single narrative strand.

As this discussion shows, the frameworks of Orientalism and African primitivism still pervade today's studies of human evolution. The narrative that has come to dominate human origins research is still drenched in a notion of superior groups, superior intelligence or capabilities, that draws from the Western views (and racist ideologies) of the past. These

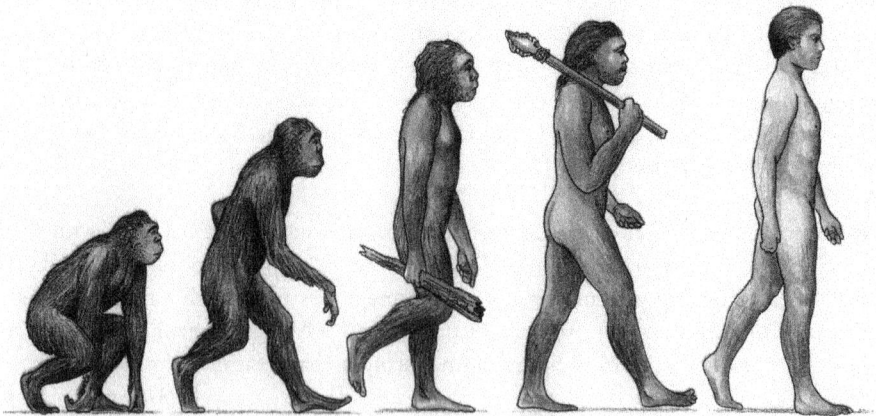

FIGURE 4.1 'Evolution of Man'. Illustrations such as this depicting the stages of human evolution typically represent the final stage as a white male

Source: Heritage Images; artist Karen Humpage ©. Reprinted with artist's permission.

FIGURE 4.2 Artistic representation of the first humans (from Marean 2015a)
Source: Scientific American © 2015. Reprinted with permission.

capabilities are also constructed to be universal and transcendental, a part of humanity's essential characteristics. Africa is now our primordial home, the site of, as Kim TallBear says, the 'biogeographical pinpoint of originality' (TallBear 2013, p. 6). Geneticists trying to reconstruct our past now look to study 'unadmixed' native populations (a genetic impossibility); Western scholars still treat living groups from former colonies as fossils from the past, and still impart notions of biological purity into their studies. What is ironic is that the Africans are, by definition, the most successful in this narrative (because humans emerged from Africa) and yet remain primitivised.

Orientalism, Afrocentrism, and the practice of palaeoanthropology today

These examples serve as good mirrors in which to reflect on the discipline of palaeoanthropology and its lingering biases. On the whole, they show that today's framing of Africa and Asia in palaeoanthropological narratives is not terribly different from what Saïd and Mudimbe described. The continued owning, shaping and defining of the meaning of Asian and African identities is part of the legacy that both scholars wrote about. The early focus on Asia as the cradle of human ancestry took place in a decidedly Orientalist context. Saïd (1978) noted that European culture managed, and even produced, the Orient – politically, sociologically, militarily, ideologically, and scientifically. The idea that an entity known as 'the East' existed in contradistinction to 'the West' was consciously and deliberately constructed by European scholars, politicians and philosophers over the course of the eighteenth to the twentieth centuries (Saïd 1978). By engaging in this discourse, Europeans were both implicitly and explicitly asserting that Asia was an unknown entity that needed to be explained, understood and defined – and they did so in European terms.

Likewise, Mudimbe noted that 'The Savage Man' of Africa was a 'brilliant invention of the 14th and 15th centuries which preceded (and shaped) the western 'discovery' of savages ... in the 16th century' (1994, p. 8). During the early decades of palaeoanthropology when the focus was on our Asian roots, Africa was relegated to a mere side-note, believed to have neither lithic nor fossil remains and therefore to play no role in human evolution at all (Smith 1935). This perception was consistent with the belief that the continent was a blank slate (*terra nullis*; Mudimbe 1994), which was essential to justifying colonial policies there. It was within this construction that our origins stories emerged.

Today's narrative sees Africa as centralised and Asia marginalised in our evolutionary origins; at other times, the inverse was true. Regardless, in the face of changing fossil, archaeological and genetic evidence, and shifting global dynamics and interests, the superiority of Westerners was maintained, and Asians and Africans othered. Initially this was an active attempt at centring Europe in the story of human origins, but as evidence percolated out that countered this hypothesis, power relations were maintained through other means. As argued above, in the case of Africa, the continued characterisation of Africans as primitive allowed Western researchers to simultaneously position Africa as the continent of origin while retaining Europeans as the 'civilised' group. They also framed the dynamics in the context of superior abilities and domination, a decidedly Western, colonialist slant. In the case of Asia, what was originally considered the most likely source for human ancestors has now been cast as an evolutionary backwater. The point is that no matter how the science plays out, the narrative that emerges always leaves one group in control, and marginalises non-European lands and their peoples.

Beyond the realms of academia, palaeoanthropological policies and practices of the last century and a half have had lasting impact on people outside the discipline, especially people descended from populations who have been othered, managed, or produced. It has perhaps most dramatically reared its head in policy disputes around repatriation and museum displays. These disputes highlight an important connection between our human origins narrative, racism and the public perception of our science. As Ros Langford eloquently pointed out (1983), we continue to study people (and their ancestors) as objects, using their bodies, defining their histories, and often taking issue with societies wanting to control their own narratives (Morell 1995; Murray & Allen 1995).

Most recently this issue has surfaced in the heated discussion by palaeoanthropologists over the repatriation and reburial of the Kow Swamp and Lake Mungo Australian remains, Kennewick Man from the Pacific Northwestern US, Tasmanian Pleistocene data (Dumont 2003; Fforde, Hubert & Turnbull 2004; McNiven & Russell 2008), and the Zambian government's request to UNESCO to return the Kabwe skull which had been immediately taken to Britain in 1921 upon its discovery (Government of the Republic of Zambia 2016). In a South African context, the scientific primitivisation of Indigenous groups has also received push-back. As a result, in August 2013, a decision was made to place all 'Bushman' life casts on display at the Iziko South African Museum in Cape Town in permanent storage (Schramm 2016). Nevertheless, following the 2015 announcement of the new species *Homo naledi*, it became clear that this linking of black people and primitiveness through the medium of palaeoanthropology still persists in the mind of the public; popular depictions linked black people – especially black leaders – with this hominin ancestor, suggesting that they were somehow less evolved (Figure 4.3).

Today's palaeoanthropologists often continue to marginalise the voices and experiences of non-Western peoples in the name of scientific inquiry which they see as unassailably objective. As Lori Hager writes:

> Based on the principles of the scientific method, 'scientific' interpretations are expected to be more than 'just stories'. They are intended to be the most logical, plausible, and objective explanations of the observable facts. And *because paleoanthropology conducts its research within the realm of 'science,' it is often assumed that it is objective and bias-free* ...
>
> *(Hager 1997, p. 3, emphasis added)*

Hager goes on to argue that, on the contrary (and like all sciences), *palaeoanthropology is neither objective nor bias-free*. This may come as some surprise to scientists, who tend to think of themselves as isolated from their socio-political context. This manifests itself in the notion that Western scientists engage in pure science, and must avoid 'identity politics'. But for palaeoanthropologists, denying the inherent hegemonic context in which they are producing knowledge means ignoring the power they have to shape what are considered the facts surrounding the identities and histories of others, as well as the responsibility they have to make space for these marginalised voices.

These examples convey how colonial ideas of owning, otherising and primitivising non-European cultures, minds and bodies, illustrated by Saïd and Mudimbe, have persisted into the present. We argue that this is primarily a reflection of the fact that scientists from former colonial countries continue to control who shapes the narrative of the human past. This persistent control is due in large part to the demographics of the field (e.g. few non-Western

FIGURE 4.3 This cartoon run in South African newspapers explicitly links *Homo naledi* and living black members of the National Prosecuting Authority as a commentary on their intelligence and abilities

Source: Cartoon by Zapiro, *The Times* © 2015. Re-published with permission.

people on high profile science projects or serving as lead authors), as will be discussed further below. Moreover, while some other branches of anthropology engage in reflexive post-colonial critiques with respect to the issue of voice, representation and power (Pels 2008), palaeoanthropology has yet to do so in any meaningful way (but see Porr & Matthews 2017). Without reflecting on the field's colonialist history, researchers continue to present these histories defined in colonial terms, implicitly (if inadvertently) reinforcing the notion that dark-skinned people are less human.

This lack of reflexivity is in part a direct outgrowth of the way science is viewed in Western societies, where scientists are the sole keepers of global knowledge (see Dumont 2003). Indigenous people's ways of knowing, their desire to control their own bodies or representation, or to define their histories, are not considered objective. The scepticism towards non-Western knowledge construction is played out in many palaeoanthropological field sites and laboratories in Africa, where the field workers and technicians are not white, and the team leaders are primarily well-funded European or American researchers from abroad who, by controlling the financial resources, also control the production of 'facts'.

This hierarchy of knowing has also been expressed in the dismissal of narratives of human evolution constructed by Asian palaeoanthropologists working in countries that have long and distinguished histories of paleoanthropological research in their own right. The Orientalist framework, in which the 'East' was cast as irrational, unvirtuous, and childlike (Saïd 1978) is still a part of palaeoanthropological science, which situates the region as a remote, stagnant evolutionary backwater with little to contribute to understanding human origins. For example, between 1950 and 2004 there was not a single session on human evolution in Asia at the annual meetings of the American Association of Physical Anthropologists. Between 1984 and 2004, the majority of research and popular news stories about human evolution in Asia centred on the stagnation of *H. erectus* there for 2 million years. Asian scholars who questioned this interpretation were dismissed as 'biased' and therefore not trustworthy (see quotes in Qiu 2016). That the same ethnocentric biases characterise Western palaeoanthropology seems to go unremarked.

Our goal here has been to demonstrate the ways in which palaeoanthropology has developed ideologically out of a colonialist past. The data, models, assumptions, and practices are all legacies of a racist agenda, centred on 'otherising' and dehumanising non-western peoples. There are remarkably few African and Asian scholars at the forefront of our field, shaping the narrative of human evolution for global consumption. And, unlike other branches of anthropology, our subfield has not truly undergone a critical re-examination of its roots. As a result, scholars in our field are largely a demographically homogeneous group, inadvertently perpetuating practices that continue to otherise and marginalise African and Asian bodies and ideas. The dangers of this should be self-evident. Not only has the lack of diversity and inclusivity in our field reduced the level of excellence and innovation overall; but it has also actively, albeit unintentionally, contributed to the racist agendas on which our field was built.

A way forward: reimagining a new narrative of human origins

Palaeoanthropology is a historical science, and cultural bias is inevitable in historical reconstructions. The problem, as Hager noted above, is that western palaeoanthropologists tend to view their science as ahistorical – as a mere uncovering of objective facts, free of any observer or implicit bias (Henke 2007). Western palaeoanthropologists have yet to fully embrace their part in owning and shaping 'otherised' bodies. As a result, the effects of the discipline's historical legacy play out at every level of our work. Western palaeoanthropologists are the primary definers of the questions asked, based on our own *a priori* assumptions (such as, there is a single entity, 'modern human', that has a single origin with a single behavioural repertoire in Africa). Western palaeoanthropologists, by and large, define the units of analysis ('Aborigines', 'Africans', etc.) and determine what roles these communities can play in shaping the scientific narrative (Marks 2001). Ultimately Western palaeoanthropologists control whose voices are given authority, and who gets to write the history of humanity.

What would a different conceptualisation of human evolution studies look like, outside of this postcolonial legacy described by Saïd and Mudimbe? We propose two primary ways that our field can engage in new approaches to constructing the narrative of human origins that will deal constructively with the issues discussed above. Both revolve around the integration of other voices and peoples into the framing of the questions, because the lack of diverse representation and diversity of voices in palaeoanthropology leads to the perpetuation of stereotypes embedded in our scientific models, often subconsciously, as we have alluded to throughout this chapter.

First, we need to embrace a more complex conceptualisation of the evolutionary mechanisms behind human origins, where regional groups cannot – and should not – be parcelled into discrete units, and where no single region dominates. This includes abandoning the search for the 'first'. The Out of Africa narrative of *H. sapiens* evolution that we discussed above is, at its heart, an adaptationist approach to considering the production of diversity. Adaptationist approaches are nearly ubiquitous in palaeoanthropology generally, despite our understanding that divergence and differences among human groups and hominin taxa frequently occur without adaptation at all (Ackermann & Cheverud 2004; Schroeder & Ackermann 2017; von Cramon-Taubadel & Weaver 2009; Weaver, Roseman & Stringer 2007). In the Out of Africa model, Africans evolve first into modern people, and it is only the African lineage that leads to modern humanity, replacing other hominins. This implies that a single group evolved special traits that provided a fitness advantage – either culturally or biologically – over those they replaced. It is an argument of domination and superiority – products of a western colonial mentality. The winners are seen as better adapted (or phrased differently evolutionarily 'superior') to whatever environmental context they were in, or moved into, than the other hominins on the landscape – a retelling of European colonial views of economic exploitation and efficiency (Porr 2014). Even when gene flow is recognised in this model, the questions are still being framed in terms of purity and impurity, evolutionarily superior to inferior, and relative success.

This whole framing of the human origins narrative as one of discrete (and adaptively different) groups that migrated, replaced or admixed, reifies meaningful group differences and hierarchies among these groups (whether recognised as populations/races or species; see Terrell 2018). It is a model that developed out of a colonialist worldview. A more complex and scientifically appropriate understanding of human history as reticulating networks that was not built on these constructs has been discussed for decades by researchers from eastern Eurasia and Oceania, and these should be brought more into mainstream discussions. These models address the role that complex (biological, cultural) processes and individual/regional diversity have played in shaping our evolutionary trajectory.

In Western science, an increasingly complex narrative around human origins is finally recognising this, although it often falls back into the same superior/inferior narrative framework as before. Nonetheless, the research is at last embracing the idea that multiple groups both within and outside of Africa contributed to the human lineage (e.g. Green et al. 2010; Kuhlwilm et al. 2016). In addition to being more inclusive, this acknowledgment of the importance of local processes is forcing western scholars to challenge what it means to be anatomically and behaviourally 'modern' (e.g. Ackermann, Mackay & Arnold 2016), which will in turn provide the intellectual space for researchers to unpack the extent to which western ideology has constructed modernness. However, this research typically fails to cite the Asian and Australian scholars who have been proposing these ideas for decades, instead attributing these 'new' ideas to the work being done by Europeans and North Americans. As we will further outline below, giving a greater platform to marginalised scholars such as these, to their studies and their models, is an important element in re-invigorating the science of palaeoanthropology.

Second, we need to abandon the representation of early humans as primitive in a way that directly links this primitiveness to living people today (e.g. Milks 2018). This representation is pervasive, from modern human origins research to museum displays to the public imagination. It reifies races and racism in a way that is damaging to the prospects of palaeoanthropology as a viable discipline. It has no doubt played a primary role in keeping people from entering the discipline, and is a major contributor to the crisis of repatriation. Dismantling this legacy can be achieved through many means, including outreach, curriculum re-development, and implicit bias training. But it is perhaps best – and most rapidly – achieved by increasing representation from marginalised groups in the primary research itself. It is well established that diverse teams result in better science (Apfelbaum, Phillips & Richeson 2014; Freeman & Huang 2014; Hong & Page 2004). The last century and a half of modern human origins research has been exemplified by the production of knowledge by a privileged – and very homogeneous – few. Efforts at diversifying the field in the United States have resulted in bodies such as the Committee on Diversity in the American Association of Physical Anthropologists (Antón, Malhi & Fuentes 2018). While this is creating an important pipeline of scholars from underprivileged communities in the US, it addresses only part of the problem. True inclusivity must provide a safe and equal platform for a wide range of voices that have historically been gate-kept from scientific space. This means publishing research by scholars from the Global South, from poor countries, and from non-Western countries that have long histories of palaeoanthropological research. Many of these communities engage in science and knowledge construction that differs from our hypothetico-deductive model, but their facts are no less well-vetted, falsifiable or repeatable.

Non-Western scientists also bring different assumptions and framings about the past and the present into the science itself, and their value systems need to be represented in order to improve the quality of our models. Chinese, Indian, and Australasian scientists, for example, so frequently dismissed as 'biased' and 'ethnocentric' have a better understanding of the unique regional processes that have shaped populations in East, South, and Southeast Asia, and Australia; that understanding should be equalised as valid in our scientific literature. African scientists – woefully underrepresented as authors on palaeoanthropological research in Africa – should be equal partners in all stages of scientific research, from constructing research questions to participating in the study design to being given lead-author control and authority over how publications resulting from the research disseminate information. And African participants in palaeoanthropology more generally should be acknowledged in official publications beyond their contributions as technicians, field workers, fossil finders and unsung heroes (e.g. Leakey Foundation 2018).

At all levels of decision making in science – in journal article reviews, grant reviews, paper authorship, and promotion letters – colonial value systems dominate. It cannot, therefore, come as a surprise – given that the people framing the questions and leading the research for the past century and a half share a common heritage, outlook and value system – that the narrative of human origins has been heavily influenced by confirmation bias (see Page 2007). By decolonising our science and making space for the voices of people who have historically been the objects of study – the 'other' – our narratives can more inclusively reflect how humanity views itself and its history. Incorporating a wider diversity of value systems and outlooks will go a long way towards correcting the problematic narratives of the past, ultimately leading us closer to the truth of our common origins.

Notes

1 An exception to this is China, where access to natural resources and collecting by foreigners was carefully controlled. For further reading on this, see Fa-ti Fan's *British Naturalists in Qing China: Science, Empire and Cultural Encounter*, Harvard University Press, 2003.
2 Although both models have changed over time in terms of how much they have emphasised gene flow, dispersals, migration, and neutral evolution, we are concerned with the ways in which they fundamentally differ in how they viewed African and Asian hominins. Out-of-Africa sees 'modern

humans' as a singular entity with an African origin; Asian populations are marginal and archaic. Multiregionalism questions the essentialist concept of 'modern' human, the singular origin in Africa, and the marginality of Asian populations.

References

Ackermann, RR & Cheverud, JM 2004, 'Detecting genetic drift versus selection in human evolution', *Proceedings of the National Academy of Sciences*, vol. 101, no. 52, pp. 17946–17951.

Ackermann, RR, Mackay, A & Arnold, ML 2016, 'The hybrid origin of "modern" humans', *Evolutionary Biology*, vol. 43, no. 1, pp. 1–11.

Antón, SC, Malhi, RS & Fuentes, A 2018, 'Race and diversity in US biological anthropology: a decade of AAPA initiatives', *American Journal of Physical Anthropology*, vol. 165, pp. 158–180.

Apfelbaum, EP, Phillips, KW & Richeson, JA 2014, 'Rethinking the baseline in diversity research: should we be explaining the effects of homogeneity?' *Perspectives on Psychological Science*, vol. 9, no. 3, pp. 235–244.

Appadurai, A 1988, 'Putting hierarchy in its place', *Cultural Anthropology*, vol. 3, no. 1, pp. 36–49.

Athreya, S 2017, 'Dead end evolutionary lineage, says the White man: the evolution of *Homo erectus* and *Homo sapiens* in Asia', Paper presented at the 86th Annual Meeting of the American Association of Physical Anthropologists.

Bowles, S 2009, 'Did warfare among ancestral hunter-gatherers affect the evolution of human social behaviors?' *Science*, vol. 324, no. 5932, pp. 1293–1298.

Bowles, S & Gintis, H 2011, *A cooperative species: human reciprocity and its evolution*, Princeton University Press, Princeton, NJ.

Bräuer, G 1984, 'The "Afro-European sapiens hypothesis," and hominid evolution in East Asia during the late Middle and Upper Pleistocene', *Courier Forschungsinstitut Senckenberg*, vol. 69, pp. 145–165.

Briggs, J 1852, 'Art. XIII – two lectures on the Aboriginal Race of India, as distinguished from the Sanskritic or Hindu Race', *Journal of the Royal Asiatic Society*, vol. 13, pp. 275–309.

Broca, P 1865, *Instructions générale pour les recherches anthropologiques (Anatomie et physiologie)*, V. Masson et fils, Paris.

Cann, RL, Stoneking, M & Wilson, AC 1987, 'Mitochondrial DNA and human evolution', *Nature*, vol. 325, pp. 31–36.

Caspari, R 2003, 'From types to populations: a century of race, physical anthropology, and the american anthropological association', *American Anthropologist*, vol. 105, no. 1, pp. 65–76.

Caspari, R 2007, 'The "Out of Africa" hypothesis', in JH Moore (ed.), *The encyclopedia of race and racism*, Gale (MacMillan Reference, USA), Detroit, MI, pp. 391–397.

Caspari, R & Wolpoff, MH 2013, 'The process of modern human origins: the evolutionary and demographic changes giving rise to modern humans', in FF Smith & J Ahern (eds), *The origins of modern humans: biology reconsidered*, John Wiley and Sons, Hoboken, NJ, pp. 355–392.

Chapais, B 2011, 'The deep social structure of humankind', *Science*, vol. 331, no. 6022, pp. 1276–1277.

Chapais, B 2013, 'Monogamy, strongly bonded groups, and the evolution of human social structure', *Evolutionary Anthropology: Issues, News, and Reviews*, vol. 22, no. 2, pp. 52–65.

Crawfurd, J 1868, 'On the supposed Aborigines of India as distinguished from its civilised inhabitants', *Transactions of the Ethnological Society of London*, vol. 6, pp. 59–71.

Cuvier, G 1817, 'Extraits d'observations faites sur le cadavre d'une femme connue à Paris et à Londres sous le nom de Vénus Hottentot', *Mémories du Muséum d'Histoire Naturelle*, vol. 3, pp. 259–274.

Dart, RA 1925, 'The present position of anthropology in South Africa', *South African Journal of Science*, vol. 22, no. 11, pp. 73–80.

Darwin, C 1871, *The descent of man and selection in relation to sex*, John Murray, London.

Darwin, J 2008, *After Tamerlane: the global history of empire since 1405*, Bloomsbury Publishing, USA.

Dennell, RW 2018, 'Where evolutionary biology meets history: ethno-nationalism and modern human origins in East Asia', in JH Schwartz (ed.), *Rethinking human evolution*, MIT Press, Cambridge, MA, pp. 229–250.

Dias, N 2012, 'Nineteenth-century French collections of skulls and the cult of bones', *Nuncius*, vol. 27, no. 2, pp. 330–347.

Dumont, CW 2003, 'The politics of scientific objections to repatriation', *Wicazo Sa Review*, vol. 18, no. 1, pp. 109–128.

Fabian, A 2010, *The skull collectors: race, science, and america's unburied dead*, University of Chicago Press, Chicago, IL.

Fforde, C, Hubert, J & Turnbull, P (eds) 2004, *The dead and their possessions: repatriation in principle, policy and practice*, One World Archaeology Series #43, Routledge, New York.

Freeman, RB & Huang, W 2014, 'Collaboration: strength in diversity', *Nature News*, vol. 513, no. 7518, p. 305.

Fu, Q, Hajdinjak, M, Moldovan, OT, Constantin, S, Mallick, S, Skoglund, P, Patterson, N, Rohland, N, Lazaridis, I, Nickel, B, Viola, B, Prüfer, K, Meyer, M, Kelso, J, Reich, D & Pääbo, S 2015, 'An early modern human from Romania with a recent Neanderthal ancestor', *Nature*, vol. 524, no. 7564, pp. 216–219.

Fu, Q, Meyer, M, Gao, X, Stenzel, U, Burbano, HA, Kelso, J & Pääbo, S 2013, 'DNA analysis of an early modern human from Tianyuan Cave, China', *Proceedings of the National Academy of Sciences*, vol. 110, no. 6, pp. 2223–2227.

Fuchs, B 2012, '"Bushmen in Hick Town": the Austrian empire and the study of the Khoesan', *Austrian Studies*, vol. 20, pp. 43–59.

Galton, F 1889, *Narrative of an explorer in tropical South Africa: being an account of a visit to Damaraland in 1851*, vol. 2, Ward, Lock & Company, London.

Galway-Witham, J & Stringer, C 2018, 'How did *Homo sapiens* evolve?' *Science*, vol. 360, no. 6395, pp. 1296–1298.

Gibbons, A 2018, *Hadza on the brink*, American Association for the Advancement of Science, Washington, DC.

Gindhart, MP 2008, 'Cro-Magnon and Khoi-San: Constant Roux's racialized relief sculptures of prehistoric artists', *Visual Resources*, vol. 24, no. 3, pp. 321–342.

Gordon, RJ 1992, 'The venal Hottentot Venus and the great chain of being', *African Studies*, vol. 51, no. 2, pp. 185–201.

Gordon-Chipembere, N 2011, *Representation and black womanhood: the legacy of Sarah Baartman*, Springer, New York.

Gould, SJ 1996, *The mismeasure of man*, Revised and expanded edn, W.W. Norton & Company, New York.

Government of the Republic of Zambia 2016, 'Zambia's quest for the return of the Broken Hill Man skull', Paper presented at the United Nations Educational, Scientific and Cultural Organisation (UNESCO) 20th Session of the Inter-Governmental Committee for Promoting the Return of Cultural Property to Its Countries of Origin or Its Restitution in Case of Illicit Appropriation.

Green, RE, Krause, J, Briggs, AW, Maricic, T, Stenzel, U, Kircher, M, Patterson, N, Li, H, Zhai, W, Hsi-Yan FM, Hansen, NF, Durand, EY, Malaspinas, A-S, Jensen, JD, Marques-Bonet, T, Alkan, C, Prüfer, K, Meyer, M, Burbano, HA, Good, JM, Schultz, R, Aximu-Petri, A, Butthof, A, Höber, B, Höffner, B, Siegemund, M, Weihmann, A, Nusbaum, C, Lander, ES, Russ, C, Novod, N, Affourtit, J, Egholm, M, Verna, C, Rudan, P, Brajkovic, D, Kucan, Z, Gusic, I, Dornichev, VB, Golovanova, LV, Laluexa-Fox, C, de la Rasilla, M, Fortea, J, Rosas, A, Schmitz, RW, Johnson, PLF, Eichler, EE, Falush, D, Birney, E, Mullikin, JC, Slatkin, M, Nielsen, R, Kelso, J, Lachmann, M, Reich, D & Pääbo, S 2010, 'A draft sequence of the Neandertal genome', *Science*, vol. 328, no. 5979, pp. 710–722.

Gregory, WK 1927, 'Did man originate in Central Asia? (Mongolia the New World, Part V)', *The Scientific Monthly*, vol. 24, no. 5, pp. 385–401.

Gregory, WK & Hellman, M 1938, 'Evidence of the Australopithecine man-apes on the origin of man', *Science*, vol. 88, no. 2296, pp. 615–616.

Haeckel, E 1876, *The history of creation. On the development of the earth and its inhabitants by the action of natural causes; a popular exposition of the doctrine of evolution in general, and of that of Darwin, Goethe, and Lamarck in particular*, trans. ER Lankester, 2nd edn, Henry S. King & Co, London.

Hager, LD 1997, 'Sex and gender in paleoanthropology', in LD Hager (ed.), *Women in human evolution*, Routledge, London and New York, pp. 1–28.

Hambly, WD 1937, 'Source book for African anthropology: Part II', *Publications of the Field Museum of Natural History. Anthropological Series*, vol. 26, no. 2, pp. 407–953.

Henderson, CE 2014, 'AKA: Sarah Baartman, the Hottentot Venus, and black women's identity', *Women's Studies*, vol. 43, no. 7, pp. 946–959.

Henke, W 2007, 'Historical overview of paleoanthropological research', in W Henke & I Tattersall (eds), *Handbook of paleoanthropology*, Springer, New York, pp. 1–56.

Hill, KR, Walker, RS, Božičević, M, Eder, J, Headland, T, Hewlett, B, Hurtado, AM, Marlowe, F, Wiessner, P & Wood, B 2011, 'Co-residence patterns in hunter-gatherer societies show unique human social structure', *Science*, vol. 331, no. 6022, pp. 1286–1289.

Hodgson, BH 1848, 'Aborigines of Central India', *Journal of the Asiatic Society of Bengal*, vol. 17, pp. 550–558.

Hong, L & Page, SE 2004, 'Groups of diverse problem solvers can outperform groups of high-ability problem solvers', *Proceedings of the National Academy of Sciences*, vol. 101, no. 46, pp. 16385–16389.

Howell, FC 1957, 'The evolutionary significance of variation and varieties of "Neanderthal" man', *The Quarterly Review of Biology*, vol. 32, no. 4, pp. 330–347.

Hrdlička, A 1904, *Directions for collecting information and specimens for physical anthropology*, vol. 39, US Government Printing Office, Washington, DC.

Hrdlička, A 1921, 'The peopling of Asia', *Proceedings of the American Philosophical Society*, vol. 60, no. 4, pp. 535–545.

Hrdlička, A 1926, 'The peopling of the Earth', *Proceedings of the American Philosophical Society*, vol. 65, no. 3, pp. 150–156.

Hrdlička, A 1927, 'The Neanderthal phase of man', *Journal of the Royal Anthropological Institute of Great Britain and Ireland*, vol. 57, pp. 249–274.

Hrdlička, A 1930, 'The skeletal remains of early man', *Smithsonian Institution Annual Report for 1928*, Smithsonian Institution, Washington, DC, pp. 593–623.

Hublin, J-J, Ben-Ncer, A, Bailey, SE, Freidline, SE, Neubauer, S, Skinner, MM, Bergmann, I, Le Cabec, A, Benazzi, S, Harvati, K & Gunz, P 2017, 'New fossils from Jebel Irhoud, Morocco and the pan-African origin of *Homo sapiens*' (Letter), *Nature*, vol. 546, no. 7657, pp. 289–292.

Huxley, TH 1863, 'On some fossil remains of man', *Evidence as to man's place in nature*, Williams and Norgate, London and Edinburgh.

Keith, A 1925, *The antiquity of man*, Williams and Norgate, London.

Keith, A 1929, 'The fossil man of Peking', *The Lancet*, vol. 214, no. 5535, pp. 683–685.

Kelly, R 2013, 'Hunter gatherers and prehistory', *The lifeways of hunter-gatherers: the foraging spectrum*, Cambridge University Press, New York, pp. 269–300.

Kopytoff, I 1987, *The African frontier: the reproduction of traditional African societies*, Indiana University Press, Bloomington.

Kuhlwilm, M, Gronau, I, Hubisz, MJ, de Filippo, C, Prado-Martinez, J, Kircher, M, Fu, Q, Burbano, HA, Lalueza-Fox, C, de la Rasilla, M, Rosas, A, Rudan, P, Kucan, Ž, Gušic, I, Marques-Bonet, T, Andrés, AM, Viola, B, Pääbo, S, Meyer, M & Siepel, A 2016, 'Ancient gene flow from early modern humans into Eastern Neanderthals', *Nature*, vol. 530, no. 7591, pp. 429–433.

Kuljian, C 2016, *Darwin's hunch: science, race and the search for human origins*, Jacana, Auckland Park, South Africa.

Langford, RF 1983, 'Our heritage – your playground', *Australian Archaeology*, vol. 16, pp. 1–6.

Le Gros Clark, WE 1947, 'The importance of the fossil Australopithecinae in the study of human evolution', *Science Progress (1933–)*, vol. 35, no. 139, pp. 377–395.

Leakey Foundation 2018, 'Fossil finders'. Available from: https://leakeyfoundation.org/category/fossil-finders/ [6 September 2018].

Leakey, LSB 1936, *Stone age Africa: an outline of prehistory in Africa*, H. Milford, Oxford University Press, Oxford.

MacCurdy, GG 1922, 'The skull from Broken Hill in Rhodesia', *American Anthropologist*, vol. 24, no. 1, pp. 97–98.

Madley, B 2005, 'From Africa to Auschwitz: how German South West Africa incubated ideas and methods adopted and developed by the Nazis in Eastern Europe', *European History Quarterly*, vol. 35, no. 3, pp. 429–464.

Marean, CW 2014, 'The origins and significance of coastal resource use in Africa and Western Eurasia', *Journal of Human Evolution*, vol. 77, pp. 17–40.

Marean, CW 2015a, 'The most invasive species of all', *Scientific American*, vol. 313, no. 2, pp. 33–39.

Marean, CW 2015b, 'Readers respond to "how we conquered the planet"', *Scientific American*. Available from: https://www.scientificamerican.com/article/readers-respond-to-how-we-conquered-the-planet/ [2 April 2019].

Marks, J 2001, '"We're going to tell these people who they really are": science and relatedness', in S Franklin & S McKinnon (eds), *Relative values: reconfiguring kinship studies*, Duke University Press, Durham, NC, pp. 355–383.

Matthew, WD 1914, 'Climate and evolution', *Annals of the New York Academy of Sciences*, vol. 24, no. 1, pp. 171–318.

Mazrui, AA 2005, 'The re-invention of Africa: Edward Saïd, V.Y. Mudimbe, and beyond', *Research in African Literatures*, vol. 36, no. 3, pp. 68–82.

McNiven, IJ & Russell, L 2008, 'Toward a postcolonial archaeology of Indigenous Australia', in RA Bentley, HDG Maschner & C Chippindale (eds), *Handbook of archaeological theories*, AltaMira Press, Lanham, MD, pp. 423–443.

Milks, A 2018, 'Making an impact', *Natural Ecological Evolution*, vol. 2, no. 7, pp. 1057–1058.

Mivart, SGJ 1873, *Man and apes; an exposition of structural resemblances and differences bearing upon questions of affinity and origin*, R. Hardwicke, London.

Morell, V 1995, 'Who owns the past?', *Science*, vol. 268, no. 5216, p. 1424.

Movius, HL 1948, 'The Lower Palaeolithic cultures of Southern and Eastern Asia', *Transactions of the American Philosophical Society*, vol. 38, no. 4, pp. 329–420.

Mudimbe, VY 1994, *The idea of Africa*, Indiana University Press and J. Currey, Bloomington and London.

Murray, T & Allen, J 1995, 'The forced repatriation of cultural properties to Tasmania', *Antiquity*, vol. 69, no. 266, pp. 871–874.

Osborn, HF 1926, 'Why Central Asia?', *Natural History*, vol. 26, pp. 263–269.

Osborn, HF 1927, 'Recent discoveries relating to the origin and antiquity of man', *Science*, vol. 65, no. 1690, pp. 481–488.

Page, SE 2007, *The difference: how the power of diversity creates better groups, firms, schools, and societies*, Princeton University Press, Princeton, NJ.

Palladino, P & Worboys, M 1993, 'Science and imperialism', *Isis*, vol. 84, no. 1, pp. 91–102.

Pels, P 1998, 'From texts to bodies: Brian Houghton Hodgson and the emergence of ethnology in India', in J van Bremen & A Shimizu (eds), *Anthropology and colonialism in Asia and Oceania*, Routledge, London and New York, pp. 65–92.

Pels, P 1999, 'The rise and fall of the Indian aborigines', in P Pels & O Salemink (eds), *Colonial subjects: essays on the practical history of anthropology*, University of Michigan Press, Ann Arbor, pp. 82–116.

Pels, P 2008, 'What has anthropology learned from the anthropology of colonialism?', *Social Anthropology*, vol. 16, no. 3, pp. 280–299.

Peringuey, L 1915, 'The bushman as a palaeolithic man', *Transactions of the Royal Society of South Africa*, vol. 5, no. 1, pp. 225–236.

Popkin, RH 1974, 'The philosophical bases of modern racism', in C Walton & JP Antón (eds), *Philosophy and the civilizing arts: essays presented to Herbert W. Schneider on his 80th birthday*, Ohio University Press, Athens, OH.

Porr, M 2014, 'Essential questions: "modern humans" and the capacity for modernity', in RW Dennell & M Porr (eds), *Southern Asia, Australia and the search for human origins*, Cambridge University Press, Cambridge, pp. 257–264.

Porr, M & Matthews, JM 2017, 'Post-colonialism, human origins and the paradox of modernity', *Antiquity*, vol. 91, no. 358, pp. 1058–1068.

Qiu, J 2016, 'The forgotten continent', *Nature*, vol. 535, no. 7611, pp. 218–220.

Reader, J 1988, *Missing links: the hunt for earliest man*, Penguin Books, London.

Roque, R 2011, 'Stories, skulls, and colonial collections', *Configurations*, vol. 19, no. 1, pp. 1–23.

Saïd, EW 1978, *Orientalism*, Random House, New York.

Scerri, EML, Thomas, MG, Manica, A, Gunz, P, Stock, JT, Stringer, C, Grove, M, Groucutt, HS, Timmermann, A & Rightmire, GP 2018, 'Did our species evolve in subdivided populations across Africa, and why does it matter?' *Trends in Ecology and Evolution*, vol. 33, no. 8, pp. 582–594.

Schramm, K 2016, *African homecoming: Pan-African ideology and contested heritage*, Routledge, London and New York.

Schrire, C 1980, 'An inquiry into the evolutionary status and apparent identity of San hunter-gatherers', *Human Ecology*, vol. 8, no. 1, pp. 9–32.

Schroeder, L & Ackermann, RR 2017, 'Evolutionary processes shaping diversity across the *Homo* lineage', *Journal of Human Evolution*, vol. 111, pp. 1–17.

Scully, P & Crais, C 2008, 'Race and erasure: Sara Baartman and Hendrik Cesars in Capetown and London', *Journal of British Studies*, vol. 47, no. 2, pp. 301–323.

Shipman, P 2001, *The man who found the missing link: Eugène Dubois and his lifelong quest to prove Darwin right*, Simon & Schuster, New York.

Shipman, P & Storm, P 2002, 'Missing links: Eugène Dubois and the origins of paleoanthropology', *Evolutionary Anthropology: Issues, News, and Reviews*, vol. 11, no. 3, pp. 108–116.

Smith, EW 1935, 'Africa: what do we know of it?', *Journal of the Royal Anthropological Institute of Great Britain and Ireland*, vol. 65, pp. 1–81.

Spencer, F & Smith, FH 1981, 'The significance of Aleš Hrdlička on "the Neanderthal phase of man": a historical and current assessment', *American Journal of Physical Anthropology*, vol. 56, no. 4, pp. 435–459.

Strkalj, G 2000, 'Inventing races: Robert Broom's research on the Khoisan', *Annals of the Transvaal Museum*, vol. 37, pp. 113–124.

Sussman, RW 2014, *The myth of race: the troubling persistence of an unscientific idea*, Harvard University Press, Cambridge, MA.

Sysling, F 2015, '"Protecting the primitive natives": Indigenous people as endangered species in the early nature protection movement, 1900–1940', *Environment and History*, vol. 21, no. 3, pp. 381–399.

TallBear, K 2013, *Native American DNA: tribal belonging and the false promise of genetic science*, University of Minnesota Press, Minneapolis.

Templeton, AR 2002, 'Out of Africa again and again', *Nature*, vol. 416, pp. 45–51.

Terrell, JE 2018, '"Plug and play" genetics, racial migrations and human history', *Scientific American*. Available from: https://blogs.scientificamerican.com/observations/plug-and-play-genetics-racial-migrations-and-human-history/ [2 April 2019].

Testart, A, Arcand, B, Ingold, T, Legros, D, Linkenbach, A, Morton, J, Peterson, N, Raju, DR, Schrire, C, Smith, EA, Walter, MS & Zvelebil, M 1988, 'Some major problems in the social anthropology of hunter-gatherers [and Comments and Reply]', *Current Anthropology*, vol. 29, no. 1, pp. 1–31.

Thorne, A 1981, 'The centre and the edge: the significance of Australian hominids to African palaeoanthropology', in REF Leakey & BA Ogot (eds), *Proceedings, 8th Pan African Congress of Prehistory and Quaternary Studies*, TILLMIAP, Nairobi, pp. 180–181.

Trinkaus, E 2005, 'Early modern humans', *Annual Review of Anthropology*, vol. 34, pp. 207–230.

Trinkaus, E & Shipman, P 1992, *The Neandertals*, Vintage, New York.

von Cramon-Taubadel, N & Weaver, TD 2009, 'Insights from a quantitative genetic approach to human morphological evolution', *Evolutionary Anthropology: Issues, News, and Reviews*, vol. 18, no. 6, pp. 237–240.

Wallace, AR 1889, *Darwinism, an exposition of the theory of natural selection, with some of its applications*, Macmillan and Company, London.

Washburn, SL 1951, 'Section of anthropology: the "new physical anthropology"', *Transactions of the New York Academy of Sciences*, vol. 13, no. 7, pp. 298–304.

Weaver, TD, Roseman, CC & Stringer, CB 2007, 'Were Neandertal and modern human cranial differences produced by natural selection or genetic drift?', *Journal of Human Evolution*, vol. 53, no. 2, pp. 135–145.

Weidenreich, F 1947, 'Facts and speculations concerning the origin of *Homo sapiens*', *American Anthropologist*, vol. 49, no. 2, pp. 187–203.

White, R 2006, 'The women of Brassempouy: a century of research and interpretation', *Journal of Archaeological Method and Theory*, vol. 13, no. 4, pp. 250–303.

Wolpoff, M & Caspari, R 1997, *Race and human evolution*, Simon and Schuster, New York.

Wolpoff, M, Wu, X & Thorne, A 1984, 'Modern *Homo sapiens* origins: a general theory of hominid evolution involving the fossil evidence from East Asia', in FH Smith & F Spencer (eds), *The origins of modern humans: a world survey of the fossil evidence*, Alan R. Liss, New York, pp. 411–483.

Woodward, AS 1922, 'The problem of the Rhodesian fossil man', *Science Progress in the Twentieth Century (1919–1933)*, vol. 16, no. 64, pp. 574–579.

Wu, X 1988, 'Comparative study of early *Homo sapiens* from China and Europe', *Acta Anthropologica Sinica*, vol. 7, pp. 287–293.

Wu, X 2004, 'On the origin of modern humans in China', *Quaternary International*, vol. 117, no. 1, pp. 131–140.

5

PRIMORDIALISING ABORIGINAL AUSTRALIANS

Colonialist tropes and Eurocentric views on behavioural markers of modern humans

Ian J. McNiven

Introduction

Scientific debates concerning the origins of modern humans (*Homo sapiens*) and their spread out-of-Africa within the past c.120–190,000 years across Eurasia and Australia focus on the three interrelated data domains of human skeletal remains, DNA, and cultural materials. Although of the same species, a curious delay exists in the anatomical expression of modernity (skeletal remains and DNA) dating back to at least c.150,000–200,000 and even c.300,000 years ago (Cann, Stoneking & Wilson 1987; Hershkovitz et al. 2018; Hublin et al. 2017; McDougall, Brown & Fleagle 2005) and material expressions of behavioural and cognitive modernity in the form of technological systems (e.g. stone flaking techniques) and symbolic systems such as body adornments (e.g. shells) which emerged cumulatively in Africa between c.80,000 and c.50,000 years ago (e.g. Klein 2008; McBrearty & Brooks 2000). This temporal mismatch may explain in part the delay in the successful movement of modern humans out-of-Africa c.50,000–70,000 years ago (which should be considered a minimum age given dates of 65,000 years in Australia, see Clarkson et al. 2017; cf. O'Connell et al. 2018). For some archaeologists, key to understanding the movement of modern humans out-of-Africa is Europe, where there exists an apparent convergence in the rapid appearance of anatomically, behaviourally, and cognitively modern humans 40,000–50,000 years ago (e.g. Mellars 1973; 2005; Mellars & Stringer 1989; see also Nowell 2010). Despite the regional specificity of this 'package', it came to represent the 'yardstick' by which behavioural modernity should be universally conceived and the standard by which the spread of modern humans across Asia and into Australia similarly should be identified and judged (e.g. Henshilwood & Marean 2003; Mellars 2006; cf. McBrearty 2003, p. 642). Yet the archaeological records of Africa (e.g. Henshilwood & Marean 2003; McBrearty & Brooks 2000), eastern Asia (e.g. Norton & Jin 2009; Szabo, Brumm & Bellwood 2007), and Australia (e.g. Brumm & Moore 2005; Davidson 2010; Habgood & Franklin 2008) have been less than forthcoming in conforming to the Eurocentric 'package' of behavioural 'traits'. In some cases, this issue of conformity has given rise to explanatory models attempting to account for an apparent breakdown or simplification of the 'package' (or elements thereof) as it advanced eastwards away from Africa and Europe and towards Australia (e.g. Clarkson 2014; Mellars 2006; 2015; see also Lycett & von Cramon-Taubadel 2008; Lycett & Norton 2010). Although adherents to these models follow objective scientific principles on the surface, these models disturbingly echo deep-seated nineteenth-century European ontological constructions of the world that underpinned the development of anthropology and archaeology and colonial expansion and expropriation of Indigenous lands in places such as Australia. Following trenchant anticolonialist critiques of past and present Eurocentric and universalising conceptualisations of human cultural development and behavioural modernity by McNiven and Russell (2005) and Martin Porr (2010; 2014; see also Porr & Matthews 2017), here I explore the colonialist underpinnings of contemporary modelling of the movement of modern humans out-of-Africa and the colonisation of Australia. The chapter focuses on the two colonial tropes of degeneration and diffusion elaborated by pioneering anthropologists and archaeologists in the nineteenth century. The degeneration trope, in its recent guise, focuses on the out-of-Africa model and its attempt to link the eastward advance of modern humans towards Australia with increasing technological simplification. The diffusion trope is illustrated by ground-edge axes which were used as a marker of human technological innovation in Europe but not so for Aboriginal Australians. Although different in approach, I argue that both tropes have the same spurious aim of primordialising Aboriginal Australians in an attempt to perpetuate the universality of Eurocentric views on behavioural markers of modern humans.

Degeneration and out-of-Africa

An important dimension to the out-of-Africa model of modern human colonisation of Eurasia and Australia is to what extent this exodus was predicated upon behavioural and cognitive developments. These developments have come to be seen as markers of fully modern humans in both a biological and cultural sense (see Mellars 2015 for an overview). The cultural repertoire expressed by modern humans in Africa c.50,000–80,000 years ago (e.g. microliths and shell beads) and those who entered Europe c.40,000–50,000 years ago (e.g. blade technologies and rock art) are seen by many as the type 'package' representing these cumulative developments. As such, other out-of-Africa peoples (i.e. Asians and Australians) whose early archaeological records do not possess these particular developments are seen to have inherited a degenerated form of the 'package' which lost key elements as it headed eastwards. Far from a modern construct, this degeneration paradigm is deeply ingrained in Western thought and epistemology and rose to prominence in European intellectual circles during the nineteenth century. To illustrate how this paradigm conceptually underpins recent discussions of the movement of behaviourally modern humans out-of-Africa, I take as a starting point Paul Mellars's 2006 *Science* paper titled '*Going east: new genetic and archaeological perspectives on the modern human colonization of Eurasia*'. Using DNA evidence for the movement of modern humans out-of-Africa by about 60,000 years ago, Mellars made much of technological similarities between cresentic microliths of southern and eastern Africa dated to around 55,000–60,000 years ago and those found in India by about 35,000 years ago. Despite the profound differences in time, Mellars saw the tradition of Indian cresentic microliths as ancestrally linked to the earlier African cresentic microlith industries both in terms of culture and genetics. Similar links were made based on shell beads and ground and incised pieces of ochre. Beyond India the story goes downhill. Mellars (2006, p. 798) stated: 'The greatest enigma in the current archaeological record lies in the lack of similarly "advanced" technologies in the areas to the east of the Indian subcontinent, and especially in the relatively well-explored areas of Australia and New Guinea.' Furthermore,

> The earliest stone-tool technologies documented across the whole of Australasia are conspicuously lacking in any trace of distinctively 'modern' or 'Upper Palaeolithic', blade-based technologies of the kind recorded from both the later African Middle Stone Age sites and the earliest modern human sites in southwest Asia and Europe.
>
> *(Mellars 2006, p. 798)*

Mellars (2015, p. 8) reiterates his stance almost ten years later: there exists 'a conspicuous "simplification" of stone-tool technology in general throughout the southern regions of southeastern Asia and in the initial colonization of the Australasian continent'. To ram home that Australian stone tool technologies are characterised by what they are not and how they are of lesser quality compared to European and African technologies, Mellars (2006, p. 798) states:

> These Australian technologies consist of very simple, flaked based industries, completely lacking in typical blade forms and apparently with little or no trace of typically Upper Palaeolithic tool forms such as end scrapers, backed blades, or burins [until] around 5000 to 7000 yr B.P.

For example, Mellars (2006, p. 799) describes 'horse hoof cores', a distinctive single platform core form found at the famous early site of Lake Mungo in western New South Wales (see Bowler et al. 1970), as possessing a 'basic flaking strategy … analogous to that of simplified forms of single-platform blade cores'.

Mellars saw the east-of-India and Australian 'simple' technologies as a 'paradox' for the theory of cultural developent underwriting the movement of modern humans out-of-Africa. In this connection, he advanced three explanations – two environmental and one cultural. The first environmental explanation posits that there existed a 'general scarcity of high-quality, fine-grained stone [e.g. chert and obsidian] for [blade-based] tool production in most areas of eastern and southeastern Asia' (Mellars 2006, p. 798). This statement is empirically wrong. Habgood and Franklin (2008, p. 212) point out that to the contrary, 'high-quality, fine-grained stone was available in parts of southern Asia and Sahul and was being used for tool production during the late Pleistocene'.

The second environmental explanation posits that coastal colonisation with subsistence practices focused on marine resources would not require complex blade-based technologies that would otherwise be needed to hunt terrestrial game and to prepare skin clothing and tents necessary in cold climates. This proposal is spurious on empirical and conceptual grounds. Empirically, Habgood and Franklin (2008, p. 212) note that evidence from south-west Tasmania indicates early reliance on hunted animals and skin clothing, and yet, blade production was not a feature of Pleistocene Tasmanian stone technologies (e.g. Cosgrove 1995; Holdaway 2004; McNiven 1994). Conceptually, Mellars (2006, p. 796) follows Carl Sauer (1962) and argues that 'a strongly coastal pattern of dispersal would make good sense in ecological and demographic terms, because this would presumably have required only limited economic adaptations from one coastal location to another'. Yet Sauer (1962, p. 45, p. 47) does not hypothesise that the 'seashore' facilitated colonisation away from Africa based on 'limited economic adaptations' but because it was an 'optimum habitat' that 'presented familiar foods and habitats'. Through a subtle language twist, Mellars changes the motivations of colonists leading to Australia from one of following a 'familiar' behavioural/cognitive pathway to one of following a pathway of least innovation and least effort.

Third, repeated founder effects and associated cultural drift resulted in, to use Mellars' (2006, p. 799) words: 'progressive loss in the complexity and diversity of cultural and technological patterns with increasing distance from their demographic point of origin' (Mellars 2015 repeats these arguments). Remarkably, Rhys Jones' (1977) Tasmanian argument of isolation and cultural loss was presented in support of this explanation. The colonialist underpinnings of Jones' degeneration thesis have been well-documented (e.g. McNiven and Russell 2005, pp. 176–177). This technological devolution was seen as 'a direct parallel to the progressive loss in the genetic diversity of the dispersing modern human populations over geographical trajectories extending from their putative African origin progressively eastward and westward' (Mellars 2006, p. 799). Recently, Chris Clarkson (2014, pp. 87–88) has taken a similar founder effects approach to construct stone artefact data from Africa eastwards across to Oceania such that it reveals a 'striking pattern' of 'declining technological diversity with distance from Africa'. To sum up, Mellars (2006, p. 799) stated: 'When viewed in these terms, the relative "simplicity" of the technology associated with the initial modern human settlement of south-east Asia and Australia becomes not merely plausible but arguably largely predictable, in demographic and cultural terms.'

What is 'largely predictable' about Mellars's degeneration model is that it harps back to late eighteenth- and nineteenth-century anthropological conceptualisations of the devolution of humanity moving away from Europe. As McNiven and Russell (2005) elaborate in their book *Appropriated Pasts*, and as numerous other colonialist critiques of anthropology and archaeology have made clear over the past two decades, European Enlightenment notions of human cultural complexity decreasing with increasing distance from Europe was, as Rhys Jones (1992, p. 754) so eloquently put it, 'a philosophy for an age of colonization'. Drawing on Blaut (1993), McNiven and Russell (2005, p. 141) detail 'how Europeans divided the world into two major cultural domains: an *inside* (European) domain representing the world's "cultural hearth" and characterised by innovation and progress, and an *outside* domain that was stagnant and unchanging ("traditional")'. This inside–outside (core–periphery) schema continued to be promulgated in the mid-twentieth century by prominent archaeologists and anthropologists. For example, Hallam Movius (1948) famously divided the Palaeolithic of Europe and southern Asia into western and eastern domains separated by a line running through India (known as the Movius Line). The western domain featured the 'progressive' 'hand-axe culture' whilst the eastern domain was a 'region of cultural retardation' featuring the 'crude' 'chopping-tool culture' (Movius 1948, p. 403, p. 409, p. 411). As Robin Dennell (2014, p. 19) notes, Movius saw Southeast Asia as 'inhabited by populations that were incapable of innovation or progress' (see also Brumm 2010). Similarly, Alfred Kroeber (1946) in his 1945 Huxley Memorial Lecture at the Royal Anthropological Institute in London elaborated the ancient Greek notion of the ecumene whereby Europe and the Near East were the cultural engine of innovation for the world. In his textbook *Anthropology*, Kroeber (1948, p. 422) stated bluntly that 'Ultramarginal to the margin that the Australians constituted were the still more backward Tasmanians.' In this light, perhaps it is not so remarkable that Mellars would include a reference to the devolution of the Tasmanians in his *Science* paper.

Mellars (2005, p. 24; 2007, p. 3; 2015, p. 6) repeatedly asserts that his Eurocentric definition of behavioural modernity was 'never intended or presented as any kind of global characterisation of "modern" behavioural patterns across Europe as whole, let alone on a more continental scale'. As others have observed, the thrust of Mellars's publications reveals otherwise (Nowell 2010, p. 440; Porr 2010, p. 28). The colonialist ancestry of Mellars's antipodean degeneration framework taps into a much bigger issue in the out-of-Africa theory of modern human dispersals that relates to the use of European and African markers of behavioural modernity. To expect that particular technological practices are somehow part of the essentialised make-up of modern humans is a legacy of nineteenth-century diffusionist frameworks for the spread of cultural traits across the globe. A distance-decay curve can be generated for most material culture traits given the geographical boundedness of most human cultural practices. As such, to use markers of the behavioural and cognitive development of modern humans in Africa such as crescentic microliths as some sort of cultural marker for the out-of-Africa spread of modern humans seems more like wishful thinking than the application of rigorous anthropological theory. It is to be expected that material expressions of modern human cultural practices will vary from region to region. The issue is not about the 'loss' of cultural traits as modern humans moved eastwards across Asia towards Australia but about peoples in different regions expressing their humanity through myriad cultural practices.

At one level, my critique of the trait diffusion approach taken by researchers such as Mellars is not new. Habgood and Franklin (2008, p. 187) pointed out that the concept of a 'package' of trait markers of modern human cultural behaviour does not stack up in the Australian context given that it took some 30,000 years for the 'package' to gradually accumulate through 'innovation' after people arrived in Australia. As such, they 'discount the idea that the "package" was lost en route to Sahul'. Alternatively, they argue that no early colonising modern humans possessed the 'package', except perhaps in places such as Africa and Europe where the contents of the 'package' were conceived and remain potentially relevant. Ironically, whether the absence of the modern human cultural 'package' by the early colonisers of Australia is conceived of as a result of loss (*sensu* Mellars) or as a result of irrelevance (*sensu* Habgood and Franklin), the end result is the same – a kind of cultural zero is created for the first peoples to enter Australia. In short, one is left wondering what cultural traits were possessed by the first colonists of Australia. This situation raises the fundamental question of whether or not the current conceptualisation of out-of-Africa migration models and the search for the geographical spread of material markers of human modernity are inherently colonialist if they continue to promote simplistic conceptualisations of the earliest ancestors of Aboriginal Australians.

Diffusionism and stone axes

Despite the characterisation of early Australian flaked stone artefact technologies in pejorative terms, Mellars (2006, p. 799) appends that the 'totally "modern" character of the burial rituals, personal ornaments, abundant use of red ochre, and elaborate ground and shaped stone axes, documented from effectively the earliest stages of colonization of Australia ... should also be kept in mind in this context'. He concedes that 'there is clearly much more to the emergence of cognitively "modern," symbolically constructed behavior than the production of typically Upper Palaeolithic stone tools' (Mellars 2006, p. 799). It is curious why

Mellars simply appends the issue of ground-edge axe manufacture by Pleistocene Australians. Perhaps it relates to the fact that earliest well-dated ground-edge axes in Europe date to the Mesolithic and c.9,500–9,300 cal BP in Ireland (Little et al. 2016). By Mellars' measure, the presence of ancient axes in Australia puts the First Australians ahead of the evolutionary game and begs the question, following Mellars' logic, of why it took so long for Europeans to take on this technology. Yet as Habgood and Franklin (2008, pp. 208–209, table 1) point out, at the time Mellars (2006) wrote his paper the earliest ground-edge axes in Australia dated to around 22,000 to 32,000 cal BP (Schrire 1982; White 1967) which was at least 20,000 years after concurrent understandings of the colonisation of Australia. As such, axes had little to do with the cultural development of peoples who first colonised Australia.

The state of play of axes in Australia has changed radically in the past couple of years following revelation of ground-edge axes at Madjedbebe rock shelter in Arnhem Land, Northern Territory, dating back to 60,000–65,000 years ago (Clarkson et al. 2017). These axes are not only the oldest known ground-edge axes in the world but are also associated with the earliest evidence for people in Australia. The Madjedbebe axes are not aberrant given that fragments of ground-edge axes dating to 35,000 cal BP and 44,000–49,000 cal BP have been found elsewhere in Arnhem Land and in the Kimberley region respectively (Geneste et al. 2010; 2012; Hiscock, O'Connor & Maloney 2016). That ground-edge axes were part of the technological repertoire of Southeast Asia is indicated by examples dating from c.32,000 to 36,000 cal BP and perhaps back to 38,000 cal BP in Japan (Tsutsumi 2012, p. 73). In both the Australian and Japanese cases, ground-edge axes are associated with the earliest evidence for human occupation of both regions. Whether ground-edge axe technology was introduced by the earliest colonisers of Australia and Japan or developed soon after arrival is unknown. While the absence of evidence for ground-edge axes pre-dating 65,000 cal BP in Indonesia and pre-dating 38,000 cal BP in Korea and China supports independent invention of ground-edge axes in Australia and Japan respectively, further excavations may change this status (Tsutsumi 2012, p. 74; cf. Bae 2017, p. S520; Lee, Bae & Lee 2017, p. 860). Whatever the case, out-of-Africa models such as elaborated by Mellars (2006) find the deep antiquity of Australian and Japanese ground-edge axes disconcerting because they discombobulate Eurocentric models of cultural development and technological 'trait' markers for the emergence of modern humans. Far from a recent issue, Australian Aboriginal ground-edge axes have challenged Eurocentric conceptions of human cultural development based on stone tools for more than 150 years.

Aboriginal Australians (as known ethnographically) employed flaked stone tools that were seen to be analogous to flaked stone tools used by Europeans during the ancient past (as known archaeologically). As is well-known, this situation was seen by nineteenth-century Europeans as revealing the undeveloped nature of Aboriginal Australians who were seen as living fossils. The use of the perceived complexity of stone tools as a marker of cultural development was foundational to the theoretical framework of social evolutionism and the development of its disciplinary instruments of anthropology (Morgan 1877; Tylor 1865) and prehistoric archaeology (Lubbock 1865; Lyell 1863). Exemplary in this regard is Edward Tylor's 1893 address to the Anthropological Institute of Great Britain and Ireland in London titled 'On the Tasmanians as Representatives of Palaeolithic Man' (Tylor 1894). It was in 'Pre-Historic Times' that John Lubbock (1865, p. 2) coined the term 'Palaeolithic period' which was characterised by flaked implements such as knives and scrapers. Lubbock (1865, p. 3, p. 60, p. 280, p. 452) contrasted the Palaeolithic period with what he famously termed the

'Neolithic period' which was characterised by 'polished' implements such as 'celts' (e.g. ground-edge axes) and represented in modern times by 'South Sea Islanders' (Melanesians and Polynesians). Seen as a 'type fossil' for the Neolithic in Europe, ground-edge axes (especially polished axes) were associated with the introduction of agriculture and the felling of forests and woodworking activities (e.g. Clark 1945; Lubbock 1865) (for recent conceptualisations of the social significance of European Neolithic axes see Bradley & Edmonds 1993; Little et al. 2016; Norton 2016, p. 21; Thomas 2013, p. 153).

Yet Tylor (1865, pp. 193, 201) also pointed out a serious problem with the nature of Australian Aboriginal stone tool technologies; namely that some groups such as those in South Australia possessed 'high-class celts' which implied a mixture of cultural traits from two entirely different stages of human development which he termed the 'Un-ground Stone Age' (cf. Palaeolithic) and the 'Ground Stone Age' (cf. Neolithic) following Lubbock. The stakes were high, for unless an explanation to account for this anomalous admixture of so-called primitive and advanced cultural traits could be found, Tylor (1865, p. 201) admitted that 'the quality of stone implements would have to be pretty much given up as a test of culture anywhere'. In short, the entire edifice of unilineal staged development that underpinned social evolutionism was in danger of collapsing. 'Fortunately', quipped Tylor (1865, p. 201), 'there is an easier way out of the difficulty':

> Polished instruments of this green jade have been, long ago or recently, one of the most important items of manufacture in the islands of the Indian Ocean and the Pacific, and the South Australians may have learnt from some Malay or Polynesian source the art of shaping these high-class weapons. The likelihood of this being their real history is strengthened by proofs we have of intercourse between Australia and the surrounding islands. Besides the known yearly visits of the trepang-fishers of Macassar to the Gulf of Carpentaria, and the appearance of the outrigger-canoe in East Australia in Captain Cook's time, there is mythological evidence which seems to carry proof of connexion far down the east coast.

By using external influence and diffusion to explain away so-called complex and advanced cultural traits such as ground-edge axes amongst Australian Aboriginal groups, Tylor was able to maintain the integrity of social evolutionism. However, this maintenance was artificial and achieved through an intellectual sleight-of-hand to ensure perpetuation of the representation of Aboriginal Australians as technologically primitive and culturally undeveloped. In short, the contrived nature of what McNiven and Russell (2005, p. 139) have termed 'colonial diffusionism' was 'necessary to keep Aboriginal Australians in their primordial place to help justify and legitimate European colonisation of Australia' (McNiven 2006, pp. 90–91).

The spurious attempt by nineteenth-century social evolutionists such as Lubbock and Tylor to conceptualise the stone tool technologies of Aboriginal Australians as primitive and undeveloped was also part of an attempt to frame the developmental history of humanity through the lens of European cultural development as revealed by archaeology. As noted above, the emerging picture of European prehistory transitioning from Palaeolithic flaked stone tools to Neolithic ground stone tools was seen as a master plan for human cultural development in general. Yet some late nineteenth-century amateur anthropologists in Australia were sceptical of the relevance of this two-phased schema for understanding Australian Aboriginal stone tool technologies. For example, in 1878 Robert Brough Smyth, a geologist with the Department of Mines in the colony of Victoria, published his two volumed magnum opus *The Aborigines of Victoria*. Like Tylor, Smyth (1878, p. I:lv) pointed out that if

> all the stone implements and weapons of the Australians be examined, one set might be put apart and classed as the equivalents of those of the Palaeolithic period of Europe, and another set as the equivalents of those of the Neolithic period.

Whereas Tylor sought to maintain the integrity of Lubbock's two-phased schema through diffusion, Smyth questioned the applicability of this European-based schema to Australia. He stated that the Australian evidence 'seem to press strongly against the theories of Sir John Lubbock' (Smyth 1878, p. I:lv). Furthermore,

> The classification made by Sir John Lubbock is confined by him to Europe, and it is based not alone in all cases on the forms of the stone implements, but also on the character of other remains that are found with them.
>
> *(1878, p. I:lv)*

For Smyth, the anomalous Australian situation required 'Lubbock to consider these facts in connection with the classification he has employed' (Smyth 1878, p. I:lv).

In his lecture to the Royal Society of New South Wales in 1889, amateur anthropologist the Rev. John Mathew explicitly referenced Smyth's concerns over the apparent incongruity of Australian Aboriginal stone tool technologies:

> The chipped stone tools of the Tasmanian are Palaeolithic, while the usual ground ones of the Australian are Neolithic, but while only the one kind (Palaeolithic) is found in Tasmania, both kinds are found side by side on the mainland, a state of things which indicates in the one case the existence of but one human stratum and in the other the existence of more than one.
>
> *(Mathew 1889, p. 351)*

However, whereas Smyth used this incongruity to question the broader applicability of Lubbock's unilinear model of cultural evolution, Mathew elaborated upon Tylor's diffusionist argument by positing that after the Tasmanians become isolated, mainland Aboriginal Australians 'were overwhelmed by a race bringing with them superior art' which included ground-edge axes (Mathew 1889, p. 350). Both Tylor's and Mathew's diffusionist views were consistent with the prevailing view of nineteenth-century anthropologists that 'savages' remained at a 'primitive level' because they had been 'prevented from advancing by exposure to adverse or less stimulating conditions' (Bowler 1992, p. 722).

During the first half of the twentieth century, Australian scholarly explanations for the so-called admixture of Palaeolithic (flaked) and Neolithic (ground) stone tools went in two directions. The first direction was taken by scholars in Victoria and South Australia and held that differences in tool form and manufacture reflected raw materials and not differences in ancestry or cultural development. Well-known anthropologist Baldwin Spencer (1901, pp. 78–79), informed by Kenyon and Sterling (1901), noted that although Aboriginal stone implements:

are at once typical of what are frequently spoken of as both Palaeolithic and Neolithic men … It must also be remembered that in many tribes both forms of implements are met with side by side. The matter is largely concerned with the kind of stone which is procurable. If only flint or quartzite can be obtained in any particular locality, then the weapons are of the chipped or flaked kind; if stone such as diorite is available, then the weapons are ground; or if both kinds of stone can be secured, then we meet with both kinds of implements.

Alfred Kenyon and Daniel Mahony (1914, p. 4 emphasis added) added that the mixture of 'palaeolithic' and 'neolithic' stone tool forms in Australia reflected the principle that 'the type of stone implement most commonly used in any particular locality is very largely influenced by the material most readily to hand, and *not by the type of culture of the maker*'. For example, the lack of 'ground-edged axes' in a region reflected local raw materials 'not being adapted for a high degree of workmanship' or producing cutting edges 'which could not be improved by grinding' (Kenyon and Mahony 1914, p. 11; see also Howchin 1934). Although this raw material determinism is equally problematic, the critique of the applicability of European frameworks to understand Australian Aboriginal stone artefact technologies remains valid.

The second direction to account for the mixture of Palaeolithic and Neolithic stone tool types in Australia was a diffusionist school which took the works of Tylor and Mathew to extreme levels. Most extreme was William Perry (1923, p. 125), a student of hyper-diffusionist Grafton Elliot Smith, who posited that 'neolithic [polished] implements', along with an array of so-called superior cultural traits, were introduced to Australia through contact with advanced peoples (the 'archaic civilization') with cultural roots back to ancient Egypt (see McNiven and Russell 2005, pp. 165–173). Indeed, Perry (1923, p. 95, pp. 98–100) posited that Aboriginal Australians learned the art of polished axe manufacture directly from interactions with visiting 'people of the archaic civilization' who were prospecting for gold. Archaeological support for Perry's visiting gold miners hypothesis is nil. Although less extreme in his diffusionist appoach, Fred McCarthy of the Australian Museum in Sydney similarly argued for an external origin for ground-edge axes in Australia:

> The presence of the ground-edge technique in Australia may be explained according to our present knowledge in two ways: 1). It was brought to the continent by the Australians before the arrival of the Papuans and Melanesians in New Guinea and north-west Pacific. 2). It diffused into Australia *via* Cape York after the coming of the Papuans and Melanesians.
>
> *(McCarthy 1940a, p. 42)*

Although McCarthy courts the idea of arrival of axes to Australia during the early years of colonisation, most of his discussions on the origin of stone axes in Australia focus on a 'Neolithic' diffusionary pathway from Southeast Asia through New Guinea via Cape York (e.g. McCarthy 1940b, p. 268; 1953, p. 250). Equally illuminating, McCarthy (1940b, p. 268) claimed 'a progressive refinement in their shape and workmanship, from the south to the north of the continent'. This claim reflected his broader belief 'that there is a progression of culture advances in Australia extending from the south-western portion of the continent northwards and north-eastwards, and also from the south-eastern portion northwards and north-westwards' (McCarthy 1940b, p. 261). With his axe diffusion model, McCarthy not only employs the classic inside–outside/core–periphery colonialist trope of degeneration and the degradation of culture moving to the extremes of the earth away from Europe, but extends its application from an inter-continental to an intra-continental scale.

Although the level to which Perry and McCarthy applied diffusionist explanations for Aboriginal material culture differed in scale, both employed 'an arbitrary and spurious categorisation of Aboriginal tool technology into locally invented ("simpler") and externally diffused ("sophisticated") elements' (McNiven 2006, p. 95). This spuriousness was expressed well by Herbert Noone (1943, p. 279), an American archaeologist who collaborated with McCarthy (e.g. McCarthy et al. 1946): 'So much evidence has been put forward to indicate that the Australian aboriginal has brought, or borrowed, many traits of his culture from overseas sources, that one is led to look for anything of his that is left.' Interestingly, Noone (1943, p. 280) stated that 'edge-grinding of flaked axes' was one of a number of stone implement types that reveal 'distinct Australian inventive genius and development'. Towards the end of his career, McCarthy (1977, p. 259) abandoned the Neolithic diffusion model in favour of local development in the wake of Carmel Schrire's (White 1967) discoveries of Pleistocene ground-edge axes in northern Australia.

Mellars (2015, p. 15) employs diffusionsim in trying to account for the 'recent, technologically "simple" hunter-gatherer societies (such as the Australian aborigines or the South African San "Bushmen" populations)'. He stated:

> Clearly, behavior, technology, and other aspects of cultural complexity are predominantly a reflection of cultural-historical processes in which successive populations build on the behavioral achievements and 'complexity' of earlier populations in ways which are frequently either constrained or stimulated by *external* environmental, demographic, and other historical factors.
>
> *(Mellars 2015, p. 15, emphasis added)*

To imply that Aboriginal Australians were unable to progress to a more complex cultural level due to a lack of external stimulation is a nineteenth-century colonial mindset and part of the intellectual baggage of social evolutionism.

Conclusion

The colonial history and legacy of prehistoric archaeology ensures that any current theoretical frameworks or analytical approaches that result in simplified representations of Australia's Aboriginal past in contrast to complex representations of the European past run the risk of being labelled colonialist (McNiven & Russell 2005). This risk is much more than fodder for postcolonial musings within the halls of academia. The consequences of such practices have real negative outcomes for contemporary Aboriginal peoples whose ancestors we study and characterise. As archaeologists we have a responsibility to be aware of the colonial history and colonialist underpinnings of our discipline. Australian archaeologists have over recent decades become acutely aware and highly sensitised to the colonial legacies of our discipline. This awareness and sensitivity has come largely from listening to and reflecting upon criticisms delivered by Aboriginal Australians of the negative impacts of archaeological practices upon their lives and identity (e.g. Colley 2002; Langford 1983; McNiven & Russell 2005; Smith 2004; Smith & Jackson 2006). In 1998, Jim O'Connell and Jim Allen wrote that the colonisation of Australia by modern humans is important in world terms because its timing has major implications for understanding when modern humans left Africa (see also O'Connell et al. 2018). Iain Davidson (2010) adds that an equally important reason to understand the colonisation process of Australia is the nature of cultural practices of these earliest Australians and the associated implications for behavioural and cognitive modernity. It is now clear that documenting and understanding these cultural practices provides a counter-narrative to Eurocentric conceptions of behavioural modernity. These Eurocentric conceptions are the legacy of nineteenth-century colonialism and its paradigmatic anthem of social evolutionism, and need to be expunged from out-of-Africa models. In this connection, Porr and Matthews (2017, p. 1065) note that 'The striking similarities that can be observed between attitudes towards human origins in contemporary academic debate and at the height of European colonialism are deeply concerning.'

It is somewhat ironic that the original colonisation sea crossing required to get to Australia may be, as Davidson and Noble (1992, p. 135) state, 'the oldest evidence for the expression of behaviour that is distinctively [modern] human'. This statement is all the more pertinent now that this colonisation process has been pushed back to at least 60,000–65,000 years ago and performed by people who may have known about ground-edge axes. Dating of the arrival of modern humans to Europe c.40,000–50,000 years ago reveals that Europe is simply a dimension of and not central to the modern human out-of-Africa story. As others have argued, the reality is that there is no 'package' of behavioural 'trait' markers of out-of-Africa modern humans but a multiplicity of regional expressions of so-called modernity as historically contingent expressions of varied environmental and social circumstances. This multiplicity is demonstrated by the unique archaeological records of Southeast Asia, Australia, and New Guinea revealing creativity and innovation (Aubert, Brumm & Taçon 2017; Balme & O'Connor 2014; Balme et al. 2009; Bellwood 2015; Brumm et al. 2017; Brumm & Moore 2005; Chase & Dibble 1990; Cosgrove, Pike-Tay & Roebroeks 2014; Davidson 2010; Gamble 2003; Henshilwood & Marean 2003; Hiscock 2013; Langley, Clarkson & Ulm 2011; Moore 2013; Norton & Jin 2009; Shea 2010, p. 13; Stern 2009; Summerhayes & Ford 2014; Szabo, Brumm & Bellwood 2007). To argue otherwise requires falling into the trap of the social evolutionist's 'simple to complex' paradigm and descending into arguments about how the first Australians were carriers of a degenerated form of the 'package' (*sensu* Mellars) or, more disturbingly, to draw the untenable conclusion that the first Australians were not behaviourally modern (Brumm & Moore 2005, p. 167; Davidson 2014, p. 247; O'Connell & Allen 2007, p. 404; cf. Sterelny 2011, p. 819). Davidson (2014, p. 250) notes cogently that 'lack of similarity does not licence writing a cultural history in terms of "failure" to achieve the goals of an illusory progress defined inductively from the record of Europe'. Eurocentric conceptualisation of a 'package' of behavioural traits diffusing (and degenerating) out-of-Africa and across the globe is a relic of nineteenth-century social evolutionism and colonialist thinking. Indeed, the very concept of 'modern behaviour' plays into this colonialist narrative, lending support to broader calls for it to be 'forgotten' (Chase 2003, p. 637), discarded (Shea 2010, p. 12), 'abandoned' (Zilhão 2010, p. 24), 'replaced' (Porr 2010, p. 28) and 'eliminated' (Garofoli 2016). As Tim Ingold (2000, ch. 21) reminds us, it is the differences between humans, and not the similarities, which make us modern.

Acknowledgments

I thank Martin Porr and Jacqueline Matthews for the kind invitation to participate in the 'Decolonisation and Human Origins' workshop. Martin Porr and Jeremy Ash provided helpful comments on an earlier draft of this chapter.

References

Aubert, M, Brumm, A & Taçon, PS 2017, 'The timing and nature of human colonization of Southeast Asia in the Late Pleistocene: a rock art perspective', *Current Anthropology*, vol. 58, no. S17, pp. S553–S566.

Bae, CJ 2017, 'Late Pleistocene human evolution in eastern Asia: behavioral perspectives', *Current Anthropology*, vol. 58, no. S17, pp. S514–S526.

Balme, J, Davidson, I, McDonald, J, Stern, N & Veth, P 2009, 'Symbolic behaviour and the peopling of the southern arc route to Australia', *Quaternary International*, vol. 202, no. 1–2, pp. 59–68.

Balme, J & O'Connor, S 2014, 'Early modern humans in island southeast Asia and Sahul: adaptive and creative societies with simple lithic technologies', in RW Dennell & M Porr (eds), *Southern Asia, Australia and the search for human origins*, Cambridge University Press, Cambridge, pp. 164–174.

Bellwood, P 2015, 'Migration and the origins of *Homo sapiens*', in Y Kaifu, M Izuho, T Goebel, H Sato & A Ono (eds), *Emergence and diversity of modern human behaviour in Paleolithic Asia*, Texas A&M University Press, College Station, pp. 51–58.

Blaut, JM 1993, *The colonizer's model of the world: geographical diffusionism and eurocentric history*, Guilford Press, New York.

Bowler, JM, Jones, R, Allen, H & Thorne, AG 1970, 'Pleistocene human remains from Australia: a living site and human cremation from Lake Mungo, western New South Wales', *World Archaeology*, vol. 2, no. 1, pp. 39–60.

Bowler, PJ 1992, 'From "savage" to "primitive": Victorian evolutionism and the interpretation of marginalized peoples', *Antiquity*, vol. 66, no. 252, pp. 721–729.

Bradley, R & Edmonds, M 1993, *Interpreting the axe trade: production and exchange in Neolithic Britain*, Cambridge University Press, Cambridge.

Brumm, A 2010, 'The Movius Line and the Bamboo hypothesis: early hominin stone technology in Southeast Asia', *Lithic Technology*, vol. 35, no. 1, pp. 7–24.

Brumm, AR & Moore, MW 2005, 'Symbolic revolutions and the Australian archaeological record', *Cambridge Archaeological Journal*, vol. 15, no. 2, pp. 157–175.

Brumm, A, Langley, MC, Moore, MW, Hakim, B, Ramli, M, Sumantri, I, Burhan, B, Saiful, AM, Siagian, L, Sardi, R & Jusdi, A 2017, 'Early human symbolic behavior in the Late Pleistocene of Wallacea', *Proceedings of the National Academy of Sciences*, vol. 114, no. 16, pp. 4105–4110.

Cann, RL, Stoneking, M & Wilson, AC 1987, 'Mitochondrial DNA and human evolution', *Nature*, vol. 325, no. 6099, pp. 31–36.

Chase, P 2003, 'Comment on "The origin of modern human behavior: critique of the models and their test implications" by CS Henshilwood and CW Marean', *Current Anthropology*, vol. 44, no. 5, p. 637.

Chase, PC & Dibble, HL 1990, 'On the emergence of modern humans', *Current Anthropology*, vol. 38, pp. 58–59.

Clark, G 1945, 'Farmers and forests in Neolithic Europe', *Antiquity*, vol. 19, pp. 57–71.

Clarkson, C 2014, 'East of Eden: founder effects and the archaeological signature of modern human dispersal', in RW Dennell & M Porr (eds), *Southern Asia, Australia and the search for human origins*, Cambridge University Press, Cambridge, pp. 76–89.

Clarkson, C, Jacobs, Z, Marwick, B, Fullagar, R, Wallis, L, Smith, M, Roberts, RG, Hayes, E, Lowe, K, Carah, X, Florin, SA, McNeil, J, Cox, D, Arnold, LJ, Hua, Q, Huntley, J, Brand, HEA, Manne, T, Fairbairn, A, Shulmeister, J, Lyle, L, Salinas, M, Page, M, Connell, K, Park, G, Norman, K, Murphy, T & Pardoe, C 2017, 'Human occupation of northern Australia by 65,000 years ago', *Nature*, vol. 547, no. 7663, pp. 306–310.

Colley, S 2002, *Uncovering Australia: archaeology, Indigenous people and the public*, Allen & Unwin, Crow's Nest, NSW.

Cosgrove, R 1995, *The illusion of riches: scale, resolution and explanation in Tasmanian Pleistocene human behaviour*, BAR International Series #608, Tempus Reparatum, Oxford.

Cosgrove, R, Pike-Tay, A & Roebroeks, W 2014, 'Tasmanian archaeology and reflections on modern human behaviour', in RW Dennell & M Porr (eds), *Southern Asia, Australia and the search for human origins*, Cambridge University Press, Cambridge, pp. 175–188.

Davidson, I 2010, 'The colonization of Australia and its adjacent islands and the evolution of modern cognition', *Current Anthropology*, vol. 51, no. S1, pp. S177–S189.

Davidson, I 2014, 'It's the thought that counts: unpacking the package of behaviour of the first people of Australia and its adjacent islands', in RW Dennell & M Porr (eds), *Southern Asia, Australia and the search for human origins*, Cambridge University Press, Cambridge, pp. 243–256.

Davidson, I & Noble, W 1992, 'Why the colonisation of the Australian region is the earliest evidence of modern human behaviour', *Archaeology in Oceania*, vol. 27, no. 3, pp. 135–142.

Dennell, RW 2014, 'East Asia and human evolution: from cradle of mankind to cul-de-sac', in RW Dennell & M Porr (eds), *Southern Asia, Australia and the search for human origins*, Cambridge University Press, Cambridge, pp. 8–20.

Gamble, C 2003, 'Comment on "The origin of modern human behavior: critique of the models and their test implications" by CS Henshilwood and CW Marean', *Current Anthropology*, vol. 44, no. 5, pp. 638–639.

Garofoli, D 2016, 'Cognitive archaeology without behavioral modernity: an eliminativist attempt', *Quaternary International*, vol. 405, pp. 125–135.

Geneste, JM, David, B, Plisson, H, Clarkson, C, Delannoy, JJ, Petchey, F & Whear, R 2010, 'Earliest evidence for ground-edge axes: 35,400±410 cal BP from Jawoyn Country, Arnhem Land', *Australian Archaeology*, vol. 71, no. 1, pp. 66–69.

Geneste, JM, David, B, Plisson, H, Delannoy, JJ & Petchey, F 2012, 'The origins of ground-edge axes: new findings from Nawarla Gabarnmang, Arnhem Land (Australia) and global implications for the evolution of fully modern humans', *Cambridge Archaeological Journal*, vol. 22, no. 1, pp. 1–17.

Habgood, PJ & Franklin, NR 2008, 'The revolution that didn't arrive: a review of Pleistocene Sahul', *Journal of Human Evolution*, vol. 55, pp. 187–222.

Henshilwood, CS & Marean, CW 2003, 'The origin of modern human behavior: critique of the models and their test implications', *Current Anthropology*, vol. 44, no. 5, pp. 627–651.

Hershkovitz, I, Weber, GW, Quam, R, Duval, M, Grün, R, Kinsley, L, Ayalon, A, Bar-Matthews, M, Valladas, H, Mercier, N & Arsuaga, JL 2018, 'The earliest modern humans outside Africa', *Science*, vol. 359, no. 6374, pp. 456–459.

Hiscock, P 2013, 'Occupying new lands: global migrations and cultural diversification with particular reference to Australia', in KE Graf, CV Ketron & MR Waters (eds), *Paleoamerican odyssey*, Department of Anthropology, Texas A&M University, College Station, pp. 3–11.

Hiscock, P, O'Connor, S & Maloney, T 2016, 'World's earliest ground-edge axe production coincides with human colonisation of Australia', *Australian Archaeology*, vol. 82, no. 1, pp. 2–11.

Holdaway, S 2004, *Continuity and change: an investigation of the flaked stone artefacts from the Pleistocene deposits at Bone Cave, Southwest Tasmania, Australia*, Report of the Southern Forests Archaeological Project, Volume 2. Archaeology Program, School of Historical and European Studies, La Trobe University, Bundoora.

Howchin, W 1934, *The stone implements of the Adelaide tribe of Aborigines now extinct*, Gillingham & Co. Ltd, Adelaide.

Hublin, JJ, Ben-Ncer, A, Bailey, SE, Freidline, SE, Neubauer, S, Skinner, MM, Bergmann, I, Le Cabec, A, Benazzi, S, Harvati, K & Gunz, P 2017, 'New fossils from Jebel Irhoud, Morocco and the pan-African origin of *Homo sapiens*', *Nature*, vol. 546, no. 7657, pp. 289–292.

Ingold, T 2000, *The perception of the environment: essays on livelihood, dwelling and skill*, Routledge, London and New York.

Jones, R 1977, 'The Tasmanian paradox', in RVS Wright (ed.), *Stone tools as cultural markers: change, evolution and complexity*, Australian Institute of Aboriginal Studies, Canberra, pp. 189–204.

Jones, R 1992, 'Philosophical time travellers', *Antiquity*, vol. 66, no. 252, pp. 744–757.

Kenyon, AS & Sterling, DL 1901, 'Australian Aboriginal stone implements. A suggested classification', *Proceedings of the Royal Society of Victoria* (New Series), vol. 13, no. 2, pp. 191–200.

Kenyon, AS & Mahony, DJ 1914, *Stone implements of the Australian Aborigine: guide to the classified collection in the Australian Room, National Museum, Public Library Buildings, Melbourne, arranged for the Australian Meeting of the British Association for the Advancement of Science*, Arnall and Jackson, Melbourne.

Klein, RG 2008, 'Out of Africa and the evolution of human behavior', *Evolutionary Anthropology*, vol. 17, no. 6, pp. 267–281.

Kroeber, AL 1946, 'The ancient oikumenê as a historical culture aggregate: the Huxley Memorial Lecture for 1945', *Journal of the Royal Anthropological Institute of Great Britain and Ireland*, vol. 75, pp. 9–20.

Kroeber, AL 1948, *Anthropology*, Revised edn, Harcourt, Brace, New York.

Langford, RF 1983, 'Our heritage – your playground', *Australian Archaeology*, vol. 16, pp. 1–6.

Langley, MC, Clarkson, C & Ulm, S 2011, 'From small holes to grand narratives: the impact of taphonomy and sample size on the modernity debate in Australia and New Guinea', *Journal of Human Evolution*, vol. 61, pp. 197–208.

Lee, HW, Bae, CJ & Lee, C 2017, 'The Korean early Late Paleolithic revisited: a view from Galsanri', *Archaeological and Anthropological Sciences*, vol. 9, no. 5, pp. 843–863.

Little, A, van Gijn, A, Collins, T, Cooney, G, Elliott, B, Gilhooly, B, Charlton, S & Warren, G 2016, 'Stone dead: uncovering early Mesolithic mortuary rites, Hermitage, Ireland', *Cambridge Archaeological Journal*, vol. 27, no. 2, pp. 223–243.

Lubbock, J 1865, *Pre-historic times, as illustrated by ancient remains, and the manners and customs of modern savages*, Williams and Norgate, London.

Lycett, SJ & von Cramon-Taubadel, N 2008, 'Acheulean variability and hominin dispersals: a model-bound approach', *Journal of Archaeological Science*, vol. 35, no. 3, pp. 553–562.

Lycett, SJ & Norton, CJ 2010, 'A demographic model for Palaeolithic technological evolution: the case of East Asia and the Movius Line', *Quaternary International*, vol. 211, no. 1–2, pp. 55–65.

Lyell, C 1863, *The geological evidences of the antiquity of man with remarks on theories of the origin of species by variation*, John Murray, London.

Mathew, J 1889, 'The Aborigines of Australia', *Journal and Proceedings of the Royal Society of New South Wales*, vol. 23, pp. 335–449.

McBrearty, S 2003, 'Comment on "The origin of modern human behavior: critique of the models and their test implications" by CS Henshilwood and CW Marean', *Current Anthropology*, vol. 44, no. 5, pp. 641–642.

McBrearty, S & Brooks, AS 2000, 'The revolution that wasn't: a new interpretation of the origin of modern human behavior', *Journal of Human Evolution*, vol. 39, pp. 453–563.

McCarthy, FD 1940a, 'A comparison of the prehistory of Australia with that of Indo-China, the Malay Peninsula and the Netherlands East Indies', in FN Chasen & MWF Tweedie, *Proceedings of the Third Congress of Prehistorians of the Far East: Singapore, 24th January–30th January*, Government Printing Office, Singapore, pp. 30–50.

McCarthy, FD 1940b, 'Aboriginal Australian material culture: causative factors in its composition', *Mankind*, vol. 2, no. 8, pp. 241–269 and vol. 2, no. 9, pp. 294–320.

McCarthy, FD 1953, 'The Oceanic and Indonesian affiliations of Australian Aboriginal culture', *Journal of the Polynesian Society*, vol. 62, no. 3, pp. 243–261.

McCarthy, FD 1977, 'The use of stone tools to map patterns of diffusion', in RVS Wright (ed.), *Stone tools as cultural markers: change, evolution and complexity*, Australian Institute of Aboriginal Studies, Canberra, pp. 251–262.

McCarthy, FD, Bramell, E & Noone, HVV 1946, 'The stone implements of Australia', *Australian Museum Memoir*, IX, Sydney.

McDougall, I, Brown, FH & Fleagle, JG 2005, 'Stratigraphic placement and age of modern humans from Kibish, Ethiopia', *Nature*, vol. 433, pp. 733–736.

McNiven, IJ 1994, 'Technological organisation and settlement in SW Tasmania after the Glacial Maximum', *Antiquity*, vol. 68, pp. 75–82.

McNiven, IJ 2006, 'Colonial diffusionism and the archaeology of external influences on Aboriginal culture', in B David, B Barker & IJ McNiven (eds), *The social archaeology of Indigenous societies*, Aboriginal Studies Press, Canberra, pp. 85–106.

McNiven, IJ & Russell, L 2005, *Appropriated pasts: Indigenous peoples and the colonial culture of archaeology*, AltaMira Press, Lanham, MD.

Mellars, P 1973, 'The character of the Middle-Upper Paleolithic transition in south-west France', in C Renfrew (ed.), *The explanation of cultural change*, Duckworth, London, pp. 255–276.

Mellars, P 2005, 'The impossible coincidence: a single-species model for the origins of modern human behavior in Europe', *Evolutionary Anthropology*, vol. 14, pp. 12–17.

Mellars, P 2006, 'Going east: new genetic and archaeological perspectives on the modern human colonization of Eurasia', *Science*, vol. 313, pp. 796–800.

Mellars, P 2007, 'Rethinking the human revolution: Eurasian and African perspectives', in P Mellars, K Boyle, O Bar-Yosef & C Stringer (eds), *Rethinking the human revolution: New behavioural and biological perspectives on the origin and dispersal of modern humans*, McDonald Institute Monographs, McDonald Institute for Archaeological Research, Cambridge, pp. 1–14.

Mellars, P 2015, 'Some key issues in the emergence and diversity of "modern" human behavior', in Y Kaifu, M Izuho, T Goebel, H Sato & A Ono (eds), *Emergence and diversity of modern human behaviour in Paleolithic Asia*, A&M University Press, College Station, TX, pp. 3–22.

Mellars, P & Stringer, C 1989, *The human revolution: behavioural and biological perspectives on the origins of modern humans*, Edinburgh University Press, Edinburgh.

Moore, MW 2013, 'Simple stone flaking in Australasia: patterns and implications', *Quaternary International*, vol. 285, pp. 140–149.

Morgan, LH 1877, *Ancient society or researches in the lines of human progress from savagery, through barbarism to civilization*, Henry Holt and Co, New York.

Movius, HL 1948, 'The Lower Palaeolithic cultures of southern and eastern Asia', *Transactions of the American Philosophical Society*, vol. 38, no. 4, pp. 329–420.

Noone, HVV 1943, 'Some Aboriginal stone implements of western Australia', *Records of the Australian Museum*, vol. 7, no. 3, pp. 271–280.

Norton, CJ & Jin, JJH 2009, 'The evolution of modern human behavior in East Asia: current perspectives', *Evolutionary Anthropology*, vol. 18, no. 6, pp. 247–260.

Norton, EJ 2016, 'Polished axes: object biographies and the writing of world prehistories', Ph.D. thesis, Department of Archaeology, University of Southampton, England.

Nowell, A 2010, 'Defining behavioral modernity in the context of Neandertal and anatomically modern human populations', *Annual Review of Anthropology*, vol. 39, pp. 437–452.

O'Connell, JF & Allen, J 1998, 'When did humans first arrive in greater Australia and why is it important to know?', *Evolutionary Anthropology*, vol. 6, no. 4, pp. 132–146.

O'Connell, J & Allen, J 2007, 'Pre-LGM Sahul (Pleistocene Australia–New Guinea) and the archaeology of early modern humans', in P Mellars, K Boyle, O Bar-Yosef & C Stringer (eds), *Rethinking the human revolution*, McDonald Institute for Archaeological Research, Cambridge, pp. 395–410.

O'Connell, JF, Allen, J, Williams, MAJ, Williams, AN, Turney, CSM, Spooner, NA, Kamminga, J, Brown, G & Cooper, A 2018, 'When did *Homo sapiens* first reach Southeast Asia and Sahul?', *Proceedings of the National Academy of the Sciences*, vol. 115, no. 34, pp. 8482–8490.

Perry, WJ 1923, *The children of the sun. A study in the early history of civilization*, Methuen & Co. Ltd, London.

Porr, M 2010, 'Identifying behavioural modernity: lessons from Sahul', *Bulletin of the Indo-Pacific Prehistory Association*, vol. 30, pp. 28–34.

Porr, M 2014, 'Essential questions: "modern humans" and the capacity for modernity', in RW Dennell & M Porr (eds), *Southern Asia, Australia and the search for human origins*, Cambridge University Press, Cambridge, pp. 257–264.

Porr, M & Matthews, JM 2017, 'Post-colonialism, human origins and the paradox of modernity', *Antiquity*, vol. 91, no. 358, pp. 1058–1068.

Sauer, CO 1962, 'Seashore – primitive home of man?' *Proceedings of the American Philosophical Society*, vol. 106, no. 1, pp. 41–47.

Schrire, C 1982, *The Alligator Rivers: prehistory and ecology in Western Arnhem Land*, Terra Australis #7, Australian National University, Canberra.

Shea, JJ 2010, 'Homo sapiens is as Homo sapiens was: behavioral variability versus "behavioral modernity" in Paleolithic archaeology', *Current Anthropology*, vol. 52, no. 1, pp. 1–35.

Smith, C & Jackson, G 2006, 'Decolonizing Indigenous archaeology: developments from down under', *The American Indian Quarterly*, vol. 30, no. 3, pp. 311–349.

Smith, L 2004, *Archaeological theory and the politics of cultural heritage*, Routledge, London and New York.

Smyth, RB 1878, *The Aborigines of Victoria: with notes relating to the habits of the natives of other parts of Australia and Tasmania*, 2 vols, John Ferres, Government Printer, Melbourne.

Spencer, B 1901, *Guide to the Australian ethnographical collection in the National Museum of Victoria*, Robert S. Brain, Government Printer, Melbourne.

Sterelny, K 2011, 'From hominins to humans: how sapiens became behaviourally modern', *Philosophical Transactions of the Royal Society B: Biological Sciences*, vol. 366, no. 1566, pp. 809–822.

Stern, N 2009, 'The archaeological signature of behavioural modernity: perspective from the southern periphery of the modern human range', in JJ Shea & DE Lieberman (eds), *Transitions in prehistory: essays in honor of Ofer Bar-Yosef*, Oxbow, Oxford, pp. 258–288.

Summerhayes, G & Ford, A 2014, 'Late Pleistocene colonisation and adaptation in New Guinea: implications for modelling modern human behaviour', in RW Dennell & M Porr (eds), *Southern Asia, Australia and the search for human origins*, Cambridge University Press, Cambridge, pp. 213–227.

Szabo, K, Brumm, A & Bellwood, P 2007, 'Shell artefact production at 32,000–28,000 BP in Island Southeast Asia: thinking across media?' *Current Anthropology*, vol. 48, no. 5, pp. 701–723.

Thomas, J 2013, *The birth of Neolithic Britain: an interpretive account*, Oxford University Press, Oxford.

Tsutsumi, T 2012, 'MIS3 edge-ground axes and the arrival of the first Homo sapiens in the Japanese archipelago', *Quaternary International*, vol. 248, pp. 70–78.

Tylor, EB 1865, *Researches into the early history of mankind and the development of civilisation*, John Murray, London.

Tylor, EB 1894, 'On the Tasmanians as representatives of Palaeolithic man', *Journal of the Anthropological Institute of Great Britain and Ireland*, vol. 23, pp. 141–152.

White [Schrire], C 1967, 'Early stone axes in Arnhem Land', *Antiquity*, vol. 41, no. 162, pp. 149–152.

Zilhão, J 2010, 'Comment on "Homo sapiens is as Homo sapiens was: behavioral variability versus behavioral modernity in Paleolithic archaeology" by J. J. Shea', *Current Anthropology*, vol. 52, no. 1, pp. 24–25.

SECTION 3

Representation, temporality and narratives of human origins

6

OLD FLAMES

Rekindling ideas of fire, humanity and representation through creative art practice

Ursula K. Frederick

The following eight pages comprise a visual essay. These images are intended to be viewed as a distinct body of work, a creative reflection on representations of early human life, considered through the lenses of fire and art. In association and following this essay, the author/ artist provides an account of her practice-led research process in developing the imagery for *Old Flames*.

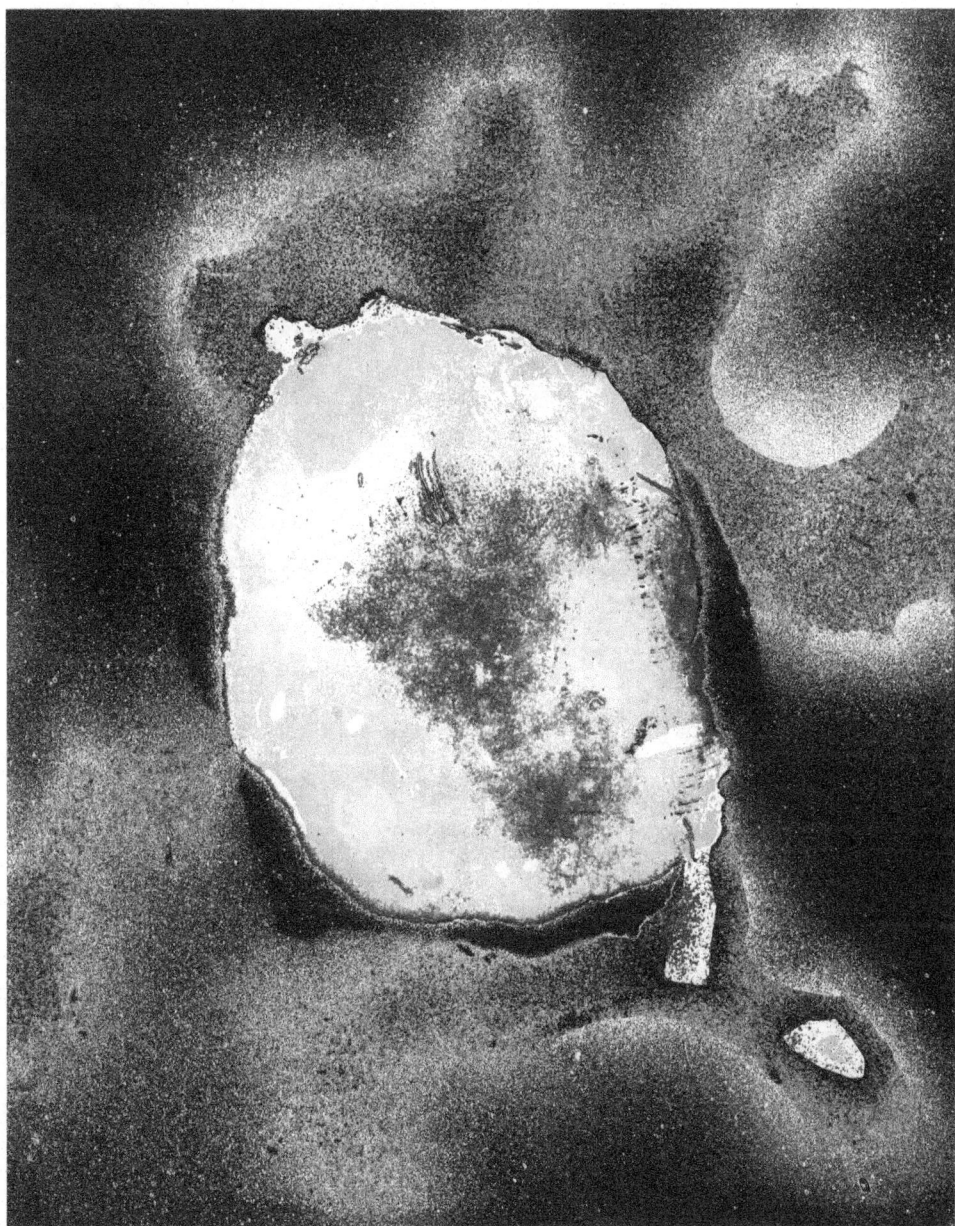

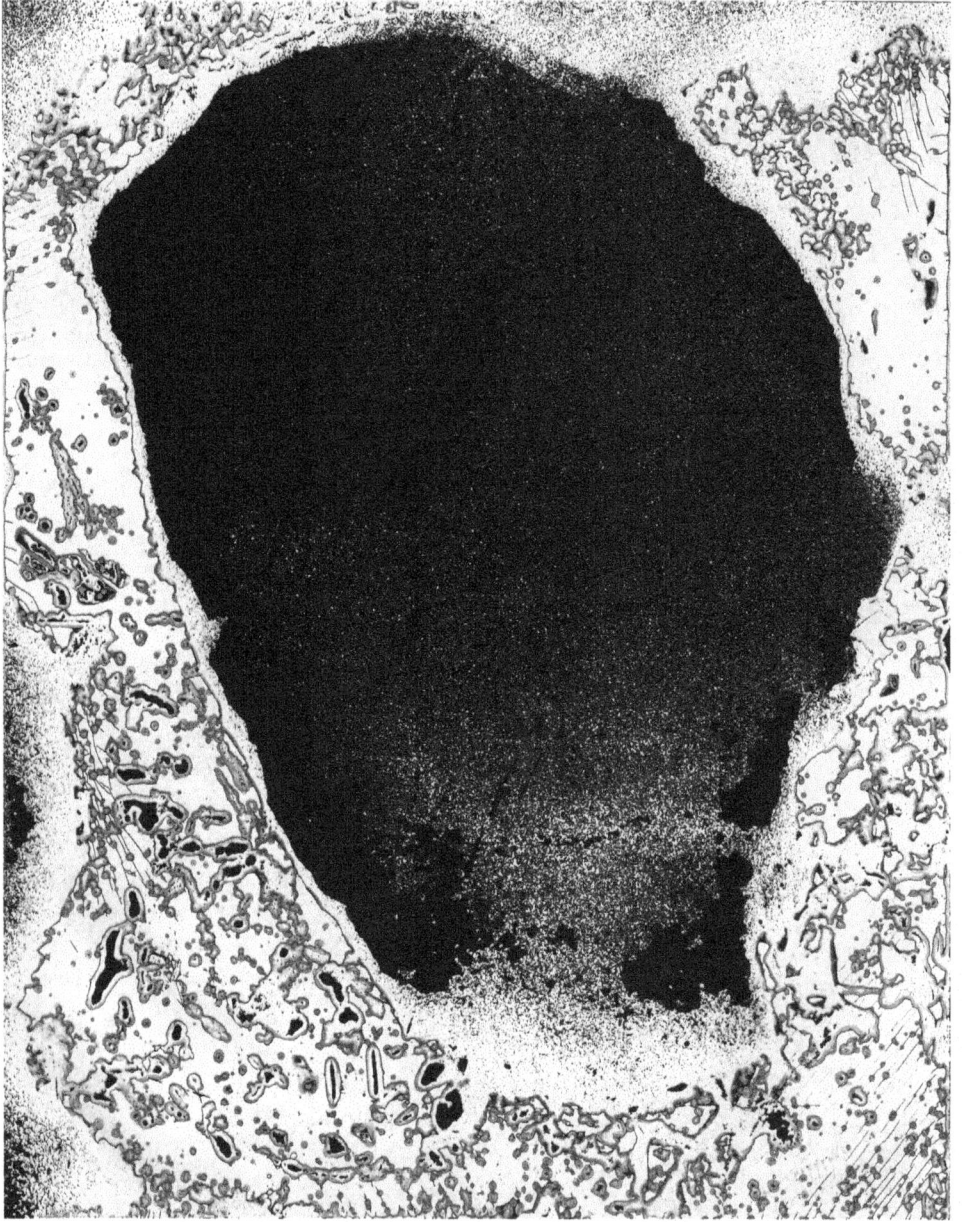

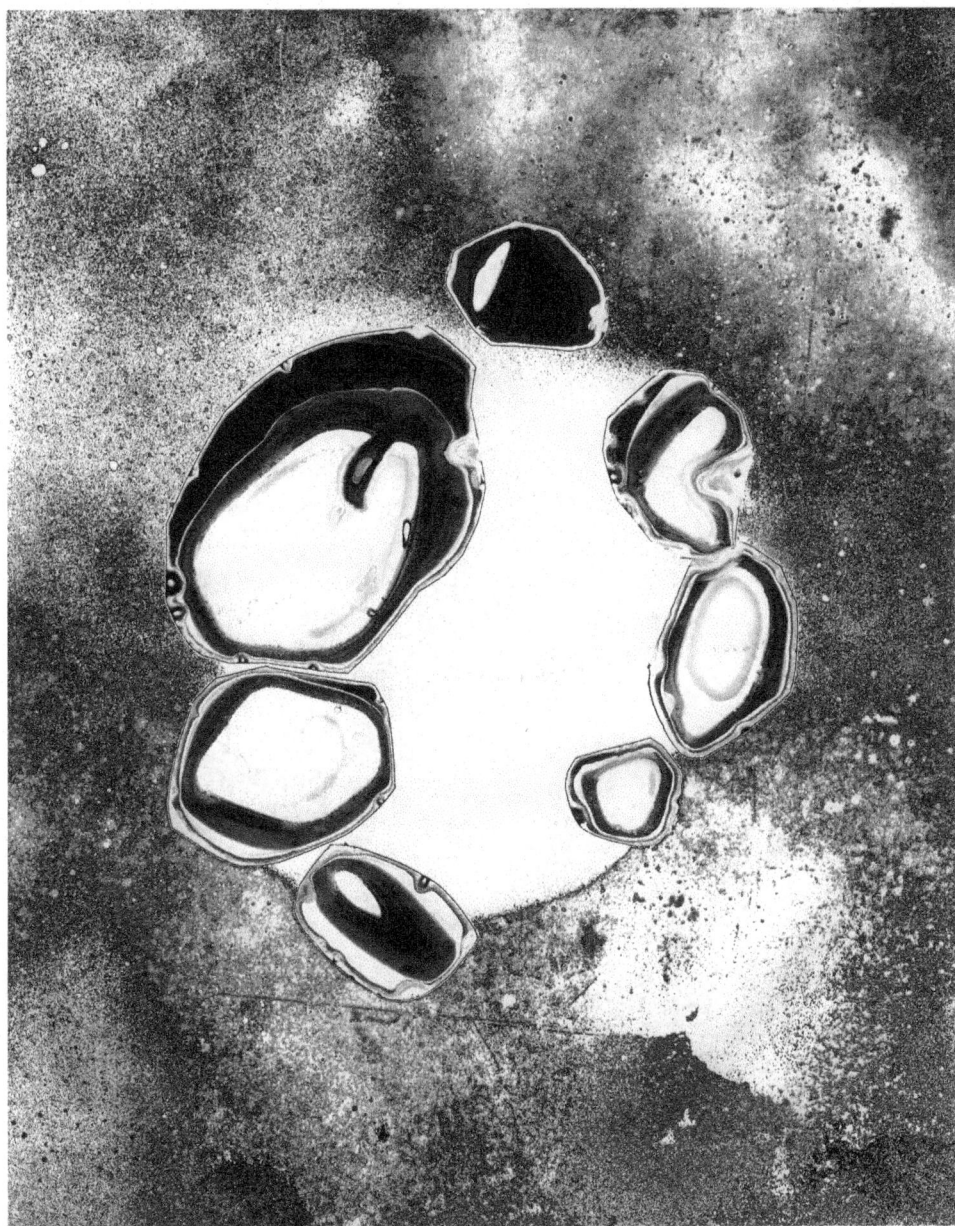

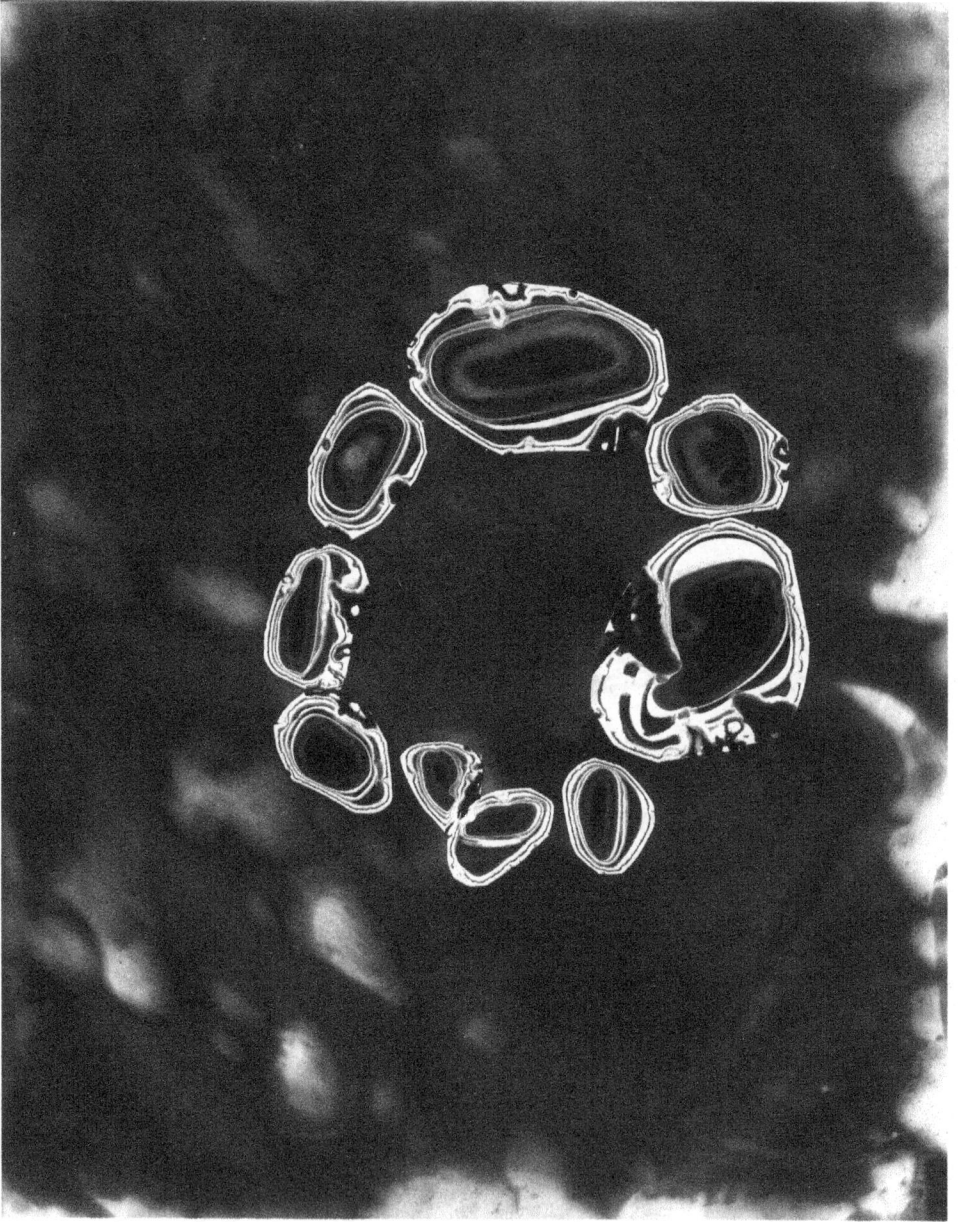

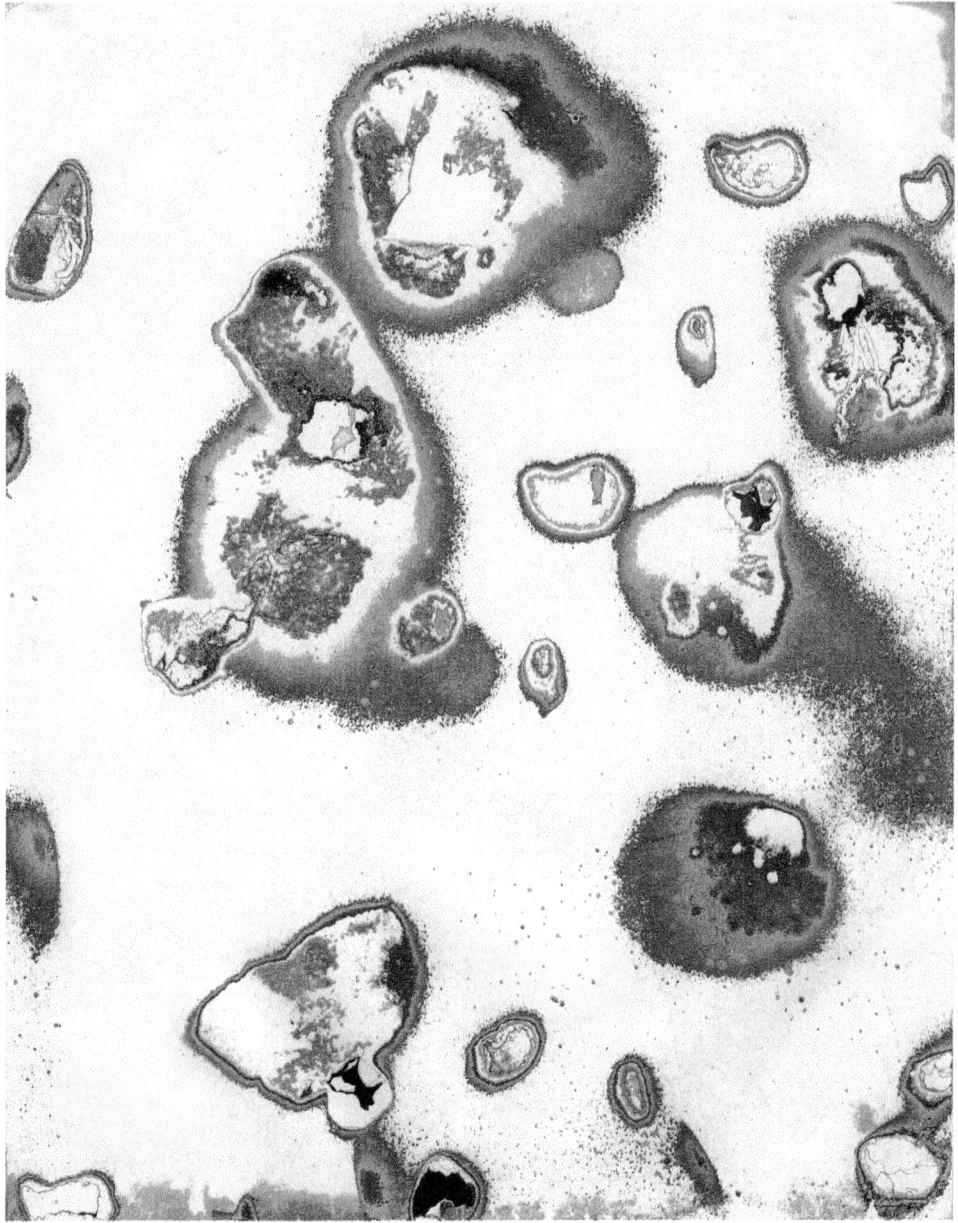

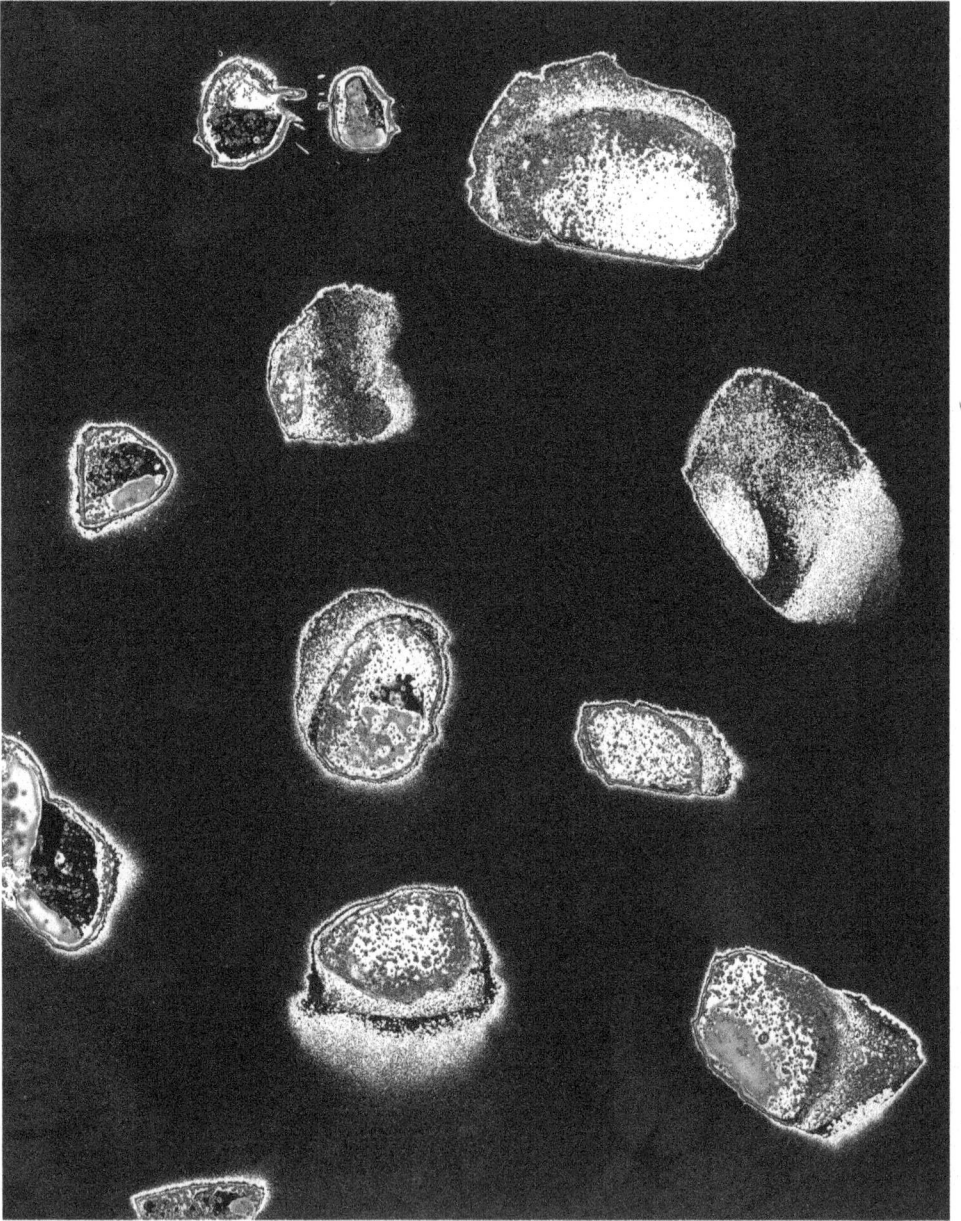

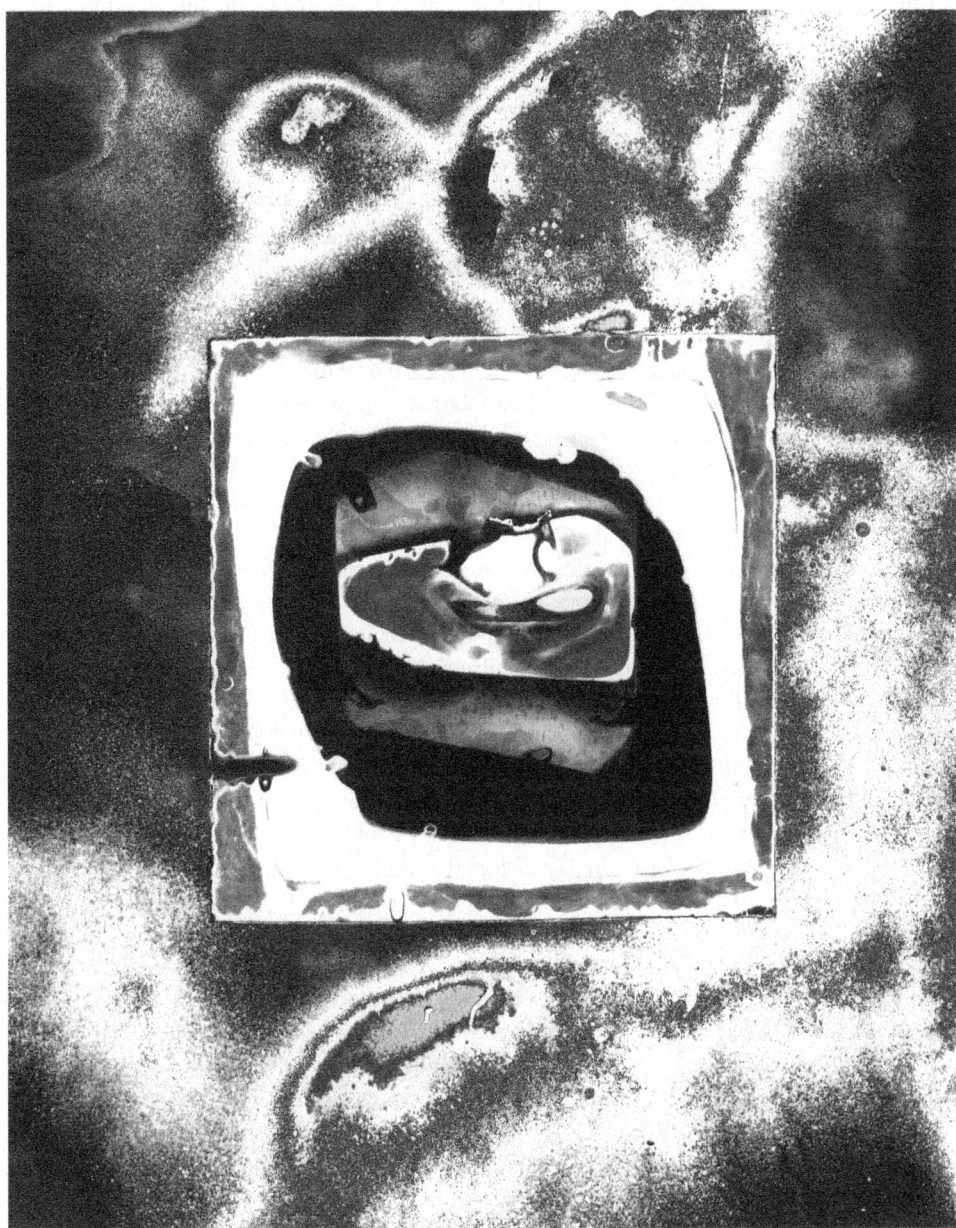

Introduction

For millennia, art has played a fundamental role in the conceptualisation and communication of knowledge regarding human origins.[1] Historically, there have been artists operating in the Western tradition who have depicted their ideas about early humans and there have been Indigenous artists who have used visual media to convey the creation stories of specific cultures. Furthermore, the figure of the artist has been a central feature in narratives of humanity's emergence. Indeed, in many visual reconstructions of human evolution the practice or presence of art serves to distinguish modern humans from other species. In short, there are various ways in which art and artists have become a persistent influence, both as subjects and producers, upon the visions of early human life with which we are most familiar.

However, we know from the scholarship undertaken to date (e.g. Conkey 1997; Gifford-Gonzalez 1993; Lucy 2002; Moser 1998) that many of these images depict an early human way of life for which there is either no known evidence or which is simply inaccurate. This is despite attempts by artists and illustrators to integrate the results of scientific research into their artwork. Due to the fact that many of the prevailing theories were deeply flawed and reconstructions were influenced by the ideologies of the time (Moser 1998), artists have played a role in perpetuating theories of evolutionary development that are both misinformed and damaging. As other authors (Berman 1999; Galanidou 2007; Gifford-Gonzalez 1993; Moser 1992; Sommer 2006) have demonstrated, the legacy of those images continues to reverberate in the reconstructions, popular perceptions, and media landscapes of the present.

Given this history and an awareness of the power that images carry it is easy to understand how an informed artist may be reluctant to engage with this topic. Yet the story of humanity and our presence in this world (often conveyed through interpretations of the body) is an enduring source of inspiration. In fact, some archaeologists (Bailey 2014; Harrison & Schofield 2010; Renfrew 2003) have suggested it is an abiding interest in the changing shape and form of human existence that unites archaeologists and artists. This shared curiosity and quest for understanding our origins is epitomised in the title of Paul Gauguin's painting *Where Do We Come From? What Are We? Where Are We Going?* (Renfrew 2003).

My purpose in emphasising the role and impact of art is, in the first instance, to suggest that any effort to undertake a decolonised approach to human origins research must take account of the visual context in which it operates. I also use it as a departure point for discussing my own art practice, in order to ask: what might a decolonised approach to imaging human origins look like as art? And more specifically, is it possible to image aspects of early human life, from the perspective of the present, without 'representing'?

In the pages that follow I outline my own creative-practice-led process of working through this challenge to present a context for viewing my series of images entitled *Old Flames*. As the title of the artwork and this chapter suggests, my approach to making these images and thinking about early human life is explored through the lens of fire.

Fire and art

For years debate has flourished over how human evolution took place and what traits signal or constitute the distinctive attributes of humanity. Although the timing and evidence is arguable, it is generally accepted that the habitual use or domestication of fire is a process that contributed significantly to human development (Roebroeks, Villa & Trinkaus 2011). Given the benefits attributed to the acquisition and control of fire espoused in both scientific discourse and mythology (Schrempp 2011) it is hardly surprising that fire features prominently in late modern and contemporary representations of early humans.

Whether rendered in the form of a lamplight, flaming torch, burning embers or simply as an amorphous glow, the presence of fire is a dominant motif in the iconography of human origins. Indeed, 'the visual theme of fire as a civilizing force' appears in the sixteenth-century engravings illustrating Vitruvius' *De architectura*, identified by Stephanie Moser as 'the earliest imagery devoted to the subject of prehistory' (Moser 1998, pp. 56–57).

In visual reconstructions of the kind analysed extensively by Moser, fire and art are often paired together, as if to clearly indicate the dawning of a set of modern behaviours. While there are examples where art activity is depicted independently of fire (e.g. Bayard's 1870 *Arts of Drawing and Sculpture during the Reindeer Epoch* and Burian's *The Dawn of Man*, 1951) it is far more common to see the 'ancestor-as-artist' working with the aid of firelight (Figure 6.1). This harnessing of art to fire implies a kind of reliance that in turn suggests a vision of art as occurring in dramatically darkened spaces.[2] Moreover, some authors have proposed that it is with the soft inconsistent flicker of the lit flame that rock art achieves its animated intent and cinematic quality (Wachtel 1993).

When viewed within a framework of human origins imagery the illuminated artist is clearly freighted with symbolism, yet there are a variety of practical and technical advances that fire brought to the lives of our early modern ancestors, including in the production of art. As well as providing light and warmth for cooking, protection, social exchange and new ways of disposing of the dead, the habitual use of fire ultimately advanced the creative potential and making skills of modern humans, by enabling new manufacturing technologies such as firing ceramics, forging metal, and so on. Moreover, as Wiessner (2014, p. 1049) suggests, firelight does not only extend the day but creates 'a qualitatively different time and space'. Perhaps this time and space enabled other modes of communication and thinking to flourish.

FIGURE 6.1 *Cro-Magnon Cave Artists at Font-de-Gaume Grotto at Les Eyzies-de-Tayac*, mural by Charles R. Knight, 1920

Source: Image reproduced with permission of the American Museum of Natural History Library.

To my mind the intersection of fire and art *and* the ambiguities associated with their emergence in human lifeways may be a productive starting point from which to approach a non-representational art practice. Fire, in particular, sparks the imagination because it is difficult to grasp. It is both 'elusive' and mesmerising in its potential and it is in the metaphor of fire that a multitude of allusions may glimmer. Anyone who has ever stared into flames will recognise the potential it provides for the mind to travel. This particular characteristic – the capacity for multivalence, imagination and abstraction – is especially relevant to my efforts, for reasons I address in the following section.

Archaeological illustrations and the representation of human origins

Through analyses of both historical and contemporary illustration scholars have demonstrated the instrumental role that visual representations play in the production, circulation, exchange and control of archaeological knowledge (Conkey 1997; Molyneaux 1997; Moser 2012; Perry 2009). Several writers have specifically noted how ideas and debates about human origins have been encapsulated as imagery, often generating inaccurate and/or ideologically-loaded stereotypes. Much of the critique to date has focussed on representations of the ancestral human form (Berman 1999; Conkey 1997; Moser 1998) and the physical body as a site for the projection of nineteenth-century anxieties around emergent evolutionary theory (Lucy 2002, p. 112). But we may also find cause for contestation in the depiction of material culture and how early humans are staged both within their surroundings and in relation to one another. In particular, scholars have interrogated the kinds of activities that are rendered in scenes of early human life.

Scenes of art production are amongst the more commonly portrayed pursuits associated with early modern humans, in fact the imaging of art creation may be regarded as 'representing the ultimate development in our evolution' (Moser 1998, p. 144). Presumably, the figure of the ancestor-as-artist has been such a central feature in narratives of humanity's emergence because of 'his'[3] capacity to engender and perform advanced mental processing and symbolic cultural behaviours. This is no more evident than in the vast array of popular imagery depicting human ancestors in the processes of making: usually in the form of painting, drawing, carving and small-scale sculpture.

Like many reconstructions of early humans these representations are problematic, not least because they perpetuate a universalised image of the artist as a white male mystic-bohemian manifesting his individual genius. Significantly, these representations also represent the very arena of cultural production *and* achievement as an exclusively male domain. Gifford-Gonzalez' (1993) analysis of dioramic representations of Cro-Magnons, for example, revealed that 90 per cent of the figures depicted creating art were male and only 10 per cent were female. This demonstrates, as Soussloff (1997) indicates, that the artist is a culturally-constructed concept. An analysis of the ancestor-as-artist figure and his attendant 'stone-age aesthetics' warrants a separate study in its own right.

Despite the great number of visual reconstructions depicting the ancestor-as-artist at work, the corpus of imagery he creates is similarly limited in scope. It is based on an iconic set of images derived from the cave and mobiliary art of the Upper Palaeolithic (Conkey 2010). By directly referencing and reiterating the art and material culture of sites like Font-de-Gaume, Altamira and Willendorf, these visual reconstructions firmly locate the birthplace of modern culture within western Europe. Never mind that some of the oldest art in the world is found on other continents (e.g. Aubert et al. 2014), some writers continue to observe 'a great awakening, very much a time of beginning for the human race ...' as evidenced by the art of Upper Palaeolithic Europe (Halverson 1987, p. 85). As Pleistocene dates on rock art and excavated deposits incorporating ancient pigments begin to accumulate in sites far beyond the European continent (Aubert, Brumm & Taçon 2017; David et al. 2013; Taçon et al. 2014) we might hope that the prevailing narrative of art's early origins in Europe is reframed to accommodate the wider archaeological evidence. However, as Moro Abadia (2015) has argued, conceptualisations of prehistoric art have been strongly influenced by disciplines other than archaeology and given the widespread circulation of Upper Palaeolithic images via academic and popular channels, and the values attributed to its naturalism, it is hard to imagine this dominant paradigm shifting anytime soon.

As writers (e.g. Galanidou 2007; Gifford-Gonzalez 1993; Moser 1998) have noted, many of the canonical images establish themes and theories that are passed down through images in subsequent decades. What is evident from their close and critical readings of visual reconstructions of human evolution is that a pretence to realism and representation plays an important role in the communication of concepts and theories. This brings me to the question of representation and the prospect of breaking through stereotypes.

Creative practice in archaeology and heritage research

Various attempts to decolonise archaeological practice and human origins research have been discussed amongst archaeologists, anthropologists and historians. One strategy proposed in the context of images is to embrace other disciplines and include new perspectives, that may 'esthetically challenge their viewers to think about the past, about what it means to be human' (Gifford-Gonzalez 1993, p. 38). Most recently an interdisciplinary approach has been advanced by archaeologists engaged with the contemporary world who see the integration of other disciplines in the process of 'doing' archaeology as a promising area of enquiry (Harrison & Schofield 2010). This position suggests that art practice may have a role to play in both the construction and dissemination of archaeological knowledge and heritage dis-course. Some archaeologists have even called upon artistic processes to demonstrate that archaeologists *construct* the past in the present (Holtorf 2004; Shanks 1997) and others have used contemporary art as a source of analogy and inspiration in their own interpretive work (Bailey 2014). Others have utilised creative processes as a means of decentring their own methodological conventions, to provoke new ways of doing fieldwork and documenting 'sites' (Bender, Hamilton & Tilley 2008; Watson 2004).

An exposure to art and a deeper understanding of the influence that imagery carries in scientific discourse and the popular imagination has led some archaeologists to rethink their own approach to visual communication. Rather than 'produce more factually accurate images' (Lovata 2008, p. 102) I am inclined to suggest, like Gifford-Gonzalez, and Bailey, that therein lies the problem. Drawing on John Berger's (1972) argument that realism in Western art has both masked and supported relations of social inequality, Gifford-Gonzalez (1993, pp. 28–29) points out realism is often read as objective truth and 'counts as a major argument in the plausibility of what is depicted'. Moreover, she argues that representational and illusionist styles of depiction are deployed in order to make speculative arguments or fictive scenarios all the more plausible as 'real facts'.

The real 'challenge is to make non-representational work and thus to avoid the restrictions that accompany the past-as-reconstruction's inherent smoothing out of reality's rough and often unpleasant ruptured surfaces' (Bailey 2014 p. 248). Is it possible to image human origins in a way that is non-representational? In the hope that a decentred art/archaeology practice may emerge, I have sought to 'embrace the non-explanatory' (Bailey 2014, p. 248) as a potential decolonising strategy.

In addition to those working from the disciplinary perspectives of archaeology and heritage research, there is a growing international body of Indigenous and non-Indigenous practitioners (artists, curators and museum professionals), as well as some institutions and arts organisations, who are actively engaging with the possibilities and challenges of art and curatorial practice as tools of decolonisation. Beyond being involved in discussions about what it actually means to decolonise curatorial spaces, practices and collections, some artists are also exploring decolonisation *as* art practice (Gamedze 2015).

Fire, photography and *Yesterday's Hearth*

My awareness of the power of imagery to both absorb and influence, to convey and inspire emotion and thought, is no doubt one of the reasons why I am personally drawn to both analysing and making artwork. Yet it also gives rise to a reflexive reluctance. It is challenging to create an art that explores fire as a fundamental influence in the development of humans and something of ongoing importance to people in the present, without reinforcing a suite of stereotypes rooted in colonialist thought. As suggested above, the non-representational may provide a way forward. Before I discuss my efforts experimenting with abstraction however, I need to discuss my experience of picturing hearths that led me there in the first place.

My first attempts to work with fire and the hearth specifically as a visual motif began as a series of photographs of extinguished campfires I encountered serendipitously in the Australian landscape. These sites of contemporary archaeology were sometimes quite discrete, a thin layer of ash resting on a grassy surface. At other times, they were more established. Before I settled on a particular approach to photographing these places, I experimented with different cameras: a prosumer Canon Digital SLR; the plastic medium format lomography Diana+; and a Hasselblad film camera with an 80mm lens. Although this achieved diverse results in clarity, colour range and mood, ultimately all three cameras retain a degree of representational veracity that is unique to photography.

My initial attention to these campfires was driven in part by an aesthetic response and by my interest in archaeologies of the contemporary world. At the time I commenced this project my research interests were focussed on contemporary archaeologies and I was curious as to where these campfires occurred and what fragments might remain in the ashes. If truth be told, as an artist part of what appealed to me about this 'site-type', if we might call it that, is that it may be seen to represent a set of practices that have endured for a very long time in one form or another.

Certainly, there are many variables which make the contemporary use of fire different to the past, not least why and how it is used and by whom; what fuel feeds the fire and how it is acquired; how fire is managed or controlled or what kind of debris we might find in the ashes, and so forth. But is it not also possible that the campfire and hearth may give rise to activities, feelings or sensations which foster a form of resemblance or point of connection?

The hearth is of course only one of many archaeological indicators of past fire practices, and as Roebroeks et al. (2011) propose, hearths are not definitively present in the archaeological record until a considerable time after the initial acquisition of fire by hominins. My interest is less in how hearths are construed as one of the 'hallmarks of humanity' (Moser 1992, p. 839) than how they may be rendered as a meeting place, both physically and conceptually, in and over time and space, between individuals and groups. Where people share stories, fictional and true, where they create a space for wonder and conversation. To see the remains of a campfire we can sense that a gathering has occurred. This is their appeal to me – the latency of conversation and creativity, the staring into the flames that provokes imaginative vision and thought.

One of the reasons why fire is a thought-provoking focus is because it is not simply anchored to one geographical point or species of origin. The fact that fire is thought to have been used by 'non-humans' in the broader evolutionary schema questions rather than affirms a discourse of human exceptionalism. In one sense then the presence and ambiguities associated with fire as motif and source of artistic inspiration may draw attention to the complexities in logic that attempt to 'describe the origin, historical development and character of humanity altogether' (Porr & Matthews 2017).

The photographs made in the series *Yesterday's Hearth* may be regarded as quite conventionally archaeological in that rather than capturing the activity in the moment, as in Olafur Eliasson's *The Large Fire Series* (1998–2005), they capture the trace of the fire only after it has occurred. This extinguishment lends an inherent pastness to the subject matter, which when aligned with photography's elegiac impulse may infuse a sense of nostalgia. But rather than see this material as dead matter (a common criticism of archaeology) or the notion of pastness as a distancing effect, I felt that it may compel the viewer to reflect on what might have occurred.

It is fair to say that although I had been inspired by the longevity of fire use in human activity, I had given little thought to what it meant in terms of human origins or how my photographs might sit within a repertoire of fire-themed artworks. In making photographs of these hearths I certainly wasn't seeking to represent 'the past' in the sense of some other contemporary artists (e.g. see Sonia Steifel in Lovata 2008). In this respect the series is distinctively different to the kind of illustrations and reconstructions produced by many artists to explicitly render past lifeways. Nor was it my goal to convey any specific message about the contemporary usage of fire (e.g. see *COOL BURN* 2016). I focussed on particular campfires because they are specific and localised instantiations of fireside activity but when grouped together or viewed in series (Figure 6.2) it is possible they may be read in comparison or as a typology and hence interpreted as a depiction of universalising experience.

I have mentioned *Yesterday's Hearth* here for the purpose of discussing my practice-led process of arriving at the present work. Precisely because of the problems posed by realism and photography's unique status as proof (Sontag 1977) I did not want it to be the focus of this chapter. It is important to note its influence, however, because it led me to reflect on my own creative practice and to wonder if it is possible to use art against image, photography against photography, not for the purpose of providing answers but to ask better questions.

One way this approach may be regarded as decolonising is because it shifts the focus of the authority from the author of the image onto its reader. Not only does the non-figurative photograph lead us away from evidentiary realism, the 'open narrative' of the non-figurative has the potential to compel the viewer to reflect and complete the image on their own

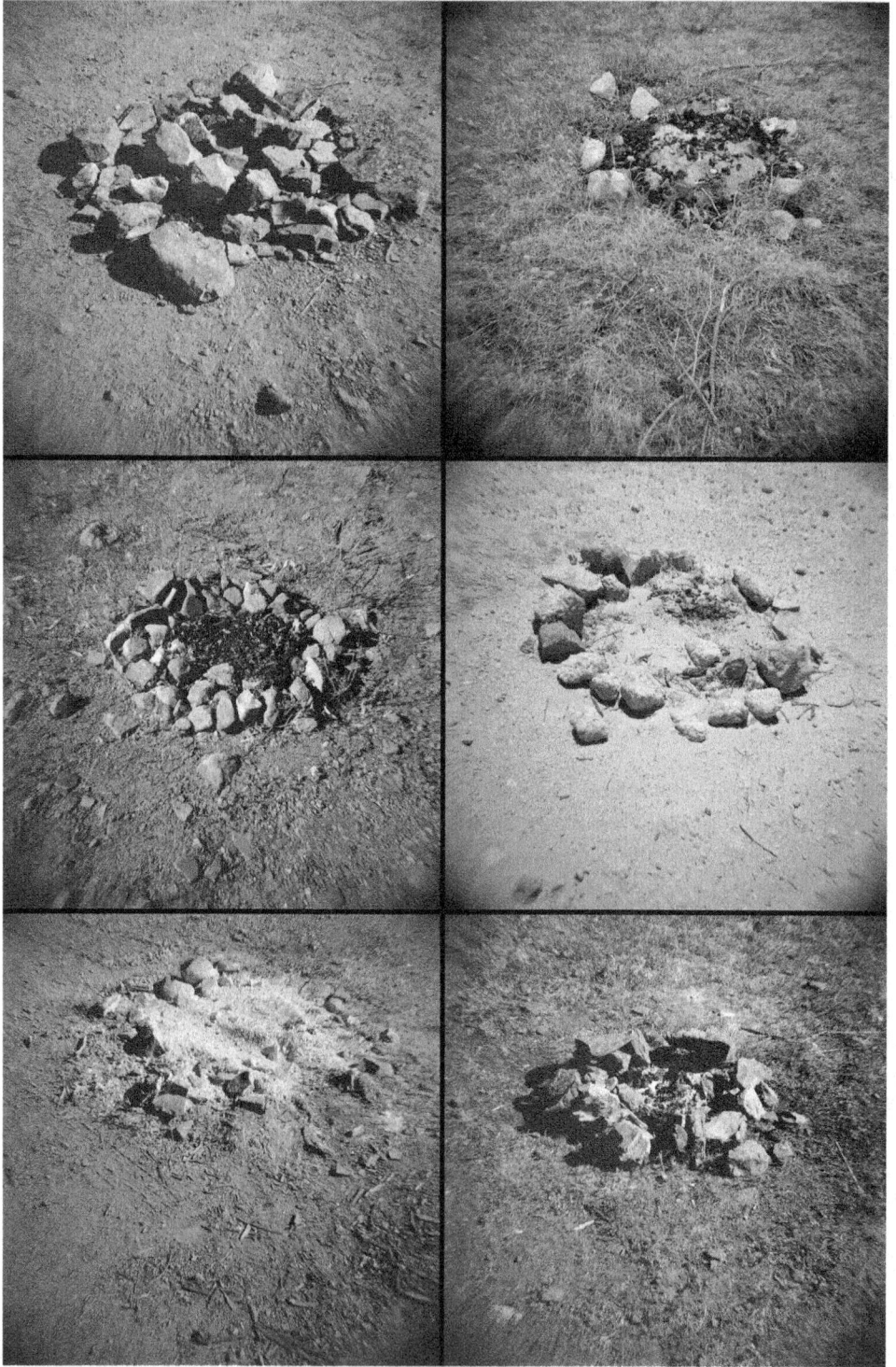

FIGURE 6.2 A selection of photographs from the series *Yesterday's Hearth*, U. K. Frederick, 2012–2016

terms. Ideally, the viewer will ask questions of the work, a provocation which starts with the specific, but which may lead out and beyond it to broader issues. What does the title of the work reflect? How important is it to the reading of the image? How was the image made? Does it matter what materials or techniques were used to make these images? What is an appropriate way to represent the impact of fire on human origins? Is it best conveyed through figurative or abstract imagery?

Stoking the flames: abstraction and the chemigram process

In order to move away from the realism of photography I turned to a field of analogue photographic practice which, with the advent of digital technologies, has come to be known as 'alternative' or 'experimental processes'. These analogue techniques include some of the oldest forms of photography and are relatively time, material and labour intensive. From its earliest history photographers have been demonstrating the expansive possibilities of the medium as 'simultaneously an investigation of reality and of the means of investigating that reality' (Rexer 2013, p. 11). In particular I focussed on a technique known as the chemigram.

In the words of Pierre Cordier, the artist who invented the technique and coined the term, the chemigram is an image produced from the reaction of chemical substances on photographic emulsions. Whereas in conventional black and white photographic printing the light sensitive paper is exposed with a negative image using light through an enlarger, with a standard chemigram there is no such 'image' exposure. Instead, the emphasis in the chemigram technique is on the processing or 'developing' and 'fixing' of the print and in the recognition that the developer will turn paper black and fixer will turn paper white.

A key principle of the chemigram process is that a coating material or *resist* applied to photographic paper will delay the effects of the photochemistry from acting on the paper. The role of resists is crucial because the presence of an image is dependent on the physical transformation of the substance coating the photographic paper as it is immersed in the baths of developer, fixer and water. An image gradually forms as the paper is moved back and forth between developer and fixer, as the resist breaks down.

Hence, while chemigrams are made from the manipulation of light sensitive papers and photochemistry, the process also incorporates a range of materials and techniques that are not used in conventional photography. In this respect the chemigram also has a relationship with drawing and painting (Anderson 2012). The chemigram does not require a 'safelight' and many artists make their chemigrams in normal room light. This can result in certain colours, predominately mauves and yellows, appearing in the print but in large part the image will have a black and white graphic appearance.

What is most important in the chemigram process is the physical nature of the resist, how it is applied and especially 'the way it is removed' (Cordier quoted in Biasino et al. 2007, p. 44). The choice of resist alone can generate enormous variation, as evidenced by the different effects of egg yolk, honey, glue, butter, and sticky tape/spray paint (Figure 6.3). Different mediums or resists have different characteristics which the chemigram not only reveals but inscribes on the photographic paper. Every substance has its own chemical structure which reacts differently to immersion and as the resist transforms it may crack, erode or simply lift away (Figure 6.4).

A resist may be left to dissolve or peel off in its own time, or the artist may intervene to speed the process. The development of the image will be affected by the temperature and

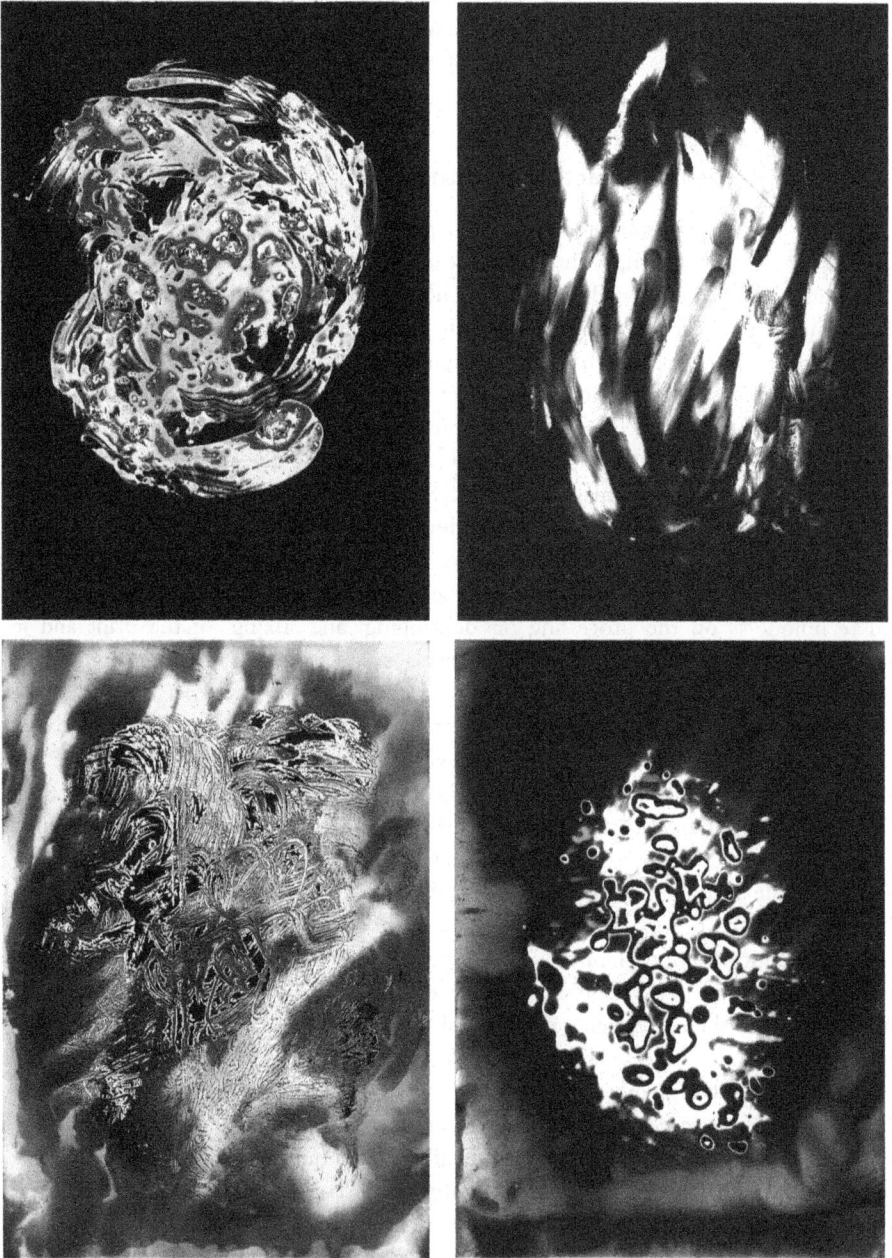

FIGURE 6.3 Chemigrams made using charcoal in egg yolk, vegemite, maple syrup, butter (clockwise from top left)

Source: Images: U. K. Frederick, 2017–2018.

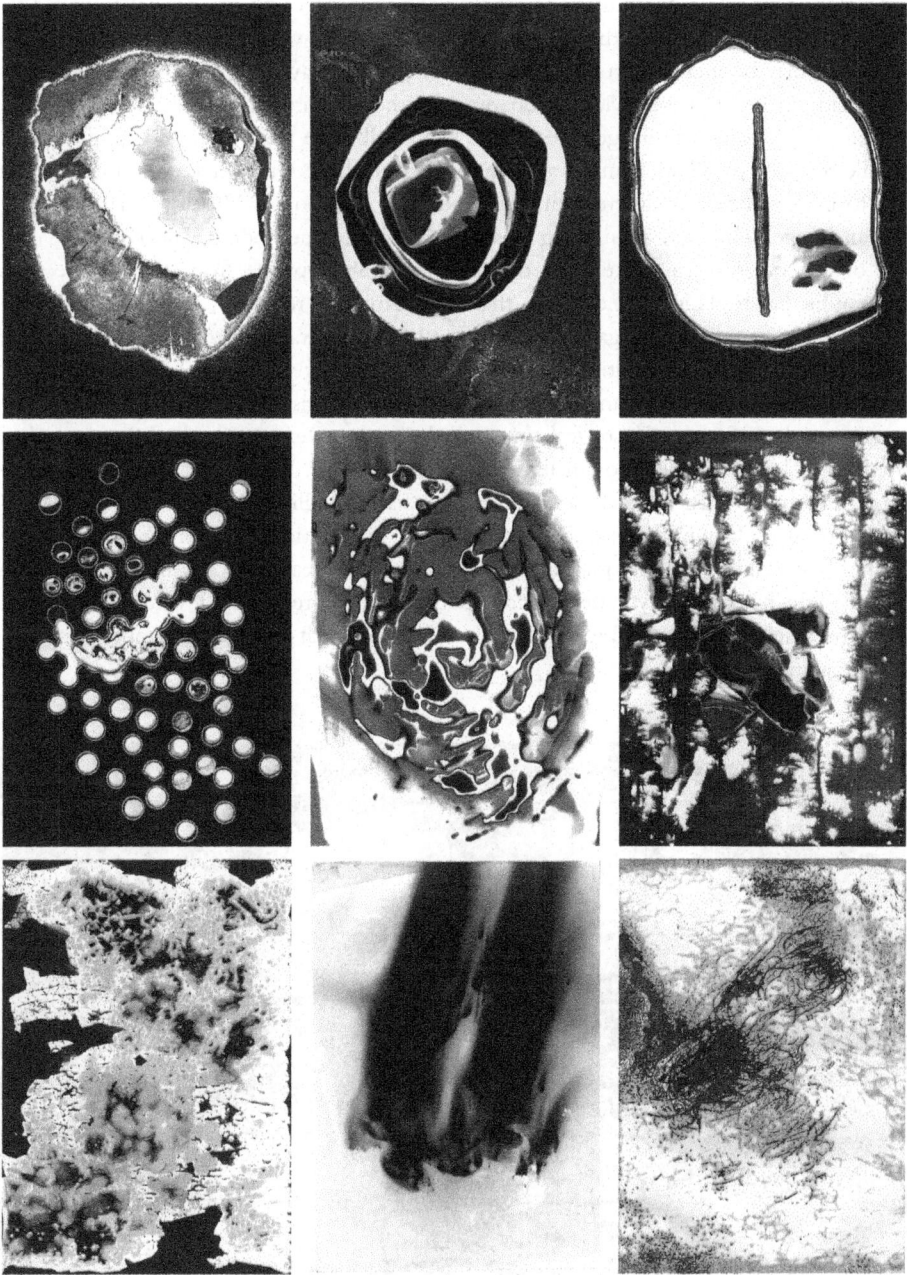

FIGURE 6.4 Chemigrams made using different materials
Source: Images: U. K. Frederick, 2017–2018.

humidity of the room, chemical baths and the water; the degree of agitation and time that the paper is immersed in each bath; and the number of times the paper is moved between the developer and fixer. In addition to manipulating the process through agitation and temperature, the artist may hasten the removal of a soft resist by wiping or washing it off whereas a hard resist may be incised, scrubbed or gradually pulled away. The edges of the resist or the breaks made in its surface provide an opening for the chemistry to enter and begin to react with the paper and as a result gestures of the hand will leave their own trace (Figure 6.5).

While there is always an element of chance, to control the image-making process the artist needs to understand how different materials perform and work with those characteristics to make an image. This way of making images is slow and methodical. Indeed, some of the more obdurate resists can take days or weeks to fully separate from the surface of the photographic paper. This is the duration that the chemigram registers rather than any referent to a given moment. In this regard it is unlike other photographic processes, and one might suggest it is even counter-intuitive or anti-thetical to how we think about photography.

Conceptually, what is relevant here is the chemigram registers the duration of its making but removes the referent of historical time and the trace of 'exterior reality' that is so deeply embedded in images made through lens-based photography. Its indexicality is instead found in the marks made with materials and the human hand. Phillippe Dasnoy (2007, p. 9) refers to the process as 'a world without a past, devoid of traditions, references, without competition … a world of inifinite graphic forms impossible to realize by any other process'. As a technique which is so deeply material and experimental and relatively devoid of conventional realism, the chemigram seemed to me the ideal medium with which to attempt re-imagining and re-imaging fire.

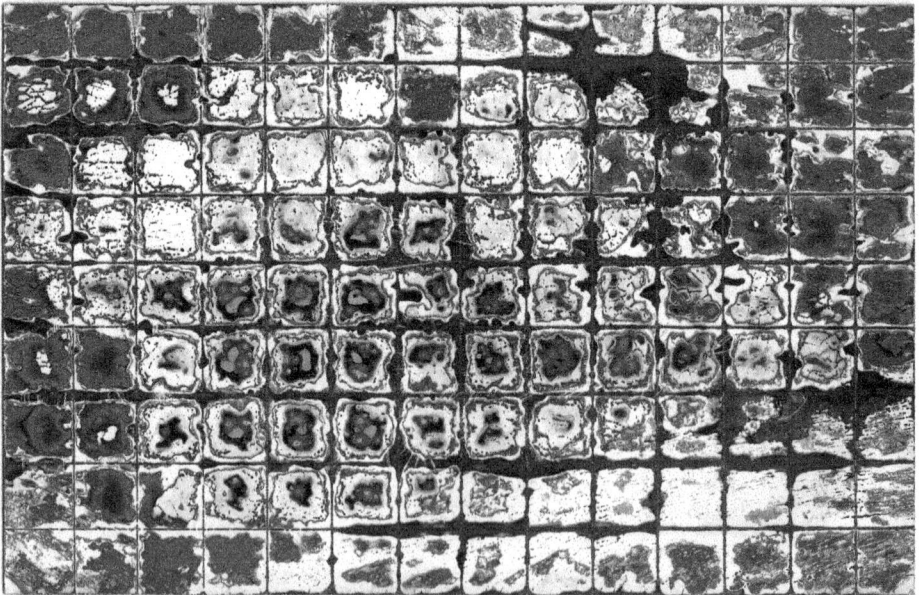

FIGURE 6.5 Chemigram showing the effect of lines incised as a grid
Source: Images: U. K. Frederick, 2017–2018.

As I noted in the previous section, the photographs in *Yesterday's Hearth* formed the inspiration and starting point for the images that compel this chapter. I looked at them after commencing my initial experimentation with the chemigram process and they helped me to develop ideas about possible shapes and compositions, as well as the materials I might bring into the mix. I thought about what materials might have been accessible to early humans: fats, proteins and various liquids. As a result, I felt compelled to trial the use of milk and honey, plant juices as well as other 'natural' products like charcoal suspended in egg yolk. But in recognition that I am not living in the past and do not wish to romanticise those materials, I also employed paint, wax, nail polish, sesame oil and vegemite. All of the materials were at my immediate disposal and came from my domestic environment: the ash from my backyard firepit; the maple syrup from the kitchen cupboard; the spray adhesive from my studio (Figure 6.5). Once I had trialled these different media and understood how they may form the impressions on the photographic paper, I used them selectively and in combination to undertake my own exploration into the themes of fire, humanity and representation.

The strident abstraction of these images is offered as a counterpoint to the representationalism so prevalent and persuasive in the visual discourse of the ancestor-as-artist figure and other imaginings of early humans. These images convey not only my own expression through engagement with the chemigram process but will hopefully urge viewers to question *how images work*. This is, as we know from ongoing critical analysis of visual traditions in archaeology, a vital pathway towards decolonising human origins research.

Conclusion

Images are integral to the practice of archaeology and art has played an important role in the formulation of ideas about human origins. In addition to illuminating persistent tropes and conventions in the visual traditions of archaeology, scholars have identified *how* ideological biases, misconceptions and evolutionary schema are woven into the images archaeologists make and use. While such critique is important, through this paper I have sought to consider whether art practice might also serve a role in human origins research.

In making *Old Flames* I have not sought to convey any particular truth but to convey instead the speculative, experimental and multivalent aspects of our research. I think of this artwork as a 'raw articulation' of the artistic and archaeological 'that embraces misunderstanding, seeks complexity, and creates what is difficult (perhaps impossible) to digest, explain, or interpret' (Bailey 2014, pp. 232–235). Much like some photographs that fail to represent, these non-representational images 'intentionally leave open our understanding', amplifying rather than constraining the possibilities of interpretation. The effect I hope, is to provoke reflection and questioning; perhaps, illuminating the role that art can play in thinking about archaeology and its use of imagery and the past more generally.

Like most artists who feel their work should stand or fall on its own merit, I have not attempted to explain *Old Flames* except to provide some context for how and why the images were made in the first place. What I will add is that the images are not based on archaeological data, though for some viewers they may bring to mind certain aspects of the 'visual language of archaeology' (Moser 1992). What the images mean, individually or as a collective, is for the viewer/reader to consider. That is, it is intended to provoke thinking about fire, photography, humanity, the challenge of representation and the *work* of art.

Acknowledgments

Ursula would like to thank the editors for the invitation to participate in the Wenner-Gren Foundation Workshop *Decolonising Human Origins* held at the University of Western Australia and the opportunity to present a creative-practice-led contribution to this volume. During the preparation of this paper Ursula received funding support through an Australian Research Council Discovery Early Career Research Award Project (DE170101351). Unless otherwise stated, all illustrations in this chapter are the work of the author, Ursula K. Frederick.

Notes

1 It is not my intention here to enter into the thorny and somewhat tired debate about what constitutes 'art', either in the past or present. Here what art is, is taken in a broad sense, see Spivey, N. *How Art Made the World*.
2 An assertion no doubt influenced by the discoveries of Upper Palaeolithic cave art.
3 This pronoun is italicized to highlight the intentionality of the gender. For analyses of gender in representations of human origins see Berman 1999; Conkey 1997; Galanidou 2007; Gifford-Gonzalez 1993.

References

Anderson, C 2012, *The experimental photography workbook: a manual of analog black & white darkroom practice*, Christina Z. Anderson, Bozeman, MT.

Aubert, M, Brumm, A, Ramli, M, Sutikna, T, Saptomo, EW, Hakim, B, Morwood, MJ, van den Bergh, GD, Kinsley, L & Dosseto, A 2014, 'Pleistocene cave art from Sulawesi, Indonesia', *Nature*, vol. 514, pp. 223–228.

Aubert, M, Brumm, A & Taçon, PSC 2017, 'The timing and nature of human colonization of Southeast Asia in the Late Pleistocene: a rock art perspective', *Current Anthropology*, vol. 58, no. S17, pp. S553–S566.

Bailey, D 2014, 'Art//archaeology//art: letting-go beyond', in IA Russell & A Cochrane (eds), *Art and archaeology: collaborations, conversations, criticisms*, One World Archaeology #11, Springer, London, pp. 231–250.

Bender, B, Hamilton, S & Tilley, C 2008, *Stone worlds: narrative and reflexivity in landscape archaeology*, Routledge, London and New York.

Berger, J 1972, *Ways of seeing*, BBC/Penguin, London.

Berman, J 1999, 'Bad hair days in the Paleolithic: modern (re)constructions of the Cave Man', *American Anthropologist*, vol. 101, no. 2, pp. 288–304.

Biasino, F, Butor, M & Cordier, P 2007, *Pierre Cordier: le chimigramme = the chemigram*, Racine, Brussels.

Conkey, M 1997, 'Mobilizing ideologies. Paleolithic "art," gender trouble, and thinking about alternatives', in LD Hager (ed.), *Women in human evolution*, Routledge, London and New York, pp. 172–207.

Conkey, M 2010, 'Images without words: the construction of prehistoric imaginaries for definitions of "Us"', *Journal of Visual Culture*, vol. 9, no. 3, pp. 272–283.

COOL BURN 2016, curated by Aleshia Lonsdale and Phoebe Cowdery. Available from: https://www.thecorridorproject.org/new-page-20 [20 October 2018].

Dasnoy, P 2007, 'Foreword', in F Biasino, M Butor & P Cordier (eds), *Pierre Cordier: le chimigramme = the chemigram*, Racine, Brussels, pp. 9–10.

David, B, Geneste, JM, Petchey, F, Delannoy, JJ, Barker, B & Eccleston, M 2013, 'How old are Australia's pictographs? A review of rock art dating', *Journal of Archaeological Science*, vol. 40, pp. 3–10.

Frederick, UK 2012–2016, *Yesterday's Hearth*, photographic series.

Galanidou, N 2007, 'In a child's eyes: human origins and Paleolithic life in children's book illustrations', in N Galanidou & LH Dommasnes (eds), *Telling children about the past: an interdisciplinary perspective*, International Monographs. University of Michigan Press, Ann Arbor, pp. 145–172.

Gamedze, T 2015, 'Decolonization as art practice', AFRICANAH.org. Available from: https://africanah.org/decolonization-as-art-practice [20 October 2018].

Gifford-Gonzalez, D 1993, 'You can hide, but you can't run: representations of women's work in illustrations of Paleolithic life', *Visual Anthropology Review*, vol. 9, no. 1, pp. 22–41.

Halverson, J 1987, 'Art for art's sake in the Paleolithic', *Current Anthropology*, vol. 28, no. 1, pp. 63–89.

Harrison, R & Schofield, J 2010, *After modernity: archaeological approaches to the contemporary past*, Oxford University Press, Oxford.

Holtorf, C 2004, 'Incavation – Excavation – Exhibition', in N Brodie & C Hills (eds), *Material engagements: studies in honour of Colin Renfrew*, McDonald Institute for Archaeological Research, Cambridge, pp. 45–53.

Lovata, T 2008, 'People make fire: archaeology and the art of Sonja Stiefel', *Public Archaeology*, vol. 7, no. 2, pp. 101–113.

Lucy, M 2002, 'Cormon's "Cain" and the problem of the prehistoric body', *Oxford Art Journal*, vol. 25, no. 2, pp. 109–126.

Molyneaux, B 1997, *Cultural life of images: visual representation in archaeology*, Routledge, London.

Moro Abadía, O 2015, 'The reception of Paleolithic art at the turn of the twentieth century: between archaeology and art history', *Journal of Art Historiography*, vol. 12, pp. 1–23.

Moser, S 1992, 'The visual language of archaeology: a case study of the Neanderthals', *Antiquity*, vol. 66, pp. 831–844.

Moser, S 1998, *Ancestral images: the iconography of human origins*, Cornell University Press, Ithaca, NY.

Moser, S 2012, 'Archaeological visualization: early artifact illustration and the birth of the archaeological image', in I Hodder (ed.), *Archaeological theory today*, Polity, Cambridge and Malden, MA, pp. 292–322.

Perry, S 2009, 'Fractured media: challenging the dimensions of archaeology's typical visual modes of engagement', *Archaeologies*, vol. 5, no. 3, pp. 389–415.

Porr, M & Matthews, J 2017, 'Post-colonialism, human origins and the paradox of modernity', *Antiquity*, vol. 91, no. 358, pp. 1058–1068.

Renfrew, C 2003, *Figuring it out. The parallel visions of artists and archaeologists*, Thames and Hudson, London.

Rexer, L 2013, *The edge of vision: the rise of abstraction in photography*, Aperture, New York.

Roebroeks, W, Villa, P & Trinkaus, E 2011, 'On the earliest evidence for habitual use of fire in Europe', *Proceedings of the National Academy of Sciences of the United States of America*, vol. 108, no. 13, pp. 5209–5214.

Schrempp, G 2011, 'Catching Wrangham: on the mythology and the science of fire, cooking, and becoming human', *Journal of Folklore Research*, vol. 48, no. 2, pp. 109–132.

Shanks, M 1997, 'Photography and archaeology', in B Molyneaux (ed.), *Cultural life of images: visual representation in archaeology*, Routledge, New York, pp. 73–98.

Sommer, M 2006, 'Mirror, mirror, on the wall: Neanderthal as image and "distortion" in early 20th-century French science and press', *Social Studies of Science*, vol. 36, no. 2, pp. 207–240.

Sontag, S 1977, *On photography*, Farrar, Straus & Giroux, New York.

Soussloff, CM 1997, *The absolute artist: the historiography of a concept*, University of Minnesota Press, Minneapolis and London.

Taçon, PSC, Tan, NH, O'Connor, S, Xueping, J, Gang, L, Curnoe, D, Bulbeck, D, Hakim, B, Sumantri, I, Than, H, Sokrithy, I, Chia, S, Khun-Neay, K & Kong, S 2014, 'The global implications of the early surviving rock art of greater Southeast Asia', *Antiquity*, vol. 88, pp. 1050–1064.

Wachtel, E 1993, 'The first picture show: cinematic aspects of cave art', *Leonardo*, vol. 26, no. 2, pp. 135–140.

Watson, A 2004, 'Making space for monuments: notes on the representation of experience', in C Renfrew, C Gosden & E DeMarrais (eds), *Substance, memory, display: archaeology and art*, McDonald Institute for Archaeological Research Monograph, Cambridge, pp. 79–96.

Wiessner, PW 2014, 'Embers of society: firelight talk among the Ju/'hoansi Bushmen', *Proceedings of the National Academy of Sciences of the United States of America*, vol. 111, no. 39, pp. 14027–14035.

7

ORIENTALISM AND ORIGINS

The search for firsts in the 'Cradle of Civilisation'

Allison Mickel

Introduction

> After the ancestors of Man learn to walk upright, on two legs, Man walks northward, Out of Africa. After a little while, he starts to build houses and settle down – ending his wild hunting and gathering ways. The place where he settles is the Middle East, or the Near East, or the 'cradle of civilization'. There, he goes on to invent the major features of civilization – agriculture, domestication of animals, writing, and governance – all of the things that later allow us to recognize him as Man.

This sequence of events, the traditional metanarrative of prehistory, is cartoonish in its simplicity. What makes it ridiculous, however, is not only the image of an independent, stoic, broad-shouldered individual striding confidently from continent to continent – but also for the sense of directionality it implies, the impression it gives that this course of history was the only logical progression of events. There is a teleology to this narrative; it is emplotted (cf. White 1987) with a certain endpoint in mind.

That endpoint, of course, is not in the Middle East. Such a metanarrative of human history, as popularly conceived, leads onward to the classical civilisations of Greece and Rome where man invents (among other things) democracy and philosophy. The story then reaches its culmination in modern European and American society, creating a narrative arc: picking up *in media res* as the morphologically modern species leaves Africa, moves through Middle Eastern ancient history, continues on to the Classical Greco-Roman world and ends in Euro-American modernity. It is a story with momentum. It is a story of resolving a series of discrete challenges, and it is a story with a resolution.

This grand narrative is pervasive and powerful. It appears, in some form, in most grade school student textbooks. It is reinforced through popular publications about archaeology and history, and it serves to underpin nationalist narratives especially in Europe and the United States (Brusius 2017; Matthews 2003; Scarre 1990; Taagepera 1978; Wailes & Zoll 1995). It appears to tell the all-encompassing, universal history of humankind, but has in fact been constructed over centuries of archaeological and historical scholarship, shaped by particular social and political contexts.

The concept of 'human origins' has been variably defined in different contexts according to divergent scientific, political and social concerns. The lack of consensus over where humans 'begin' is apparent even within contemporary archaeology, where biological anthropology seeks evidence of human characteristics in hominid ancestors from millions of years ago, while scholars such as Colin Renfrew (2006) argue for a more recent origin point 60,000 years ago as the beginning of a new and distinct human evolutionary process from what came before.

In late eighteenth-century Europe, the definition of origins centred on the distinctive characteristics of Western civilisation, and excavation was the chosen mode of inquiry for investigating origins thus defined. The interest in the origins of recognisably Western society was entangled, of course, with an imperialist desire for expansion. If researchers could demonstrate a cultural, ancestral link to the lands being dug into, the states sponsoring this research could defend taking over these territories. Archaeology was thereby enrolled to justify conquest over regions in terms of a rightful reclamation, rather than a violent military invasion (Bahrani 1998; García 2007).

Early excavations accordingly focused especially on sites mentioned in the Bible and other ancient texts deemed to be part of the cultural inheritance of Europe. Félicien de Saulcy, for instance, started excavating in Jerusalem in 1860, imagining himself to be uncovering the tombs of the House of David (de Saulcy 1865). Fifteen years prior, Sir Austen Henry Layard had begun excavating at Nimrud with an intention of identifying which Biblical city the ruins represented (Layard 1849). And from 1870 to 1890, Heinrich Schliemann excavated the mound at Hissarlik in Turkey, searching for evidence that it had once been the ancient city of Troy (Schliemann 1875). Locating these sites was integral to building up the historical narrative explaining how modern Western civilisation came to be.

The ways in which these early excavations proceeded further illuminates how the sites were meant to slot unproblematically into the unilinear narrative of the development of Western society. The digging strategies of the earliest archaeologists notoriously slashed through phases of occupation later than the particular period of interest, destroying evidence of more recent Arab, Persian, and Muslim communities. Layard, for example, famously tunnelled along the walls that he located at Nimrud in pursuit of artefacts and art objects that he could send back to the British Museum (Chevalier 2012; Larsen 1996). Moreover, the movement of artefact assemblages from sites in the Middle East to museums in the West is a physical embodiment of the vision of progress that structured early archaeological fieldwork. While these objects were invented and created in the Middle East, they were seen as rightfully belonging in the hallowed institutions of European and American museums. Accordingly, they were shipped to these museums abroad. These physical objects functioned as concrete illustrations of the imagined 'torch of civilisation', passing from the Middle East onward to the West – and importantly, leaving gaps in the assemblages and sites that remained in the countries where they were found.

But the memoirs, diaries, letters, and publications of early archaeologists working in the Middle East prefigured this emptiness, this sense of loss, in the way they wrote about the people and landscapes they encountered over the course of archaeological fieldwork. They portrayed the land as barren and the people as having fallen from grace, as having degenerated from the glorious ancient civilisations of the distant past. In the 1880s, for instance, the Babylonian Exploration Fund's team of Americans traveling through Iraq (then a province of the Ottoman Empire) in search of Babylonian remains described the people they encountered as 'vilely dirty', 'half-savage people', 'degraded', and evidence of 'evolution in reverse' (Kuklick 1996, pp. 46–47). Nineteenth-century explorers and scholars routinely refused to believe that the contemporary people they encountered could be the direct descendants of the builders of great civilisations like Assyria, Babylon, Nubia, and Pharaonic Egypt and sought alternative explanations for how the contemporary communities could have arrived to the region through some later, separate processes (Kendall 1996; Wynn 2007).

Their rhetoric framed the Middle East as a place paused in time, or worse: a place that had slipped backward from the peak of culture and civilisation that archaeological excavation sought to uncover. Early archaeological research and publications thereby placed the Middle East on an alternative time scale from that which led to contemporary societies in Europe and the United States. This out-of-time temporal definition constructed the Middle East solely as the site for the *origins* of civilisation – the place where key societal inventions and transformations occurred, but not the place where it continued to emerge, grow, and change. The Middle East, through this rhetoric, became identified as the ancestral 'cradle of civilisation', but not civilisation's current, fully-fledged home and habitat.

The first use of the term, 'the cradle of civilisation', is generally traced to French historian Charles Rollin's *Ancient History*, first published in 1734, a period of rife competition between Britain and France for colonial expansion, particularly in North America and the Caribbean. In his text, Rollin referred to Egypt as the place 'that served at first as the cradle (if I may be allowed the expression) of the holy nation' (1879, p. ii). He went on, however, to state that Egypt 'afterwards was a severe prison, and a fiery furnace to it [the holy nation]', reflecting a prevailing ideology justifying European colonialism – the notion that non-Western societies had somehow regressed and degraded, that righteousness was alien to the places and communities invaded for imperialist aims (Rollin 1879, p. ii). The context surrounding the very first known use of this phrase illustrates the problematic implications of searching for a birthplace of civilisation. The location, so identified, becomes nothing *more* than its birthplace, cast thereafter as an anti-home, a region that is categorically hostile to the development and flourishing of human society.[1]

Despite these colonialist origins and implications, however, this turn of phrase has continued to appear in both vernacular and academic contexts. Its meaning has expanded far beyond Egypt, referring equally to the area between the Tigris and Euphrates Rivers – but sometimes as well all of the land between these two areas (e.g. Maisels 1993). Such language evokes powerful, persisting imagery, with connotations that continue to affect conceptions of the ancient and contemporary Middle East. Indeed, many scholars have pointed out and critiqued the notion of the Middle East as the birthplace of civilised society. In the section that follows, I first attempt (and fail) to define the cradle geographically, then review the insights of others who have problematised the persisting phrase. From there, I argue that archaeology – through the physical and discursive processes of fieldwork, publication, and publicisation – aids in entrenching the view of the Middle East as the site of civilisation's origins but an inhospitable place for its long-term development. The longtime hunt for evidence that pushes back ever further the earliest dates of key human inventions, the retrieval of such material evidence from a landscape characterised otherwise as barren and hostile, the separation of the remarkable antiquities in Western museum displays from the places and layers of soil that are used to identify the early inventions and transformations of human societies – all of these construct the Middle East spatially and temporally as the place where human civilisation began but did not belong. Archaeological storytelling and fieldwork practices reinforce one another in a visible, physical, and politically powerful way, making the 'cradle of civilisation' more than a metaphor.

Critiques of the cradle

Where exactly is the cradle of civilisation? What are its boundaries? It is nearly impossible to find maps of the so-called 'cradle of civilisation' – speaking to the indefinite nature of this term. Somewhat more common – especially in media dedicated to popular Biblical history, K-12 lesson planning, and Wikipedia – are maps of the 'Fertile Crescent', a related and commonly co-occurring term for the areas of the Middle East where settled life, agriculture, and animal domestication occurred (Bible History Online 2002; NormanEinstein 2005; Smith 2017; ThingLink 2017).

But even with this apparently easier-to-define term, contemporary maps do not agree on the boundaries of the Fertile Crescent (see Figure 7.1). Most indicate a region with shading that extends from the southern tip of contemporary Israel, bending northward through Lebanon and into Syria, then follows the path of the Tigris and Euphrates rivers to the Persian Gulf. Some, however, stop just short of the Gulf coastline. Other maps continue through the Sinai Peninsula into Egypt. A few maps highlight two separate regions, raising the question of whether two separate areas can be 'the' Fertile Crescent. Some maps of the Fertile Crescent include Cyprus; others don't. Several of them reach up into the Anatolian plateau of Turkey. The extents of the map vary in all directions, and there seems to be no agreement over whether the eastern end of the Fertile Crescent lies on the southern, northern, or western coastline of the Persian Gulf (in contemporary Iran, Iraq, Kuwait, or Saudi Arabia).

This is because the Fertile Crescent is not real, outside of these maps and the scholarly disciplines and historical circumstances that create them. Neither is the cradle of civilisation. Both of these terms are instead examples of what Edward Said called 'imaginative geography' (1979, p. 57), representations of place created through scholarly practices and colonial discourse. Said analysed how this practice of imaginative geography produced the Orient. In this process: 'a line is drawn between two continents. Europe is powerful and articulate; Asia is defeated and distant' (1979, p. 57; see also Scheffler 2003).

Said argued that Orientalist scholars used this imaginative geography and its attendant literary, academic, and artistic modes of expression to define both territorially and culturally what constituted 'the Orient'. Through maps made, travel memoirs published, and paintings exhibited, European colonial powers created a place with specific physical and societal features that not only justified but necessitated colonialism and cultural re-education. European study and representation of this region bred 'the commonly-held view of the Orient as a geographical space to be cultivated, harvested, and guarded' (Said 1979, p. 219).

Said used the language of geography intentionally, retaining focus on the construction of place through the Orientalist project. The imaginative geography of the Orientalist enterprise included not only the boundary-making inherent in colonial cartography and in the establishment of the classically xenophobic us vs. them binary – but also the interpretation of features of the Middle Eastern landscape as containing meaning for understanding the social history and contemporary culture of communities in this region. The silence and sterility of desert landscapes, for instance, fortified assertions that the region was empty, devoid of

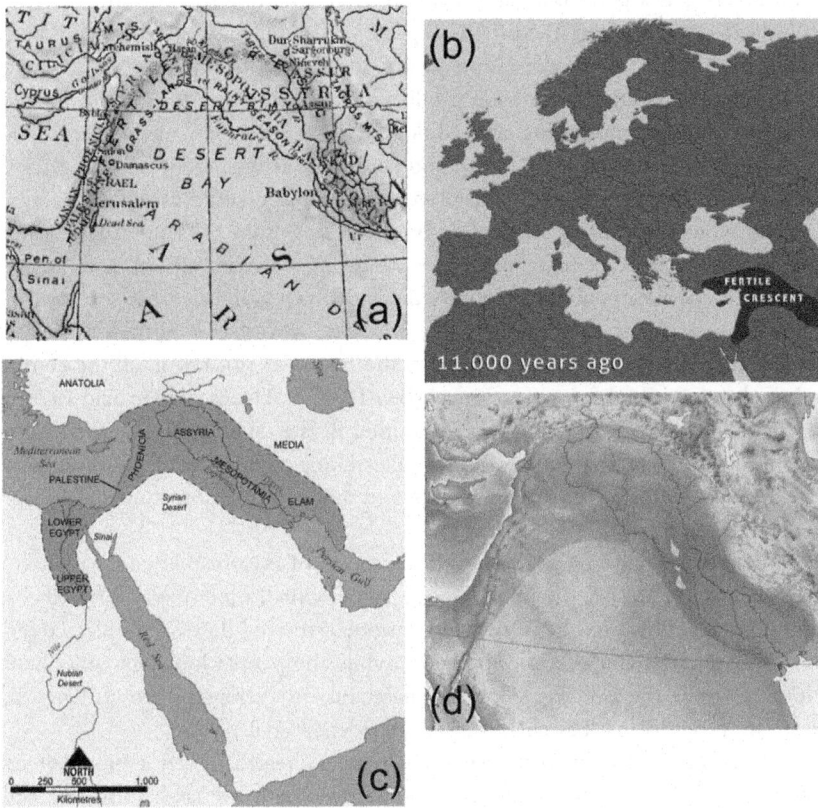

FIGURE 7.1 Four maps showing the diversity of geographical definitions afforded to the 'Fertile Crescent'. All are labelled as maps of the Fertile Crescent, but have very different territorial extents, with some but not all including parts of Egypt, Turkey, and Cyprus

Source: From: (a) Breasted 1916, p. 100–101; (b) Wikirictor 2017; (c) NormanEinstein 2005; (d) Sémhur 2011.

culture and vibrancy. 'Barrenness' expanded from a label used to describe the perceived ecological void to a metaphor for the historical and moral development of society in the Middle East. The landscape was viewed as a window into the ancient past; the desert silence as an invitation for Orientalist scholars to speak (Said 1979, p. 173).

And the writers who did fill this apparent silence, who represented the places and people of the Middle Eastern region back to European audiences – they imbued the sands and winds of this landscape with timelessness. Contemporary Middle Eastern people and their homes could not escape antiquity as their defining characteristic. In this imaginative geography, contemporary places became ancient times.

T. E. Lawrence (popularly known as 'Lawrence of Arabia' despite spending many more years of his life in the United Kingdom than in the Arab world), in a 1918 letter to V. W. Richards, emphasised that Arab society 'is the old, old civilisation, which has refined itself clear of household gods, and half the trappings which ours hastens to assume. The gospel of bareness in materials is a good one, and it involves apparently a sort of moral bareness, too' (Garnett 1938, p. 244, as cited in Said 1979, p. 228). Lawrence wrote the physical onto the moral, seeing the longevity of occupation in this region as a history of stripping away built structures and tangible objects alongside guiding belief systems and virtued principles. The imaginative geography constituting the Middle East was fundamentally about place and landscape – but it was not *just* about place and landscape. It was about how far back in time the metaphorical meanings read into that place and landscape could extend.

The way in which Orientalist scholars derived meaning from the landscape of the Middle East itself is particularly apparent in the writings of political official and archaeologist Gertrude Bell. In her memoir of her travels through Syria and Palestine, she mused, 'How many thousand years this state of things has lasted, those who shall read the earliest records of the inner desert will tell us, for it goes back to the first of them, but in all the centuries the Arab has bought no wisdom from experience' (Bell 1907, p. 244, as cited in Said 1979, p. 229). For Bell, the archaeological record – literally buried in the desert as it is – would illuminate the long history of life in the region by illustrating the lack of meaningful societal development over millennia. The physical sand and soil in this region contained the scientific evidence of stagnation.

Bell's ruminations tie the concrete and areal aspects of imaginative geography to a temporal imagining of the region, one like an hourglass in which time moves forward constantly but almost imperceptibly. In the Orientalist vision, layers of dust accumulate over earlier layers of dust as decades and centuries press on, while the people look the same, behave the same. Nothing – not the landscape nor its inhabitants – develops or grows. They are both immune to the progress that has characterised Occidental civilisation.

It is this temporal figuration that Zainab Bahrani addressed in her critique of the term 'Mespotamia' and its relationship to the idea of the cradle of civilisation. According to Bahrani:

> In historical scripture, then, the Mesopotamian past is the place of world culture's first infantile steps: first writing, laws, architecture, and all the other firsts that are quoted in every student handbook and in all the popular accounts of Mesopotamia ... then described as being 'passed' as a 'torch of civilization' to the Greco-Roman world. If Mesopotamia is the cradle of civilization, and civilization is to be understood as an organic universal whole, then this Mesopotamia represents human culture's infancy.
>
> *(Bahrani 1998, p. 162)*

Bahrani examined educational volumes and museum exhibits on Mesopotamian archaeology and pointed out that these texts very often fail to recognise the wider contemporaneous sociopolitical circumstances under which such archaeological work proceeds, or even at the very least to make clear that many of the artefacts and discoveries come from contemporary Iraq. Within archaeological and historical literature, she observed that 'Mesopotamia is not to be associated with Iraq as it [Mesopotamia] can only inhabit a temporal, not a terrestrial space' (1998, p. 163). The Orientalist view of history, the grand linear narrative of the development of civilisation, constructs and constrains the Middle East not only in the spatial terms Said identified, but also by imagining analogous boundaries between past and present and locking the region into an eternal past while Western civilisations reflect the present (and future). The Fertile Crescent and the Cradle of Civilisation exist as perpetually underdeveloped, in a never-ending state of infancy in comparison to the fluorescence and complexity of classical societies and beyond.

These terms are unsurprisingly as difficult to locate within a calendrical timeline as they are impossible to outline on a map; the cradle of civilisation is more often linked to various kingdoms and empires like the Sumerian civilisation or the Egyptian dynasties than to particular centuries or millennia. The cradle of civilisation escapes absolute dating. The amorphous and flexible nature of this term allow it to be defined contextually, by the narratives in which it appears and by the storytellers who craft those narratives.

Given that the still-dominant metanarratives about the development of civilisation are rooted in the European colonial endeavour, the origins of many of the phrases that are still used to refer to the ancient Near East retain the legacy of a cultural moment in which the sciences and the humanities worked together to justify colonial expeditions by framing the Middle East as ancient through an exaggeration of spatial distance and a freezing of time. Margarita Díaz-Andreu García recognised this playing with time as a core strategy for motivating European conquest generally:

> Imperialism fostered the remodelling of discourses about the past of areas beyond their boundaries. People beyond the core of imperial Europe were perceived as static, needing guidance from the dynamic entrepreneurial European classes to stimulate their development or to regain – in the case of the countries where ancient civilisations had occurred – their lost impetus.
>
> *(García 2007, p. 128)*

The rhetorical origins of the notion of the cradle of civilisation were structured and determined by the social and political intentions of the nineteenth-century European colonial powers. And while the criticism has certainly and justifiably been made that archaeology as a discipline has not sufficiently decolonised its practices or interpretive approaches (Hamilakis 2016; Haber 2012; Shepherd 2002), the narratives written today about the development of human society are no longer in the sponsored service of overtly imperial agendas.

Still, anthropology and archaeology retain the ability to manipulate timelines and place human subjects into constructed temporal frameworks. Johannes Fabian's *Time and the Other* argued that this is in fact at the core of the anthropological project – that 'allochronism' (2014, p. 32) is foundational to ethnography. Fabian defined allochronism as the denial of coevalness (having a shared age and time). He argued that establishing such allochronism continues to represent a fundamental aspect of anthropological research and writing, that part of the making of the anthropological subject *still* involves building the alternative time-scale on which one imagines this subject to exist. Simply put, anthropology 'is a science of other men in another Time' (2014, p. 143). And for Fabian, this is a persisting legacy of anthropology's early interconnections with the Western colonial enterprise.

Contemporary archaeology shares with cultural anthropology such an ongoing rhetoric of allochronism. In the Middle East, specifically, archaeological research continues to generate stories about the past that reproduce and even reinforce much of this spatiotemporal construction of the region as the 'cradle of civilisation' – whether or not this language appears explicitly. For Fabian, looking at anthropology, much of the allochronism he recognised was reproduced in particular through ethnographic writing. For me, the alternative time-scale of the Middle East comes from *both* text and embodied work. I argue that the analytical and material strategies of current archaeological practice are mutually reinforcing one another as they fortify many of the claims on which the cradle of civilisation and its associated view of human development are founded.

The search for firsts

In 2017, the following stories about archaeological discoveries were reported by popular media outlets: the earliest evidence for humans altering the geology of the planet found in the Dead Sea (Malewar 2017), ancient grains revealing the development of the earliest cities in Mesopotamia (Jakobsen 2017), the earliest evidence of eggplant seeds in Israel (Hasson 2017), in Northern Israel the earliest evidence of a ritual feast (Munro 2017), stone tools found in Saudi Arabia that may reveal when early humans left Africa (Jarus 2017), and the earliest evidence of winemaking which was discovered in Georgia but is strangely subtitled as the 'discovery of 8,000 year old wine production in ancient Middle East'[2] (Bettam 2017). Each one of these stories emphasised the way in which a given archaeological discovery pushed back in time what we understand about the development of human history. Each one illustrated the ability of the Middle Eastern region to provide insight into the beginnings of human society. Each one suggested that this land contains the secrets to understanding the ancient story of how humans discovered, invented, and experimented their way to civilisation.

These stories are only a few of their kind from 2017. Every year, new stories like this are published internationally. Readers are excited by the knowledge that familiar practices – like gathering to share a meal with friends or drinking wine – are old, older, possibly innate. Reading an article like this simultaneously satisfies and ignites public curiosity; the curtain to the past is drawn back for a moment, locating in a specific place and time the origins of a particular practice or behaviour, while at the same time offering a reminder of the enormity of what remains unknown about the human past.

At the same time, however, the construction of the past as a mysterious expanse and the drive to study it, map it, classify it, know it are not innocent, objective, or universally shared. Historically, some pasts have been conceived as more mysterious than others, while some people have had both more power and motivation than others to investigate the past – and the Middle East has typically been one of the regions subject to exploration and study by foreign researchers. Indeed, the first chapter of Said's *Orientalism* is entitled 'Knowing the Oriental', and opens with a consideration of the ways in which the colonial occupation relied essentially on research and scholarship, 'and not primarily with military or economic power' (Said 1979, p. 32). In the colonial vision, knowledge 'means surveying a civilisation from its origins to its prime to its decline – and of course, it means *being able to do that*' (Said 1979, p. 32).

This re-entrenchment of power hierarchies through the accumulation of particular types of knowledge (and the practices that lead to these sorts of knowledge) sorts nations and regions into categories. Places which apparently possess the means to solve historical problems, to overcome barriers to understanding, to penetrate the enigmatic character of the past are separated from places which represent the raw material to be studied, which lack the means to transform the layers of soil into answers about the ancient past. The Middle East as a region has traditionally been framed as the latter, more specifically as the container of the clues to the beginnings of recognisable human civilisation. This characterisation is so robust and solid that it becomes difficult to imagine such clues being located outside of the Middle

East. This is why, perhaps, the discovery of the earliest evidence of winemaking was reported as being in the 'ancient Middle East', although the remains were found in southeastern Georgia, a country which is almost never included as part of the contemporary Middle East.

The discursive construction of the Middle East as a direct window into the past, as time-lessly timeless, is prevailing and potent, and it is not relegated solely to reporting on archaeological finds. For instance, Susan Pollock has shown how American news coverage of the war in Iraq during the early 2000s used these same tropes in order to garner public support for the war. She argued that:

> Readers were encouraged to recall, or form, a sense of identification with the ancient past of Iraq ... This strategy was made explicit through appeals to 'firsts', those inventions credited to ancient Mesopotamia and also judged basic to our modern civilization.
>
> *(Pollock 2009, p. 84)*

More recently, Sophus Helle formulated a similar critique of US television coverage of the Da'esh insurgence, suggesting that this coverage too deploys the same Orientalist tropes to imply the unchanging nature of the Middle East. The rhetoric of such reporting conveys the idea that the contemporary problems of the area have always been an integral part of life there. As a touchstone, Helle interrogated the satirical use of the invented term 'Mess O'Potamia' on Jon Stewart's *The Daily Show*, saying:

> The messiness of Mess O'Potamia is ... figured as somehow endemic to the country, revealed as part o' the name of the geographical region itself, from antiquity to the present moment. It is not a mess in 'Potamia', brought there by, say, external colonial interests, but a mess of it and thus belonging to Iraq as part of its essence, across millennia.
>
> *(2016, p. 306)*

Such popular portrayal of the Middle East as existing outside of historical development and illustrating the essential character of the past is as unchanging as the caricature itself. Centuries after the first colonial forays into the region, media rhetoric subtly reinforces this same idea. And the widely-disseminated and broadly-read headlines of archaeological discoveries of 'first' or 'earliest' evidence of one or another civilised practice are a strong and persisting component of the continuing curation of this association.

Academic work, while most often more nuanced and less dramatic in publication, still plays a role in the perpetuation of this tradition. Each of the stories listed above represents a public-oriented translation of a peer-reviewed article, and examining the versions written for scientific audiences reveals definite differences in the language and narrative of the search for firsts from those in the popular science genre. Whereas a *Tech Explorist* article reported that the 'earliest evidence of human impact on Earth's geology has been found in the Dead Sea' (Malewar 2017), the corresponding piece in *Global and Planetary Change* was titled 'Increased sedimentation following the Neolithic Revolution in the Southern Levant' (Lu et al. 2017). The original, peer-reviewed *Nature Plants* article on the agricultural economy that fostered urbanisation in northern Mesopotamia (Styring et al. 2017) did not attempt to link these archaeological insights to a clearer understanding of life in cities today, as the *ScienceNordic* report for a public audience did (Jakobsen 2017). Even Natalie Munro's own public-oriented publication (2017) of her discovery of ritual feasting before agriculture emphasises much more strongly the connection between feasting in the past and 'lighting Hanukkah candles', for instance, than the *PNAS* article she co-authored (Munro & Grossman 2010). After all, academic literature does not need to work nearly as hard as popular media to demonstrate the contemporary relevance of archaeology. One might be tempted to conclude that scientific publications as a category do less to reify the Orientalist vision of the Middle East as a clear window through which to view the origins of human civilisation.

Scholarly and popular audiences, of course, do share a real interest in pinpointing exactly when inventions and developments occurred in history. The 'search for firsts' satisfies pressing scientific questions which happen to correspond to issues that fascinate non-specialist audiences. These types of discoveries are recognised academically *and* celebrated publicly – and rightly so. They are momentous, they take an immense amount of work and expertise to analyse and verify, and they can challenge established understandings about history.

There are certainly textual strategies at play particularly in the popular reporting on such 'first' moments in human civilisation. These stories often rely on and reinforce the idea of a single, shared human past and an equally unified concept of what constitutes civilisation. They locate the origins of the behaviours that characterise (especially Western) civilisation in the Middle Eastern soil most often – or at least, these stories attract a great deal of attention even as current scholarly evidence suggests the independent origination of many key developments such as farming and writing (Fuller et al. 2011; Senner 1991). And so, they perpetuate rather than challenge the Orientalist rhetorical construction of the Middle East as a time capsule of evidence of the origins of civilisation.

Meanwhile, the disciplinary practices of archaeology add a concrete, material presence to the production and persistence of the cradle of civilisation idea. The physical processes that constitute archaeological research complement the language and the focus of the texts reporting on the discovery of first steps in the Middle East, conveying a sense of tangible truth to the idea of the region as an archive and to the idea of the 'torch of civilisation' passing to the West after the earliest (mis)steps of human society. In the following section, I discuss these material and disciplinary strategies in order to demonstrate that archaeology continues to reify these same conceptions; it is not merely the public portrayal of archaeology which is problematic but also many integral aspects of disciplinary practice, which must be recognised and addressed actively in order to challenge the continuing legacy of the way in which archaeological study has long produced a Middle East.

Region as relic

In Pollock's (2009) examination of the discursive practices of newspaper coverage on the war in Iraq, she articulated how reporters' emphasis on the ancient history of the region – and its imagined links to contemporary American society – led American readers to feel a sense of ownership over the Iraqi landscape. She went on to argue that the material objects and structures deemed worthy of military protection added strongly to this sense of ownership. 'When cultural heritage is treated as consisting of material objects and material objects are understood as things that can be owned', Pollock (2009, p. 89) stated, 'it is an easy step to view heritage as a commodity like any other that can be bought and sold'. The location of heritage or history in particular artefacts and built sites enables an intangible, felt claim to the Middle Eastern past to become tangible and linked to conventional notions of property. And the discipline of archaeology readily provides these material elements.

Excavations produce objects – things that can be touched and held, things that become identified as history itself, things that accordingly give the impression that the past can likewise be transported and handled (Figure 7.2). Archaeologists recover collections of objects that can be sorted and ported to laboratories, depots, and museums often far from their original location. The 'torch' of civilisation thereby transforms from an abstract metaphor into concrete items such as pottery, paintings, tablets, figurines, seeds and animal bones. These objects, following excavation and analysis, are removed from their original location and frequently exported to laboratories, museums, collections, and galleries abroad. One no longer has to imagine the historical momentum of ideas disseminating westward; it has been borne out physically through the movement of physical objects – tangible manifestations of ancient civilisation – from deserts and mounds and the soil of the Middle East to the recognisable elite and intellectual spaces of contemporary civilisation.

The concrete materiality of these artefacts, however, does not come with a concomitant inflexibility with regard to interpretation. Artefacts are fragmentary and enigmatic (Figure 7.2). They do not assert their own stories, or resist their adoption into certain narratives rather than others. It is therefore easy to interpret these sorts of assemblages for what they reveal about the longevity of essential behaviours and practices that are culturally familiar to Western audiences. Artefacts therefore perform a rather ironic role wherein their physicality offers the substance to reinforce the abstract narratives and interpretations which they are drawn into. Historic interpretation relies on their materiality to act as a perceptible, weighty demonstration of grand-scale, theoretical arguments. Archaeological excavation uncovers

FIGURE 7.2 Archaeology produces objects that make it possible to hold, sort, and transport the past, but these objects are also enigmatic and do not tell their own stories
Source: Photograph by A. Mickel.

such real-world referents which can be not only pointed to, but held, turned over, tested, smelled, photographed, and measured as evidence for ideas about the past.

Furthermore, as mobile as archaeological fieldwork makes the artefacts once they are recovered and released from the earth – both physically and analytically – enormous emphasis is placed on determining with security the exact location from which each these objects come. Precise provenance is essential; artefacts and deposits are recorded in a three-dimensional Cartesian grid. This practice, while undeniably crucial to rigorous scientific practice, also has its political associations. For instance, Susan Cohen (2014) has noted how the development of stratigraphic excavation in the late nineteenth century served to underpin the Biblical stories that many early archaeologists sought to prove. She argued that the ability of archaeology to provide tangible identification through excavation of the z-axis enabled visual presentations and maps of the Biblical past to be made with the support of 'hard' data (Cohen 2014, p. 7). The effect, in other words, was equivalent to that produced through the excavation of material objects which are attached to abstract grand narratives. Ideas are invested with the potency of seemingly solid empirical data. The scientific methods and language of systematic archaeological excavation allow the mystery of ancient texts to be rooted firmly in mathematics and geography.

Likewise, the metanarrative of civilisation's westward development is given the weight and concreteness of scientific fact when linked into a stratigraphic grid. It is no longer general but specific; the supposed beginnings of recognisable human society suddenly have coordinates and elevation. Maps and matrices can then be used to interpret stories about the long-term development of human society all over again, as if reaching the same conclusions rationally and objectively.

Beyond the rhetorical moves made possible by the materiality of artefacts and by the mathematics of mapping, the act of archaeological excavation additionally adds a physical, embodied reality to the idea that the origins of civilisation lie in the Middle Eastern region. Through the difficult, laborious process of excavation, the evidence of the origins of human civilisation is revealed to be deeply rooted under meters of Middle Eastern sand. In many locations, more recent periods are often dug past, frequently less closely documented and published than the periods of interest to the guiding story of the development of human civilisation (Abu El-Haj 2001; Milwright 2010). Public interest and archaeological research questions create a target for the excavation, so that diggers are looking in particular for ancient evidence illustrating how the hallmarks of contemporary Western civilisation came to be. Methodologies are designed to answer specific research questions and it is well observed in archaeology that some periods – including those revolutionary 'firsts' – are supported with more funding and more research projects than others. The expedient excavation of the upper layers then enacts the words of Gertrude Bell more than 100 years ago; the stratigraphic layers that do not answer questions about the origins of civilisation are less closely examined and therefore seem emptier.

By default, then, there are periods – physical stratigraphic layers – about which less is known than others. These periods and layers appear, perhaps, 'barren', in the words of T. E. Lawrence, especially compared to the 'earliest records of the inner desert', in Bell's. They may be dry, and sandy, and they signify the passage of time rather than humankind advancing itself. And if these periods reflect some kind of historical barrenness, a temporal barrenness correlating with the desolate desert of the Orientalist vision, then the evidence that archaeologists and the public are interested in represents a historical fertility that can be found deep within the earth. Archaeological excavation, digging down into the earth and bringing to light this evidence of productivity, performs a sort of reverse planting. Instead of placing things that will grow into the soil, excavation rescues evidence of growth and humanity's future development *from* the soil. Archaeological work empties the earth of the evidence of these landmark moments.

In this way, archaeological excavation adds an embodied realism to the rhetorical construction of the Middle Eastern landscape as barren, as incapable of developing. Targeted excavations ignore the more recent evidence of development past the moment of particular interest. Piles of discarded sand grow and finally, when the particular material evidence of historical transformation is located, it is taken away, elsewhere, for further study and possible display. Holes are backfilled, and the landscape returns to looking as timeless and unchanging as colonial explorers once described (Figure 7.3). The many implements and technologies that characterise the modern practice of archaeology further underscore the radical gap between the past and the present in this particular area, and the discovery of ancient evidence of a recognisable human society is wrapped into a narrative of contemporary cutting-edge science.

Through this process, hard evidence is produced to reinforce the teleological metanarrative of the 'cradle of civilisation' while the landscape is gradually emptied of these (sometimes literal) seeds of evidence. New stories, more complex stories, stories that evince the differential development that took place from the early innovations being uncovered – these sorts of stories become increasingly difficult to produce. The physical process of archaeological evidence is one which can easily be adapted to add structure and substance to longstanding ideas about progress and primitivism. It physically alters the landscape so that ideas about barrenness and stunted development which colonial scholars interpreted to be at play in the Middle East gain weight, while a material and historical wealth in Western institutions and in archaeology becomes much easier to see. Through archaeological excavation, the narrative

FIGURE 7.3 Backfilling an excavated trench protects the uncovered remains from erosion or vandalism, and may discourage potential looters from continuing to dig further in this location. At the same time, it fills these trenches with the kind of soft, sterile sand that Orientalists imagined the Middle East to be filled with, and creates the image of the timeless, unchanging landscape that they described

Source: Photographs by A. Mickel.

which guided so much early archaeological work manages to reshape the land and produce a body of tangible supposed evidence which, whether intentionally or not, reaffirms persisting colonialist and supremacist understandings of the Middle Eastern region.

I have intended here to illustrate the ways in which the material practices of archaeological excavation affirm and lend a physicality to the textual practices by which the Middle East is framed as the 'cradle of civilisation'. I do not, however, mean to suggest that all archaeological fieldwork participates in these processes equally, or to imply that archaeological excavation is malicious, or to ignore the changes in the discipline that have occurred to mitigate the practices I describe (i.e. the emergence of stratigraphic excavation, single-context recording, and the end of *partage*). To be sure, destructive excavation practices in search of art pieces or particular pieces of evidence have decreased on academic research projects, and more antiquities remain in the countries where they were uncovered than for much of the discipline's history. My argument is not to suggest that archaeological work is intentionally designed to corroborate colonial textual constructions of the Middle East, or that it is irredeemable, or to paint all archaeological work in the same way.

Instead, I am arguing that examining the powerful teleological narrative of the development of Western civilisation in terms of its rhetorical components and traction should be paired with a careful inquiry into the embodied, material practices that lend this narrative life and land. The persistence of the idea of the 'cradle of civilisation' is certainly due in large part to its continual stoking in art and writing, but there are also real-world movements of people and things that make the narrative visible and physical. Archaeological excavation, for the most part, continues to function in this way. It continues to foster the conception of the Middle East as the once-hospitable home for humanity's first steps into civilisation, before progressing onward and outward.

It is possible, however, to imagine how an intentional focus on these practices and behaviours – coupled with an unrelenting, intensified commitment to destabilising the discursive power of the cradle of civilisation narrative – could engender alternative material realities. One can imagine ways in which archaeological excavation might be used to resist this dominating metanarrative; people, things, and practices could be rearranged so as to lend substance and form to novel and nuanced images of the Middle East. Language and practice might be bound together in ways that challenge the unilineal conception of the development of human civilisation that continues to cast the Middle East as a location solely for origins, to describe and demonstrate the complex and vibrant histories which have come out of the 'Fertile Crescent' and the silt and sand beyond. In the following, concluding section, I explore some possibilities for such new material practices in archaeology and the narratives to match.

Conclusion: rocking the cradle

As I argue for the urgency of disrupting the cradle of civilisation model of history, it is essential to clarify that I am not advocating for taking the story of origins away from the regions with which it has been identified. After all, seeking alternative origins for biological humanity or for recognisable civilisation in exclusively European or white contexts is a longstanding practice tied to explicitly racist intentions. The Piltdown Hoax is an obvious example, in which a skull allegedly found between 1908 and 1912 in Sussex, England was supposed to be the 'missing link' between humans and apes and used to show that northern

Europeans were therefore the most evolved among humans on earth (Goulden 2009; Stocking 1990). The skull was discovered to be a fake, underscoring the stakes of the connection between human origins and place. Before the Piltdown Hoax was Isaac de la Peyrère's widely accepted text *Prae-Adamitae* (1655) which argued that the different races on earth did not even come from the same Biblical creation event. The idea circulated widely and was used to justify and advance racist theories regarding human difference circulating at the time (Barkun 1997). In much more recent history, of course, Adolf Hitler used archaeological and historical research into the origins of human civilisation to make arguments for the superiority of Aryan biology and language (Arnold 2006; Jones 1997; Renfrew 1990, p. 4). And so, what I am suggesting is not to wrest the rhetoric of origins from the Middle East and instead look for origins in places that will reinforce dangerous, white supremacist ideologies – but rather to complicate the concept of origins, to write and enact narratives of history that are spatially and temporally complex, that resist the allochronism and teleology of traditional historical metanarratives.

In this, I am in agreement with Alfredo Gonzalez-Ruibal when he acknowledged that this has been a concern with archaeology 'for over half a century', but that 'the discourses of origins and civilisation still prevail in the cultural imagination of the West' (Gonzalez-Ruibal 2010, p. 40). For Gonzalez-Ruibal, 'it is the task of archaeologists to keep fighting these stereotypes and decolonising discourses, not only in academia, but at a popular level' (2010, p. 40).

Some scholars have offered suggestions as to how that fight might proceed. For historian of science Mirjam Brusius, what is needed is to produce histories of archaeology which

> impede the recurrence of nineteenth century tropes by showing that collecting itself is a racial discourse – one which has established notions of difference between those who collected (Occidental) and those whose objects were collected (Oriental).
>
> *(2017, p. 389)*

The way out, according to Brusius, lies in investigating the roots of the practices that entrench imagined dichotomies between the developed and what came before. Revealing the legacy of artefact retrieval, exposing the ways in which this practice was always infused with politics and prejudice, is critical to disentangling contemporary archaeological fieldwork from its relationship with centuries of collecting. We must expand our thinking and discussion of archaeology's persisting attachments to racialised histories of quests to accumulate antiquities.

For archaeologist Reinhard Bernbeck, the key is in the histories that archaeologists participate in writing. 'A remedy', for Bernbeck (2005, p. 113) 'would be the construction of non-directional, truly historical alterities'. Crafting narratives that mobilise historical narratives to challenge the dominant, unilinear mode of thinking is a way of decolonising discourse, at both an academic and a popular level. It upsets the notion that historical development moved spatially towards the sunset, instead accounting for the more realistic notion of simultaneous-cross continent flourishing.

Alternative histories do not cast change in the guise of progress, or continuation of practices and behaviours as stagnation. Writing histories like these requires recognition that the persistence of traditional lifeways entails day-to-day active decision-making, just as periods of change and invention do. People in all places, in all time periods, have responded to various environmental, social, and historical challenges, whether those responses necessitate invention or enduring practices at any given moment in time. Writing the past in this way is the archaeological equivalent of Fabian's (2014, p. 165) 'meeting the Other on the same ground, in the same Time'. Archaeology's challenge is distinct from cultural anthropology in that we are faced not only with ethnographers' refusal of contemporaneity with the communities they study, but rather with the complete distortion of space and time that links the Middle Eastern past with the Euro-American present, rather than the Middle Eastern present.

Alternative histories recognise that all regions have originated some cultural traditions and traits, but not others, and alternative histories do not cannibalistically claim the 'earliest evidences' of particular behaviours so that they fit a narrative of white supremacy. The long-term, long-distance, and complex interactions between regions are analysed rather than some kind of 'train track' view of history, in which geographically-defined groups appear to be on predefined paths that operate mostly separately until one group ultimately dominates the other and continues onward. Truly alternative histories may break with the fundamental linear conception of time, as scholars such as Uzma Z. Rizvi, Gavin Lucas, and James McGlade have proposed (Lucas 2004; McGlade 1999; Rizvi 2013).

But as I have argued here, in addition to writing alternative narratives of history that challenge the unilineal concept of progress, archaeologists must be responsible for revising their material practices in order to substantiate and concretise such alternative narratives. Like ethnographers, for archaeologists to motivate new ideas around time and history, there must be a united transformation of both language and praxis (cf. Fabian 2014, p. 161). Specifically, archaeologists must work against the inherent tendencies of archaeological excavation to be extractive, to move material out of the places where they are found, to embody the act of 'bringing to light' the specific evidence of hallmarks of history.

In contexts outside of the Middle East, archaeologists have done exciting, transformative work where their excavation methodologies subvert dominating narratives. On excavations involving the cultural heritage of Native American communities, scholars such as Kent G. Lightfoot, Katherine M. Dowdall, and Otis O. Parrish (who is himself a member of the Kashaya Pomo tribe) have carried out research projects that, for instance, dramatically prioritise remote sensing over excavation in accordance with the wishes of some tribes to minimise or completely avoid disturbance of objects and ancestors (Lightfoot 2006a; 2006b). Or, for example, on the collaborative excavation that Dowdall and Parrish describe between the California Department of Transportation and the Kashaya Pomo tribe, the scientific methods were very much wrapped together with sacred practices such that the excavation and the assemblage it created became as much about ceremony as about artefact retrieval (Dowdall & Parrish 2003).

Transformative methodologies like these challenge the relationships that archaeologists create between themselves, places, and objects. They engender new possibilities for the movements of artefacts and the meanings attached to them. They change the way that archaeologists approach the site, touch the earth, handle the objects – and it is impossible to imagine that tangible change at every level of the archaeological process can happen without impacting how archaeologists and, in turn, the public conceive of assemblages, sites, and the past. Engaging in transformative practices and writing alternative histories also entails removing the black box around what happens to objects when the excavation has concluded. The Follow the Pots project illustrates the urgent need for attention to this issue within the archaeological discipline; this project studies how a range of stakeholders – including archaeologists, museum administrators, and antiquities dealers – acquire and use pots and grave goods from Early Bronze Age sites in the southern Levant (Kersel 2015; 2017). The project directors place emphasis on the 'second life' of these artefacts, the complex roles they play for people and in narratives in the present. Follow the Pots muddies the idea that artefacts 'belong' in a museum and reveals the multiplicity of identities that they take on and the range of directions they can and do move in after excavation. It becomes increasingly difficult, in the light of this sort of work, to visualise the simple one-way movement of artefacts mimicking the supposed movement of civilisation's development.

Only by pairing new imaginaries in narrative with parallel practices will frameworks like the 'cradle of civilisation' be changed. The construction of the Middle East in this way is more than an idea, and more than a historical set of behaviours. As I have argued here, the conception of the Middle East as the bed of human civilisation's origins but nothing further is continually established and upheld by a combination of descriptions, images, stories, and practices. Projects and initiatives like the ones I describe here work together to disentangle the persistent, consistent construction of the Middle Eastern region by challenging all of these factors all at once. They create the possibility of an alternative vision of the Middle East, not as the repository for evidence of the origins of human civilisation, but as a complex region with diffuse borders and the home of diverse communities with histories that overlap, conflict, combine, and continue into the present.

I make this argument not only on the basis of justice and equity – that the refusal of a dynamic and forceful history in the Middle East performs epistemic and political violence on contemporary Middle Eastern communities – but also because of the ironic realisation that allowing the perpetuation of the cradle mythology actually fosters stagnation in understandings of past and present human communities. Examine, simply, the most recent use of the cradle of civilisation terminology that I could locate in print, which comes from a 2017 self-published book entitled *The Legacy of Abdel Fatah al-Sisi and Cairo's Military Dictatorship: A Study of Democratic Deficit, Human Rights Abuses and Militarism in the Arab Republic of Egypt*. The author, identified as Dr Mark O'Doherty, stated repeatedly in the book:

> Egypt was once a cradle of civilization of the highest spiritual integrity but has regrettably descended today into a country of military dictatorship and blatant human rights violations.
>
> *(2017, p. 9)*

Recall the earliest example of the phrase, Charles Rollin's assertion in 1879, that:

> Egypt 'served at first as the cradle (if I may be allowed the expression) of the holy nation' but 'afterwards was a severe prison, and a fiery furnace to it'.
>
> *(1879, p. iv)*

It is striking how similar the two examples are, separated as they are by more than 150 years. Both quotes use the concept of the cradle of civilisation as a benchmark by which to measure the alleged degeneration of contemporary Middle Eastern society. Both are making use of classic Orientalist tropes of suggesting the modern Middle East possesses the morals and cultural traits that should be avoided at all costs. And both imply an ideal unilineal direction for cultural evolution.

But it is in fact the isometry between these two quotes – and the broader conceptions of the origins of human civilisation that they represent – that reflects an unchanging time-lessness, and one that should galvanise archaeologists and our allies into transforming our methods and the stories we tell. The stasis lies not in the dunes of the Arabian desert but rather in the conceptions that still circulate regarding whose origins lie underneath those sands. After almost two centuries of accumulation of archaeological data which should enable new stories to be told about the past, it should be shocking to observe instead the perpetuation of the same myths of degeneration, in nearly exactly the same language. Archaeology as a field may have changed in obvious ways since the nineteenth century, but those same changes do not seem to have affected the imagined relationship between place and time in the Middle East that emerged in the earliest decades of the discipline.

The voices of Rollin and O'Doherty, speaking in unison between 1850 and 2017, illustrate the lack of new, imaginative, vibrant conceptions of human history, at least as pertaining to the Middle East. This is disturbing, disappointing, distressing. And it lays out a challenge for archaeologists, practitioners of a discipline that subsists on drawing out the nuances and contours of the past and advancing understandings of history. The need is accordingly apparent, not just for fuller or more creative writing strategies in the discipline, or for more accurate and ambitious methodologies, but for *joint* material and discursive transformations aimed at liberating historical subjects – and ourselves – from the stagnant cradle of civilisation paradigm and all that comes with it. Archaeologists must engage with the same intensity that drove our nineteenth-century counterparts – but working now to construct and support new narratives, new practices, and new metaphors that oppose simplification, linearity, and Orientalism in the search for the origins of civilisation.

Notes

1 I should note that the 'Cradle of Humankind', which refers to a UNESCO World Heritage Site in South Africa where a number of hominid fossils have been discovered and identified, has been used to connote a similar idea of being a homeland to which non-Africans might return, but on a very different basis. Boloka (1999), Taylor (2004), and Naidu (2008) have shown that the 'Cradle of Humankind' trope is instead used to suggest that this location holds some kind of ancestral, maternal, ecological knowledge about how humans can live in harmony with nature, rather than the barren hostility attached to the Middle Eastern region. Both of these phrases, however, share a similar distortion of spatio-temporality and a similar suggestion of regional stasis, as opposed to a pace of human development in parallel with other areas of the world.
2 While archaeological research on the Caucasus is often included in publications and professional meetings on the ancient 'Near East', in general 'the Middle East' does not usually include countries further north than Turkey.

References

Abu El-Haj, N 2001, *Facts on the ground: archaeological practice and territorial self-fashioning in Israeli society*, University of Chicago Press, Chicago, IL.
Arnold, B 2006, '"Arierdämmerung": race and archaeology in Nazi Germany', *World Archaeology*, vol. 38, no. 1, pp. 8–31.
Bahrani, Z 1998, 'Conjuring Mesopotamia: imaginative geography and a world past', in L Meskell (ed.), *Archaeology under fire: nationalism, politics and heritage in the Eastern Mediterranean and Middle East*, Routledge, London, pp. 159–174.

Barkun, M 1997, *Religion and the racist right: the origins of the Christian identity movement*, University of North Carolina Press, Durham, NC.

Bell, G 1907, *The desert and the sown*, William Heinemann, London.

Bernbeck, R 2005, 'The past as fact and fiction: from historical novels to novel histories', in S Pollock & R Bernbeck (eds), *Archaeologies of the Middle East: critical perspectives*, Vol. 4, Blackwell, Malden, MA, pp. 97–122.

Bettam, S 2017, 'Archaeologists find earliest evidence of winemaking', *University of Toronto News*. Available from: https://www.utoronto.ca/news/archaeologists-find-earliest-evidence-winemaking [2 April 2019].

Bible History Online 2017, 'Map of the ancient fertile crescent'. Available from: www.bible-history.com/maps/maps/map_ancient_fertile_crescent.html [2 April 2019].

Boloka, GM 1999, 'African renaissance: a quest for (un)attainable past', *Critical Arts*, vol. 13, no. 2, pp. 92–103.

Breasted, JH 1916, *Ancient times, a history of the early world: an introduction to the study of ancient history and the career of early man*, Ginn, Boston.

Brusius, M 2017, 'Hitting two birds with one stone: an afterword on archeology and the history of science', *History of Science*, vol. 55, no. 3, pp. 383–391.

Chevalier, N 2012, 'Early excavations (pre-1914)', in DT Potts (ed.), *A companion to the archaeology of the Near East*, Vol. 1, Wiley-Blackwell, Chichester, pp. 48–69.

Cohen, S 2014, 'Mapping the z-axis: early archaeological engagement with time and space in the ancient Near East', *Bulletin of the History of Archaeology*, vol. 24, no. 13, pp. 1–13.

de la Peyrère, I 1655, *Prae-Adamitae*.

de Saulcy, F 1865, *Voyage en terre sainte*, Libraire Academique, Paris.

Dowdall, KM & Parrish, OO 2003, 'A meaningful disturbance of the earth', *Journal of Social Archaeology*, vol. 3, no. 1, pp. 99–133.

Fabian, J 2014, *Time and the other: how anthropology makes its object*, Columbia University Press, New York.

Fuller, DQ, Willcox, G & Allaby, RG 2011, 'Cultivation and domestication had multiple origins: arguments against the Core Area Hypothesis for the origins of agriculture in the Near East', *World Archaeology*, vol. 43, no. 4, pp. 628–652.

García, MD-A, 2007, *A world history of nineteenth-century archaeology: nationalism, colonialism, and the past*, Oxford University Press, Oxford.

Garnett, D 1938, *The letters of T.E. Lawrence of Arabia*, Spring Books, London.

González-Ruibal, A 2010, 'Colonialism and European archaeology', in J Lydon & UZ Rizvi (eds), *Handbook of postcolonial archaeology*, Left Coast Press, Walnut Creek, CA, pp. 37–47.

Goulden, M 2009, 'Boundary-Work and the human–animal binary: Piltdown Man, science and the media', *Public Understanding of Science*, vol. 18, no. 3, pp. 275–291.

Haber, AF 2012, 'Un-disciplining archaeology', *Archaeologies*, vol. 8, no. 1, pp. 55–66.

Hamilakis, Y 2016, 'Decolonial archaeologies: from ethnoarchaeology to archaeological ethnography', *World Archaeology*, vol. 48, no. 5, pp. 678–682.

Hasson, N 2017, 'Earliest evidence of eggplants in Israel found in 1,000-year-old Jerusalem garbage pit', *Haaretz*, 16 November.

Helle, S 2016, 'The return of Mess O'Potamia: time, space, and politics in modern uses of Ancient Mesopotamia', *Postcolonial Studies*, vol. 19, no. 3, pp. 305–324.

Jakobsen, RK 2017, 'Ancient grain reveals the development of the earliest cities', *ScienceNordic*, 3 October.

Jarus, O 2017, 'Ancient axes, spear points may reveal when early humans left Africa', *LiveScience*, 27 December.

Jones, S 1997, *The archaeology of ethnicity: constructing identities in the past and present*, Routledge, London.

Kendall, T 1996, 'The American discovery of Meroitic Nubia and the Sudan', in N Thomas (ed.), *The American discovery of Ancient Egypt*, Los Angeles County Museum of Art, Los Angeles, CA, pp. 151–168.

Kersel, MM 2015, 'An issue of ethics? Curation and the obligations of archaeology', *Journal of Eastern Mediterranean Archaeology and Heritage Studies*, vol. 3, no. 1, pp. 77–79.

Kersel, M 2017, 'Object movement: UNESCO, language and the exchange of Middle Eastern artifacts', in J Anderson & H Geismar (eds), *The Routledge companion to cultural property*, Routledge, New York.

Kuklick, B 1996, *Puritans in Babylon: the ancient Near East and American intellectual life, 1880–1930*, Princeton University Press, Princeton, NJ.

Larsen, MT 1996, *The conquest of Assyria: excavations in an antique land 1840–1869*, Routledge, London.

Layard, AH 1849, *Nineveh and its remains*, John Murray, London.

Lightfoot, KG 2006a, 'Rethinking archaeological field methods', *News from Native California*, vol. 19, no. 3, pp. 21–24.

Lightfoot, KG 2006b, 'Experimenting with low impact field methods', *News from Native California*, vol. 19, no. 4, pp. 16–19.

Lu, Y, Waldmann, N, Nadel, D & Shmuel, M 2017, 'Increased sedimentation following the Neolithic revolution in the southern Levant', *Global and Planetary Change*, vol. 152, pp. 199–208.

Lucas, G 2004, *The archaeology of time*, Routledge, London.

Maisels, CK 1993, *The Near East: archaeology in the 'cradle of civilization'*, Routledge, London.

Malewar, A 2017, 'Earliest evidence of human impact on earth's geology has been found in the Dead Sea', *Tech Explorist*. Available from: https://www.techexplorist.com/earliest-evidence-human-impact-earths-geology-found-dead-sea/5801/ [7 June 2017].

Matthews, R 2003, 'Year Zero for the archaeology of Iraq', *Papers from the Institute of Archaeology*, vol. 14, pp. 1–6.

McGlade, J 1999, 'The times of history: archaeology, narrative and non-linear causality', in T Murray (ed.), *Time and archaeology*, Routledge, London, pp. 139–163.

Milwright, M 2010, *An introduction to Islamic archaeology*. Edinburgh University Press, Edinburgh.

Munro, N 2017, 'An archaeological dig in Israel provides clues to how feasting became an important ritual', *The Conversation*. Available from: https://theconversation.com/an-archaeological-dig-in-israel-provides-clues-to-how-feasting-became-an-important-ritual-86370 [27 December 2017].

Munro, ND & Grosman, L 2010, 'Early evidence (ca. 12,000 BP) for feasting at a burial cave in Israel', *Proceedings of the National Academy of Sciences of the United States of America*, vol. 107, no. 35, pp. 15362–15366.

Naidu, M 2008, 'Creating an African tourist experience at the Cradle of Humankind world heritage site', *Historia*, vol. 53, no. 2, pp. 182–207.

NormanEinstein 2005, 'File: Fertile Crescent Map.Png', *Wikimedia Commons*. Available from: https://commons.wikimedia.org/wiki/File:Fertile_Crescent_map.png [2 April 2019].

O'Doherty, M 2017, *The legacy of Abdel Fatah Al-Sisi and Cairo's military dictatorship: a study of democratic deficit, human rights abuses and militarism in the Arab Republic of Egypt*, Lulu.com, Morrisville.

Pollock, S 2009, 'Archaeology goes to war at the newsstand', in S Pollock & R Bernbeck (eds), *Archaeologies of the Middle East: critical perspectives*, Blackwell, Malden, MA, pp. 78–96.

Renfrew, C 1990, *Archaeology and language: the puzzle of Indo-European origins*, Cambridge University Press, Cambridge.

Renfrew, C 2006, 'Becoming human: the archaeological challenge', *Proceedings of the British Academy*, vol. 139, pp. 217–238.

Rizvi, UZ 2013, 'Creating prehistory and protohistory: constructing otherness and politics of contemporary Indigenous populations in India', in PR Schmidt & SA Mrozowski (eds), *The death of prehistory*, Oxford University Press, Oxford, pp. 141–160.

Rollin, C 1879, *The ancient history of the Egyptians, Carthaginians, Assyrians, Babylonians, Medes, and Persians, Macedonians, and Grecians*, Vol. 1, American Book Exchange, New York.

Said, EW 1979, *Orientalism*, Vintage Books, New York.

Scarre, C 1990, 'The western world view in archaeological atlases', in P Gathercole & D Lowenthal (eds), *The politics of the past*, Routledge, London, pp. 11–18.

Scheffler, T 2003, '"Fertile Crescent", "Orient", "Middle East": the changing mental maps of Southwest Asia', *European Review of History: Revue Europeenne d'Histoire*, vol. 10, no. 2, pp. 253–272.

Schliemann, H 1875, *Troy and its remains; a narrative of researches and discoveries made on the Site of Ilium, and in the Trojan Plain*, John Murray, London.

Sémhur 2011, 'File: Fertile Crescent.png', *Wikimedia Commons*. Available from: https://commons.wikimedia.org/wiki/File:Fertile_Crescent.png [2 April 2019].

Senner, WM 1991, *The origins of writing*, University of Nebraska Press, Lincoln.

Shepherd, N 2002, 'Heading south, looking north: why we need a post-colonial archaeology', *Archaeological Dialogues*, vol. 9, no. 2, pp. 74–82.

Smith, A 2017, 'Learning history as his story: the Fertile Crescent', *Come Fill Your Cup*. Available from: http://comefillyourcup.com/2016/02/28/learning-history-as-his-story-the-fertile-crescent/ [2 April 2019].

Stocking, GW 1990, *Bones, bodies and behavior: essays in behavioral anthropology*, vol. 5, University of Wisconsin Press, Madison.

Styring, AK, Charles, M, Fantone, F, Hald, MM, McMahon, A, Meadow, RH, Nicholls, GK, Patel, AK, Pitre, MC & Smith, A 2017, 'Isotope evidence for agricultural extensification reveals how the world's first cities were fed', *Nature Plants*, vol. 3, no. 6, pp. 170–176.

Taagepera, R 1978, 'Size and duration of empires: systematics of size', *Social Science Research*, vol. 7, no. 2, pp. 108–127.

Taylor, B 2004, 'A green future for religion?' *Futures*, vol. 36, no. 9, pp. 991–1008.

ThingLink 2017, 'Fertile crescent interactive Map'. Available from: https://www.thinglink.com/scene/706128691062636545 [2 April 2019].

Wailes, B & Zoll, AL 1995, 'Civilization, barbarism, and nationalism in European archaeology', in PL Kohl & C Fawcett (eds), *Nationalism, politics and the practice of archaeology*, Cambridge University Press, Cambridge, pp. 21–38.

White, H 1987, *The content of the form: narrative discourse and historical representation*, Johns Hopkins University Press, Baltimore, MD.

Wikirictor 2017, 'File: Europe agricultural Revolution.gif', *Wikimedia Commons*. Available from: https://en.wikipedia.org/wiki/File:Europe_agricultural_revolution.gif [2 April 2019].

Wynn, LL 2007, *Pyramids & nightclubs: a travel ethnography of Arab and Western imaginations of Egypt, from King Tut and a colony of Atlantis to rumors of sex orgies, urban legends about a marauding prince, and blonde belly dancers*, University of Texas Press, Austin.

8

THE BEAST WITHOUT

Becoming human in the science fiction of H. G. Wells

John McNabb

Introduction

This paper is the second of two on the subject of H. G. Wells' engagement with human evolution, and how it was reflected in his scientific journalism and science fiction writing. The first paper (McNabb 2015) focused on the theme of the 'beast within' and covered the 1890s up to and including the novelisation of *The Island of Doctor Moreau* in 1896. This paper will cover the period from *Moreau* to 1901. After this date Wells' writing changed (Mackenzie & Mackenzie 1987; Philmus & Hughes 1975). He no longer focused on scientific romances. He began to position himself as the prophet of a new social order, his writing reflecting his developing interests in sociology and his belief in the need for radical social change.

In this paper I will continue to focus on the idea of the beast within, but I will slant it towards one of the volume's main themes, 'becoming human'. I will look at the juxtaposition of human and animal in Wells' work, as well as a selection of the work of other writers from this period, see Table 8.1.

In a volume of this nature it is important to emphasise that many of the research agendas pursued today are rooted in those dating to the very foundations of human origins research. In Britain this means an engagement with the British imperial past enmeshed in a context of perceived racial and social superiority. Just what was it that allowed the imperial generations to feel that they were a better class of humanity than the Indigenous peoples they colonised? Popular fiction of the time perfectly reflects the context, agendas (and concerns) that the colonial mentality confronted (Taylor 2017).

I will pick up where I left off in the earlier Wells article.

One of the most dramatic and emotive pieces of Palaeolithic art ever discovered is the *Löwenmensch*, the lion man. Human representations in European Upper Palaeolithic cave art are rare and contested (Bahn & Vertut 1997), but this therianthrope figurine is unambiguous (Figure 8.1). Ongoing restoration of the figure has not changed the powerful visual impact of the piece. It is still a bipedal lion headed creature, standing erect and with its arms down at its sides. It is neither fully human, nor wholly animal but something in between.

TABLE 8.1 A personal selection of H. G. Wells' fiction and scientific journalism with a human evolutionary theme or related to Palaeolithic archaeology, between 1896 and 1901. The table is not intended to be definitive. Significant contributions to human evolutionary studies are included in the far right column. See text for details

Year	Month	HGW and human origins or Palaeolithic link	HGW and evolutionary theme	Selected novels and stories of HGW	Other debates and relevant items
1896	January			'Under the Knife'	
	February				Abstract of Dubois's Dublin lecture published in RAI journal.
	March				Kropotkin in *Nineteenth Century*
	April		'Concerning the Nose' 'Intelligence on Mars'	*The Island of Doctor Moreau* published as a novel.	
	May		'The Origin of the Senses'		
	June				Prestwich dies. Slowly, the eolith campaign begins to lose impetus, though many are still committed to concept of 'Tertiary Man'.
	July				
	August			'In the Abyss'	
	September				Harrison displays eoliths at Guildhall, London. Clement Reid reports on excavations at Hoxne to B.A.A.S. in Liverpool.
	October	'Human Evolution an Artificial Process'			
	November				Earliest papers by K Pearson on evolution from 1894 in *Phil. Trans. R. Soc.*
	December				

Year	Month	HGW and human origins or Palaeolithic link	HGW and evolutionary theme	Selected novels and stories of HGW	Other debates and relevant items
1897	January	'The Acquired Factor'			
	February	'Morals and Civilization'			
	March				Between 1896 and 1900 Karl Pearson and colleagues published a series of articles in *Proceedings of the Royal Society of London*, and the *Philosophical Transactions of the Royal Society of London Series A*. Clement Reid reports on excavations at Hitchin to Royal Society.
	April		'Human Evolution'	April–December: *War of the Worlds* in Pearson's Magazine.	
	May			May–November: *A Story of the Stone Age* in *The Idler*.	
	June			*The Invisible Man* published in *Pearson's Weekly* June–August 1897. Novel of same name published later in 1897.	
	July				*Ancient Stone Implements*, John Evans, 2nd edition.

Year	Month	HGW and human origins or Palaeolithic link	HGW and evolutionary theme	Selected novels and stories of HGW	Other debates and relevant items
1898	January			The War of the Worlds published as a novel.	
	September				E. B. Tylor read paper on survival of Palaeolithic in Tasmania to, BAAS Bristol. There were two main series: Mathematical Contributions to the Theory of Evolution, and Data for the Problem of Evolution in Man.
	November			'When the Sleeper Wakes' begins in The Graphic, concludes February 1899.	
1899	May			When the Sleeper Wakes published as a novel.	
1900	May				Bateson unveils Mendel's work to Royal Horticultural Society. All were biometrical articles published as contributions to the Royal Society's biometrics committee.
	September				J. Paxton Moir & E.B. Tylor read papers on Tasmanian stone tools to BAAS Bradford. After 1897 biometricians slowly lost control of the committee to Bateson and saltationists

Year	Month	HGW and human origins or Palaeolithic link	HGW and evolutionary theme	Selected novels and stories of HGW	Other debates and relevant items
	February (?)				After 1900 Pearson sought alternative journals in which to publish biometric work. 'The Bicycle and Crime'; 'Lombroso', in *Pall Mall Magazine*.
	December			December 1900–August 1901: *The First Men in the Moon* in *The Strand Magazine*.	
1901	November			*The First Men in the Moon* published as a novel.	After 1900 Bateson and saltationists dominate studies of heredity. Now being called Mendelians.

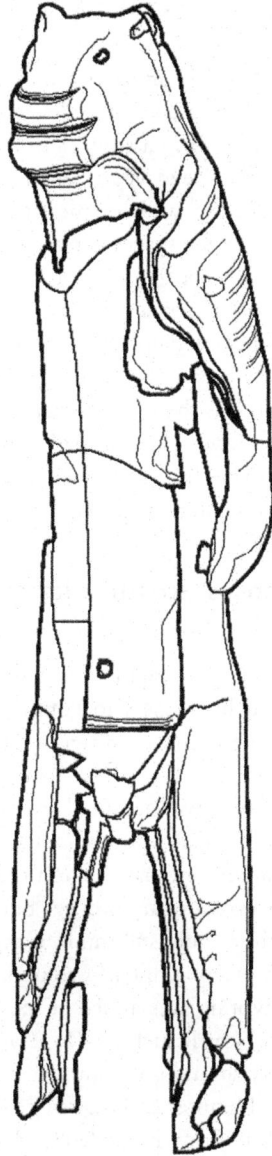

FIGURE 8.1 Drawing of the *Löwenmensch* by Penny Copeland. The original *Löwenmensch* statuette is housed at the Ulmer Museum, Ulm, Germany

It was discovered in a recessed chamber at the back of a cave, the Hohlenstein-Stadel cave in the Lone Valley in the Swabian Alb Mountains, Germany. Its placement in the dark recess of a back chamber is thought to be deliberate (Porr 2015). The most recent dates (Kind et al. 2014) place it at 39,000–41,000 (calBP), and it was carved from the tusk of a woolly mammoth. It is associated with Aurignacian artefacts, the earliest material culture made by modern humans in Western Europe.

So how do we explain this astonishing artefact?

Although other interpretations should take precedence (Hussain & Floss 2015; Porr 2015) for me, the *Löwenmensch* is a creature from a story, a story that fused the real world with an imaginary one, although it may have been very real to the story tellers. It was a story told while the firelight flickered against the walls of the cave. It is a creature not born of our world, yet still a part of it, inhabiting the spaces between the dancing shadows where human imagination first took root. It was a popular story too. A small *Löwenmensch*, some 2.5 cm in height, was found in the cave Hohle Fels near Schelkingen, also in the Swabian Jura, possibly 32,000 years in age. A third is suggested to come from Geissenklösterle (Hussain & Floss 2015). So, this was a story that was widely told, perhaps handed down the generations.

We can think of the *Löwenmensch* as the earliest science fiction story yet discovered. It is a creature from an imaginative world, yet one that had impact in our own – perhaps like our own stories it had the power to shape human thought and action. Through its own story it challenged the division between human and animal.

H. G. Wells, scientific romances, scientific journalism, and human origins, 1896–1901

This challenge is exactly what Wells was attempting with *The Island of Doctor Moreau* (Wells 1896). In this story he challenged his readers to confront their own understanding of the animal–human dichotomy by asking them to engage with the evolutionary mechanisms that transformed the one into the other.

By the 1890s the fact of evolution was accepted by most scientists and the public alike, even if the thought of an animal heritage was distasteful. For Victorian England, becoming human meant putting the dark prehistoric past behind them. For many people Darwin had replaced special creation with the evolutionary process, but this was OK because it still placed humans at the top of the tree – they could still think of themselves as special. Deep time was a pair of binoculars with which to view a distant evolutionary horizon from a safe distance.

Much of H. G. Wells' early writing was aimed at exploding this complacency (McLean 2009; Philmus & Hughes 1975). Novels such as *The Time Machine* (1895) spoke directly to this. Humanity and English society should not assume it was special, inevitable, or permanent (McLean 2009; McNabb 2015; Philmus & Hughes 1975). Any number of things could happen to knock Victorian hubris from its pedestal; degeneration, continued adaptation, overwhelming natural or artificial disasters, even parallel evolution.

Forcing the reading public to confront the reality of evolutionary change perhaps explains why the critical reaction to *The Island of Doctor Moreau* was so negative (Mackenzie & Mackenzie 1987). Many like Chalmers Mitchell writing in *The Saturday Review* railed at the brutality in Moreau's transformative process – it wasn't art (Chalmers Mitchell 1896). He echoed other reviewers who contested the emphasis on pain as a moulding force in emergent humanity. Like his mentor T. H. Huxley, Wells saw evolutionary change through natural selection as 'selection by death', so the pain inherent in Moreau's vivisection is a metaphor for the evolutionary process itself. In fact, the character of Moreau can be seen as a metaphor for evolution, as a number of Wellsian scholars have pointed out; the Mackenzie's noted that in the chapter entitled 'Doctor Moreau Explains' (Mackenzie & Mackenzie 1987, p. 125) Moreau opines 'The study of Nature makes man at least as remorseless as Nature.' The vivisectionist is utterly indifferent to the suffering he creates – like natural selection he is only concerned with process. There is a nice irony in the fact that Moreau is ultimately killed by one of his own creations, the *Löwenmensch*-like puma.

In the same chapter Moreau asserted:

> This store men and women set on pleasure and pain ... is the mark of the beast upon them, the mark of the beast from which they came.
>
> *(Wells 2005, p. 74)*

In fact, the purpose of Moreau's experiments is to raise humanity above the level of its bestial heritage altogether. Moreau sees pain as the link to the past, an evolutionary warning system no longer useful to an evolving humanity. By attempting to do away with it in his creations, he is seeking to free humanity from its heritage. So here is a view of humanity that transcends ancestry – free of the chains of time. But Wells does not allow his readers any comfort. All of Moreau's experiments fail, the beast within reclaims them. Moreau becomes a victim of his own process.

In other words, the beast cannot be taken out of humanity. If vivisection represented evolutionary change, then Wells was telling his readers that the animal within was still there. Evolution had not removed it, and cultural and social evolution had not buried it as deeply as people wanted to believe.

The 1890s saw considerable debates on just what exactly the mechanisms of evolutionary change were (Bowler 2003; McNabb 2012; 2015). *Moreau* is Wells' statement that at least some of these mechanisms wouldn't work. Lamarckian theories, the inheritance of acquired inherited characteristics, are explicitly stated to be absent in the beast-men's progeny; Moreau's process itself represents saltation – evolution in rapid jumps across generations. The failure of the process signals the failure of such quick fixes. Although not explicitly stated, what remains is natural selection. There is no doubt in my mind that Wells was a firm believer in natural selection, and under the tutelage of Huxley understood its contingent nature and the importance of randomness and variation. Too much of his fiction and scientific journalism reflects this to be otherwise. However, I suspect that like many others at the time, he just felt that it didn't answer every question. What for example was the evolutionary significance of baldness (*Pall Mall Gazette*, 1 March 1895)?

By the time of the publication of *Moreau* (April 1896) Wells had already come to his own conclusions on human evolution. Although published some six months after the novel, his article 'Human Evolution an Artificial Process' was possibly written, but certainly envisaged before *Moreau*, probably in the time intervening between the abandonment of the first draft of the novel in December 1894, and the completion of the second draft in June 1895 (Philmus 1993).

In 'Human Evolution an Artificial Process' (*Fortnightly Review*, October 1896) Wells argued that the human body was a result of natural selection (explicitly stated as such), but that since the Upper Palaeolithic there had been no further evolutionary changes in our physical form. The same applied to humanity's innate nature. We are still given to the same rages lusts and passions as Upper Palaeolithic 'savages'. So natural selection had fashioned both the modern human body, which he called the 'culminating ape', and the human mind, but not enough time had passed since the Palaeolithic for these two inherited aspects of humanity to change. Where evolution had progressed, but not through selection, was in the development of the mind itself – but in particular in the understanding of concepts. Critically, this was facilitated through the development of speech. The 'artificial man' was a product of development in the 'acquired factor'. This was the web of social ideas – concepts – that enmeshed an individual. In particular concepts of social morality kept the culminating ape in its place and allowed the artificial man to emerge. Morality here was more of a conception of doing the right thing than a set of specific do's and don'ts. Education and the example of other moral individuals, role models in effect, served to reinforce the ascendency of the acquired factor.

For Wells becoming human was the same as becoming moral in the sense of the social and ideational evolution he proposed in 'Human Evolution an Artificial Process' and then backed up with other articles – 'The Acquired Factor' (*The Academy*, January 1897) and 'Morals and Civilization' (*Fortnightly Review*, February 1897). His view of human evolution coalesced as he finished *Moreau* off – it is no wonder then the novel charts the failure of non-selectionist process to effect rapid change in physical bodies and especially in minds, even if gifted with the power of speech.

The concept that physical evolution in humans had stopped with the Palaeolithic was not a new one, nor was the notion that evolutionary change had shifted its focus to the human mind (Huxley 1894a; Kidd 1894; 1895; Morris 1890; Wallace 1889). The idea that social morality was the glue that would hold an unreconstructed prehistoric nature in check had also been mooted elsewhere. The idea may well have been planted in Wells' head by his old teacher T. H. Huxley through his prestigious Romanes Lecture in 1893 (Huxley 1894a; 1894b). Nonetheless, this concept of human evolution and what it meant to be human informed much of Wells' writing after this point, but perhaps because of resolving his uncertainties his interest in publishing scientific and evolutionary journalism lessened. Just prior to *Moreau*'s publication he defended selectionist interpretations for otherwise curious physical and mental features ('Concerning the Nose' – *The Ludgate*, April 1896; 'The Origin of the Senses' – *The Saturday Review*, May 1896), and the contingent character of evolution ('Intelligence on Mars' – *The Saturday Review*, April 1896). In terms of short stories with an evolutionary slant, there was very little after *Moreau*. 'Under the Knife; (*New Review*, January 1896), a tale of an out-of-body experience, had a passing reference to the human senses having had an evolutionary origin; 'In the Abyss' (*Pearson's Magazine*, August 1896), one of Wells' cleverest short stories, introduces an undersea race who believed all the human flotsam and jetsam (*sensu lato*) that sank below the waves was manna from the gods. The story epitomises Wells' warnings that parallel evolution may have fashioned some other race, ready to challenge humanity's sense of its deserved destiny.

The fragility of humanity was a theme Wells continued to pursue in the post-*Moreau* years. Two of his most famous novels are relevant here. *The War of the Worlds*, one of the greatest science fiction stories ever written, was published between April and December 1897 in *Pearson's Magazine*, and the novel in January of the following year. The story is now a familiar one. The earth is invaded by Martians who sweep away the might of the British Empire and all human resistance in a matter of weeks. Yet they evolved on a world where there were no bacteria, no 'putrefaction', and ultimately succumb to infection. Following the pitiless law of evolution, humanity should have perished at the hands of a technologically and cognitively superior species. We are saved, but only by the merest chance.

The Martians are following an evolutionary imperative. Mars was to the Victorians one of the 'older worlds of space', a planet already in decline with its natural resources exhausted. The Martians were forced to invade in order to ensure their own survival. The strong came to earth to prey on the weak – this is part of their heritage. Their food source on Mars was a bipedal humanoid species with siliceous skeletons. A few were brought to earth in each of the Martian cylinders as food for the journey. Like humans on earth, the Martians were the dominant species of their world, evolved from creatures similar to ourselves, yet they too faced extinction.

The second story of relevance here is *The Invisible Man*, published in *Pearson's Weekly* between June and August 1897; the novelisation was published later the same year. The story concerns a scientist experimenting with chemicals and light reflection, who discovers the secret of invisibility. There is no obvious human evolution connection in the novel, but the Mackenzie's make a valid point (Mackenzie & Mackenzie 1987). The scientist, Griffin, choses 'power over wisdom' and so loses his moral compass. The result is a descent into brutality and indifference to the suffering of others – in other words he regresses toward the primitive. He reverts to the culminating ape wilfully eschewing the acquired factor. In that sense Griffin is a powerful reminder of the absolute necessity of the acquired factor. The beast within actually lies too close to the surface for complacency. McLean (2009) astutely observes that the village mob also become atavistic as they brutally beat Griffin to death in the street.

I will finish this section with 'A Story of the Stone Age' (*Idler*, May–September 1897). Not as well-known as Wells' later Neanderthal story 'The Grisly Folk' (*Storyteller Magazine*, April 1921), this is nevertheless one of the most important Victorian examples of prehistoric fiction (Ruddick 2009). Eudena, a young Palaeolithic female, is pursued by Uya the Cunning, the leader of the tribe. She flees and is joined by a young male Ugh-lomi who kills Uya. After many adventures, Ugh-lomi becomes Eudena's mate and the tribe's leader. What is key in this story is the factual background to the landscape setting of the story, and the picture of prehistoric life it presents. Wells had an interest in Palaeolithic archaeology, he wrote a number of articles engaging with it, and positively reviewed Worthington Smith's classic *Man the Primeval Savage* (McNabb 2015; Smith 1894; Wells 1894). The physical landscape of the story is Palaeolithic Sussex. Mention is made of the Wealden mountains to the east, a range of mountains believed to have existed in eolithic times (see below). A remnant of their foothills was thought to survive as the North Downs of Kent. The broader southern English Pleistocene geography is sketched out in the beginning of the story (Dawkins 1880) and remains remarkably accurate even today (McNabb 2007).

It is the picture of Palaeolithic life that it presents that is perhaps most important. This was precisely what the public would have believed the Palaeolithic was like. The individuals in the tribe are alternatively brave and cowardly, more animal in their moral outlook than human, they are venal and delight in the misery of others since it is not their own. Life is hard and brutal. This is Huxley's vision, selection by death, 'nature red in tooth and claw', borrowing from Tennyson. In 'Human Evolution an Artificial Process' Wells had argued that one of the ways in which the acquired factor was maintained was through desire to emulate gifted individuals – those who moved the moral environment onwards. It was a notion he received criticism for (Perry Coste 1897a; 1897b; Wells 1897a). Ugh-lomi is one of these 'great men', and though she suffers from the Victorian (and Wellsian?) prejudice against women, Eudena too differs from the other women in her tribe. Both are described as 'exceptionally' straight limbed for their time, and in becoming Ugh-lomi's mate as opposed to just his woman, the foundations of Victorian gender relations are forged. Ugh-lomi invents the first composite tool, a hafted flint axe, and is the first to ride a horse. He comes to epitomise the human domination of the natural world by killing a cave bear and a lion, the chief predators of the time. The brutality of our primitive forebears is underlined in the last few sentences as the narrator tells us that despite becoming the tribe's leader, Ugh-lomi is eventually killed and eaten, the implication being by his own people.

This picture of Palaeolithic life would have been familiar to the public from other works which presented the same imagery. Stanley Waterloo's *The Story of Ab* (novel published 1897) is a good example, and Ruddick details more (Ruddick 2009). This was (and remains?) the public's view of what Stone Age life was like. Popular factual texts on human evolution and prehistory (Büchner 1894; Clodd 1895; Laing 1892; McNabb 2012) would have provided grist for this mill.

Palaeolithic archaeology and anthropology in the last half of the *fin de siècle* decade

It is important to briefly place the ideas discussed above in their broader context before returning to Victorian literary concerns with the beast within. The reports of the British Association for the Advancement of Science (BAAS) and the contents pages of the *Journal of the Anthropological Institute of Great Britain and Ireland* represent the most informative weathervanes for what was hot and what was not in research between 1896 and 1901. The former, described as the 'parliament of British science', was an annual meeting held in different UK cities every year, and occasionally abroad, to discuss topics of current interest. Section H was entirely dedicated to anthropology. A report of all the papers from each meeting, as well as the reports of its various scientific committees were published annually. The London based Anthropological Institute was the premier scientific society for the study of the human past. Often papers given in the BAAS were published in greater detail in the *Journal*. It will be recalled that neither prehistoric archaeology nor Palaeolithic archaeology/human origins were considered separate disciplines at this time. Both came under the broad mantle of anthropology – the 'science of man'.

Both the BAAS meetings and the annual AI journals focused heavily on ethnology both at home and abroad, with a particular interest in those peoples colonised by the British Empire. Anthropology was very much seen as the handmaiden of imperial expansion (Stocking 1971; 1987). British, European, and world prehistory equally figured in both publications. Anthropometrical papers and contributions to its methodology were common, an important part in the classification of the empire's subject peoples – a key first step in efficient governance and subjugation.

For hominin discoveries the latter part of the fin de siècle decade was not a particularly exciting time. Eugene Dubois' *Pithecanthropus erectus* road show around the philanthropic societies of Europe had finished in London with a talk and demonstration of the remains to the AI on 25 November 1895. Interest in the fossil was kept alive by a summary of Dubois' talk in Dublin published in the *Journal* in February 1896, and a popular article by Peter Kropotkin the science writer for the prestigious periodical *The Nineteenth Century*

(Kropotkin 1896) which was widely read. A paper was read to the BAAS in Liverpool in September 1896 on the *Pithecanthropus* femur by Dr D. Hepburn, but after that the fossil dropped off the radar, at least for these two publications. The Galley Hill skeleton (McNabb 2015; Newton 1895) had also dropped out of the spotlight. Its enduring significance was that as a later prehistoric interment of a modern human (but not recognised as such at the time), it contributed to the belief that Palaeolithic humans were essentially modern looking. In 'A Story of the Stone Age', Ugh-lomi and Eudena are distinguished in appearance from Uya, whose description is much more brutish and Neanderthal-like. Nevertheless the illustrations to these stories usually presented them all as more human than simian (i.e. *Pithecanthropus*-like), helping to shape the view that the modern human form had very ancient roots (Keith 1895; Ruddick 2009). The only other possible Palaeolithic human remains found in Britain during this period was the Orwell skull, reported to the BAAS in Glasgow by Nina Layard in 1901. It was dredged out of peat from the base of the river Orwell near Ipswich. For nine months it sat on top of a pole on the dredger. It too was later prehistoric.

The search for a viable mechanism to explain heredity had originally been embedded in anthropology, but by the 1890s the fledgling sciences of genetics and evolutionary biology had captured the field. At the BAAS between 1896 and 1901, only a single paper on Lamarckism was presented, and only one on saltation (the former by Cossar-Ewart, the latter by Iles, both at the BAAS, in Toronto in 1897). Heredity was conspicuously absent from the *Journal*. Elsewhere, in the biological journals, heredity was actively discussed, for example in the pages of *Natural Science*. In Britain, the majority of research on heredity was presented via the increasingly bitter feud between the biometricians (continuous variation pro-natural selection) and the saltationists (discontinuous variation and anti-selection) at the Royal Society (Gillham 2001; Gillham 2015). It is during this period that William Bateson, a leader in the saltation camp, first presented the newly rediscovered work of Gregor Mendel to the British scientific community. The saltationists moved in quickly to consolidate their hold on the Royal Society's committee on heredity (Table 8.1) and claim Mendel as proof positive that heredity worked in leaps and bounds. Soon to be called Mendelians, the saltationists dominated evolutionary biology from that point onwards.

Archaeologically, there was little of major interest in the latter half of the 1890s. A long running debate on how many glaciations and interglacials there had been, and where in the chronostratigraphic sequence Pleistocene humans should be located rumbled on. Excavations by Clement Reid at Hoxne were reported to the BAAS Committee on 'The Relation of Palaeolithic Man to the Glacial Epoch' in September of 1896 at Liverpool. Clement Reid reported on excavations at Hitchin to the Royal Society in March the following year (Reid 1897). The Hitchin project was intended to test the results from Hoxne. Both sites told essentially the same story. Handaxe-making humans post-dated the last major evidence for glacial activity (the chalky boulder clay), and at Hoxne could be shown to have post-dated a second and later cold period too. The obsession of early twentieth-century Palaeolithic archaeologists with chronostratigraphic sequences had its roots in this debate (McNabb 1996; O'Connor 2007), and an opening salvo was fired by Dr Allen Sturge at the Glasgow BAAS in 1901. BAAS committees investigated the Pleistocene sites of Uphill near Weston-super-Mare (BAAS 1898 at Bristol and 1899 at Dover), and attempted to finally solve the question of whether eoliths were found at depths within remnant spreads of gravel on the North Downs of Kent (BAAS 1895 at Ipswich). The results were ambiguous.

The eolith question, so prominent in the first half of the decade was beginning to lose momentum. In part this was because the debate had reached methodological stalemate, but also because of the death of Sir Joseph Prestwich, the influential champion of the eophiles (Ellen 2011; Ellen & Muthana 2010; McNabb 2012; 2015; O'Connor 2003; 2007). Only a single eolithic paper was published in the JAI between 1895 and 1901 (Shrubsole 1895), although they got a mention as being part of the older gravels present at the Oxfordshire handaxe site of Wolvercote (Bell 1900). A. M. Bell, the discoverer of the site, gave a paper on the same subject at the 1900 BAAS at Bradford. The only other archaeological papers of a Palaeolithic character were by Henry Stopes, initial announcements of discoveries at Swanscombe, Kent, a site that would come into prominence with the new century (Stopes 1899; 1900).

The eolithic debate had centred on small stones found on the surface of very ancient deposits on the North Downs in Kent. Their fortuitous shapes were thought to have been recognised by early humans as potential tools and used as such. They pre-dated the glacial period (the chalky boulder clay of Hitchin and Hoxne) and had been transported down to their present position by rivers draining the very Wealden mountains that Ugh-lomi and Eudena fled to when escaping Uya. Wells got his chronology a little mixed here. Eoliths were thought to be evidence for ancestors in the Tertiary – the period of *Pithecanthropus*, unless Wells, following Arthur Keith (1895), accepted that the modern human form had a very deep antiquity. Had eoliths been found at depth in these old gravel spreads (as above) it would have provided powerful support for their being genuine tools, rather than just fortuitously shaped surface stones which their detractors asserted they were.

Eoliths had an input into another aspect of anthropology debated at the BAAS and in the *Journal*. In the first half of the decade E. B. Tylor, founding father of anthropology and developer of its first theoretical paradigm, evolutionary anthropology (Stocking 1987; Stocking 1995; Tylor 1865; 1881), had argued that the Tasmanian Aboriginal people had been the equivalent in development of the eolith makers as their tools were the same (Tylor 1894a; 1894b; 1895). Although he never quite stated it openly (and his prose is often ambiguous), his writings strongly imply he believed the Tasmanians were an eolithic people – in terms of their stone tool manufacture. He termed them 'pre-drift' on a number of occasions while emphasising the primitiveness of their unifacially retouched scrapers. He returned to this theme toward the end of the decade.

There were interesting tensions in the use of the Tasmanians as examples of primitiveness. Their non-lithic technology and diverse cultural repertoire was 'far from primitive', but their stone tools were nevertheless thought to be representative of the earliest stage in development (Tylor 1900). In these later communications (BAAS Bristol 1898; Bradford in 1900) Tylor proposed that the Tasmanian stage of evolution had once been found across all of Australia (Tylor 1898; 1900). It had then been displaced by new people coming in. Specifically, hafted ground stone axe makers from New Guinea, representing the Neolithic stage of development, although this never reached Tasmania.

Evolutionary anthropology asserted that cultural evolution was by sequential developmental stages. Different Indigenous people, in different parts of the world, could be living at differing levels of development at the same time. That all people everywhere experienced broadly the same developmental sequence was explained by a psychic unity common to all humans. But Tylor never really explained the mechanism of change from one stage to the next, preferring to leave it to the convenient idea of invasion by new people or new ideas.

By the late 1890s this was deeply unsatisfactory and under attack. It's easy to see why Tylor felt the Tasmanian evidence was so important. It provided a near-living laboratory of people in different stages of cultural evolution, contemporary with each other, and also explained cultural change by diffusion from elsewhere. What empowered Tylor's theories was the widespread belief that the Tasmanians were an extinct people. Thus, primitiveness had succumbed to the inevitability of progress and domination by superior cultures. In reality the Tasmanians were anything but extinct (Taylor 2017).

However, evolutionary anthropology also meant characterising Indigenous people as living fossils. Once objectified and therefore de-humanised, people could be studied as academic propositions – the major function of anthropometrics. At the same time this served to increase the sense of distance between Europeans as the epitome of evolutionary progress and their remote past.

The literary context of the last half of the fin de siècle decade

In this section I will contextualise the interpretations of Wells and the anthropological and archaeological background described above. The novels and stories used here are well known and unsurprisingly embedded in a huge body of scholarship encompassing a very wide range of textual criticism. I have not attempted to engage with much of this as it penetrates levels of meaning that are not relevant to this essay. Some excellent texts which cover at least some of the topics in more depth can be found in the following (Glendening 2007; Karschay 2015; Mighall 1999).

Fin de siècle literature was preoccupied with transformations and the passage into modernity (Pearson 2007). This meant an equally strong emphasis on the primitive. This often took the form of the relationship between animal and human. Many of the scientific romances of fin de siècle literature reflected the uncertainty of where the line should be drawn to separate the bestial past from civilised modernism.

Time was thought of as progressive (McNabb 1996), and this notion lay at the heart of the Victorian world view. If popular literature reflected this, it was only because scientists were telling the writers it was so, with the possible exception of H. G. Wells. Biological theory included the concept of atavism, the birth of physical throwbacks reflecting earlier ancestral stages. These were living proofs of the sequential and developmental character of time and evolution. Atavism was a major trope in literature, as we shall see (Brantlinger 1985; Mighall 1999). This in turn was reinforced by the widespread acceptance amongst scientists and embryologists of the doctrine of recapitulation. Each stage in the growth of an embryo reflected the adult form of one of its ancestral stages of development, summarised in the phrase 'ontogeny recapitulates phylogeny'. A good example of physical atavism is provided by Arthur Conan Doyle in the first Sherlock Holmes story, 'A Study in Scarlet' (*Beeton's Christmas Annual*, December 1887). Watson's description of the odious Enoch J. Drebber of Cleveland virtually identifies him as a simian avatar, which his behaviour confirms. Other villains in later stories receive the same treatment.

The synergy between these and evolutionary anthropology is obvious. The potential for contemporaneity between different cultural stages had the additional consequence of bringing the past and the present into direct contact with each other (Reid 2005), intruding the primitive and prehistoric into Victorian modernity as Moreau had tried to do with his creations. This too is a major trope in late Victorian fiction, reflecting a similar concern amongst the general public. Tylor (1873) believed that certain ancient cultural practices tended to live on into the modern world long after their utility had vanished. He called them survivals. They were in effect cultural avatars and proof of the sequential evolution of social systems. He famously considered the Victorian obsession with spiritualism a prehistoric survival into modern times (Reid 2005; Tylor 1873).

Heart of Darkness (Conrad 1973) is a justly famous story. It was published in three parts in 1899 in *Blackwood's Magazine* between February and April, and as a novella in *Youth: a Narrative and Two Other Stories* (1902). Like all of Conrad's work it is subtle and open to interpretation on many levels. Earlier literary criticism saw it as an indictment of colonialism and European exploitation, which it is. But more recently African scholarship has concentrated on the novella's portrayal of black Africans and their dehumanisation, also true. I see this in some of the links Conrad makes between Africans and 'primitives'. For me the book is about the Victorian fear of the beast within, and just how close to the surface the beast really was. This was present in Huxley's Romanes lecture and Wells' 'Human Evolution an Artificial Process', as well as in *The Island of Doctor Moreau* and *The Invisible Man*.

In *Heart of Darkness*, Marlow, the narrator, is hired as a river boat captain by an unnamed Continental trading company to navigate an unnamed river in Africa. Up-river there are rumours that the company's most able officer, Mr Kurtz, has run into trouble. His trading station is one of the most profitable ivory stations the company has, and he himself is considered an exceptional man – the very best 'sort' of European in Africa.

The impenetrable and limitless African forest becomes a metaphor for the past as Marlow journeys further up river, two months in all. The river journey itself stands for the passage backwards in time. He feels the pull of the primordial forest. As they steam by villages, the people come out and dance to drum rhythms:

> The steamer toiled along slowly on the edge of a black and incomprehensible frenzy. The prehistoric man was cursing us, praying to us, welcoming us – who could tell? ... We could not understand because we were too far and could not remember, because we were traveling in the night of first ages, of those ages that are gone, leaving hardly a sign – and no memories.

And a little further on:

> No, they were not inhuman. Well you know, that was the worst of it – this suspicion of their not being inhuman ... but what thrilled you was just the thought of their humanity – like yours – the thought of your remote kinship with this wild and passionate uproar.
>
> *(Conrad 1973, p. 51)*

The racism is evident, but it is rooted in an anthropological view of the past in the present. Marlow increasingly feels the pull of the forest. He becomes aware that his reaction to the drum rhythms is an atavism because he shares a common kinship with the African villagers (in my opinion an example of Tylorian psychic unity), although his European hubris will not allow him to acknowledge the immediacy of that kinship. The tension here is in Marlow's comprehension of as well as his struggle with his kinship with the African peoples he is sailing past.

When they finally arrive at Kurtz's station they find he has 'gone native' as the phrase used to be. He is in a relationship with an African woman, has participated in 'unspeakable' ceremonies, willingly embraced African life and religion. This is the first level of his betrayal – he has abandoned his European heritage. But in willingly embracing his own atavistic nature Kurtz's betrayal goes much deeper. He frees himself of any of the moral restrictions of the civilised present. He had sanctioned murder. Like Griffin in *The Invisible Man* the acquired factor is abandoned and the culminating ape allowed to break free.

> [the] mute spell of the wilderness – that seemed to draw him to its pitiless breast by the awakening of forgotten and brutal instincts, by the memory of gratified and monstrous passions.
>
> *(Conrad 1973, p. 94)*

If Kurtz, the best that European education and breeding had to offer, could fall so completely what chance had lesser mortals? The moral environment of the acquired factor was not enough to hold the back the past, the distance between animal and human, primitive and modern, proved to be shallow.

In Conan Doyle's *The Hound of the Baskervilles* we have a different take on this theme. The story appeared first in *The Strand Magazine* (August 1901–April 1902), and the novel in 1902. Here we see the power of heredity and the past to influence the present. Heredity is the thread which joins the two. Once again the story is well known and need not be dwelt upon in detail. It has been the subject of considerable scholarly interest (see Mighall 1999 for references and discussion). Sherlock Holmes and Dr Watson are hired by a country physician from Dartmoor, Dr Mortimer, to safeguard the new tenant of Baskerville Hall, Sir Henry Baskerville. His uncle, Sir Charles Baskerville died under mysterious circumstances and Mortimer is afraid that a similar fate awaits the new heir.

From the outset atavism and anthropology are set at the heart of the story. Dr Mortimer is a student of degeneration and atavism as his publication list reveals. He is also an anthropologist confident in ascribing racial origins to a skull. This sets the tone for the remainder of the novel. Mighall suggests the brooding moors with their scattering of prehistoric monuments assume the status of a character in the plot (Mighall 1999) – another example of injecting the past into the present, and it is fitting that Seldon, the Notting Hill murderer, finds his death on the moor in the jaws of the hound. Watson's description of Seldon is suitably prehistoric and bestial – he had an 'animal face, all seamed and scored with vile passions'. The hound is as much an atavistic character as Seldon is himself; both die on the moor. Mighall highlights the irony in Seldon escaping the gallows, and being sent to Dartmoor instead, precisely because his atavistic character was recognised and he was deemed not responsible for his actions.

Unveiling the true culprit, Holmes shows Watson a painting of the evil Sir Hugo Baskerville whose iniquities laid the curse of the hound on his descendants. Watson realises the features of old Sir Hugo are those of Stapleton, the real culprit, who is in reality a Baskerville:

> 'Yes, it is an interesting instance of a throw-back, which appears to be both physical and spiritual.'
>
> *(Conan Doyle 1989, p. 533)*

Stapleton has not only inherited Sir Hugo's looks, but his cruel and evil nature as well. The actual curse is not the hound but the tainted bloodline. Stapleton inherited his looks and temperament from his own father, Sir Charles' younger brother, Rodger Baskerville. We are not told what his crimes were, but they forced him to flee to South America where he was believed to have died childless. In *The Hound* heredity and its power to reassert atavistic tendencies underscore the fear of how near to the surface the animal/human boundary actually lies (McNabb 2017). Unlike Mr Kurtz whose atavism was triggered by the African forest, Stapleton was born bad. Here then is another Victorian anxiety; the primitive could be sitting right next to you on the Clapham omnibus and you'd never know it.

From the power of heredity to influence the modern world, we move to the animal/human divide itself. Laura Otis constructs a convincing parallel between *Moreau* and *Pygmalion* (Otis 2009). Although George Bernard Shaw's *Pygmalion* was written between March and June 1912, the idea had been first developed in 1897, a year after *Moreau* was published. Both were transformation novels (*Pygmalion* appeared in book form in 1916) in which the primitive is changed into the modern.

Betting that he can pass off a London streetwise flower seller as a duchess, Henry Higgins, a phonetics professor, teaches Eliza how to speak properly. He wins his bet at the cost of her respect and happiness. Otis catalogues a number of instances where Eliza and/or the working class are caricatured as primitives; Eliza is forced to take a bath, as dirty she cannot be considered human. Otis then notes how the rhetoric of the Salvation Army and the social reformers of Victorian London functioned to dichotomise the filth-ridden poor as somehow inhuman and unclean, juxtaposed to the civilised modern and well-scrubbed middle classes.

Both Moreau and Higgins are uninterested in the subjects of their experiments, seeing them as just that. Once the intellectual challenge is over, Higgins has no further interest in Eliza and is unconcerned as to her future. Both Higgins and Moreau place a significant emphasis on speech. Otis (2009) reminds her readers that for many Victorian scientists, speech had to come first, since without it complex thought could not evolve. In science and in literature speech was one of the lines drawn to distinguish animal from human. But both *Pygmalion* and *Moreau* seem to dispute this. The beast-men had the power of speech, but never evolved cognitive complexity. They had their 'laws' (injunctions against acting like animals) which they had to learn by rote and repeat out loud, but they struggle to keep the laws and eventually they lose the power of speech. Ultimately speech is not transformative. Though Eliza does learn the refined speech of polite society, she returns to her former life where there is no use for it and so it has no power to further her transformation.

So what Moreau has failed to understand is that speech without real understanding is useless. It is not enough to repeat the 'law' parrot fashion. You have to understand why it is important (McNabb 2015). The acquired factor is not just acquired culture, it is a meaningful engagement by the agent in understanding why we are all better off with social morality than without it. This was why Wells emphasised the role of education in instilling the acquired factor. That level of understanding can only be achieved through teaching and constant positive reinforcement through social frame working (emulation). Wells understood this (Wells 1896; 1897b).

I will end with vampires.

Previous to *The Origin of Species* in 1859, vampires were a pretty tame bunch, but empowered by evolutionary theory they took on a new life. *Carmilla* (*The Dark Blue*, December 1871– March 1872), by J. S. Le Fanu, is one of the founding stories of the genre, and introduced the lesbian vampire to an eager Victorian world. The link with evolution is slight, but G-L. L. Comte de Buffon (1707–1788) is mentioned in passing as Carmilla talks about the essentialist nature of organisms. As the caterpillar feeds on grubs until it transforms into the butterfly, so the vampire feeds on humans. That is its nature. For Carmilla the true transformation is to convert Sapphic love into the eternal.

The real connection comes with Robert Louis Stevenson's *Olalla* (Stevenson 2016 [orig. 1885]), first published in *The Court and Society Review* for December 1885. A wounded English officer convalesces at an isolated *residencia* in the Spanish mountains during the Peninsular War. He falls in love with the mysterious daughter of the house, who is descended from a noble family, now fallen on hard times. When the young officer cuts his wrist badly he goes to the *Señora* of the house, Olalla's mother. Until this moment she has been a lethargic figure; translated into the modern idiom Stevenson's prose presents her as a person with special needs. But suddenly she is a dynamic force, sinking her teeth into the officer's wrist 'to the bone' and drinking his blood. The young man is only saved by the timely intervention of Olalla, and her brother. Olalla explains. Her family had once been great, but regression had set into the bloodline and they degenerated:

> beauty was still handed down, but no longer the gushing wit nor the human heart; the seed passed on, it was wrapped in flesh, the flesh covered the bones, but they were the bones and flesh of brutes, and their mind was as the mind of flies.
>
> *(Stevenson 2016, p. 134)*

Heredity is the curse here. Physically, her family always resemble their ancestors, down to the last detail, they retain their physical beauty, but they also inherit an atavistic behaviour. The blood drinking of the mother is couched in terms of a primitive inheritance and the link to bestiality is clearly drawn.

In the post-Darwinian world this is an interesting story, and although appropriated by vampire fandom, it is to be wondered why Stevenson did not explicitly reference vampirism. It is implied rather than made explicit. It is possible to read the story purely as one of hereditary degeneration and atavism, and only possible after 1859. 'Man has risen', says Olalla, 'if he has sprung from the brutes, he can descend again to the same level' (Stevenson 2016, p. 133). In the preceding quote Olalla asserts 'the seed passed on' – there are shades of Weismann's eternal germ plasm here (McNabb 2015; Weismann 1882). Olalla is as yet untouched by her mother's curse, but her fear is that it will eventually overtake her also. Here then is another anxiety of the Clapham omnibus passenger – if you were uncertain about the person sitting next to you, then how could you be so sure about yourself? If we cannot distinguish between the avatars and the angels, will our unknown family history rise to claim us too, as it did Moreau's beast-men?

If we define our humanity by comparison with the Other, then vampires are a perfect mirror within which to explore what it is the Other tells us about ourselves. We are everything they are not. The most famous is of course Count Dracula. Published in 1897 (Stoker 2011 [orig. 1897]), *Dracula* is a corpse whose bones have been incessantly picked over by literary theorists.

> Critics connect him, for example, to foreign Others of diverse stripes, to infectious disease, to criminality, to rampant capitalism as well as to anti-capitalism, to an intransigent

aristocracy, and, most commonly, to transgressions of conventional sexuality and gender construction.

(Glendening 2007, p. 108)

He is a commentary upon Protestantism, on Catholicism, on Irish Nationalism, he's gay, he's straight, he is a statement on the Celtic Fringe. The list goes on.

From my reading of this novel it is evolutionary anthropology that underpins the story's basic premise. Dracula is not an atavar *sensu stricto*, he has not regressed to a more primitive state. He is locked into one moment in the past, his knowledge mirroring the time he made his pact with the devil and transformed. There is a familiar tension here. As a vampire he is a creature of the superstitious past, yet he lives in the modern world. He validates the contemporaneity of past and present together in one body and powerfully undermines the idea of a past humans have left behind. Glendening (2007) presciently notes that as a shape shifter (human-bat-hound) Dracula obscures the animal (past bestial primitive)/human (modern evolved) divide. To the Victorian, Dracula epitomises the threat of 'moral disorder' that the primitiveness of the Other represents (Glendening 2007). The contrasting modernity of the vampire hunters is often highlighted by their use of short hand, typewriters, wax audio recording cylinders and repeating rifles. But Dracula has the power to create other vampires, so the threat of the bestial heritage could spread, like a disease. It may be a contagion that is difficult to fight. Just as Marlow was drawn by the rhythm of the drums, so Jonathan Harker is drawn to want the vampire's kiss when he meets the 'weird sisters' in Castle Dracula. He is both repelled and attracted by them (Glendening 2007). Once again, the veneer of the acquired factor proved thin.

Perhaps even more unsettling to Victorian hubris was Dracula's evolution. The Count was planning on moving to London. He was acquiring property in the city and elsewhere and researching the modern world. He was a threat to it. In this sense the novel fits well with the popular invasion trope which began with G. T. Chesney's 'The Battle of Dorking' published in *Blackwood's Magazine* in May 1871, with the added twist that it is the past which is invading the present (Carroll 2016).

In terms of the evolutionary anthropology, it is Mina Harker and Professor Van Helsing who make the link, and critics have discussed it extensively. Dracula is described as having a 'child-brain' as compared with the 'man-brain' of Van Helsing and the other vampire hunters. Since he was transformed, Dracula's brain and intellect have been in stasis, while the rest of humanity has been developing – another nod to Tylor's universal psyche of humanity, and the unrealised potential of the 'primitive' brain. This is underscored by Dracula's ability to learn about the modern world. Under the theory of recapitulation children were considered to be atavistically behavioural criminals (Davie 2003; Gould 1984). This theme was taken further by what became known as the Italian school of criminal anthropology, whose most prominent member was Cesare Lombroso, and he is referenced in the novel. He developed the theory (rooted in recapitulation) that criminality was atavistic, a behavioural throwback to prehistoric times. Habitual criminals were hereditary criminals. Anthropometrics could identify the habitual criminal. Their atavistic nature came with series of inherited physical traits that always gave the primitive away. Harker's description of the count (see Table 8.2) maps nicely onto Lombroso's list. Although the British medical establishment did not accept Lombroso's inherited concept of criminality, or its physical manifestations, atavistic criminality and Lombroso were discussed at the BAAS and in the pages of the *Journal* across the

TABLE 8.2 Physical features associated with Lombroso's view of hereditary criminal atavism and those features attributed to Count Dracula by Bram Stoker

Physical features described by Lombroso as being atavistic (after Davie 2003)		Dracula
Eyes	Cold, immobile, glassy Bloodshot or bloodthirsty	
Nose	Aquiline, hooked Always prominent	Thin with high bridge ✓ Aquiline ✓
Jaw	Robust	Broad, strong ✓
Ears	Long	Pale, very pointed ✓
Cheekbones	Wide	Firm, thin
Teeth	Canines highly developed	Sharp, protrude over lip ✓
Lips	Thin	Ruddy, cruel mouth
Hair	Frizzy, abundant, dark Often no beard	Scanty at temples, profuse elsewhere ✓

See Gould 1984 for a similar table.

1890s. Cranfield and Davie both assert that Lombroso's general views would have struck a chord with the Victorian public who would have instinctively felt them to be true (Cranfield 2013; Davie 2003).

In our terms, criminality is more evidence of the invasion of the past into the present. Children were atavistic criminals too in Lombroso's view (Ellis 1890; Galton 1890). Mina and Van Helsing both realise that with a criminal's child-like brain Dracula will fall back on old habits. To escape his enemies the vampire will return to his Transylvanian castle, and that is how he is caught and ultimately killed. There is a nice tension here between the relationship between past vs present. Transylvania, like the forest in *Heart of Darkness*, is a peripheral place whose liminality allows the past to persist. As Marlow travels back in time as he moves further up river, so does Jonathan Harker and later the vampire hunters as they penetrate deeper into Transylvania. In effect Stoker flips the trope here: the moderns invade the past to successfully kill it. On the other hand, Marlow and crew fail, they have to flee the past with Kurtz's body. Stoker's transformation is positive, modernity ultimately triumphs; as it does in *The Hound of the Baskervilles*. Conrad's darker vision of transformation is negative, the past triumphs over the present.

So, in *Dracula*, the difference between the vampiric other and a modern person was cognitive flexibility, a familiar item on contemporary check lists of what represents modernity. It was beyond criminals and vampires. In terms of modern research this places the eponymous count squarely in the list of pre-modern hominins.

Conclusion

What made the Victorian man on the Clapham omnibus human?

His belief in his own modernity did, and it was linked to his skin colour, his Britishness, and his membership of a divinely sanctioned imperial political system whose superiority was proven by the very fact of its success. It was also linked to progress. The modern man was a scientific man, a technological man – both features of cognitive flexibility. The proof was all around. The stuccoed porticoes of Whitehall dominated the mud huts of Africa and Australia.

Human origins research in Victorian and Edwardian Britain was about showing this. Initially the explanation for superiority had been God, but then evolution came along. However, a wilful misreading of evolution (that it created perfection – something Darwin never asserted) allowed the Victorians to replace the divine with natural selection. So white Europeans, and the British imperial man on the bus remained at the top of the tree. Ask him to define superiority (yes, him) and he would point to himself in the mirror.

But there was a problem. Sure, we had evolved, but just how far had we really come? This was what haunted the Victorians in the last decade of Victoria's reign. If atavism and recapitulation brought the biological past into the biological present, then Tylorian survivals brought the cultural past into the cultural present. Biology, archaeology and anthropology did more than just establish a dark primordial heritage, they asserted its presence in the modern world. The 'fantastic literature' of the age engaged this anxiety. Fiction dwelt on the possibility that such a heritage could rise up to drag you back into the shadows at the rear of the cave. What clearer proof was there than to take one of the eastbound London buses, and within only a few miles of Whitehall were the slums of Whitechapel, from whose degraded and atavistic inhabitants had come Jack the Ripper.

In the century and more between the early fiction of H. G. Wells and his contemporaries, and today, research agendas in human origins have changed and developed. But many of those core questions about just what makes us human, and how modernity contributed to that, remain the same – and in many instances are still unanswered.

The Victorians and Edwardians feared we carried the past within us. The vampire's kiss was, in reality, something that stripped you of your humanity, it took away your modernity and left you a helpless slave to an innate past. The dark forest of Mr Kurtz and the Dartmoor of the *Hound* did the same. So how far has modern science freed us of these anxieties? The truth is it hasn't. The worst of the Victorians' fears have actually been realised as we now know that we do carry our past within us. Fragments of the genomes of Neanderthals, Denisovans, Mesolithic hunters and Neolithic farmers are present in living peoples. There are hints of even older genomes too. DNA is the new vampire's kiss.

And so, to the *Löwenmensch*. It is a character in a story, one that spans our world and another. It is a story from the shadows because that is where it was found. Was it placed there to protect our world or to bring it harm from another? We will never know, but like the tales of ancient evils that beset the present, it comes from a story that had anxiety set at its heart. It was there for a reason, so perhaps we should put it back were we found it?

References

Bahn, PG & Vertut, J 1997, *Journey through the Ice Age*, Weidenfeld and Nicolson, London.

Bell, AM 1900, 'On the occurrence of flint implements of palaeolithic type on an old land-surface in Oxfordshire, near Wolvercote and Pear-Tree Hill, together with a few implements of plateau types', *Journal of the Anthropological Institute of Great Britain and Ireland*, vol. 30, p. 81.

Bowler, PJ 2003, *Evolution the history of an idea*, University of California Press, London.

Brantlinger, P 1985, 'Imperial gothic: atavism and the occult in the British adventure novel 1880–1914', *English Literature in Transition*, vol. 28, pp. 243–252.

Büchner, L 1894, 'The origin of mankind', *Fortnightly Review*, vol. 55, pp. 74–82.

Carroll, S 2016, 'Resurrecting Redgauntlet: the transformation of Walter Scott's nationalist revenants in Bram Stoker's Dracula', in B Tredennick (ed.), *Victorian transformations: genre, nationalism and desire in nineteenth-century literature*, Routledge, London, pp. 116–131.

Chalmers Mitchell, P 1896, 'Mr Wells's "Dr. Moreau"', *The Saturday Review*, vol. 11, April, pp. 368–369.

Clodd, E 1895, *The story of primitive man*, George Newnes, London.

Conan Doyle, A 1989, *The original illustrated 'Strand' Sherlock Holmes: the complete facsimile edition*, Wordsworth Editions, Ware, Hertfordshire.

Conrad, J 1973, *Heart of darkness*, Penguin Modern Classics, Harmondsworth.

Cranfield, JL 2013, 'Arthur Conan Doyle, H. G. Wells and the Strand Magazine's long 1901: from Baskerville to the Moon', *English Literature in Transition, 1880–1920*, vol. 56, pp. 3–32.

Davie, N 2003, 'Criminal man revisited? Continuity and change in British criminology, c1865–1918', *Journal of Victorian Culture*, vol. 8, pp. 1–32.

Dawkins, WB 1880, *Early man in Britain and his place in the tertiary period*, Macmillan, London.

Ellen, R 2011, 'The place of the Eolithic controversy in the anthropology of Alfred Russel Wallace', *The Linnean*, vol. 27, pp. 22–33.

Ellen, R & Muthana, A 2010, 'Classifying "Eoliths": how cultural cognition featured in arguments surrounding claims for the earliest human artefacts as these developed between 1880 and 1900', *Journal of Cognition and Culture*, vol. 10, pp. 341–375.

Ellis, H 1890, *The criminal*, Walter Scott, London.

Galton, F 1890, 'Criminal anthropology', *Nature*, vol. 42, pp. 75–76.

Gillham, NW 2001, *Sir Francis Galton: from African exporation to the birth of eugenics*, Oxford University Press, Oxford.

Gillham, NW 2015, 'The battle between the miometricians and the Mendelians: how Sir Francis Galton's work caused his disciples to reach conflicting conclusions about the hereditary mechanism', *Science and Education*, vol 24, pp. 61–75.

Glendening, J 2007, *The evolutionary imagination in late Victorian novels: an entangled bank*, Ashgate, Aldershot.

Gould, SJ 1984, *The mismeasure of man*, W.W. Norton, New York.

Hussain, ST & Floss, H 2015, 'Sharing the world with mammoths, cave lions and other beings: linking animal human interactions and the Aurignacian belief world', *Quartär*, vol. 62, pp. 85–120.

Huxley, TH 1894a, 'Evolution and ethics: the Romanes Lecture 1893', in TH Huxley (ed.), *Collected essays by T.H. Huxley, volume 9: evolution and ethics and other essays*, Macmillan, London, pp. 46–86.

Huxley, TH 1894b, 'Prolegomena', in TH Huxley (ed.), *Collected essays by T.H. Huxley, volume 9: evolution and ethics and other essays*, Macmillan, London, pp. 1–45.

Karschay, S 2015, *Degeneration, normativity, and the gothic at the fin de siècle*, Palgrave Macmillan, London.

Keith, A 1895, 'Pithecanthropus erectus: a brief review of human fossil remains', *Science Progress*, vol. 3, pp. 348–369.

Kidd, B 1894, *Social evolution*, Macmillan, London.

Kidd, B 1895, 'Social evolution', *The Nineteenth Century*, vol. 37, pp. 226–240.

Kind, C-J, Ebinger-Rist, N, Wolf, S, Beutelspacher, T & Wehrberger, K 2014, 'The smile of the lion man: recent excavations in Stadel Cave (Baden-Württemberg, south-west Germany) and the restoration of the famous Upper Palaeolithic figure', *Quartär*, vol. 16, pp. 129–145.

Kropotkin, P 1896, 'II. The erect ape-man', *The Nineteenth Century*, vol. 39, pp. 425–432.

Laing, S 1892, *Human origins*, Chapman and Hall, London.

Mackenzie, N & Mackenzie, J 1987, *H.G. Wells: the time traveller*, Hogarth Press, London.

McLean, S 2009, *The early fiction of H.G. Wells*, Palgrave Macmillan, Basingstoke.

McNabb, J 1996, '4. Through the looking glass: an historical perspective on archaeological research at Barnfield Pit, Swanscombe, ca.1900–1964', in B Conway, J McNabb & N Ashton (eds), *Excavations at Barnfield Pit, Swanscombe, 1968–1972*. Occasional Papers of the British Museum #94, Trustees of the British Museum, London, pp. 31–51.

McNabb, J 2007, *The British lower Palaeolithic: stones in contention*, Routledge, London.

McNabb, J 2012, *Dissent with modification: human origins, Palaeolithic archaeology and evolutionary anthropology in Britain 1859–1901*, Archaeopress, Oxford.

McNabb, J 2015, 'The beast within: H. G. Wells, *The Island of Doctor Moreau*, and human evolution in the mid-1890s', *Geological Journal*, vol. 50, pp. 383–397.

McNabb, J 2017, 'Anthropology by gaslight: Sherlock Holmes, Conan Doyle and the anthropology of detection at the Victorian fin de siècle', *World Archaeology*, vol. 49, pp. 728–751.

Mighall, R 1999, *A geography of Victorian gothic fiction*, Oxford University Press, Oxford.

Morris, C 1890, 'From brute to man', *The American Naturalist*, vol. 24, pp. 341–350.

Newton, ET 1895, 'On a human skull and limb-bones found in the Palaeolithic terrace-gravel at Galley Hill, Kent', *Quarterly Journal of the Geological Society of London*, vol. 51, pp. 505–527.

O'Connor, A 2003, 'Geology, archaeology, and "the raging vortex of the 'Eolith' controversy"', *Proceedings of the Geologists' Association*, vol. 114, pp. 255–262.

O'Connor, A 2007, *Finding time for the old Stone Age*, Oxford University Press, Oxford.

Otis, L 2009, 'Monkey in the mirror: the science of Professor Higgins and Doctor Moreau', *Twentieth Century Literature*, vol. 55, pp. 485–509.

Pearson, R 2007, 'Primitive modernity: H. G. Wells and the prehistoric man of the 1890s', *The Yearbook of English Studies*, vol. 37, pp. 58–74.

Perry Coste, FH 1897a, 'Human evolution I: according to Mr H. G. Wells', *Natural Science*, vol. 10, pp. 184–187.

Perry Coste, FH 1897b, 'Untitled note', *Natural Science*, vol. 10, p. 244.

Philmus, RM 1993, *H.G. Wells: The Island of Doctor Moreau. A variorum text*, University of Georgia Press, Athens, GA.

Philmus, RM & Hughes, DY (eds) 1975, *H.G. Wells: early writings in science and science fiction*, University of California Press, London.

Porr, M 2015, 'Beyond animality and humanity: landscape, metaphor and identity in the early Upper Palaeolithic of Central Europe', in F Coward, R Hosfield, M Pope & F Wenban-Smith (eds), *Settlement, society and cognition in human evolution*, Cambridge University Press, Cambridge, pp. 54–74.

Reid, C 1897, 'The Palaeolithic deposits at Hitchin and their relation to the glacial epoch', *Proceedings of the Royal Society of London*, vol. B287, pp. 535–570.

Reid, J 2005, 'Robert Louis Stevenson and the "romance of anthropology"', *Journal of Victorian Culture*, vol. 10, pp. 46–71.

Ruddick, N 2009, *The fire in the stone: prehistoric fiction from Charles Darwin to Jean M. Auel*, Wesleyan University Press, Middletown, CT.

Shrubsole, OA 1895, 'On flint implements of a primitive type from old (pre-glacial) hill-gravels in Berkshire', *Journal of the Anthropological Institute of Great Britain and Ireland*, vol. 24, pp. 44–49.

Smith, WG 1894, *Man the primeval savage: his haunts and relics from the hill-tops of Bedfordshire to Blackwall*, Stanford, London.

Stevenson, RL 2016 [1885], 'Olalla', in G Cavendish (ed.), *Horror tales*, Solis Press, Tunbridge Wells, pp. 104–140.

Stocking, GW 1971, 'What's in a name? The origin of the Royal Anthropological Institute (1837–1971)', *Man*, vol. 6, pp. 369–390.

Stocking, GW 1987, *Victorian anthropology*, Free Press, New York.

Stocking, GW 1995, *After Tylor: British social anthropology 1888–1951*, University of Wisconsin Press, Madison.

Stoker, B 2011 [1897], *Dracula*, Collins Classics, HarperCollins, London.

Stopes, H 1899, 'On the discovery of Neritina Fluviatilis with a Pleistocene fauna and worked flints in high terrace gravels of the Thames Valley', *Journal of the Royal Anthropological Institute*, vol. 29, pp. 302–303.

Stopes, H 1900, 'Unclassified worked flints', *Journal of the Anthropological Institute of Great Britain and Ireland*, vol. 30, pp. 299–304.

Taylor, R 2017, *Into the heart of Tasmania. A search for human antiquity*, Melbourne University Press, Melbourne.

Tylor, EB 1865, *Researches into the early history of mankind and the development of civilization*, John Murray, London.

Tylor, EB 1873, *Primitive culture*, 2nd edn, John Murray, London.

Tylor, EB 1881, *Anthropology. An introduction to the study of man and civilization*, Macmillan, London.

Tylor, EB 1894a, 'On some stone implements of the Australian type from Tasmania', *Report of the sixty-fourth meeting of the British Association for the Advancement of Science held at Oxford in August 1894*, John Murray, London, p. 782.

Tylor, EB 1894b, 'On the Tasmanians as representatives of Palaeolithic man', *Journal of the Anthropological Institute of Great Britain and Ireland*, vol. 23, pp. 141–152.

Tylor, EB 1895, 'On the occurrence of ground stone implements of Australian type in Tasmania', *Journal of the Anthropological Institute of Great Britain and Ireland*, vol. 24, pp. 335–340.

Tylor, EB 1898, 'On the survival of Palaeolithic conditions in Tasmania and Australia, with especial reference to the modern usage of unground stone implements in West Australia', *Report of the sixty-eighth meeting of the British Association for the Advancement of Science held at Bristol in September 1898*, John Murray, London, pp. 1014–1015.

Tylor, EB 1900, '37. On the stone age in Tasmania, as related to the history of civilization', *Journal of the Anthropological Institute of Great Britain and Ireland*, vol. 30, pp. 33–34.

Wallace, AR 1889, *Darwinism. An exposition on the theory of natural selection with some of its applications*, Macmillan, London.

Weismann, A 1882, *Studies in the theory of descent*, trans. R Meldola, Sampson Low, London.

Wells, HG 1894, 'Flint implements old and new', *Pall Mall Gazette*, vol. 58, April 3rd, p. 4.

Wells, HG 1896, 'Human evolution, an artificial process', *Fortnightly Review*, vol. 60, October, pp. 590–595.

Wells, HG 1897a, 'Human evolution III. Mr Wells replies', *Natural Science*, vol. 10, pp. 242–244.

Wells, HG 1897b, 'Morals and civilization', *Fortnightly Review*, vol. 61, February, pp. 263–268.

Wells, HG 2005 [1896], *The island of Doctor Moreau*, Penguin Classics, Penguin, London.

9

THE TEMPORALITY OF HUMANITY AND THE COLONIAL LANDSCAPE OF THE DEEP HUMAN PAST

Martin Porr

Introduction

Archaeology is fundamentally connected to notions of time, origins and history. The history of archaeology as an academic discipline is closely tied to the establishment of the geological antiquity of the world and, subsequently, the antiquity of humanity (Stavrinaki 2018b). This well-known history also relates to the close connections between archaeology and the modern ideological, discursive, economic and political structures in Europe in the eighteenth and nineteenth century (Trigger 1984; 1989). These aspects have been critically discussed within archaeology for some time, although one can argue that the respective critique has so far failed to have a substantial impact on archaeological method and theory (Lucas 2005). Modern archaeology, indeed, remains a deeply modern practice and exercise (Thomas 2004). Elsewhere in this volume, the close connections between the Western modern project and the project of archaeology have been discussed as well as the entanglements of these projects and the phenomenon of colonialism. Within the overall framework of this volume, the aim of this chapter is to explore related aspects with a focus on notions of time and temporality.

The growth of the modern global system since the fifteenth century was connected to increasingly accelerated dialectical changes in social and political attitudes and practices, as well as orientations towards the natural world, knowledge and reasoning (Moore 2015; 2016). These developments had fundamental effects on the perception and understanding of humanity's past and present, which are, in turn, related to changes in attitudes towards time, causal processes and history. Here, I want to establish a critical perspective on these processes and discuss their impact on the understanding of the deep human past. I argue that these aspects are relevant on a variety of levels, ranging from the very long-term to the micro-dynamics of social interactions and human relationships with the natural environment. I make a preliminary case that these aspects can be related to deep social, discursive and perceptual structures that are a consequence of the establishment of the global system of capitalism and the related experience of global colonialism. As such, they continue to have an impact on the construction of the deep history of humanity until the present day, and I want to raise critical questions about the applicability of this frame of reference for understanding the whole of humanity's past and present.

The temporality of modernity and humanity: social and historical perspectives

The notion of time is one of the thorniest and most paradoxical areas of scientific inquiry and philosophical considerations. Even though it is a central aspect of human experience, consciousness, perception, communication, social interactions and technology, time remains an elusive philosophical and metaphysical entity. However, modernity itself as an economic, historical and social phenomenon has been closely connected to a specific understanding and construction of time. As Mignolo (2011, p. 163) argued: '"Time" became a central rhetorical figure in the self-definition and self-fashioning of modernity: modernity is a "time" based concept.' Such a view is reflective of the development of an understanding of time as a homogeneous, quantifiable and linear dimension that is unaffected by spatial differences and human experience. The main proponent of this concept was Isaac Newton (1643–1727), who developed an absolute understanding of space and time as fundamentally independent from objects and events. Time progresses evenly and homogeneously in one direction from the past towards the future. It has been traditionally stressed by historians of science that this view of time was dialectically connected to fundamental socio-economic developments in Europe from the seventeenth century onwards:

> Modernity, it is said, arose, first, as the temporality of modern science, in which mathematically expressed laws apply uniformly across time and space, and, second, as the temporality of the nation-state, in which laws apply with perfect uniformity throughout its territory, in which politics are national in scope, citizenship a unifying status, and history the story of the nation's self-liberation.
>
> *(Reddy 2016, p. 326)*

Throughout the nineteenth century, the need for temporal integration and coordination of social and economic processes in the nation states of Europe and their colonies became an increasingly urgent task for governments, originally driven by the introduction of steam train networks. It appears consequently ironic that during these dramatic and accelerating socio-economic changes, the scientific understanding of time seemingly dramatically diverged from its social construction and everyday experience in the Western world. With the theory of relativity, Albert Einstein (1879–1955) famously rejected the Newtonian absolute conception of time and space according to which both are separate, uniform and unchanging. In contrast, since Einstein, time has been understood as a fourth spatial dimension and the usual dichotomy of space and time is collapsed into the single term 'space-time'. According to Einstein, time is relative to motion and space-time is relative to the motion of an observer (Barad 2007, p. 437). Together with quantum physics, the special and the general theory of relativity have established an understanding of time that is vastly removed from its Western 'common-sense' experience. This applies, for example, to the experience of the present, the distinction of past and future, the irreversibility of processes, and the relationships between causes and effects (Riggs 2015, pp. 49–50; Rovelli 2018). It needs to be stressed that these developments are not just an issue of elementary particles and cosmological phenomena. Within modern physics, many elements are understood only to exist relative to an observer or a measuring mechanism. This means that technological, social and cultural aspects participate in the construction of the so-called natural environment of human beings and our knowledge about it (Barad 2007; 2011).

The experience of temporality in connection with the phenomenon of modernity appears to be largely a reflection of the necessities of coordinating economic relationships of production and consumption within a capitalist framework and the nation state. These aspects became particularly significant during the nineteenth century with the introduction of new technologies of time measurement, production and transport and the globalisation of colonial networks of resource extraction and trade (Galison 2003). Just when physics undermined the Western and Newtonian metaphysics of time, the necessities of colonialism and military organisation enhanced the experience of a homogeneous temporality that operates and progresses independently from location and place. Equally, space itself is given a mathematical and universal quality, independent from its contents, and formalised with the introduction of the global latitude/longitude system and other measurement systems (Zerubavel 1982). Following the seminal argument of Anderson (2006) in *Imagined Communities*, 'the very possibility of imagining the nation' depends on this modern type of temporality 'in which simultaneity is, as it were, transverse, cross-time, marked not by prefiguring and fulfilment, but by temporal coincidence, and measured by clock and calendar' (Reddy 2016, p. 327).

Not surprisingly, the development of the European nation state also had a significant impact on the experience and interpretation of human history and the past more generally. The necessity to create a unified and homogeneous community in the present necessitated a projection of its characteristics into the past. The consequence is the strategic creation of triumphal narratives of nation-building that pass over any

> traumas and divisive conflicts of the sort best passed over by any political community that hopes to imagine itself as a unified body. [...] As Ernest Renan remarked in 1882, 'forgetting, I would even say historical error, is essential to the creation of a nation'.
>
> *(Smail & Shryock 2013, pp. 710–711)*

Therefore, the creation of defined spatial boundaries around the nation states in Europe from the eighteenth century onwards was supplemented by the creation of mythical boundaries in time.

At the same time, more general ideological changes were taking place that had an impact transnationally. The ideologies that were adopted by and shared between these nation states were also projected backwards and transformed into origin narratives of modernity or modern humanity itself. These shared elements are broadly understood as the ideas and conceptions of Enlightenment thought that were characterised – despite many differences – by the core aspects of humanism, rationalism, individualism and materialism. Stoczkowski (2002) has argued in his seminal study of 'myth, imagination and conjecture' in the study of human origins that these aspects of the philosophies of the eighteenth century crystallised intellectual elements that had persisted in European culture for more than two millennia and remained influential over more than 200 years, despite a radically expanding knowledge about global archaeological evidence. Paired with the Newtonian understanding of time (driven by socio-economic conditions and experiences), these elements amounted to the specific Western and modern understanding of human history that was created in conjunction with the discovery during the nineteenth century of the Earth's antiquity and humanity's deep past. It was characterised by a unilineal and progressive view of an ascendency of humanity from simple beginnings towards technological and social complexity as represented by European contemporary societies.

A wide range of authors have critically engaged with these aspects in the context of the origin and research history of Western historical disciplines (Lucas 2005; Shryock & Smail 2011b; Trigger 1989). The extension of the depth of human history and the time revolution in the mid-nineteenth century caused a split and fragmentation in the treatment of the past. While before the 1860s, the human and the natural sciences had constituted a single field of enquiry a distinction was now made between ancient and modern history, with respective epistemologies and interpretative frames of reference. This shift amplified the essential distinction between humanity and nature that had been a part of the Western tradition for millennia. Shryock and Smail (2011a, p. 18) have argued that this rift was 'a deliberate intellectual and epistemological move' that was bound up with the establishment of the discipline of history in academia itself. In any case, this understanding cemented a qualitative distinction between history and prehistory in the linear development of humanity through time and towards Western civilisation. Together with the distinction between nature and culture it severed history and evolution from each other as separate domains with their own causal regimes and processes. This movement connected fundamentally to the Western commitment to human exceptionalism and it further emphasised the Western idea of humanity's history as a journey out and towards increased control of nature.

However, at the same time, the newly discovered temporal depth of human history required explanation. As has been stressed elsewhere, it was the framework of Darwinian evolution that provided the explanatory framework, reflecting the experience and living conditions of the nineteenth century (e.g. Barta 2005). While Darwinian evolution (as developed by C. Darwin, T. Huxley, A. Wallace and E. Haeckel) forcefully proposed a materialist vision of nature without any overarching direction or meaning, these latter aspects were less clear-cut in the case of the treatment of humanity itself. Ingold (2004) has drawn attention to the fact that modern approaches to human evolution have been consistently characterised by constant tensions and paradoxes between continuity and discontinuity from the eighteenth century Enlightenment philosophies to the present day. The main reason for these contradictory issues is the continuity of the dualistic understanding of the universal and essential exceptionality of humanity that needs to be maintained despite the recognition of the fundamental connections between humanity and nature (Porr 2014). However, the distinction between humanity and nature was (and still is) an illusion, an imagination that itself dissolves natural, historical and cultural elements (Fuentes & Visala 2016; Sahlins 2008). The distinction is a boundary created between modernity and the Other. In temporal terms, it is the distinction between the modern and the pre-modern. As Smail and Shryock (2013, p. 711) have argued, in this exercise, modernity firmly remains the ultimate centre of reference: 'The result is a center-periphery model of history that strips the past of its autonomy and renders it provincial.'

This observation can clearly be extended to other historical periods as well (Fazioli 2017). It draws attention to the fact that modernity is itself a representation that generates its own starting point in the form of tradition (Cooper 2007). This process is ongoing, flexible, political and historically contingent. For the discussion below, it becomes important to acknowledge that with these developments, the past or the origins of modernity do not become a historical period that is enclosed in the past: 'Rather, it is a narrative space auto-populated by features that define temporal Otherness for the self-consciously modern observer' (Smail & Shryock 2013, p. 713). In fact, modernity becomes as much an unstable and contested condition as any other form of social identity. Humans can slip in and out of modernity, while objects, animals and natural phenomena can slip in and out of humanity. They oscillate between animality and humanity, between the animate and the inanimate. These determinations remain contested and subject to changing circumstances and boundary maintenance processes. How could it be otherwise in a world that is fluid and characterised by innumerable intersecting processes and temporalities?

These aspects can be observed in several interrelated areas that have been perceived as liminal or transitory in the narrative of human becoming: apes and hunter-gatherers. Corbey (2005) has put together a convincing overview of the shifting views of the great apes in modern Western history, especially since the eighteenth century. He effectively demonstrated that besides an enormous increase in empirical knowledge, research into and attitudes towards great apes are characterised by

> an alternation of humanising and bestialising moves with respect to both apes and humans, a persistent quest for unambiguousness and human purity [...] an enduring activity of drawing, policing, displacing, denying, and bridging the metaphysical, religious, and moral boundaries between humans and their closest relatives in nature.
>
> *(Corbey 2005, p. 1)*

Comparable elements can be traced in the concern with hunting and gathering people, who are variously constructed as belonging either to the realm of nature or humanity or existing in an unstable condition between them (Barnard 2014; Ingold 2000; Pluciennik 2014). These cases are informed by the necessity to negotiate the relationship between human exceptionalism and human unity and the deep temporalisation of nature. What is humanity's place in and apart from nature and how must this be thought as a temporal process?

The Darwinian revolution during the nineteenth century did not fundamentally question the ideas of human exceptionalism and humanity's ascent out of nature (Porr 2014). In the light of the recognition of the deep ancestry of humanity, this created a range of contradictions and paradoxes. How can there be a teleological structure in human evolution if the processes of variation and selection are random and reward short-term advantages? How can something completely new and unique arise from purely natural factors and material processes (McDonald Pavelka 2002)? The idea of human exceptionalism was itself paradoxical, because it was equally applied to the basic and universal abilities for language and symbolic communication on the one hand and restricted to European modern rationality and values on the other. These observations draw attention to the fact that the described liminalities and boundaries are in fact reflections of processes of self-determination, identity creation and boundary maintenance of modern Western society itself. They are reflections of changing relationships with the environment and changing views of nature, which in turn necessitated a renegotiation of what it means to be human. The understanding of nature and humanity are different sides of the same coin (Descola 2013).

Accordingly, during the nineteenth century, the attitude towards the historicity of humanity changed, along with the attitude towards humanity's temporality. While Western society constructed itself as being as far away as possible from the origin of humanity, animality was never far away. This follows the logic outlined above that modernity is a concept that is actually temporally heterogeneous (Smail & Shryock 2013). Each human individual was perceived as a compound being with parts that relate to different aspects of humanity's phylogeny. In the first half of the nineteenth century, this orientation was a factor of

Hegel's historical philosophy of Subjective Spirit, which is the realm of freedom that needs to overcome the causal necessities of nature. As the latter is never finally overcome, spiritual freedom involves constantly overcoming natural necessity (Moellendorf 1992, p. 249). Darwin himself famously wrote that despite the human 'god-like intellect', 'man still bears in his bodily frame the indelible stamp of his lowly origin' (Darwin, quoted in Corbey 2005, p. 67). Humanity's struggle with the legacy of multiple temporalities in bodies and brains was also a key element of the work of Sigmund Freud, possibly the most influential psychologist of all time. Freud elaborated most clearly the idea that the boundary between animality and humanity is located within each human individual (Corbey 1991). Maintaining this boundary becomes a struggle against the predicament of primitive 'man', who had a mind that was inconsistent, childish, confused, deficient in foresight, and inclined to confuse facts with fantasy. Every individual consequently must repeat the struggle of humanity's ascent out of animality: 'Evolutionary progress implied the domestication of man's bestial nature, the taming of the beast within, the triumph of reason in the transcending of brute creation' (Corbey 2005, p. 83).

Freud and Darwin both reflected the socio-economic conditions of their times, but they also did more than that. They turned their situated experience into natural history. In their influential writings, they transformed history into nature. In this way, their thinking gained the authority of universal applicability and inevitability (Sahlins 1996). In each case and despite crucial differences, they assumed that the modern individual was the product of a unique temporality in which ontogeny mirrors the phylogeny of the whole species. The modern individual has not only to succeed in the ascent from animality to humanity. It also must fight back the constant threat of animality from within itself. The development of the modern individual is consequently a deeply moral affair that is, nevertheless, given a naturalistic and universal dimension. Wagner has argued that it is a peculiarity of the Western tradition to link the idea of the 'human' as a natural and biological phenomenon with a set of moral assumptions. Consequently, '"becoming human" in our tradition is a moral task for the individual as well as an evolutionary one for the species, and the resolution to treat these two aspects as the same thing has given our study of man's origins its teleological and moralistic overtones' (Wagner 2016, p. 133). Freud and Darwin's views, as well as the understanding of Western morality during the eighteenth and nineteenth century, were formed by their own socio-economic conditions and experiences, which were, in turn, shaped by modern European colonialism and the imaginary ethnography and history of the world it had created (Barta 2005). It is those aspects and their temporality that will be discussed next.

The temporality of colonialism

Barta (2005) has argued that it is largely forgotten that Darwin was intimately familiar with colonial atrocities and the processes of colonial exploitation. During his journey on *HMS Beagle*, Darwin described a range of violent episodes in South America and Australia and the consequences these had on the Indigenous population. How did Darwin experience and interpret these insights into the ongoing 'worldwide human catastrophe' (Barta 2005, p. 118)? Darwin's opposition to slavery is often emphasised and celebrated by his supporters. However, while he was unconventional and revolutionary in the realm of science, he was less so in terms of political and social issues. He retained the worldview of his time and class. He also was convinced that the advance of civilisation was inevitable and a natural process. Consequently, he tended to interpret the effects of colonial exploitation, the disappearance of people and cultures, as a consequence of the progressive mechanisms of history (Brantlinger 2003). During his voyage on the *Beagle*, Darwin wrote that 'besides several evident causes' a 'mysterious agency' seems to be responsible for the destruction he observed. He knew what the 'evident causes' were, but he also naturalised the overall process of European colonisation and appropriation: 'The varieties of man seem to act on each other in the same way as different species of animals, the stronger always extirpating the weaker' (Darwin, quoted in Barta 2005, p. 125). At the same time, he was intrigued and fascinated by the opportunities for economic development that were opened by the demise of Indigenous people. Reflecting the attitudes of the wealthy British class during the nineteenth century, he also welcomed the new world of productivity that was created by European colonialism. In a comment on the frontier violence during his travels into the interior of Tierra del Fuego, he wrote: 'If this warfare is successful, that is if all the Indians are butchered, a grand extent of country will be available for the production of cattle, and the valleys ... will be most productive of corn' (Darwin, quoted in Barta 2005, p. 120). There is little doubt that these attitudes were very much the rule among the privileged class during the nineteenth century. They contain a problematic admixture of assumptions about natural and human causes as well as an implicit ignorance of human agency and intentions and their socio-economic conditions. They are also indicative of the different temporalities that colonialism established, in which it operated, and which provided a moral framework of justification.

The development of the modern global colonial economic and political system during the eighteenth and nineteenth centuries necessitated the coordination of the production and movement of goods and people on an unprecedented scale. It created a global system of political and economic centre–periphery relationships between Europe and the rest of the world. To a certain degree, it can be argued that this development is a complex enlargement and extension of the socio-economic processes connected to the rise of the modern European nation state, which also necessitated the development of spatial-temporal coordination and unification on an unprecedented scale (Mignolo 2011, pp. 160–162). It also coincided with the development of a new historical philosophy in Europe. During the Enlightenment period, the constitutive dichotomies between nature/culture and modernity/tradition were restructured within a framework of an abstract but also a progressive temporality. Temporal progression became the most important dimension to understand human variability. While in earlier periods, a hierarchy between a centre (usually Europe) and a periphery also was recognised and interpreted hierarchically, it did not receive a temporal or historical significance. 'Natural history' in the tradition of Pliny the Elder described the present condition in spatial terms and not because of historical developments or evolution. Nature did not have a history; it had a physiognomy (Bredekamp 2012, p. 16). The German philosopher Immanuel Kant complemented this understanding in 1775 with a temporal component, *naturalis historia*, that related to the historical understanding of natural phenomena in addition to spatial and classificatory description (Bredekamp 2012, p. 17). Kant also formalised the idea that humanity is undergoing a progressive universal secular history that moves towards the realisation of its 'natural capacities'. This understanding was juxtaposed over Kant's view of the differences between the human races (e.g. Allais 2016) and, accordingly, that 'civilisation can only be defined, implemented, and guided by the white man who is in Europe at the present moment of a linear, historical time. [...] *time* became the central factor in making and recasting colonial difference' (Mignolo 2011, p. 163).

From this understanding (itself a product of the experience of colonialism from a safe and privileged distance), a moral power discourse with reference to a universal metaphysical principle was constructed that denied the largest part of humanity a life in the present. This discourse is encapsulated in Fabian's (1983) seminal notion of the 'denial of coevalness'. This unusual term was intended to reflect the paradoxical understanding that people might be living contemporaneously and inhabiting the same space, but they are still regarded to exist in different historical periods and, therefore, are not of the same time. It refers to the German term *Gleichzeitigkeit*, which can equally mean contemporaneity and simultaneity/synchronicity (Fabian 1983, p. 31). The classification of people and societies according to typological time and chronological schemes becomes a powerful way of characterising the Other. It also is a powerful way of creating difference and distance. Fabian was very clear about the fact that the denial of coevalness is a deeply political act that is entangled in the power relationships of modernity/colonialism. Fabian developed his approach in the framework of a systematic analysis of the practices of the discipline of (social) anthropology. However, the latter only reflected and enhanced features and tendencies that structured the complex development of capitalism and colonialism and its transformation of the understanding of time and history. Mignolo (2011) has argued that this intellectual complex and its different stages from the sixteenth century to the present should be subsumed under the notion of coloniality, and in its global reach and effects 'coloniality at large' (Mignolo & Walsh 2018). The understanding of time and history served to structure a wide range of notions, value judgements and practices:

> Modernity and tradition, progress and stagnation, city and country, speed and slow motion, and so on were distinctive temporal features of the second stage of the modern/colonial world. [...] Progress, a weapon of the civilising mission, was the key rhetorical figure in the nineteenth century.
>
> *(Mignolo 2011, p. 163)*

As was outlined in the previous section, the distinctions that were created in this way were only superficially clear-cut and hierarchical; the reality was far more complicated. Distance from the centre was equated with distance in time and proximity to the origin of humanity and, therefore, nature. However, the reality was rather that a narrative space was created that intersected with everything everywhere and structured the experience of people everywhere. Practices and items in the West could be termed 'mythological' or 'archaic' or 'primitive', which served as means of distinction and distance irrespective of the geographical location in relation to the centre (Fabian 1983, p. 30). Consequently, a whole range of dialectical oppositions between humanity/animality, tradition/modernity, culture/nature, fast/slow and so on were created that related temporalities to each other that operate at different scales – from the everyday to the depths of human history. For example, the South was not only constructed as primitive and backwards along the scale of history; it was also the place of 'slow speed' that lives 'a slow time, while the North is the location of speed, progress and living by the "clock"' (Mignolo 2011, p. 173). These ideas are reflections of the realities of the global socio-economic structure of the colonial period from the eighteenth to the twentieth century. Most individuals found themselves entangled in competitive processes that put them more and more under pressure. People experienced this as an acceleration of time. Benjamin Franklin's famous dictum 'time is money' reflected the need to maximise labour time against production outcomes. Success became dependent on the idea that to go faster is to win (and of course you accept that winning is the name of the game), that you not only have to produce more (of whatever you produce) but that you have to do it first.

(Mignolo 2011, p. 177)

These developments not only characterised the socio-economic shifts within European nations. They also formed one of the key aspects of the experience of colonialism outside of Europe and, consequently, became the target of anti-colonial critique. For example, Mishra (2013) has collected and discussed a range of significant contributions from Asian contexts from the nineteenth and early twentieth century that was experienced by the European ruling class as a time of self-confident progress. It was particularly the 'great speed of change' and a resulting feeling of helplessness that was commonly expressed. Japanese novelist Natsume Sōseki (1867–1916) wrote:

The new waves come one after another from the West … It is as if, before we can enjoy one dish on the table, or even know what it is, another dish is set before us … We cannot help it; there is nothing else we can do.

(quoted in Mishra 2013, p. 43)

Other writers emphasised the sobering effects of the creation of a 'Darwinian universe of conflict between individuals, classes and nations' that produced materialistic people, who constantly desire ever-new things and are at the same time constantly being frustrated (Mishra 2013, p. 210). However, the experience and assessment were at the same time deeply conflicted and ambiguous. While traditions were destroyed and devalued, people in colonised or otherwise affected countries could hardly resist the extraordinary dominance of the West and often lamented their own 'backwardness'. These processes were the product of the unique nature of European colonialism that was equally a political and economic endeavour as well as an intellectual, moral and spiritual subordination (Mishra 2013, p. 45).

As mentioned above, a range of authors have analysed the role of (social) anthropology itself in these contexts. Particularly French- and English-speaking anthropology is today widely regarded as a product of European colonialism and has reflected, amplified and shaped colonial structures and their experience. Particularly during the 1980s, these aspects have received extensive critical attention. Key elements have been a critique of the production of anthropological knowledge and the representation of the Other (Clifford & Marcus 1986). Through this critique, anthropologists have attempted to transform their work from a tool of intercultural misrepresentation into a movement of cultural critique (Marcus & Fischer 1986) and, more recently, a practice of the decolonisation of thought (Viveiros de Castro 2014). The basis of these developments was a critique of Western epistemology or, rather, a critique of the claims of universal applicability of Western/scientific epistemology. In this context, Mignolo (2011, p. 172) has argued that it is particularly the Western notion of time that caused 'history' and 'science' to acquire a hegemonic force and allowed 'the erasure or devaluation of other forms of knowledge'. Fabian's seminal book *Time and the Other* (1983) is generally regarded as one of the first systematic elucidations of the role of time in anthropology's construction of its research subjects in the field and in literary form (see also Gell 1992; Gosden 1994). For example, in *Time and the Other*, Fabian argued that the ethnographic description and the construction of an ethnographic present tend to remove the

Other from the flow of time and denied the possibility of change. Furthermore, Fabian critiqued literary practices of abstraction and the selective omission of fieldwork communications that created a distance between the research subjects, the author and the reader. This temporal logic was referred to as 'allochronism' and through the creation of different temporalities, it denied the condition of coevalness (Birth 2008, p. 4). These elements currently form integral aspects of anthropological intellectual practice. Beyond the effects of the crisis of representation and the critique of the production of knowledge, the engagement with the discipline's implicit and explicit temporal frames forms a constitutive criterion of the mainstream of the discipline (Hodges 2008; James & Mills 2005; Kockelman & Bernstein 2012; Munn 1992).

The critical and reflexive assessment of the role of time in anthropological discourse has also opened new avenues for understanding and appreciating temporality cross-culturally. This movement included a critical deconstruction and reassessment of the dichotomy between Western linear time concepts and traditional cyclical understandings of time (Mignolo 2011, pp. 170–171; Rifkin 2017). In the case of Aboriginal Australia, it is now widely acknowledged that the anthropological concept of the 'Dreamtime' has problematic romantic and exotic dimensions to it and is a product of European colonial appropriation and generalisation (Perkins 1998; Stanner 1958; Wolfe 1991). Based on long-term collaborative research, the concept of Dreaming has been expanded and deepened in recent decades. It is no longer understood as a unified concept, but reflective of the dialectic between Aboriginal philosophies and lifeways, which cannot be divorced from the experience and understanding of landscape (James 2015; Rose 1996). As Rumsey (1994) has argued, Dreaming is not to be understood as the inability to understand linear time or history, but a particular economy of inscriptive and interpretive practices through which 'country' becomes 'story'. Expositions like these open less deterministic and restrictive cross-cultural and anthropological explorations of the treatment and construction of time (Rifkin 2017). They also enable taking serious convergences between Western/scientific approaches and Indigenous philosophies within 'a universe busy with different spatio-temporal systems' (Strang 2015, p. 103). As such, they are also significant for a critical assessment of time in archaeology and the temporalisation of human origins.

The barbarian and the primitive: time and archaeology

In recent years, a range of publications have provided valuable insights into the historical and recent treatment of time in archaeology (Holdaway & Wandsnider 2008; Lucas 2005; Murray 1999). It is therefore not necessary to revisit this history in detail here. One of the key elements of the founding mythology of archaeology is its inherent connection to the development of a linear modern understanding of time and the discovery of 'deep time' in the nineteenth century (Stavrinaki 2018a). The latter enabled the recognition of the deep antiquity of the earth as well as humanity. There can be little doubt that the origins of archaeology are broadly entangled in the establishment of the modern world and the worldview of modernity. Together with anthropology, the discipline shaped, reflected and amplified the understanding of the temporality of humanity's past and present. Archaeology's theoretical framework and methodologies can only be understood in relation to the fundamental modern structures of perception and interpretation outlined above, particularly a homogeneous understanding of space and time (Thomas 2004). However, as part of the origin narrative of modernity, archaeology is similarly affected by the complex temporal structure of modernity as well as the resulting paradoxes and contradictions.

As outlined above, during the eighteenth century an important shift took place in the interpretation of global human difference. It became temporalised. The Other was no longer foremost located in space but now also in time. This crucial change transformed the 'barbarians' from classical times into 'primitives'. This movement is connected to the understanding of a progressive temporality in which humanity moves from simple beginnings towards a more sophisticated future. Significantly, this process was understood as a movement out of nature towards civilisation, and both conditions were foremost distinguished by the presence or absence of material technologies. The increased mastery and exploitation of nature through technology became the underlying distinctive theme. So-called primitives were regarded as being traditional and closer to nature, while 'civilised' people were at the peak of culture and were modern in their advanced understanding of nature (Mignolo 2011, pp. 155–156). These views are usually connected to the prevalent progressive chronological schemes that have dominated archaeology and anthropology in a dialectical fashion during most of the nineteenth and twentieth centuries.

There is probably no introductory text to archaeology that does not give prominent space to the observation that during the eighteenth century and early nineteenth century people had little understanding of the depth of the antiquity of human existence that was independent of reference to classic historical sources or the Bible (Daniel 1950; 1975). Probably, the most famous example in this context are the events that are related to the establishment of the Three Age System by C. J. Thomsen at the Danish National Museum. With reference to the prehistoric collection, the first director of the Museum, Rasmus Nyerup, had declared in 1806 that:

> everything which has come down to us from heathendom is wrapped in a thick fog; it belongs to a space of time which we cannot measure. We know that it is older than Christendom, but whether by a couple of years or a couple of centuries, or even by more than a millennium, we can do no more than guess.
>
> *(as quoted in Eggert 2001, pp. 31–33)*

The Three Age System gave earlier ideas about the history of humanity a systematic temporal and methodological dimension. It formalised the priority of the significance of technological aspects in the measurement of progress between different societies. The Three Age System was the first formal scheme to view archaeological evidence within formal stages of progressive development. Furthermore, from the first expositions of this scheme, the formal analysis of the different stages (or Ages) was connected to a moral assessment that connected Europe's deep past with reports on Indigenous people. Eggert (2001, p. 42) quotes from Thomsen's *Leitfaden* (1837, p. 58), in which he writes about the 'Stone Age' 'that this is the earliest time, in which we find that people already lived in our country and that there is no doubt that these people must have had similarities with savages'. In 1825, Thomsen wrote in a letter:

> It appears clear to us that the whole of Northern Europe was inhabited during a very early period by very similar and very raw tribes. That these latter are very similar to the wild North American Indians in a lot of respects is obvious. They were warlike, lived in

the forests, had no or only little knowledge of metals, were divided in bands and were partly annihilated, partly enslaved, partly pushed towards the furthest ends of the world or most distant places.

(as quoted in Eggert 2001, p. 42)

From the earliest recognition of the depth of human antiquity a link was established to cultural and moral development over time that was also expressed spatially. The peripheries of the known world were seen as the peripheries of history. Needless to say, these relationships were constructed from the perspective of Europe as the centre. This view remained very stable throughout the establishment of archaeology during the nineteenth century and into the twentieth century. Eggert (2001, p. 42) consequently concluded that the developments that are visible during that time are mostly methodological refinements and elaborations rather than fundamental conceptual changes of much more general and older ideas. This period also experienced an integration of cultural-evolutionist and teleological interpretations. Anthropology and archaeology clearly mirrored and supported each other in the application of a social evolutionary framework. Particularly during the nineteenth century, close intellectual connections existed between archaeological chronologies and explanations and the schemes put forward by E. B. Tylor and L. H. Morgan. Particularly Morgan's scheme of the successive stages of savagery, barbary and civilisation proved to be influential. It had a crucial impact on Karl Marx and subsequently Gordon V. Childe. In the twentieth century, another evolutionary schema emerged in this tradition, based on the complexity of social structure (Bands, Tribes, Chiefdoms, States). It remains a dominant paradigm of deep time social change, particularly in the United States (Lucas 2005, p. 12).

Through this overall typological model of history, archaeology's focus remains on periodisation and chronology. Following Althusser's critique of Marx, Lucas (2005, pp. 12–13) has argued that in this form archaeological narratives reproduce totalising forms of history that suppress the specifics of individual cases and contexts. As such, they are indeed connected to universalising approaches to history that are part of the politics of global European hegemony and colonialism (Thomas 1993; 2004). Not surprisingly, this aspect played a (small) part in the context of the processualism/post-processualism debate (Shanks & Tilley 1987). Most current discussions have diversified considerably and have engaged with a broad range of topics inspired by philosophical, geographical and anthropological approaches to memory, temporality and historical interpretation (Lucas 2015; Olivier 2011; 2013; Witmore 2014b). A significant influence has also been a rethinking of the character of material objects, their causalities and temporalities (McGlade 1999; Olsen 2010; Olsen et al. 2012; Witmore 2007; 2014a). These engagements contain many valuable aspects that could be taken further in future critical evaluations. For example, Latour's critique of the Western idea of nature in opposition to modern science and humanity is an ongoing influence in this context. Latour (1993; 2004) famously argued that this understanding is a modern politically-driven illusion, which also generates an understanding of human history as a natural past. It appears that this critique can be productively linked to a critical challenge of the reduction of archaeology's engagement with the dimension of time to methodological aspects of radiometric dating techniques, their application and contexts, which can be equated with the aim of identifying absolute ages for different aspects of the archaeological record and assigning them places in a virtual spatio-temporal grid. These developments are certainly driven by the increasingly scientific orientation of archaeology and are particularly prevalent in deep time archaeology (i.e. Palaeolithic archaeology and palaeoanthropology). González-Ruibal (2013) has criticised the modernist orientations of archaeological inference with respect to time as unreflected and methodologically-driven. This critique is part of a wider recent discussion about the modernist ontological and epistemological basis of archaeology and, as such, is of relevance for the topic of this chapter. Hence, I will come back to some of the above-mentioned contributions below.

Bailey (e.g. summary in 2007) has discussed the necessity in archaeology to consider time perspectivism when dealing with the archaeological record. He referred to the observation that the archaeological record is always constituted by a range of different temporalities that operate at a range of scales. Consequently, the concept of clear-cut chronological stages or phases appears to be problematic in the light of these considerations. In his discussions, Bailey did not have a specific critical and political dimension in mind. However, these observations draw attention both to the contradictions that characterise the project of modernity itself, its origin narrative and its mirroring in archaeological practice and interpretation. On the one hand, archaeology's practice is actually foreign to the idea of completeness and totality; archaeology's objects of study are fragmentary and often accidental assemblages. On the other hand, archaeology gains its authority from the claim of reconstructing actual history in its totality, providing an understanding of the structure and order behind the disjunction, messiness and chaos. In this sense, archaeology repeats the paradoxes of the epistemic violence that characterises the colonial encounter with the Other and the creation of modernity's own origin mythology. For example, in this context Verdesio (2013, p. 170) highlighted that it has, in fact, been very difficult to find any unequivocal example of a chiefdom transforming into a state either in the archaeological or ethnographic record – despite the continuing popularity of the respective social evolutionary scheme claiming just this.

Dawdy (2010) has argued that one of the unintended effects of the extensive criticism of earlier social evolutionary schemas has in fact been a propagation of the fundamental temporal rupture between modernity and pre-modernity. The rejection of the denial of coevalness produces a temporal flattening of human diversity, which is all included in modernity. This movement, however, now reinforces the concept of modernity as an essential and incomparable period of human history with unique and powerful social forces: 'Modernity is allowed to be essentialized even if nothing else is' (Dawdy 2010, p. 764). With reference to Walter Benjamin, Dawdy (2010 pp. 767–769) suggested that archaeology should reject the uniqueness of modernity as well as the ideas of a progressive temporality and separate chronological entities or phases. Benjamin recognised that the temporality of modernity and its insistence on the new was an illusion. The new only could exist in the presence and persistence of the old. Temporality consequently was always constructed dialectically from the past and the present. Benjamin recognised that relicts from the past formed the source material for utopian visions of the present and the future, which both demonstrated the power of the material environment as well as the necessity for critique (e.g. of the mythic history of modernity itself).

The colonial temporality of the deep human past

One of the most significant and prestigious fields of archaeological research has recently been the search for the origins of so-called behavioural modernity or behaviourally modern humans. The concept itself originated in the late 1980s and it has undergone a series of transformations until the present day. It is not possible to engage with these aspects in greater detail here (Caspari & Wolpoff 2013; Kaifu et al. 2015; Mellars et al. 2007). However, one key element that has been structuring these debates has been the shift from an anatomical or taxonomic definition of modern humans to a behavioural and/or cognitive one (Nowell 2010). Several authors within and outside of archaeology have productively criticised the current understanding of modern human origins (Garofoli 2016; Ingold 2000; Porr 2014; Roberts 2016). Here, I extend the discussion above and concentrate on its temporal aspects and entanglements with historically recent views in the context of European capitalism and colonialism. To a certain extent, I want to critique the intellectual relationships between the historical notion of modernity and the evolutionary deep time concept that has been proposed within archaeology and palaeoanthropology. In its most recent form, it was first formulated by Noble and Davidson (1991) and related to the presence of language and symbolic communication. These elements are viewed to be the key component in the emergence of 'people like us' or humans expressing the present and historically known behavioural variability. A very similar understanding was also formulated by Mellars and Stringer in their introduction to the seminal volume *The Human Revolution* (Mellars & Stringer 1989). In these early contributions, a crucial tension already became apparent between an essential biological capacity that is supposedly shared by all modern humans and the variability of behavioural and material expressions (Porr 2014). The inference of the former through the latter became a major area of debate and it was plagued by a problematic Eurocentrism, because the European Upper Palaeolithic evidence was generally used as a global benchmark in this respect. Several authors from Australia, for example, criticised this orientation already from an early stage (Cosgrove & Pike-Tay 2004; Davidson & Noble 1992; Porr 2010).

However, possibly the most influential contribution in this respect was put forward in the context of the African archaeological record by McBrearty and Brooks (2000). They argued for a slow accumulation of so-called modern traits during the African Middle Stone Age and against a revolutionary understanding of modern human origins. They explicitly wanted to shift the focus away from Europe and its Upper Palaeolithic record. It has been noted, however, that this shift was only partially successful because the defining traits of modern humanity that were put forward remained closely linked to the original formulation and based on the European evidence. However, they also created an implicit dichotomy between an essential human capacity for modern behaviour and widely dispersed material expressions that signal the presence of this capacity (Porr 2014). While the former is assumed to be a defining characteristic of human beings and shared by all members of the species, the latter are widely dispersed in time and space. Consequently, the essence of humanity has a different temporality from its material expressions.

The effects of this understanding correspond to a large extent to some key mechanisms outlined above about the relationship between modernity and premodernity (Smail & Shryock 2013). Both categories are presented as chronological and sequential as well as within a presence/absence logic. In reality, however, they are dispersed across the past and present. They are neither periods nor stages. They are socially constructed features of objects, places and (human) bodies. Within the dialectic between an essential and indivisible capacity of humanity and the variability of material cultural expressions, it is possible to locate the realisation of the former through the latter almost anywhere in time and space. This understanding is responsible for the notion of the Sapiens Paradox, which refers to the perceived time lag between the origins of human cognitive potentials and their material realisation in complex societies (Renfrew 1996; 2008). It is also responsible for the conjecture that only in the modern Western world has humanity fully realised its innate potential. Apparently, only in the modern Western world, humanity has achieved the full and proper use of its potential (Porr & Matthews 2017).

The teleology that is constructed in this way is a product of the generation of origin phenomena. Gamble (2007) has argued that 'origins research' is the main driver and justification for the study of the Palaeolithic and the deep human past. According to his analysis, it leads to the creation of 'Originsland', which is a construction of the past as a mirror image of the present. This construction is guided by today's interests, values and research agendas. Originsland can take many different forms, because it is the product of present attitudes and desires: 'a time and space that is defined by many different interests across the arts as well as the sciences and by beliefs that are variously rational and relational, common-sense and based on faith' (Gamble 2007, p. 61).

It is important to note that this understanding depends on an essentialist ontology, in which time is external to the workings of human behaviour and development. Such an understanding is deeply entangled with fundamental aspects of archaeological thinking (Alberti 2016). Time cannot affect the essences that came into existence in Originsland. They must be preserved in an unchanged form until the present day for this research agenda to have any meaning (Porr 2014). Despite the advances of empirical science, the narratives of human origins remain foremost a product of an essentialist logic that is ultimately a product of the modern Western ontology:

> origins questions have not changed under the weight of data supplied by those same academic disciplines that arose to feed our curiosity. [...] the current wealth of facts, scientifically arrived at, were servicing the same philosophical conjectures about the origins of humanity that had been inherited from Hobbes and Rousseau.
>
> *(Gamble 2007, p. 60)*

If one wanted to select a year from which Palaeolithic archaeology, human evolutionary studies and palaeoanthropology became integrated into the endeavour of academic archaeology, 1859 would probably not be a bad choice. This was the year of the publication of Darwin's *Origin of Species* and it is also the year in which human antiquity was further extended with stratigraphic discoveries in the gravels along the Somme River (Gamble & Kruszynski 2009). The concern with the human past extended to an embrace of biology, geology and palaeontology. Despite this extension, we find that established ideas about the role and notion of time remained unchanged, and this seems to be the case almost until the present day. In recent years, it has become more and more popular to criticise the Darwinian image of the branching tree as a metaphor for evolutionary processes. Rather, the favourite metaphor now seems to be the braided river or the muddy delta (Hawks 2016; Shreeve 2015). Both images have been put forward to consider the possibility of the division and reconnection of population branches as well as the possibility of gene exchanges between branches or populations. The focus is on the idea that the braided stream also holds the potential that its different parts can not only diverge but also converge. However, the metaphor of the river (of time) is of course significant on further levels. The image of the river transports the idea of constant movement in one direction, the flow of time is a constant but ultimately external background to human history and evolution. However, this idea also contains an inherent contradiction or inconsistency in the treatment of time. On the one hand it appears that the hominin species are the different streams of the river themselves, but on the other, the river or time appears to transport hominin species into the present. The latter is described here as the river's mouth, where it is flowing into the ocean, which in turn gives the impression of today's endless and deep possibilities and complexities that can be contrasted with the narrow and restricted passages of the river itself. Following the river back to its source, we arrive at its origin point. The metaphor of the river unwittingly but almost perfectly encapsulates the idea of an inevitability of the flow of time that moves from simple origins to a complex presence. The river, therefore, also encapsulates the idea of the 'origin point and the cone of research', which illustrates the assumption of an unfolding of complexity over time (Gamble 2007, pp. 62ff.). As mentioned above, these arguments can only work within an essentialist framework in which time is understood as external to the actual workings of human behaviour and development, so that time does not affect essences that came into existence at some point in the past and are subsequently preserved unchanged into the present (Porr 2014).

The deep human past further becomes a mirror image of the present in that the essential traits that are regarded as most significant are primarily formulated in socio-economically and historically specific, modernist terms. For Palaeolithic archaeology this means that measurement of proximity to modernity is overwhelmingly formulated in technological terms. The latter follows again a global and universal logic in which so-called innovations are accumulated over the course of global human evolution in a fashion that emulates the metaphor of the river of time mentioned above. The most highly developed human beings of the present retain inside their self all the achievements of humanity's ascent in a layered fashion around their essential human core that is supposedly shared by all 'behaviourally modern humans', the capacity for modernity (Porr 2014). This understanding is necessarily translated into a spatio-temporal landscape in current narratives of human evolution that show reflections both of colonial views of humanity's essential characteristics as well as its spatio-temporal imagination. The idea of an essential core of humanity leads to the necessity of identifying the origin location in both time and space. But the actual realisation of the essence of humanity can easily be located elsewhere, both in time (present/modernity) and in space (Western civilisation). However, the characterisation of the core of humanity is also deeply entangled with the understanding of temporality; although the latter is not related to long-term developments, but rather to the micro-dynamics of the use and evaluation of time.

Since the development of the New Archaeology or Processual Archaeology, the dominant explanatory framework to study human evolution or Palaeolithic hunter-gatherers is a variant of human behavioural or evolutionary ecology. This framework is built onto the basic assumption that 'the goal of the forager should be to forage optimally, that is, to maximize the net *rate* of food intake' (Kelly 1995, p. 54). As Kelly explained, a central assumption of the optimisation between input and output relationships of energy as the basis of human behaviours gives time a central role: 'the optimization assumption is integral to behavioural ecological studies that direct themselves to *how people allocate their time* among competing activities' (Kelly 1995, p. 55 [emphasis added]). This quote demonstrates that time in this framework is regarded as 'something that can be spent or saved, used profitably or wastefully, hoarded or squandered' (Ingold 2000, p. 327). It is a resource, a currency, which requires careful management. However, time in this framework is also seen and understood as being external to social relationships and its fundamental character is not altered by its use by human beings or other organisms.

Ingold (2000, p. 326) has drawn attention to the fact that this understanding of time is a product of 'the temporal logic of capitalist production', which systematically neglects the social dimension of every human activity and subjects everything – including time – to a process of commodification and supposedly independent evaluation between supply and demand, input and output. The universal currency that would allow such an evaluation is of course money and it is no surprise then that the idea of 'time is money' has a long tradition within Western thought and goes at least back to the eighteenth century and the rise of industrial capitalism. From the eighteenth century onwards was, of course, also the period of the establishment of Enlightenment thought and as 'a child of the Enlightenment, neoclassical economics developed as a science of human decision-making and its aggregate consequences, based on the premise that every individual acts in pursuit of rational self-interest' (Ingold 2000, p. 27).

This latter assessment has of course been discussed extensively in the study of more recent historical periods and sociology (e.g. Graeber 2001; 2011). However, what emerges in relation to the study of human evolution and human origins appears as a much more fundamental imposition of temporal regimes as it is connected to supposedly universal features of nature and biological evolution. Just as the supposed temporal location of the colonised in the great scheme of human history and evolution was used to denigrate their ways of life, the assumed rationalist temporality of human existence in the deep past has a colonialist dimension, because it denies any causality of the fundamental differences between socially constructed temporalities that are intertwined with social relationships. Control of the temporality of human lives and the temporality of social relationships were of course important dimensions of colonial exploitation and control (Ashcroft, Griffiths & Tiffin 2006; Fabian 1983). As was discussed above, the imposition of temporal regimes was, and continues to be, a mechanism to exert power and domination in social and economic interactions.

Conclusions

Within Palaeolithic and deep time archaeology, previous research has critically engaged with the treatment of time in a limited way. This assessment has, for example, focused on the epistemology of the creation of archaeological periods and stages (Roebroeks & Corbey 2001) and these respective practices have been linked to normative and hegemonic processes (Murray 2001). Here, I want to encourage a continuation and deepening of these considerations with a specific focus on the social construction of time and its links to colonial practices and ideologies. I have argued that the social construction of time played a crucial role in colonial processes. There exists a complex dialectic between the construction of the overall course of history and the understanding of the micro-dynamics of social interactions and relationships with the environment. Within historical colonial contexts, the understanding of the merciless temporality of history, that caused certain societies to succeed and others to fail, was translated into the imposition of particular temporal schemes of control and oppression. Reference to the former implicitly or explicitly provided justification for the latter. In the construction of humanity's deep past, it is possible to discern similar elements and reflections. The micro-dynamics of past hominins and humans are assessed within a framework that is linked to the temporal experience of the modern world and to a universalist understanding of a progressive history. Both temporalities are connected by notions of material improvement and competition that originated as a major discursive force within Western modernity that has been fuelling colonial ideologies.

The decolonisation of the temporality of the deep human past must consequently critically assess these underlying influences and must counter them to produce a more diversified past. The current dominant orientation produces universalist and teleological variants of the temporality of the deep human past that do not fully consider the social construction of time. It also fails to fully account for the variabilities that can be observed between societies in their attitudes to time. Therefore, the critique of deep time archaeology as 'origins research' (Gamble & Gittins 2004) is linked to the universalist project of modernity that denies the existence of deep forms of alterity and difference (Thomas 2004). As such, this critique is deeply connected to the project of decolonisation. The answer to this critique can consequently not be similarly universalist counter-narrative or counter-scheme. Answers can only be found in the opening of inquiries to diversity, alterity and creativity. Answers can only be found in acknowledging the entanglement of temporality in social and cultural processes that are shaped, created and formed through real human practices:

> What we mean by 'time', and the thing that stands behind this whole landscape of cycles, the situational, the innately human, the movement and evolution of 'natural force' and the phenomenal world, is the inventive dialectic – the contradictory, paradoxical, and moving aspect of culture.
>
> *(Wagner 2016, p. 75)*

In continuation of this theme and as briefly mentioned above, recent discussions in archaeology of time and temporality provide some important connections and points of departure to further explore and critique the colonial dimension of time in the study of human origins. However, only a few contributions can be discussed here. Lucas (2015) has recently provided an important critical assessment of the concept of contemporaneity in archaeology. In most current analyses, two objects or aspects of the archaeological record are regarded as contemporaneous when it can be demonstrated that they belong to the same period or section of time. In the Palaeolithic, for example, those periods can either be defined culturally (e.g. Acheulean, Aurignacian, Middle Palaeolithic, Middle Stone Age etc.) or radiometrically in absolute terms (e.g. 75–65ky BP). This understanding establishes the contemporaneity of objects or events in relation to a unit of time. Furthermore, it defines the temporal relationship between two objects in relation to an external linear as well as segmented view of time. The significance of objects is consequently established with reference to a hegemonic scheme that also defines relationships of significance with reference to temporal progression. Objects within a time period can consequently still be interpreted as being out of time. Some elements can be viewed as progressive and some as archaic. In fact, Lucas argued that the complexity and flow of human life and its entanglement with the material world makes material anachronistic elements inevitable. Consequently, no archaeological period is ultimately pure or whole. It is a retrospective evaluation and value judgement, which emphasises some elements at the expense of others. Objects or features are only perceived as anachronistic as long as history is understood to be divided into a series of temporal periods with specific defining features (Lucas 2015, p. 9). Rather, contemporaneity should be approached through the interrelationship between objects themselves. In this way, the idea of temporal periods becomes secondary (or obsolete), and the focus is placed on the mutual constitution of objects and their intertwined and variable causalities and influences. The centre of analysis becomes the persistence and decay of objects, their multiple temporalities. As a consequence, the archaeology that is envisioned here is relational, multi-subject and multi-temporal (Lucas 2015, p. 15). In a similar spirit, McGlade (1999, p. 144) has argued that archaeology must aim for a radical rejection of its legacy of providing 'a practical methodology for interpreting the linear passage of time'. In contrast, it is suggested that archaeology should embrace the complex temporal nature of social phenomena and the non-linearity of historical phenomena.

These explorations can be linked to key propositions of the postcolonial critique, its rejection of universalist schemes and an emphasis on local conditions and histories. Witmore (2013; 2014b) has recently argued that the linear evaluation of the past and its sorting into eras, periods or epochs is not a consequence of the past itself but a negotiation between political and economic decisions in the present and objects suggestive of the past, which, in turn, participate in these exchanges about what can and cannot be said. As Shanks and Tilley (1992, pp. 53–54) have argued, the placement of past societies into typological sequences contributed to the homogenisation of past variability and the politicisation of time. Witmore (2013, p. 131) stressed that archaeology is mostly concerned with *chronos*, an understanding of time that is separate from events and objects, emphasising classification and the establishment of interchangeability. He also emphasised that this understanding suppresses the pluritemporal mixture of processes characterising human life. There is a continuing recognition of human life as entangled in a multitude of temporalities of endurance and destruction, 'witnessed in the intertwining of ephemerality and repetition, of perpetual perishing and incessant novelty, of never-ending accumulation and duration'. The decisions that underlie different representations of the past are a product of implicit or explicit political decisions, which can be understood as the *chronopolitics* of archaeological reasoning (Witmore 2014b). Archaeology is not so much the study of the (deep) past. Rather, it is the study of memory, materiality and temporality operating in the present: 'A site or an artefact is never wholly contained within the past. It is a product of a dynamic past-present continuum and, as every historical process, its study is affected by considerations of the future' (Olivier 2013, p. 122; see also Olivier 2011).

Since its establishment during the eighteenth and nineteenth centuries, the deep past has occupied an important position within and among Western intellectual traditions. The deep past also always had a complex and contradictory existence. Stavrinaki (2018a) has argued that prehistory, the deep human past, continues to return to haunt the present. Prehistory is referred to in political debates, speculative philosophical thought and contemporary art. These attempts are united by an underlying search for origins and, hence, attempts to make the present legible. They are reflective of the inextricable link between prehistory and modernity. The Enlightenment's ambition to consolidate histories into a monolithic History continues until the present day. One of the key motivations and themes of deep time archaeology is to find and uncover the defining moments and events of human history and evolution. It equally fuels academic and popular imagination. In the famous entry sequences of *2001: A Space Odyssey*, the use of the first bone tool in human evolution is seamlessly linked with space travel technology (Porr 2005). More recently, the film *Lucy* linked the earliest hominins of more than 3 million years ago with the potential of the human mind to become detached from the human body and continue a more powerful existence within the global data networks (Besson 2014). Technology defines humanity and is the implicit force that shapes history and evolution. In each case, the origin of humanity is linked with humanity's destiny in the future. History becomes a realisation of humanity's original potential. These are artistic reflections of the modern understanding of the character and temporality of humanity that transcend spatial and temporal difference and alterity. They refer to attempts to assert a more definite past, one made more real than others through the mechanisms of modern science. These interrelationships between academic and artistic visions are reflective of modern utopian visions. They are also colonial visions that interpret human difference and control the definition of history and humanity. Hence, these processes are reflective of the chronopolitics of human evolutionary studies (cf. Witmore 2014b).

The critical revision of these epistemological structures will open up new opportunities to attack inequalities and falsehoods. They will enhance social justice through acts of remembrance and an embrace of the pluritemporal (Witmore 2014b). The importance for the discussion in this paper is located in the recognition that these considerations cut across entrenched nature/social/culture divides. Together with Barad (2007, p. 183), we should consequently not just be interested in altruistically advocating for the subaltern. It also does not mean to give up the aims and objectives of scientific reasoning. We rather must accept the intertwined nature of ethics, knowing and being. This acceptance is why we need an ongoing process like decolonisation that is not divorced from ontological and epistemological concerns because it is the confluence of all these aspects through which we make and mark all knowledge.

References

Alberti, B 2016, 'Archaeologies of ontology', *Annual Review of Anthropology*, vol. 45, pp. 163–179.

Allais, L 2016, 'Kant's racism', *Philosophical Papers*, vol. 45, no. 1–2, pp. 1–36.

Anderson, B 2006, *Imagined communities: reflections on the origin and spread of nationalism*, Verso, London.

Ashcroft, B, Griffiths, G & Tiffin, H (eds) 2006, *The post-colonial studies reader*, 2nd edn, Routledge, London.

Bailey, G 2007, 'Time perspectives, palimpsests and the archaeology of time', *Journal of Anthropological Archaeology*, vol. 26, pp. 198–223.

Barad, K 2007, *Meeting the universe halfway: quantum physics and the entanglement of matter and meaning*, Duke University Press, Durham, NC.

Barad, K 2011, 'Nature's queer performativity', *Qui Parle: Critical Humanities and Social Sciences*, vol. 19, no. 2, pp. 121–158.

Barnard, A 2014, 'Defining hunter-gatherers: enlightenment, romantic and evolutionary perspectives,' in V Cummings, P Jordan & M Zvelebil (eds), *The Oxford handbook of the archaeology and anthropology of hunter-gatherers*, Oxford University Press, Oxford, pp. 43–54.

Barta, T 2005, 'Mr Darwin's shooters: on natural selection and the naturalizing of genocide', *Patterns of Prejudice*, vol. 39, no. 2, pp. 116–137.

Besson, L (dir.) 2014, *Lucy*, motion picture, TF1 Films Production, London.

Birth, K 2008, 'The creation of coevalness and the danger of homochronism', *Journal of the Royal Anthropological Institute (N.S.)*, vol. 14, pp. 3–20.

Brantlinger, P 2003, *Dark vanishings: discourse on the extinction of primitive races, 1800–1930*, Cornell University Press, Ithaca, NY.

Bredekamp, H 2012, *Antikensehnsucht und Maschinenglauben. Die Geschichte der Kunstkammer und die Zukunft der Kunstgeschichte*, Klaus Wagenbach, Berlin.

Caspari, R & Wolpoff, MH 2013, 'The process of modern human origins: the evolutionary and demographic changes giving rise to modern humans', in FH Smith & JCM Ahern (eds), *The origins of modern humans: biology reconsidered*, John Wiley, New York, pp. 355–391.

Clifford, J & Marcus, GE (eds) 1986, *Writing culture. The poetics and politics of ethnography*, University of California Press, Berkeley.

Cooper, F 2007, *Colonialism in question. Theory, knowledge, history*, University of California Press, Berkeley.

Corbey, R 1991, 'Freud's phylogenetic narrative', in R Corbey & JTL Leerssen (eds), *Alterity, identity, image. Selves and others in society and scholarship*, Rodopi, Amsterdam, pp. 37–56.

Corbey, R 2005, *The metaphysics of apes. Negotiating the animal–human boundary*, Cambridge University Press, Cambridge.

Cosgrove, R & Pike-Tay, A 2004, 'The Middle Palaeolithic and Late Pleistocene Tasmania hunting behaviour: a reconsideration of the attributes of modern behaviour', *International Journal of Osteoarchaeology*, vol. 14, pp. 321–332.

Daniel, G 1950, *A hundred years of archaeology*, Gerald Duckworth, London.

Daniel, G 1975, *A hundred and fifty years of archaeology*, Gerald Duckworth, London.

Davidson, I & Noble, W 1992, 'Why the first colonisation of the Australian region is the earliest evidence of modern human behaviour', *Archaeology in Oceania*, vol. 27, pp. 135–142.

Dawdy, SL 2010, 'Clockpunk anthropology and the ruins of modernity', *Current Anthropology*, vol. 51, no. 6, pp. 761–793.

Descola, P 2013, *Beyond nature and culture*, Chicago University Press, Chicago, IL.

Eggert, MKH 2001, *Prähistorische Archäologie. Konzepte und Methoden*, A. Francke Verlag, Tübingen.

Fabian, J 1983, *Time and the other. How anthropology makes its object*, Columbia University Press, New York.

Fazioli, KP 2017, *The mirror of the medieval. An anthropology of western historical imagination*, Berghahn, New York.

Fuentes, A & Visala, A (eds) 2016, *Conversations on human nature*, Left Coast Press, Walnut Creek, CA.

Galison, PL 2003, *Einstein's clocks, Poincaré's maps. Empires of time*, W.W. Norton, New York.

Gamble, CS 2007, *Origins and revolutions. Human identity in earliest prehistory*, Cambridge University Press, Cambridge.

Gamble, CS & Gittins, E 2004, 'Social archaeology and origins research: a Paleolithic perspective', in L Meskell & RW Preucel (eds), *A companion to social archaeology*, Blackwell, Malden, MA, pp. 96–118.

Gamble, CS & Kruszynski, R 2009, 'John Evans, Joseph Prestwich and the stone that shattered the time barrier', *Antiquity*, vol. 83, pp. 461–475.

Garofoli, D 2016, 'Cognitive archaeology without behavioral modernity: an eliminativist attempt', *Quaternary International*, vol. 405, pp. 125–135.

Gell, A 1992, *The anthropology of time. Cultural constructions of temporal maps and images*, Berg, Oxford.

González-Ruibal, A 2013, 'Reclaiming archaeology', in A González-Ruibal (ed.), *Reclaiming archaeology: beyond the tropes of modernity*, Routledge, New York, pp. 1–30.

Gosden, C 1994, *Social being and time*, Blackwell, Oxford.

Graeber, D 2001, *Toward an anthropological theory of value*, Palgrave, New York.

Graeber, D 2011, *Debt: the first 5,000 years*, Melville House, New York.

Hawks, J 2016, 'Human evolution is more a muddy delta than a branching tree', *Aeon*. Available from: https://aeon.co/ideas/human-evolution-is-more-a-muddy-delta-than-a-branching-tree [27 May 2019].

Hodges, M 2008, 'Rethinking time's arrow: Bergson, Deleuze and the anthropology of time', *Anthropological Theory*, vol. 8, pp. 399–429.

Holdaway, S & Wandsnider, L (eds) 2008, *Time in archaeology: time perspectivism revisited*, University of Utah Press, Salt Lake City.

Ingold, T 2000, *The perception of the environment: essays in livelihood, dwelling and skill*, Routledge, London.

Ingold, T 2004, 'Beyond biology and culture. The meaning of evolution in a relational world', *Social Anthropology*, vol. 12, no. 2, pp. 209–221.

James, D 2015, '*Tjukurpa* time', in A McGrath & MA Jebb (eds), *Long history, deep time. Deepening histories of place*, ANU Press, Canberra, pp. 33–46.

James, W & Mills, D (eds) 2005, *The qualities of time: anthropological approaches*, Berg, Oxford.

Kaifu, Y, Izuho, M, Goebel, T, Sato, H & Ono, A (eds) 2015, *Emergence and diversity of modern human behavior in Paleolithic Asia*, Texas A&M University Press, College Station.

Kelly, RL 1995, *The foraging spectrum: diversity in hunter-gatherer lifeways*, Smithsonian Institution Press, Washington DC and London.

Kockelman, P & Bernstein, A 2012, 'Semiotic technologies, temporal reckoning, and the portability of meaning. Or: modern modes of temporality – just how abstract are they?', *Anthropological Theory*, vol. 12, no. 3, pp. 320–348.

Latour, B 1993, *We have never been modern*, Harvard University Press, Cambridge, MA.

Latour, B 2004, *Politics of nature: how to bring the sciences into democracy*, Harvard University Press, Cambridge, MA.

Lucas, G 2005, *The archaeology of time*, Routledge, London.

Lucas, G 2015, 'Archaeology and contemporaneity', *Archaeological Dialogues*, vol. 22, no. 1, pp. 1–15.

Marcus, GE & Fischer, MMJ (eds) 1986, *Anthropology as cultural critique: an experimental moment in the human sciences*, University of Chicago Press, Chicago, IL.

McBrearty, S & Brooks, AS 2000, 'The revolution that wasn't: a new interpretation of the origin of modern human behavior', *Journal of Human Evolution*, vol. 39, pp. 453–563.

McDonald Pavelka, MS 2002, 'Change versus improvement over time and our place in nature', *Current Anthropology*, vol. 43, pp. S37–S44.

McGlade, J 1999, 'The times of history: archaeology, narrative and non-linear causality', in T Murray (ed.), *Time and archaeology*, Routledge, London, pp. 139–163.

Mellars, P, Boyle, K, Bar-Yosef, O & Stringer, C (eds) 2007, *Rethinking the human revolution: new behavioural and biological perspectives on the origin and dispersal of modern humans*, McDonald Institute for Archaeological Research, Cambridge.

Mellars, P & Stringer, C 1989, 'Introduction', in P Mellars & C Stringer (eds), *The human revolution: behavioural and biological perspectives in the origins of modern humans*, Edinburgh University Press, Edinburgh, pp. 1–14.

Mignolo, WD 2011, *The darker side of western modernity. Global futures, decolonial options*, Duke University Press, Durham, NC.

Mignolo, WD & Walsh, CE 2018, *On coloniality: concepts, analytics, praxis*, Duke University Press, Durham, NC.

Mishra, P 2013, *From the ruins of empire. The revolt against the west and the remaking of Asia*, Penguin, London.

Moellendorf, D 1992, 'Racism and rationality in Hegel's philosophy of subjective spirit', *History of Political Thought*, vol. 13, no. 2, pp. 243–255.

Moore, JW 2015, *Capitalism in the web of life. Ecology and the accumulation of capital*, Verso, London.

Moore, JW (ed.) 2016, *Anthropocene or capitalocene? Nature, history, and the crisis of capitalism*, PM Press, Oakland.

Munn, ND 1992, 'The cultural anthropology of time: a critical essay', *Annual Review of Anthropology*, vol. 21, pp. 93–123.

Murray, T 2001, 'On "normalizing" the Palaeolithic. An orthodoxy questioned', in R Corbey (ed.), *Studying human origins. Disciplinary history and epistemology*, Amsterdam University Press, Amsterdam, pp. 29–43.

Murray, T (ed.) 1999, *Time and archaeology*, Routledge, London.

Noble, W & Davidson, I 1991, 'The evolutionary emergence of modern human behaviour: language and its archaeology', *Man (N.S.)*, vol. 26, no. 2, pp. 223–253.

Nowell, A 2010, 'Defining behavioral modernity in the context of Neandertal and anatomically modern human populations', *Annual Review of Anthropology*, vol. 39, no. 1, pp. 437–452.

Olivier, L 2011, *The dark abyss of time: memory and archaeology*, Altamira Press, Lanham, MD.

Olivier, L 2013, 'The business of archaeology is the present', in A González-Ruibal (ed.), *Reclaiming archaeology: beyond the tropes of modernity*, Routledge, New York, pp. 117–129.

Olsen, B 2010, *In defense of things. Archaeology and the ontology of objects*, Altamira Press, Lanham, MD.

Olsen, B, Shanks, M, Webmoor, T & Witmore, C 2012, *Archaeology: the discipline of things*, University of California Press, Berkeley.

Perkins, M 1998, 'The "Dreamtime" as colonial discourse', *Time and Society*, vol. 7, no. 2, pp. 335–351.

Pluciennik, M 2014, 'Historical frames of reference for "hunter-gatherers"', in V Cummings, P Jordan & M Zvelebil (eds), *The Oxford handbook of the archaeology and anthropology of hunter-gatherers*, Oxford University Press, Oxford, pp. 55–68.

Porr, M 2005, 'The making of the biface and the making of the individual', in CS Gamble & M Porr (eds), *The Hominid individual in context. Archaeological investigations of Lower and Middle Palaeolithic landscapes, locales and artefacts*, Routledge, London, pp. 68–80.

Porr, M 2010, 'Identifying behavioural modernity: lessons from Sahul', *Bulletin of the Indo-Pacific Prehistory Association*, vol. 30, pp. 28–34.

Porr, M 2014, 'Essential questions. Modern humans and the capacity for modernity', in RW Dennell & M Porr (eds), *Southern Asia, Australia and the search for human origins*, Cambridge University Press, Cambridge, pp. 257–264.

Porr, M & Matthews, JM 2017, 'Post-colonialism, human origins and the paradox of modernity', *Antiquity*, vol. 91, no. 358, pp. 1058–1068.

Reddy, WM 2016, 'The Eurasian origins of empty time and space: modernity as termporality reconsidered', *History and Theory*, vol. 55, pp. 325–356.

Renfrew, C 1996, 'The sapient behaviour paradox: How to test for potential?', in P Mellars & K Gibson (eds), *Modelling the early human mind*, McDonald Institute for Archaeological Research, Cambridge, pp. 11–15.

Renfrew, C 2008, *Prehistory: the making of the human mind*, Modern Library, New York.

Rifkin, M 2017, *Beyond settler time: temporal sovereignty and indigenous self-determination*, Duke University Press, Durham, NC.

Riggs, PJ 2015, 'Contemporary concepts of time in Western science and philosophy', in A McGrath & MA Jebb (eds), *Long history, deep time: deepening histories of place*, ANU Press, Canberra, pp. 47–66.

Roberts, P 2016, '"We have never been behaviourally modern": the implications of material engagement theory and metaplasticity for understanding the Late Pleistocene record of human behaviour', *Quaternary International*, vol. 405, pp. 8–20.

Roebroeks, W & Corbey, R 2001, 'Biases and double standards in palaeoanthropology', in R Corbey & W Roebroeks (eds), *Studying human origins. Disciplinary history and epistemology*, Amsterdam University Press, Amsterdam, pp. 67–76.

Rose, DB 1996, *Nourishing terrains: Australian Aboriginal views of landscape and wilderness*, Australian Heritage Commission, Canberra.

Rovelli, C 2018, *The order of time*, Allen Lane, London.

Rumsey, A 1994, 'The Dreaming, human agency and inscriptive practice', *Oceania*, vol. 65, no. 2, pp. 116–130.

Sahlins, M 1996, 'The sadness of sweetness. The native anthropology of western cosmology', *Current Anthropology*, vol. 37, no. 3, pp. 395–428.

Sahlins, M 2008, *The western ilusion of human nature*, Prickly Paradigm Press, Chicago, IL.

Shanks, M & Tilley, C 1987, 'Abstract and substantial time', *Archaeological Review from Cambridge*, vol. 6, pp. 32–41.

Shanks, M & Tilley, C 1992, *Reconstructing archaeology*, Routledge, London.

Shreeve, J 2015, 'This face changes the human story. But how?', *National Geographic*. Available from: https://news.nationalgeographic.com/2015/09/150910-human-evolution-change/ [27 May 2019].

Shryock, A & Smail, DL 2011a, 'Introduction', in DL Smail & A Shryock (eds), *Deep history: the architecture of past and present*, University of California Press, Berkeley, pp. 16–26.

Shryock, A & Smail, DL (eds) 2011b, *Deep history: the architecture of past and present*, University of California Press, Berkeley.

Smail, DL & Shryock, A 2013, 'History and the "Pre"', *American Historical Review*, vol. 118, no. 3, pp. 709–757.

Stanner, WEH 1958, 'The Dreaming', in W Lessa & E Vogt (eds), *Reader in comparative religion: an anthroplogical approach*, Harper and Row, New York, pp. 158–167.

Stavrinaki, M 2018a, 'All the time in the world', *Artforum*, vol. 56, no. 7, pp. 202–214.

Stavrinaki, M 2018b, '"We escape ourselves": the invention and interiorization of the age of the earth in the nineteenth century', *Res: Anthropology and Aesthetics*, vol. 69–70, pp. 20–37.

Stoczkowski, W 2002, *Explaining human origins. Myth, imagination and conjecture*, Cambridge University Press, Cambridge.

Strang, V 2015, 'On the matter of time', *Interdisciplinary Science Reviews*, vol. 40, no. 2, pp. 101–123.

Thomas, J 1993, 'Discourse, totalization, and "the Neolithic"', in C Tilley (ed.), *Interpretative archaeology*, Berg, Oxford, pp. 357–394.

Thomas, J 2004, *Archaeology and modernity*, Routledge, New York.

Trigger, B 1984, 'Alternative archaeologies: nationalist, colonialist, imperialist', *Man*, vol. 19, pp. 355–370.

Trigger, B 1989, *A history of archaeological thought*, Cambridge University Press, Cambridge.

Verdesio, G 2013, 'Indigeneity and time. Towards a decolonization of archaeological temporal categories and tools', in A González-Ruibal (ed.), *Reclaiming archaeology. Beyond the tropes of modernity*, Routledge, New York, pp. 168–180.

Viveiros de Castro, E 2014, *Cannibal metaphysics. For a post-structural anthropology*, Univocal, Minneapolis, MN.

Wagner, R 2016, *The invention of culture*, 2nd edn, University of Chicago Press, Chicago, IL.

Witmore, C 2007, 'Symmetrical archaeology: excerpts of a manifesto', *World Archaeology*, vol. 39, no. 4, pp. 546–562.

Witmore, C 2013, 'A question of chronopolitics', in A González-Ruibal (ed.), *Reclaiming archaeology. Beyond the tropes of modernity*, Routledge, New York, pp. 130–144.

Witmore, C 2014a, 'Archaeology and the new materialisms', *Journal of Contemporary Archaeology*, vol. 1, no. 2, pp. 203–246.

Witmore, C 2014b, 'Chronopolitics and archaeology', in C Smith (ed.), *The encyclopedia of global archaeology*, Springer, New York, pp. 1471–1476.

Wolfe, P 1991, 'On being woken up: the Dreamtime in anthropology and in Australian settler culture', *Comparative Studies in Society and History*, vol. 33, pp. 197–224.

Zerubavel, E 1982, 'The standardization of time: a sociohistorical perspective', *American Journal of Sociology*, vol. 88, no. 1, pp. 1–23.

SECTION 4

National, political and historical dimensions of human origins

10

THE FAR WEST FROM THE FAR EAST

Decolonisation and human origins in East Asia: the legacy of 1937 and 1948

Robin Dennell

Introduction

Narratives about origins – whether human, agricultural or urban – are often framed in terms of centres and peripheries, whereby centres are deemed important areas of innovation and development, and the peripheries are seen as marginal in importance. These narratives are based primarily upon archaeological (and fossil skeletal evidence, in the case of human origins), and current explanatory frameworks. Often, these narratives are judgmental, in that those in centres are seen as 'advanced', and those in the peripheries as 'backward' or 'conservative'. Sometimes they reflect the political and national outlook of the narrator; always, they are embedded in the social and economic conditions of their time.

When reflecting upon the writings of those who worked in a colonial or imperial era, it is easy with the benefit of hindsight to dismiss or judge much of their writing as racist or arrogant about the apparent superiority of the colonial rulers, and the inferior status of the ruled. It is also easy to view their work as naïve in comparison with what we know today. What is much more difficult, but necessary, is to see the world through their eyes, and to understand why they explained their data the way they did. We see these figures now in the past; at the time, they were looking to the future. Here, I examine two narratives about human evolution in East Asia that continue to exert a huge influence in palaeoanthropology, and a third that is specific to China. All three were rooted in research undertaken in East Asia before World War II (WWII), particularly at the site of Choukoutien (now Zhoukoudian),[1] near Beijing, where large number of fossil specimens of an extinct hominin named *Sinanthropus pekinensis* (now known as *Homo erectus*) were found after their first discovery in 1924. Central to all three narratives involving Choukoutien, although in very different ways, are notions about centres of importance and authority, and peripheries that were less important. I focus on two years – 1937 and 1948 – as major watersheds for those studying human origins, and for the societies to which they belonged in both 'the West' and in China. I try to show the worlds they inhabited in 1937 and 1948, and how the world that emerged in 1948 would have been unimaginable to those who studied human origins in 1937. I try also to explain how and why the views on the early Palaeolithic and human origins in East Asia were frozen in time for around 50 years after 1948 as consequences of decolonisation and post-WWII political developments. Finally, I suggest how we might now start afresh, 70 years after these views were first articulated.

The term 'decolonisation' is used in this chapter in two ways. The first is more accurately called 'de-colonialisation' and refers to the historical events by which we entered a post-colonial and post-imperial age following the independence of former imperial possessions, particularly those in South Asia of the former British territories of British India, and in Southeast Asia of the former Dutch colonies of what is now Indonesia. Although China was never a colony or imperial possession, the creation of the PRC (People's Republic of China) in 1949 marked a major break with Western powers, and in that sense was part of the process of de-colonialisation. 'Decolonisation' also refers to the intellectual legacies of colonialism and imperialism which often persist long after colonial and imperial territories became independent.

First, we can briefly survey the world of 1937.

The world of 1937

As a selection of headline news from 1937: on 20 January, Roosevelt was sworn for a second term as president of the USA; on 23 January, Stalin's show trial in Moscow of the Anti-Soviet Trotskyite Centre began; Frank Whittle ground-tested the first jet engine on 12 April; on 26 April, Guernica, Spain, was bombed by the Condor Legion of the Luftwaffe; the Hindenburg airship caught fire on 6 May, on 12 May 1937, George VI was crowned king and emperor, the Golden Gate, California – then the world's longest suspension bridge – was opened on 27 May; the following day, Neville Chamberlain became prime minister of Britain; on 2 July, Emilia Earhart (and navigator Fred Noonan) disappeared somewhere over the Pacific during Earhart's attempt to become the first woman to fly around the world; Spam[2] made its debut on 5 July, on 12 December Japanese bombers sank the American gunboat USS *Panay* outside Nanking, and *Snow White and the Seven Dwarfs* had its premiere on 21 December as the first technicolour full length animated cartoon. On 25 December and at the age of 70, Arturo Toscanini conducted the NBC Symphony Orchestra on radio for the first time. Musically, 1937 was a good year, with Benny Goodman, Duke Ellington, Ella Fitzgerald, and Fred Astaire at their best.

The main foreign news for readers in Britain, France and the USA were the continuing civil war in Spain, and the outbreak of war in China. However, although war clouds were undoubtedly gathering in 1937, the British Empire still seemed secure, as did the French Empire in Indo-China and Africa, and the Dutch empire in the East Indies. For the Chinese, 1937 was the year that Japan invaded: on 7 July, the Marco Polo Bridge incident marked the beginning of WWII in Asia; the Japanese captured Peiping (now Beijing) on 8 August, Shanghai on 9 November, and Nanking on 13 December, with appalling numbers of civilian casualties. By the end of 1937, the Japanese had over-run the eastern seaboard of China, so the only way the USA could send aid to the Chinese Nationalists was via the Burma Road that ran from Lashio to Kunming. Regarding the consequences of the Japanese invasion on palaeoanthropology, 1937 was the year that work at Choukoutien was terminated after three of the workers were killed by the Japanese army (Jia Lanpo & Huang Weiwen 1990, p. 153).

Also that year, Dorothy Garrod and Dorothy Bate published *The Stone Age of Mount Carmel*, which summarised the results of their excavations at Mount Carmel between 1929 and 1934 in what was then British Palestine and is now Israel. In November 1937, Hallam Movius (1907–1987) arrived in Burma (now Myanmar) with his wife Nancy and the geologist Helmut de Terra (1900–1981) to undertake a survey of the Irrawaddy in order to find Palaeolithic material that could be incorporated into a framework of Pleistocene climatic change as indicated by river terraces. In December they were joined by the French Jesuit and palaeontologist Pierre Teilhard de Chardin (1881–1955), who had been researching the Chinese Palaeolithic and Pleistocene since 1922, and who had been involved in the analysis of the faunal and lithic material from the excavations at Choukoutien. In February 1938, Terra ('his own geological party') drove from Mandalay to Lashio and the Chinese border, ostensibly to look for Pleistocene formations[3] (Movius 1943). In the late summer of 1938, Franz Weidenreich (1942, p. 61) travelled from Beijing to Java to meet Ralph von Koenigswald (1902–1982) and compare notes on *Sinanthropus* and *Pithecanthropus*. This resulted in a reciprocal visit by von Koenigswald, and joint papers (von Koenigswald & Weidenreich 1939; von Koenigswald & Weidenreich 1938).

Palaeoanthropology in 1937

Three features relevant to Choukoutien are conspicuous about palaeoanthropology in 1937. The first is that the fossil record of our early evolution was extremely meagre. The only fossil specimens that were accepted by most figures of authority (at least in Britain) as evidence of the earliest phases of human evolution were those of *Eoanthropus* from Piltdown, England *Pithecanthropus* from Java, and *Sinanthropus* from Choukoutien. These were all thought to date from the Early Pleistocene and thus be at most ca. 1 million years old, although in the absence of chronometric dating their estimated ages were no more than guesstimates. Piltdown tended be ignored by non-British specialists as an early hominin,[4] which reduced the earliest part of the human fossil record to only *Pithecanthropus* and *Sinanthropus*. (Specimens such as the Mauer mandible, and cranial fragments from sites such as Broken Hill (Kabwe), Ngandong, Steinheim and Swanscombe were seen as representative of later stages of human evolution). In 1937, almost no-one accepted the Australopithecine material found in South Africa by Raymond Dart (1893–1988) and Robert Broom (1866–1951) as hominin; as seen below, widespread recognition did not occur until after 1937. The second feature is that the small number of specialists researching early human evolution usually worked in isolation and tended to be anatomists such as Sir Arthur Keith (1866–1955) and Sir Grafton Elliot Smith (1871–1937) in the UK, Marcellin Boule (1861–1942) in France, and Franz Weidenreich (1873–1948) in Beijing. None showed any interest in genetics, ecology or variation, but instead gave most attention to morphological details on particular specimens that were often very minor. As a result, by 1937, around 13 genera of extinct hominins were recognised.[5] The third feature that stands out in 1937 about the study of human origins is that Central Asia – variously defined as China, Tibet, Mongolia and the Gobi Desert – was seen by many as the probable 'cradle of humankind' rather than Africa.

I have previously argued (Dennell 2001) that 1937 was the high-water mark for those who championed the importance of East Asia for studying human origins. Several researchers before WWII regarded East Asia as a centre of human evolution, and Africa as marginal. Landmark publications were those by Osborn (1910; 1915), Matthew (1915) and Davidson Black (1925 and particularly, 1934), who oversaw the study of the *Sinanthropus* specimens from Choukoutien until his untimely death in 1934.[6] Choukoutien was undoubtedly the most important site worldwide in human origins research in 1937, and discoveries there aroused immense international interest, especially following the discovery of the first skull in 1929, and the first artefacts in 1931. Java was also generating important new evidence, such as the child's skull at Mojokerto in 1936, and the cranium known as *Pithecanthropus* II[7] and two mandibles at Sangiran in 1937, and the skulls excavated at Ngandong in 1931–1933 that were classed as *Homo* or *Javanthropus soloensis* (Oppenoorth 1932).

British interest in these discoveries are discussed at length by Manias (2015). These were covered as news items in many newspapers and discussed at scientific meetings. The weekly magazine *The Illustrated London News* covered several discoveries for a more up-market readership than the tabloids, with pieces covered by experts such as the two most eminent in Britain at the time, Sir Arthur Keith (the main protagonist of Piltdown) and Sir Grafton Elliot Smith, who is perhaps better (or worse) remembered for his ideas about hyper-diffusionism of civilisation from Egypt. These pieces give reasonable overviews of how early human evolution was envisaged, and how new discoveries added to that understanding. For example, in 1929, Smith published a piece entitled *The Peking Man: A New Chapter in Human History* on the discovery of two mandibles from Choukoutien. He noted (unlike other authors at that time) the role played by Chinese researchers C. C. Young (Zhongjian Yang, 1897–1979) and Mr W. C. Pei (Pei Wen-Zhong, 1904–1982). For Smith, the two main issues were the relation of these new finds to the Piltdown specimen, and whether there was a pattern to human evolution. He thus refers to Piltdown, *Sinanthropus* and *Pithecanthropus* as 'experimental types of mankind'. He draws attention to the fact that these all come from the margins of Eurasia ('the vast domain of man') and proposes that their last common ancestor must have lived long before them for such differences to become apparent: in his curious and colourful phrasing,

> A variety of experimental types of the human family, grotesque caricatures of mankind, must have been roaming about in the heart of the great continent, at the time when Nature was throwing the jetsam and flotsam of her failures into Java, Sussex and China.

He ends by noting that the ape-like features of the new mandibles indicate that 'the association of an ape-like jaw such as Mr. Dawson found at Piltdown, with a primitive human skull was not impossible'. He reported next on the discovery of the first skull from Choukoutien at the end of 1929 (Smith 1930), again paying tribute to W. C. Pei for his care in its excavation. He compared it to both *Pithecanthropus* and Piltdown, and notes it differed substantially from the latter (hardly surprising as the Piltdown cranial fragment was from a modern human).

Manias further points out that the initial discoveries were generally seen in an optimistic light as showing human progress, but as the international situation worsened, especially in Europe with the rise of Nazism, assessments about the nature of human evolution grew more pessimistic, with doubts about human ability to rid itself of violence and intolerance. In this, evidence that the late Pleistocene inhabitants of Upper Cave – excavated in 1934 – had died violent deaths, and that *Sinanthropus* may have been a cannibal, reinforced views that humanity had a dark and deeply-entrenched nature.

A preoccupation with human races was another conspicuous feature of British palaeoanthropology before WWII. Sir Arthur Keith incorporated the 'Mongoloids' into a branch in which modern races originated in the late Pliocene (see Figure 10.1) and maintained their

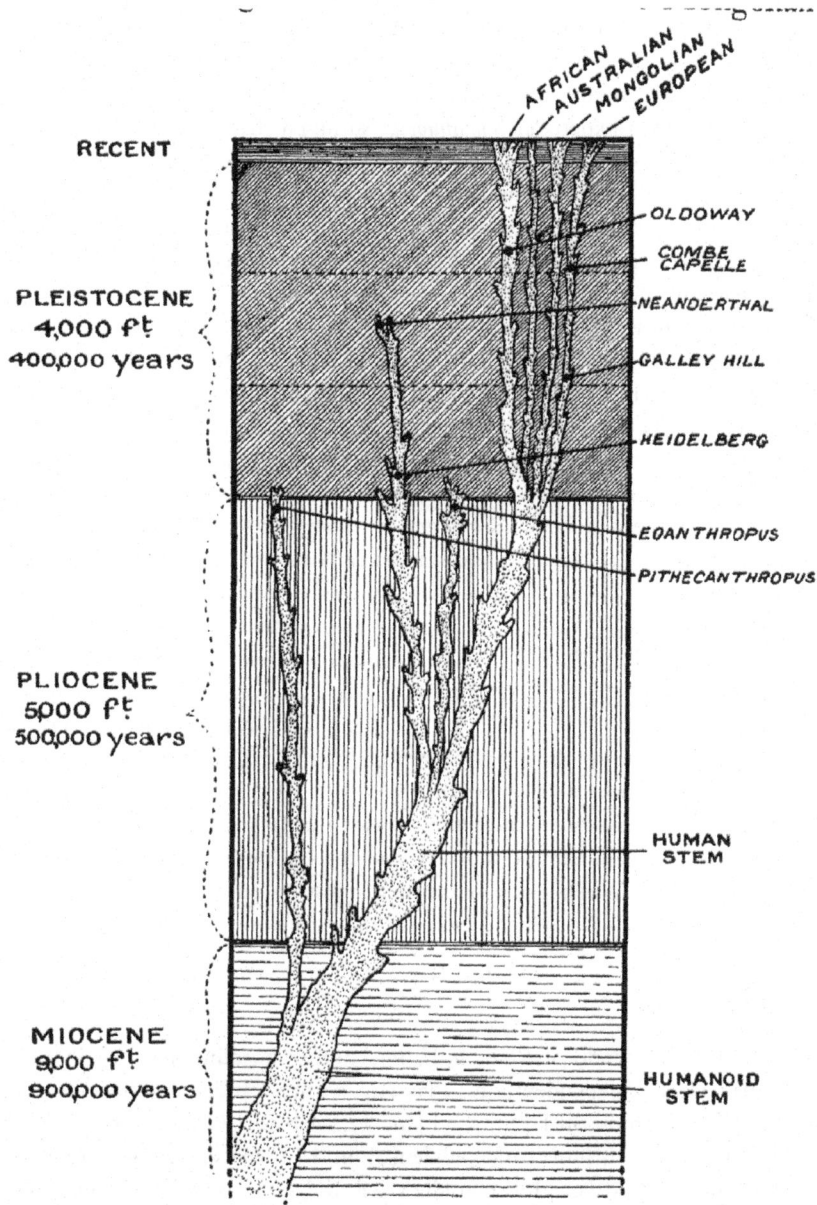

FIG. 187.—Genealogical tree of man's ancestry. The depth of the deposits and the duration of the geological periods are based on estimates published by Professor Sollas.

FIGURE 10.1 Sir Arthur Keith's (1916) view of human evolution. Note the inclusion of *Eoanthropus*, a.k.a. the Piltdown specimens that were shown to be a hoax in 1953; and Keith's view that racial types originated at the beginning of the Pleistocene

Source: Keith 1916, Figure 187 (best efforts have been made to obtain permission for the reproduction of this image).

separateness by mutual repulsion. For him, 'The whole length of the Pleistocene does not seem sufficiently long for the purpose' of differentiating Negroes from Europeans (Keith 1916, pp. 256–257). Sir Grafton Elliot Smith, who visited Choukoutien in 1930 and thereby became a self-proclaimed expert on *Sinanthropus*, surmised that races were more recent and perhaps originated around the time that Neanderthals became extinct but were nonetheless profoundly different and inferior to modern Europeans. As an example of his line of thought, 'Those anthropologists who use the retention of primitive features in the European as an argument to exalt the Negro to equality with him are neglecting the clear teaching of comparative anatomy' (Smith 1924, p. 51).

What is now curious is that British academics saw themselves as central figures of authority over the significance of Choukoutien when the reality was that the British were wholly irrelevant to that research. In a way, it is perhaps emblematic of Britain's over-inflated view of its importance. Choukoutien was most definitely not a British story. The initial discovery was made by an Austrian (Zdansky), and the Swedes Anderson and Bohlen; the funding was Swedish and American via the Rockefeller; the main anatomists were the Canadian Davidson Black, and then the German Franz Weidenreich; dating and geological studies came from Chardin and Barbour[8]; the artefacts were studied by Chardin, with input from Breuil, and the non-hominin fauna was studied by Pei. Although Davidson Black and Weidenreich receive most attention in Western accounts, Choukoutien was a Chinese excavation, undertaken and directed by the Chinese, with limited Western involvement except when hominins were found. In Java, the main external funding came from the Carnegie Foundation, and even in British India, it was largely American money that funded Terra and Patterson's fieldwork in 1935–36 and the discovery of *Ramapithecus* at Haritiyanglar.

To summarise, excavation at Choukoutien ceased in 1937; Movius and Terra concluded their fieldwork in Burma in 1938; and Dutch research in Java ceased in 1939. The outbreak of war in China in 1937, in Europe in 1939, and the Pacific in 1941 halted all research in East and Southeast Asia. When peace resumed in most of Europe in 1945, the world had changed beyond recognition in many regions, as shown below.

The world of 1948

If we move now to the world of 1948, and a selection of headline news for that year: on 4 January, Burma became independent; on 17 January, a truce was declared between Indonesian nationalists and Dutch troops in Java; on 30 January, Mahatma Gandhi was assassinated by a Hindu nationalist following India's independence; on 4 February, Ceylon became independent; on 28 February, the last British soldiers left India; on 3 April, Truman signed the Marshall plan which authorised $5 billion of aid for 16 countries; the World Health Organisation was established on 7 April, on 1 May, the People's Democratic Republic of Korea (PDRK) was founded; on 15 May, the British mandate in Palestine terminated and Chaim Weizmann became the first president of Israel on 16 May, on 15 June, the first issue of *renmin ribao*, the People's Daily, appeared; the Malayan insurgency started on 18 June, and the Berlin blockade on 24 June; on 26 July, Truman signed Executive Order 9981 to desegregate US armed forces; the Republic of South Korea was established on 15 August, and on 10 December, the Universal Declaration of Human Rights was adopted by the UN General Assembly. Despite all that, 1948 was the year in which apartheid began in South Africa. Musically, Arturo Toscanini made his television debut; Al Johnson was voted best male vocalist of the year; and Columbia Records introduced its long playing $33^{1}/_{3}$ rpm phonograph format.

This period was now a post-imperial era: India, Pakistan, Ceylon (now Sri Lanka), Burma (now Myanmar), North and South Korea were now independent, and Israel had emerged from the British mandate in Palestine; France was losing its grip on Indo-China, and the Dutch were about to lose what is now Indonesia.[9] The Philippines had also been granted independence from the USA in 1946. For foreign news in 1948 in Britain, France and the USA, the main stories were the early stages of the Cold War, the Berlin airlift, the end of the British mandate in Palestine, and the continuing civil wars in Greece and China. For the Chinese, 1948 was the year in which Chinese Communists formed the North China People's Republic on 30 September, and defeated the nationalists in Mukden on 30 October, which marked the beginning of the end of the civil war for the Nationalists.

The study of human origins in 1948

What is fascinating about the gap between 1937 and 1948 is how the study of human origins between those years developed at different rates and from different directions. On the one hand, the transition to peace allowed the publication of material that would have been published much earlier, notably that by Movius and Weidenreich, but on the other hand, new developments overshadowed their importance. To take the new developments first:

The 1947 Pan-African Congress of Prehistory and Archaeology

The 1st Pan-African Congress on Prehistory and Archaeology was held in Nairobi in January 1947 and was a major milestone in the study of African prehistory. It was organised by Louis Leakey, the Abbé Breuil was elected president, and Robert Broom as vice-president. *Nature, Science, L'Anthropologie* (Anon 1947; Phillips 1947; Oakley 1947) and other journals reported favourably on it. Much attention was paid to the australopithecine material found by Dart and Broom, and Wilfred Le Gros Clark presented his observations on the significance of these specimens (see below). As an indication of how views were changing, Wendell Phillips (1947, p. 613), who reported on the meeting for *Science*, ended his account with the comment that: 'The majority of delegates were sympathetic toward Darwin's view that Africa was the probable cradle of man. Whether or not this view is correct, within Africa there are still great possibilities for far-reaching contributions to the study of man's beginnings.' Africa, rather than Asia, was now being seen as where humanity may have originated.

The rise of the australopithecines

Dart published the Taung find of *Australopithecus africanus* in 1925 but was overshadowed by Black's publication of *Sinanthropus* in 1927. For the next ten years, Choukoutien enjoyed the world's attention. Two developments helped Dart to convince sceptics by 1948 about the importance of the Taung baby. The first was the contribution of Robert Broom, whose interest in palaeontology had been heightened by Dart, and who discovered the type specimen of *Australopithecus transvaalensis* at Sterkfontein in 1936 and *Paranthropus robustus* at Kromdraai in 1938 and thus showed that Taung was not an isolated find (see Broom 1937; 1938a; 1938b; 1938c). In 1946, Broom and Schepers (1946) published their monograph on the 'fossil ape-man of South Africa' so there was now detailed information in the public domain. Broom made further discoveries at Swartkrans in 1948, where he showed that *Australopithecus* and *Homo* were contemporary, and Dart (1948a; 1948b) also published his first papers on Makapansgat. Second, Dart now received outside support. As he commented in 1940, 'Like criminals in certain countries, advocates of the unexpected are naturally suspect until others appear who can prove their dependability' (Dart 1940, p. 169). The ones who appeared were the American palaeontologist William Gregory and dental specialist Milo Hellman (1938; 1939a; 1939b; 1939c; 1940), who took the trouble of visiting South Africa in 1938 to examine the fossil material at first hand, and broadly confirmed Dart's original observations.[10] An equally significant visit was paid in 1947 by Wilfred Le Gros Clark, Professor of Anatomy at Oxford, who also examined the material, and declared emphatically in Dart's favour (Le Gros Clark 1946). Gregory, Hellman and Clark had four invaluable assets: first, they were immensely experienced in their field; second, they came from highly prestigious institutions (the American Museum of Natural History for Gregory and Hillman; Oxford University for Le Gros Clark); and third, they were distinguished figures in their own right (Gregory had been a member of the American Academy of Science since 1927; Hellman was a former vice-president of the New York Academy of Sciences; and Le Gros Clark was elected to the Royal Society in 1935); and fourthly and probably most importantly of all, they had studied the fossil specimens for themselves and could thus write with first-hand knowledge. When Weidenreich published his synthesis of human evolution in 1946, his positioning of *Gigantopithecus* at the base of the human tree (see Figure 10.3 below) was already outdated by the intervention of Gregory, Hellman and Clark.

The New Biology

The study of human origins was revolutionised in the early post-war years by the 'New Biology' in the United States. Instead of regarding each fossil cranial material as a distinct type of early humanity, this school emphasised the importance of population variability, and in so doing, ruthlessly lumped into the same taxon specimens that had previously been regarded as distinct at the species and even generic level. Led by the ornithologist Ernst Mayr, the geneticist Theodosius Dobzhansky and the palaeontologist Gaylord Simpson, the human tree was reduced from 17 species and genera to merely three – *Homo transvaalensis* (i.e. the Australopithecines), *Homo erectus*[11] and *Homo sapiens*. In so doing, they also asserted the primacy of bipedalism over brain enlargement as the hallmark of early human evolution, which left Piltdown even more exposed as an anomaly.[12]

Nazism and WWII also helped force a re-evaluation of the significance of racial differences, and indeed, whether races could be defined biologically. Biology could no longer escape politics. In the United States, one writer who used his talents fully was Ashley-Montagu[13] in his 1942 book *Man's Most Dangerous Myth: The Fallacy of Race*. The racial differences that seemed so deeply-rooted and significant to pre-war authorities such as Keith and Smith were now seen as recent, and biologically trivial. To quote Ashley-Montagu's (1945, p. 192) *An Introduction to Physical Anthropology*, differences between races 'are seen to be of a significance which does not render any one of the groups either biologically superior or inferior to the other … They assist us to demonstrate the essential unity – not difference of mankind.'

With this background in mind, we can now review the syntheses of Movius and Weidenreich.

Movius and his synthesis of 1948

In his synthesis, *The Lower Palaeolithic Cultures of Southern and Eastern Asia*, Movius (1948) summarised what was then known about the early Palaeolithic in Africa, Europe and Asia. As such, it was ambitious, and attempted to pull together what was known before 1939, as well as new data that had been acquired in East Asia, some of which Movius had managed to publish during WWII (Movius 1943). As is well known, Movius drew a profound contrast between the early Palaeolithic records of Africa, Europe, Western Asia and India on the one hand, and China and Southeast Asia on the other: the former was characterised by Acheulean, bifacial handaxes, and the latter area by simple, unstandardised flake and core assemblages (see Figure 10.2). In his conclusions, Movius (1948, p. 411) wrote of East Asia that it 'cannot be considered in any sense as "progressive" from a cultural point of view'; the tools are

> relatively monotonous and unimaginative assemblages of choppers, chopping tools, and hand-adzes ... as early as Lower Palaeolithic times, southern and eastern Asia was a region of cultural retardation ... it seems very unlikely that this vast area could ever have played a vital and dynamic role in early human evolution ... Very primitive forms of Early Man apparently persisted there long after types at a comparable stage of physical evolution had become extinct elsewhere.

There are two aspects that are relevant here: first, was he factually correct? And second, was his judgement about cultural retardation justified?

(i) The factual evidence

As implied by the title of Movius's (1948) paper, Movius discussed the Pleistocene chronology and lower Palaeolithic evidence from Java, Northwest (British) India, Burma, China and mainland Southeast Asia. Unsurprisingly, he relied heavily upon his colleagues Chardin (26 citations), von Koenigswald (22 citations) and Terra (20 citations). Weidenreich was cited 14 times. The main lower Palaeolithic evidence for Northwest India was the Soanian, which Terra and the English archaeologist Thomas Paterson had identified in 1935 along what Terra had identified as terraces along the Soan Valley (Terra and Paterson 1939). The Soanian had four phases; and like the Anyathian, was a flake and core assemblage throughout. The so-called 'pre-Soan' artefacts were likely geofacts (Stiles 1978). In East Asia, he cited the material he had helped collect from gravel deposits along the Irrawaddy that he termed Anyathian, which Terra claimed was on each of the four terraces he identified along the Irrawaddy. The Anyathian had a three-phase Early and a two-stage Late phase (but no middle phase). Handaxes were absent, and according to Movius, the artefacts were simply flakes and cores. Many were made from fossil wood. The total size of the collections was only 600–650, and the earliest would almost certainly be classed as geofacts today (see Dennell 2014a). None of these artefacts was in a stratified context.

For Southeast Asia, the main evidence came from Java, which Movius, Chardin and Terra visited in 1938 after finishing their fieldwork in Burma. Their most important contact was Ralph von Koenigswald, who had been employed since 1930 as a geologist and palaeontologist by the Geological Services of Netherlands India; Chardin had met him in Java in 1935.

VOL. 38, PT. 1, 1948 SUMMARY AND CONCLUSIONS 409

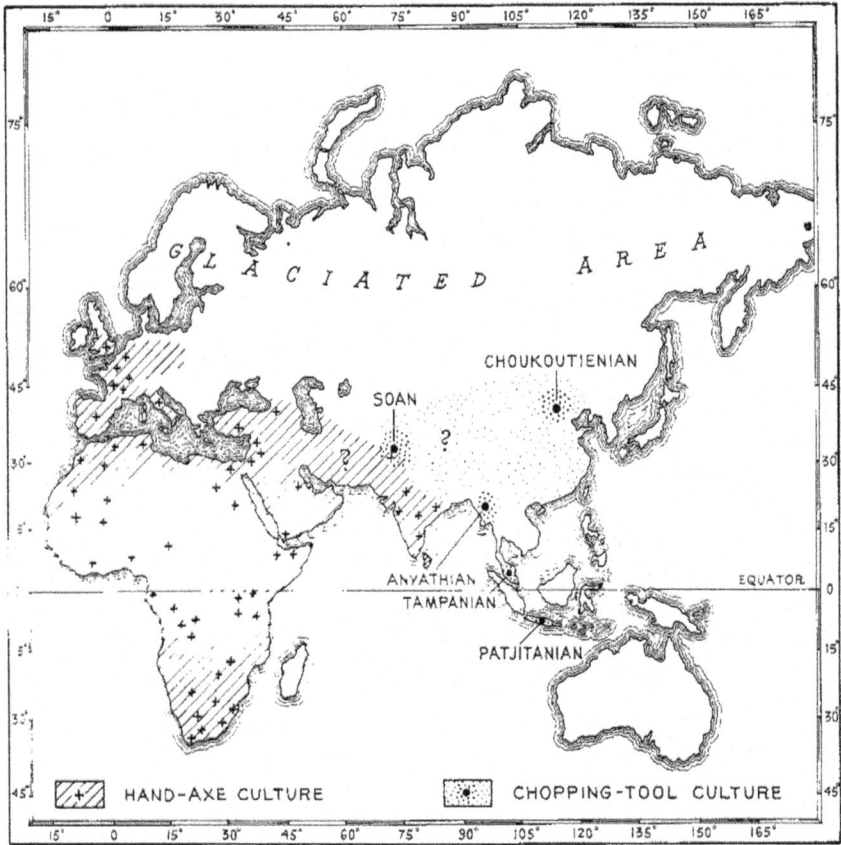

MAP 4. The distribution of Lower Palaeolithic hand-axe and chopping-tool cultures in the Old World during Late Middle Pleistocene times.

FIGURE 10.2 Movius's (1948) synthesis of the early Palaeolithic of Africa, Asia and Europe. As is well-known, he contrasted flake and core assemblages of East and Southeast Asia with Acheulean bifacial assemblages of India, Africa and Europe. Note the inclusion of the Soanian in northern British India (now Pakistan) that Terra and Paterson identified from the fieldwork in 1935, and the omission of flake assemblages such as the Clactonian in Northwest Europe

Source: Movius 1948, Map 4 (reproduced with permission from the American Philosophical Society).

Von Koenigswald's main contribution to the archaeological discussions that took place with Chardin and Movius in 1938 concerned the artefacts he had collected in 1935, when he (von Koenigswald 1936) collected examples of flaked stone from the hilltop surface of a conglomerate at Kampong Ngebung, in the Sangiran area, and attributed them to *Pithecanthropus* (see von Koenigswald & Ghosh 1973). Later that year he also collected artefacts along a dry water course near Pajitan on the south coast of Java, as well as from a boulder conglomerate in the river bank (von Koenigswald 1936). As the conglomerate was tilted, he thought it had to be at least as old as the strata at Trinil. The artefacts he collected included some that he classed as Chellean handaxes, and because of their crude appearance he argued that the conglomerate from which they came must also have been very ancient. (He was not the only one at the time to employ that type of circular argument: Terra had done the same in both the Punjab and the Irrawaddy Valley.) Terra (1943, pp. 456–457) attributed the Sangiran artefacts to the Upper Pleistocene as he thought them too advanced for *Pithecanthropus*, and the Pacitan artefacts to the late Middle Pleistocene. (Much later, Bartstra [1983, p. 429; 1985] attributed them to the Late Pleistocene.)

Additionally, there were a small number of artefacts collected in 1943 under appalling conditions by van Heekeren, a Dutch geologist who was then a prisoner of the Japanese and working on the notorious Thailand railway; Heekeren (1948) later elevated this small assemblage into a Fingnoan variant of the Early Palaeolithic. In Malaya, Kota Tampan was known from a brief publication (Collings 1938) and cited by Movius as the type site of the Tampanian. For China, Chardin was the crucial link. He had been involved in the excavations at Choukoutien for many years and was one of the few Western specialists who had seen the stone artefacts. He would have been able in 1937 and 1938 to inform Movius that handaxes were absent, and that the artefacts were overwhelmingly simple flakes and cores. During WWII Chardin (1941) had also published a brief report on this evidence that Movius cited. It is important to note that in 1948, Choukoutien was the only Middle Pleistocene archaeological site that had been investigated in China.

Movius was extremely thorough in his coverage of the evidence from India, Burma, China and Southeast Asia, but much less so for other regions. Evidence from Africa, Europe and Western Asia was mentioned briefly on page 410 in the final discussion, and there is no specific reference to any European material. His most important omission was the evidence for unstandardised flake and core assemblages (a.k.a. Clactonian) from Britain and Northwest Europe. These were first identified at the type site of Clacton by Hazeldean Warren in the 1920s (e.g. Warren 1926), and in France by Breuil (1932). For Movius, recent relevant publications would have been by Breuil (1932) on the Clactonian and the French evidence; Oakley and Leakey (1937), who proposed a four-stage division at Clacton; and Paterson (1937), who recognised five variants at Barnham St Gregory, and who also studied the Soanian with Terra in 1935. The site of Markkleeberg, Germany, was also known about in 1948 as it was discovered in 1895. If Movius had included this material, he would have had to acknowledge that simple flake and core assemblages were not unique to East Asia. Indeed, Oakley (1949, p. 49) proposed that the Clactonian was related to the assemblages from Choukoutien that Movius had described in his 1948 paper (see Pettitt & White 2012, p. 174).

(ii) Was his judgement about cultural retardation justified?

The main criticism that can be levelled at Movius is his sweeping condemnation of East Asia as 'a region of cultural retardation'.[14] There was no evident reason why hominins who used handaxes were more 'advanced' than those who did not. Why was the West seen as 'dynamic'? I suggest the main reason was the influence of Chardin, who had already published along those lines. For example, Chardin (1941, p. 60) suggested that 'in contrast with the already "steaming" West, Early Pleistocene Eastern Asia seems to have represented … a quiet and conservative corner amidst the fast advancing human world', by which he meant regions where handaxes were used. Rather quaintly, when one considers that the Chinese name for China, Zhongguo, means Central Country, Chardin thought that the Palaeolithic of China was conservative 'on account of its marginal geographical position': marginality depends of course upon where one defines the centre. He further asserted that 'East Asia gives the impression of having acted (*just as [in] historical China and in sharp contrast with the Mediterranean world*) as an isolated and self-sufficient area, closed to any major human migratory wave' (1941, pp. 86, 88, emphasis added). (Movius [1948, p. 411] cited this quotation in his own paper). This European perception of China as isolated, self-sufficient and sealed behind its Great Wall betrays an alarming degree of ignorance about China's dynastic history, which includes several periods when it was as cosmopolitan and expansionist as many Mediterranean states before 1800: 'The idea of a changelessly static East Asia, at any rate, is a fantasy, sustained only by a lack of historical knowledge' (Holcombe 2011, p. 160). In seeing China as geographically marginal and historically static, Chardin can be accused of allowing his Eurocentric views of geography and history to prejudice his interpretations of the early Palaeolithic of East Asia. Movius can also be criticised for being insufficiently critical of Chardin. Both can be criticised for imposing their stereotypic views of 'the Orient' (see e.g. Said 1978; 2004) upon its remote past (see also Dennell 2014b).

Would Movius have been so negative about East Asia if he had included the Clactonian and similar assemblages from Northwest Europe? If he had, would he also have seen Britain and France as 'a region of cultural retardation'? Or might he have agreed with Breuil's (1932) suggestion that there were parallel cultural phylae of handaxe and non-handaxe industries in the lower Palaeolithic? Although we cannot now determine what he might have written if he had included the Clactonian in his synthesis, there is little doubt that he helped to marginalise East Asia in Western perceptions of the region.

At this point, we can consider Weidenreich's (1946) multi-regional view of human evolution.

Weidenreich and multi-regional evolution

Franz Weidenreich replaced Davidson Black in 1935 as honorary director of the Cenozoic Research Laboratory of the Geological Survey of China[15] following the latter's premature death in 1934 at the age of 50. In that role, he assumed the principal responsibility for the study of the hominin fossil specimens from Choukoutien. Weidenreich had been trained in a different intellectual tradition and was more interested in human development than origins. From 1899 to 1901 he served under Gustav Schwalbe (1844–1916) at Strasburg; Schwalbe studied the Neanderthal remains from Krapina, Croatia, and concluded that Neanderthals were a transitional form to *H. sapiens*. This put him at odds with Marcellin Boule, who studied the Neanderthal remains from La Ferrassie and La Chapelle-aux-Saints and concluded that Neanderthals were an extinct side branch of humanity. As is well known, Weidenreich's detailed examination of the cranial remains from Choukoutian and his previous extensive anatomical expertise led him to propose a multi-regional view of human evolution in which our species emerged in Africa, Europe and Asia from an indigenous background of different species and avoided speciation by constant gene flow between populations. His view was summarised in the famous – or infamous – trellis figure he published (see Figure 10.3) in *Apes, Giants and Man* (Weidenreich 1946). As noted above, Weidenreich ignored the Piltdown specimens and placed *Gigantopithecus* as the basal member of the hominin lineage rather than the South African australopithecine material that had by now been recognised as hominin. Because the fossil record for human evolution was so poor when Weidenreich was writing, Choukoutien was the only place where there was a sequence that could be traced from a basal stem (*Sinanthropus*) to the present via an early form of our own species (see Figure 10.3). According to Weidenreich, the human remains from Upper Cave (excavated in 1934) showed affinities to *Sinanthropus* but also to those he classified as Mongolians[16] (with traits such as shovel shaped incisors, and an Inca bone) as well as to Eskimos (now known as Inuit). This implied a deep ancestry of both peoples and could be interpreted (or misinterpreted) as extending Chinese identity deep into the Pleistocene. By using the crucial link between modern Chinese, Upper Cave and Locality 1, it was possible to extend the origins of the Chinese people back into the Upper Pleistocene, and then to *Sinanthropus* in the Middle Pleistocene (see Wolpoff and Caspari 1997 for an excellent and sympathetic account of Weidenreich's work).

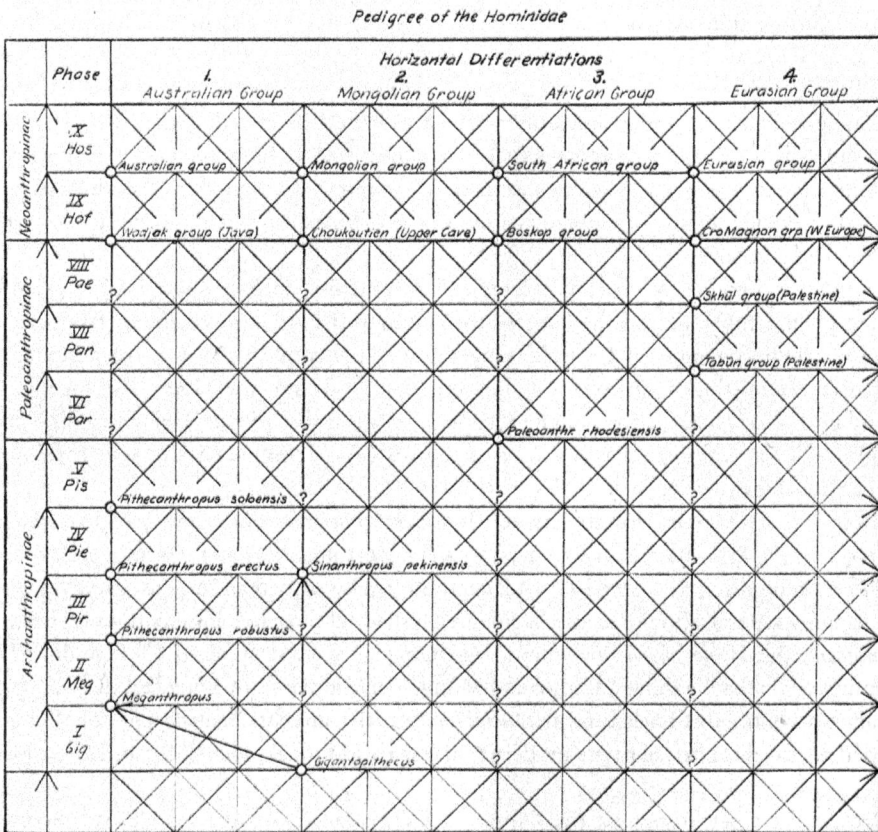

FIGURE 10.3 Weidenreich's model of multi-regional evolution. Note first that he placed the Chinese *Gigantopithecus* at the base of the hominin lineage rather than the South African australopithecines. Second, in his figure, the modern Mongolian group is shown as directly descended from Choukoutien Upper Cave and *Sinanthropus pekinensis*. His scheme could thus be interpreted as showing that modern Chinese are the direct descendants of *Sinanthropus*

Source: Weideneich 1946, Figure 30 (reproduced with permission from the University of Chicago Press).

For its time, it was a remarkable synthesis, especially for a researcher who was then 75 years old. The simple point that multi-regional evolution is still debated 70 years later indicates his enduring influence. Later in this chapter, I evaluate its current status, but at this point we can turn to a different and specifically Chinese narrative that can be traced back to Weidenreich's multi-regional model.

Multi-regionalism with Chinese characteristics

Western contacts with China were broken off after 1949 (apart from the Soviets, until 1960), so that Chinese researchers had to build on ideas that were developed before 1937 (see Shen, Zhang & Gao 2016). The ending of American influence in mainland China, and Mao's anti-imperialist foreign policy, resulted in the 'Bamboo Curtain', and China's isolation from the West, with the USSR and later North Korea and Albania as its only allies. Chinese isolation increased further following the Sino–Soviet split in 1960, and the turmoil created by the Great Leap Forward (and ensuing Great Famine) and the Cultural Revolution of the 1960s. The severance of contact between China and the outside world thus marooned a generation of Chinese researchers who could only warily tread their own path (Shen, Zhang & Gao 2016) and hope to avoid censure by whichever political storm blew their way. The thawing of China's isolation from the wider international community, and the USA, in particular, started after President Nixon's visit to Beijing in 1972, but did not really begin to take effect until the Deng Xiao Ping era of the 1990s.

The most important feature of Weidenreich's scheme for Chinese researchers was that the Chinese people could be seen as entirely the product of local developments. By using the crucial link between modern Chinese, Upper Cave and Locality 1 at Choukoutien, it was possible to extend the origins of the Chinese people back into the Upper Pleistocene, and then back to *Sinanthropus* in the Middle Pleistocene. It was that part of Weidenreich's scheme of multi-regional evolution that was used as the basis for a completely different narrative of ethno-nationalism (see Dennell 2018a).

This specifically Chinese narrative about their deep past grew out of pre-WWII research at Choukoutien, and also the trauma of Japanese occupation after 1937 and the ending of civil war with the Communists' victory of 1949. It is a more complex story than Movius's, and there is no single landmark publication. Because Weidenreich showed morphological continuity between *Sinanthropus*, the *Homo sapiens* specimens from Upper Cave and modern Chinese (as well as continuity with what he called Eskimos and Mongolians), it is not surprising that this was read as indicating a continuous lineage from *Sinanthropus* to the present. *Sinanthropus* could thus be regarded as directly ancestral to the modern Chinese nation. As Reader (1990, p. 111) explains,

> In the West, scientists treat the Chinese fossil evidence as part of the broad picture of human evolution worldwide; in China, it is part of national history – an ancient and fragmentary part, it is true, but none the less one that is called upon to promote a unifying concept of unique origin and continuity within the Chinese nation.

Multi-regionalism to ethno-nationalism

The proposition that *Sinanthropus* was the direct ancestor of the modern Chinese nation needs to be understood in the context of its time. First, there are undoubted similarities between the Upper Cave *H. sapiens* remains and those of *Sinanthropus*, even if we would see these now as plesiomorphic, i.e. shared primitive features. Second, by 1940, the existence of China was under severe threat from the Japanese, and in 1949, the newly-founded PRC was faced with the problems of ruling a huge country that had been traumatised by eight years of Japanese occupation (14 years in the case of Manchuria), over two decades of civil war, and was also confronted by hostile Western powers. *Sinanthropus* thus became a useful device for stressing the unity and deep historic roots of the Chinese people (see Yen 2014; Sautman 2001; Schmalzer 2008). This was not an original idea: according to Dikötter (2015, p. 85), Chinese archaeologist Lin Yan in 1940 cited *Sinanthropus* as proof that the Chinese race had inhabited the Middle Kingdom from the earliest stage of human history. (As we shall see later by reference to the 2008 Olympic Games, this official view remains unchanged.)

Following Engels' essay of 1876 (translated into Chinese in 1928, Schmalzer 2008, pp. 60–61), *Sinanthropus* also served socialism in showing the primacy of human labour, particularly (in the Mao era) male strength, as *Sinanthropus* (unlike *Pithecanthropus*) had mastered the ability to make tools (Schmalzer 2008). These 'messages' of the deep antiquity and unity of the Chinese people, and the primacy of human labour were disseminated to as many as possible through visits to the Zhoukoudian museum by mass groups from schools, army and work units (Schmalzer 2008, p. 153) as a way of promoting national and social cohesion.

The post-1948 legacy

After World War II, it was impossible for Western researchers to resume human origins and related research in China and in South and Southeast Asia. The PRC after 1949 and Myanmar after 1948 were strongly anti-Western, and the Dutch were no longer welcome in Indonesia. When India and Indonesia became independent, the British and Dutch lost the research institutes[17] that had undertaken much of the pre-war research in British India and the former Dutch East Indies. At home, both Britain and the Netherlands faced enormous problems of post-war reconstruction and were unable or unwilling to fund fieldwork in their former Asian territories. Although France retained nominal control over Indo-China (Vietnam, Laos, Cambodia), it became increasingly difficult to conduct field research after 1945, and impossible after it lost control of Vietnam in 1954.

Developments post-WWII in South, Southeast and East Asia varied country by country under new management. The most impressive was in China, where fieldwork at Choukou-tien was resumed only a few weeks after the founding of the PRC in 1949 (Jia & Weiwen 1990, p. 191), and continued throughout the 1950s and 1960s. (As a clear indication of change, new finds of hominins were now studied by Chinese, not Western, specialists; see e.g. Woo Ju-Kang 1966.) It helped that there was a core of university-educated and experienced researchers (notably Pei-wen Zhong and Jia Lan-po) who had acquired the necessary research and management skills at Choukoutien. Although few in number and with (by current standards) miniscule research budgets, they were able to recruit a new generation of researchers and generate new data from their own field projects, notably excavations at sites such as Dingcun, Xujiayao, Lantian, Shuidonggou and Yuanmou in the 1950s and 1960s, and the Nihewan Basin in the 1970s. Because most of this research was published in Chinese, it went largely unnoticed in the West, but it laid the foundations for what we now know about the Chinese Palaeolithic.

In India, despite its enormous problems of poverty, Palaeolithic research was undertaken in the 1950s and 1960s by Indian researchers (with some input from Frederick Zeuner and Bridget Allchin); see Sankalia (1978). In Indonesia, some fieldwork continued at Sangiran in the 1950s and 1960s (see Jacob 1978). In Pakistan, Siwalik research did not restart until the late 1970s, when American teams began work in the Salt Range (see e.g. Barry et al. 1980), and the Dutch started research in Azad Kashmir, Pakistan (Hussain et al. 1992). Terra and Paterson's fieldwork of 1935 was not rechecked and followed up until the 1980s with my own work with Helen Rendell in the Soan Valley some 45 years later (Dennell & Rendell 1991; Rendell, Dennell & Halim 1989). In Indonesia, work at Sangiran accelerated after Dutch and Japanese teams started collaborative projects in the 1970s (see e.g. Hyodo et al. 1993; Leinders et al. 1985). In Burma, the 1937–1938 fieldwork by Terra and Movius has never been re-assessed although I have judged it from my own experience of how Terra worked in British India and see little reason to maintain their conclusions (Dennell 2014a). In former Indo-China, there was an even longer hiatus before French researchers returned (see e.g. Demeter et al. 2017). In contrast, in Europe and Africa, most pre-WWII fieldwork was reappraised fairly rapidly – there are probably no areas of Africa where fieldwork published in 1937 was still regarded as the basic work on the subject 50 years later. As Movius (1978, p. 354) himself pointed out, in the 30 years since the publication of his synthesis, no significant new Early Palaeolithic evidence had been produced in East Asia.[18]

An additional reason why human origins research in East and Southeast Asia stalled after 1948 was that Africa became the main area of interest. As seen above, this shift was already well under way after Gregory, Hellman and Clark had validated the australopithecine specimens as hominin in the 1940s. After 1959–60, with Leakey's discoveries at Olduvai Gorge of *Zinjanthropus* and *Homo habilis*, public and academic attention shifted to Africa. It helped that East Africa was politically stable and pro-Western (compared with East Asia) as well as largely Anglophone. The relocation of the 'cradle of humankind' from East Asia to East Africa seemed well justified by the constant stream of new discoveries, often resulting from US funding and research projects. By the 1960s, East and Southeast Asia no longer appeared interesting or exciting; most importantly, these regions were no longer generating new data for a Western audience. In any case, Movius had already stigmatised East and Southeast Asia as culturally retarded regions that had played no significant role in human evolution. Consequently, it scarcely merited attention. As Athreya (2010) has pointed out, between 1950 and 2003, there was not a single session on Asian palaeoanthropology by the annual meetings of the American Association of Physical Anthropologists.

The 1948 legacy in China

For the Chinese, isolation from the West lasted for almost 50 years from 1937 to the 1980s. The ethno-nationalism that emerged in China in the 1940s continued to the present as the official viewpoint of how the Chinese defined themselves. This is shown graphically by the opening ceremony of the Olympic Games in Beijing in 2008. The last leg of the Olympic torch to the Bird's Nest Stadium was from Zhoukoudian. As stated in the *People's Daily* (*renmin ribao*), the official newspaper of the Chinese government, Zhoukoudian was 'once inhabited by the ancestors of the Chinese' and the Olympic Games marks a long awaited moment. This glorious historical moment congeals with the unswerving pursuit of a people; it records *the steadfastly progressive steps of a nation*; and is filled with true desires of the Chinese sons and daughters for friendship and peace with peoples of the world.

(italics mine)

The choice of Zhoukoudian was significant and deliberate in two ways: first, because Peking Man was one of the first to use fire (according to Chinese archaeologists, and contra Weiner et al. 1998) – thus establishing a link with the Olympic Torch – and second, it is still presented in China by the official media as the direct ancestor of the modern Chinese[19] (see Dennell 2018a).

Discussion: where we are now

For those studying human origins in East Asia, it was not just World War II that interrupted their research but its aftermath: the decolonisation of the former imperial possessions in British India and the Dutch East Indies; the lessening of power in French Indo-China; the Cold War; and, the 'Bamboo Curtain' that isolated China from the West until the 1990s. Because of the discontinuity in research, the work of Movius and of Weidenreich before and immediately after WWII still provide the starting points of research in the twenty-first century. This is completely unlike Europe and Africa, where pre-WWII fieldwork rarely survived unchallenged into the 1990s.

In the twenty-first century, we need to reappraise the models of Movius and Weidenreich in the light of current evidence to evaluate whether they are still fit for purpose.

With the evidence now available – and which was not available to Movius or Chardin – we now know that there are Middle Pleistocene (Acheulean) bifaces in China and Korea. Examples in China are Dingcun (Yang, Huang & Hou 2014), Lantian, the Luonan Basin (Wang 2005), Yunxian level 3 (Lumley et al. 2008) and the Danjiangkou Reservoir Region (Li et al. 2014); and in the Korean peninsula, Kumpari, Chuwoli, and Kawoli and Chongokni in the Imjin-Hantan River Basin (IHRB) in South Korea contain Acheulean types of bifaces (Norton et al. 2006). Handaxes that are probably late Middle or early Late Pleistocene in age are also reported from numerous localities in Sumatra, Java, Bali, Lombok, Sulawesi and Halmahera (Simanjuntak, Sémah & Gaillard 2010). We also now recognise that 'the Acheulean' is largely an open-air phenomenon, and that bifaces are rare in caves – e.g. Yarimburgaz, Atapuerca Gran Dolina, Kudaro, and Azyk, so their absence at Zhoukoudian should not be surprising. Non-bifacial flake assemblages are also known across Eurasia – examples are known from Central Asia (Vishnyatsky 1999), Tajikistan (Ranov 1995), Bizat Ruhama (Israel) (Zaidner 2003), the Clactonian, Bilzingsleben, Schöningen, Vertesszollos in Northwest and Central Europe, and the earliest assemblages from Atapuerca (Carbonell et al. 1995; Parés et al. 2005) and the Orce Basin (Toro Moyano et al. 2011) in Spain. The challenge is thus a wider one of explaining lithic variability across the Eurasian landmass, rather than of seeing two monolithic blocks of bifacial and non-bifacial assemblages (see Dennell 2016; 2018b). Breuil's (1932) suggestion that there were parallel phyla of lithic traditions in the Early Palaeolithic fits the current evidence from Eurasia better than Movius's mutually exclusive areas of biface and non-biface assemblages.

What is remarkable is that the Movius Line still continues to provide the dominant framework for interpreting the Early Palaeolithic of South and East Asia. This is all the more surprising because it was factually incorrect due to the omission of the Clactonian and similar assemblages from Northwest Europe (as noted above). Although the notion of a 'Movius Line sensu stricto' is no longer accepted, many researchers support the idea of a 'Movius Line sensu lato' that accommodates the presence of some bifaces in East and Southeast Asia without seriously violating the basic concept (see e.g. Lycett & Bae 2010). This author (Dennell 2016) and Bar-Yosef (2015) are currently in a minority in recommending that the Movius Line is outmoded as a useful framework.

It is now evident that the fossil record for *H. sapiens* is complex outside Western Europe, where a simple replacement model of Neanderthals by our species is still (largely) valid. The African record is growing in complexity, with very early examples such as Jebel Irhoud attributed to our species 300 ka (Richter et al. 2017), yet apparently co-existing with the very primitive-looking *Homo naledi* (Dirks et al. 2017). In Southeast Asia, *Homo floresiensis* (a.k.a. 'the hobbit') has been a game changer as a previously unsuspected type of hominin that is known only (so far) from the island of Flores, Indonesia, and which became extinct ca. 50 ka (Sutikna et al. 2016). *H. sapiens* may have been in Java as early as the last interglacial ca. 125–110 ka, depending upon the identification of a premolar tooth as *H. sapiens* (Storm et al. 2005) and not *H. erectus* (Polanski, Marsh & Maddux 2016) and its association with a tropical forest. Our species is present in Laos at Tam Pan Ling between ca. 44 ka and 63 ka (Demeter et al. 2012), Sumatra at Lida Ajer between 63 ka and 73 ka (Westaway et al. 2017), and Niah ca. 45 ka (Barker et al. 2007).

The Chinese fossil skeletal record shows a more complex picture than a simple one of an undifferentiated population of *H. erectus* being replaced in a single immigration event by *H. sapiens*. As example, 'the suite of traits exhibited by Dali could be indicative of a local transition between *H. erectus* and *H. sapiens* that included some influence from Western Eurasian populations during the Middle Pleistocene' (Wu & Athreya 2013, p. 154). The crania from Xuchung, ca. 125–100 ka show a mix of different characters (Li et al. 2017), and the mandible from Zhirendong (ca. 60–100 ka) may also indicate hybridisation between late *H. erectus* and incoming *H. sapiens* (Dennell 2010; Liu et al. 2010). In contrast, teeth from Daoxian, dated to 80–100 ka, appear fully modern *H. sapiens* (Dennell 2015; Liu et al. 2015). In North China, immigration by *H. sapiens* appears to have occurred much later, as the earliest clear indication of our species is the individual from Tianyuandong near Beijing (Shang et al. 2010). The seemingly archaic-looking cranium from Salkhit, Mongolia (Lee 2014) and the crania from Longlin, Southwest China (Curnoe et al. 2012) also imply the retention of primitive features in populations that were isolated over long periods. The evidence from south and central China increasingly suggests deep, structured populations with complex histories, and that from North China implies an immigration event ca. 40 ka. The model now emerging of human evolution in China is one of 'continuity with hybridisation' (see Liu et al. 2010) that involves both indigenous and immigrant populations, and interactions between the two.

This complexity is compounded by genetic evidence that indicates a considerable amount of interbreeding between *H. sapiens*, Neanderthals, and Denisovans (a population recently identified by its ancient DNA (aDNA) from the cave of Denisova, Siberia, and a likely sister clade of Neanderthals; see Krause et al. 2010 and Reich et al. 2010). Studies of Neanderthal aDNA show that there is some (c. 2–4 per cent) of Neanderthal DNA in all modern non-Africans, i.e. those in Europe and Asia and their descendent populations in the Americas and Australia (Sankararaman et al. 2014). Genetic evidence suggests that there was an 'inter-breeding bonanza' (Callaway 2016) between *H. sapiens*, Neanderthals and Denisovans. As Kuhlwilm and colleagues (2016, p. 429) observe, there was:

> admixture among archaic and modern human populations, including gene flow from Neanderthals into modern humans outside Africa, Denisovan gene flow into the ancestors of present-day humans in Oceania and mainland Asia, gene flow into the Denisovans from Neanderthals and, possibly, gene flow into the Denisovans from an unknown archaic group that diverged from the other lineages more than one million years ago.

In recent years, Weidenreich's model of multi-regional evolution across Asia, Europe and Africa has been largely replaced by the ROA (recent Out of Africa) model, whereby our species originated in Africa and then replaced Neanderthals in Europe and *H. erectus* and other hominin species in Asia. However, it would be premature to dismiss his views as an interesting historical anachronism. To recapitulate the basic components of his model: Weidenreich envisaged a series of metapopulations (or sub-groups of the total population) of hominins across Asia, Europe and Africa. Most gene flow (i.e. mating) took place within a metapopulation, but some also occurred between metapopulations, thereby avoiding speciation. The total population composed of these metapopulations was therefore structured in the sense that it was not a panmictic population in which mating was random across the entire range but comprised a series of sub-groups. At a continental level, his concept of a structured population comprising different metapopulations that occasionally interbred is a useful way of envisaging the origin of our species in Africa: instead of a single place of origin, it seems now more likely that our species emerged as a result of gene flow within and between different metapopulations (see e.g. Scerri 2018; Stringer 2016). Similarly, in China, the fossil evidence now indicates a complex picture of different metapopulations that were sufficiently self-contained to develop their own morphs – or skeletal idiosyncrasies – but exchanged genes with neighbouring metapopulations and thereby avoided speciation. This scenario is borne out by the recent genetic evidence for gene flow between Neanderthals, Denisovans and *H. sapiens* that was mentioned above. This type of multi-regionalism for Africa and East Asia does not exclude the possibility of immigration as that simply introduces (at least initially) another metapopulation that could exchange genes with the indigenous metapopulations and produce hybrid forms. In other words, on the scale of Europe, Africa and East Asia, the replacement ROA model is a valid model for explaining how our species eventually replaced all contemporary indigenous hominin populations, but a multi-regional model on the smaller scale of sub-Saharan Africa or East Asia that admits gene exchange between indigenous and immigrant populations is also valid, as implied by the 'continuity with hybridization' model. In short, it is possible to integrate the two, even though they were once presented as mutually incompatible (see e.g. Stringer & Andrews 1988; Stringer 2001; Thorne & Wolpoff 1992). We are now a long way from a polarised debate between Weidenreich's ideas about multi-regional evolution and simple replacement models. Instead, the population history of China (and Southeast Asia) is likely to have been complex, with numerous immigration events that interacted with local, structured metapopulations with deep histories. Weidenreich's model is therefore still useful at a regional or sub-continental level, but not at the scale of the entire Old World that he originally envisaged

On a positive note, there have been two welcome developments in the last 20 years that mark the end of the 'Bamboo Curtain'. The first is that the Palaeolithic of the 'Far East' – China and Southeast Asia – is no longer regarded as marginal, isolated or backward, but is instead seen as a major and integral part of the Palaeolithic world. The second is that Chinese researchers now interact on an equal basis with non-Chinese colleagues and take their rightful place in a global community.

Concluding comments

Decolonisation takes many forms and has many consequences. In the context of much current writing about decolonisation, the emphasis is to expose the biases and prejudices of those who worked and wrote in colonial times, and to note how these biases and prejudices reverberate and continue into the present. Regarding the individuals mentioned in this chapter, we can detect biases towards East Asia, particularly by Chardin and Movius in the way the 'Far East' was dismissed as marginal, backward and culturally retarded. The racist views of authorities such as Elliot Smith and Arthur Keith also provide obvious examples of how the rulers can look down upon the ruled and misuse their authority and scientific expertise to legitimate their prejudices. These are thankfully exceptions, and none of the other figures mentioned in this paper expressed any opinions in their writing that we would find politically or socially biased today. Instead, they emerge as individuals who did their best to describe and explain the material that they studied. As in any generation, some emerge as more diligent or enthusiastic than others, but overall, they emerge as sympathetic and decent people.

Decolonisation in South, Southeast and East Asia after WWII had a profound impact on the study of human origins in that it ended Western palaeoanthropological fieldwork in what had been British India, the Dutch East Indies, and French Indo-China for at least a generation. The emergence of the People's Republic of China in 1949 was part of decolonisation in that it ended the unequal patron–client relationships that patterned Western involvement before 1937.[20] It is only in the last 20 years or so that human origins research in East and Southeast Asia has become re-integrated into a global academic community. Importantly, current research in these regions is now undertaken by Indigenous researchers, sometimes working in collaboration, and on an equal basis, with Western researchers. Because so much of what we think about human evolution in East Asia is grounded in research undertaken in a colonial and imperial era, it is all the more important that we try to understand those who researched at that time, how and why they reached their conclusions, and the world in which they operated. Only by taking this history seriously will we be able to develop contemporary research without the biases and prejudices of the past.

Notes

1 I refer to this site as Choukoutien for research undertaken before the establishment of the Peoples' Republic of China (PRC) in 1949, and as Zhoukoudian for subsequent research, following the reforms of the Chinese script in the PRC. Research-wise, Choukoutien was used by both Movius and Weidenreich in their 1948 and 1946 publications respectively.

2 For millennials, Spam in 1937 was a type of tinned pork, not the junk emails that now clog our inboxes.

3 The road from Lashio to Kunming was 715 miles long, with two lanes and a cobbled surface. It was constructed by 200,000 labourers in 1937 and early 1938 (Webster 2004, p. 24), so had only

recently been completed when Terra drove along it. As it was now the main supply route of military aid to the Chinese Nationalists, one wonders if Terra had been asked to provide a first-hand account of its condition.

4 As early as 1915, Gerrit Miller described Piltdown as a chimpanzee jaw fortuitously mixed with a human skull. William Gregory (1916) supported Miller's assessment of the molar. Had Miller written 'orangutan jaw deliberately mixed' he would have been spot on. Weidenreich (1947, p. 192) commented 'everybody now doubts its authenticity'.

5 In alphabetical order: *Atlantropus helmei, Atlanthropus mauritanicus, Australopithecus africanus, Cyanthropus rhodesiensis, Eoanthropus dawsoni, Homo heidelbergensis, Homo neanderthalensis, Homo spelaeus, Javanthropus soloensis, Meganthropus palaeojavanicus, Palaeoanthropus palestinensis, Palaeoanthropus heidelbergensis, Pithecanthropus erectus, Plesianthropus transvaalensis, Protanthropus neanderthalensis, Sinanthropus pekinensis, Telanthropus capensis* (see Tattersall 2012).

6 Under the agreement between the Peking Medical College and the Rockefeller Foundation (which financed the college), the excavation and analysis of the non-human fauna were the responsibilities of Chinese researchers, but a Western scientist would be responsible for studying any human remains. This caused understandable bitterness: to quote Jia Lanpo (1980, p. 22) 'In recognition of a $80,000 donation to the project by the Rockefeller Foundation, the reactionary Chinese government at that time had gone to the length of relinquishing the right to study these human remains found on its own territory.'

7 *Pithecanthropus* I was the specimen found by Dubois at Trinil in 1891.

8 George Barbour (1890–1977) is an overlooked figure in pre-WWII research in China. He was Scottish by birth, moved to the USA, then to China from 1920 to 1932, where he collaborated with Chardin on fieldwork in North China, including Choukoutien. He returned to the USA in 1937 and taught geology at Cincinnati until 1960. Post-WWII, he worked extensively in Africa (including the australopithecine sites in the Transvaal), and was probably the only figure from that era to have worked extensively in both China and Africa. See Barbour (1977).

9 The Dutch finally ceded independence to Indonesia on December 27, 1949 with the exception of Netherlands New Guinea, which the Netherlands retained until 1963.

10 Following the visit by Gregory and Hellman, Dart was invited to address the American Association of Physical Anthropologists in 1939 as part of the celebration of the 70th birthday of Aleš Hrdlička, the first president of the Association.

11 Weidenreich (1940, p. 383) anticipated this development. In this paper, he discussed the value of generic terms, and proposed that 'Instead of *Pithecanthropus erectus* we should speak of *Homo erectus javanensis. Sinanthropus pekinensis* should be replaced by *Homo erectus pekinensis* or *sinensis* … I want only to broach the question here but not to enter into a special discussion'.

12 Piltdown was finally exposed as a fraud in 1953 by Kenneth Oakley, Joseph Weiner and Wilfred LeGros Clark.

13 Ashley-Montagu (1905–1999) was born in London's East End as Israel Ehrenberg. Evidently a polymath, he studied psychology under Karl Pearson, and anthropology under Eliot Smith and Bronislav Malinowski, as well as informally under Arthur Keith. He emigrated to the USA in 1931, changed his name to Montague Francis Ashley Montagu, and taught at Columbia, Rutgers and various other universities until dismissed for his political views. He also played a major role in the drafting of the UNESCO Statement on Race (1950). As a Jew, he would have been acutely aware of the lethal consequences of racial classifications.

14 It is easy now to see Movius's pronouncements on East Asia as 'a region of cultural retardation' (Movius 1948, p. 411) as judgmental and even racist in articulating Western superiority over 'the Orient', but I do not know of any criticism of these views in Movius's lifetime.

15 The Cenozoic Research Laboratory was housed in Peking Medical College, which is still there in its original building despite the phenomenal growth and modernisation of Beijing in recent years. Somewhat incongruously for a Communist state, it contains a bust of J. D. Rockefeller, the ruthless capitalist turned philanthropist who provided the key funding.

16 It is not at all clear from Weidenreich's account what he meant by the term 'Mongolian'. Present-day 'Mongolians' are multi-ethnic and multi-linguistic, and widely distributed outside the modern Republic of Mongolia. I suspect that he was referring to cranial specimens that were labelled as 'Mongolian' and which may have come from Central Asia, Mongolia, Inner Mongolia (China), Siberia, or Tibet. In other words, the term 'Mongolian' was as imprecise as labelling a cranial specimen as 'negro' or 'Caucasian'.

17 For example, for the British, the Archaeological Survey of India, and the Geological Survey of India, and for the Dutch, the Geological Survey of the Dutch East Indies.

18 Hutterer (1977, p. 39) likewise asserted that 'the evidence for palaeolithic cultures in Southeast Asia is very meagre, often highly ambiguous, and in many cases quite useless'.

19 This use of the fossil hominin record to promote a type of ethno-nationalism is not unique to China. It is worth noting that Woodward (1948) entitled his book on Piltdown *The Earliest Englishman*. More recently, in 2017 Cyril Ramaphosa, the deputy president of South Africa, kissed a reconstruction of *Homo naledi*'s face at a news conference at the Maropeng Cradle of Humankind in Magaliesburg, South Africa (see google images/cyril ramaphosa, naledi).

20 As part of decolonisation, the extra-territorial rights of the British and most other countries only ended in 1943; previously, Europeans could not be tried in a Chinese court for any criminal offence.

Acknowledgements

I am very grateful to the editors for inviting me to contribute to this volume, and to Sheela Athreya for her constructive criticisms of an earlier draft of this chapter. The editors and Linda Hurcombe are also thanked for their comments.

References

Anon 1947, 'The Pan-African Congress on prehistory', *Nature*, vol. 159, p. 216.

Ashley-Montague, MF 1942, *Man's most dangerous myth: the fallacy of race*, Columbia University Press, New York.

Athreya, S 2010, 'Book review: *The Palaeolithic settlement of Asia* by Robin Dennell', *American Journal of Anthropology*, vol. 142, pp. 501–502.

Barbour, H 1977, 'Memorial to George Brown Barbour 1890–1977', The Geological Society of America. Available from: www.geosociety.org/documents/gsa/memorials/v09/Barbour-GB.pdf [2 January 2019].

Barker, G, Barton, H, Bird, M, Daly, P, Datan, I, Dykes, A, Farr, L, Gilbertson, D, Harrisson, B, Hunt, C, Higham, T, Kealofer, L, Krigbaum, J, Lewis, H, McLaren, S, Paz, V, Piper, P, Pyatt, B, Rabett, R, Reynolds, T, Rushworth, G, Stephens, M, Stringer, C, Thompson, J & Turney, C 2007, 'The "Human Revolution" in lowland tropical Southeast Asia: the antiquity and behavior of Anatomically Modern Humans at Niah Cave (Sarawak, Borneo)', *Journal of Human Evolution*, vol. 52, pp. 243–261.

Barry, JC, Behrensmeyer, AK & Monoghan, M 1980, 'A geologic and biostratigraphic framework for Miocene sediments near Khaur village, northern Pakistan', *Postilla*, vol. 183, no. 1, pp. 1–19.

Bartstra, G-J 1983, 'Some remarks upon fossil man from Java, his age, and his tools', *Bydragen to de Taal-Land-and Volkenkunde*, vol. 139, pp. 421–434.

Bartstra, G-J 1985, 'Sangiran, the stone implements of Ngebung, and the palaeolithic of Java', *Modern Quaternary Research in SE Asia*, vol. 9, pp. 99–113.

Bar-Yosef, O 2015, 'Chinese Palaeolithic challenges for interpretations of Palaeolithic archaeology', *Anthropologie*, vol. 53, no. 1–2, pp. 77–92.

Black, D 1925, 'Asia and the dispersal of primates', *Bulletin of the Geological Society of China*, vol. 4, pp. 133–183.

Black, D 1927, 'Further hominid remains of lower Quaternary age from the Chou-kou-tien deposit', *Nature*, vol. 120, p. 954.

Black, D 1934, 'The Croonian Lecture: On the discovery, morphology, and environment of *Sinanthropus pekinensis*', *Philosophical Transactions of the Royal Society of London*, vol. 123, pp. 57–120.

Breuil, H 1932, 'Les industries à éclats du Paléolithique ancien 1: le Clactonien', *Préhistoire*, vol. 1, pp. 148–157.

Broom, R 1937, 'Discovery of a lower molar of Australopithecus', *Nature*, vol. 140, p. 681.

Broom, R 1938a, 'More discoveries of Australopithecus', *Nature*, vol. 141, pp. 828–829.

Broom, R 1938b, 'The Pleistocene anthropoid apes of South Africa', *Nature*, vol. 142, pp. 377–379.

Broom, R 1938c, 'Further evidence on the structure of the South African Pleistocene anthropoids', *Nature*, vol. 142, pp. 897–899.

Broom, R & Schepers, GWH 1946, *The South African fossil ape-men: the Australopithecinae*, Transvaal Museum Memoirs #2. New edition: AMS Press, New York, 1978.

Callaway, E 2016, 'Evidence mounts for interbreeding bonanza in ancient human species', *Nature News*, 17 February. Available from: doi:10.1038/nature.2016.19394 [3 April 2019].

Carbonell, E, Bermúdez de Castro, JM, Arsuaga, JL, Díez, JC, Rosas, A, Cuenca-Bescós, G, Sala, R, Mosquera, M & Rodríguez, XP 1995, 'Lower Pleistocene hominids and artifacts from Atapuerca-TD6 (Spain)', *Science*, vol. 269, pp. 826–829.

Chardin, PT de 1941, 'Early man in China', *Institut de Géo-Biologie, Pékin*, vol. 7, pp. 1–100.

Collings, HD 1938, 'Pleistocene site in the Malay Peninsula', *Nature*, vol. 142, pp. 575–576.

Curnoe, D, Xueping, J, Herries, AIR, Kanning, B, Taçon, PSC, Zhende, B, Fink, D, Yunseng, Z, Hellstrom, J, Luo, Y, Cassis, G, Bing, S, Wroe, S, Shi, H, Parr, WCH, Shengmin, H & Rogers, N 2012, 'Human remains from the Pleistocene-Holocene transition of Southwest China suggest a complex evolutionary history for East Asians', *PLoS One*, vol. 7, https://doi.org/10.1371/journal.pone.0031918.

Dart, RA 1925, '*Australopithecus africanus*: the man-ape of South Africa', *Nature*, vol. 115, pp. 195–199.

Dart, RA 1940, 'The status of Australopithecus', *American Journal of Physical Anthropology*, vol. 26, pp. 167–186.

Dart, RA 1948a, 'The Makapansgat proto-human *Australopithecus prometheus*', *American Journal of Physical Anthropology*, vol. 6, no. 3, pp. 259–284.

Dart, RA 1948b, 'The adolescent mandible of *Australopithecus prometheus*', *American Journal of Physical Anthropology*, vol. 6, no. 4, pp. 391–412.

Demeter, F, Shackelford, LL, Bacon, A-M, Duringer, P, Westaway, K, Sayavongkhamdy, T, Braga, J, Sichanthongtip, P, Kamdalavong, P, Ponche, J-L, Wang, H, Lundstrom, C, Patole-Edoumba, E & Karpoff, A-M 2012, 'Anatomically Modern Human in Southeast Asia (Laos) by 46 ka', *Proceedings of the National Academy of Sciences USA*, vol. 109, no. 36, pp. 14375–14380.

Demeter, F, Shackelford, L, Westaway, K, Barnes, L, Duringer, P, Ponce, J-L, Dumoncel, J, Sénégas, F, Sayavongkhamdy, T, Zhao, Z-X, Sichanthongtip, P, Patole-Edoumba, E, Dunn, T, Zachwieja, A, Coppens, Y, Willerslev, E & Bacon, A-M 2017, 'Early Modern Humans from Tam Pà Ling, Laos: fossil review and perspectives', *Current Anthropology*, vol. 58, no. S17, pp. S527–S538.

Dennell, RW 2001, 'From Sangiran to Olduvai, 1937–1960: the quest for "centres" of Hominid origins in Asia and Africa', in R Corbey & W Roebroeks (eds), *Studying human origins: disciplinary history and epistemology*, Amsterdam University Press, Amsterdam, pp. 45–66.

Dennell, RW 2010, 'Early *Homo sapiens* in China', *Nature*, vol. 468, pp. 512–513.

Dennell, RW 2014a, 'Hallam Movius, Helmut de Terra, and the Line that never was: Burma, 1938', in K Boyle, RJ Rabett & C Hunt (eds), *Living in the landscape: essays in honour of Graeme Barker*, McDonald Institute for Archaeological Research, Cambridge, pp. 11–34.

Dennell, RW 2014b, 'East Asia and human evolution: from cradle of mankind to cul-de-sac', in RW Dennell & M Porr (eds), *Southern Asia, Australia and the search for human origins*, Cambridge University Press, Cambridge, pp. 8–20.

Dennell, RW 2015, '*Homo sapiens* in China by 80,000 years ago', *Nature*, vol. 526, pp. 647–648.

Dennell, RW 2016, 'Life without the Movius Line', *Quaternary International*, vol. 400, pp. 14–22.

Dennell, RW 2018a, 'Where evolutionary biology meets history: ethno-nationalism and modern human origins in East Asia', in JP Schwartz (ed.), *Rethinking human evolution*, MIT Press (Vienna Series in Theoretical Biology), Cambridge, MA and London, pp. 229–250.

Dennell, RW 2018b, 'The Acheulean assemblages of Asia: a review', in R Gallotti & MM Mussi (eds), *The emergence of the Acheulean in Africa and beyond*, Springer, Cham, pp. 194–214.

Dennell, RW & Rendell, H 1991, 'De Terra and Paterson, and the Soan flake industry: a perspective from the Soan Valley, Pakistan', *Man and Environment*, vol. 16, no. 2, pp. 91–99.

Dikötter, F 2015, *The discourse of race in modern China*, Hurst and Company, London.

Dirks, PHM, Roberts, EM, Hilbert-Wolf, H, Kramers, JD, Hawks, J, Dosseto, A, Duval, M, Elliott, M, Evans, M, Grün, R, Hellstrom, J, Herries, AIR, Joannes-Boyau, R, Mahhubela, TV, Placzek, CJ,

Robbins, J, Spandler, C, Wiersma, J, Woodhead, J and Berger, LR 2017, 'The age of *Homo naledi* and associated sediments in the Rising Star Cave, South Africa', *eLife*, vol. 6, p. e24231.

Engels, F 1950 [1876], *The part played by labor in the transition from ape to man*, International Publishers, New York.

Gregory, WK 1916, 'Note on the molar teeth of the Piltdown mandible', *American Anthropologist*, New Series, vol. 18, no. 3, pp. 384–387.

Gregory, WK & Hellman, M 1938, 'Evidence of the Australopithecine man-apes on the origin of man', *Science*, vol. 88, pp. 615–616.

Gregory, WK & Hellman, M 1939a, 'Fossil man-apes of South Africa', *Nature*, vol. 143, pp. 25–26.

Gregory, WK & Hellman, M 1939b, 'The dentition of the extinct South African man-ape Australopithecus (Plesianthropus) transvaalensis Broom. A comparative and phylogenetic study', *Transvaal Museum*, vol. 19, pp. 339–373.

Gregory, WK & Hellman, M 1939c, 'The South African fossil man-apes and the origin of the human dentition', *Journal of the American Dental Association*, vol. 26, pp. 558–564.

Gregory, WK & Hellman, M 1940, 'The upper dental arch of Plesianthropus transvaalensis Broom, and its relations to other parts of the skull', *American Journal of Physical Anthropology*, vol. 26, pp. 211–228.

Gregory, WK & Hellman, M 1945, 'Revised reconstruction of the skull of Plesianthropus transvaalensis Broom', *American Journal of Physical Anthropology*, vol. 3, pp. 267–275.

Heekeren, van HR 1948, 'Stone age discoveries in Siam', *Proceedings of the Prehistoric Society*, vol. 14, pp. 24–32.

Holcombe, C 2011, *A history of East Asia*, Cambridge University Press, Cambridge.

Hussain, ST, Bergh, GD van den, Steensma, KJ, Visser, JA de, Vos, J de, Arif, M, Dam, J van, Sondaar, PY & Malik, SB 1992, 'Biostratigraphy of the Plio-Pleistocene continental sediments (Upper Siwaliks) of the Mangla-Samwal Anticline, Azad Kashmir, Pakistan', *Proceedings of the Koninkijke Nederlandse Akademie van Wetenschappen*, vol. 95, no. 1, pp. 65–80.

Hutterer, KL 1977, 'Re-interpreting the Southeast Asian palaeolithic', in J Allen, J Golson & R Jones (eds), *Sunda and Sahel: prehistoric studies in Southeast Asia, Melanesia and Australia*, Academic Press, London, pp. 31–71.

Hyodo, M, Watanabe, N, Sunata, W, Susanto, EE & Wahyono, H 1993, 'Magnetostratigraphy of hominid fossil bearing formations in Sangiran and Mojokerto, Java', *Anthropological Science*, vol. 101, no. 2, pp. 157–186.

Jacob, T 1978, 'New finds of Lower and Middle Pleistocene hominines from Indonesia and an examination of their antiquity', in F Ikawa-Smith (ed.), *Early Paleolithic in South and East Asia*, Mouton, The Hague, pp. 13–22.

Jia, L 1980, *Early man in China*, Foreign Languages Press, Beijing.

Jia, L & Weiwen, H 1990, *The story of Peking Man: from archaeology to mystery*, Oxford University Press, Oxford.

Keith, A 1916, *The antiquity of man*, Williams and Norgate, London.

von Koenigswald, GHR 1936, 'Early Palaeolithic stone implements from Java', *Bulletin of the Raffles Museum (Singapore)*, vol. B1, pp. 52–60.

von Koenigswald, GHR & Ghosh, AK 1973, 'Stone implements from the Trinil beds of Sangiran, Central Java', *Proceedings of the Koninklijke Nederlandse Akademie van Wetanschappen*, vol. B76, no. 1, pp. 1–17.

von Koenigswald, GHR & Weidenreich, F 1938, 'Discovery of an additional Pithecanthropus skull', *Nature*, vol. 142, p. 715.

von Koenigswald, GHR & Weidenreich, F 1939, 'The relationship between *Pithecanthropus* and *Sinanthropus*', *Nature*, vol. 144, pp. 926–929.

Krause, J, Fu, Q, Good, JM, Viola, B, Shunkov, MV, Derevianko, AP & Pääbo, S 2010, 'The complete mitochondrial DNA genome of an unknown hominin from southern Siberia', *Nature*, vol. 464, pp. 894–897.

Kuhlwilm, M, Gronau, I, Hubisz, MJ, Filippo, C de, Prado-Martinez, J, Kircher, M, Fu, Q, Burbano, HA, Lalueza-Fox, C, Rasilla, M de la, Rosas, A, Rudan, P, Brajkovic, D, Kucan, Z, Gušic, I,

Marques-Bonet, T, Andrés, AM, Viola, B, Pääbo, S, Meyer, M, Siepel, A & Castellano, S 2016, 'Ancient gene flow from early modern humans into Eastern Neanderthals', *Nature*, vol. 530, pp. 429–433.

Lee, S-H 2014, '*Homo erectus* in Salkhit, Mongolia?', *HOMO – Journal of Comparative Human Biology*, vol. 66, pp. 287–298.

Le Gros Clark, WE 1946, 'Significance of the Australopithecinae', *Nature*, vol. 157, pp. 863–863.

Leinders, JJM, Aziz, F, Sondaar, PY & de Vos, J 1985, 'The age of the hominid-bearing deposits of Java: state of the art', *Geologie en Mijnbouw*, vol. 64, pp. 167–173.

Li, H, Li, C & Kuman, K 2014, 'Rethinking the "Acheulean" in East Asia: evidence from recent investigations in the Danjiangkou Reservoir Region, central China', *Quaternary International*, vol. 347, pp. 163–175.

Li, Z-Y, Wu, X-J, Zhou, L-P, Liu, W, Gao, X, Nian, X-N & Trinkaus, E 2017, 'Late Pleistocene archaic human crania from Xuchang, China', *Science*, vol. 355, pp. 969–972.

Liu, W, Jin, C, Zhang, Y, Cai, Y, Xing, S, Wu, J, Cheng, H, Edwards, RL, Pan, W, Qin, D, An, Z, Trinkaus, E & Wu, X 2010, 'Human remains from Zhirendong, South China, and modern human emergence in East Asia', *Proceedings of the National Academy of Sciences USA*, vol. 107, pp. 19201–19206.

Liu, W, Martinón-Torres, M, Cai, Y-J, Xing, S, Tong, H-W, Pei, S-W, Sier, MJ, Wu, X-H, Edwards, RL, Cheng, H, Li, Y-Y, Yang, X-X, Castro, MB de & Wu, X-J 2015, 'The earliest unequivocally modern humans in southern China', *Nature*, vol. 526, pp. 696–699.

Lumley, H de, Batalla i Llasat, G, Cauche, D, Notter, O, Yanxian, L, Tianyuan, L and Feng Xiao, B 2008, 'L'industrie du Paléolithique inferieur du site de l'homme de Yunxian', in H de Lumley & L Tianyuan (eds), *Le site de l'homme de Yunxian: Quyuanhekou, Quingpu, Yunxian, Province du Hebei*, CRNS Editions Recherche sur les Civilisations, Paris, pp. 467–583.

Lycett, SJ & Bae, CJ 2010, 'The Movius Line controversy: the state of the debate', *World Archaeology*, vol. 42, pp. 521–544.

Manias, C 2015, '*Sinanthropus* in Britain: human origins and international science, 1920–1939', *British Society for the History of Science*, vol. 48, no. 2, pp. 289–319.

Matthew, WD 1915, 'Climate and evolution', *Annals of the New York Academy of Science*, vol. 24, pp. 171–318.

Miller, GS 1915, 'The jaw of the Piltdown Man', *Smithsonian Miscellaneous Collections*, vol. 65, no. 12, pp. 1–31.

Movius, HL 1943, 'The stone age of Burma', *Transactions of the American Philosophical Society*, vol. 32, pp. 341–393.

Movius, HL 1948, 'The lower Palaeolithic cultures of southern and eastern Asia', *Transactions of the American Philosophical Society*, vol. 38, no. 4, pp. 329–420.

Movius, HL 1978, 'Conclusions', in F Ikawa-Smit (ed.), *Early Paleolithic in South and East Asia*, Mouton, The Hague, pp. 351–355.

Norton, CJ, Bae, K, Harris, JWK & Lee, H 2006, 'Middle Pleistocene handaxes from the Korean Peninsula', *Journal of Human Evolution*, vol. 51, no. 5, pp. 527–536.

Oakley, KP 1947, 'Le premier congrès Pan-Africain de Prehistoire (Nairobi, 1947)', *L'Anthropologie*, vol. 51, pp. 251–262.

Oakley, K 1949, *Man the toolmaker*, British Museum of Natural History, London.

Oakley, KP & Leakey, MD 1937, 'Report on excavations at Jaywick Sands, Essex (1934), with some observations on the Clactonian industry, and on the fauna and geological significance of the Clacton channel', *Proceedings of the Prehistoric Society*, vol. 3, pp. 217–260.

Oppenoorth, WEF 1932, '*Homo (Javanthropus) soloensis*: een Pleistocene Mensch van Java', *Scientific Proceedings of the Mining Company of the Dutch East Indies*, vol. 20, pp. 49–75.

Osborn, HF 1910, *The age of mammals in Europe, Asia and North America*, Macmillan, New York.

Osborn, HF 1915, *Men of the Old Stone Age: their environment, life and art*, Charles Scribner's Sons, New York.

Parés, JM, Pérez-González, A, Rosas, A, Benito, A, Bermúdez de Castro, JM, Carbonell, E & Huguet, R 2005, 'Matuyama-age lithic tools from the Sima del Elefante site, Atapuerca (northern Spain)', *Journal of Human Evolution*, vol. 50, pp. 163–169.

Paterson, TT 1937, 'Studies on the palaeolithic succession in England no. 1: the Barnham sequence', *Proceedings of the Prehistoric Society*, vol. 3, pp. 87–135.

Pettitt, P & White, M 2012, *The British Palaeolithic: human societies at the edge of the Palaeolithic world*, Routledge, London and New York.

Phillips, W 1947, 'The first pan-African congress on prehistory', *Science*, vol. 105, pp. 611–613.

Polanski, JM, Marsh, HE & Maddux, SD 2016, 'Dental size reduction in Indonesian *Homo erectus*: implications for the PU-198 premolar and the appearance of *Homo sapiens* on Java', *Journal of Human Evolution*, vol. 90, pp. 49–54.

Ranov, VA 1995, 'The "Loessic Palaeolithic" in South Tadjikistan, Central Asia: its industries, chronology and correlation', *Quaternary Science Reviews*, vol. 14, pp. 731–745.

Reader, J 1990, *Missing links*, Penguin, London.

Reich, D, Green, RE, Kircher, M, Krause, J, Patterson, N, Durand, EY, Viola, B, Briggs, AW, Stenzel, U, Johnson, PLF, Maricic, T, Good, JM, Marques-Bonet, T, Alkan, C, Fu, Q, Mallick, S, Li, H, Meyer, M, Eichler, EE, Stoneking, M, Richards, M, Talmov, S, Shunkov, MV, Derevianko, AP, Hublin, J-J, Kelsom, J, Slatkin, M & Pääbo, S 2010, 'Genetic history of an archaic hominin group from Denisova Cave in Siberia', *Nature*, vol. 468, pp. 1053–1060.

Reich, D, Patterson, N, Kircher, M, Delfin, F, Nandineni, MR, Pugach, I, Ko, AM-S, Ko, Y-C, Jinam, TA, Phipps, ME, Saitou, N, Wollstein, A, Kayser, M, Pääbo, S & Stoneking, M 2011, 'Denisova admixture and the first modern human dispersals into Southeast Asia and Oceania', *American Journal of Human Genetics*, vol. 89, pp. 516–528.

Rendell, HM, Dennell, RW & Halim, M 1989, 'Pleistocene and Palaeolithic investigations in the Soan Valley, Northern Pakistan', *British Archaeological Reports International Series*, vol. 544, pp. 1–346.

Richter, D, Grün, R, Joannes-Boyau, R, Steele, TE, Amani, F, Rue, M, Fernandes, P, Raynal, J-P, Geraads, D, Ben-Neer, A & Hublin, J-J 2017, 'The age of the hominin fossils from Jebel Irhoud, Morocco, and the origins of the Middle Stone Age', *Nature*, vol. 546, pp. 293–296.

Said, EW 1978, *Orientalism*, Pantheon Books, New York.

Said, EW 2004, 'Orientalism once more', *Development and Change*, vol. 35, no. 5, pp. 869–879.

Sankalia, HD 1978, 'The early palaeolithic in India and Pakistan', in F Ikawa-Smith (ed.), *Early Paleolithic in South and East Asia*, Mouton, The Hague, pp. 97–128.

Sankararaman, S, Mallick, S, Dannemann, M, Prüfer, K, Kelso, J, Pääbo, S, Patterson, N & Reich, D 2014, 'The genomic landscape of Neanderthal ancestry in present-day humans', *Nature*, vol. 507, no. 7492, pp. 354–357.

Sautman, B 2001, 'Peking Man and the politics of palaeoanthropological nationalism in China', *Journal of Asian Studies*, vol. 60, no. 1, pp. 95–124.

Scerri, EML, Thomas, MG, Manica, A, Gunz, P, Stock, J, Stringer, CB, Grove, M, Groucutt, HS, Timmermann, A, Rightmire, PG, d'Errico, F, Tryon, C, Drake, N, Brooks, A, Dennell, R, Durbin, R, Henn, B, Lee-Thorp, J, deMenocal, P, Petraglia, MD, Thompson, JC, Scally, A & Chikhi, L 2018, 'Did our species evolve in subdivided populations across Africa, and why does it matter?', *TREE (Trends in Ecology and Evolution)*, vol. 33, no. 8, pp. 582–594.

Schmalzer, S 2008, *The people's Peking Man: popular science and human identity in twentieth-century China*, University of Chicago Press, Chicago, IL.

Shang, H, Tong, H, Zhang, S, Chen, F & Trinkhaus, E 2010, 'An early modern human from Tianyuan Cave, Zhoukoudian, China', *Proceedings of the National Academy of Sciences USA*, vol. 104, pp. 6573–6578.

Shen, C, Zhang, X & Gao, X 2016, 'Zhoukoudian in transition: research history, lithic technologies, and transformation of Chinese Palaeolithic archaeology', *Quaternary International*, vol. 400, pp. 4–13.

Simanjuntak, T, Sémah, F & Gaillard, C 2010, 'The Palaeolithic in Indonesia: nature and chronology', *Quaternary International*, vol. 223, pp. 418–421.

Smith, GE 1924, *The evolution of man*, Oxford University Press, Oxford.

Smith, GE 1929, 'The Peking Man: a new chapter in human history', *Illustrated London News* [London, England] 19 October, p. 672.

Smith, GE 1930, 'A new basis for the study of human evolution', *Illustrated London News*, [London, England] 8 February, p. 210.

Stiles, D 1978, 'Palaeolithic artefacts in Siwalik and post-Siwalik deposits of northern Pakistan', *Papers of the Kroeber Anthropological Society*, vol. 53–54, pp. 129–148.

Storm, P, Aziz, F, de Vos, J, Kosasih, D, Baskoro, S, Ngaliman & van den Hoek Ostende, LW 2005, 'Late Pleistocene *Homo sapiens* in a tropical rainforest fauna in East Java', *Journal of Human Evolution*, vol. 49, pp. 536–545.

Stringer, C 2001, 'Modern human origins – distinguishing the models', *African Archaeological Review*, vol. 18, pp. 67–75.

Stringer, CB 2016, 'The origin and evolution of *Homo sapiens*', *Philosophical Transactions of the Royal Society B*, vol. 371, no. 20150237, pp. 1–12.

Stringer, C & Andrews, P 1988, 'Genetic and fossil evidence for the origin of modern humans', *Science*, vol. 239, pp. 1263–1268.

Sutikna, T, Tochieri, MW, Morwood, MJ, Saptomo, W, Jatmiko, E, Due Awe, R, Wasisto, S, Westaway, KE, Aubert, M, Bo, L, Jian-xin, Z, Storey, M, Alloway, BV, Morley, MW, Meijer, HJM, van den Bergh, GD, Grün, R, Dosseto, A, Brumm, A, Jungers, WL & Roberts, RG 2016, 'Revised stratigraphy and chronology for *Homo floresiensis* at Liang Bua in Indonesia', *Nature*, vol. 532, pp. 366–369.

Tattersall, I 2012, 'Paleoanthropology and evolutionary theory', *History and Philosophy of Life Sciences*, vol. 34, pp. 259–282.

Terra, H de 1943, 'Pleistocene geology and early man in Java', *Transactions of the American Philosophical Society*, vol. 32, pp. 437–464.

Terra, H de & Paterson, T 1939, *Studies on the Ice Age in India and associated human cultures*, Carnegie Institute Publications 493, Washington DC.

Thorne, AG & Wolpoff, MH 1992, 'The multiregional evolution of humans', *Scientific American*, vol. 266, no. 4, pp. 76–83.

Toro Moyano, ID, Cauche, D, Celiberti, V, Grégoire, S, Lebegue, F, Hélène Moncel, M & Lumley, H de 2011, 'The archaic stone tool industry from Barranco León and Fuente Nueva 3, (Orce, Spain): Evidence of the earliest hominin presence in southern Europe', *Quaternary International*, vol. 243, pp. 80–91.

Vishnyatsky, LB 1999, 'The Paleolithic of Central Asia', *Journal of World Prehistory*, vol. 13, no. 1, pp. 69–122.

Wang, S 2005, *Perspectives of Hominid behaviour and settlement patterns: study of the Lower Palaeolithic sites in the Luonan Basin, China*, British Archaeological Reports International Series #1406, Archaeopress, Oxford.

Warren, SH 1926, 'The classification of the Lower Palaeolithic with especial reference to Essex', *The South-Eastern Naturalist*, pp. 38–51.

Webster, D 2004, *The Burma Road*, HarperCollins, New York.

Weidenreich, F 1940, 'Some problems dealing with ancient man', *American Anthropologist*, vol. 42, no. 3, pp. 375–383.

Weidenreich, F 1942, 'Early man in Indonesia', *Journal of Asian Studies*, vol. 2, no. 1, pp. 58–65.

Weidenreich, F 1946, *Apes, giants and man*, University of Chicago Press, Chicago, IL.

Weidenreich, F 1947, 'Facts and speculations concerning the origin of *Homo sapiens*', *American Anthropologist*, New Series, vol. 49, no. 2, pp. 187–203.

Weiner, S, Qinqi, W, Goldberg, P, Liu, J & Bar-Yosef, O 1998, 'Evidence for the use of fire at Zhoukoudian, China', *Science*, vol. 281, pp. 251–253.

Westaway, KE, Louys, J, Awe, RD, Morwood, MJ, Price, GJ, Zhao, JX, Aubert, M, Joannes-Boyau, R, Smith, TM, Skinner, MM, Compton, T, Bailey, RM, van den Bergh, GD, de Vos, J, Pike, AWG, Stringer, C, Saptomo, EW, Rizal, Y, Zaim, J, Santoso, WD, Trihascaryo, A, Kinsley, L & Sulistyanto, B 2017, 'An early modern human presence in Sumatra 73,000–63,000 years ago', *Nature*, vol. 548, pp. 322–325.

Wolpoff, M & Caspari, R 1997, *Race and human evolution: a fatal attraction*, Simon and Schuster, New York.

Woo, J-K 1966, 'The skull of Lantian Man', *Current Anthropology*, vol. 7, no. 1, pp. 83–86.

Woodward, AS 1948, *The earliest Englishman*, Watts and Co, London.

Wu, X & Athreya, S 2013, 'A description of the geological context, discrete traits, and linear morphometrics of the Middle Pleistocene hominin from Dali, Shaanxi Province, China', *American Journal of Physical Anthropology*, vol. 150, pp. 141–157.

Yang, SX, Huang, WW & Hou, YM 2014, 'Is the Dingcun lithic assembly a "chopper-chopping tool industry", or "Late Acheulian"?' *Quaternary International*, vol. 321, pp. 3–11.

Yen, H-P 2014, 'Evolutionary Asiacentrism, Peking Man, and the origins of Sinocentric Ethno-centrism', *Journal of the History of Biology*, vol. 47, pp. 585–625.

Zaidner, Y 2003, 'The use of raw material at the Lower Palaeolithic site of Bizat Ruhama, Israel', in M Burdukiewicz & A Ronen (eds), *Lower Palaeolithic small tools in Europe and the Levant*, British Archaeological Reports, International Series #1115, Oxford, pp. 121–132.

11

INTERPRETATIVE SHIFTS IN UNDERSTANDING THE PREHISTORIC SETTLEMENT OF THE INDIAN SUBCONTINENT

Comparing Western and Indian historical perspectives

Parth R. Chauhan

Introduction

Its geographic context and ecological diversity make the Indian Subcontinent an ideal and promising region for palaeoanthropological research in Asia. In fact, the location of the region in the centre of the Old World has encouraged many attempts (both empirical and theoretical) to establish various cultural, biogeographic and faunal links between regions to the east and west of the Subcontinent (e.g. Mishra et al. 2010; Misra 2001a; Sankalia 1974). The case for the longest prehistoric dispersal to India has also been made between southern Africa and India, including onwards to Australasia (the southern route hypothesis as discussed below) (e.g. Dennell & Petraglia 2012; Dennell & Porr 2014; Petraglia et al. 2010). The idea of colonisation of the Indian Subcontinent continues to permeate even younger time periods and cultures, such as the Harappan/Indus Valley civilisation. One of the related main debates (i.e. the historical Aryan debate), as with the Palaeolithic evidence, continues to revolve around the geographic source and ethnicity of these populations, or whether they represent external colonisers or indigenous populations (e.g. Dhavalikar 2007). The prehistory of the region has been known and regularly highlighted since the nineteenth century (Misra 2001a) and predominantly includes stone tool assemblages from various time periods ranging from the Lower Palaeolithic to the Neolithic. In the absence of fossil evidence, palaeoanthropologists have had to rely primarily on the stone assemblages and the growing evidence of genetic data from modern indigenous and migrating populations (e.g. Athreya 2017; Endicott 2007; Majumder 1998).

This paper provides a broad historical overview how different types of evidence have been utilised by both Western and South Asian researchers to infer the presence of different hominin species and dispersals into the Indian Subcontinent. Individual lithic technologies are not discussed in detail as that is outside the scope of this paper, but are rather utilised to illustrate attempts to identify colonisation events and processes of local development. Much of the research in the region has been influenced directly by trending research topics at the global level over the decades. Historical perspectives (e.g. Dennell 2000–2001) show a major increase in foreign involvement in Indian prehistory following Independence, as both independent and collaborative projects. For example, the last two decades have witnessed a surge of research at various sites across Eurasia focusing on modern human dispersals and alleged interactions with pre-existing archaic hominin populations, the latter driven by new DNA studies demonstrating extensive gene flow across continents as well population movements (see Dennell & Petraglia 2012; Dennell & Porr 2014; Groucutt et al. 2015a).

At the broadest level, our perceptions of prehistoric colonisation have altered significantly since the British Colonial period, where previously simplified interpretations have made way for complex population interactions as well as technological innovations and replacements. Although all techno-chronological periods have been addressed in the past, the dominant debate currently centres around the post-Acheulean prehistoric evidence, particularly in relation to the appearance of our species in the Subcontinent and the technologies they most likely brought with them (see Chauhan 2016). One of the most profound observations and current issues is the intellectual and academic bias faced by Asian researchers (whether based abroad or in Asia) in global palaeoanthropology and how certain projects or publications are expected to conform to Western theories, concepts and interpretations, particularly about dispersals of *Homo sapiens* from Africa (see Athreya 2019 for a personal account). In that respect, there have been growing Indian movements to emerge from long-established Western shadows of intellectual thought and interpretations, which is gradually leading to more objective and balanced perspectives on the regional palaeoanthropological records.

Lower Palaeolithic colonisations

Prior to the discovery of stone tools, the story of human evolution in India started in the 1830s with the chance discovery of primate fossils in the Siwalik Hills of northern India (see Kennedy 2000 for a detailed historical account). Additional fossil specimens were also later recovered from the Pakistan and Nepal Siwaliks and some were respectively classified as *Ramapithecus* and *Sivapithecus* (among others) and thought to have migrated from Europe and Africa prior to 7 Ma. In the 1930s, some of the fossil specimens were given *hominid* status by Lewis (1937), a view met with criticism and doubt until the mid-1960s when it was brought back into the palaeoanthropological limelight by E. L. Simons and D. Pilbeam as the (then-known) earliest hominid. However, following comparisons of new – and more complete – fossil specimens recovered in the 1970s and demonstration of a *late* ape–hominin divergence by molecular biologists, the hominid status of select Siwalik species was revised (again led by D. Pilbeam) to an ape species ancestral to modern-day orangutans. Post-cranial specimens recovered in the 1970s also clearly demonstrated that *Sivapithecus* was not bipedal. Since then, however, there appears to have been a reluctance or hesitation from select South Asian scholars and institutions to fully accept the Western rejection of its hominin status. This observation is informally based on obscure Indian literature and regional museum exhibits that show *Sivapithecus* as being bipedal. This revision may need to be updated in regional textbooks and other academic sources as well. The Siwalik Hills reigned as the exclusive geographic domain of these controversial ape species since the 1830s, until recently recovered finds were reported from Gujarat in western India, thus extending its home range (Bhandari et al. 2018). The Siwalik Hills fossil vertebrate evidence combined with the historical importance of the tropics for human evolution had other important roles to play in world prehistory in the nineteenth century. Some of the earliest and most famous pioneering work was done by Hugh Falconer before 1855, after which he returned to England where he similarly started investigating the River Thames for its gravels and mammalian fossil fauna (see Paddayya 2015). Likewise, he visited numerous cave sites across Europe and in this flurry of enthusiastic activity, including short academic communications and intellectual interactions, collectively and indirectly accelerated the establishment of prehistoric research in Europe.

The first historical discovery of (Lower) Palaeolithic archaeological evidence in India was made in the late nineteenth century and is credited to Robert Bruce Foote, who first recognised handaxes at Pallavaram, Tamil Nadu (Sankalia 1974). That phase was a major turning point for global prehistoric studies as it marked several historical milestones including the discovery of the first Neanderthal fossils in the early nineteenth century (Drell 2000), the first *H. erectus* fossils in the late nineteenth century (Anton 2003) and the first formal recognition of the Palaeolithic period through the discovery of the Acheulean in the late eighteenth century (Frere 1800) – incidentally all from Europe and Asia and not Africa. Indeed, the discovery of the handaxes in France stimulated numerous discoveries in various parts of the Old World, including the first known Indian handaxes in 1863. Because the Oldowan was not formally discovered and reported until the early twentieth century in Africa (i.e. Leakey 1936), Acheulean bifaces were considered to be the oldest prehistoric evidence in all these respective regions. The then academic trend and emphasis in a search for the roots of humanity lay prominently in Asia until the now famous discoveries made in Africa from the beginning of the twentieth century and onwards. Indeed, these discoveries of Oldowan sites throughout the twentieth century in Africa (Schick & Toth 2006) as well as the early recognition of the Clactonian in England (see White 2000), possibly encouraged both Western and Indian researchers to identify similar pre- or non-Acheulean entities in India, albeit at different times. For instance, a pre-Acheulean technology based on pebbles and cobbles was first proposed for the Indian subcontinent in the form of the Soanian industry in what is now northern Pakistan (de Terra & Paterson 1939). This suggested a different cultural group had colonised that part of the Subcontinent and comparable technologies at select sites in the Indian Siwalik zone were labelled as *Gulerian* as a regional culture separate from the Acheulean (e.g. Lal 1963). The initial impetus for a Yale–Cambridge team to work in the Soan region was provided by the intellectual climate of Palaeolithic archaeology in Britain at the time (see Dennell 1990). Later work by the British Archaeological Mission to Pakistan (BAMP) in the 1980s resulted in a major revision of de Terra and Paterson's interpretations of the Soanian evidence (see Rendell & Dennell 1985; Rendell, Dennell & Halim 1989). Subsequently, multiple lines of evidence including a comparison of Soanian and Acheulean technology (Gaillard 1995), landscape geoarchaeology (Chauhan 2008), surveys of dated geological features (Soni & Soni 2005) and a comparative morphometric analysis (Lycett 2007) clearly revealed that the majority of Soanian assemblages, if not all, represent post-Acheulean technologies (Gaillard & Mishra 2001).

Subsequent claims for a pre-Acheulean occupation have come from the Siwalik Hills in the northern zones of Pakistan and India and from the Narmada Valley of central India. Unfortunately, all these claims have various scientific problems because of a lack of excavated and dated material, dubious contexts or insufficient evidence (Chauhan 2009). Two researchers (A. P. Khatri and J. Armand) working separately in the Narmada Valley even reported two indigenous cultural entities based on their respective excavations: the Mahadevian at Mahadeo Piparia and the Durkadian at Durkadi. Khatri (1962; 1966) equated the former to the Oldowan and interpreted it as a technological predecessor to the Indian

Acheulean. Later investigations (Sen & Ghosh 1963; Supekar 1968) refuted Khatri's claim of a Mode 1 to Mode 2 transition here. A similar claim to that of Khatri's was made more systematically through controlled excavations by Armand (1983). At both sites, a large amount of non-biface artefacts were recovered in stratified contexts and comprised of cores, choppers, flakes, 'protobifaces', and other formal tool types. While Mahadeo-Piparia was estimated to be early Middle Pleistocene in age, Durkadi was interpreted to be about 1 Ma in relative age; this view was mostly based on geo-stratigraphic and typological grounds and later disproved (Chauhan, Sathe & Shaik 2013). At one of the Bhimbetka rockshelters, Wakanker (1973) proposed that the Acheulean horizon was underlain by a 'pebble-tool' horizon, both being separated by a sterile layer, which may or may not reflect technological progression between the two traditions. Such sterile layers in between different technological entities have been reported from almost all known multi-cultural sequences (see Chauhan 2009) and may simply represent complicated geological histories and/or site abandonment, thus making it notoriously difficult to clearly recognise population continuity versus replacement. Another explanation may be that populations did not change over time, but their associated technologies did, reflecting changing adaptations due to a number of possible factors. Later research at Bhimbetka by Misra (1985) failed to support such claims for a pre-Acheulean industry in this area. The oldest palaeoanthropological evidence in the subcontinent was recently reported from the Siwalik region of Masol near Chandigarh in northern India. This controversial evidence includes cut-marked fossils and 'simple' choppers, both interpreted to be about 2.6 Ma (Malassé 2016). However, the archaeological integrity of the cut-marks and the contextual integrity of the lithics are yet to be convincingly demonstrated. In fact, the scientific significance of this discovery has been undermined by internal academic bias: the (controversial) results of this largely French-dominated project were all published in a French journal. Although the evidence from Riwat and Pabbi Hills remains the best studied (see Chauhan 2010a), unequivocal pre-Acheulean evidence in South Asia has yet to be excavated from primary fine-grained contexts and well-dated, such as key examples in other parts of the Old World. In any case, all these investigations and reports suggested a pre-Acheulean technological/cultural presence in the Subcontinent, possible attributed to *H. erectus* or its predecessor such as *H. habilis* or *H. ergaster*, depending on the age of the concerned site(s). As mentioned earlier, this is a historical consequence of the intellectual dependency on African and/or European evidences.

The main tool-types and features used to historically recognise a pre-Acheulean hominin occupation by both Indian and Western researchers has included the following: (i) an Oldowan-like tool-kit similar to the African evidence; (ii) absence of large flake and bifacial elements; and (iii) stratification of the evidence *below* Acheulean level(s). In the later decades, this evidence was further supplemented (by both Western and South Asian researchers) by (iv) geochronological results from contexts older than the regional Acheulean (e.g. Rendell, Hailwood & Dennell 1987); and (v) non-lithic evidence such as cut-marked bones. Attempts to demonstrate a transition between the Oldowan-like and Acheulean technologies in the region invoked the recognition of *proto-bifaces* in the studied assemblages. Today, this term and concept has been abandoned in Indian Palaeolithic archaeology.

Terms that were historically utilised to recognise the Acheulean as a distinct technology for the first time in the Subcontinent include 'chipped stone implements', 'well-shaped oval implements', 'pointed weapons', 'spear heads', 'axes' and 'hatches', as compared with the then well-known distinctly shaped stones from Europe (Foote 1866, p. 9) and handaxes, cleavers and bifaces, though not classified as such at the time, were physically described in detail. Due to the sheer abundance of the lithic evidence in southern India and its historical precedence, Acheulean assemblages were also classed as 'Madrasian' and the 'Madras Handaxe Tradition' for almost a century by some researchers. From the typological similarities with the few known European assemblages, it was surmised that both sets of evidence must have been made by the same 'people' and during shared climatic conditions. In the early twentieth century, the terms 'coup de poing' (for handaxe) and Acheulean were established by the Western researchers in the Soan Valley of modern-day Pakistan (e.g. de Terra, Teilhard de Chardin & Paterson 1936; de Terra 1939) though the term 'Chelles-Acheul culture' was also being utilised decades later (e.g. Khatri 1966). Another way African and European connections and comparisons were being made in the 1930s was by recognising 'Victoria West', 'Vaal' and 'Micoquian' typological elements in southern India (e.g. Cammiade & Burkitt 1930; Krishnaswami 1938). Specialised and modern typological terms were well-established in the discipline and literature from the mid-1900s onwards: handaxe, cleaver, pick, biface, and so forth. In recent decades, the term 'Large Flake Acheulean' was introduced abroad and within India to distinguish the larger Lower Palaeolithic biface assemblages from the smaller Middle Palaeolithic biface assemblages. It is notable that the first proper Palaeolithic excavations in the Subcontinent were undertaken by Indian archaeologists at Kuliana in Mayurbhanj (Bose & Sen 1948), although previous work may have included 'section-scrapings'. This paved the way for subsequent contextual and spatial investigations in other regions of India, while the prehistory of Nepal was not properly studied until the 1980s, indeed by a Westerner (e.g. Corvinus 1996). In addition to the growing number of Indian prehistorians following India's Independence, Western researchers continued to carry out investigations at prehistoric sites including Acheulean occurrences through excavations and surface studies from the 1950s to 1980s. It is notable that many of these were done independently (e.g. F. Zeuner in Gujarat, J. Armand at Durkadi, J. Jacobson in the Raisen District of Madhya Pradesh, G. Corvinus at Chirki-on-Pravara in Maharashtra and F. R. and B. Allchin at multiple locations) rather than through collaborations with Indians; the latter rule was established by the Archaeological Survey of India only in recent decades. The oldest unequivocal evidence in South Asia is currently represented by the Acheulean evidence, which is now known to extend from 1.5 Ma in the very region where the first Indian Acheulean was discovered (Pappu et al. 2011) and end at about 120 Ka (Haslam et al. 2011) or 100 Ka (Blinkhorn et al. 2013). Historically, this technology has been predominantly associated with *H. erectus* as hominin fossil evidence increased at Acheulean sites across the Old World from the 1950s onwards. It is interesting that this association continued throughout all phases of Acheulean studies, despite the later recognition and application of such divisions as Early, Middle and Late Acheulean technologies. In other words, different species were generally not considered by researchers to be associated with different Acheulean phases in the Subcontinent, except for Misra (2001b, p. 226):

> The technological shift from the Early to Late Acheulian seems more marked than that from the Late Acheulian to the Middle Palaeolithic. This shift may well have coincided with the biological transition from *Homo erectus* to archaic *Homo sapiens*.

However, based on growing evidence outside India (e.g. Goren-Inbar & Saragusti 1996; Mendez-Quintas et al. 2018), it is highly possible that there were at least two Acheulean dispersals into the region, thus possibly representing different species at different times (*H. erectus* with Early Acheulean and other archaic species such as *H. heidelbergensis* with the Late Acheulean). The timing of technological change or transition from Early to Late Acheulean appears to have an intermediate phase, possibly reflecting mixing of local populations and technologies with incoming ones. The undiagnostic, poorly dated and sparse hominin fossil evidence (see Athreya 2007) does not enable any clear links with specific Acheulean colonisation events, despite a reported fossil-handaxe association (Salahuddin 1986–1987; also see Patnaik et al. 2009). Despite this interpretative limitation of the Hathnora cranium, Sonakia and de Lumley (2006) considered the possibility of regional evolution of *H. sapiens* in India from the preceding *H. erectus* populations. Interestingly, another French–Indian collaboration has suggested the same for a cranium recovered from the Orsang Valley of Gujarat, despite inconsistent ages between 50 Ka to 5 Ka from two different dating methods on the sediments and on the specimen respectively (Chamyal et al. 2011). In comparison to research on the younger time periods, particularly in pursuit of *Homo sapiens* dispersals and evolution, the Lower Palaeolithic evidence in South Asia requires increased attention to pinpoint the true presence/absence of the Oldowan and to better understand the factors of change for the local developments of the Acheulean after initial arrival and to identify subsequent dispersal(s), if any.

The Indian Middle Palaeolithic: indigenous, introduced or both?

The Indian Middle Palaeolithic was first classified in the early 1900s as Series II (Cammiade & Burkitt 1930) and formally labelled in the 1950s by H. D. Sankalia (*Nevasian*) and numerous sites have been reported since then (Kennedy 2000; Pal 2002). Sankalia (1974) first compared the Indian evidence with the African Middle Stone Age based on the presence of distinct prepared core technologies (and possibly influenced by his education in England); however, the tripartite 'Palaeolithic' system eventually prevailed in India from the 1970s onwards.

Historically, it has been considered to be both indigenous and introduced, one of the main reasons being that it spatially, chronologically and technologically overlaps with the terminal Acheulean. In the past, it has been associated by various researchers with both indigenous archaics as well as incoming moderns, and only recently has it come to prominence in relation to the evolution and (an earlier) dispersal of prehistoric modern human populations across the Old World. In addition to prepared cores and Levallois elements, the decreased size of bifaces and increase in flake tools were also gradually utilised to recognise and define the Middle Palaeolithic, followed by blades and projectile points. In the last two decades, this technology has been increasingly considered (by one particular research group) to be associated with the initial arrival of *H. sapiens* soon after 100 Ka (e.g. Blinkhorn & Petraglia 2014; 2017; Haslam et al. 2010a; 2010b; Petraglia 2007; Petraglia et al. 2007), thus challenging the traditional hypothesis (see Mellars et al. 2013) of an initial arrival with microlithic technology. For example, Blinkhorn, Achyuthan and Ajithprasad (2015) identified Nubian technological elements in the Middle Palaeolithic of the Thar Desert and associate it with possible modern human dispersals from Africa.

This ongoing debate is confounded by the lack of hominin fossils and the lack of adequate genetic data from living populations. Complicating matters further is the recent chronological extension of the Indian Middle Palaeolithic to 385 Ka (Akhilesh et al. 2018), possibly a general trend that seems to have occurred at multiple locations across the Old World between 400 and 300 Ka instead of originating in Africa as previously thought. This early age completely changes the historical narrative to date and makes it difficult to continue associating this technology exclusively with *H. sapiens*, although the youngest evidence may be attributed as such, as it extends to 38 Ka (Petraglia et al. 2012). Therefore, in terms of colonisation events, the older Middle Palaeolithic possibly represents the innovation of indigenous archaics while evidence younger than 100 Ka or 77 Ka may have been brought by the first modern human populations to disperse into the region. At the moment, a genetic signature for such an event is lacking in modern Indian populations (see Chauhan, Ozarkar & Kulkarni 2015), possibly suggesting that either a majority of the Middle Palaeolithic evidence belongs to archaics or that the earliest arriving moderns were too low in number for biological/genetic continuity. Due to the lack of absolute dates and detailed comparative lithic analyses, technological change within the entire Middle Palaeolithic (385 Ka to 38 Ka) across the Subcontinent remains poorly understood. Nonetheless, it is generally agreed upon that the Lower-Middle Palaeolithic transitional evidence comprises of a mixture of large and small bifaces with an increase in flake tools such as scrapers; while the more advanced Middle Palaeolithic is devoid of bifaces and shows a marked increase in classic Levallois elements, blades and other flake tools.

It is possible that just as with the Late Acheulean, the Indian Middle Palaeolithic represents a mixture of similar technologies adapted by different species at different times. The complexity of population movements and technological replacements at a pan-Indian level is reflected in the uneven nature of the current evidence: early Middle Palaeolithic seems to be appearing at 385 Ka in southern India (Akhilesh et al. 2018) while a Late (Large Flake) Acheulean continues to at least 120–100 Ka across northern India and is presumably associated with archaic *Homo* (Haslam et al. 2011; Blinkhorn et al. 2013). In other words, it appears to take over 200 kyrs for the Large Flake Acheulean to disappear completely across the Subcontinent. However, the inconsistency and challenge in interpreting some sites as either Late Acheulean or (early) Middle Palaeolithic by different researchers over time need to be appreciated, as pointed out by Akhilesh et al. (2018) for the Patpara evidence from Son valley. Additionally, the same proponents that link the Indian Middle Palaeolithic with dispersing moderns (e.g. Blinkhorn et al. 2013; Haslam et al. 2010b; Petraglia et al. 2007) have published contradicting papers outlining a gradual and local transition from the Indian Late Acheulean to the early Middle Palaeolithic (e.g. James & Petraglia 2009; Petraglia et al. 2003; Shipton et al. 2013).

Only absolute dates from multiple sites across the Subcontinent can validate any of these hypotheses, but the issue raises the tantalising possibility of more than one species overlapping during this Acheulean transition. In addition to *H. erectus* being associated with the Acheulean record, recent typo-technological studies of Mousterian assemblages in Pakistan (Biagi & Starnini 2014) have again highlighted the possible presence of Neanderthals in the Subcontinent (Ghosh 1974; Misra 2001b). Similar examples of unexpected techno-biological colonisation and decolonisation have been forthcoming from within Africa and Europe. For example, it was generally presumed that most African Middle Stone Age evidence younger than 300–200 Ka probably belonged to *H. sapiens*; however, the dating of *H. naledi* to ~250 Ka suggests a more complex occupational history (Dirks et al. 2017). In the same manner, it was traditionally assumed that Europe was predominantly occupied by Neanderthals after about 350 Ka but a report of a rich Large Flake Acheulean assemblage from Spain suggests otherwise (Mendez-Quintas et al. 2018). Growing palaeoanthropological evidence suggests parallel evolution of the anatomically modern form across the Old World: the possible pan-

African appearance of *Homo sapiens* (Scerri et al. 2018), Neanderthals in Europe and West Asia, some Chinese fossils such as the Dali specimen (Athreya & Wu 2017) and so forth. Indeed, patterns of both biological and technological evolution after ~400 Ka appear to be synchronised at a global level, a fact rendering the South Asian record all the more relevant. The only exception is eastern Asia, where Levallois technologies are marginal (see Schick 1994), a pattern that may eventually change following more focused surveys.

The enigmatic 'Upper Palaeolithic' and early Mesolithic phases

The Indian Upper Palaeolithic and Mesolithic phases were formally recognised as early as the 1880s, primarily based on broad similarities with the then-known European record (e.g. Brown 1889; Cammiade & Burkitt 1930; see Kennedy 2000 for detailed reviews). From his excavations at Billa Surgum caves, R. B. Foote compared the recovered archaeological material with the Magdalenian of Europe (Murty 1979). It was also then thought that microliths originated in India and spread to other parts of the Old World (see Kennedy 2003) and were subsequently classified as Series IV in the technological sequence ordered by Cammiade and Burkitt (1930). These techno-typological similarities included the presence of blades, burins and bone tools at numerous sites, which were all collectively associated – without a doubt – with *H. sapiens* (e.g. Kennedy 2003; Misra 2001a; Sankalia 1974). In the same vein, rock art and other evidence for symbolic behaviour such as beads, microliths and the conspicuous exploitation of perishable materials (e.g. bone, ivory, wood, antler, ostrich eggshells) were interpreted fairly early (late 1880s) to be associated with modern humans, although it took several decades to establish a typological framework for the formal and standardised tool types including both non-geometric and geometric shapes. This notion was gradually supported by the growing fossil evidence for modern humans at several Mesolithic sites in India and Sri Lanka (Kennedy 1999). It is also notable that historically, the Indian Middle Palaeolithic was first compared with African evidence while the Upper Palaeolithic was first compared with European evidence. Prior to the 1950s, Upper Palaeolithic assemblages were not considered as prominent components of a formal phase in India as it was debated whether the Indian lithic record should be classified according to the African or European systems (Kennedy 2000). Since then, however, our understanding of the Upper Palaeolithic–Mesolithic transition has become complicated owing to the earliest microlithic occurrence being extended to 45 Ka (Mishra et al. 2013). Seshadri (1962) was one of the first scholars to consider an indigenous development of the Upper Palaeolithic from the preceding 'Levalloisian' (see Murty 1979). Sali (1989) was another scholar to recognise this complex transition at Patne where he further divided the Upper Palaeolithic into Early and Late phases. In most recent years, the South Asian Upper Palaeolithic has been linked with the African Later Stone Age as a possible source region (Mellars et al. 2013). Contrasting views suggest that Indian microliths were innovated as an adaptive response (Clarkson et al. 2018) as a part of globally parallel/convergent evolution (Groucutt et al. 2015b). This echoes the results of Lewis, Perera and Petraglia (2014) who compared two South African and Sri Lankan microlithic datasets and challenged Mellars et al. (2013) regarding typo-morphological similarity verses diversity. Other scholars have even attempted to deconstruct the archaeological integrity of some of the most important type-localities historically used to define the South Asian Upper Palaeolithic, such as the Kurnool caves and associated sites (Haslam et al. 2010c). These researchers are of the opinion that some previously described Upper

Palaeolithic artefacts (e.g. by R. B. Foote, M. L. K. Murty, and T. Reddy) may represent natural rock spalls that mimic artefacts. Based on coastal surveys in Saurashtra (Costa 2012) and a reassessment of the only-reported 'Upper Palaeolithic' evidence in Gujarat (Allchin 1973), Costa (2011) demonstrated that the site, Visadi, represents a Mesolithic occurrence and thus, there is no clear Upper Palaeolithic technological evidence in the entire state of Gujarat, the presumed main coastal peninsular entry point to India. At a wider scale, between approximately 95 Ka and 20 Ka, there is considerable stepwise techno-chronological and geographic overlap respectively, between terminal Middle Palaeolithic (including those with and without diminutive bifaces), Upper Palaeolithic and early Mesolithic technologies. Such an integrated and widespread overlap hints at complex indigenous or regional transitions of these technologies, although it is not impossible that they were also intermittently mixed with 'in-dispersing' counterparts and also possibly hominin species. To reconcile all these issues including technological overlap and regional differences between the Indian evidence from its African and European counterparts, James and Petraglia (2005) proposed the term 'Late Palaeolithic', actually first introduced by Sali (1985) around 1960. However, this classificatory term overlooks sites/assemblages (largely undated) that are *exclusively* comprised of blade-based tools larger than three centimetres (i.e. marked absence of Middle Palaeolithic and microlithic elements), and thus may have been prematurely introduced and not comprehensively applicable at the pan-Indian level. In summary, the existence of the Upper Palaeolithic in the Subcontinent continues to be challenged at various levels and through different types of observations. While the primary problem has been identifying and dating *exclusive* Upper Palaeolithic sites across the region, it provisionally appears that the phase was both geographically and chronologically restricted. One factor or explanation for the decreased or marginal presence of this technology is increased aridity across the Subcontinent (Misra 2001b). Indian researchers directly attempted to establish the antiquity of Indian rock art within the Upper Palaeolithic by linking green paintings with a green nodule excavated at Bhimbetka (Wakanker 1983). Although rock art is abundant across the Subcontinent, its temporal roots remain unclear and a review by James and Petraglia (2005) highlights the relative scarcity of symbolic behaviour in India compared to Europe and Africa. One of the first evolutionary and behavioural links made between the Indian Upper Palaeolithic and modern-day hunter-gatherer populations was through an excavated prehistoric shrine at Baghor in north-central India (Kenoyer et al. 1983). Since then, numerous genetic studies on select tribal groups have supported this terminal Palaeolithic–early Mesolithic legacy, since at least the last 60–50 kyrs. When viewed as a whole, the South Asian Upper Palaeolithic requires greater focused research on its transition from the late Middle Palaeolithic, its typo-technological exclusivity, chronological range, patterns of regional manifestations and subsequent transition to the Mesolithic. Along with the Mesolithic, this phase also needs to be archaeologically investigated to pinpoint the beginnings of symbolic behaviour and behavioural modernity in the Subcontinent. For the Mesolithic proper, we need to understand such information as factors for the transition from non-geometric to geometric microliths and the differential nature of microlithic dispersals across the Subcontinent.

Discussion and conclusions

The above historical perspective demonstrates how our perceptions of hominin colonisation have been intermittently altered for over a century following new discoveries and comparisons with the global evidence (Table 11.1). The intellectual concepts of *multiple technological dispersals* and *interbreeding between species* were rarely addressed or considered in the early stages of prehistoric research in the Subcontinent. Until the mid-1900s, most evolutionary scenarios included a simple dichotomy of early *Homo* populations subsequently replaced (via dispersals or regional evolution) by *H. sapiens* (generally through regional evolution). This notion has its roots in the single-species hypothesis prevalent for Europe and Africa at the time. Emphasis and criteria for the identification of hominin dispersals have changed over the decades in the Indian Subcontinent. In the earliest phase of prehistoric research, researchers (both Western and Indian) were primarily influenced by the discoveries made in Europe (e.g. Clactonian, Upper Palaeolithic). Broad interpretations made during the second phase of prehistoric research involved more direct connections with Africa (e.g. Oldowan, Acheulean) although cases for an indigenous development of the Oldowan have also been made. While both these phases recognised indigenous transitions at various levels, external cultural and geographic links were also invoked. Finally, the latest phase of research includes interpretative and theoretical scenarios involving both dispersals from Africa as well as indigenous evolutionary transitions within the Subcontinent.

Regarding the appearance of *Homo sapiens* and associated lithic transitions in the Subcontinent, the concerned criteria have evolved or increased over the decades. The earlier phases placed greater emphasis on the associating modern humans more with the Upper Palaeolithic and Mesolithic phases, historically based on European evidence. In recent decades, this link started to include new criteria such as the presence of symbolic behaviour and detailed analytical comparisons of lithic attributes with the African evidence. One major outcome of foreign involvement in the last two decades is the partial deconstruction of past conceptual frameworks regarding indigenous technological innovations (i.e. the Upper Palaeolithic was reclassified as the Late Palaeolithic, and the Middle Palaeolithic became associated with incoming modern humans from Africa). This interpretation has been further enhanced by recognising the respective diversity in global microlithic assemblages suggesting independent convergent evolution, while the Middle Palaeolithic is thought to be introduced by dispersing African *Homo sapiens*. Regardless of these changes, it is evident that respective research trends, personal interests and methodological approaches between South Asian and Western palaeoanthropologists both diverged and converged from the beginning. This is partly reflected in the terms introduced to recognise regional prehistoric cultures by both Western and South Asian researchers: Soanian, Gulerian, Mahadevian, Durkadian, Madrasian and Nevasian.

One aspect that is not clear, however, is whether joint publications resulting from international collaborations between South Asian and Western scholars have all been *intellectually* balanced. It is possible that in some projects – if not all – Western concepts, perspectives and interpretations have dominated in the final interpretations of the archaeological data (i.e. maintaining intellectual control of a project due to the supplied funding, scientific methods and access to or knowledge of intellectual information not easily available in the Subcontinent), even though the data were generated collaboratively by both sides. If this is the case, some South Asian palaeoanthropologists may have been intellectually (and methodologically) marginalised at times over the decades since Independence. For instance, Joseph (2018) highlighted the change of opinion of R. Korisettar (in Haslam et al. 2017, in an Indian volume edited by Korisettar) as compared to an older paper in *Science* (Petraglia et al. 2007) regarding the link between *Homo sapiens* and the Middle Palaeolithic evidence at

TABLE 11.1 Historical trends in evidence types and associated interpretations in relation to recognising prehistoric colonisation events in the Indian Subcontinent

Technology	Historical views	Current status
Possible Oldowan or pre-Acheulean	• Reported at various sites since the 1960s and respectively dated to 2.6 Ma to 0.9 Ma. • All viewed as dispersal into region, though indigenous cultural/industrial names given for some assemblages (i.e. Soanian; Gulerian; Mahadevian; Durkadian). • Evidence: lithics, cut-marked fossil bones. • Candidate species: *H. erectus, H. habilis,* early *Homo.*	• Pakistan Siwalik evidence best studied (2.2–0.9 Ma) but remains controversial. • Cut-marked fossil bones (controversial) from Masol, India are oldest at 2.6 Ma. • No unequivocal Oldowan presence confirmed, through well-dated excavations in fine-grained primary contexts. • Candidate species: Open.
Early Acheulean	• Reported at various sites since the 1860s. • Cultural classification included Abbevillian, Chellian, Chelles-Acheul, coup-de-poing, Madrasian, Madras Handaxe Tradition, Acheulian, Acheulean. • Viewed as a dispersal into the region. • Candidate species: *H. erectus.*	• Oldest evidence securely dated to 1.5 Ma. • Still viewed as a dispersal into the region. • Candidate species: *H. erectus?*
Middle and Late Acheulean	• Broadly viewed as part of initial Acheulean dispersal into the region. • Viewed separately from Early Acheulean only after mid-1900s. • Viewed as indigenous development from the preceding Early Acheulean. • Candidate species: Traditionally *H. erectus.* The Hathnora cranium was observed to be stratigraphically associated with Late Acheulean handaxes and has been variably interpreted to be, or compared with advanced *H. erectus, H. heidelbergensis, H. neanderthalensis,* archaic *H. sapiens* and *H. sapiens.* However, its taxonomy (now *Homo* sp.) and age remain uncertain.	• Youngest evidence dated to 120 Ka and overlaps with earliest Middle Palaeolithic. • Still viewed as having developed from preceding Early Acheulean. • However, some assemblages may represent additional Acheulean dispersal(s) into the region. • Hence mixture of indigenous and incoming technologies. • Candidate species: Multiple (e.g. *H. erectus, H. heidelbergensis*).
Middle Palaeolithic	• Formally recognised since the 1950s (Nevasian). • Traditionally interpreted as having developed indigenously. • Challenge of distinguishing from terminal Acheulean noted by various researchers. • Earlier age range unclear and overlapping with both terminal Acheulean and Upper Palaeolithic assemblages. • Candidate species: Multiple, including *H. neanderthalensis* (for the Mousterian in Pakistan) and *H. sapiens.*	• New age range for this technology is 385 Ka–38 Ka. • Entire record may be a mixture of both indigenous and dispersed technologies over time. • Oldest evidence suggests indigenous development from Late Acheulean at broadly the same time (400–300 Ka) as some other Old World regions. • Temporally and spatially overlapping with terminal Acheulean, Upper Palaeolithic or microlithic technologies. • Debate continues over whether the younger evidence (~90–77 Ka) represents the earliest *H. sapiens* dispersal into the region. • Candidate species: Initially indigenous archaic *Homo* followed by *H. sapiens?*

Technology	Historical views	Current status
Upper Palaeolithic	• First recognised formally in the 1880s and early 1900s based on broad similarities with European evidence (i.e. blades, burins, bone tools). • Thought to represent dispersals into the region. • Candidate species: *H. sapiens*.	• Status as an exclusive entity/phase questioned, due to lack of absolute dates for exclusive sites and chronological overlap with other technologies. • Chronologically and geographically overlaps with preceding Middle Palaeolithic and succeeding microlithic technologies. • Indigenous development has been proposed from select sites (i.e. Patne) but evidence is limited. • Candidate species: *H. sapiens*.
Microlithic or Mesolithic	• First recognised formally in the 1880s based on broad similarities with European evidence. • Thought to represent the technology of the first *H. sapiens*. • Stratigraphic results from Patne suggests indigenous evolution; the sequence remains undated. • Candidate species: *H. sapiens*.	• Age ranges from 45 Ka up to Colonial period. • Currently debated whether it's introduced into the region through dispersals or innovated indigenously due to environmental changes. • May represent a second dispersal of H. sapiens and/or a mixture of both indigenous and dispersed technologies over time. • Candidate species: *H. sapiens*.

Jwalapuram. Another factor that can affect the intellectual reputation (and hence marginalisation?) of South Asian archaeologists and their data and interpretations at the international level (also see Athreya 2019 for bias against Asian researchers abroad) is the way they disseminate their own independent research results. With a few exceptions, most South Asian researchers continue to restrict their publications to national and regional journals and edited volumes, many of which are not easily accessible to Western researchers or have low impact factors. In addition, not all Indian journals or edited volumes have a reliable and objective review process (see Kennedy 2003) and often accept poorly written papers. Informal personal communication with some Indian colleagues regarding all of this has revealed a number of reasons for not publishing internationally: that they are incapable of publishing in international venues due to English language problems, or that their project, data and interpretations are not robust enough. Some others are of the opinion that publication in international journals is not required or they simply do not deem it necessary.

While all research should be ideally published in both international and national platforms, consistent imbalanced dissemination results in their respective students continuing the same biased 'tradition'. Similar opinions and issues exist regarding unsuccessful international grant applications, in addition to some Indian researchers opining that such agencies (and even international journals) appear to favour Western researchers and are biased against Indian ones. On the positive side in recent years, some promising Indian students have independently secured international grants for their research. This brief discussion has highlighted a number of issues that need to be dealt with in India: balanced international collaborations; control of intellectual property rights; proper publication at multiple levels; and the use/ misuse of intellectual data through high profile publications for the sake of academic publicity, promotions and additional grants – all part of the academic juggernaut. Historically, classification and interpretations from the global Palaeolithic evidence was intellectually controlled by France and Britain until the 1960s (Dennell 1990). Such 'intellectual colonialism' has been recently highlighted by Porr and Matthews (2017) who caution against such a path during our quest for the archaeology of becoming human. This sentiment of avoiding such research bias is further resonated by Athreya (2018) who supports balanced ethnic diversity in palaeoanthropological research (also see Athreya and Ackermann in this volume) contra to an example pointed out by Chauhan (2010b). Another growing challenge that persists in decolonising previous interpretations is addressing *prehistoric* cultural identity or being able to distinguish between *African*, non-African and indigenous lithic technologies and associated behaviours. When hominin groups and their technologies dispersed from Africa to India (or to any region for that matter), it is not apparent what change (if any) took place along the way and how many generations the dispersal required. For instance, perhaps the *youngest and most direct* source(s) of Palaeolithic–Mesolithic technologies dispersing into India were the Arabian Peninsula and/or the Levant instead of Africa directly. Ultimately, *all* technologies following the Early Acheulean are strong candidates for being both indigenous to and/or introduced into the Subcontinent (e.g. Late Acheulean, Middle Palaeolithic, Upper Palaeolithic and microlithic). It is also unclear whether the Subcontinent was utilised as a dispersal corridor for *any* of the populations responsible for these technologies, as the records in the east and southeast of the region do not match. Future multidisciplinary datasets (genetic, archaeological and palaeontological) combined with *balanced* collaborations between South Asian and international researchers will better reveal the nuanced patterns of human evolution in this part of the Old World.

Acknowledgements

I thank the editors for inviting me to contribute to this exciting volume (and for their patience), and my colleagues and students for the stimulating discussions over the years on the various topics addressed in this paper. I also thank the following reviewers for their positive comments and constructive suggestions which improved the original draft considerably: Sheela Athreya, Dilip K. Chakrabarti and K. Paddayya.

References

Akhilesh, K, Pappu, S, Rajapara, HM, Gunnell, Y, Shukla, A-D and Singhvi, AK 2018, 'Early Middle Palaeolithic culture in India around 385–172 ka reframes Out of Africa models', *Nature*, vol. 554, pp. 97–101.

Allchin, B 1973, 'Blade and burin industries of West Pakistan and Western India,' in N Hammond (ed.), *South Asian archaeology*, Duckworth, London, pp. 39–50.

Antón, SC 2003, 'Natural history of *Homo erectus*', *Yearbook of Physical Anthropology*, vol. 46, pp. 126–170.

Armand, J 1983, *Archaeological excavations in the Durkadi Nala: an early Palaeolithic pebble-tool workshop in central India*, Munshiram Manoharlal Publishers, Delhi.

Athreya, S 2007, 'Was *Homo heidelbergensis* in South Asia? A test using the Narmada fossil from central India', in MD Petraglia & B Allchin (eds), *The evolution and history of human populations in South Asia*, Springer Press, New York, pp. 137–170.

Athreya, S 2017, 'Major issues in South Asian prehistory and early history: a view from the genome', in R Korisettar (ed.), *Beyond stones and more stones*, The Mythic Society, Bangalore, pp. 150–179.

Athreya, S 2018, 'Picking a bone with evolutionary essentialism', *Anthropology News*, vol. 59, no. 5, pp. e55–e60.

Athreya, S 2019, '"But you're not a *real* minority": the marginalization of Asian voices in paleoanthropology', *American Anthropologist*, vol. 121, no. 2, pp. 472–474.

Athreya, S & Ackermann, RR 2019, 'Colonialism and narratives of human origins in Asia and Africa', in M Porr & JM Matthews (eds), *Interrogating human origins: decolonisation and the deep past*, Archaeological Orientation Series, Routledge, Abingdon.

Athreya, S & Wu, X 2017, 'A multivariate assessment of the Dali hominin cranium from China: morphological affinities and implications for Pleistocene evolution in East Asia', *American Journal of Physical Anthropology*, vol. 164, pp. 679–701.

Bhandari, A, Kay, RK, Williams, BA, Tiwari, BN, Bajpai, S & Hieronymus, T 2018, 'First record of the Miocene hominoid Sivapithecus from Kutch, Gujarat state, western India', *PLoS ONE*, vol. 13, no. 11, p. e0206314.

Biagi, P & Starnini, E 2014, 'The Levallois Mousterian assemblages of Sindh (Pakistan) and their relations with the Middle Palaeolithic of the Indian Subcontinent', *Archaeology Ethnology and Anthropology of Eurasia*, vol. 42, no. 1, pp. 18–32.

Blinkhorn, J, Achyuthan, H & Ajithprasad, P 2015, 'Middle Palaeolithic point technologies in the Thar Desert, India', *Quaternary International*, vol. 382, pp. 237–249.

Blinkhorn, J, Achyuthan, H, Petraglia, MD & Ditchfield, P 2013, 'Middle Palaeolithic occupation in the Thar Desert during the Upper Pleistocene: the signature of a modern human exit out of Africa?' *Quaternary Science Reviews*, vol. 77, pp. 233–238.

Blinkhorn, J & Petraglia, MD 2014, 'Assessing models for the dispersal of modern humans to South Asia', in RW Dennell & M Porr (eds), *Southern Asia, Australia and the search for human origins*, Cambridge University Press, New York, pp. 64–75.

Blinkhorn, J & Petraglia, MD 2017, 'Environments and cultural change in the Indian Subcontinent: implications for the dispersal of *Homo sapiens* in the Late Pleistocene', *Current Anthropology*, vol. 58, no. S17, pp. S468–S479.

Bose, NK & Sen, D 1948, *Excavations in Mayurbhanj*, Calcutta University, Calcutta.

Brown, JA 1889, 'On some small highly specialized forms of stone implements found in Asia, North Africa and Europe', *Journal of Royal Anthropological Institute*, vol. 18, pp. 134–139.

Cammiade, LA & Burkitt, MC 1930, 'Fresh light on the Stone Age in southeast India', *Antiquity*, vol. 4, pp. 327–339.

Chamyal, LS, Dambricourt Malasse, A, Maurya, DM, Raj, R, Juyal, N, Bhandari, S, Pant, RK & Gaillard, C 2011, 'Discovery of a robust fossil *Homo sapiens* in India (Orsang Valley, Lower Narmada Basin, Gujarat): possible continuity with Asian *Homo erectus*', *Acta Anthropologica Sinica*, vol. 2, pp. 158–191.

Chauhan, PR 2008, 'Soanian lithic occurrences and raw material exploitation in the Siwalik Frontal zone, northern India: a geoarchaeological approach', *Journal of Human Evolution*, vol. 54, no. 5, pp. 591–614.

Chauhan, PR 2009, 'The South Asian paleolithic record and its potential for transitions studies', in M Camps & PR Chauhan (eds), *Sourcebook of paleolithic transitions: methods, theories and interpretations*, Springer, New York, pp. 121–139.

Chauhan, PR 2010a, 'The Indian subcontinent and "Out of Africa I"', in J Fleagle, J Shea & R Leakey (eds), *Out of Africa I: the first hominins of Eurasia*, Paleobiology and Paleoanthropology Series, Springer Press, pp. 145–164.

Chauhan, PR 2010b, 'Book Review of *The Evolution and History of Human Populations in South Asia: Inter-Disciplinary Studies in Archaeology, Biological Anthropology, Linguistics and Genetics*, M. D. Petraglia & B. Allchin (eds)', *PaleoAnthropology*, pp. 64–71. doi:10.4207/PA.2010.REV81.

Chauhan, PR 2016, 'A decade of paleoanthropology in the Indian Subcontinent (2005–2015)', in G Schug & S Walimbe (eds), *Companion to South Asia in the past*, Wiley Blackwell, Chichester, pp. 32–50.

Chauhan, PR, Ozarkar, S & Kulkarni, S 2015, 'Genes, stone tools, and modern human dispersals in the center of the Old World', in K Yōsuke, I Masami, T Goebel, S Hiroyuki & A Ono (eds), *Emergence and diversity of modern human behavior in Paleolithic Asia*, Texas A&M University Press, College Station, pp. 94–113.

Chauhan, PR, Sathe, V & Shaik, S 2013, 'A short note on prehistoric reinvestigations at Durkadi, central India', *Indian Journal of Physical Anthropology and Human Genetics*, vol. 32, no. 1, pp. 185–193.

Clarkson, C, Petraglia, MD, Harris, C, Shipton, C & Norman, K 2018, 'The South Asian Microlithic: *Homo sapiens* dispersal or adaptive response?', in E Robinson & F Sellet (eds), *Lithic technological organization and paleoenvironmental change*, Springer International Publishing, Basel, pp. 37–61.

Corvinus, G 1996, 'The prehistory of Nepal after 10 years of research', *Bulletin of the Indo-Pacific Prehistory Association*, vol. 14, pp. 43–55.

Costa, AG 2011, 'A techno-typological reassessment of an alleged Upper Paleolithic assemblage from Visadi (Northwestern India)', Poster presented at The Paleoanthropology Society meetings, Minneapolis, April 2011.

Costa, AG 2012, 'A Pleistocene passage to India: the palaeoanthropology of early human settlement in coastal western India', Ph.D. Thesis, Indiana University, Bloomington.

Dennell, RW 1990, 'Progressive gradualism, imperialism and academic fashion: Lower Palaeolithic archaeology in the 20th century', *Antiquity*, vol. 64, no. 244, pp. 549–558.

Dennell, RW 2000–2001, 'Palaeolithic studies in India since Independence: from an outsider's point of view', *Bulletin of the Deccan College Post-Graduate and Research Institute*, vol. 60–61, pp. 175–187.

Dennell, RW & Petraglia, MD 2012, 'The dispersal of *Homo sapiens* across southern Asia: how early, how often, how complex?' *Quaternary Science Reviews*, vol. 47, pp. 15–22.

Dennell, RW & Porr, M (eds) 2014, *Southern Asia, Australia and the search for human origins*, Cambridge University Press, Cambridge.

Dhavalikar, MK 2007, *The Aryans: myth and archaeology*, Munshiram Manoharlal, New Delhi.

Dirks, PHGM, Roberts, EM, Hilbert-Wolf, H, Kramers, JD, Hawks, J, Dosseto, A, Duval, M, Elliott, M, Evans, M, Grun, R, Hellstrom, J, Herries, AIR, Joannes-Boyau, R, Makhubela, TV, Placzek, CJ, Robbins, J, Spandler, C, Wiersma, J, Woodhead, J & Berger, LR 2017, 'The age of *Homo naledi* and associated sediments in the Rising Star Cave, South Africa', *eLife*, vol. 6, p. e24231.

Drell, JRR 2000, 'Neanderthals: a history of interpretations', *Oxford Journal of Archaeology*, vol. 19, no. 1, pp. 1–24.

Endicott, P 2007, 'Genetic evidence on modern human dispersals in South Asia: Y chromosome and mitochondrial DNA perspectives: the world through the eyes of two haploid genomes', in MD Petraglia & B Allchin (eds), *The evolution and history of human populations in South Asia*, Springer Press, Dordrecht, pp. 229–244.

Foote, RB 1866, 'On the occurrence of stone implements from various parts of Madras and North Arcot Districts', *Madras Journal of Literature and Science*, Third Series, part 2, pp. 1–35.

Frere, J 1800, 'Account of flint weapons discovered at Hoxne in Suffolk', *Archaeologia*, vol. 13, pp. 204–205.

Gaillard, C 1995, 'An Early Soan assemblage from the Siwaliks: a comparison of processing sequences between this assemblage and of an Acheulian assemblage from Rajasthan', in S Wadia, R Korisettar & VS Kale (eds), *Quaternary environments and geoarchaeology of India: essays in honour of Professor S.N. Rajaguru*, Geological Society of India, Bangalore, pp. 231–245.

Gaillard, C & Mishra, S 2001, 'The Lower Palaeolithic in South Asia', in F Semah, C Falgueres, D Grimaud-Herve & A Semah (eds), *Origin of settlements and chronology of the Palaeolithic cultures in Southeast Asia*, Semenanjung, Paris, pp. 73–91.

Ghosh, AK 1974, 'Denticulates in India: examination of a type concept', *Journal of the Hong Kong Archaeological Society*, vol. 5, pp. 47–56.

Goren-Inbar, N & Saragusti, I 1996, 'An Acheulian biface assemblage from Gesher Benot Ya'aqov, Israel: indications of African affinities', *Journal of Field Archaeology*, vol. 23, no. 1, pp. 15–30.

Groucutt, HS, Petraglia, MD, Bailey, G, Scerri, EML, Parton, A, Clark-Balzan, L, Jennings, RP, Lewis, L, Blinkhorn, J, Drake, NA, Breeze, PS, Inglis, RH, Deves, MH, Meredith-Williams, M, Boivin, N, Thomas, MG & Scally, A 2015a, 'Rethinking the dispersal of *Homo sapiens* out of Africa', *Evolutionary Anthropology*, vol. 24, no. 4, pp. 149–164.

Groucutt, HS, Scerri, EML, Lewis, L, Clark-Balzan, L, Blinkhorn, J, Jennings, RP, Parton, A & Petraglia, MD 2015b, 'Stone tool assemblages and models for the dispersal of *Homo sapiens* out of Africa', *Quaternary International*, vol. 382, pp. 8–30.

Haslam, M, Clarkson, C, Petraglia, MD, Korisettar, R, Bora, J, Boivin, N, Ditchfield, P, Jones, S & Mackay, A 2010a, 'Indian lithic technology prior to the 74,000 BP Toba super- eruption: searching for an early modern human signature', in KV Boyle (ed.), *Upper Palaeolithic revolution in global perspective: essays in honour of Paul Mellars*, McDonald Institute for Archaeological Research, Cambridge, pp. 73–84.

Haslam, M, Clarkson, C, Petraglia, MD, Korisettar, R, Jones, S, Shipton, C, Ditchfield, P & Ambrose, SH 2010b, 'The 74 ka Toba super-eruption and Southern Indian Hominins: archaeology, lithic technology and environments at Jwalapuram Locality 3', *Journal of Archaeological Science*, vol. 37, pp. 3370–3384.

Haslam, MD, Korisettar, R, Petraglia, MD, Smith, T, Shipton, C & Ditchfield, P 2010c, 'In Foote's steps: the history, significance and recent archaeological investigation of the Billa Surgam caves in Southern India', *South Asian Studies*, vol. 26, no. 1, pp. 1–19.

Haslam, M, Oppenheimer, S & Korisettar, R 2017, 'Out of Africa, into South Asia: a review of archaeological and genetic evidence for the dispersal of *Homo sapiens* into the Indian Subcontinent', in R Korisettar (ed.), *Beyond stones and more stones*, The Mythic Society, Bangalore, pp. 117–149.

Haslam, M, Roberts, RG, Shipton, C, Pal, JN, Fenwick, JL, Ditchfield, P, Boivin, N, Dubey, AK, Gupta, MC & Petraglia, M 2011, 'Late Acheulean hominins at the Marine Isotope Stage 6/5e transition in north-central India', *Quaternary Research*, vol. 75, no. 3, pp. 670–682.

James, HVA & Petraglia, MD 2005, 'Modern human origins and the evolution of behavior in the later Pleistocene record of South Asia', *Current Anthropology*, vol. 46, pp. S3–S27.

James, HVA & Petraglia, MD 2009, 'The Lower to Middle Palaeolithic transition in South Asia and its implications for hominin cognition and dispersals', in M Camps & PR Chauhan (eds), *Sourcebook of Paleolithic transitions: methods, theories and interpretations*, Springer Press, Netherlands, pp. 255–264.

Joseph, T 2018, *Early Indians: the story of our ancestors and where we came from*, Juggernaut Books, New Delhi.

Kennedy, KAR 1999, 'Paleoanthropology of South Asia', *Evolutionary Anthropology*, vol. 8, no. 5, pp. 165–185.

Kennedy, KAR 2000, *God-apes and fossil men: paleoanthropology of South Asia*, University of Michigan Press, Ann Arbor.

Kennedy, KAR 2003, 'The uninvited skeleton at the archaeological table: the crisis of paleoanthropology in South Asia in the twenty-first century', *Asian Perspectives*, vol. 42, no. 2, pp. 352–366.

Kenoyer, JM, Clark, JD, Pal, JN & Sharma, GR 1983, 'An Upper Palaeolithic shrine in India?', *Antiquity*, vol. 57, no. 220, pp. 88–94.

Khatri, AP 1962, 'Mahadevian: an Oldowan pebble culture of India', *Asian Perspectives*, vol. 6, no. 1, pp. 186–197.

Khatri, AP 1966, 'Origin and evolution of hand-axe culture in the Narmada Valley (Central India)', in D Sen & AK Ghosh (eds), *Studies in prehistory (Robert Bruce Foote Memorial Volume)*, Firma K.L. Mukhopadhyay, Calcutta, pp. 96–121.

Krishnaswami, VD 1938, 'Environmental and cultural changes of prehistoric man near Madras', *Journal of the Madras Geographic Association*, vol. 13, pp. 58–90.

Lal, BB 1963, 'India', *Asian Perspectives*, vol. 7, no. 1/2, pp. 27–38.

Leakey, LSB 1936, *Stone Age Africa*, Oxford University Press, London.

Lewis, GE 1937, 'Siwalik fossil anthropoids', Ph.D. Thesis, Yale University, New Haven, CT.

Lewis, L, Perera, N & Petraglia, MD 2014, 'First technological comparison of Southern African Howiesons Poort and South Asian Microlithic industries: an exploration of inter-regional variability in microlithic assemblages', *Quaternary International*, vol. 350, pp. 7–25.

Lycett, S 2007, 'Is the Soanian techno-complex a Mode 1 or Mode 3 phenomenon? A morphometric assessment', *Journal of Archaeological Science*, vol. 34, pp. 1434–1440.

Majumder, P 1998, 'People of India: biological diversity and affinities', *Evolutionary Anthropology*, vol. 6, no. 3, pp. 100–110.

Malassé, DA 2016, 'The first Indo-French Prehistorical Mission in Siwaliks and the discovery of anthropic activities at 2.6 million years', *Comptes Rendus Palevol*, vol. 15, pp. 281–294.

Mellars, P, Gori, KC, Carr, M, Soares, PA & Richards, MP 2013, 'Genetic and archaeological perspectives on the initial modern human colonization of southern Asia', *Proceedings of the National Academy of Sciences*, vol. 110, no. 26, pp. 10699–10704.

Mendez-Quintas, E, Santonja, M, Pérez-González, A, Duval, M, Demuro, M & Arnold, LJ 2018, 'First evidence of an extensive Acheulean large cutting tool accumulation in Europe from Porto Maior (Galicia, Spain)', *Scientific Reports*, vol. 8, p. 3082.

Mishra, S, Chauhan, N & Singhvi, AK 2013, 'Continuity of microblade technology in the Indian subcontinent since 45 ka: implications for the dispersal of modern humans', *PLoS ONE*, vol. 8, p. e69280.

Mishra, S, Gaillard, C, Hertler, C, Moigne, A-M & Simanjuntak, T 2010, 'India and Java: contrasting records, intimate connections', *Quaternary International*, vol. 223, pp. 265–270.

Misra, VN 1985, 'The Acheulian succession at Bhimbetka, Central India', in VN Misra & P Bellwood (eds), *Recent advances in Indo-Pacific prehistory*, Oxford/IBH, New Delhi, pp. 35–47.

Misra, VN 2001a, 'Prehistoric human colonization of India', *Journal of Biosciences*, vol. 26, no. 4, pp. 491–531.

Misra, VN 2001b, 'Archaeological evidence of early modern human occupation in South Asia', in PV Tobias, R Raath, JA Moggi-Cecchi & GA Doyle (eds), *Humanity from African Naissance to coming millenia*, Firenze University Press, Firenze, pp. 223–230.

Murty, MLK 1979, 'Recent research on the Upper Palaeolithic phase in India', *Journal of Field Archaeology*, vol. 6, no. 3, pp. 301–320.

Paddayya, K 2015, 'Birth of prehistory in Europe: the India connection grâce à Hugh Falconer', *Man and Environment*, vol. 40, no. 1, pp. 82–93.

Pal, JN 2002, 'The Middle Palaeolithic culture of South Asia', in S Settar & R Korisettar (eds), *Indian archaeology in retrospect: archaeology and interactive disciplines*, Manohar and Indian Council of Historical Research, New Delhi, pp. 67–83.

Pappu, S, Gunnell, Y, Akhilesh, K, Braucher, R, Taieb, M, Demory, F & Thouveny, N 2011, 'Early Pleistocene presence of Acheulian hominins in South India', *Science*, vol. 331, pp. 1596–1600.

Patnaik, R, Chauhan, PR, Rao, MR, Blackwell, BAB, Skinner, AR, Sahni, A, Chauhan, MS & Khan, HS 2009, 'New geochronological, palaeoclimatological and Palaeolithic data from the Narmada Valley hominin locality, central India', *Journal of Human Evolution*, vol. 56, pp. 114–133.

Petraglia, MD 2007, 'Mind the gap: factoring the Arabian Peninsula and the Indian subcontinent into out of Africa models', in P Mellars, O Bar-Yosef, K Boyle & C Stringer (eds), *The human revolution revisited*, McDonald Institute Archaeological Publications, Cambridge, pp. 383–394.

Petraglia, MD, Ditchfield, P, Jones, S, Korisettar, R & Pal, JN 2012, 'The Toba volcanic super-eruption, environmental change, and hominin occupation history in India over the last 140,000 years', *Quaternary International*, vol. 258, pp. 119–134.

Petraglia, MD, Haslam, M, Fuller, DQ, Boivin, N & Clarkson, C 2010, 'Out of Africa: new hypotheses and evidence for the dispersal of *Homo sapiens* along the Indian Ocean Rim', *Annals of Human Biology*, vol. 37, pp. 288–311.

Petraglia, MD, Korisettar, R, Boivin, N, Clarkson, C, Ditchfield, P, Jones, S, Koshy, J, Lahr, MM, Oppenheimer, C, Pyle, D, Roberts, R, Schwenninger, J-L, Arnold, L & White, K 2007, 'Middle Paleolithic assemblages from the Indian subcontinent before and after the Toba super-eruption', *Science*, vol. 317, no. 5834, pp. 114–116.

Petraglia, MD, Korisettar, R & Schuldenrein, J 2003, 'Landscapes, activity, and the Acheulean to Middle Paleolithic transition in the Kaladgi Basin, India', *Journal of Eurasian Prehistory*, vol. 1, no. 2, pp. 3–24.

Porr, M & Matthews, JM 2017, 'Post-colonialism, human origins and the paradox of modernity', *Antiquity*, vol. 91, no. 358, pp. 1058–1068.

Rendell, H & Dennell, RW 1985, 'Dated Lower Palaeolithic artefacts from northern Pakistan', *Current Anthropology*, vol. 26, no. 3, p. 393.

Rendell, H, Hailwood, W & Dennell, RW 1987, 'Magnetic polarity stratigraphy of Upper Siwalik Sub-Group, Soan Valley, Pakistan: implications for early human occupance of Asia', *Earth and Planetary Science Letters*, vol. 85, pp. 488–496.

Rendell, HM, Dennell, RW & Halim, MA 1989, *Pleistocene and palaeolithic investigations in the Soan Valley, northern Pakistan*, British Archaeological Reports Vol. 554, Archaeopress, Oxford.

Salahuddin, RKG 1986–1987, 'On the archaeological association of the fossil hominid from Hathnora, Madhya Pradesh, India', *Asian Perspectives*, vol. 27, no. 2, pp. 193–203.

Sali, SA 1985, 'The Upper Palaeolithic culture at Patne, District Jalgaon, Maharashtra', in VN Misra & P Bellwood (eds), *Recent advances in Indo-Pacific prehistory*, Oxford & IBH Publishing Co., New Delhi, pp. 137–145.

Sali, SA 1989, *The Upper Palaeolithic and Mesolithic cultures of Maharashtra*, Deccan College Post-Graduate and Research Institute, Pune.

Sankalia, HD 1974, *The prehistory and protohistory of India and Pakistan*, Deccan College and Postgraduate Research Institute, Pune.

Scerri, EML, Thomas, MG, Manica, A, Gunz, OM, Stock, JT, Stringer, C, Grove, M, Groucutt, HS, Timmermann, A, Rightmire, P, d'Errico, F, Tryon, CA, Drake, NA, Brooks, AS, Dennell, RW, Durbin, R, Henn, BM, Lee-Thorp, J, deMenocal, P, Petraglia, MD, Thompson, JC, Scally, A & Chikhi, L 2018, 'Did our species evolve in subdivided populations across Africa, and why does it matter?' *Trends in Ecology and Evolution*, vol. 33, no. 8, pp. 582–594.

Schick, KD 1994, 'The Movius line reconsidered', in RS Corruccini & RL Ciochon (eds), *Integrative paths to the past*, Prentice Hall, Englewood Cliffs, NJ, pp. 569–596.

Schick, K & Toth, N 2006, 'An overview of the Oldowan Industrial Complex: the sites and the nature of their evidence', in N Toth & K Schick (eds), *The Oldowan: case studies into the earliest Stone Age*, Stone Age Institute Press, Gosport, pp. 3–42.

Sen, D & Ghosh, AK 1963, 'Lithic culture: complex in the Pleistocene sequence of the Narmada Valley, Central India', *Rivista Di Scienze Prestoriche*, vol. 18, pp. 3–23.

Seshadri, M 1962, 'Stone Age tools from Salvadgi, Bijapur District Mysore State', *Journal of the University of Mysore*, vol. 25, no. 2, pp. 1–5.

Shipton, C, Clarkson, C, Pal, JN, Jones, SC, Roberts, RG, Harris, C, Gupta, MC, Ditchfield, PW & Petraglia, MD 2013, 'Generativity, hierarchical action and recursion in the technology of the Acheulean to Middle Palaeolithic transition: a perspective from Patpara, the Son Valley, India', *Journal of Human Evolution*, vol. 65, no. 2, pp. 93–108.

Sonakia, A & de Lumley, H 2006, 'Narmada *Homo erectus*: a possible ancestor of the modern Indian', *Comptes Rendus Palevol*, vol. 5, no. 1, pp. 353–357.

Soni, AS & Soni, VS 2005, 'Palaeolithic tools from the surface of optically stimulated luminescence dated alluvial fan deposits of Pinjaur Dun in NW sub-Himalayas', *Current Science*, vol. 88, no. 6, pp. 867–871.

Supekar, SG 1968, 'Pleistocene stratigraphy and prehistoric archaeology of the Central Narmada Basin', Ph.D. Thesis, Deccan College Postgraduate and Research Institute, Pune.

de Terra, H 1939, 'The Quaternary terrace system of Southern Asia and the age of man', *Geographical Review*, vol. 29, no. 1, pp. 101–118.

de Terra, H & Paterson, TT 1939, *Studies on the Ice Age in India and associated human cultures*, Carnegie Institute Publication #493, Carnegie Institute, Washington, DC.

de Terra, H, Teilhard de Chardin, P & Paterson, TT 1936, 'Joint geological and prehistoric studies of the Late Cenozoic in India', *Science*, vol. 83, no. 2149, pp. 233–236.

Wakanker, VS 1973, 'Bhimbetka excavations', *Journal of Indian History*, vol. LI, no. 1, pp. 23–33.

Wakanker, VS 1983, 'The oldest works of art?' *Science Today*, vol. 20, pp. 43–48.

White, M 2000, 'The Clactonian question: on the interpretation of core-and-flake assemblages in the British Lower Paleolithic', *Journal of World Prehistory*, vol. 14, no. 1, pp. 1–63.

12

OUR EARLIEST ANCESTORS

Human and non-human primates of North America

Paulette F. Steeves

My place in this story

Tansi (hello), my name is Paulette Steeves, I am a Cree-Metis scholar, a descendant of First Nations people of the Western Hemisphere, from the area we now know as Canada. My research is framed in Indigenous Method and Theory, Indigenous ways of knowing, being, and doing. In Indigenous research, respect, reciprocity, and relationality are central to all that we do. Thus, I present this introduction as a respectful way of creating a relationship with the reader before I share my story. Indigenous scholars often present their research as storytelling; this reflects where the storytellers are in their lives (Wilson 2008). '"Location" in Indigenous research, as in life, is a critical starting point' (Sinclair 2003, p. 122). The story I tell in this research focuses on the decolonisation of knowledge production regarding humans and the deep past of their ancestral primates.

In an Indigenous methodology, stories do the work of decolonisation. Aman Sium and Eric Ritskes (2013, pp. II–III) argue 'Stories are decolonization theory in its most natural form', they 'are resurgent moments, which reclaim epistemic ground that was erased by colonialism'. The research ceremony that is the basis of this story weaves through different understandings of the past, through ancient oral traditions, and through archaeological and palaeontological collections and stories, which inform us in the present. Some of what I share in this story is based on my journey through graduate school and my 2015 dissertation, 'Decolonizing Indigenous Histories: Pleistocene Archaeology Sites of the Western Hemisphere (the Americas)' (Steeves 2015).

This introduction and telling of my place in this story provide the reader with information that is essential to understanding the story (Kovach 2009) and allows the reader to know of any possible bias that may be linked to my place in life and the story. For non-Indigenous people, unfamiliar with Indigenous ways, this creates a space for understanding. For Indigenous people and scholars, shared understandings are central to providing people with knowledge that opens spaces to decolonise minds, hearts, and communities.

Introduction

Stories of hominid evolution that have been taught throughout all levels of education are written from a Eurocentric view of the past, with a focus on politics, power and control in the present. Throughout this chapter I discuss *hominin*, the group consisting of modern humans, extinct human species, including *Ardipithecus, Australopithecus, Paranthropus*, and all modern human immediate ancestors, and *hominid*, the group consisting of modern and extinct humans, chimpanzees, gorillas and orangutans, and primate ancestors. Traditionally educational materials on hominid evolution do not often, if ever, present a detailed accounting of the human and primate past on a global scale despite numerous academic articles reporting on this topic. Discussions on the possibilities of human evolution and the evolution of our primate ancestors on continents outside of Africa are often ignored as they challenge the status quo of decades-old tropes of human evolution embedded within Western universities. Re-telling the stories and re-framing them to include discussions from communities outside of Western science would create a much more diverse and informed view of the past. Decolonising literature on the human past would allow people to begin to decolonise their worldviews and to expand their knowledge.

In my experience teaching college students, I have found they are often not aware of the colonised frames of educational literature and programs. Students have been taught to trust the authority of those in positions of power over them, specifically to trust so called academic or scientific authority. The first thing I tell all my students in every class, is that they have not only an opportunity to challenge authority, they also have a duty to challenge authority. Class readings and discussions on colonialism begin a long process of lifting layers of colonial oppression in education that, unbeknown to students, have been woven through their worldviews. Violence is often woven through Eurocentrically framed educational literature, disguised as unbiased scientific authority. Students are most often blinded and silenced, trapped under nets of cognitive imperialism woven through and normalised in their everyday lives.

In many Indigenous communities, there is a saying, *we have been here forever* (Calloway 2004), which links people to their homelands across time. Another Indigenous saying shared by many First Nations and Native American communities is, *we are all related* (Battiste 2007). According to Western scientists' theories of evolution, all life grew from an ancestral life form that evolved in the warm waters of a primordial sea (Futuyma 2005). Regarding the Indigenous peoples of the Western Hemisphere, many of their stories tell about how they have been here since time immemorial. Calloway (2004) linked oral traditions to community histories that hold knowledge of how the people emerged into the worlds, identity, and histories. In origin stories, people were 'given ceremonies and rituals that enabled them to find their place on the continent' (Deloria & Lytle 1984, p. 8). In consideration of a group of first people whose distinct identities, culture, and traditions grew from their relationship to their homelands, it could be said they have been here forever. For Indigenous people, forever may mean from their physical creation, or from the beginning of their cultural identities in a specific place; 'an emergence into a precise cultural identity' (Silko 1996, p. 272).

Indigenous people have an unalienable right to tell their history and their stories in their own voice and their own ways of knowing. Indigenous discourse challenges academic hegemony, which maintains the traditional privileging of non-Indigenous written sources in knowledge production of the Indigenous past (Steeves 2015; Wilson 2008). Western scientists have studied human evolution for a few hundred years. Indigenous people have told origin stories and taught generations of their communities about human evolution and humans' place in the world for thousands of years.

In this chapter, I discuss primate and human evolution and migrations that often remain unreported in general textbooks. First, I discuss early proto-primates, as modern humans' earliest ancestors, *Purgatorius coracis (S.W. Saskatchewan), Pandemonium dis,* and *Purgatorius unio* (Montana) (Scott, Fox & Redman 2016), because where the earliest proto-primates arose and where they migrated to, has the distinct possibility of informing our understanding of later hominin migrations. The earliest proto-primate fossils are dated to times just after the Cretaceous-Palaeogene extinction event 16, around 66–65 million years ago (Scott et al. 2016). VanValen and Sloan (1965) have discussed the evidence for Palaeocene primates in North America based on their field work in Montana.

> Field work in 1964 in eastern Montana by a party from the University of Minnesota has resulted in the discovery of six primate teeth from the early Paleocene Purgatory Hill local fauna (4) in the Tullock Formation and one tooth from the latest Cretaceous Harbicht Hill local fauna (4) in the Hell Creek Formation. These teeth represent two species of a new genus. The Cretaceous species was contemporaneous with at least six species of dinosaurs and in fact was recovered from the same stream channel sand as was a main part of the mounted skeleton of Triceratops in the American Museum of Natural History (A.M.N.H. No. 5033).
>
> *(VanValen & Sloan 1965, p. 743)*

Second, I discuss recent evidence of new hominin fossils that have challenged our understanding of modern human evolution (Pääbo 2015). This recent fossil evidence, supported by genetics research, highlights changing paradigms that expand our understanding of the Multiregional Theory of human evolution. Third, I discuss long-standing denials of Pleistocene human migrations between the Eastern and Western Hemispheres and pre-Last Glacial Maximum arrival of humans in the areas of the Western Hemisphere that we now know as the Americas. Overall, I discuss our earliest human ancestors, recently discovered fossil hominins, new knowledge of human migrations on a global scale, and Palaeolithic sites in the Western Hemisphere (the Americas). Throughout these discussions I am focused on decolonising knowledge production framed within national, political, and historical discourses of the human past.

Decolonising minds and Western constructs of the past

As an academic, it is important to introduce students to critical thought and to create safe spaces to openly discuss the possibilities of other stories of the human past. It is not as if we have already discovered everything there is to know about human and primate evolution. It is more likely there is a lot we have yet to learn. The possibilities of furthering research in the field of human evolution are just beginning to be understood; thus, discussions of decolonisation of knowledge production in this field are paramount to furthering knowledge of the human past.

It is also paramount to discuss how we arrived at this point in research and education of the past. Thus, it is equally important to discuss the academy, research, and education framed in national and colonial modes of politically correct and safe knowledge. Knowledge framed in discourses of agnotology have kept generations of people and researchers in varying states of 'colonialism of the mind' (Dugassa 2011) where critical thought is discouraged and limited. Through a silencing of critical thought, historical knowledge production supporting national ideologies of power and control of the past remain embedded in the present. The where, when, and how of modern human evolution and human migrations on a global scale are framed in words that are never value-free. Research discussions and findings are tethered to state ideologies and institutions.

Western constructs of human evolution have often been framed in epistemologies of agnotology discussed as 'how knowledge has not come to be' and 'how ignorance is produced through neglect, secrecy, suppression, destruction of documents, unquestioned tradition, and sociopolitical selectivity' (Proctor & Schiebinger 2008, p. 5). Discussions of the human past have been centred in Western universities and thought; though not necessarily universal thought. Deconstructing discussion of human evolution is fundamental to decolonising knowledge production of the human past. To decolonise any area of knowledge production, we must understand how knowledge came to the specific point from which we seek to decolonise it. Thus, we must discuss colonisation because colonial discussions and frames of Eurocentrically-based knowledge production of the past often remain woven through control of the present.

Ramon Grosfoguel (2013, p. 74) questioned how the knowledge of a few had achieved such epistemic privilege and superiority in knowledge production:

> How is it possible that the canon of thought in all the disciplines of the Social Sciences and Humanities in the *Westernized University* is based on the knowledge produced by a few men from five countries in Western Europe (Italy, France, England, Germany and the USA)?
>
> *(Grosfoguel 2013, p. 74, original emphasis)*

When one or numerous groups of people colonise another group in any way, including their knowledge production, there are genocides or rather epistemicides that take place as part of colonial processes of oppression. Boaventura de Sousa Santos (2010) discussed the extermination of knowledge and ways of knowing as 'epistemicide'. In European colonisation of Indigenous peoples, genocide was carried out through ideologies of epistemicides, the erasure and outlawing of other ways of knowing. Canada recently admitted to this in apologies to First Nations peoples regarding boarding and residential schools (Government of Canada 2008). In residential schools in Canada and the United States, children were beaten and punished if caught speaking their own languages; the intent was to destroy Indigenous cultures, a process Marie Battiste discussed as cognitive imperialism (Battiste 2013).

Grosfoguel (2013) addressed the pretensions of knowledge based in such a small area as being discussed within discourses of universality, yet Western knowledge stems from a small base of Western Europe. This leaves out the realities of most the world, of all people of colour, of all Indigenous nations and communities, whose knowledge is diverse, vast, and ancient. When we are made aware of the cost of colonisation within knowledge production and its devastating impacts upon Indigenous people, we can begin to understand the dire and immediate need for knowledge to be decolonised across all areas of Western society and Western-centred universities. In decolonising research discussions of the human past, academics and researchers must learn to weave other ways of knowing, being and doing, into their worldviews. There are many ways of knowing and many ways of telling stories based on observations, testing, data, and knowledge. Western scientists have told stories through a so-called positivist or 'emotion-free' unbiased science based on quantitative and qualitative data. However, it has been argued that an unbiased science is not even possible (Chilisa 2012). We all have biases and we cannot take them off when we sit down to write our stories: the human heart, mind, and soul do not work that way. We can learn from other ways of knowing, being and doing and we can weave other ways of knowing throughout our discussions, literature, research, and worldviews.

Western scientists have a history of being very emotional at times about owning and being credited for their research in all areas of academia, including stories of the past. There is often a great deal of academic and financial capital at stake in the owning of research stories, including those regarding human evolution, such as the Out-of-Africa or the Mitochondrial Eve story. The traditional and ongoing discussion of human evolution is an old one, linking all events of importance in human and primate evolution to beginnings in Africa (Begun 2015). While Africa is important to stories of human and primate evolution, it is only one part of a much bigger story, and the evidence of primate evolution outside of Africa is not often included in general anthropological textbooks or discussed in general media.

In research framed by respect, relationality, and reciprocity, as in Indigenous methodology, I strive to learn, to unravel the stories of others and honour their traditions. We must remember that the stories do not belong to us and that reciprocity, that is giving back to communities, is desired over all else. Regarding human evolution, the story belongs to the world, to many nations of people who have their own stories and who have every right to have their stories respected, included and acknowledged. In writing this story, I hope that Western scientists will come to understand that it is OK if there are other stories told through other ways of knowing. Regarding the human past, I have learned other stories from many Indigenous people. I have come to know that Indigenous people's stories do not do harm to Western scientists or other people. The same cannot be said of Eurocentric stories told by Western researchers who colonise the production of knowledge about the past. Words are not value free (Steeves 2015), they come laden with a high cost and have historically been used as weapons of genocide, and epistemicide. It is words applied through colonial thought that become seeds of racism and ignorance through agnotology.

In some Indigenous communities, genesis stories tell how Turtle Island was built on the back of a turtle (Watts 2013). Many Indigenous communities of North America refer to the continent as Turtle Island. Four-legged, two-legged, winged, finned, crawlers and rooted beings, the waters that flowed and danced with the moon, were all here long before humans. When Sky Woman fell from the sky, there was no land, only water. Some oral traditions tell stories of the first human (Watts 2013), others about groups of people that emerged from different levels of the underworld (Zolbrod 1987). The story of Sky Woman and the clans who save her is beautifully told by Indigenous writers in many publications, and I will leave that story for them to tell. I wanted to briefly mention it here as a way of introducing readers to oral traditions that also tell us about the deep history of the earth and human evolution:

> One day the clans looked up and saw a being falling from the sky, they knew she needed a place to land. Swans flew up and spread out their wings to catch the creature and slow her fall from the sky. One by one members from the different clans took turns and dived deep into the water looking for dirt to put on the turtle's back, to make land

for the first human, Sky Woman (Watts 2013). Many of those who tried to find dirt beneath the deep water were not successful, and some never returned. Eventually one brought back a small fist full of mud; it was placed on Turtle's back where it grew and spread out to create Turtle Island. Before Sky Woman from the sky, there were no people on earth, only the non-human clans (Watts 2013).

Indigenous people's oral histories tell in metaphorical and unforgettable ways of the ancient histories of earth. Indigenous people and Western scientists both tell similar stories about the beginning of time; however, Indigenous people's stories are thousands of years older than those told by Western scientists. Stories told by Western scientists, and by Indigenous people, include that in the beginning of time the earth was covered in water, a place from which the first life formed and grew. Both Indigenous people's oral traditions and much later Western scientists' stories agree that many clans were here on the earth long before humans. Western scientists have never understood Indigenous oral traditions, as the histories and stories told by Indigenous people are very sophisticated and framed in Indigenous languages and ways of knowing, being, and doing, in relationality and respect for all beings place in life. By all beings I refer to all clans, the rocks, soils, trees, and rooted clans, the winged, finned, crawlers, sliders, two-footed and four-footed clans, the mountains, waters, and winds. Western scientists have never considered the stories told by Indigenous peoples to be records of historical events in part because the language and sophistication was at a much higher level than Westerners had ever encountered. However, some Western geologists are now beginning to pay attention to oral traditions and have recently begun to acknowledge that they are stories of actual geological and environmental events in deep time (Ludwin et al. 2007).

Not all Indigenous oral traditions are factual histories; some stories were meant to entertain or to educate on morals and ethical behaviour. Western people do much the same; they also have different types of stories for different purposes. Academics and Western scientists write many stories about how they think things were and why they need funding to prove they are correct. The goal is to receive research funds, carry out research, improve the human condition or add to educational knowledge production, and bolster one's academic career. With these goals in mind some Western scientists have made up a few wild and wholly unsubstantiated stories and received research funding and academic credit. Academics such as Jared Diamond, for example, who has won many awards for his writing through publications. Yet Diamond was also sued by the very Indigenous people he wrote about for making up false stories about them being violent (Society Matters 2010). There are costs associated with research findings, often for Indigenous people and places and for the public in general, but that is another story entirely and another book yet to be written. To be fair, many Western and Indigenous researchers get large grants and do great things that support health, human rights and environments for the betterment of all people. It is not necessarily the funding process that is problematic, but the ethical practices of some academics and researchers.

Research funds come with stipulations and expectations. Academic researchers have felt the sting of rejection and a loss of funds when their research findings are rejected, or their analysis contradicted socially constructed discourses guarded by the ghosts of imperial institutions. Research on human evolution is a competitive area, where researchers are expected to have a working relationship with experts in all areas of the world. Demands and the necessity of academic capital drive many researchers' claims of having found the earliest, the first, or the only. Funding institutions hand out millions of dollars with the expectations of being linked to intellectual breakthroughs and ground-breaking research findings; the first, the earliest, the oldest, the biggest, the one thing that grabs the most attention and fame. These expectations linked to funding have worked to create false theories presented as concrete facts that act as roadblocks to further understanding and discoveries. In theories of modern human evolution, such claims historically made the human past in the context of some geographical areas impossible to consider or to discuss. Though the situation is slowly beginning to change, evidence of human and primate evolution on a global scale in general textbooks is often ignored in favour of simplistic linear views of the past. I had to wonder when I first read about tiny proto-primates in the Americas, how it was that I had never learned of this in my classes on human evolution. Undaunted, I sought out this intriguing primate history on my own.

Our earliest ancestors

When I discuss human evolution with students, I first ask them, where did early hominins evolve? They answer correctly, Africa. I then ask if they know whom modern humans share a common ancestor with, they usually correctly state primates. Then I ask them where primates evolved, from their earliest basal forms, and they always answer this incorrectly by saying Africa. Our earliest ancestors, according to specialists in the field of primatology and palaeontology, have been found in the Western Hemisphere, in areas we know today as the badlands of Montana, in Wyoming and southern Saskatchewan. Whitten and Nickels (1983) acknowledged Africa as the birthplace of the genus *Homo*, our immediate ancestors. However, they further argued that the rise of primates took place in North America.

The earliest proto-primates, *Purgatorius coracis (S.W. Saskatchewan), Pandemonium dis* and *Purgatorius unio* (Montana) (Rose & Bown 1982; Scott, Fox & Redman 2016) and later proto-primates and Eu-primates, once roamed much of the area we now know as North America (Rose, Godinot & Bown 1994). Evidence from palaeontology sheds light on how far back in time we can trace mammalian evolution and migration on a global scale. Tracing mammalian migrations on a global scale highlights the possibilities for human migrations across time, in areas where evidence of early humans is minimal, erased, or questioned. Distributional and fossil evidence suggests that proto-primates originated in North America (Klein 1989). Palaeocene (66 Ma–56 Ma) primates have been reported from Montana and Wyoming (VanValen & Sloan 1965). Later Eocene (56 Ma–33.9 Ma) primate fossils came mainly from Western North America and Western Europe; some are also known from Asia (Rose & Bown 1982). Richard Fox and Craig Scott (2011) published on a newly discovered and oldest member of the Purgatorius family from Saskatchewan, as the earliest known primate:

> Here we describe *Purgatorius coracis* n. sp. from the Ravenscrag Formation, at the Rav W-1 horizon, Medicine Hat Brick and Tile Quarry, southwestern Saskatchewan. This horizon occurs within C29R, making *P. coracis* the earliest known primate while strengthening the evidence that plesiadapiforms, and hence primates, originated and underwent their initial evolutionary diversification in North America.
>
> *(Fox & Scott 2011, p. 537)*

Examples of the earliest member, *Purgatorius ceratops*, are from the Late Cretaceous (145 Ma–66 Ma) and Early Palaeocene (66 Ma–56 Ma), (Silcox et al. 2005) and are found exclusively in

North America (Van Valen & Sloan 1965). However, with further research and sampling in the field, we must remain open to the possibilities of early proto-primate evolution taking place in both the Western and Eastern hemispheres.

> While the Southeast Asian location of the closest living relatives of primates might suggest an Asian origin for the order (Beard 2004), the North American location of most primitive plesiadapiforms supports a North American origin instead (Bloch et al. 2007). This may be a product, however, of much greater sampling of the fossil record in North America. Indeed, there is now a relatively primitive plesiadapiform known from Asia (*Asioplesiadapis youngi*, Fu et al. 2002).
>
> *(Silcox 2014, p. 1)*

Areas of the Western and Eastern hemispheres, now known as North America and Europe, split apart around 80 million years ago (Cox 2000). On the northwestern side of the Western Hemisphere, a broad swath of land measured 57 miles across and connected the Northern, Eastern and Western Hemispheres. This area we know as Beringia was bisected by melting glacial water and ice near the end of the last glacial maximum around 11,000 to 10,000 years ago (Clark & Mix 2002). We do not know if the earliest proto-primates arose in many areas of the world, or at first in the Western Hemisphere then migrated to other continental areas and eventually to the Eastern Hemisphere., We do know that the majority of early proto-primate fossils have been found in the northern Western Hemisphere in areas we now know today as the badlands of Montana and Wyoming, and in southern Saskatchewan. These are all areas that were at one time under the waters of the Cannonball Sea, which had bisected the Western Hemisphere (North America) from north to south during the Maastrichtian of 77.1–66 Ma.

Ni et al. (2013, p. 64) discussed a rare, well preserved, 55 million-year-old Haplorrhine fossil found in China, noting that, '*A. achilles* may well mirror that of other phylogenetically basal primates.' A co-author of the Ni et al. paper, Christopher Beard, was quoted in a subsequent *New York Times* article (Wilford 2013) as saying that, 'We've heard of the "out of Africa" theory of human evolution, but that's recent history. So, there may now be the "into Africa" problem.' John Wilford (2013), who authored the *New York Times* article, asked 'How and when did some primates finally make it to Africa, which was an island until as recently as 16 million years ago, to set in motion the emergence of the human species?' 'There is evidence that 38 million years ago, some primates had apparently crossed the open water to colonise the African continent' (Wilford 2013). Wilford further wrote that:

> They also agreed that findings strongly supported Asia, not Africa, as the most likely continent of primate origins. No known primate fossils of such antiquity have been found in Africa, which the anthropoids eventually did colonize, evolving into *Homo sapiens* only about 200,000 years ago.
>
> *(Wilford 2013, p. A4)*

I have to point out that in the article by Ni et al. 2013, 'The Oldest Known Primate Skeleton and Early Haplorhine Evolution' and Wilford's (2013) coverage of it in the *New York Times* there was no mention of the earlier Palaeogene Plesiadapiforms which have been found in the area of the Western Hemisphere that we now know as North America. In Ni et al. 2013, the phylogeny of mammals, the 55 Ma primate skeleton from China shows that Plesiadpiforms (55–65 Ma) are ancestral to later primates both *strepsirrhini* and *haplorhini*. Given that the oldest dated Plesiadpiforms come from areas we know as Saskatchewan, Montana and Wyoming, and that the Palaeocene (55.8–65.5 Ma) primates set in motion the later emergence of the human species, it could be argued that the Western Hemisphere (North America) is most likely the area where the most basal of our earliest primate ancestors evolved. From the fossil evidence, it seems that as Plesiadpiforms found in areas of the Western Hemisphere date to the Palaeogene (55.8–65.5 Ma) and that North America is the most likely continent of primate origins, not Asia or Africa. We also need to keep in mind that around 65 Ma, when the dinosaurs died off thus facilitating the rise of smaller mammals, parts of the Eastern and Western Hemisphere were still connected as Laurisa. There may have been Palaeocene primates or Plesiadapiforms in the eastern and western areas of Laurisa, which are now known as North America, Eurasia, and Western Europe respectively. There have been ongoing debates between palaeontologists for decades regarding the phylogeny of early primate species and the most likely global location of early primate or proto-primate evolution.

Michael Heads (2010) offered a model of early primate evolution and biogeography based on molecular phylogenetics, variance and plate tectonics. Heads (2010) did not support Plesiadpiforms as ancestral to primates from a centre of origin at Garbani Channel, Montana. However, he allowed that a literal interpretation of the fossil record does support the view that primates evolved from Plesiadapiforms. Heads drew attention to many interesting areas of primate evolution. Primate evolution was most likely a long drawn out process, predating and the currently known oldest fossils by millions of years. The oldest known primate fossils represent the minimal age for proto-primates or Plesiadapiforms (Heads 2010).

I have no preference for where primates evolved. However, I do argue that it is important that all the available data and or facts published in an academic research area be discussed in educational literature. This allows students and others to think for themselves, and draw their own conclusions, based on available peer reviewed and published data. This capacity for critical thought is, after all, how great leaps in science and understanding originate.

When we know in which timeframes mammals and/or primates made intercontinental migrations, we can track their evolution across time and space. After all, if mammals and primates migrated to and from certain areas then so too could have early hominins or humans.

Palaeogeography is critical to our understanding of early intercontinental migrations. Water levels at times during the Palaeocene and Eocene where much lower than they are today and facilitated land connections between continental and island mainland areas. Global temperatures and ecosystems changed across time to create grassland and forest where once glaciers and tundra capped the land. Views of the past beyond ice age glaciers can be very interesting; where San Francisco's Golden Gate Bridge now spans a broad and substantial body of water, is an area where mammoths one roamed through fields of deep grass. The telling signs of very tall boulders polished only near their top edges, inform us that mammoths previously lived in the area and were fond of rubbing their itchy hides along the boulders' top edges and thus polishing them (Erickson & Parkman 2010).

Changing paradigms of human evolution

Changing paradigms of human evolution and multiregional theories of modern human evolution are supported by recent discoveries of fossil hominins and by genetic research. The main tenets of the Mitochondrial Eve hypothesis or the Out-of-Africa hypothesis have been seriously challenged by the discovery of new fossil hominins and through genetic research. In the Out-of-Africa or Mitochondrial Eve hypothesis, Cann et al. (1987) argued that *Homo sapiens* arose in Africa and migrated to Asia and Europe, replacing all other archaic *Homo sapiens*.

1. The ancestors of modern humans arose in one place, Africa (Cann 1987).

Did *Homo sapiens* originate in Africa? Many specialists in the field agree that they did. Is this the only continental land mass the fossil remains of *Homo sapiens* have been found? No, they are also known from fossil remains at sites in the Eastern Hemisphere now known as the Middle East and Asia; although most scholars agree that their earliest forms have been found in Africa.

2. Homo sapiens *ultimately migrated out of Africa and replaced all other human populations, without interbreeding with other archaic groups of* Homo sapiens *(Cann 1987).*

To claim that archaic *Homo sapiens* outside of Africa went extinct, to facilitate the Out-of-Africa or Ancestral Eve hypothesis, is far too simplistic, and from fossil and genetic evidence we now know that did not happen.

In the Multi-Regional Continuity hypothesis of modern human evolution, Alan Thorne and Milford Wolpoff (1992) argued that after *Homo erectus* left Africa and dispersed into other areas, regional populations slowly evolved into modern humans. Some level of gene flow between geographically separated populations prevented speciation, after the dispersal (Thorne & Wolpoff 1992).

Yes, we now know from genetic evidence that Neanderthal, Denisovans, and *Homo sapiens* shared genes (gene flow between geographically separated populations).

3. All living humans derive from the species Homo erectus *that left Africa nearly 2 million years ago (Thorne & Wolpoff 1992).*

Did *Homo sapiens, Homo erectus*, Neanderthals, and Denisovans share a common African ancestor, *Homo erectus*? Most scholars agree, yes.

4. Natural selection in regional populations, ever since their original dispersal, is responsible for the regional variants (sometimes called races) we see today (Pääbo 2015).

This seems to be agreed upon across all species.

5. The emergence of Homo sapiens *was not restricted to any one regional location but took place throughout the entire geographic range where humans lived (Pääbo 2015).*

Modern humans, *Homo sapiens sapiens*, are descendants of archaic populations including *Homo sapiens*, Neanderthals, and Denisovans. Archaeological sites provide evidence of archaic populations throughout the Eastern Hemisphere.

Gao et al. (2010) reviewed the Out-of-Africa and multiregional theory, and the continuity-with-hybridisation theory of human evolution, and posited that:

> the origin and evolution of modern humans is a complex issue. While controlled by genetic forces, the progress of evolution was also affected by cultural and social factors. Researchers should consider not only common characteristics of human groups living in one area, but also variations caused by adaptations of different human populations to different environmental conditions. As a result, no single universal model can explain the diversity of human evolutions.
>
> *(Gao et al. 2010, p. 1938)*

Researchers are now reevaluating the Out-of-Africa hypothesis that claimed all modern humans are descended from one small group that came out of Africa and replaced all other hominins on a global scale. This reevaluation is due in part to the discovery of evidence for previously unknown hominins, namely Denisovans, known from fragmented fossil remains found in present-day Siberia (Dillehay 2000), and genetic evidence which shows that some modern humans carry genetic materials of Neanderthals, Denisovans and another yet unknown ancestor (Dillehay 2000). In recent changes to the understanding and discussion of modern human evolution, we are informed that there is often a lot we do not know, and thus an acknowledgment of our own ignorance is an important starting point for growth within the field and for decolonising knowledge production.

Early people in Turtle Island (the Americas)

For over a century many archaeologists have denied that humans arrived in the Americas earlier then the end of the last glacial maximum, around 11,000–12,000 years ago (Adovasio & Page 2002). Archaeologists who claimed to have found earlier sites with the required evidence of human manufactured implements or tools, undisturbed stratigraphy, and C14 dates older than 11,200 years BP were most commonly, if not always, dismissed out of hand. Recently a few earlier sites such as Monte Verde in Chile, excavated and reported by Tom Dillehay (2000), and Meadowcroft in Pennsylvania reported by James Adovasio and Jake Page (2002), have been accepted as archaeological sites dated to earlier than 12,000 years ago.

However, some archaeologists still defend recent dates of initial human migrations to the Western Hemisphere. For over a century the possibilities of humans having reached the Western Hemisphere prior to the end of the last glacial maximum have been denied. Funding for research on earlier sites was scarce. How did such restrictive thoughts and policing of the past of the Americas come to be? Discussions denying the humanity and intellectualism of Indigenous people of the Western Hemisphere were common between initial colonisation and the turn of the twentieth century. Federal institutions such as the Smithsonian under the watchful eye of Ales Hrdlička initially supported an unsubstantiated theory that 'Indians' had only been in the Americas for 3,000 years (Hrdlička et al. 1912). In 1927 Jesse Figgins from the Colorado Museum of Natural History, now known as the Denver Museum of Nature and Science, argued, after finding fluted stone tools with the fossil remains of an extinct species of Bison in New Mexico, that people had been in the Americas for at least 10,000 years (Figgins & Cook 1927).

For the last eight decades, the dates for initial human migrations into the Western Hemisphere were argued to be only 10,000 to 12,000 years before the present (BP). This view has recently changed, but only by a few thousand years to around 14,000–15,000 years ago near the end of last glacial maximum. I argued in my 2015 dissertation (Steeves 2015) that humans have been in the Americas as early as 60,000 years BP and possibly much earlier. I based my argument on published archaeological reports on sites dated from 11,200 years to over 200,000 years BP, and seven years of experience in field work including two seasons of working only on pre-12,000 years BP sites in North America. There are reports of archaeology sites in the Americas that date to over 100,000 years BP. The majority of the sites I have reviewed date to between 11,200 and 40,000 years BP, with the oldest dating to over 200,000 years ago. However, in research and archaeological excavations we must keep an open mind, as we actually know very little regarding the human past, specifically of the Western Hemisphere.

Recently, Steve Holen et al. (2017) published a paper on the Cerutti Mastodon Site, which is located just northeast of San Diego, California; they argued that mastodon remains with human workmanship from the site dated to over 130,000 years ago. The Cerutti site formerly known as the Hwy 54 site, was one of three sites from which I studied the artefacts, materials and literature for my 2015 dissertation. A team of researchers waited patiently for years to date the mastodon remains from the Cerutti site, until they felt the science of dating had improved to a point that it could not easily be questioned; their patience paid off. The Cerutti Mastodon Site report was published in *Nature* in 2017 and was included in a discussion of the best 100 stories of the year in *Discover* magazine. The Cerutti Mastodon Site was discovered inadvertently during a road building project in Southern California; it was not the only archaeology site found during that project – over 100 were uncovered and recorded. Thomas Demere et al. (1995) analysed the site area to determine if there was a pattern of spirally fractured bone around two large stones found at the site. Demere et al. (1995) found that spirally fractured bone was concentrated around the two large stones: a pattern, he stated, which is similar to that recorded at the La Sena and Lovewell sites in the Great Plains of North America. The project was initially funded by the public; however, the unusual taphonomy of the specimen and the threat of destruction and loss due to highway construction required further funding, which was provided by the National Geographic Society (NGS # 4971–93), the California Department of Transportation (Caltrans; contract # 11C841 to the San Diego Natural History Museum), and a gift from John and Christie Walton of National City, California (Demere et al. 1995).

In 2011, I began to study the literature of Pleistocene archaeological sites in both North and South America that dated to over 11,200 years BP. It did not take long to amass a database of sites that met or exceeded the required archaeological evidence, dating and stratigraphy to be accepted as valid sites. Many sites, no matter the dates, have issues and secondary testing and dating may be carried out; that does not automatically make them unacceptable as an archaeology site. Archaeological sites with signs of human technology and/or presence that date to over 11,200 years BP are those that we should be paying attention to if we are truly interested in discerning the human history of the Western Hemisphere. I have reviewed the published record of over 300 pre-11,200 years BP sites in both North and South America. Many are in regions where sites with similar artifacts and dated to within a few hundred to a few thousand years of each other have been recorded. This is not surprising as we know that early humans had to travel across the land to reach inland areas, and family groups or communities often expanded across time and space. We also know that most archaeology sites are inadvertently discovered in areas where construction disturbs deposits left by previous inhabitants; that leaves a great deal of North and South America as unknown, archaeologically speaking. When I began researching Pleistocene archaeological sites in the Americas, I was aware of only a few pre-11,200 years BP or pre-Clovis sites. These included Monte Verde in Chile, Pedra Furada in Brazil, Pikimachay in Peru, the Manis Site in Washington State, Cactus Hill in Virginia, Coats Hinds in Tennessee, Meadowcroft in Pennsylvania, Pendejo Cave in New Mexico, and the La Sena site in Nebraska. These sites are thousands of miles apart and are dispersed across the Western Hemisphere. In further literature research I became aware of hundreds of published and dated pre-11,200 years BP archaeological sites or pre-Clovis sites, which created a path of human links to the land across time and space. This is what we might expect to see, as humans had to stop and spend time in many places to reach areas where well documented sites have been reported, such Monte Verde in Chile, La Sena in Nebraska, and Meadowcroft in Pennsylvania.

I wanted to determine just how many pre-Clovis sites had been published in academic literature over the last 60–80 years. This question began what I am now sure will be a life-long pursuit. I was amazed by the number of reports that have been written and published. I have located over 300 reports, and through those I now know of many more that have been reported over the last 80 years. I also searched the literature for critiques of these sites. I expected to find many, as the majority of pre-Clovis sites have been considered problematic by archaeologists who argue against pre-Clovis sites (Fidel 1992; Haynes 1980). I found only a few published critiques of pre-Clovis sites, and those critiques were successfully answered after further testing of site materials (Adovasio et al. 1998; Dillehay 1999). There were a few other critiques, however, that were argued by Bryan & Gruhn (2003) to be based on opinions rather than research or scientific data. Archaeologists base their stories of human migrations and communities on artefacts that are often compared to similar technologies. Recent developments in science have expanded our understanding of archaeological evidence of early human diets and cultural practices, adding to the stories that archaeologists tell. However, there are many stories of the human past told by many people; Indigenous people tell histories based on oral traditions which are rich archives of firsthand knowledge.

In oral traditions, Indigenous people discuss the past and the beginning of life just as Western science does, but in an Indigenised way framed by vibrant stories that can never be forgotten. Many clans were living on the earth long before humans. Western scientists also discuss this, through a linear evolutionary frame across time. A video on the Nova website (NOVA 2018) leads viewers through the human past, linking them to their earliest ancestors. In this video, we are told that the oldest known human and primate ancestors have been found in the badlands of Montana and Wyoming. The Indigenous peoples' saying that 'we have been here forever' can be said to be 'literally' supported by Western palaeontology and science. Yes, from what we know to date, hominins and early humans arose in the Eastern Hemisphere, Africa, Asia, and Europe. However, their primate ancestors arose in North America as early as 65 million years ago. Yes, primates later left the Western Hemisphere, now known as northern North America, and their descendants, *Homo sapiens*, later returned to recolonise the continents of the Western Hemisphere, both North and South America. Many Indigenous people consider all species to be relations; 'we are all related' – that story does no harm to anyone. Many Western scientists believe that we are not all related, yet their own research into the Big Bang and a primordial beginning of life, tells us that we are. Scientifically speaking, I think the Indigenous people are correct here.

In consideration of a group of first peoples whose distinct identities, culture, and traditions grew from their relationship to their homelands, it can be said they have been here forever. For Indigenous people, forever may mean from their physical creation, or from the beginning of their cultural identities in a specific place on the land (Steeves 2015); 'an emergence into a precise cultural identity' (Silko 1996, p. 272). Indigenous people have an unalienable right to tell their history and their stories in their own voice and their own ways of knowing. Indigenous discourse challenges academic hegemony which maintains traditional privileging of non-Indigenous written sources in knowledge production of the Indigenous past (Wilson 2005).

Nationalistic, historical and politicalised discourses of the human past

Discussing structures of power Lloyd Lee (2010, p. 33) argued that 'important critiques of existing scholarship have revealed Western scholarship to be simply another kind of imperialism that re-inscribes existing structures of power'. In work focused on decolonising Western knowledge production, open discussions are central to building spaces from which to deconstruct colonially framed literature on the human past. In deconstructing colonial histories of the human past, we open discussions from which we may learn where we came from, and how we got to where we are today. Thus, in understanding knowledge production of the past, we learn of power and control in the present. It is only then that we learn of the paths we may take to rebuild the future.

Many questions remain unanswered regarding the support for or acceptance of one theory of modern human evolution over another. There are questions regarding the acceptances of archaeology sites of early humans in some continental areas and not others, of stone tools which are identical being acknowledged as humanly constructed tools on one continent (Africa) and eco-facts of nature on another (North America). Why do some academics and researchers cling so stubbornly to the Out-of-Africa theory and the Clovis First theory when the main tenets of these theories have been disproven? Volumes could be written on this topic, foregrounding discussion on assumed links between ancient and contemporary people and communities, lands as *terra nullius* as opposed to ancient, Old Worlds and so-called New Worlds, and the importance of mammalian migrations for the possibilities of human evolution and migrations. Cristobal Gnecco and Patricia Ayala (2011, pp. 13–14) addressed the erasure of Indigenous achievements and knowledge as being appropriated by 'members of elites that despised the Indians as a "brutal paradox"'.

I have found that it is not just the achievements of Indigenous people that nationalist storytellers despised (Gnecco & Ayala 2011), it is also their homelands and their places of origin, their humanity and ancient histories on lands desired by empires. Many times, I have read of and heard so-called voices of authority deny that anything of importance ever developed in or evolved or migrated from the Western Hemisphere (the Americas) to other areas of the world. I have seen the most ancient art of the Indigenous peoples of the Western Hemisphere credited to other people who brought their memories and abilities with them from the Eastern Hemisphere (Europe). Archaeologists spent decades looking for the source of the Western Hemisphere's sophisticated stone technologies (Clovis tools) in areas of the Eastern Hemisphere, and never found even one. Recent archaeological discussions have acknowledged that Clovis technologies have never been found outside of the Western Hemisphere and were developed in the Western Hemisphere. The earliest human ancestors, primates, and North America's prominent place in many areas of human evolution and migrations remains buried in Eurocentric knowledge production. Nothing of importance to human migrations on a global scale is discussed as possibly linked to the Western Hemisphere.

There have recently been many changes to theories we teach on human evolution. Beyond any other change in our understanding of the human past, the recent discoveries of previously unknown hominins and interbreeding between archaic hominins should inform us of our own ignorance. There are many things we do not know the answers to; they are often yet to be discovered. However, we do know about the history of nationalism, colonialism, genocide, and erasures of humanity. We have no excuse for not discussing them and working to make positive changes. We know that nation states maintain power and control over the human past, over the erasure of Indigenous identities and the importance of Indigenous communities' links to their homelands.

Eyes wide open or eyes wide shut

In today's world of numerous journals and social media outlets, an academic or anyone who teaches in secondary or tertiary education would have to willfully keep their eyes wide shut to not include a lesson on colonisation and decolonisation. To not include a discussion on the time and place of early of early humans and early human ancestors in a curriculum on human evolution is to exclude important aspects of the students' learning experience. Thus, the ongoing use of colonised literature on human and primate evolution across time and place must be willful. Humans had crossed open bodies of water before 80,000 years ago and had successfully colonised areas of the Eastern Hemisphere, including the continent that is now known as Australia. We have not given early modern humans the credit they deserve for their skills in exploration, adaptation, and survival. Ongoing denials and erasures of the human past in specific global areas is due in part to long embedded national, political, and historical dimensions of colonisation within knowledge production. Some textbooks and literature still present a discussion of early primates of South America accidentally rafting there from Africa (Larsen 2008). Where is the physical, archaeological or palaeontological evidence for such a scenario? Is there a primate skeleton in a tree on a small island, in a museum somewhere? There is no such evidence, yet it is presented as fact in textbooks. Stankiewicz et al. (2006) studied possible ways of primate migrations between continental areas: rafts, vegetation, cyclones; they concluded that the widely accepted rafting theory is not valid at the theoretical or applied levels. A raft coming from Africa would drift back to the mainland. Animals would not survive transport by cyclones even if it did happen. The chances of successful dispersal are ludicrously small Stankiewicz et al. (2006, p. 231).

Heads (2010) discussed theories of sweepstakes dispersals that would have primates surviving weeks- or months-long accidental voyages to colonise new continental land mass areas. Heads proposed a molecular, vicariance, and plate tectonics model, where primates originated from a widespread global ancestor (Archonta) that differentiated 185 Ma, into Northern, Southern, and two Southeast Asian groups, and argued that thus there is no need for a sweepstakes migration hypothesis (Stankiewicz et al. 2006). Primate distribution is discussed as a result of the breakup of Pangea, a plate tectonics phylogeny and vicariance

(Stankiewicz et al. 2006). Heads (2010) offered a new idea on early primate evolution and links it to place and time of plate tectonics. He also cited discussions regarding the absurdity of hypotheses that discuss any possibility of New World primates rafting from Africa to South America (Stankiewicz et al. 2006). Critical thought goes a long way in clearing the fog of colonial discussion and exposing agnotology in academia and higher education. I neither support nor critique Heads' model. I do allow that he has raised many good points and offered a very fresh view of the possibilities of early primate evolution. Most palaeontologists agree on one thing: there are centres of origin. It just so happens that the majority of proto-primate fossils found to date have been located in the Western Hemisphere.

Why is the history of our earliest primate ancestors cohabiting with *Triceratops* (Fox & Scott 2011) in North America not discussed in educational materials? When I discuss this with students, they are amazed and so eager to dive into the subject matter. Some scholars have reported on palaeo-environments and palaeo-species, highlighting the movements of four-legged mammals intercontinentally. However, the vehement denial of Pleistocene archaeology sites in the Americas has been described as a battle ground: 'the archaeology of America is more like a battle field than a research topic' (L. L. Cavalli-Sforza, quoted in Churchill 2005, p. 266). If funding were made available equally to studies of human and primate migrations in the Western Hemisphere, as they are in the Eastern Hemisphere, there is not telling what we may yet discover. Palaeontological studies have provided the evidence for mammalian migrations between the Eastern and Western Hemispheres for millions of years. It seems since time immemorial there has been two-way traffic across land connections between the Eastern and Western Hemispheres. Horses, sabre-tooth cats, camels and other mammals arose in North America and migrated to Asia, Europe, and Africa. Mammoth, bison, elk, and others arose in the Eastern Hemisphere and migrated to the Western Hemisphere.

Recent debates on human and primate evolution are being informed by genetics, renewed questioning and field work. This is evident in the recent findings from the Jebel Irhoud site in Morocco. Hublin et al. (2017) argued that hominin fossils from the Jebel Irhoud site that date to as early as 315,000 ± 34 thousand years ago have a mosaic of cranial features aligned with modern humans and a more primitive endocranial neurocranial morphology. The research by Hublin et al. (2017) challenges the single area or Mitochondrial Eve, Garden of Eden hypothesis, and spreads the evolution of modern humans across time and the area we know today as Africa from the southeast to the northwest. In recent research by Fuss et al. (2017), the authors argued that *Graecopithecus* is possibly the oldest known hominin. *Graecopithecus* fossil remains have been found near Pyrgos Vassilissis (Greece) and Azmaka (Bulgaria). Fuss et al. (2017) discussed the taxonomic distinction a partial root fusion and canine root reduction as providing evidence of possibly the oldest known hominin. Böhme et al. (2017) questioned the where, when and why of major splits in the hominid line and suggested that *G. freyberge* is potentially the oldest known hominin. According to Böhme et al. (2017, p. 1) their 'results suggest that major splits in the hominid family occurred outside Africa'.

Research by many scholars including Fuss et al. (2017), Böhme et al. (2017), and Begun (2015) have discussed possible candidates for pre-human primates, and a split between *Homo* and *Pan* taking place in areas outside of the continent we know today as Africa. This opens the history of human and primate evolution to a vast area of the Eastern Hemisphere. At some point in the research process, someone may also find links between proto-primates and their migrations between Eastern and Western hemispheres, as the oldest yet know proto-primate fossils are from the North America.

It is also very interesting regarding the evolution of life, that the first life form to crawl up out of the ocean onto land did so in an area of the northeastern Western Hemisphere. To be more specific, in an area known as the Joggins Fossil Cliffs in Nova Scotia, Canada, which is a UNESCO World Heritage Site. This amazing and ancient fossil cliff is on the southern shore of the Cumberland Bay. This is the most easterly area of the larger Bay of Fundy, and the cliffs are right across from where I lived while writing this article in 2016–2017. I can look out from the edge of Sackville, New Brunswick and see Joggins Fossil Cliffs every day. Charles Lyell visited Joggins Fossil Cliffs in 1842 and proclaimed that 'the finest example in the world of a natural exposure in a continuous section ten-miles-long, occurs in the sea cliffs bordering a branch of the Bay of Fundy in Nova Scotia' (Joggins Fossil Institute 2019). Charles Darwin discussed the Joggins Fossil Cliffs in his book *The Origin of the Species* (1859), and in 1859, William Dawson reported to the Geological Society yet another discovery, *Hylonomus lyelli*, meaning 'forest dweller', named in honour of Lyell, his mentor and friend. It remains the earliest known amniote in the fossil record. *H. lyelli* has been discussed as the earliest reptile to crawl up out of the ocean; it lived 312 million years ago during the Late Carboniferous period; it is the ancestor of later reptiles, dinosaurs and mammals. Thus, it could be argued that all two-legged and four-legged life we know today evolved from a common ancestor known from the fossil record of Joggins, Nova Scotia in Canada, on Mi'kmaq traditional territories within North America. (Though to be exact, scientists label the area dated to 312 million years ago as Pangea, where current day Prince Edward Island and Nova Scotia were connected to a land area currently known as Morocco.) Our most primitive or earliest ancestors have been here forever, once living and now as fossils.

Advancements in genetic research have allowed an unprecedented view into the past, challenging and changing stories of human evolution in many ways. It is now clear that there was interbreeding between archaic *Homo sapiens*, Neanderthals and Denisovans, and at least one other unknown hominin species (Pääbo 2015). However, it was not too long ago that students were taught that archaic *Homo sapiens* and Neanderthals could not interbreed, as there were not the same species. For decades, academic scholars have, in many ways and fields of study, taught conjecture or hypothesis as scientific fact. There is nothing wrong with telling students that we do not yet have all the answers. Teaching students that what we know and what we do not know is not the end of the questioning: it is important to create a strong field of critical thought in the academy. When we leave out important facts and or areas of study, we do an injustice to an already colonially burdened system of education. It is amazing to see how quickly discussions on human evolution have recently changed and expanded our knowledge of the human past. However, many areas of the past remain bound by colonial restraints of time and place, denying civilisation, life, culture and humanity to Indigenous people and places. While it is great to see the recent changes and challenges to the status quo of discussions on human evolution, we have a long way to go within academia to create safe, open spaces for discussion of human evolution on a global scale.

Conclusion

It is clear from fossil evidence that where four-legged mammals go, so too do two-legged ones. It was never impossible for modern or archaic hominins to have migrated from the Eastern to the Western Hemisphere or the Western to the Eastern Hemisphere. It has been made impossible via colonial politics controlling the when and where of human evolution. I am not saying that hominins either did or did not migrate between the Eastern and Western Hemisphere at any given time. It is evident hominins were present in areas we know today as Asia and Siberia as early as 2 million years ago, and that mammals have been migrating between areas we know today as Siberia and Alaska for millions of years. What I am saying is that due to politics and colonisation, not many researchers have looked for early humans in the Western Hemisphere (the Americas). Those that did so intentionally, or who accidentally found sites earlier than 11,000–12,000 years BP, faced decades of ridicule and overly harsh critiques.

It is not science when certain locations of proto-primate evolution are not being discussed, when there is a blocking of funds for research in specific geographical areas, and when there is the threat of academic destruction for daring to look for early human sites in a given geographical area. This is not science, it is imperial control of the past and asserting power over the present and future. It is an embedded imperial and colonial control over history with a focus on creating socially acceptable memories of Indigenous people in empty lands discussed as *terra nullius*. Academics and researchers have a very difficult time gaining access to resources to study the human past in lands long claimed to be empty of humans prior to very recent dates on a global scale. New research is funded because there are other possibilities, because we do not know all there is to know about the human past.

Other ways of knowing, being, doing and telling stories support a more robust under-standing of the past and are pivotal to understanding the present and future. We should teach students that we are intelligent enough to understand, rather than deny, other ways of knowing, being and doing. When we put our minds together to learn from each other and to work to make the world a better place for all people only then will we begin to build a robust understanding of the human past. Though there is a lot to yet be unravelled regarding human evolution, we can claim with some certainty a few very basic points. We know that discussions of the human past within academia have historically been, and often remain, constrained by what defines a safe and acceptable discussion in a global social context. Stephen Jay Gould addressed the social context of science, arguing that:

> science must proceed in a social context and must be done by human beings emmeshed in the constraints of their culture, the throes of surrounding politics, and the hopes and dreams of their social and psychological construction.
>
> (Gould 2001, p. 7)

It is clear, that due to historical and ongoing colonisation of lands and people, that the time and place of many of the world's Indigenous peoples has been ignored in discussions of humanity's past and present. It is also evident, that Indigenous people hold a great deal of knowledge of their place within the world; as one of many clans. Academics and researchers have known for decades that some of their peers create stories based on speculation that they call hypotheses, which take on a life of their own as fact, yet often remain unsubstantiated. We also know that as scientists we can do much better. We can create safe spaces for a weaving of Western and Indigenous ways of knowing, being and doing. We can create a praxis in which all voices and knowledges have a place in discussing and contributing to human history and knowledge of human evolution on every continent. We can openly acknowledge our place and our possible bias in research and allow others to be aware of our place in the process. In teaching, academics can become aware of agnotology, of what is missing in their curriculum and their education, and fill in those missing bits to create a more substantial and informed pedagogy. Regarding human evolution, there have recently been some very good examples of research discussions resulting from remaining open minded and seeking knowledge that is outside of traditional linear stories of the human and primate past. Pivotal to advancing research on human evolution are discussions of colonisation and work towards decolonising and re-writing stories of the human and primate past on a global scale.

References

Adovasio, J, Donahue, D, Stuckenrath, R & Pedler, R 1998, 'Two decades of debate on Meadowcroft Rock Shelter', *North American Archaeologist*, vol. 19, no. 4, pp. 317–341.

Adovasio, JM & Page, J 2002, *The first Americans. In pursuit of archaeology's greatest mystery*, Random House, New York.

Battiste, M 2007, 'Research ethics for protecting Indigenous knowledge and heritage, institutional and research responsibilities', in N Denzin & MD Giardina (eds.), *Ethical futures in qualitative research: decolonizing the politics of knowledge*, Left Coast Press, Walnut Creek, CA, pp. 111–132.

Battiste, M 2013, 'You can't be the doctor if you're the disease: eurocentrism and Indigenous renaissance', CAUT Distinguished Academic Lecture.

Battiste, M 2017, *Decolonizing education: nourishing the learning spirit*, Purich Publishing Limited, Saskatoon, Canada.

Beard, C 2004, *The hunt for the dawn monkey: unearthing the origins of monkeys, apes, and humans*, University of California Press, Berkeley.

Begun, DR 2015, *The real planet of the apes: a new story of human origins*, Princeton University Press, Princeton, NJ.

Bloch, JI, Silcox, MT, Boyer, DM and Sargis, EJ 2007, 'New Paleocene skeletons and the relationship of plesiadapiforms to crown-clade primates', *Proceedings of the National Academy of Sciences*, vol. 104, no. 4, pp. 1159–1164.

Böhme, M, Spassov, N, Ebner, M, Geraads, D, Hristova, L, Kirscher, U, Kötter, S, Linnemann, U, Prieto, J, Roussiakis, S, Theodorou, G, Uhlig, G & Winklhofer, M 2017, 'Messinian age and savannah environment of the possible hominin Graecopithecus from Europe', *PLoS ONE*, vol. 12, no. 5, p. 0177347.

Bryan, AL & Gruhn, R 2003, 'Some difficulties in modeling the original peopling of the Americas', *Quaternary International*, vol. 109, pp. 175–179.

Calloway, CG 2004, *First Peoples: a documentary survey of American Indian history*, Bedford/St. Martin's Press, New York.

Cann, RL 1987, 'In search of Eve', *The Sciences*, vol. 27, no. 5, pp. 30–37.

Cann, RL, Stoneking, M & Wilson, AC 1987, 'Mitochondrial DNA and human evolution', *Nature*, vol. 325, no. 3, pp. 31–36.

Chilisa, B 2012, *Indigenous research methodologies*, Sage, Los Angeles, CA.

Churchill, W 2005, *Since predator came: notes from the struggle for American Indian liberation*, AK Press, Oakland, CA.

Clark, PU & Mix, AC 2002, 'Ice sheets and sea level of the Last Glacial Maximum', *Quaternary Science Reviews*, vol. 21, no. 1, pp. 1–7.

Cox, CB 2000, 'Plate tectonics, seaways and climate in the historical biogeography of mammals', *Memórias do Instituto Oswaldo Cruz*, vol. 95, no. 4, pp. 509–516.

Deloria, V Jr & Lytle, C 1984, *The nations within: the past and future of American Indian sovereignty*, Pantheon, New York.

Demere, T, Cerutti, RA & Majors, PC 1995, *San Diego Natural History Museum Hwy 54 Mastodon Site final report*, Prepared for Cal. Trans. District 11.

de Sousa Santos, B 2010, *Las epistemologías del sur*, Siglo XXI, Mexico.

Dillehay, TD 1999, 'The late Pleistocene cultures of South America', *Evolutionary Anthropology: Issues, News, and Reviews*, vol. 7, no. 6, pp. 206–216.

Dillehay, TD 2000, *The settlement of the America: a new prehistory*, Basic Books, New York.

Dugassa, BF 2011, 'Colonialism of mind: deterrent of social transformation', *Sociology Mind*, vol. 1, no. 2, pp. 55–64.

Erickson, R & Parkman, EB 2010, 'Mammoth rocks and the geology of the Sonoma Coast', Northern California Geological Society. Available from: www.ncgeolsoc.org/wp-content/uploads/2018/01/2010-1_Geology-Sonoma-Coast_MASTER.pdf [3 April 2019].

Fidel, SJ 1992, *Prehistory of the Americas*, 2nd edn, Cambridge University Press, Cambridge.

Fidel, SJ 1999, 'Artifact provenience at Monte Verde, confusion and contradictions', *Discovering Archaeology*, vol. 1, no. 6, pp. 1–12.

Figgins, JD & Cook, HJ 1927, *The antiquity of man in America*, American Museum of Natural History, Washington DC.

Fox, R & Scott, C 2011, 'A new, Early Puercan (earliest Paleocene) species of Purgatorius (plesiadapiformes, primates) from Saskatchewan, Canada', *Journal of Paleontology*, vol. 85, no. 3, pp. 537–548.

Fu, J, Wang, J & Tong, Y 2002, 'The new discovery of the Plesiadapiformes from the early Eocene of Wutu Basin, Shandong Province', *Vertebrata Pal. Asiatica*, vol. 40, no. 3, pp. 219–227.

Fuss, J, Spassov, N, Begun, DR & Böhme, M 2017, 'Potential hominin affinities of Graecopithecus from the Late Miocene of Europe', *PLoS ONE*, vol. 12, no. 5, p. e0177127.

Futuyma, DJ 2005, *Evolution*, Sinauer, Sunderland, MA.

Gao, X, Zhang, X, Yang, D, Shen, C & Wu, X 2010, 'Revisiting the origin of modern humans in China and its implications for global human evolution', *Science China Earth Sciences*, vol. 53, no. 12, pp. 1927–1940.

Gnecco, C & Ayala, P 2011, 'What is to be done? Elements for a discussion', in C Gnecco & P Ayala (eds.), *Indigenous peoples and archaeology in Latin America*, Left Coast Press, Walnut Creek, CA, pp. 11–27.

Gould, SJ 2001, 'Humbled by the genome's mysteries', *New York Times*, 19 February. Available from: https://www.nytimes.com/2001/02/19/opinion/humbled-by-the-genome-s-mysteries.html [5 January 2019].

Government of Canada 2008, 'Statement of apology to former students of Indian Residential Schools'. Available from: https://www.aadnc-aandc.gc.ca/eng/1100100015644/1100100015649 [5 January 2019].

Grosfoguel, R 2013, 'The structure of knowledge in westernized universities: epistemic racism/sexism and the four genocides/epistemicides of the long 16th century', *Human Architecture: Journal of the Sociology of Self-Knowledge*, vol. 11, no. 1, pp. 73–90.

Haynes, CV 1980, 'The Clovis culture', *Canadian Journal of Anthropology*, vol. 1, no. 1, pp. 115–121.

Heads, M 2010, 'Evolution and biogeography of primates: a new model based on molecular phylogenetics, vicariance and plate tectonics', *Zoologica Scripta*, vol. 39, no. 2, pp. 107–127.

Holen, SR & May, DW 2002, 'The La Sena and Shaffert mammoth sites', in DC Roper & RK Blasing (eds.), *Medicine Creek: seventy years of archaeological investigations*, University of Alabama Press, Tuscaloosa, pp. 20–36.

Holen, SR, Deméré, TA, Fisher, DC, Fullagar, R, Paces, JB, Jefferson, GT, Beeton, JM, Cerutti, RA, Rountrey, AN, Vescera, L & Holen, KA 2017, 'A 130,000-year-old archaeological site in southern California, USA', *Nature*. vol. 544, no. 7651, pp. 479–483. doi:10.1038/nature22065.

Hrdlička, A, Holmes, WH, Willis, B, Wright, FE & Fenner, CN 1912, *Early man in South America*, no. 52, US Government Printing Office., Washington DC.

Hublin, JJ, Ben-Ncer, A, Bailey, SE, Freidline, SE, Neubauer, S, Skinner, MM, Bergmann, I, Le Cabec, A, Benazzi, S, Harvati, K & Gunz, P 2017, 'New fossils from Jebel Irhoud, Morocco and the pan-African origin of *Homo sapiens*', *Nature*, vol. 546, no. 7657, pp. 289–292.

Joggins Fossil Institute 2019, 'Joggins Fossil Cliffs: early researchers and finds'. Available from: http://jogginsfossilcliffs.net/cliffs/history/ [5 January 2019].

Klein, RG 1989, *The human career: human biological and cultural origins*, University of Chicago Press, Chicago, IL.

Kovach, M 2009, *Indigenous methodologies: characteristics, conversations, and contexts*, University of Toronto Press, Toronto.

Larsen, CS 2008, *Our origins: discovering physical anthropology*, W.W, Norton, New York.

Lee, LL 2010, 'Navajo transformative scholarship in the twenty-first century', *Wicazo Sa Review*, vol. 25, no. 1, pp. 33–45.

Ludwin, RS, Smits, GJ, Carver, D, James, K, Jonientz-Trisler, C, McMillan, AD, Losey, R, Dennis, R, Rasmussen, J, De Los Angeles, A, Buerge, D, Thrush, CP, Clague, J, Bowechop, J & Wray, J 2007, 'Folklore and earthquakes: Native American oral traditions from Cascadia compared with written traditions from Japan', *Geological Society, London, Special Publications*, vol. 273, no. 1, pp. 67–94.

Ni, X, Gebo, DL, Dagosto, M, Meng, J, Tafforeau, P, Flynn, JJ & Beard, KC 2013, 'The oldest known primate skeleton and early haplorhine evolution', *Nature*, vol. 498, pp. 60–64.

Nova 2018, 'Meet your ancestors', Public Broadcasting Service. Available from: https://www.pbs.org/wgbh/nova/evolution/meet-your-ancestors.html [5 January 2019].

Pääbo, S 2015, 'The diverse origins of the human gene pool', *Nature Reviews Genetics*, vol. 16, pp. 313–314.

Proctor, R & Schiebinger, L 2008, *Agnotology: the making and unmaking of ignorance*, Stanford University Press, Stanford, CA.

Rose, KD & Bown, TM 1982, 'New plesiadapiform primates from the Eocene of Wyoming and Montana', *Journal of Vertebrate Paleontology*, vol. 2, no. 1, pp. 63–69.

Rose, KD, Godinot, M & Bown, TM 1994, 'The early radiation of Euprimates and the initial diversification of Omomyidae', in JG Fleagle & RF Kay (eds.), *Anthropoid origins*, Springer, Boston, pp. 1–28.

Scott, CS, Fox, RC & Redman, CM 2016, 'A new species of the basal plesiadapiform Purgatorius (mammalia, primates) from the early Paleocene Ravenscrag Formation, Cypress Hills, southwest Saskatchewan, Canada: further taxonomic and dietary diversity in the earliest primates', *Canadian Journal of Earth Sciences*, vol. 53, no. 4, pp. 343–354.

Silcox, MT 2014, 'Primate Origins and the Plesiadapiforms', *Nature Education Knowledge*, vol. 5, no. 3 p. 1.

Silcox, MT, Bloch, JI, Sargis, EJ & Boyer, D 2005, 'Euarchonta Dermoptera, Scandentia, Primates', in KD Rose & JD Archibald (eds.), *The rise of placental mammals*, Johns Hopkins University Press, Baltimore, MD, pp. 127–144.

Silko, LM 1996, 'Landscape, history, and the Pueblo imagination', in C Glotfelty & H Fromm (eds.), *The ecocriticism reader: landmarks in literary ecology*, University of Georgia Press, Athens, GA and London, pp. 264–275.

Sinclair, R 2003, 'Indigenous research in social work: the challenge of operationalizing worldview', *Native Social Work Journal*, vol. 5, pp. 117–139.

Sium, A & Ritskes, E 2013, 'Speaking truth to power: Indigenous storytelling as an act of living resistance', *Decolonization: Indigeneity, Education and Society*, vol. 2, no. 1, pp. i–x.

Society Matters 2010, 'Jared Diamond sued by Indigenous people', 17 November. Available from: http://societymatters.org/2010/11/17/jared-diamond-sued-for-45-million/ [5 January 2019].

Stankiewicz, J, Thiart, C, Masters, JC & Wit, MJ 2006, 'Did lemurs have sweepstake tickets? An exploration of Simpson's model for the colonization of Madagascar by mammals', *Journal of Biogeography*, vol. 33, no. 2, pp. 221–235.

Steeves, PF 2015, 'Decolonizing Indigenous histories: Pleistocene archaeology sites of the Western Hemisphere', Ph.D. thesis, State University of New York at Binghamton.

Thorne, AG & Wolpoff, MH 1992, 'The multiregional evolution of humans', *Scientific American*, vol. 266, no. 4, pp. 76–83.

Van Valen, L & Sloan, RE 1965, 'The earliest primates', *Science*, vol. 150, no. 3697, pp. 743–745.

Watts, V 2013, 'Indigenous place-thought and agency amongst humans and non-humans (First Woman and Sky Woman go on a European world tour)', *Decolonization, Indigeneity, Education & Society*, vol. 2, no. 1, pp. 20–34.

Whitten, P & Nickels, MK 1983, 'Our forebears' forebears', *The Sciences*, vol. 23, no. 1, pp. 20–29.

Wilford, JN 2013, 'Palm-size fossil resets primates' clock, scientists say', *New York Times*, 5 June. Available from: https://www.nytimes.com/2013/06/06/science/palm-size-fossil-resets-primates-clock-scientists-say.html [3 April 2019].

Wilson, S 2008, *Research is ceremony: Indigenous research methods*, Fernwood Publishing, Halifax, Nova Scotia.

Wilson, WA 2005, *'Remember this!' Dakota decolonization and the Eli Taylor narratives*. University of Nebraska Press, Lincoln and London.

Zolbrod, PG 1987, *Diné bahane': the Navajo creation story*, University of New Mexico Press, Albuquerque.

13

'IF WE ARE ALL AFRICAN, THEN I AM NOTHING'

Hominin evolution and the politics of identity in South Africa

Amanda Esterhuysen

Introduction

South Africa is renowned for its fossil hominin finds. Interest in the fossil specimens has been created, in equal part, by a number of well-preserved specimens, and the often-charismatic personalities who with confidence and persistence continue to make discoveries and keep the science in the public eye. Often the tales of discovery become household knowledge, because the announcement of each find is a well-choreographed media event. The scientific import is simplified for the public and usually takes the form of the 'first', 'oldest', 'most-complete' and/or 'new species', and the media performance includes an impressive display of technological innovations either used to make the discovery, or to scan and reconstruct the finds.

The hominin fossils are found predominantly in dolomitic cave infills in the interior of South Africa. The first discoveries date back to the early phase of gold mining on the Witwatersrand. Initially gold was extracted from the weathered surface zone of the exposed gold reefs through coarse crushing and the use of mercury amalgam, but once deeper sulphidic ores were reached, the amalgam method became inefficient and uneconomic (Katz 1995; Tutu, McCarthy & Cukrowska 2008). The boom years were thus followed by a short period in the early 1890s, when mines and associated dumps of untreated tailings started to be abandoned (Katz 1995). The industry was revived through the introduction of the MacArthur-Forrest cyanidation process in 1892, which created an immediate demand for lime. Limestone quarries sprung up in areas of exposed dolomite, and the search for travertine exposed subterranean caves and vast collections of fossils. Scientists began to work in collaboration with mine foremen who sent them examples of the rich fossiliferous deposits, and when with further advances in gold extraction the demand for lime ceased, mined caves continued to be worked by scientists (Kuykendall & Štrkalj 2007, p. 37). The ensuing years produced a string of important finds that placed South Africa at the forefront of studies in hominin evolution. These included: the discovery of an infant *Australopithecus africanus* in 1924, the first adult Australopithecine (1936), *Paranthropus robustus* (1938), the most complete skull of *Australopithecus africanus* (Mrs Ples) (1947), *Australopithecus prometheus* (1948, 1999), *Homo ergaster*

(1953), *Homo habilis* (1976), *Australopithecus sediba* (2010) and *Homo naledi* (2013).[1] Each find has shifted the boundaries of the discipline, reset the chronologies (currently the early hominins date to between 300,000 and 3.6 million BP), provided new insights into complex evolutionary pathways, and tested the credibility of the science.[2]

In its formative years palaeoanthropology and archaeology enjoyed considerable political support; it was a source of national pride and fast became internationally competitive (Dubow 1995; 2007). However, while scientists working in South Africa developed the science locally, using and creating new terminology, their early interpretations were influenced by Western thinking that at the time was firmly invested in categorising, differentiating and ordering people (Fabian 1983). In the first part of the chapter I present two different responses to hominin evolution voiced after the end of apartheid, and during the period in office of successive ANC presidents Nelson Mandela, Thabo Mbeki, and Jacob Zuma, each with their own influence on schooling, science development and heritage. The first is a reaction against the use of hominin evolution and associated sites to develop a historical narrative common to both white and black people, a reconciliatory step towards a new nationalism. The second is a bold rejection of hominin evolution, not as an affront to religion, but as a Western science. Each illustrates how the lived reality of South Africans has affected acceptance of and tolerance for the politics of new nationalism and created a mistrust of Western science. The second part of the chapter examines more closely the history of the growth of palaeoanthropology and archaeology and its complicity in racialising and supporting the differential treatment of people based on colour. It shows how the uptake of hominin evolution in schools and some universities has been partly hindered through religious misgivings, but the main source of resistance from students at universities is attendant to an impatience with and lack of transformation in the field.

Part I: two responses

Response one: 'If we are all African, then I am nothing.'

This unsettling, but incontrovertible statement, was made by a young black teenager participating in the finals of a South Africa-wide school competition in 2002. The theme 'Our Roots are Speaking', was intended to stimulate a debate about 'Heritage: History, Values and Creativity', and was part of a larger government initiative to try to encourage learners and teachers to become involved in and recognise the value of teaching and learning about history.[3] Following in the footsteps of President Nelson Mandela, Thabo Mbeki, elected in 1999, recognised the socio-political role that heritage could play in promoting reconciliation, and the need for a new historical memory that would invoke pride, humanity and a sense of achievement amongst all its peoples. Patriotism and nation-building was to be achieved through a number of different government departments and initiatives. The National Heritage Resources Act (NHRA 25 of 1999) took the lead in stressing the role of heritage in healing and providing material and symbolic restitution for a country with a schizophrenic, highly racialised national memory. Prior to 1999 the national heritage landscape was dominated by colonial art, architecture, and science (Deacon & Pistorius 1996), and African heritage occupied a different historic space. After 1999 sites declared under the new Act were more representative of an African past, and the material and oral evidence was intended to give rise to a new black African historiography,[4] highlight the social injustice of the apartheid years, and emphasise the historic struggle of the ANC. A new narrative was needed to re-define what it meant to be South African, and this storyline would find its way into schools through the Ministerial History project promoted by the then minister of education, the late Kadar Asmal. Thabo Mbeki flew the banner of an African Renaissance which focused the national narrative on the rediscovery of a glorious precolonial past. He acknowledged oral history as a valid source of information, and valorised African intellectuals and indigenous knowledge systems (see for example Mbeki 1996; 2005). After 1999 he was able to project South Africanism further back in time to an African *naissance* through the listing of the hominin fossil sites of Sterkfontein, Swartkrans, Kromdraai and associated sites as a World Heritage Site. South Africa appropriated the Out-of-Africa origins story – i.e. that Africa gave rise to the earliest hominins and to modern humans – through site branding, and the Sterkfontein Valley sites, and later two other fossil sites in different provinces were christened the 'Cradle of Humankind World Heritage Site' (COH WHS). The World Heritage Site was both a source of national pride and international relevance. African *naissance* and the Out-of-Africa hypothesis provided a means of debunking the myth that 'nothing good ever came out of Africa' (Tobias 2002, pp. 6, 10) and Mbeki demonstrated his political support by attending the announcement of the discovery of 'Little Foot' – a near complete australopithecine fossil from Sterkfontein Caves, which currently holds the title of being the oldest and most complete fossil found in southern Africa. Later, when opening Maropeng, the COH WHS official centre, Mbeki recited a lyrical speech in which he situated Africa, and South Africa firmly at the centre of history, and provided a moment in time when all people shared a past (Bonner, Esterhuysen & Jenkins 2007b, p. 276; Naidu 2008):

> I would ask you to be very still. If we are very still, we will hear, if we really listen, these rocks and stones speaking to us today.
>
> They are the voices of our distant ancestors, who still lie buried in them. The voices of my ancestors and yours!
>
> You see, in Africa, things are seldom what they seem. And so I would say to everyone, welcome home!
>
> *(Thabo Mbeki, Official opening of the Maropeng Visitors centre,*
> *at the Cradle of Humankind, Gauteng, 7 December 2005)*

It was against this celebration of universal Africanism and South African nationalism that the student made her pronouncement.

Response two: 'No one will dig old monkey bones to back up a theory that I was once a baboon – sorry.'

This second response was tweeted on 12 September 2015 by former General Secretary of the Congress of South African Trade Unions, Zwelinzima Vavi, during the announcement of *Homo naledi* in Johannesburg.

At an education and heritage symposium held in March 2009, the ANCs chief whip Dr Mathole Motshekga referred to the COH WHS as 'the cradle of baboons', and like Zwelinzima Vavi lashed out following the announcement of *Homo naledi* to dismiss Lee Berger's Rising Star finds as pseudo-science, and an affront to Africans.

'This thing is inconsistent with reality and supports the theory that we are subhuman. That's why Africans aren't respected by the rest of the world,' he said.

He explained the western materialist theory, which states that 'we are subhumans who developed from the animal kingdom. Therefore they (the west) gave us the title of subhuman beings to justify slavery and colonialism.'

(Report on an interview with eNCA, 11 September 2015, Botha 2015)

The South African Council of Churches (SACC) also came out in support of Vavi's tweet, and while one might expect the church to come out against human evolution, the overwhelming impression was that the Council of Churches added the charge of racism to bolster their theological argument against hominin evolution. Just as the SACC historically had denounced religiously justified racism, they now turned against evolution as a racist science. Whether their motives were doctrinal or political, there is little contention that in pre- and apartheid South Africa, scientifically and religiously justified racism ran in parallel. At a conference of educators held in 1996, white educationists with a strong Christian upbringing disclosed their conviction that they had been created while black people evolved.[5] During workshops held in the black townships of Soweto and Kagiso it became evident that black people regarded activities at Sterkfontein with suspicion because they believed the motive behind the excavation was to prove that the 'blacks' had evolved from apes. Hominin evolution thus not only touched on religious sensitivities but cut to the core of South African identity politics. While the church was castigated during the Truth and Reconciliation Commission, science, for its part, was never called to book.

The 'inferiority' mentioned in the quote arose not from a point of ignorance about science – as many respondents to the twitter feed and news articles suggested (see for example, MMO-Champion 2018) – it resulted from a deep history of science being used to create a difference between black and white bodies.

Part II: a history

Christian National Education (CNE) as a pedagogic framework was adopted by the Afrikaner nationalists after 1948 to reinforce a racist creationist ideology. CNE explicitly set out to Christianise *all* South Africans, but the rationale for 'Christianising' different 'races' differed. A conservative Afrikaner Nationalist interpretation of the Bible provided ideological rationalisation for racial separation (Dubow 1992) and was taught to White children so that they could understand race relations, economic disparity and appreciate their god-ordained superiority (Christie 1991, pp. 185–186). Black and Coloured people were regarded as 'tribal', untamed heathens (Jeppe 1946, p. 1758), and needed to be guided by the White man to Christianity to 'secure him against his own heathen and all kinds of ideologies which promise him sham happiness ...' (Christian National Education Policy 1949, Articles 14 & 15, quoted in Enslin 1984, p. 140). The Christian Bible was regarded as the foundation of the curriculum, and all teachers wanting to teach in public schools were obliged to be trained in biblical instruction. Evolution was excluded from all school curricula before 1994, and some universities, whilst teaching palaeontology and archaeology, did little to promote it beyond the academy, while museums that included displays on evolution were obliged to provide an alternative creationist interpretation (Bonner, Esterhuysen & Jenkins 2007b, p. 276). However, while the use of religion to justify the legalisation of slavery and apartheid is by now a familiar refrain, to fully appreciate the resentment of evolutionary science one needs to reflect on how the pre- and apartheid government drew readily on the palaeo-sciences to support racism and inequality (Dubow 1992; 1995).

Wallerstein (2003) explained how after the French Revolution 'equality' was redefined by the liberal state to create different categories of citizens in order to protect the classes, and to manage the transformation of the 'barbarian to civilised' (Wallerstein 2003, pp. 650–653). The 'hierarchy of stages', derived largely from the work of social evolutionists like Morgan (1877, p. 13), presented a global template for social change that started at 'savagery' and progressed to 'civilisation'. These ideas remained central to archaeological thought until after the Second World War (see for example Childe 1950; for an overview, Gosden 1999, p. 64). In South Africa during the early part of the twentieth century the scientific and cultural organisations helped to shape and bolster the emergent White nation state (Dubow 2007, p. 15), by ensuring that whiteness was tied to advancement and progress. This was in part supported by archaeological 'evidence' that black people were in a state of degeneration or had become trapped at different developmental stages of evolution (Trigger 1989). In a section of a speech delivered in London in 1917, Jan Smuts drew on archaeological examples to illustrate his discussion about the South African 'racial experiment' and associated risks:

> We know that on the African Continent at various times there have been attempts at civilisation. We read of a great Saracen civilisation in Central Africa, and of the University of Timbuctoo, to which students came from other parts of the world. Rhodesia also shows signs of former civilisation. Where are those civilisations now? They have all disappeared, and barbarism once more rules over the land ...
>
> *(Smuts 1917, p. 76)*

In 1925, Smuts, while president of the South African Association for the Advancement of Science, coined the phrase 'cradle of mankind'. However, unlike Mbeki who tried to use the concept to build a new South Africa, Smuts saw it as an opportunity to promote White domination (Bonner 2007, pp. 1–2; Dubow 2007). He saw in one 'the leading race of the world, while the other, though still living ... a mere human fossil verging to extinction' (quoted in Schlanger 2003, p. 9). While these ideas are easily dismissed as being outdated and typical of the period, one cannot overlook the social and economic consequences.

Economic growth in South Africa depended on maintaining a 'backward' and an advanced sector (Wolpe 1972, p. 433) to ensure an unlimited supply of cheap labour, and these sectors were scientifically engineered along racial lines. Job reservation laws were promulgated from 1911, particularly in the mining sector, to place a ceiling on progression and development of black workers (Moodie 2005). Although by 1920 the economic and political power of the capitalist sector had succeeded in this (Wolpe 1972, p. 433), theories about social development continued to be used to fix groups of people in time and space (Fabian 1983). Africans were studied, and their practices and behaviours often reduced to the crudest racial stereotypes and categories (Crush 1994; Mamdani 2012; Parnell 2003). By 1926 the use of black Africans in any skilled position was illegal (Allen 1992; Lang 1986), and job reservation ensured that social progress was measured against a colour bar. Of course, as Bonner (2007, p. 205) pointed out, it is ironic that whites 'so endowed with powers of civilization' needed artificial protection, or that they needed scientific programmes specifically designed to rehabilitate poor whites between 1925 and 1930 (Clynick 2007, pp. 261–264).

In short, black South Africans became excluded from politics, and stripped of their rights as individuals and citizens (Agamben 1998, p. 90). To justify this inequality, the difference between black and white bodies had to be constantly reinforced. African people in the rural areas were regarded as wild and untamed (Moodie 2005), and the Khoisan were treated as curiosities to be exhibited in city centres (Gordon 1999). In the urban areas, as studies of the spatial engineering (Ally & Lissoni 2012; Parnell 2003) and the history of black people on the mines attest, black bodies became synonymous with disease, sexuality and brutality (Breckenridge 1998; Crush 1994; Moodie 2005). Race and racial fear were given meaning through the agency of human beings within these historical and social contexts (Roediger 1994, p. 2), and politics, science and religion made it morally acceptable, natural and normal (Butler 2004; Grant & Jungkunz 2016, p. 4). It is notable that during his term of office President Mbeki was very sensitive and susceptible to the association of African bodies with promiscuity and disease, and he justified his support of the AIDS dissidents partly through his attitude to Western treatment, and its use of African bodies for experimentation (Comaroff 2007, p. 214).

After the Second World War the invention of radiometric dating changed the age of the earth and added considerable time depth to Africa. Thousands of years became millions of years and the earliest African innovation predated anything in Europe by many thousands of years. It proved what many scientists had expected, that hominins had evolved in Africa. This knowledge, however, did not do much to change misconceptions of Africa's degenerated state, nor did it reverse the rationale of classifying people according to ethnic units to underscore difference and separation. In her study of presentations of hominin evolution in museums, Scott (2007, p. 234) sardonically sums up how Europeans continue to protect and project their own advancement at the expense of 'primitive' Africans. Many people of European ancestry, like Smuts before them, are happy to accept that Africa is the cradle of humankind as long as Europe is seen as the 'evolutionary finishing school' (Scott 2007, p. 234).

Presentations of the past in museums have been heavily criticised for giving material expression to racist stereotypes, and for lending them credibility they do not deserve (Bachelard 1964; Davidson 1998, pp. 145–159). Equally, illustrations in both 'scientific' and popular books on human evolution have been critiqued for the racist and androcentric messages that they persistently convey (see for example, Wiber 1998). It has been long recognised that the notion of the linear march of progress or the 'ascent of man' is 'woefully flawed' (Gould 1989) yet it remains one of the more popular ways of depicting the evolution of 'man'. Apart from being scientifically incorrect, these illustrations still convey the disturbing subtext that progress is synonymous with being a white male (Wiber 1998). Wiber (1998, p. 2) and Scott (2007) have both highlighted how, in depictions of emerging *Homo sapiens*, the early hominid forms are more 'ape-like' and 'Negroid in feature', while representations of later hominins exhibit less hair and become fair skinned. Wiber (1998) adds that displays of early stone tools also support the message of linear progress. The result being that:

> Primates and modern hunter/gatherer populations are coded as primitive while euro-American whiteness and explicitly masculine technology act as conventions of progress; these codes are pervasive an element of reconstructive scientific illustrations …
>
> *(Wiber 1998, p. 2)*

These stereotypes still persist in representations of hominins in the Cradle of Humankind today. In 1999, amidst much protest from scientists, the Cradle of Humankind's Management Authority chose a logo that contained the 'march of progress'. In an attempt to placate the academics a breast was added to the front figure in an effort to feminise an otherwise obviously European male. Eventually the parade of hominins was shortened to three figures. In the museum's display hairy and naked dark-skinned, ape-like models of the early hominins still result in finger pointing, name-calling and embarrassment amongst local visitors. In popular publications and school textbooks, there is slippage between the idea that objects can be regarded as units of ethnic identity, associated ancient DNA being representative of that ethnic group, and ethnic groups being dealt with as separate breeding units (Kreita & Kittles 1997, p. 535). This generally minimises the 'reality of variation', and more problematically continues to project the Khoisan as fixed and unchanging 'proto-Africans' (Kreita & Kittles 1997, p. 539).

Part III: discussion

The anger expressed by the teenager in 2002 arose out of years of segregated, inferior education and a society that reified whiteness. In her mind, to be African was to have endured a specific and oppressive past, a past that had defined her present profoundly. Her identity, like that of politicians Zwelinzima Vavi and Mathole Motshekga, exists in opposition to the Western constructions of African history and of African people. Their sense of self is imbricated with slavery, colonialism and apartheid (see Mbembe & Rendall 2002 for broader discussion on the construction of African identity), and this identity cannot be erased or appropriated to appease or make Europeans feel at home.

In 1996 the then Deputy Director of Curriculum Development asked researchers to investigate whether hominid evolution could be taught in the classroom. Specifically, to investigate how social science teachers felt about teaching this 'sensitive' topic and to assess whether pupils could cope with the content (Esterhuysen & Smith 1998). At the time the only 'official' information that had been made available to social science teachers by the Department of Education (1995) comprised two paragraphs that reduced hominin/human evolution to the discovery of *Australopithecus africanus* by Professor Raymond Dart and 'other discoveries' at similar sites. The focus had been carefully placed on the discoveries and not on hominin evolution at all.

Research was carried out in ten primary schools and ten secondary schools. At the time schools were still racially segregated and a local museum curator who spoke a number of different languages was enlisted to translate the content. In this way researchers were able to compare learners' and teachers' responses across the colour divide. From the study it was apparent that issues around 'race' and 'colour' were important to black learners, but less so to white learners (Esterhuysen & Smith 1998), and the researchers suggested that this was possibly due to the 'naturalisation of whiteness' (Roediger 1994, p. 19).

Twenty years later, first-year students enrolled in an English-speaking university were asked to 'write a history of South Africa, in the way you see, remember or understand it' (Angier 2017). All of these students had left school between 2010 and 2015 and had studied history up to Grade 12 and attended integrated schools. The researcher found that histories written by white students more often included human origins. They included the Cradle of Humankind and emphasised a common past at the expense of the more recent period of apartheid. By contrast black students started their stories in the twentieth century, and focused on the formation of the ANC, the Sharpville massacre, the Soweto uprisings and the first democratic election (Angier 2017, p. 162). Angier concluded that black and coloured learners reflected on race in a way that white learners do not, and that 'lived experience [was] at least as powerful as the official curriculum in shaping historical consciousness' (Angier 2017).

Although religion is still regarded as the barrier to understanding evolution, studies carried out amongst trainee and in-service teachers suggest that the problem is more complex. For example, a survey among biology teachers at historically Afrikaans-speaking universities was carried out to gauge their willingness to teach the topic, and their knowledge of evolution. The results showed that while the majority claimed to be religious, and most rejected the theory of evolution, most participants displayed a poor understanding of and harboured many misconceptions about evolution (Abrie 2010). A study carried out in 2016 amongst 336 pre- and in-service english and biology teachers in KwaZulu-Natal, South Africa, demonstrated that teachers with a religious affiliation held nuanced and diverse views. For example, it was found that Protestants tend to be more creationist than Catholics, Hindu teachers experienced no conflict at all, and that a substantial proportion believed it possible to hold different views at same time (Stears et al. 2016, p. 8). This research also indicated that teachers were happy to teach the evolution of living organisms but tried to avoid teaching hominin evolution (Stears et al. 2016, p. 1). This predisposition was supported by a focus group study carried out in 2017 to test the level and suitability of materials to be exhibited at the Cradle of Humankind Exhibition Centre in Maropeng. Teachers were most comfortable with evolution at the molecular level (DNA), and less so with hominin evolution. Amongst the reasons listed was that the socio-political context in South Africa is making it increasingly more difficult for teachers and lecturers to introduce primitive 'ape-like' creatures as ancestors in Africa. The tropes associated with primitivism and Africanism are painful triggers in what is a racially charged society and are no longer tolerated. For example, in 2016 popular satirical cartoonist Zapiro was publicly castigated for depicting the National Prosecuting Authority's director as President Zuma's organ grinding monkey (Staff Reporter 2017), and in the same year a real estate agent was heavily fined by the Equality Court for hate speech, which included calling black people monkeys (Le Roux 2016). More recently (2018) a popular DJ was fired for calling a black politician a monkey on the radio (Timeslive 2018).

In universities hominin evolution is still monopolised by white, often foreign researchers. The universal importance of the science is used to justify and mobilise international interest, funding and networks. But in South Africa it still carries the burden of history, and many of its tropes and popular constructions continue to create a barrier for young black scientists. Some black researchers justify doing 'white' science through an Africanist lens, and in some cases find acceptance by summoning African belief systems and ancestral ties.[6] Many find it distasteful that African history still achieves prominence and acceptance through the work of white intellectuals, and the call for the decolonisation of science is becoming louder. Along with calls to pull down 'apartheid' statues, there has been an appeal for Western science to be thrown out so that Africans can start from scratch.[7] Further, calls to 'cut the throat of whiteness'[8] have been taken up by more populist political proponents.

The question is, how does one begin to decentre what is quintessentially a European intellectual space and remove the social and psychological barriers that prevent black scholars from participating in palaeoscience? The historical baggage cannot be ignored and the role that evolutionary science played in reinforcing difference and inequality, particularly in South Africa, needs to be given more than just an apologetic nod, it requires deconstructing and recasting the language and idiom of the science.

In 1986 Professor Njabulo Ndebele delivered a lecture at the Jubilee Conference of the English Academy of South Africa on the 'evolving place of English' in South Africa given the various colonial and economic interests that it served (Ndebele 1987, p. 3). At that time Ndebele pointed out that talk about 'reform' and 'change', from the vantage point of white South Africans, revolved around what black people needed to 'be speedily introduced to' to 'become "responsible" citizens of the future' (Ndebele 1987, p. 8). It was 'premised not on what the whites of South Africa may have to unlearn' but on the '"humanization" of the oppressed according to the specifications of South African capital' and stipulations of the 'international corporate world' (Ndebele 1987, p. 8). The assumption that racism in science will disappear through the speedy training of black palaeoscientists is similarly flawed. It will take a new vocabulary to disentangle the associations of 'whiteness' with 'progress', 'super-iority', and 'normality', and a considered re-imagining of the discursive and visual explanations of the science in a way that does not offer redemption to white South Africans at the expense of black South Africans.

Conclusion

Resistance to human evolution in South Africa has resulted from a long and complex history of racism and inequality buttressed by both science and religion. The transformation in palaeoanthropology has been slow despite or because of new jingoistic narratives and lack of transformation. Palaeosciences will need to address barriers faced by black scholars and recast the disciplines so that new generations of black palaeoscientists can find acceptance and be celebrated as evolutionary scientists within South Africa.

Notes

1 Key publications include Dart (1948); Broom et al. (1950); Broom & Robinson (1952); Brain (1958); Tobias (1965); Partridge et al. (1999); Berger et al. (2010); Clarke (2013); Berger et al. (2015).
2 These would include criticism of Dart's 'man the hunter hypothesis' by Brain (1981), and critique of Berger's claim for early ritual at Rising Star (Val 2016).
3 The Ministerial History project was launched in 2001. Values and democracy promoted the teaching of archaeology and evolution as part of history.
4 The late professor Kadar Asmal, then minister of education, undertook to place a textbook on Apartheid in every classroom.
5 Presented on behalf of the SAAA Education Standing Committee. Conference of the Historical Association of South Africa and the South African Association for History Teaching, Potchefstroom, January 1996.
6 Dr Nonhlanhla Vilakazi, one of the few palaeontologists with a Ph.D., is also a sangoma and regards the analysis of ancient bones in the same light as throwing the bones through divination.
7 During student protests in 2016, along with the calls for university fees to be lowered, students called for Western science to be done away with. One event that took place at UCT became highly publicised on YouTube (UCT Scientist 2016) and stimulated much debate.
8 Julius Malema, leader of the Economic Freedom Fighters, repeatedly alludes to the politics of whiteness, and made the call to 'cut the throat' of whiteness at the launch of the party's election campaign on 3 March 2018.

References

Abrie, AL 2010, 'Student teachers' attitudes towards and willingness to teach evolution in a changing South African environment', *Journal of Biological Education*, vol. 44, no. 3, pp. 102–107.

Agamben, G 1998, *Homo sacer*, trans. D Heller-Roazen, Stanford University Press, Stanford, CA.

Allen, VL 1992, *The history of the black mineworkers in South Africa: volume one*, The Moor Press, Keighley.

Ally, S & Lissoni, A 2012, 'Let's talk about Bantustans', *South African Historical Journal*, vol. 64, no. 1, pp. 1–4.

Angier, K 2017, 'In search of historical consciousness: an investigation into young South Africans' knowledge and national histories', *London Review of Education*, vol. 15, no. 2, pp. 155–173.

Bachelard, G 1964, *Poetics of space*, Orion Press, New York.

Berger, LR, de Ruiter, DJ, Churchill, SE, Schmid, P, Carlson, KJ, Dirks, PHGM & Kibii, JM 2010, '*Australopithecus sediba*: a new species of *Homo*-like australopith from South Africa', *Science*, vol. 328, no. 5975, pp. 195–204.

Berger, LR, Hawks, J, de Ruiter, DJ, Churchill, SE, Schmid, P, Delezene, LK, Kivell, TL, Garvin, HM & Williams, SA 2015, '*Homo naledi*, a new species of the genus *Homo* from the Dinaledi Chamber, South Africa', *eLife*, vol. 4, no. 09560.

Bonner, P 2007, 'The racial paradox: Sterkfontein, Smuts and segregation', in P Bonner, A Esterhuysen & T Jenkins (eds), *A search for origins. Science, history and South Africa's 'cradle of humankind'*, University of the Witwatersrand Press, Johannesburg, pp. 201–205.

Bonner, P, Esterhuysen, A & Jenkins, T (eds) 2007a, *A search for origins. Science, history and South Africa's 'cradle of humankind'*, University of the Witwatersrand Press, Johannesburg.

Bonner, P, Esterhuysen, A & Jenkins, T 2007b, 'Voice of politics, voice of science: politics and science after 1945', in P Bonner, A Esterhuysen & T Jenkins (eds), *A search for origins. Science, history and South Africa's 'cradle of humankind'*, University of the Witwatersrand Press, Johannesburg, pp. 275–278.

Botha, B 2015, '*Homo naledi* promotes Africans as subhuman'. Mathole Motshekga, eNCA. Available from: www.enca.com/south-africa/homo-naledi-promotes-africans-subhuman-mothole-motshekga [29 March 2018].

Brain, CK 1958, *The Transvaal ape-man-bearing cave deposits*, Transvaal Museum Memoir #13, Transvaal Museum, Pretoria.

Brain, CK 1981, *The hunters or the hunted*, Chicago University Press, Chicago, IL.

Breckenridge, K 1998, 'The allure of violence: men, race and masculinity on the South African goldmines 1900–1950', *Journal of Southern African Studies*, vol. 24, no. 4, pp. 669–693.

Broom, R, Robinson, JT & Schepers, GWH 1950, *Sterkfontein ape-man Plesianthropus*, Transvaal Museum Memoir #4, Transvaal Museum, Pretoria.

Broom, R & Robinson, JT 1952, *Swartkrans ape-man Paranthropus crassidens*, Transvaal Museum Memoir #6, Transvaal Museum, Pretoria.

Butler, J 2004, *Precarious life. Powers of mourning and violence*, Verso, London.

Childe, VG 1950, 'The urban revolution', *The Town Planning Review*, vol. 21, no. 1, pp. 3–17.

Christie, P 1991, *The right to learn*, 2nd edn, SACHED/Ravan Press, Johannesburg.

Clarke, R 2013, '*Australopithecus* from Sterkfontein Caves, South Africa' in K Reed, J Fleagle & R Leakey (eds), *The paleobiology of Australopithecus. Vertebrate paleobiology and paleoanthropology*, Springer, Dordrecht, pp. 105–123.

Clynick, T 2007, 'White South Africa's weak sons: poor whites and the Hartebeespoort dam', in P Bonner, A Esterhuysen & T Jenkins (eds), *A search for origins. Science, history and South Africa's 'cradle of humankind'*, University of the Witwatersrand Press, Johannesburg, pp. 248–274.

Comaroff, J 2007, 'Beyond bare life: AIDS, (bio)politics, and the neoliberal order', *Public Culture*, vol. 19, no. 1, pp. 197–219.

Crush, J 1994, 'Scripting the compound: power and space in the South African mining industry', *Environment and Planning D: Society and Space*, vol. 12, no. 3, pp. 301–324.

Dart, R 1948, 'The Makapansgat proto-human Australopithecus Prometheus', *American Journal of Physical Anthropology*, vol. 6, pp. 259–283.

Davidson, P 1998, 'Museums and the reshaping of memory', in C Coetzee & S Nuttall (eds), *Negotiating the past: the making of memory in South Africa*, Oxford University Press, Cape Town, pp. 143–160.

Deacon, J & Pistorius, P 1996, 'Introduction and historical background to the conservation of monuments and sites in South Africa', in J Deacon (ed.), *Monuments and sites – South Africa*, ICOMOS, Colombo, Sri Lanka.

Department of Education, Curriculum Technical Sub-committee: History Sub-committee 1995, *History support materials standards 3–7*, Government Press, Pretoria.

Dubow, S 1992, 'Afrikaner nationalism, apartheid and the conceptualization of race', *Journal of African History*, vol. 33, no. 2, pp. 209–237.

Dubow, S 1995, *Scientific racism in modern South Africa*, Cambridge University Press, Cambridge.

Dubow, S 2007, 'White South Africa and the South Africanisation of science: humankind or kinds of humans', in P Bonner, A Esterhuysen & T Jenkins (eds), *A search for origins. Science, history and South Africa's 'cradle of humankind'*, University of the Witwatersrand Press, Johannesburg, pp. 9–12.

Enslin, P 1984, 'The role of fundamental pedagogics in the formulation of education policy in South Africa', in P Kallaway (ed.), *Apartheid and education. The education of Black South Africans*, Ravan Press, Johannesburg, pp. 139–147.

Esterhuysen, AB & Smith, J 1998, 'Evolution: "the forbidden word"', *South African Archaeological Bulletin*, vol. 53, pp. 135–137.

Fabian, J 1983, *Time and the other: how anthropology makes its object*, Columbia University Press, New York.

Federasie van Afrikaanse Kultuurvereeniginge 1948, *Instituut vir Christelike-Nationale Onderwys, Beleid*, Johannesburg.

Gifford-Gonzalez, D 1993, 'You can hide but you can't run: representations of women's work in illustrations of Palaeolithic life', *Visual Anthropology Review*, vol. 9, no. 1, pp. 23–41.

Gordon, RJ 1999, 'Scene(s) at the exhibition: Bain's 'Bushmen' at the Empire Exhibition, 1936', in B Lindfors (ed.), *Africans in show business*, Indiana University Press, Bloomington, pp. 266–289.

Gosden, C 1999, *Anthropology and archaeology. a changing relationship*, Routledge, London & New York.

Gould, SJ 1981, *The mismeasure of man*, Penguin Books, London.

Gould, SJ 1989, *Wonderful life. The Burgess Shale and the nature of history*, W.W. Norton, New York.

Grant, J & Jungkunz, VG 2016, *Political theory and the animal/human relationship*, State University of New York Press, Albany.

Jeppe, CWB 1946, *Gold mining on the Witwatersrand: volume two*, Cape Times Ltd, Cape Town.

Katz, EN 1995, 'Outcrop and deep level mining in South Africa before the Anglo-Boer War: reexamining the Blainey thesis', *Economic History Review*, vol. XLVIII, no. 2, pp. 304–328.

Kreita, SOY & Kittles, RA 1997, 'The persistence of racial thinking and the myth of racial divergence', *American Anthropologist*, vol. 99, no. 3, pp. 534–544.

Kuykendall, K & Štrkalj, G 2007, 'A history of South African palaeoanthropology', in P Bonner, A Esterhuysen & T Jenkins (eds), *A search for origins. Science, history and South Africa's 'cradle of humankind'*, University of the Witwatersrand Press, Johannesburg, pp. 28–49.

Lang, J 1986, *Bullion Johannesburg: men, mines and the challenge of conflict*, Jonathan Ball, Johannesburg.

Le Roux, I-M 2016, 'Court hands Penny Sparrow R5000 fine', EWN. Available from: https://ewn.co.za/2016/09/12/R5000-fine-or-12-months-in-prison-for-Penny-Sparrow [3 April 2019].

Mamdani, M 2012, *Define and rule: native as political identity*, South African edn, Witwatersrand University Press, Johannesburg.

Mbeki, TM 1996, 'Statement of Deputy President T. M. Mbeki, on behalf of the African National Congress, on the occasion of the adoption by the Constitutional Assembly of the Republic of South Africa Constitutional Bill 1996', Cape Town, 8 May 1996. Available via https://www.youtube.com/watch?v=r7VX83JXnbo [accessed 30/09/2019].

Mbeki, TM 2005, 'Official speech at the opening of the Maropeng Visitor Centre at the Cradle of Humankind World Heritage Site', Gauteng, 7 December 2005. Available via https://www.polity.org.za/article/mbeki-opening-of-maropeng-visitor-centre-07122005-2005-12-08 [accessed 30/09/2019].

Mbembe, JA & Rendall, S 2002, 'African modes of self-writing', *Public culture*, vol. 14, no. 1, pp. 239–273.

MMO-Champion 2018, 'South Africa's new human ancestor, Homo neledi, sparks racism row', Discussion thread. Available from: https://www.mmo-champion.com/threads/1866011-South-Africa-s-new-human-ancestor-Homo-neledi-sparks-racism-row [2 April 2019].

Moodie, TD 2005, 'Maximum average violence: underground assaults on the South African gold mines, 1913–1965', *Journal of Southern African Studies*, vol. 31, no. 3, pp. 547–567.

Morgan, LH 1877, *Ancient society, or researches in the lines of human progress from savagery through barbarism to civilization*, Macmillan, London.

Naidu, M 2008, 'Creating an African tourist experience at the Cradle of Humankind World Heritage Site', *Historia*, vol. 53, no. 2, pp. 182–207.

Ndebele, NS 1987, 'The English language and social change in South Africa', *English Academy Review*, vol. 4, no. 1, pp. 1–16.

Parnell, S 2003, 'Race, power and urban control: Johannesburg's inner city slum-yards, 1910–1923', *Journal of Southern African Studies*, vol. 29, no. 3, pp. 615–637.

Partridge, TC, Shaw, J, Heslop, D & Clarke, RJ 1999, 'The new hominid skeleton from Sterkfontein, South Africa: age and preliminary assessment', *Journal of Quaternary Science*, vol. 14, no. 4, pp. 293–298.

Roediger, DR 1994, *Towards the abolition of whiteness*, Verso, London.

Schlanger, N 2003, 'The Burkitt affair revisited. Colonial implications an identity politics in early South African prehistoric research', *Archaeological Dialogues*, vol. 10, no. 1, pp. 5–26.

Scott, M 2007, *Rethinking evolution in the museum: envisioning African origins*, Routledge, London & New York.

Smuts, JC 1917, *War-time speeches. A compilation of public utterances in Great Britain*, George H. Doran, New York.

Staff Reporter 2017, 'Five Zapiro cartoons that may have crossed the line', *Huffington Post*. Available from: https://www.huffingtonpost.co.za/2017/04/11/five-zapiro-cartoons-that-may-have-crossed-the-line_a_22035267/ [3 April 2019].

Stears, M, Clément, P, James, A & Dempster, E 2016, 'Creationist and evolutionist views of South African teachers with different religious affiliations', *South African Journal of Science*, vol. 112, no. 5–6, pp. 1–10.

Timeslive 2018, 'Radio station fires Sasha Martinego for referring to Julius Malema as a "monkey"'. Available from: https://www.timeslive.co.za/news/south-africa/2018-10-02-radio-station-fires-sasha-martinengo-for-referring-to-julius-malema-as-a-monkey/ [4 October 2018].

Tobias, PV 1965, '*Australopithecus, Homo habilis*, tool-using and tool-making', *South African Archaeological Bulletin*, vol. 20, pp. 167–169.

Tobias, PV 2002, 'Africa: the cradle of humanity', in H Bajinath & Y Singh (eds), *Rebirth of science in Africa: a shared vision for life and environmental sciences*, Umdaus Press, Pretoria, pp. 1–12.

Trigger, BG 1989, *A history of archaeological thought*, Cambridge University Press, Cambridge.

Tutu, H, McCarthy, TS & Cukrowska, E 2008, 'The chemical characteristics of acid mine drainage with particular reference to sources, distribution and remediation: the Witwatersrand Basin, South Africa as a case study', *Applied Geochemistry*, vol. 23, pp. 3666–3684.

UCT Scientist 2016, *Science must fall?* YouTube video, 13 October. Available from: https://www.youtube.com/watch?v=C9SiRNibD14 [3 April 2019].

Val, A 2016, 'Deliberate body disposal by hominins in the Dinaledi Chamber, Cradle of Humankind, South Africa?' *Journal of Human Evolution*, vol. 96, pp. 145–148.

Vavi, Z [@Zwelinzima1] 2015, 'Science is materialism – it's facts that can be proven. No one will dig old monkey bones to back up a theory that I was once a baboon – sorry', Twitter post, 12 September, 10:41 p.m.

Wallerstein, I 2003, 'Citizens all? Citizens some! The making of the citizen', *Comparative Studies in Society and History*, vol. 45, no. 4, pp. 650–679.

Wiber, MG 1998, *Erect men, undulating women. The visual imagery of gender, 'race' and progress in reconstructive illustrations of human evolution*, Winfrid Laurier Press, Ontario.

Wolpe, H 1972, 'Capitalism and cheap labour-power in South Africa: from segregation to apartheid', *Economy and Society*, vol. 1, no. 4, pp. 425–456.

Zihlman, A 1989, 'Woman the gatherer: the role of women in early hominid evolution', in S Morgan (ed.), *Gender and anthropology. Critical reviews for research and teaching*, American Anthropological Association, Washington DC, pp. 21–40.

SECTION 5

The construction of genetic facts

14

NAMING THE SACRED ANCESTORS

Taxonomic reification and Pleistocene genomic narratives

Jonathan Marks

Introduction

This paper represents part of a broader intellectual project attempting to embrace human evolution under the general theoretical umbrella of anthropology. In particular, human evolution is a theory of kinship, producing origin narratives with particular epistemic assumptions: naturalism (that the natural order can be bracketed and studied separately from the supernatural order), rationalism (that knowable processes are preferable as explanations within the natural order than unknowable miracles), empiricism (that theory is supported or superseded by data), and the overarching goal of maximum accuracy (Marks 2015; 2016a; 2017).

All of these are cultural assumptions which have evolved in modern times, and help to demarcate science, even while being often frustratingly polysemic. The origin narratives with which we work in science are subject to these constraints, and nevertheless also have considerable leeway (Landau 1991). Some special leeway is usually accorded in the area of taxonomy, or how we classify ourselves and our ancestors. Much of the history of physical anthropology has involved constructing (pseudo-)taxa of modern peoples and ancient hominids and attempting to creatively associate them with one another.

The nested hierarchy of Linnaeus (1758) provided a powerful tool for describing the natural order. It was a fundamentally relativising proposition – that all species should be organised according to their similarities to one another, rather than according to how similar they are to people, implicit in the ancient *scala naturae*. A century later, Darwin argued persuasively that the underlying structure of nature's system was provided by common descent; species were more or less similar to one another because of their shared ancestries. The fact that classification and phylogeny are related, however, leaves the nature of that relationship unproblematised. Should phylogenetic reconstructions be based on classifications (Sneath & Sokal 1962); should classifications be based on phylogenetic reconstructions (Eldredge & Cracraft 1980); or should phylogenetic reconstructions and classifications be broadly consistent with one another, without obsessing too much about it (Mayr 1969; Simpson 1961)?[1]

Clearly there is a bit more to this than the nineteenth-century appreciation that patterns of species similarity are generally derived from species history. I will argue here that understanding scientific classification as it relates to human diversity and ancestry is part of an anthropology that sees the study of organising or classificatory principles as a window on the native's (in this case, the scientist's) view of the world (Bowker & Star 2000; Durkheim & Mauss 1903). In this way, intellectual decolonisation can begin in part by exoticising the processes and products of scientific taxonomy. For a simple but critical example, today the most basic natural unit of living primates, the species, has undergone a subtle but crucial change in the last generation, which has permitted an explosive growth in the number of recognised primate species – circa 1990 there were about 170 of them, while today there are about 450. Where a few decades ago a primate species was a unit of ecology and gene pools, it is now a unit of conservation and political action, and consequently is an implicitly more biopolitical than biological unit. Whether the newer tallies are inflated and wrong (Groves 2014; Rosenberger 2012; Tattersall 2007) misses the point; we are now tallying different things than we used to. Arguing about whether primate species are 'real' now is fruitless, for the species itself has been reconceptualised. Thus, whatever reality a modern primate species occupies is a different reality than that of a primate species of 40 years ago. Conservation issues drive modern primate taxonomy, and if we recognise those issues as paramount (and who would fail to, aside from a cold-hearted pedant?), then we must conceptualise primate species not as abstract gene pools, but as differentiated lineages meriting legal recognition and protection – and identify close to 500 of them. Primate species here are not facts of nature by any means, but facts of nature/culture.[2]

Taxa and pseudo-taxa in human evolution

Another significant arena of narrative construction is rooted in palaeoanthropological taxonomy, where we have traditionally differentiated between 'splitters' and 'lumpers'. The former 'splits' a fossil assemblage into many species, downplaying anatomical differences due to sex, age, geography, polymorphism, or pathology, and overstating taxonomic distinctions. The latter does the opposite, underestimating the taxonomic variation represented by a collection of fossils, and 'lumping' them into too few species by overstating the other sources of anatomical variation. The taxonomic practice is strategic, however, and not nearly as capricious as it is often made to sound. Consider professional advancement, where the reward system is structured very differently for finding 'the first X' instead of 'the second Y or Z'. Science, after all, advances by the perception of novelty. Or consider national pride, where finding a new species for your country can help situate it in the global history of our species. We know that such considerations helped stimulate the acceptance and ascendance of Piltdown man in England a century ago (Spencer 1990). Today, with Spain's *Homo antecessor*, Indonesia's *Homo floresiensis*, Kenya's *Homo rudolfensis*, South Africa's *Homo naledi*, and many others, the science is more democratised – with more key sites, more key museums, more key specimens, and more key curators. Further, the most basic study of the fossils is a cladistic analysis, which only works above the species level, where two fossils that share a particular feature can be presumed to have inherited the feature from a common ancestor, and not to have received the common feature through hybridisation. Consequently, if you want your cladistic analysis to work, to appear to be valid, you need to be working with species. In short, there exists a cultural economy in palaeoanthropology that distinctly favours 'splitting' over 'lumping' and is only hinted at in the study of the history of other species.

The crucial distinction between palaeoanthropology and palaeontology lies in the fact that the palaeoanthropologist studies our ancestors, who are universally sacred (in the general anthropological sense); and is engaged in the process of naming the ancestors, which is invariably filled with symbolic power. It cannot be taken lightly as a cultural act, and helps distinguish biological anthropology for the hybrid field it is. From the presumption that fossil human species are just like other species, except that they happen to be ours, palaeoanthropological taxonomy has been very contested for a very long time. G. G. Simpson (1945, p. 288), reviewing mammalian systematics, observed that the biological training in palaeoanthropology was generally medical anatomy rather than zoology, and was prepared to throw up his hands in mock frustration: 'Perhaps it would be better for the zoological taxonomist to set apart the family Hominidae and to exclude its nomenclature and classification from his studies.'

In addition to the *Sinanthropus pekinensis* ('Peking Man') and *Pithecanthropus erectus* ('Java Man'), which existed at the time Simpson wrote, today we have *Australopithecus prometheus* and *Homo soloensis*, who may be real and not-real simultaneously. The reality of *Sinanthropus pekinensis* lay in the fossil sample it designated, and likewise with *Pithecanthropus erectus*; they represented once-alive animals, who participated in our ancestry. But they didn't represent distinct taxonomic elements, supraspecific lineages, or gene pools; today we see them both as *Homo erectus*. In other words, their reality as zoological species was entirely illusory. They were not units of nature, but units of story, the story of our ancestry. The interesting scientific question is epistemological: can we actually know how many species of hominins there were? If so, then why the disagreement? And if not – if the actual answer is under-determined by the fossil record itself – then what constitutes an authoritative scientific macroevolutionary narrative?

Why does this matter? Because it shapes the narrative we construct. The lumper narrative is a story about one or a few lineages cohering and surviving; while the splitter narrative is a story about many lineages diversifying and going extinct. One narrative has the human genus like the trunk of a mighty oak; and the other narrative has the human genus like the branches of the tree, spreading outward as they bifurcate.

Certainly, there were species in our ancestry. There was an ecological and genetic reality, but that reality cannot be captured in the Linnaean framework at our disposal. The perception of a pattern where there is no pattern – a hot streak at the roulette wheel or a face on Mars – is called apophenia. Any biological anthropologist can create a list of species that they do not think are real, but which some scholars insist on using anyway; and the list of non-existent fossil human species can be considered as an expression of apophenia, seeing fossil species that are not really there. The act of creating one's own ancestors is a universal and mythological practice. It is familiar through kinship studies in any number of ways: adoption, marriage, emphasising some ancestors (e.g. a patriline) over others, name-changing, and good old-fashioned imaginative invention. The problem is not, as Simpson imagined, incompetent biological taxonomy; it is not biological taxonomy at all. In this case, hominin species are the bricolage – the raw narrative elements – for constructing our scientific origin story; to imagine them as inhabiting the same reality as other kinds of zoological species is the mistake. And it is a mistake of a familiar sort – the blindness to one's own cultural assumptions when trying to impose order upon the world.

Race as genetic apophenia

The symbolling human mind makes sense of things through the linguistic processes of naming, aggregating, and analogising. And just as *Homo soloensis* might sound misleadingly similar to *Peromyscus maniculatus* (the deer mouse), *Drosophila melanogaster* (the fruit fly) and *Ursus spelaeus* (the extinct giant cave bear), it nevertheless is a different kind of thing. For there is in fact little difference between the non-existent *Homo soloensis* (which nevertheless denotes a group of Indonesian fossils, similar to *Homo erectus* earlier and *Homo sapiens* later), and the non-existent *Homo mongolus* (which nevertheless denoted east Asian peoples to the biologist Ernst Haeckel in 1868). Neither is a biologically real species, yet both serve as intellectual place-holders in part of a scientific ancestry narrative. In fact, most of the species names we see in palaeoanthropology do not designate biologically real units of nature and are thus unreal ancestor figures (White 2008). In a different origin story, the imaginary ancestor might be named Noah, or Mother Corn Spirit (Marks 2016b).

The study of human diversity and origins is thus biopolitical in ways that other sciences are not. By narrating the authoritative story of who we are and where we came from, biological anthropology assumes properties and responsibilities that are quite distinctive and different from those in cognate fields, notably evolutionary biology. Failing to acknowledge the difference has been a source of considerable confusion, with especially pernicious results at the microevolutionary level. In the mid-eighteenth century, for example, Linnaeus formalised the division of humans into colour-coded, continental subspecies – establishing a formal framework by which the homogeneous and civilised Europeans could be contrasted against the world's other human subspecies, effectively harmonising the science of natural history with the politics of colonialism. Scarcely a generation later, Buffon's informal term 'race' came to be used synonymously with Linnaeus's formal subspecies. Throughout the nineteenth century, increasingly loose usages of the word permitted races to be identified in local communities, nations, regions, continents, extended families, tribes, physical forms, and of course, the Jews.

Early twentieth-century anthropologists tried to introduce rigour into the term by restricting it to the continents, and secondarily to geographically localised physical types. This was accompanied by a radical reconception of the naturalistic basis of race. In the nineteenth century, race was an essential property, a part of you. In the twentieth century, race became a population that you were a part of. Through mid-century, the major geographical categories were still considered to be equivalent to zoological subspecies. But empirically human races were so nebulous as naturalistic entities that some scholars suggested jettisoning the term 'race' in favour of 'ethnic group' (Huxley & Haddon 1936; Montagu 1942). And the 1950s saw the increasing reconceptualisation of human biological diversity in non-taxonomic terms. The British physical anthropologist Joseph Weiner (1957, p. 80) could describe the human species 'as constituting a widespread network of more-or-less interrelated, ecologically adapted and functional entities'. By 1962, genetic anthropologist Frank Livingstone could epigrammatically declare that studying the biological diversity over the human species, 'There are no races, there are only clines.' A decade later, geneticist Richard Lewontin would demonstrate that even the clinal variation constituted a small part of human biological diversity, the great bulk of which was actually cosmopolitan or polymorphic, with the same genetic variants being found everywhere.

Thus, by the 1980s, it was clear that even the natural or biological component to human population diversity was not taxonomically structured. Race was as much a taxonomic fiction as any other way of classifying people. Race, as a natural unit of the human species, was nearly as elusive as the more obviously biologically fictive classificatory categories of nation, religion, or favourite football team – any of which could well mean the difference between life and death in the appropriate context. Race was politically valuable and socially important, but did not describe the empirical patterns of human biological variation. At best, it afforded a contrast among the people from the most geographically distant regions – East Asians, Northern Europeans, West Africans – but even so, it would fail to classify most of the living peoples of the world. Indeed, the physical heterogeneity of the peoples within any continental landmass made the taxonomic status of continental mega-populations intractable (Coon 1939; Huxley 1931; Ripley 1899; Seligman 1930). One could arbitrarily subdivide human populations into as many races, sub-races, and sub-sub-races as one chose, but the practice revealed nothing about the intrinsic natural partitioning of the human species, for the human species was not intrinsically partitionable in a rigorous, non-arbitrary way.

The lesson for twenty-first-century anthropology is the cumulative wisdom of two centuries of human taxonomy: human variation and race are different things, and do not map well onto each other. To study human variation is to identify its major patterns as (1) cultural; (2) epigenetic or developmental; (3) polymorphic or cosmopolitan; (4) clinal; and (5) local – the object of scientific analysis and interpretation. To study race, on the other hand, is to identify the assumptions inherent in any taxonomic practice, and the injustices that emerge from systems of classifying people – analysing law, history, politics and the quest for an Enlightenment ideal of equality in the face of political injustice – a humanistic endeavour.

And yet, genetics did not enter significantly into that realisation. From the 1920s into the 1960s, geneticists consistently claimed not only to have found races, but to have found *better* races – more objective, more real, more meaningful, and more authoritative – than anybody else's races. Using the ABO blood group, now considered paradigmatically non-racial, geneticists quickly divided the human species into European, Intermediate, Hunan, Indo-manchurian, Africo-Malaysian, Pacific-American, and Australian (Snyder 1926). Anthropologists found these clusters of very limited utility, since the ABO blood group frequencies actually vary within a fairly limited range, and consequently this criterion united some disparate peoples and divided some close relatives. The 'Hunan' group, for example, included the people of Poland; but if there is anything at all to racial groups, the people of Poland and the people of China would be expected to be in different ones. Some decades later, geneticist William C. Boyd published a definitive human genetic racial classification, identifying five races of Europe, but only one each from Africa and Asia, as well as Indo-Dravidians (i.e. south Asians), American Indians, and four Pacific races, for a total of thirteen (Boyd 1963). The imposition of qualitative boundaries on quantitative variation, and the failure to recognise the cultural value inherent in identifying, say, five kinds of European but only one kind of African, led to the paper being largely ignored. Physical anthropologists were already rethinking the ontology of race (Livingstone 1962).

This genetic paradox is of epistemological and historical interest: how could geneticists find and use racial groupings as natural analytic categories when the data now preclude the identification of such groupings? And indeed, this is the tip of an intellectual iceberg, which may be considered an example of apophenia, the imposition of meaningful form upon meaningless pattern – like seeing a camel in a cloud formation, as Hamlet suggested, or the face of Jesus on a tortilla. Although human population genetics now denies the existence of racial clusters in the human gene pool, when geneticists expected to find race, they were nevertheless able to (Schneider 1995). But races were not there; hence the apophenia (seeing non-existent patterns); geneticists were seeing features of the human gene pool that were no more real than seeing a face in the surface geology of Mars. Nor were the geneticists able to tell; that is to say, the patterns were there regardless of whether or not the patterns were actually there.

In the 1960s, the geneticist Luca Cavalli-Sforza made a bold claim. Applying early multi-variate statistical techniques to make trees from genetic data, he found that such a tree clustered his African samples together with his European samples, and separately from his Asian samples. The gene pools of the peoples of the Old World thus appeared to divide fundamentally along an East–West axis. Moreover, this pattern was different from the one he obtained when he constructed a tree by a similar process, but with anatomical data. Anatomically, those peoples divided along a North–South axis, with EurAsians-versus-Africans constituting the deepest bifurcation of the tree (Cavalli-Sforza & Edwards 1964). Since these two historical narratives were mutually exclusive, he concluded self-servingly that the anatomy narrative was wrong, and the genetic narrative was right: In the dim past, perhaps 40,000 years ago, the ancestors of the Asians bade farewell to their EurAfrican kin and headed eastward (Cavalli-Sforza 1974).

Although rhetorically strong in its validation of genetic data over anatomical data as a more authoritative source of inferences about human prehistory, nevertheless the conclusion was not terribly robust. Other genetic datasets and other statistical techniques produced other trees, even the dismissed anatomical tree, which linked EurAsians versus Africans (Nei & Roychoudhury 1981).

But if the pattern we now see in the data – geographic similarities among populations, but no qualitative breaks, particularly at the boundaries of continents; and Africans subsuming other populations – indeed is true, then there is no question whether the earliest split among Europeans, Asians and Africans was between EurAfricans and Asians or between EurAsians and Africans. In the famous phrase of the physicist Wolfgang Pauli, it is not even wrong. The answer is not wrong; the premodern view of the human gene pool and its history that frames the question is wrong. The answer, *any* answer, is consequently nonsense. Thus, the geneticists have been particularly vulnerable to the problem of assuming and identifying taxonomic structure in the human species where in fact none exists and have been able to analyse and dispute the relationships of entities that do not really exist in nature.

In other words, no classifications of the human species accurately describe a species composed of a few significant natural, geographically-based divisions, with homogeneity within and heterogeneity between, those divisions. Any classification of the human species encodes primarily symbolic, not empirical, information. We can thus see it as a folk taxonomic practice: establishing and treating categories of people as if they were naturalistic categories, equivalent to, but smaller than, the Order Rodentia, Superfamily Cercopithecoidea, or Class Mammalia. But these human categories thus established are not biological taxa; they are biocultural pseudo-taxa.

The human boundary

Neanderthals lie outside the range of human variation, which marks them as both zoological and mythological objects: our closest extinct relatives, or humans lacking some essential features of humanity. It might be just a chin and forehead that they lack, but perhaps also the incest taboo, or the ability to grasp the subjunctive mood, or being able to follow the street signs and make correct change. Whatever can be imagined as an essential feature of the human condition, and ambiguous in the fossil record, can in principle be projected upon the

Neanderthals and then subtracted. This has been done for features as fundamental as full bipedalism in the scientific literature and is a staple of science fiction.

We know that by 32,000 years ago, Neanderthals were extinct, supplanted by people with foreheads, chins, and linear body builds, first seen in Africa perhaps 150,000 years earlier. But we don't know why. And this literature is replete with possible answers (e.g. Shipman 2015). Although 100,000 years ago our ancestors and Neanderthals lived nearly indistinguishable lives, our narratives about them are shaped by the inescapable fact that we know what the future holds for them. Something will go terribly wrong for those Neanderthals over the next 70,000 years. The big question is what – and this in turn leads to the broadest narrative about Neanderthals, as tragically flawed and doomed.

The slightly smaller question is, what would it be like to meet one? We do find Neanderthals and anatomically modern human at the same sites, overlapping in time. You can imagine that encounter by simply identifying with the people physically like you, with chins and foreheads. Nevertheless, the division of Pleistocene Europeans into Neanderthals and moderns is a zoological narrative that may have little relation to the actual human groups that existed. After all, we have no idea what value either Neanderthals or moderns of 60,000 years ago would place on your forehead and chin. Do you socialise with people on the basis of their head shape? What constitutes difference is, of course, culturally defined; as are the behavioural consequences of perceiving difference. In one time and place you might not interact with people you perceive as different; while in another time and place it might not be such a social or political stigma. Imposing our zoological distinctions upon people of tens of thousands of years ago, and inscribing our meanings upon those populations, produces an inescapably ethnocentric narrative of the deep past. If you were time-transported back into that age, you would probably be just as alien to the forehead-and-chin people as to the non-forehead-and-chin people. You would not know how to communicate, behave, or decorate yourself appropriately to be accepted by any group – modern or Neanderthal – and there is no reason to think that you would be any worse off with, or perceived as more alien by, the Neanderthals.

Denying people their essential humanity is a familiar practice as well amongst the living and real. Consequently, contemporary political discourses can help us identify our own biases toward those extinct populations. The fact that Neanderthals lie outside the known range of human variation has a historical analogy; after all, in 1492, so did Native Americans – and it took a papal bull called *Sublimus Dei* (and occasionally called by related Latin variants), issued in 1537 by Pope Paul III, to establish them formally as fully human to Europeans.

With Neanderthals, the scientific question is again whether to expand the range of human variation to embrace them, or to let them stand in perpetual contrast to the form and state of humanity. Neanderthals are important because if there is a boundary between microevolution and macroevolution constituted by speciation (Gould 2003), then Neanderthals sit right on that boundary. But are there any practical implications for the answer to the question, 'Were Neanderthals our species or a different species?', especially given that the answer seems to be under-determined by the data and that the species is a contested bio-political category in the first place? Indeed, there is something at risk. If we see Neanderthals as a separate subspecies then there is no taxonomic place within which to exoticise or essentialise diverse peoples, for the subspecies is as low as it gets. On the other hand, if the Neanderthals are a species, then that opens up the taxonomic space in which to reify human diversity. And since culture abhors a vacuum, it might be reasonable to consider that as an additional variable in formulating one's ultimately arbitrary taxonomic decision about the Neanderthals.

Thus, the story of human diversity and the story of human ancestry are really parts of the same scientific story and are both entangled in the political history of colonialism. Much of the charm of mitochondrial Eve in the 1980s was that since we did not find mega-geographical clusters, race was not a feature of the human gene pool, and further, since all human mitochondrial DNA appeared to be a subset of African mitochondrial DNA, we are all Africans under the skin – a narrative of modern brotherhood superimposed upon the fictive ancestor, mitochondrial Eve. This narrative harmonised strongly with the newer data and non-taxonomic interpretations of human diversity. Anthropologists had increasingly come to understand human prehistory as being characterised by extensive genetic contact among populations (Wolf 1982). This in turn suggests that the most powerful post-Darwinian image – the tree – might not be applicable to the human species.

Physical anthropologist Earnest Hooton, in the first half of the twentieth century, had actually used the circulatory system as his metaphor of choice, connecting the human 'races' as a capillary network (Hooton 1946, p. 652). Franz Weidenreich (1947) instead used the railroad trellis as his metaphor of choice. Other relevant metaphors include the rhizome, web or mesh, and braided stream (Ackermann, Mackay & Arnold 2016); these microevolutionary narratives are not tree-like. This is particularly important in the case of humans, because we have powerful false cultural narratives of isolation and purity; while of course populations are different from one another, but only quantitatively.

Thus, while human genetics is a very active site of meaning-production, the meaning may well be independent of reality. In the 1980s, researchers saw three waves of migration into the Americas from North Asia in the genetic data (Greenberg, Turner & Zegura 1986). Researchers no longer see that pattern in those data. Behavioural genetics is rife with correlations, spurious or otherwise, that have implied the transitory existence of 'super-male' XYY syndrome (Jacobs et al. 1965) and 'the gay gene' (Hamer et al. 1993). Anthropologists have given the name 'biosociality' to the new kinship narratives that emerge from shared genetic patterns (Gibbon & Novas 2007; Rabinow 1992). And once again, this is apophenia – seeing things that aren't there. It is about perception and meaning, and its domain is the natural/cultural, not simply the natural.

Neoliberal recreational genomics

Perhaps the most unexpected consequence of the Human Genome Project has been the development of recreational ancestry testing, which yield some examples of the new biosociality (Bolnick et al. 2007). Not legally able to sell direct-to-consumer genomic testing for medical purposes in the US, companies have been obliged to rebrand their data as primarily stories of the ancestry of their clients. This is an ostensibly scientific service that nevertheless is accompanied by disclaimers about its lack of reliability or authority. One company explains, 'Currently 23andMe has several features that can reveal genetic evidence of Native American ancestry, although they are not considered a confirmatory test or proof of such ancestry in a legal context' (23andMe 2019). Another pitches to prospective consumers with generic stories of ancient ancestral migrations, based on the geographic correlates of the customer's genetic markers. But just in case the consumer is curious, 'This is not a genealogical study, and your DNA trail may not lead to your present-day location. Rather, your results will reveal the anthropological story of your ancestors – where they lived and how they migrated around the world over tens of thousands of years' (National Geographic 2019).

One genetic test (for the 'Cohanim Modal Haplotype') purports to tell clients whether they have the Y-chromosome of Moses (Roots for Real 2019).[3] That chromosome is also the Y-chromosome of Adam, however, although never advertised as such – through the genealogies in Genesis 5 (Adam to Noah), Genesis 11 (Noah to Abraham), and Exodus 6 (Abraham to Moses). Presumably geneticists, like creationists, get to choose arbitrarily which parts of the Bible they care to take at face value. Biblical literalists notwithstanding, the ontological status of Moses is on a par with that of Odysseus, yet if anyone purported to develop a genetic test for descent from wily Odysseus, you would properly suspect a scam.

Another test purports to reconnect African-Americans with their ancestral African tribe using mitochondrial DNA (mtDNA), putting a romanticised and commercial spin on the scientific reification of African ancestry (African Ancestry Inc. 2019). But mtDNA only identifies one of the thousands of ancestors you had in the year 1700. Moreover, peoples of Africa are poorly sampled and overlap one another substantially in their genetic composition. One could hardly anticipate a unique match to a single population, except as a direct consequence of very poor sampling. Finally, the relationship of ethnic labels of today to the gene pools of 300 years ago is very unclear, but certainly the idea that the ethnic labels of today can be translated unproblematically into the Africa of 300 years ago is unlikely to be true. And of course, the meanings of kinship to Africans and to Americans armed with DNA results are quite different.

Another genetic identity on the market involves the mtDNA of Europeans, and their statistical cluster into a small number of deduced lineages, whose inferred founders are known as 'The Seven Daughters of Eve'. Here, clients are assigned to one or another lineage descended from a fictive 25,000-year-old 'clan mother' (Oxford Ancestors 2019). Yet, demographic modellers have shown that human pedigrees collapse into one another by about 10,000 years ago (Rohde, Olson & Chang 2004). That is to say, everyone has so many ancestors (figuring 4 generations per century and 100 centuries yields 2 to the 400th power lineal ancestors in that generation, a ridiculously large number) and there were so few people alive back then (10 million?), that we must all be descended from the same pool of ancestors as recently as 10,000 years ago. It is simply the only way to cram so many theoretical ancestors into so few real bodies. Consequently, if we just limit ourselves to Europeans, I may have the mtDNA of 'Clan Mother Ursula' from 25,000 years ago, but we are all her descendants, and someone else may well have more of her DNA in their nuclear genomes than I do.

The biosocial meanings are real, regardless of the nature of the genetic patterns – real, trivial, or spurious. Kinship resides in the zone of the natural/cultural, because it involves the creation of relatedness often in defiance of biology. Kinship bends biology. The principal issues here arise from imagining the patterns as inhering in genetics or nature, when they are really patterns of kinship or nature/culture. Genomics in a neo-liberal economy is particularly susceptible to such apophenia, because there may be money in scientifically recreating an imaginary past and inserting a customer into it.

The other achievement of mitochondrial Eve was that she reinvented the concepts of heredity and ancestry in ways that go against commonsense and biological ideas about those, and additionally turned out to be marketable. Mitochondrial DNA is very unusual and quite different from nuclear or chromosomal DNA – the DNA we usually think of – in two crucial ways. First, at fertilisation chromosomal DNA is provided equally by both parents, but mitochondria and their DNA are provided almost exclusively by the egg – thus, to a geneticist, you are a mitochondrial clone of your mother and unrelated to your father (Ankel-Simons & Cummins 1996). Second, whether mutations are good or bad for you is less important than the sex ratio of your children. If you have ten offspring, you are doing fine in the Darwinian world of nuclear genomic DNA; but if they are all boys, then you are mitochondrially extinct. So, this is DNA and it is heredity, but it is neither ancestry nor even evolution in any familiar way.

As we noted earlier, if we estimate four generations per century, then around the year 1700, say twelve generations ago, you had two to the twelfth power, or over 4,000 lineal ancestors, of which mitochondrial DNA tracks one. In the time of Charlemagne, 50 generations ago, you had about a quadrillion ancestors, as did everyone else (Hitt 2005). The vast majority of your ancestors are common and shared, meaning that you are inbred and related to the rest of our species. But significantly, biological inheritance at the individual or group level more or less breaks down this far back in time because of too many theoretical ancestors, and too few people alive at the time.

Very ancient DNA

The hottest research field in the study of human evolution is currently the study of ancient DNA, from bones that have not yet fully fossilised, and retain some cellular matter. The application of such technologies to Neanderthals would be very meaningful, even though Neanderthals went extinct over 30,000 years ago.

The initial analysis of Neanderthal mitochondrial DNA showed it to be slightly outside the range of modern human variation, as indeed they are anatomically. Moreover, the notation of difference harmonised well with a 'splitter' view of the classification of Neanderthals, and the earliest Neanderthal mtDNA analyses emphasised the lack of genetic connection between Neanderthals and ourselves, and assigned them species status (Krings et al. 1999). Subsequent analyses of nuclear DNA, on the other hand, come rather to emphasise a small bit of Neanderthal DNA that is indeed polymorphic in humans (present in some people, but not in others), and infer it to be introgression into the human gene pool. For a fee, companies will now determine how much (up to about 5 per cent) of your DNA is from Neanderthals.

The 'Denisovans' are the newest introgressors into our gene pool, named for the Siberian cave that yielded an isolated finger bone (and later, two teeth) from which DNA was extracted. Initial analyses of the mtDNA indicated that it was equidistant from humans and Neanderthals (Krause et al. 2010), but more recent nuclear genomic studies show it to be a variant Neanderthal. For a fee, you can also find out how much of the Denisovans is in your DNA.

This turns out to be a particularly creative reification since the 'Denisovans' are only known from the DNA in the Siberian finger and teeth, and are only accessible to the geneticist. A toe bone, from the same location as the teeth and finger, turned out to have ordinary Neanderthal DNA (Prüfer et al. 2014). Yet the living people with the greatest similarity to Denisovan DNA come from Papua New Guinea. In fact, geographically, to get from Siberia (where the finger bone is from) to New Guinea (where the greatest genetic similarities to the finger bone are found today), you have to go through a lot of peoples who have no detectable genetic similarities at all to the Denisovan finger bone. In a dendritic, taxonomic framework, this is very difficult to make sense of. Here we see 'Denisovans' and Neanderthals as sister taxa, more closely related to one another than either is to modern humans. But the comparison in the scientific literature itself is a bit misleading, since the terminal taxa for 'Denisovans' and 'Neanderthals' are specimens, while the terminal taxa for 'modern humans' are those old familiar monophyletic continental populations. So, the scientific narrative becomes the Denisovans spread widely over Asia, and migrating and interbreeding with New Guineans, and being subsequently swamped out in their original homeland (Reich et al. 2011). Or as *Science* magazine put it, 'one group [of modern humans] mixed with Denisovans … on the way to Melanesia' (Gibbons 2011, p. 394).

Or else, perhaps the pattern is spurious (Qin & Stoneking 2015), and this is another example of genomic apophenia. Indeed, looking a bit harder, geneticists subsequently found some Denisovan DNA in peoples geographically between the Siberian cave and Papua New Guinea and have begun crafting new stories that invoke 'two pulses of … admixture' (Browning et al. 2018, p. 53).

There are very divergent narratives that can be constructed from the genomic data. The splitter narrative involves essentially marauding bands of Ice Age rapists, bestialising our ancestors, while the lumper narrative sees the Neanderthal and Denisovan contribution to our species as part of the connectedness of diverse human gene pools, which can now be seen as a 'metapopulation' (Pääbo 2015). In this sense, a palaeoanthropological species is thus a natural/cultural unit, a narrative element, or the bricolage (Lévi-Strauss 1962) of the scientific origin story for our species. We know little of the ancient human gene pool, except that it was probably much more diverse than it is now, since chimpanzees and gorillas seem to have far more genetic diversity than we do (Prado-Martinez et al. 2013). 'Human' here would consequently denote a loose network of diverse gene pools, connected over time and through space, of which we all partake today, if slightly unevenly. This has always been at least as much about the hermeneutics of human evolution as it is about the empirics of human evolution.

Conclusion

The scholarly study of one's own ancestors and relatives involves reflexivity, not objectivity; and is an anthropological, not a biological, exercise. A century of crafting narratives of human evolution from the analysis of genetic data has shown it to be invariably a highly culture-bound process, which yields a highly culture-bound story. Today's scientific narrative from the field of ancient DNA studies reinscribes an old colonial framework upon the data to make sense of its patterns – racial invasions – although perhaps conceptually more benign than a century ago (Reich 2018). The conflation of populations with races, and the difficulty in quantitatively modelling population dynamics without the assumption of primordial purity, have contributed to a new scientific narrative in which 'the Denisovans', 'the Neanderthals', and 'the moderns' are all discrete pseudo-taxonomic entities.

While prehistoric human populations must have been structured, the trend of recent scholarship has been to decouple samples and specimens from taxonomies. Thus, Weiner's (1957, p. 80) image of the human species 'as constituting a widespread network of more-or-less interrelated, ecologically adapted and functional entities' can be profitably extended through time, without having to rely on pre-modern pseudo-taxonomic science. Rather than the discrete branches of a tree, human ancestry is better served with more complex and dynamic metaphors.

Notes

1 Obsessing about phylogenetic classifications can lead to the absurdity of declaring humans to be fish, since 'fish' is a paraphyletic category, embracing both tuna and coelacanths, although coelacanths are more closely related to us than to tuna. Acknowledging the difference between the statements, 'humans arose from fish' and 'humans are fish' is critical here. By the same phylogenetic argument by which humans are apes, humans are also monkeys, prosimians, and fish, which beggars the very prospect of zoological classification.
2 This is not to say that other species do not have biopolitical content, but simply that the biopolitics of human relatives and ancestors is different and more pronounced.
3 'The priestly caste of the Cohanim are thought to have the same Y chromosome as the biblical Moses, because Aaron, Moses' brother, founded this priesthood, whose duties traditionally pass from father to son. The Cohanim Y type identified in groundbreaking analysis by the team of Prof. David Goldstein and colleagues agrees with the biblical tradition, and a simple Y test using our database search can confirm whether a Cohen male indeed carries the Cohen Y type' (Roots for Real 2019).

References

23andMe 2019, 'Can 23andMe Identify Native American Ancestry?'. Available from: https://customer care.23andme.com/hc/en-us/articles/202906870-Can-23andMe-identify-Native-American-ancestry- [5 January 2019].

Ackermann, RR, Mackay, A & Arnold, ML 2016, 'The hybrid origin of "modern" humans', *Evolutionary Biology*, vol. 43, pp. 1–11.

African Ancestry Inc. 2019, 'Why choose African ancestry?' Available from: http://africanancestry.com/ home/ [5 January 2019].

Ankel-Simons, F & Cummins, JM 1996, 'Misconceptions about mitochondria and mammalian fertilization: implications for theories on human evolution', *Proceedings of the National Academy of Sciences, USA*, vol. 93, pp. 13859–13863.

Berger, LR, Hawks, J, de Ruiter, DJ, Churchill, SE, Schmid, P, Delezene, LK, Kivell, TL, Garvin, HM, Williams, SA, DeSilva, JM, Skinner, MM, Musiba, CM, Cameron, N, Holliday, TW, Harcourt-Smith, W, Ackermann, RR, Bastir, M, Bogin, B, Bolter, D, Brophy, J, Cofran, ZD, Congdon, KA, Deane, AS, Dembo, M, Drapeau, M, Elliott, MC, Feuerriegel, EM, Garcia-Martinez, D, Green, DJ, Gurtov, A, Irish, JD, Kruger, A, Laird, MF, Marchi, D, Meyer, MR, Nalla, S, Negash, EW, Orr, CM, Radovcic, D, Schroeder, L, Scott, JE, Throckmorton, Z, Tocheri, MW, VanSickle, C, Walker, CS, Wei, P & Zipfel, B 2015, '*Homo naledi*, a new species of the genus *Homo* from the Dinaledi Chamber, South Africa', *eLife*, vol. 4, p. e09560.

Boas, F 1911, *The mind of primitive man*, Macmillan, New York.

Bolnick, DA, Fullwiley, D, Duster, T, Cooper, RS, Fujimura, J, Kahn, J, Kaufman, J, Marks, J, Morning, A, Nelson, A, Ossorio, P, Reardon, J, Reverby, S & Tallbear, K 2007, 'The science and business of genetic ancestry testing', *Science*, vol. 318, pp. 399–400.

Bowker, G & Star, S 2000, *Sorting things out: classification and its consequences*, MIT Press, Cambridge, MA.

Boyd, WC 1963, 'Genetics and the human race', *Science*, vol. 140, pp. 1057–1065.

Browning, SR, Browning, BL, Zhou, Y, Tucci, S & Akey, JM 2018, 'Analysis of human sequence data reveals two pulses of archaic Denisovan admixture', *Cell*, vol. 173, pp. 53–61.

Cann, RL, Stoneking, M & Wilson, AC 1987, 'Mitochondrial DNA and human evolution', *Nature*, vol. 325, pp. 31–36.

Cavalli-Sforza, LL 1974, 'The genetics of human populations', *Scientific American*, vol. 231, pp. 81–89.

Cavalli-Sforza, LL & Edwards, A 1964, 'Analysis of human evolution', in S Geerts (ed.), *Proceedings of the 11th International Congress of Genetics*, Pergamon Press, Oxford, pp. 923–933.

Coon, CS 1939, *The races of Europe*, Macmillan, New York.

Davenport, CB 1928, 'Race crossing in Jamaica', *The Scientific Monthly*, vol. 27, pp. 225–238.

Durkheim, É & Mauss, M 1903, 'De quelques formes de classification: contribution à l'étude des représentations collectives', *Année Sociologique*, vol. 6, pp. 1–72.

Eldredge, N & Cracraft, J 1980, *Phylogenetic patterns and the evolutionary process: method and theory in comparative biology*, Columbia University Press, New York.

Gibbon, S & Novas, C 2007, *Biosocialities, genetics and the social sciences: making biologies and identities*, Routledge, New York.

Gibbons, A 2011, 'A new view of the birth of *Homo sapiens*', *Science*, vol. 331, pp. 391–394.

Gould, SJ 2003, *The structure of evolutionary theory*, Harvard University Press, Cambridge, MA.

Greenberg, JH, Turner, CG & Zegura, SL 1986, 'The settlement of the Americas: a comparison of the linguistic, dental, and genetic evidence', *Current Anthropology*, vol. 27, pp. 477–497.

Groves, CP 2014, 'Primate taxonomy: inflation or real?', *Annual Review of Anthropology*, vol. 43, pp. 27–36.

Haeckel, E 1868, *Natürliche Schöpfungsgeschichte*, Reimer, Berlin.

Hamer, D, Hu, S, Magnuson, V, Hu, N & Pattatucci, A 1993, 'A linkage between DNA markers on the X chromosome and male sexual orientation', *Science*, vol. 261, pp. 321–327.

Herrnstein, R & Murray, C 1994, *The bell curve*, Free Press, New York.

Hitt, J 2005, 'Mighty white of you: racial preferences color America's oldest skull and bones', *Harper's Magazine*, July, pp. 39–55.

Hooton, EA 1931, *Up from the ape*, Macmillan, New York.

Hooton, EA 1946, *Up from the ape*, 2nd edn, Macmillan, New York.

Huxley, J 1931, *Africa view*, Chatto and Windus, London.

Huxley, J & Haddon, AC 1936, *We Europeans*, Harper and Brothers, New York.

Jacobs, P, Brunton, M, Melville, M, Brittain, R & McClemont, W 1965, 'Aggressive behavior, mental subnormality and the XYY male', *Nature*, vol. 208, pp. 1351–1352.

Krause, J, Fu, Q, Good, JM, Viola, B, Shunkov, MV, Derevianko, AP & Pääbo, S 2010, 'The complete mitochondrial DNA genome of an unknown hominin from southern Siberia', *Nature*, vol. 464, pp. 894–897.

Krings, M, Geisert, H, Schmitz, RW, Krainitzki, H & Pääbo, S 1999, 'DNA sequence of the mitochondrial hypervariable region II from the Neandertal type specimen', *Proceedings of the National Academy of Sciences*, vol. 96, pp. 5581–5585.

Landau, M 1991, *Narratives of human evolution*, Yale University Press, New Haven, CT.

Lévi-Strauss, C 1962, *The savage mind*, University of Chicago Press, Chicago, IL.

Lewontin, RC 1972, 'The apportionment of human diversity', *Evolutionary Biology*, vol. 6, pp. 381–398.

Linnaeus, C 1758, *Systema naturæ*, 10th edn, Lars Salvius, Stockholm.

Livingstone, FB 1962, 'On the non-existence of human races', *Current Anthropology*, vol. 3, pp. 279–281.

Lordkipanidze, D, Ponce de León, MS, Margvelashvili, A, Rak, Y, Rightmire, GP, Vekua, A & Zollikofer, CPE 2013, 'A complete skull from Dmanisi, Georgia, and the evolutionary biology of early *Homo*', *Science*, vol. 342, pp. 326–331.

Malinowski, B 1929, 'Kinship', *Encyclopaedia Britannica*, 14th edn, vol. 13, pp. 403–409.

Marks, J 1996, 'The legacy of serological studies in American physical anthropology', *History and Philosophy of the Life Sciences*, vol. 18, pp. 345–362.

Marks, J 2012, 'The origins of anthropological genetics', *Current Anthropology*, vol. 53, no. S5, pp. S161–S172.

Marks, J 2015, *Tales of the ex-apes: how we think about human evolution*, University of California Press, Berkeley, CA.

Marks, J 2016a, 'The units of scientific anthropological origin narratives', *Anthropological Theory*, vol. 16, pp. 285–294.

Marks, J 2016b, 'A tale of ex-apes: whence wisdom?', *Philosophy, Theology and the Sciences*, vol. 3, pp. 152–174.

Marks, J 2017, 'What if the human mind evolved for nonrational thought? An anthropological perspective', *Zygon*, vol. 52, pp. 790–806.

Mayr, E 1969, *Principles of animal taxonomy*, Harvard University Press, Cambridge, MA.

Meyer, M, Kircher, M, Gansauge, M-T, Li, H, Racimo, F, Mallick, S, Schraiber, JG, Jay, F, Prüfer, K, de Filippo, C, Sudmant, PH, Alkan, C, Fu, Q, Do, R, Rohland, N, Tandon, A, Siebauer, M, Green, RE, Bryc, K, Briggs, AW, Stenzel, U, Dabney, J, Shendure, J, Kitzman, J, Hammer, MF, Shunkov, MV, Derevianko, AP, Patterson, N, Andrés, AM, Eichler, EE, Slatkin, M, Reich, D,

Kelso, J & Pääbo, S 2012, 'A high-coverage genome sequence from an archaic Denisovan individual', *Science*, vol. 338, pp. 222–226.

Montagu, A 1942, *Man's most dangerous myth: the fallacy of race*, Columbia University Press, New York.

National Geographic 2019, 'GENO 2.0 FAQ: about the project'. Available from: https://genographic.na tionalgeographic.com/faq/about-project/#is-this-a-genealogy-study [5 January 2019].

Nei, M & Roychoudhury, AK 1981, 'Genetic relationship and evolution of human races', in MK Hecht, B Wallace & GT Prance (eds), *Evolutionary Biology*, Plenum, New York, pp. 1–59.

Osborn, HF 1926, 'The evolution of human races', *Natural History*, vol. 26, pp. 3–13.

Oxford Ancestors 2019, 'Maternal ancestry'. Available from: www.oxfordancestors.com/content/view/ 35/55/ [5 January 2019].

Pääbo, S 2015, 'The diverse origins of the human gene pool', *Nature Reviews Genetics*, vol. 16, pp. 313–314.

Prado-Martinez, J, Sudmant, PH, Kidd, JM, Li, H, Kelley, JL, Lorente-Galdos, B, Veeramah, KR, Woerner, AE, O'Connor, TD, Santpere, G, Cagan, A, Theunert, C, Casals, F, Laayouni, H, Munch, K, Hobolth, A, Halager, AE, Malig, M, Hernandez-Rodriguez, J, Hernando-Herraez, I, Prufer, K, Pybus, M, Johnstone, L, Lachmann, M, Alkan, C, Twigg, D, Petit, N, Baker, C, Hormozdiari, F, Fernandez-Callejo, M, Dabad, M, Wilson, ML, Stevison, L, Camprubi, C, Carvalho, T, Ruiz-Herrera, A, Vives, L, Mele, M, Abello, T, Kondova, I, Bontrop, RE, Pusey, A, Lankester, F, Kiyang, JA, Bergl, RA, Lonsdorf, E, Myers, S, Ventura, M, Gagneux, P, Comas, D, Siegismund, H, Blanc, J, Agueda-Calpena, L, Gut, M, Fulton, L, Tishkoff, SA, Mullikin, JC, Wilson, RK, Gut, IG, Gonder, MK, Ryder, OA, Hahn, BH, Navarro, A, Akey, JM, Bertranpetit, J, Reich, D, Mailund, T, Schierup, MH, Hvilsom, C, Andres, AM, Wall, JD, Bustamante, CD, Hammer, MF, Eichler, EE & Marques-Bonet, T 2013, 'Great ape genetic diversity and population history', *Nature*, vol. 499, pp. 471–475.

Prüfer, K, Racimo, F, Patterson, N, Jay, F, Sankararaman, S, Sawyer, S, Heinze, A, Renaud, G, Sudmant, PH, de Filippo, C, Li, H, Mallick, S, Dannemann, M, Fu, Q, Kircher, M, Kuhlwilm, M, Lachmann, M, Meyer, M, Ongyerth, M, Siebauer, M, Theunert, C, Tandon, A, Moorjani, P, Pickrell, J, Mullikin, JC, Vohr, SH, Green, RE, Hellmann, I, Johnson, PLF, Blanche, H, Cann, H, Kitzman, JO, Shendure, J, Eichler, EE, Lein, ES, Bakken, TE, Golovanova, LV, Doronichev, VB, Shunkov, MV, Derevianko, AP, Viola, B, Slatkin, M, Reich, D, Kelso, J & Pääbo, S 2014, 'The complete genome sequence of a Neanderthal from the Altai Mountains', *Nature*, vol. 505, pp. 43–49.

Qin, P & Stoneking, M 2015, 'Denisovan ancestry in East Eurasian and Native American populations', *Molecular Biology and Evolution*, vol. 32, pp. 2665–2674.

Rabinow, P 1992, 'Artificiality and enlightenment: from sociobiology to biosociality', in J Crary & S Kwinter (eds), *Zone 6: Incorporations*, Zone Books, New York, pp. 234–252.

Reich, D 2018, *Who we are and how we got here: Ancient DNA and the new science of the human past*, Pantheon, New York.

Reich, D, Patterson, N, Kircher, M, Delfin, F, Nandineni, MR, Pugach, I, Ko, AM-S, Ko, Y-C, Jinam, TA & Phipps, ME 2011, 'Denisova admixture and the first modern human dispersals into Southeast Asia and Oceania', *American Journal of Human Genetics*, vol. 89, pp. 516–528.

Ripley, WZ 1899, *The races of Europe*, D. Appleton, New York.

Rohde, DLT, Olson, S & Chang, JT 2004, 'Modelling the recent common ancestry of all living humans', *Nature*, vol. 431, pp. 562–566.

Roots for Real 2019, 'DNA'. Available from: www.rootsforreal.com/dna_en.php [5 January 2019].

Rosenberger, AL 2012, 'New world monkey nightmares: science, art, use, and abuse (?) in Platyrrhine taxonomic nomenclature', *American Journal of Primatology*, vol. 74, pp. 692–695.

Schneider, WH 1995, 'Blood group research in Great Britain, France, and the United States between the world wars', *Yearbook of Physical Anthropology*, vol. 38, pp. 87–114.

Seligman, C 1930, *Races of Africa*, Henry Holt, New York.

Shipman, P 2015, *The invaders: how humans and their dogs drove Neanderthals to extinction*, Harvard University Press, Cambridge, MA.

Simpson, GG 1945, 'The principles of classification and a classification of mammals', *Bulletin of the American Museum of Natural History*, vol. 85, pp. 1–349.

Simpson, GG 1961, *Principles of animal taxonomy*, Columbia University Press, New York.

Sneath, PHA & Sokal, RR 1962, 'Numerical taxonomy', *Nature*, vol. 193, pp. 855–860.

Snyder, L 1926, 'Human blood groups: their inheritance and racial significance', *American Journal of Physical Anthropology*, vol. 9, pp. 233–263.

Spencer, F 1990, *Piltdown: a scientific forgery*, Oxford University Press, New York.

Tattersall, I 2007, 'Madagascar's lemurs: cryptic diversity or taxonomic inflation?', *Evolutionary Anthropology*, vol. 16, pp. 12–23.

Weidenreich, F 1947, 'Facts and speculations concerning the origin of *Homo sapiens*', *American Anthropologist*, vol. 49, pp. 135–151.

Weiner, JS 1957, 'Physical anthropology: an appraisal', *American Scientist*, vol. 45, pp. 79–87.

White, TD 2008, 'Review of "The last human: a guide to twenty-two species of extinct humans", by G. J. Sawyer and Viktor Deak', *Quarterly Review of Biology*, vol. 83, pp. 105–106.

Wolf, E 1982, *Europe and the people without history*, University of California Press, Berkeley.

15

TRADITIONAL OWNER PARTICIPATION IN GENETIC RESEARCH

A researcher perspective

Craig Muller and Joe Dortch

Introduction

Between 2013 and 2016, researchers from the University of Western Australia, the University of Copenhagen and Griffith University, conducted an ancient populations research project using DNA samples from Aboriginal[1] participants. This was published as *A Genomic History of Aboriginal Australia* (Malaspinas et al. 2016). These researchers included us, respectively, Muller, a historian experienced in Australian native title and lately human origins research, and Dortch, an archaeologist who has worked with Aboriginal people across Western Australia. Our purpose in this chapter is to outline our experience in discussing scientific and Indigenous knowledge systems with Australian Indigenous participants in human origins research. While we began the research with a particular scientific viewpoint, we were well aware of contrasting Indigenous viewpoints, and initially unsure how dialogue between them would evolve. We present our experiences and preliminary conclusions in the belief that they are of interest to all those working in cross-cultural research and especially in human origins.

The use of genetics as a means to research ancient populations in Australia began after such work was well under way in Europe and North America, and as late as 2010 comparatively little such research had occurred (van Holst Pellekaan 2013). A result of the slow start in Australia is a sense of cautiousness, as Indigenous people and researchers feel for the best way forward in what is viewed as a somewhat unknown situation whose novelty brings with it some trepidation and wariness.

The *Genomic History of Aboriginal Australia* project led on from the sequencing of the first full Aboriginal genome in 2011 (Rasmussen et al. 2011). In that first study, the researchers decided to seek endorsement for the research from those who would be most affected by the findings, the local Aboriginal people. The DNA used was from a sample of hair collected in the Western Australian Goldfields in 1923, held at the Duckworth Laboratory at Cambridge before being sent to the Center for GeoGenetics, University of Copenhagen, for sequencing by a research team led by Eske Willerslev. This sample was selected because it had a clear provenance and was deemed to originate from a person who would not have non-Aboriginal admixture. The Goldfields region is on the western edge of the arid Australian interior and in

1923 was the frontier of non-Aboriginal settlement. At that time, first contacts between Aboriginal and non-Aboriginal people were still being made – a process not complete until the 1970s. Alfred Haddon, the anthropologist who collected the hair sample, most likely identified the donor as being of solely Aboriginal ancestry.

Obtaining consent for the study was an involved process. The identity, including the language group affiliation, of the person who donated the hair was unknown and so neither direct descendants nor membership of a specific group could be ascertained. It was therefore considered that the proper body to make the decision about the research was the Board of Directors of the Goldfields Land and Sea Council (GLSC). The GLSC is the Aboriginal representative body for the Goldfields region and the directors are elected by the Aboriginal members who belong to the numerous different language groups of the region. This process established a preferred model where researchers would seek in every instance to undertake direct and ongoing consultations with potential participants and their representative organisations, a model that has been endorsed by Indigenous peoples elsewhere in the world (Callaway 2017).

Publication of the resultant research article in October 2011 (Rasmussen et al. 2011) was well received by Aboriginal people in the Goldfields (Logan 2012). It was presented as a result for all of Aboriginal Australia. Then, a number of senior figures, including GLSC Board members and other cultural leaders outside the organisation, expressed the desire to take the research further to look at Aboriginal pre-history at a more nuanced, regional level. The GLSC endorsed this further research and the collaboration that had begun between the relevant Aboriginal communities and researchers set the pattern for subsequent work that expanded on this initial project.

The fieldwork for a genomic history of Aboriginal Australia

A decision was made by researchers and endorsed by representative Aboriginal organisations that the genome history study would build a dataset from the participation of volunteer Aboriginal groups and individuals. This shift from getting DNA from museum-held objects to obtaining it from community participants focused the project's emphasis on fieldwork and communication and opened direct and personal relationships.

The project occurred at the interface between Western scientific and traditional Indigenous knowledge systems. Within both systems, the claim to epistemological authority is made through the methodology of empiricism, evidence-based data and observation, though there are significant differences in the way knowledge is viewed and used – differences that are not always recognised and/or respected. Retrieving usable DNA from ancient samples is difficult: accolades are won with laboratory effort, technical skills and publication of complex data. These efforts result in statements of identity about the person or persons from whom the DNA was recovered but are undertaken at far remove from those who may have a vested interest in them. Likewise, Aboriginal knowledge and worldviews are unfamiliar to many geneticists. The disjuncture of knowledge systems and the use of highly specialised research methods created significant issues that needed to be addressed, while the collection of data from individuals also raised questions about the relationship between individual autonomy and collective cultural authority.

There were few pre-existing Australian protocols for such research. While the ethics of medical research are clearly defined, there were no guidelines specific to ancient populations genetic research with volunteer community members. We developed a process and protocols based on: the 2011 experience; input from Aboriginal individuals and representative organisations; the research guidelines set by the Australian Institute of Aboriginal and Torres Strait Islander Studies (AIATSIS); and the United Nations Declaration on the Rights of Indigenous Peoples 2007 statement on Indigenous Free, Prior and Informed Consent (FPIC).[2]

We then sought meaningful engagement with Aboriginal communities. Initial meetings were held with a few key individuals to find out whether a particular group might be interested in joining the research. When it was clear this was the case, follow-up meetings were held with representative organisations. These discussions with representative bodies focussed on the likely outcomes of the research.

Whenever it was possible, a senior person from the participating language group was engaged. This person was in each case known to all the individuals who were subsequently approached. The use of such consultants both facilitated the researchers gaining an understanding of the group's interests and concerns and allowed participants a personal and culturally appropriate avenue of communications. The consultants' contributions were recognised through co-authorship (Malaspinas et al. 2016).

There followed the critical process of consultation with individuals who were interested in participating as DNA sample donors. Each was contacted personally, so that detailed discussions could be conducted with them.

Two specific concerns that clearly needed to be addressed were uncertainty about the field and laboratory methodologies, and about the possible uses of the likely outcomes. Part of the attempt to demystify genetic research had two of the GLSC Board members travelling to Copenhagen to visit the Center for GeoGenetics to see the physical basis of the scientific authority that was asserted. These individuals then made themselves available to discuss the research with other interested Aboriginal people.

Potential participants in the new, expanded study were introduced to and told the background of those Australian-based researchers involved in the project, and given extensive information about the overseas researchers and the institute they represented and background in the ancient populations genetic research that had occurred to date. They were told how such research is undertaken, including how the samples would be collected and treated, the expected timeframe before results would be available, and what the subsequent information might constitute.

Each person was given ample opportunity to comment on, ask about or make suggestions about the project. It was also considered important to discuss what the likely results might be so that each individual and group could assess properly the likely social and cultural impact. Participants were also made aware that results would be published but that their identities would remain anonymous and that they could withdraw from the study at any time, including after samples were donated, without having to offer any explanation for their decision. Having been approached and had the project discussed by a recognised elder in a personally, culturally and socially appropriate way, each person was then left to make the decision whether or not to participate.

As noted, the critical threshold for the involvement of each person was that these discussions resulted in obtaining FPIC. When the researchers and Aboriginal consultants were satisfied that this was being given, signed consent forms – drafted in plain English – were obtained and each individual was filmed giving her or his consent orally as extra and different evidence of consent.

To protect anonymity, the filmed consents are held securely and cannot be viewed by anyone outside the immediate research team. If there is a challenge to the process of getting consent an arrangement will have to be made that a mutually acceptable third party views the films and confirms that consent was freely given.

Return visits were scheduled with each individual to discuss results when these became available. Thus, the data generated by the research is returned to these participants and – in generalised form – to their representative organisations for their use and benefit.

Developing direct relationships with more than 80 Indigenous individuals (including the cultural consultants) helped to establish mutual respect, ensured there was full and equitable participation in good faith and maintained communications. This provided a better means to safeguard individual rights. Some previous genetic research has been published using DNA collected third-hand, where the donating individuals poorly understood the work being done and in at least two cases were actually never told about it (Callaway 2017; Kowal & Anderson 2012; Redd & Stoneking 1999).

Repeat discussions with participants allowed updating on progress. Such discussions also meant that Aboriginal viewpoints were more easily identified and incorporated. This included input into preferred methodologies and shaping of outcomes. In the case of the former, for example, a number of groups stated it was desirable for the senior person from each major family in the group to give the DNA sample. Outcomes were then directed towards the extended family and language group level.

Ancient populations research uses multiple lines of inquiry. Dates from genetic research need to take into account archaeological and palaeo-climatic data, for example. There is space, too, for Aboriginal cultural knowledge and oral traditions to be incorporated. Participants have given researchers – now and in the past – information about kinship, cultural and linguistic connections.

These insights applied particularly to known, recent connections but occasionally went further back. For example, the research found that there were strong connections in the past between Aboriginal groups in the Pilbara and those in the Western Desert regions. This information echoes in close detail the much earlier Western Desert *Wati Kutjara* – the Two Men – origins story. As recorded by anthropologist Norman Tindale in the 1930s and 1960s (Tindale 1936; 1966), the account says that during the Dreaming (creation time) the eponymous two men, accompanied by a group of women (that is, a migrating group capable of reproducing), came to the Western Desert from the northwest, the direction of the Pilbara. In this instance, quite clearly, genetic studies have merely confirmed existing Aboriginal knowledge in a new form.

Contentious issues with the research

Study participants relayed previous experiences suggesting that the successful establishment of trust-based relationships during the Genomic History research project would rely on addressing a number of contextual issues where Aboriginal people have been given cause to mistrust research in the past. These issues are discussed as follows.

1: past uses of genetic research in Australia

At the turn of the century, the Human Genome Project was criticised for its approach to genetic research with Aboriginal peoples (Dodson & Williamson 1999). Elsewhere, genetic research has occurred using Aboriginal DNA samples that would now be considered to have questionable ethical provenance (Callaway 2017; Redd & Stoneking 1999).

However, the discussions we held with Aboriginal people suggested to us that in the 12 or so years following the Human Genome Project, the climate surrounding DNA research has changed for many Indigenous people – people appeared to be more familiar with the concept and more receptive as a result. Since the turn of the century, DNA research has been covered in commercial media and we encountered sentiment in the communities that genetic research specifically targeted to Aboriginal people should be considered (see also Kowal 2013). Many participants in the Genomic History project were able to identify specific desired outcomes for their DNA analysis – most often the pursuit of more information about kinship connections.

2: colonialist political and economic framework

There are in Australia significant remnants of a colonialist political and economic framework in which research has been used against Aboriginal interests. This extends to the most recent major endeavour to address Aboriginal disadvantage, the legal system of native title that has operated since the Australian High Court's Mabo decision of 1992. Native title allows Aboriginal groups to reclaim rights in their traditional country, but while it has delivered benefits it is a complex and onerous system to negotiate. The process places a premium on where the ancestors of Aboriginal people lived and who constitutes the claimant group. Claimants must show group membership and ongoing attachment to the area of country they are claiming while respondents argue, too often successfully, that such connections are broken or that the claimants and their ancestors were not originally from that country (Barker 2015; Lindgren 2007; Olney 1998).

Native title litigation outcomes often include statements about claimants' identities based on research by non-Aboriginal people which are often at odds with how the claimants see themselves and sometimes deleterious to their interests. Many Aboriginal people are involved in the native title process and feel deeply the issues it raises. It was clear to us that there was widespread concern that potentially here was another means for externally exerting detrimental identity definitions. We were often met with the questions, 'what if the DNA says we're not from this area?' or 'will the DNA tell us who should be in our group?'

In response, it was explained that DNA could not define membership of a group. Rather, DNA could only show there were (or were not) connections to people in other areas but not whether or not any individual was from any particular region. These explanations seemed readily understood by participants, who will often characterise themselves, their families and their ancestors as being far-ranging geographically. That is, people understand the idea of DNA crossing landscapes and cultures.

While it seemed in our dealings that people easily compartmentalised the different research agendas, there is nonetheless a lingering suspicion about the ends to which research will be put. Not surprisingly, people resist having outsiders telling them who they are when it does not agree with their own conceptions. An obvious way to address this is to have Aboriginal communities and individuals involved in shaping the research parameters. This occurred in, for example, the way Aboriginal people made the original requests to expand on the 2011 sequencing of the hair sample from the Goldfields into research with whole groups.

3: the distant past is politicised

Even the ancient Aboriginal past in Australia has sometimes been highly contested. An illustrative example occurred in the 1990s, when Aboriginal Ranger land management programs and joint management of National Parks and other protected areas were being established across Australia. At the same time, the idea that the early occupants of Australia caused the extinction of Australian megafauna entered the popular realm. One unforeseen consequence was conflict over land use, with some non-Aboriginal interests arguing that Aborigines lacked land-management credentials as a result (Nakashima 2000). This line of reasoning was based on what may or may not have happened between 20,000 and 40,000 years ago.

More recently, opponents have argued against Indigenous recognition in the Australian constitution on the basis that Aboriginal people were not the first in this country (Yaxley 2015). The claim lacks any scientific credibility: the genetic evidence here supports the Aboriginal viewpoint, showing a continuous Aboriginal lineage for 2,500 generations. Even so, it reminds us that even the distant past will be pressganged into ideological service.

4: contested research outcomes

Findings by non-Indigenous researchers may conflict with the knowledge held by Indigenous peoples, an issue that proved to be the most significant for the researchers involved in this project.

There are many pasts. The Aboriginal past is personal and spiritual, and it is not viewed in the same way as it is in other cultures. There is no delineated hierarchy of ages in Aboriginal epistemology – no Pleistocene and Holocene – as there is for most non-Aboriginal researchers, a legacy of Western Enlightenment preference for scientific classification, and one which implies discontinuity. Instead, there is among Aboriginal people an immediacy of connection to the distant past; it is part of the present. Aboriginal Dreaming begins at the point back in time where no personal(ised) information about ancestors is known. Ancestors who have faded into the past and become increasingly mythological are still considered an integral part of family and culture no matter when they lived and ancestral generations are not imagined in a linear way, extending like stepping stones infinitely laid out behind us. The different attitude is illustrated in the Western Desert word *thamu*, which means both grandfather and grandchild (Wangkanyi Ngurra Tjurta Aboriginal Corporation Language Centre 2001/2002). When the 2011 results were released, we were publicly reminded by Aboriginal people that they have the longest continual occupancy in their areas of country of any populations in the world (Logan 2012). This notion has been reinforced by genetic research since (Tobler et al. 2017).

We were mindful that there could be mixed reactions to the results of this research project. As we conducted the broader Australian Aboriginal genome project between 2013 and 2016, extensive consultations were held with Aboriginal Australian groups and individuals across the country. We observed a common theme emerging that reminded us of how the Aboriginal past has been colonised: the past we were explaining was not the past Aboriginal people knew. It became evident to us in our research that the idea of imposing one version of the past on another could be seen as an exercise in neo-colonialism.

This regular sticking point focussed on the theory that the origins of all modern humans lie in Africa, a theory which genetic research endorses. Although it was stressed repeatedly that the project would avoid challenging people's explanations of their origins it was unavoidable that current scientific theory would be discussed.

Over the course of two years, we talked to hundreds of Aboriginal people about genetic research, across the broad cultural and socio-economic diversity that characterises Aboriginal Australia, and only a handful indicated they accepted the Out-of-Africa theory. The overwhelming majority were strong and steadfast in their opposition to the idea. The majority of project participants expressed views that can be summed up by one statement that, 'We have been here since time began.' This sentiment is often expressed by Aboriginal Australians in contexts outside the research we were doing. It was a reminder that the ontology of all Aboriginal societies is autochthonous; where language group members believe that their deepest origins lie within Australia and usually (though not always) within the country the group now occupies.

In some instances, the opposition to Out-of-Africa was confrontational; most people, however, seemed content to ignore the non-Aboriginal researchers prattling on about African origins. This attitude was understood by us to be a polite way of refuting the theory. Then, over repeated discussions, overt resistance to statements about African origins tended to dissipate but this was not taken to mean participants had been swayed by the evidence but rather that it signalled we should discontinue that part of the discussion. It suggested a divergence in worldviews that might never be fully resolved. The question was what approach we should take.

We stressed that we did not intend to challenge the knowledge Aboriginal people held about their origins, yet this presented difficulties because the different ways of explaining Aboriginal origins are seemingly at odds. That is, while benefits were provided for all involved in the research and although Aboriginal people had advocated for the research to occur, it nonetheless took place as a scientific endeavour: empirical testing of theory. We, as advocates of Western scientific theory, were entering the Aboriginal intellectual domain, as non-Aboriginal people have done across every sphere of life, often with extreme bias or malign intent, since at least the seventeenth century.

It seemed there were two alternative approaches to this. First, as researchers we could insist on the primacy of the scientific origins accounts (accounts that personally we hold to be true). This would be confrontational but controversy over theories of human origins is not new. It is hardly necessary to reiterate that there has been a long history of often acrimonious debate between proponents of scientific explanations and those who hold other theories about human origins (e.g. Larson 2006). Some in the scientific community are actively engaged in debunking religious belief on this issue (e.g. Rennie 2002). This usually occurs within the confines of Western epistemology as negative critiquing of belief that is not fact-based and is therefore inferior to knowledge based on fact. That is, there is a widespread belief that using the 'tools of science' is the best way to test whether a model of reality is supported by observations made by separate, independent observers: science holds that not all truths are equal and not everyone's reality is deserving of respect (Shermer 2012).

However, there are some characteristics unique to the meeting of Aboriginal and non-Aboriginal belief systems that require careful consideration. First, there has been an unequal power relationship between settlers and Aboriginal people in Australia in explaining Aboriginal origins. Christianity has long been associated with colonialism (e.g. Carey 2011) and has exerted a powerful influence on at least some of the Aboriginal groups who participated in this genetics study (e.g. Morgan 1985). One result has been the attempted undermining of

Aboriginal culture (Haebich 2000), including a concerted challenge to replace origins accounts (although there has always been resistance to such attempts, see Reynolds 1996).

This unequal relationship is potentially replicated by scientific research. Science has long been assumed to have both power and universality (e.g. Christophorou 2009; Cobern & Loving 2001) and may be indifferent to local society and culture (Jarvie 1995). We had taken the genetic research to the communities and so, even though there were requests for us to do so, we were the proactive party. Our approaches required Aboriginal people to consider an alternative origins account to that which they held strongly. However, the guiding principles of the project were to create research partnerships, build relationships and attempt to avoid the antagonism that had occurred at times in the past, and pushing the primacy of scientific accounts was antithetic to these aims. In this, we were taking an approach that derived from our personal experiences, including in particular histories of working with Aboriginal groups previously; it mirrored that promoted in recent years by collaboration-minded archaeologists such as Sonia Atalay (2012).

An alternative approach could have us accept that Aboriginal and science-based origins accounts are of equal worth. Rather than dismissing Aboriginal origins accounts as merely myth we could accept them as being held by their proponents as truths of equal value to the truths that are put forward from scientific research. Such an approach was eminently suitable to the discussions we were having but it requires explanation, because on face value it seems to be an acceptance of an extreme relativist position. Following Boas (1887) more than a century ago, cultural relativism became a popular, and enduring, heuristic tool in the humanities, in particular anthropology (e.g. Nagengast & Turner 1997; Phillips 2007). By this doctrine, all world views are equally valid; reality is culturally relative (e.g. Herskovits 1972) but this is something that has long rankled many researchers in the fields of science (e.g. Bernard 1950; Bernstein 2011).

An equal relationship between Aboriginal participants and scientific researchers requires that each have respect for the position of the other. That in turn requires there be equal respect for differing knowledge systems. To hold that intellectual position honestly it was worthwhile examining the way each origin theory was held by its proponents.

In Western scientific epistemology, the ways in which the world is perceived are hierarchised. Knowledge, based on rationalism, occupies the highest echelon; belief, faith, emotion and imagination are less trustworthy because they cannot be proven empirically. Since Descartes, through Leibnitz and the British Empiricists, particularly Locke and Hume, faith (i.e. belief) and reason (i.e. knowledge) have been increasingly separated (Alston 1998), with faith or myth relegated to a lesser status. This is embodied in our language. In common terms, knowledge is defined as 'recognition ... acquaintance with a fact or facts' (Oxford University Press 2002, p. 1511); belief is 'trust, confidence; faith' (Oxford University Press 2002, p. 213). That is, belief is not based on fact but on supposition which is as likely to be unfounded as not.

Respect for different knowledge systems is now accepted and promoted by many researchers (e.g. Atalay 2012; Mignolo 2012). In Australia, historically, this has not been the case. Positioning Aboriginal epistemologies as being founded on something other than knowledge has seen them debased. Early ethnographic writings on Aboriginal societies referred to Aboriginal origins accounts as myths (e.g. Spencer and Gillen 1898). At the same time, theories of social Darwinism and the idea that there existed a hierarchy of races that placed Aboriginal Australians at the bottom (Attwood 1989; Haller 1971; Sussman 2014) permeated non-Aboriginal settler society in Australia.

These streams of thought coalesced into attitudes that Aboriginal origins accounts were myths in the sense of being fictitious, lacking credibility and of little worth (Berndt and Berndt 1988, p. 241). So did Europeans tend to see the Dreaming stories as preposterous (Stanner 2010, p. 62), and such superstition and mysticism, in opposition to rationalism and science, ruling all aspects of Aboriginal thought (Stanner 2010). By supposing that Aboriginal explanations of origins are belief-based rather than knowledge-based, that they inhabit the irrational (Other), while science is the very embodiment of the rational, Aboriginal explanations are accorded a lower status than scientific explanations. This intellectual positioning has allowed non-Aboriginal people to impose their knowledge systems on Aboriginal people. From this intellectual position, non-Aboriginal settlers have practiced epistemological colonialism, importing and imposing their knowledge systems in Australia, rather than adapting to and incorporating Aboriginal knowledge. For example, the Australian landscape now bears stark evidence of the unforeseen consequences: clearing of vast areas of native vegetation for European-style agriculture has resulted in erosion and salinification on a massive scale, with salinity alone affecting more than 1 million hectares, or 12 percent, of Western Australia's farmland (Western Australian Department of Agriculture 2017).

In reviewing competing origins accounts it could be asked whether some are knowledge-based and others belief-based. Scientists now 'know' that all modern humans originated in Africa. We 'know' that some 75,000 years ago the first group left Africa and began a journey to Australia, arriving approximately 53,000 years ago (Rasmussen et al. 2011). We have very recently at the time of writing 'learned' that the early Australian population spread across the continent rapidly, within perhaps 2,000 years (Tobler et al. 2017). The words 'know' and 'learned' are put in inverted commas not to place caveats upon them but merely to highlight that the origins accounts being described are considered to be knowledge rather than myth/belief. These accounts are 'knowledge' because they are based on analysis of empirical data, analysis which is verifiable.

For some time, many scientists argued that modern humans evolved independently in different regions of the world (Wolpoff, Wu & Thorne 1984). Then, when it was settled that we all have our origins in Africa it was argued – strongly on both sides – whether there were one or multiple exodus events. In both cases, as with scientific ideas previously, theories were held as knowledge. However, even within that we call the scientific, rationalist epistemology, differing and incompatible theories can be drawn from the same set of comprehensive data (Quine 1970, p. 179) and none may be falsifiable. Indeed, it has been argued that the difference between widely accepted and not widely accepted theories is how well each is advocated (Feyerabend 1975; Lakatos 1970) to the point where if two theories or models predict accurately the same events they can be considered equally real and we are free to choose between them (Hawking & Mlodinow 2010).

This leads us to ask how Aboriginal origins accounts are actually held: as knowledge or as belief? Plato proposed that for an idea to be held as knowledge three criteria had to be satisfied: the idea has to be believed; it has to be true; and the belief in it has to be justified. That is, a person knows something if, and only if, that something is true, the person believes it, and that person is justified in believing it (that is, there is good reason to believe). This demonstration, known as the Tripartite Analysis of Knowledge, was a widely accepted definition until it came under criticism in the mid-twentieth century (Gettier 1963). Yet while the theory as a whole is less secure now, the three elements of it are still considered necessary foundations for the holding of knowledge (Ichikawa & Steup 2017).

Such criticisms did not address a specific problem: in a post-colonial context the criterion of 'justified' in the definition of knowledge is subjective and culturally specific. If it cannot be so easily determined, across a cultural divide, whether or not a belief is justified, then equally non-Indigenous researchers cannot presume to be sure what is and is not knowledge within an Indigenous society.

Science is described as a metanarrative (Lyotard 1984), an all-encompassing model of explaining the world. Scientific knowledge satisfies two criteria that have encouraged this description: scientific theories can be falsified (Popper 2014) (that is, experiments can be replicated and data reused and if different results occur then the proposed theory is not substantiated) and science can generate new knowledge (Kuhn & Hawkins 1963), and as a consequence provides an unlimited explanatory model. This has tended to elevate scientific knowledge above other knowledge systems, but the criteria have been established by thinkers within those systems and do not account for the way knowledge systems are held by Indigenous peoples.

Ethnographic research in Australia suggests that Aboriginal people have a different perspective on what is knowledge and what is myth. Origins accounts are considered objectively verifiable and they are accepted as true to such an extent that the people who hold the knowledge are accorded societal rights by the rest of the people within that system in recognition of the veracity and importance of that knowledge (Bern 1979; Myers 1986). Holding beliefs does not earn societal rights in Aboriginal societies; only holding knowledge can do so and only because within those systems that knowledge is regarded as universal – true for the entire system.

Australian anthropologist W. E. H. Stanner (2010, p. 62) described the Dreaming as being held in mythology but lived in reality, where there is no separation of Dreaming and day-to-day life. Kenneth Maddock (1982) referred to Aboriginal 'knowledge of a remote "totemic geography"'. That is, the Dreaming is part of the knowledge system and origins accounts are known as the everyday world is known; that is, they are empirically known.

As Aboriginal people know their landscape, so they know the explanations for the way the land, and its inhabitants – plants, animals and people – arrived there. In this way, the landscape itself is observable data. The objection that Aboriginal people did not observe the landscape being created and therefore accounts of its origins are not empirical has been equally met with the retort that neither did the geneticist who studies ancient populations observe people leaving Africa approximately 75,000 years ago (Rasmussen et al. 2011). Because origins accounts are linked intricately with physical sites, they are considered verifiable by the people who have the knowledge. This fits the definition of model-dependent realism (Hawking & Mlodinow 2010) where, when an explanatory model provides a satisfactory explanation of events, it can be ascribed as being true.

Other prominent researchers have placed Aboriginal accounts in the realm of knowledge not myth. Mid-twentieth century ethnographers Roberts and Mountford declared that what they called Aboriginal myths were 'accepted as a record of absolute truth' (1969, p. 10). Specific examples come from Western Desert language groups, of which some members were participants in the genetics research project. Ethnographer Norman Tindale travelled to the Warburton Range in 1966 gathering information from the Western Desert language groups living there (Tindale 1966). One of his informants, a local elder, told him of the *malu tjukurrpa* (Kangaroo Dreaming) track, a creation story that is embodied along a specific route and incorporates specific sites. The elder then recounted the story of the first contacts made between his family and the earliest non-Aboriginal people, explorers and prospectors who arrived in the desert in the early twentieth century. Both accounts were tendered as events that occurred in the past of which the elder had knowledge. Tindale's account (1966, pp. 171–172, p. 182) of the major origin story in the Western Desert, the *wati kutjara* referred to above, likewise shows it is held as knowledge rather than belief:

> The Wati Kutjara … of the Ngadadjara tribespeople are also known to the Julbara people (of Laverton district) as Pundur Kutjara (pundu=man) … Now the Wati Kutjara possessed a group of women who were known as Kunkarunkara … Panatapia … is the first place [the *wati kutjara*] were known to have discovered or brought into being … it is known that the two men visited many other places and had other adventures.

Fred Myers recorded of the Pintubi of the Western Desert that having rights to an area of country involves knowing the stories, rituals, songs and designs for the important places in that country (Myers 1986). It is much the same for the Nyungar of Australia's southwest. As one of the most thorough anthropological studies of that group (Palmer 2016, p. 195) noted:

> Narratives relating to specific places … serve to explain how the creative forces evident in the Dreaming, when the activities reported in the narratives are considered to have taken place, resulted in modifications to the landscape. The narrative event is explicatory text. The knowledge of the narrative is an indication to others of the possession of an understanding of Noongar [Nyungar] cosmological processes.

On this basis, Aboriginal origins accounts do provide a successful, truthful explanation, equal in value to the explanations offered by genetic research. They are a strong and viable explicatory text in Aboriginal thought that alternative accounts are not seen as a challenge. It was apparent during our discussions on the genetics research project that those Aboriginal people who participated were not averse to new knowledge. Therefore, it was not the newness of the genetics origins accounts that caused them to be rejected but that they were not considered equally proven as knowledge.

When these knowledge systems met in the context of DNA research it was squarely in the realm of post-colonial politics. In our discussions about ancient populations research with Aboriginal groups we were conscious of avoiding consigning the explanations we were hearing to being less true than the scenarios that the DNA research suggested. Personally, we hold the accounts that are told by the scientific data to be true (albeit they have changed over time as new data has become available or old data is re-examined). We accept Out-of-Africa as being factual. We also accepted that Aboriginal origins accounts are factual for Aboriginal people. However, we wished to treat both systems as equally valid, a shift in the way Australian Aboriginal knowledge systems have been viewed by the majority of non-Indigenous people. The implication of Aboriginal epistemology being knowledge-based – not belief-based – is that it is not enough to treat Indigenous and Western knowledge as being of equal worth but kept separate. It is not enough for Western researchers to treat Indigenous knowledge with respect but still as being the Other. The two knowledge systems must be synthesised, to the extent possible.

If we focus on specific issues, this is not an easy task. Is it possible, for example, to reconcile the two origins accounts? If they were to be treated as being of equal standing, as we accepted, should we downplay the Out-of-Africa part of the story of Aboriginal settlement in Australia in an attempt to please Aboriginal audiences? Should we state that here was an alternative story to Aboriginal origins accounts and it was there for examination if desired? Or should we try a third approach? A theoretical synthesis is possible. In the context of the meeting of Indigenous and scientific explanations of origins, the scientific explanation of time is that it is a construct of the human mind and does not exist independently (e.g. Smolin 2015). It can be argued that history began in Australia with the arrival of the first people. In this sense at least, Aboriginal origins accounts are not incompatible with the scientific explanation. In practice, however, contradictions remain, and with them tensions in the intellectual relationships between researchers and Indigenous participants. We responded to the opposition to Out-of-Africa by telling accounts that began with the initial arrival in Sahul (greater Australia and New Guinea), although it felt somewhat restrictive not talking about what we knew.

Project participants were particularly interested in language group connections to country and family histories. It has been stated that Western societies view kin connections vertically; a result of the increasing importance of inheritance since approximately the fourteenth century, and that Aboriginal societies see their kinship connections horizontally. It is most important to know who alive today that one is related to, a result of the need to be able to share resources in times of scarcity. It was clear in our discussions about preliminary research results that receiving information about kinship was still a very strong motivation for Aboriginal people to participate in the research. Where researchers were focussed on connections across time, for the Aboriginal study participants it was equally or more important to know about current kinship connections across space, even those that the non-Aboriginal researchers considered to be very distant relationships.

Many of the connections that genetics revealed were those already familiar to Aboriginal people. In these cases, the new information was limited perhaps to showing the time depth of such connections. But some information was evidently new to participants – connections indicated by common haplogroups being found on opposite sides of the country, for example. Almost always, these were inquired about with considerable interest, although as yet definitive answers cannot be given.

Occasionally, learning about previously unknown or hazily known kinship connections exerted a powerful response. As is typical across Australia, many of those Aboriginal people who participated in this project have family histories that involve removals from family and country and even massacre of family members as recently as two or three generations ago. The effect has been profound on the makeup of extended families. This history added a layer of complexity to new information about kinship connections. A few people inquired about making contact with the people indicated as distant relatives. These requests are being considered although meeting them presents difficulties as the anonymity of all participants must be maintained.

Some evidence of the success in focussing, at least in part, on kinship connections came late in the project when various people who had not participated in the original DNA sampling came forward to request that they too have their DNA analysed.

Conclusion

The ancient populations DNA research project undertaken between 2013 and 2016 aimed to add knowledge to both Aboriginal people and the scientific research community. To the former, it provided some new information (and a lot of supportive knowledge to what was already known to some degree) about kinship and connections to country. For scientists, it added considerably to scientific understanding of human origins, the first arrival to Sahul and the process of populating of that continent. Integral to the consultation and field research processes was the need to address the issue that genetic researchers and Indigenous people did not agree on significant research outcomes. Considerable effort was made to address this on a practical level by ensuring that the different sets of knowledge were respected as theories of equal worth. On our part, it was primarily necessary to propose and discuss the research with a personal sense of humility that showed a genuine respect for alternative worldviews. Ultimately, extensive common ground was found between Aboriginal people and researchers, with both wanting to know more about long-term population histories on a regional, language group basis. In this way, some of the pitfalls that might occur in a major cross-cultural research endeavour in a post-colonial environment were avoided.

Notes

1 In this chapter, the term Aboriginal refers to Indigenous peoples of Australia (but not Torres Strait); Indigenous refers to First Peoples generally.
2 FPIC is a standard benchmark for many Aboriginal representative organisations in Australia; where: 'Free' means the decision-making must be free of coercion or pressure; 'Prior' means that adequate discussion about the decision has taken place before the decision is made; and 'Informed' is the requirement that the participant understands the nature of the project, including the past or future context in which the research and the likely outcomes sit.

Acknowledgements

The authors would like to acknowledge the individuals and Aboriginal organisations who participated in and assisted with the research, in particular Darren Injie, Betty Logan, Aubrey Lynch, Doc Reynolds and the directors and staff of the Goldfields Land and Sea Council. We would also like to acknowledge the support of our colleagues at the University of Copenhagen's Center for GeoGenetics, in particular Eske Willerslev and Anna-Sapfo Malaspinas; and Martin Porr and Jacqueline Matthews for organising the 'Decolonising Human Origins' workshop and inviting us to present the paper that was the basis of this chapter.

References

Alston, WP 1998, 'History of philosophy of religion', in E Craig (ed.), *The Routledge Encyclopedia of Philosophy*, Routledge, New York, pp. 238–248.
Atalay, S 2012, *Community-based archaeology: research with, by, and for Indigenous and local communities*, University of California Press, Berkeley.
Attwood, B 1989, *The making of the Aborigines*, Allen & Unwin, Sydney.
Barker, J 2015, *CG (deceased) on behalf of the Badimia People v State of Western Australia (No 2) [2015]*, FCA 507, Federal Court of Australia. Available from: www.judgments.fedcourt.gov.au/judgments/Judgments/fca/single/2015/2015fca0507 [15 February 2018].
Bern, J 1979, 'Ideology and domination: toward a reconstruction of Australian Aboriginal social formation', *Oceania*, vol. 50, no. 2, pp. 118–132.
Bernard, J 1950, 'Can science transcend culture?', *The Scientific Monthly*, vol. 71, no. 4, pp. 268–273.

Berndt, RM & Berndt, CH 1988, *The world of the first Australians: Aboriginal traditional life: past and present*, Aboriginal Studies Press, Canberra.

Bernstein, RJ 2011, *Beyond objectivism and relativism: science, hermeneutics, and praxis*, University of Pennsylvania Press, Philadelphia.

Boas, F 1887, 'Museums of ethnology and their classification', *Science*, vol. 9, no. 589, pp. 126–128.

Callaway, E 2017, 'South Africa's San people issue research code', *Nature*, vol. 543, no. 7646, p. 475.

Carey, HM 2011, *God's empire: religion and colonialism in the British world, c. 1801–1908*, Cambridge University Press, Cambridge.

Christophorou, LG 2009, 'The universality of science: limits and needs', *Proceedings from the International Council for Science (ICSU)*, European members annual meeting, Podgorica, Montenegro, 29–30 September.

Cobern, WW & Loving, CC 2001, 'Defining "science" in a multicultural world: implications for science education', *Science Education*, vol. 85, no. 1, pp. 50–67.

Dodson, M & Williamson, R 1999, 'Indigenous peoples and the morality of the Human Genome Diversity Project', *Journal of Medical Ethics*, vol. 25, no. 2, pp. 204–208.

Feyerabend, P 1975, *Against method*, Verso, London.

Gettier, EL 1963, 'Is justified true belief knowledge?' *Analysis*, vol. 23, no. 6, pp. 121–123.

Haebich, A 2000, *Broken circles*, Fremantle Press, Fremantle, WA.

Haller, JS 1971, *Outcasts from evolution: scientific attitudes of racial inferiority, 1859–1900*, Southern Illinois University Press, Carbondale & Edwardsville.

Hawking, S & Mlodinow, L 2010, *The grand design*, Bantam Books, New York.

Herskovits, MJ 1972, *Cultural relativism*, Random House, New York.

Ichikawa, JJ & Steup, M 2017, 'The analysis of knowledge', *Stanford Encyclopedia of Philosophy*. Available from: https://stanford.library.sydney.edu.au/entries/knowledge-analysis [21 February 2018].

Jarvie, IC 1995, 'Cultural relativism'. Available from: www.yorku.ca/jarvie/online_publications/CultRel.pdf [1 September 2017].

Kowal, E 2013, 'Orphan DNA: Indigenous samples, ethical biovalue and postcolonial science', *Social Studies of Science*, vol. 43, no. 4, pp. 577–597.

Kowal, E & Anderson, I 2012, 'Genetic research in Aboriginal and Torres Strait Islander communities: continuing the conversation: discussion paper', Lowitja Institute. Available from: http://dro.deakin.edu.au/view/DU:30064989 [15 February 2018].

Kuhn, TS & Hawkins, D 1963, 'The structure of scientific revolutions', *American Journal of Physics*, vol. 31, no. 7, pp. 554–555.

Lakatos, I 1970, 'Falsification and the methodology of scientific research programmes', in I Lakatos & A Musgrave (eds), *Criticism and the growth of knowledge*, Cambridge University Press, Cambridge, pp. 91–196.

Larson, EJ 2006, *Evolution: the remarkable history of a scientific theory*, Modern Library Chronicles, no. 17. Modern Library, New York.

Lindgren, J 2007, *Harrington-Smith on behalf of the Wongatha People v State of Western Australia (No 9) [2007]*, FCA 31, Federal Court of Australia. Available from: www.austlii.edu.au/cgibin/sinodisp/au/cases/cth/FCA/2007/31.html?stem=0&synonyms=0&query=Harrington-Smith [9 January 2014].

Logan, D 2012, 'Chairperson's report', *Goldfields Land and Sea Council Aboriginal Corporation (Representative Body) 2011–12 Annual Report*. Kalgoorlie, WA.

Lyotard, J-F 1984, *The postmodern condition: a report on knowledge*, vol. 10, University of Minnesota Press, Minneapolis.

Maddock, K 1982, *The Australian Aborigines: a portrait of their society*, 2nd edn, Penguin, Ringwood VIC, Australia.

Malaspinas, A-S, Westaway, MC, Muller, C, Sousa, VC, Lao, O, Alves, I, Bergström, A, Athanasiadis, G, Cheng, JY, Crawford, JE, Heupink, TH, Macholdt, E, Peischl, S, Rasmussen, S, Schiffels, S, Subramanian, S, Wright, JL, Albrechtsen, A, Barbieri, C, Dupanlup, I, Levikivskyi, IP, Moreno-Mayar, JV, Ni, S, Racimo, F, Sikora, M, Xue, Y, Agakhanian, FA, Brucato, N, Brunak, S, Campos, PF, Clark, W, Ellingvåg, S, Fourmile, G, Gerbault, P, Injie, D, Koki, G, Leavesley, M, Logan, B, Lynch, A, Matisoo-Smith, EA, McAllister, PJ, Mentzer, AJ, Metspalu, M, Migliano, AB, Murgha, L,

Phipps, ME, Pomat, W, Reynolds, D, Ricaut, F-X, Siba, P, Thomas, MG, Wales, T, Wall, CM, Oppenheimer, SJ, Tyler-Smith, C, Durin, R, Dortch, J, Manica, A, Schierup, MH, Foley, RA, Lahr, MM, Bowern, C, Wall, JD, Mailund, T, Stoneking, M, Nielsen, R, Sandhu, MS, Excoffier, L, Lambert, DM & Willerslev, E 2016, 'A genomic history of Aboriginal Australia', *Nature*, vol. 538, pp. 207–214.

Mignolo, W 2012, 'Decolonizing Western epistemology/building decolonial epistemologies', in A Isasi Díaz & E Mendieta (eds), *Decolonizing epistemologies. Latina/o theology and philosophy*, Fordham University Press, New York, pp. 19–44.

Morgan, M 1985, *A drop in a bucket: the Mount Margaret story*, United Aborigines Mission, Williamstown.

Myers, FR 1986, *Pintubi country, Pintubi self: sentiment, place, and politics among Western Desert Aborigines*, University of California Press, Berkeley.

Nagengast, C & Turner, T 1997, 'Introduction: universal human rights versus cultural relativity', *Journal of Anthropological Research*, vol. 53, no. 3, pp. 269–272.

Nakashima, D 2000, 'Burning questions: shaping landscapes with Aboriginal fire-interview with Professor Marcia Langton', *Natures Sciences Sociétés*, vol. 8, no. 1, pp. 50–56.

Olney, J 1998, *The Members of the Yorta Yorta Aboriginal Community v The State of Victoria [1998]*, FCA 1606, Federal Court of Australia. Available from: www.austlii.edu.au/cgi-bin/viewdoc/au/cases/cth/FCA/1998/1606.html [24 September 2018].

Oxford University Press 2002, *Shorter Oxford English dictionary: on historical principles*, 5th edn, WR Trumble & A Stevenson (eds), Oxford University Press, Oxford.

Palmer, K 2016, *Noongar people, Noongar land: the resilience of Aboriginal culture on the South West of Western Australia*, AIATSIS Research Publications, Canberra.

Phillips, PJJ 2007, *The challenge of relativism: its nature and limits*, Continuum, London.

Popper, K 2014, *Conjectures and refutations: the growth of scientific knowledge*, Routledge, London.

Quine, WV 1970, 'On the reasons for indeterminacy of translation', *Journal of Philosophy*, vol. 67, no. 6, pp. 178–183.

Rasmussen, MG, Wang, X, Lohmueller, Y, Rasmussen, KE, Albrechtsen, S, Skotte, A, Lindgreen, L, Metspalu, S, Jombart, M, Kivisild, T, Zhai, T, Eriksson, W, Manica, A, Orlando, A, de la Vega, L, Tridico, FM, Metspalu, S, Nielsen, E, Ávila-Arcoz, K, Moreno-Mayar, M, Muller, JV, Dortch, C, Gilbert, J, Lund, MTP, Wesolowska, O, Karmin, A, Weinert, M, Wang, LA, Li, B, Tai, J, Xiao, S, Hanihara, F, van Driem, T, Jha, G, Ricaut, AR, de Knijff, F-X, Migliano, P, Gallego Romero, AB, Kristiansen, I, Lambert, K, Brunak, DM, Forster, S, Brinkmann, P, Nehlich, B, Bunce, O, Richards, M, Gupta, M, Bustamante, R, Krogh, CD, Foley, A, Lahr, RA, Balloux, MM, Sichertiz-Pontén, F, Villems, T, Nielsen, R, Wang, J & Willerslev, E 2011, 'An Aboriginal Australian genome reveals separate human dispersals into Asia', *Science*, vol. 334, no. 6052, pp. 94–98.

Redd, AJ & Stoneking, M 1999, 'Peopling of Sahul: mtDNA variation in aboriginal Australian and Papua New Guinean populations', *The American Journal of Human Genetics*, vol. 65, no. 3, pp. 808–828.

Rennie, J 2002, '15 answers to creationist nonsense', *Scientific American*, American edition, vol. 87, no. 1, pp. 78–85.

Reynolds, H 1996, *Dispossession: black Australians and white invaders*, no. 5, Allen & Unwin, Sydney.

Roberts, A & Mountford, CP 1969, *The dawn of time: Australian aboriginal myths in paintings*, Rigby Ltd, Australia.

Shermer, M 2012, *The believing brain: from spiritual faiths to political convictions – how we construct beliefs and reinforce them as truths*, Robinson, London.

Smolin, L 2015, 'Is time real or an illusion?' *Science Focus*. Available from: www.sciencefocus.com/qa/time-real-or-illusion [21 February 2018].

Spencer, B & Gillen, FJ 1898, *The native tribes of Central Australia*, Cambridge University Press, New York.

Stanner, WEH 2010, *The Dreaming and other essays*, 2nd edn, Black Inc. Agenda, Collingwood, Australia.

Sussman, RW 2014, *The myth of race: the troubling persistence of an unscientific idea*, Harvard University Press, Cambridge, MA.

Tindale, NB 1936, 'Legend of the Wati Kutjara, Warburton Range, Western Australia', *Oceania*, vol. 7, no. 2, pp. 169–185.

Tindale, NB 1966, 'Journal of a trip to Western Australia in search of tribal data by Norman B. Tindale 1966', South Australian Museum Series AA 338/1/27. Adelaide, SA.

Tobler, R, Rohrlach, A, Soubrier, J, Bover, P, Llamas, B, Tuke, J, Bean, N, Abdullah-Highfold, A, Agius, S, O'Donoghue, A, O'Loughlin, I, Sutton, P, Zilio, F, Walshe, K, Williams, AN, Turney, CSM, Williams, M, Richards, SM, Mitchell, RJ, Kowal, E, Stephen, JR, Williams, L, Haak, W & Cooper, A 2017, 'Aboriginal mitogenomes reveal 50,000 years of regionalism in Australia', *Nature*, vol. 544, no. 7649, p. 180.

van Holst Pellekaan, S 2013, 'Genetic evidence for the colonization of Australia', *Quaternary International*, vol. 285, pp. 44–56.

Wangkanyi Ngurra Tjurta Aboriginal Corporation Language Centre 2001/2002, *Wangkatha dictionary*, Kalgoorlie, WA.

Western Australian Department of Agriculture 2017, 'Soil salinity'. Available from: https://www.agric. wa.gov.au/climate-land-water/soils/managing-soils/soil-salinity [26 January 2018].

Wolpoff, MH, Wu, XZ & Thorne, AG 1984, 'Modern *Homo Sapiens* origins: a general theory of Hominid evolution involving the fossil evidence from east Asia', *The origins of modern humans*, Liss, New York, pp. 411–483.

Yaxley, L 2015, 'Senator David Leyonhjelm questions if Aboriginals were first occupants of Australia; says it would be "bizarre" to put into Constitution', *ABC News*. Available from: www.abc.net.au/news/2015-06-25/david-leyonhjelm-raises-doubts-over-aboriginal-occupants/6572704 [6 February 2018].

INDEX

Aboriginal Australians 44–5, 100, 101; belief systems, Aboriginal and non-Aboriginal, meeting of 316–17; colonial legacies and representations of 105–6; diffusionist approach to stone tool forms of 104–5; 'Dreamtime' of 193; evolutionary craniometry and 64; flaked stone tools used by 101–2; genetic research and engagement with Aboriginal communities 312; genome project (2013–2016) 315–16; knowledge and worldviews of 311; material at hand explanation for stone tool forms 104; origins of, accounts of 318–19, 319–20; origins of, explanations of 316; 'primitive' nature of 58; primordialisation of 96–106; Ranger land management programs 315; science-based origins accounts of 317–18, 320–21; stone tool technologies of, problems with 102–4

The Aborigines of Victoria (Smyth, R.B.) 103

Abrie, A.L. 286

Abu El-Haj, N. 150

The Academy 168

Acheulean bifacial assemblages 220, 241–2, 242–3, 243–4, 245, 249, 251

Ackermann, R.R. & Cheverud, J.M. 88

Ackermann, R.R., Mackay, A & Arnold, M.L. 80, 88, 302

Adas, M. 61

Adovasio, J., Donahue, D, Stuckenrath, R & Pedler, R. 269

Adovasio, J.M. & Page, J. 267

Africa: Africanness, roots and 280–81; Afrocentrism and palaeoanthropology today 84–7; ancestors of modern humans in 266; Broken Hill skull from Zambia 75; colonial narratives of 'human origins,' emergence from 73–6; homogenisation of 72–3; 'human origins,' African models of 80–81; 'othering' of 72–3; in palaeoanthropological narratives, centralisation of 84; 'primitive' Africa as framework for 'human origins' 82–4; root of humanness, support for 79; 'Savage Man' of, invention of 84; theory of origins of modern humans in 315–16; *Zinjanthropus* and *Homo habilis,* Leakey's discoveries at Olduvai Gorge of 226

The Idea of Africa (Mudimbe, V.Y.) 72

African Ancestry Inc. 303

Agamben, G. 60, 284

agriculture, effects of 38

AIDS 284

Akhilesh, K., Pappu, S, Rajapara, H.M, Gunnell, Y, Shukla, A.-D. et al. 244, 245

Al-Hussainy, A. & Matthews, R. 42

Alberti, B. 4, 198

Alberti, B. & Marshall, Y. 4

Alberti, B, Fowles, S, Holbraad, M, Marshall, Y & Witmore, C.L 4

Allais, L. 190

Allbrock, M. & McGrath, A. 9

Allchin, B. 226, 243, 247

Allchin, F.R. 243

Allen, J. 106

Allen, V.L. 283

allochronism, rhetoric of 145–6

Ally, S. & Lissoni, A. 284

Alston, W.P. 317

Althusser, L. 195

American Association of Physical Anthropologists 87

analogue techniques 131

anatomical humanism 59

ANC (African National Congress) 280, 281, 286